# Lecture Notes in Computer Science 11582

Commenced Publication in 1973
Founding and Former Series Editors:
Gerhard Goos, Juris Hartmanis, and Jan van Leeuwen

Vincent G. Duffy (Ed.)

# Digital Human Modeling and Applications in Health, Safety, Ergonomics and Risk Management

## Healthcare Applications

10th International Conference, DHM 2019
Held as Part of the 21st HCI International Conference, HCII 2019
Orlando, FL, USA, July 26–31, 2019
Proceedings, Part II

 Springer

*Editor*
Vincent G. Duffy
Purdue University
West Lafayette, IN, USA

ISSN 0302-9743          ISSN 1611-3349   (electronic)
Lecture Notes in Computer Science
ISBN 978-3-030-22218-5          ISBN 978-3-030-22219-2   (eBook)
https://doi.org/10.1007/978-3-030-22219-2

LNCS Sublibrary: SL3 – Information Systems and Applications, incl. Internet/Web, and HCI

This Springer imprint is published by the registered company Springer Nature Switzerland AG
The registered company address is: Gewerbestrasse 11, 6330 Cham, Switzerland

# Foreword

The 21st International Conference on Human-Computer Interaction, HCI International 2019, was held in Orlando, FL, USA, during July 26–31, 2019. The event incorporated the 18 thematic areas and affiliated conferences listed on the following page.

A total of 5,029 individuals from academia, research institutes, industry, and governmental agencies from 73 countries submitted contributions, and 1,274 papers and 209 posters were included in the pre-conference proceedings. These contributions address the latest research and development efforts and highlight the human aspects of design and use of computing systems. The contributions thoroughly cover the entire field of human-computer interaction, addressing major advances in knowledge and effective use of computers in a variety of application areas. The volumes constituting the full set of the pre-conference proceedings are listed in the following pages.

This year the HCI International (HCII) conference introduced the new option of "late-breaking work." This applies both for papers and posters and the corresponding volume(s) of the proceedings will be published just after the conference. Full papers will be included in the *HCII 2019 Late-Breaking Work Papers Proceedings* volume of the proceedings to be published in the Springer LNCS series, while poster extended abstracts will be included as short papers in the HCII 2019 *Late-Breaking Work Poster Extended Abstracts* volume to be published in the Springer CCIS series.

I would like to thank the program board chairs and the members of the program boards of all thematic areas and affiliated conferences for their contribution to the highest scientific quality and the overall success of the HCI International 2019 conference.

This conference would not have been possible without the continuous and unwavering support and advice of the founder, Conference General Chair Emeritus and Conference Scientific Advisor Prof. Gavriel Salvendy. For his outstanding efforts, I would like to express my appreciation to the communications chair and editor of *HCI International News,* Dr. Abbas Moallem.

July 2019                                                                                   Constantine Stephanidis

# HCI International 2019 Thematic Areas
## and Affiliated Conferences

Thematic areas:

- HCI 2019: Human-Computer Interaction
- HIMI 2019: Human Interface and the Management of Information

Affiliated conferences:

- EPCE 2019: 16th International Conference on Engineering Psychology and Cognitive Ergonomics
- UAHCI 2019: 13th International Conference on Universal Access in Human-Computer Interaction
- VAMR 2019: 11th International Conference on Virtual, Augmented and Mixed Reality
- CCD 2019: 11th International Conference on Cross-Cultural Design
- SCSM 2019: 11th International Conference on Social Computing and Social Media
- AC 2019: 13th International Conference on Augmented Cognition
- DHM 2019: 10th International Conference on Digital Human Modeling and Applications in Health, Safety, Ergonomics and Risk Management
- DUXU 2019: 8th International Conference on Design, User Experience, and Usability
- DAPI 2019: 7th International Conference on Distributed, Ambient and Pervasive Interactions
- HCIBGO 2019: 6th International Conference on HCI in Business, Government and Organizations
- LCT 2019: 6th International Conference on Learning and Collaboration Technologies
- ITAP 2019: 5th International Conference on Human Aspects of IT for the Aged Population
- HCI-CPT 2019: First International Conference on HCI for Cybersecurity, Privacy and Trust
- HCI-Games 2019: First International Conference on HCI in Games
- MobiTAS 2019: First International Conference on HCI in Mobility, Transport, and Automotive Systems
- AIS 2019: First International Conference on Adaptive Instructional Systems

# Pre-conference Proceedings Volumes Full List

1. LNCS 11566, Human-Computer Interaction: Perspectives on Design (Part I), edited by Masaaki Kurosu
2. LNCS 11567, Human-Computer Interaction: Recognition and Interaction Technologies (Part II), edited by Masaaki Kurosu
3. LNCS 11568, Human-Computer Interaction: Design Practice in Contemporary Societies (Part III), edited by Masaaki Kurosu
4. LNCS 11569, Human Interface and the Management of Information: Visual Information and Knowledge Management (Part I), edited by Sakae Yamamoto and Hirohiko Mori
5. LNCS 11570, Human Interface and the Management of Information: Information in Intelligent Systems (Part II), edited by Sakae Yamamoto and Hirohiko Mori
6. LNAI 11571, Engineering Psychology and Cognitive Ergonomics, edited by Don Harris
7. LNCS 11572, Universal Access in Human-Computer Interaction: Theory, Methods and Tools (Part I), edited by Margherita Antona and Constantine Stephanidis
8. LNCS 11573, Universal Access in Human-Computer Interaction: Multimodality and Assistive Environments (Part II), edited by Margherita Antona and Constantine Stephanidis
9. LNCS 11574, Virtual, Augmented and Mixed Reality: Multimodal Interaction (Part I), edited by Jessie Y. C. Chen and Gino Fragomeni
10. LNCS 11575, Virtual, Augmented and Mixed Reality: Applications and Case Studies (Part II), edited by Jessie Y. C. Chen and Gino Fragomeni
11. LNCS 11576, Cross-Cultural Design: Methods, Tools and User Experience (Part I), edited by P. L. Patrick Rau
12. LNCS 11577, Cross-Cultural Design: Culture and Society (Part II), edited by P. L. Patrick Rau
13. LNCS 11578, Social Computing and Social Media: Design, Human Behavior and Analytics (Part I), edited by Gabriele Meiselwitz
14. LNCS 11579, Social Computing and Social Media: Communication and Social Communities (Part II), edited by Gabriele Meiselwitz
15. LNAI 11580, Augmented Cognition, edited by Dylan D. Schmorrow and Cali M. Fidopiastis
16. LNCS 11581, Digital Human Modeling and Applications in Health, Safety, Ergonomics and Risk Management: Human Body and Motion (Part I), edited by Vincent G. Duffy

34. CCIS 1033, HCI International 2019 - Posters (Part II), edited by Constantine Stephanidis
35. CCIS 1034, HCI International 2019 - Posters (Part III), edited by Constantine Stephanidis

**http://2019.hci.international/proceedings**

# 10th International Conference on Digital Human Modeling and Applications in Health, Safety, Ergonomics and Risk Management (DHM 2019)

Program Board Chair(s): **Vincent G. Duffy,** *USA*

- Stephen Baek, USA
- André Calero Valdez, Germany
- H. Onan Demirel, USA
- Stephen J. Elliott, USA
- Afzal A. Godil, USA
- Ravi Goonetilleke, Hong Kong, SAR China
- Akihiko Goto, Japan
- Hossam Haick, Israel
- Hiroyuki Hamada, Japan
- Dan Högberg, Sweden
- Thorsten Kuebler, USA
- Noriaki Kuwahara, Japan
- Byung Cheol Lee, USA
- Kang Li, USA
- Claudio Loconsole, Italy
- Masahide Nakamura, Japan
- Sergio Nesteriuk, Brazil
- T. Patel, India
- Caterina Rizzi, Italy
- Beatriz Santos, Portugal
- Juan A. Sánchez-Margallo, Spain
- Meng-Dar Shieh, Taiwan
- Leonor Teixeira, Portugal
- Renran Tian, USA
- Anita Woll, Norway
- Kuan Yew Wong, Malaysia
- S. Xiong, Korea
- James Yang, USA
- Rachel Zuanon, Brazil

The full list with the Program Board Chairs and the members of the Program Boards of all thematic areas and affiliated conferences is available online at:

http://www.hci.international/board-members-2019.php

# HCI International 2020

The 22nd International Conference on Human-Computer Interaction, HCI International 2020, will be held jointly with the affiliated conferences in Copenhagen, Denmark, at the Bella Center Copenhagen, July 19–24, 2020. It will cover a broad spectrum of themes related to HCI, including theoretical issues, methods, tools, processes, and case studies in HCI design, as well as novel interaction techniques, interfaces, and applications. The proceedings will be published by Springer. More information will be available on the conference website: http://2020.hci.international/.

General Chair
Prof. Constantine Stephanidis
University of Crete and ICS-FORTH
Heraklion, Crete, Greece
E-mail: general_chair@hcii2020.org

**http://2020.hci.international/**

# Contents – Part II

## Health Dialogues

## Health Games and Social Communities

# Contents – Part I

**Work Modelling and Industrial Applications**

**Risk Assessment and Safety**

# Models in Healthcare

# Digital Transformation of Prostate Cancer Pathway and Optimizing Patient Experience, Patient Safety and Clinical Professionalism

Joan Cahill[1]([✉]) [iD], Ben Turney[2], Sean Wetherall[3], Haseeb Khan[3],
Maurice McGrath[3], and Igor Widlicki[3]

[1] School of Psychology, Trinity College Dublin (TCD), Dublin 2, Ireland
cahilljo@tcd.ie
[2] Churchill Hospital, Oxford University Hospital (OUH), Oxford, England
[3] Oneview Healthcare, Blackrock Business Park, Blackrock, Block 2,
Dublin, Ireland

**Abstract.** This paper presents the preliminary findings of an ongoing human factors re-search project addressing the digital transformation of the prostate cancer path-way to optimize patient experience, patient safety and clinical professionalism. The proposed technology attempts establish an appropriate balance between focusing on (1) cure/cancer treatment outcomes and (2) quality of life. Preliminary research indicates that this technology provides an opportunity to influence the behavior and actions of clinicians, enhancing professionalism and impacting on patient experience and patient safety.

**Keywords:** Patient experience · Oncology pathways ·
Electronic health records · Staff professionalism

## 1 Introduction

### 1.1 Introduction to Problem

Prostate cancer is the most common malignancy in men with an estimated 21% prevalence among new cancer cases in males for 2016 [1]. Since many forms of cancer are chronic yet highly survivable, the definition of successful treatment has shifted toward maximizing the quality of life of individuals diagnosed with cancer for as long as they live. Given the excellent survival rates, patients undergoing clinical treatment for prostate cancer often focus on patient-centered outcomes of care to guide treatment choices, such as rates of urinary incontinence (UI) or irritative voiding symptoms and erectile/sexual dysfunction (ED) [2].

Patient centered approaches have replaced physician centered care approaches. Some argue that the concept of patient centered care might be replaced with the concept of person-focused care [3]. More recently, there has been a move towards relationship centered care [4–6]. As human beings are social beings [7, 8], fostering and maintaining positive social relationships is essential to well-being. Further, this positively impacts on health outcomes.

V. G. Duffy (Ed.): HCII 2019, LNCS 11582, pp. 3–22, 2019.
https://doi.org/10.1007/978-3-030-22219-2_1

Patient experience spans the physical, social and emotional experience of the patient, while in hospital. It reflects the 'occurrences and events that happen independently and collectively across the continuum of care' [9]. A positive patient experience is underpinned by concepts of dignity and respect for patients. Further, it involves the treatment of patients and their families as 'partners in care' and associated clinical decision making [10].

The National Health Service (NHS) in the United Kingdom (UK) has defined a ten-year plan to put patient experience at center of NHS work [11]. In relation to enhancing patient experience, the NHS had defined several goals. These include: (1) involving patients and families in treatment decisions, (2) treating the patient with dignity and respect, (3) reducing delays in diagnosis and treatment, (4) avoiding unnecessary treatment, (5) providing patients with access to information about their care and (6) the consideration of patient interest and wellbeing in treatment decisions [11]. According to the findings of the NHS patient experience survey for 2017, most of the people with cancer also feel positive about the care they receive (respondents gave an average rating of 8.8) [12]. Interestingly, survey findings highlight the key role played by the Cancer Nurse Specialist [12]. However, this research has identified several areas for improvement – including improvements in relation to staff teamwork, the provision of patient access to care plans and attention to the 'patient voice' [12].

Cancer multidisciplinary teams (MDTs) are well established worldwide. In breast cancer care, the contribution of cancer specialist nurse in relation to the holistic assessment of patient needs been associated with improved patient experience and quality of life [13].

Surgery is associated with certain risks (for example, infection), that need to be carefully managed in relation to vulnerable populations [14]. To this end, where possible, non-invasive treatments are proposed (for example, drugs treatments instead of surgery). In parallel, there has been a move to locate certain oncology treatments in the community (i.e. patients having treatments at primary care centers), to better manage infection risks. From a patient and information technology perspective, this requires more information integration and co-ordination between hospital and community services.

The concept of a networked approach to cancer care is important to ensure that each element of the patient pathway operates in an integrated manner.

Teamwork and communication issues have been cited as root causes in adverse events in healthcare [15]. As defined by Dixon-Woods and Pronovost, patient safety depends upon open communication, trust and effective interdisciplinary teamwork [16].

## 1.2 New Technologies

Electronic health records (EHR's) provide access to patient health related information in digital format. These records capture the state of a patient across time and can be shared across different health care settings. Currently, these records capture have a biomedical focus and do not provide a holistic perspective on the patient (i.e. there is no attention to the provision of information about patient ability, need, preferences etc.).

New Medical Oncology Clinical Information System (MOCIS) are currently being introduced. Such systems are being integrated with existing electronic heath records. Recent research undertaken by Sicotte et al. (2016) indicates that the utilization of electronic medical records (EMR) in clinical pathways can reduce waiting times for patients, improve workflow integration in medical and radiation oncology [17]. This in turn has implications in relation to patient outcomes.

### 1.3   Conceptualizing Human Factors Research Problem

Staff professionalism has an impact on patient experience and patient safety. The digital transformation of the prostate cancer pathway provides the opportunity to influence the behavior and actions of clinicians, to enhance staff professionalism and thereby impact on patient experience and safety.

Accordingly, the human factors problem to be addressed is multi-dimensional and can be conceptualized at four levels

1. Human factors problems pertaining to the oncology pathway design.
   This includes process efficiency, sharing of information between different team-members, management of breaches and the use of the clinical nurse specialist role within the pathway.
2. Human factors problems pertaining to clinical professionalism.
   This includes issues pertaining to clinical teamwork, MDT teamwork problems, staff burnout, role definition and perception.
3. Human factors problems pertaining to the patient in the pathway.
   This includes (a) patient experience and quality of life, (b) patient safety and (c) patient outcomes.
4. Information management problems and the Human Machine Interaction (HMI) design of new information technology.
   This includes problems pertaining to poor integration of hospital and community pathways, weaknesses in relation to the existing design of electronic health records, issues pertaining to information sharing in relation to clinical workflows for oncology care, difficulties obtaining information about patient suitability for drugs trials, HMI design issues with existing tools etc.

### 1.4   Paper Overview

This paper presents the preliminary findings of an ongoing human factors research project addressing the digital transformation of the prostate cancer pathway to optimize patient experience, patient safety and clinical professionalism. This research is being undertaken at Churchill Hospital, Oxford University Hospitals (OUH), Oxford, UK. It involves a multidisciplinary collaboration between clinicians, researchers and software developers at Churchill Hospital/OUH, Trinity College Dublin, (TCD) and Oneview Healthcare. First the methodology is presented. The key findings are then outlined. The proposed electronic pathway solution is then presented. Following this, the proposed solution is discussed, and some preliminary conclusions drawn.

## 2 Methodology

### 2.1 Objectives and Research Questions

The primary objective of this research is advance a new digital pathway for prostate cancer which will provide key benefits for patients (i.e. patient experience, patient safety) and for staff (i.e. teamwork and professionalism). The proposed research has three high level goals:

1. To engage in stakeholder evaluation research to define an optimum care pathway linking to certain key clinical areas of focus (i.e. medical professionalism, patient experience, patient safety, patient education and compliance and standardization of care).
2. To evaluate the existing Oxford Pathway workflows from the perspective of (1).
3. To identify and validate new technology features/workflows for the Oxford Pathways software, to promote (1).

The following research questions have been defined:

1. How might this new technology address the key areas of clinical focus?
2. What are the key problems pertaining to (1) professionalism and (2) patient experience and safety, to be addressed by this new technology?
3. In relation to (1) professionalism and (2) patient experience and safety, what are the key process gates and states to focus on?
4. In relation to patients, what are the requirements for new technology to support specific states at key process gates, considering the key clinical areas of focus?
5. In relation to staff, what are the requirements for new technology to support specific states at key process gates, considering the key clinical areas of focus?
6. What are the human machine interaction (HMI) design requirements for the proposed technology at different process gates (see 3)?
7. What is an appropriate implementation plan for the new technology?

### 2.2 Overview of Research Design and Research Phases

Enhancing patient experience concerns all stakeholders. To this end, this research adopts a stakeholder evaluation approach to requirements elicitation and user interface design [18]. The study design combines several qualitative human machine interaction (HMI) design frameworks/methods, including realist ethnography [19, 20], persona-based design [21] and participatory design [22].

Overall, requirements specification and system development involves several iterative activities pertaining to (1) personae specification, (2) requirement elicitation, (3) design and prototyping and (4) evaluation. Human factors research considers patients with different treatment paths and outcomes (including palliative). Overall, it spans clinical activity and patient experience across different process gates defined in the care pathway.

As indicated in Table 1 below, research activity is structured into three overall research phases. Each phase is associated with different research sub-phases.

**Table 1.** Research phases & status

| Phase | # | Title | Description | Schedule | Status |
|---|---|---|---|---|---|
| 1 | 1 | Requirements gathering | Field research with key stakeholders (interview and observations with clinical team – N = 10, two phases of codesign workshops with clinical team N = 15) | 2017/2018 | Complete |
| | 2 | Development of software & user interface prototypes | Specification of data architecture | | |
| | 3 | Preliminary evaluation of prototypes | Co-design/evaluation of prototypes with stakeholders – N = 10) | | |
| 2 | 1 | HF analysis | Literature review. Analysis of stakeholder requirements (phase 1) HF evaluation of software prototypes (phase 2) Specification of process gates, target behaviors and information flows (patient and clinical team) Specification of personae and requirements | 2018 | Complete |
| | 2 | Redesign: prototypes 2 | Development of prototypes for key process gates • Schedule consultation • Tele-med/consultation • MDT/diagnosis • Treatment meeting | | |
| 3 | 1 | Participatory co-design with end users | Co-design with patients and clinicians | To do | 2019 |
| | 2 | Implementation and evaluation | Implementation and evaluation in hospital setting | | |
| | 3 | Final prototype | Final specification of prototypes | | |

## 2.3 Participants

Stakeholder evaluation research involves the participation of five participant groups – (1) medical staff, (2) patients, (3) family members, (4) cancer support volunteers and (5) health informatics experts. In relation to (1), this comprises Clinicians, Nurses, Care Assistants, & Administrative staff. In relation to (2), this includes patients on the Prostate Cancer Care Pathway.

## 3   Findings

### 3.1   Clinical Areas of Focus and Technology Goals

In line with the clinical areas of focus outlined previously, the overall approach is to develop technology which (1) promotes patient experience and wellness and (2) is premised on supporting real-time communication between staff, between staff and patients, and between staff and families.

The clinical areas of focus should underpin all enhancements to the EHR. Accordingly, human factors principles associated with these areas of focus can be translated into goals for the emerging technology.

Several Human Factors Goals have been identified. These are:

- Equal access to healthcare services for all patients
- Equal opportunities for the best outcomes for all patients
- Responsive service
- Provision of a safe service
- Provision of a caring/compassionate service
- Patient focus/patient at the center of care
- Patient treated as a person and not a set of symptoms
- Patients educated about their prognosis, treatment plan and outcomes
- Patients receive appropriate written information about their prognosis and treatment plan
- Patients involved in decision making about their treatment
- Patients have a voice that is heard
- Patient dignity addressed
- Patient privacy addressed
- Effective health service
- Efficient health care delivery
- Improve team situation awareness
- Improve MDT decision making
- Address compliance in relation to process
- Reduce errors
- Promote a safe environment where team members can raise concerns
- Reduce delays in diagnosis and treatment and unnecessary treatment
- Consideration of patient interest and wellbeing in treatment decisions.

### 3.2   High Level Process Map and Process Gates for Patient and Clinical Team

Table 3 below provides an overview of the high-level prostate cancer pathway/process. As indicated in Table 3, specific processes are classified in relation to an overall type (i.e. prevention, detection etc.). Certain processes can be further sub-divided into subprocesses. For the purpose of the initial technology demonstration, it has been agreed to focus on a subset of these processes – see 3 to 9 as indicated in Table 3 below.

**Table 2.** High level process

| # | Classification | High level process | Sub process | Focus for preliminary demonstration |
|---|---|---|---|---|
| 1 | Prevention | Prevention (patient awareness and education) | | No |
| 2 | Detection | Self-referral/A & E/GP referral (PSA blood test and digital rectal examination) | | |
| 3 | Patient entered in system | Referral received by hospital | | Yes |
| | | Patient info, referral info & history added to EPR system | | |
| 4 | Consultation | Pathway manager schedule consultation and assign type | Contact patient and assess situation | |
| | | | Assign to tele-med or face to face | |
| | | Initial consultation (face to face or tele-med) with urologist | | |
| 5 | Diagnosis | Diagnostic testing | MRI and recording of results | |
| | | | Biopsy | |
| | | MDT | | |
| 6 | Treatment | Schedule treatment meeting with patient or perform benign tele-med with patient | | |
| | | Discussion & agreement on treatment plan | | |
| | | Treatment | | No |
| 7 | Discharge | | | |
| 8 | Aftercare | | | |
| 9 | Monitoring in the community | Monitoring | | |
| | | Follow-up/recurrence | | |
| 10 | Palliative care | | | |
| 11 | Clinical learning | | | |

**Table 3.** States to be achieved (clinical professionalism)

| States to promote/support | States to manage/mitigate & reduce | States to avoid |
|---|---|---|
| Teamwork | Fear of speaking out | Poor teamwork |
| Understanding the patient and the context of that patient's illness | Not understanding the patient and the context of that patient's illness | Avoiding relating to patient/understanding the patient |
| Listening to patient story - diseases, their new problem, their social situation, and their beliefs | Not listening to patient story | Patient story not considered by team |
| Effective team communications | Not reporting issues around care | Poor communication |
| Team situation awareness | Patient wishes not considered | Team members not speaking out |

An initial workflow was specified in relation to work activity pertaining to gates 3 to 9. This is depicted in Fig. 1 below.

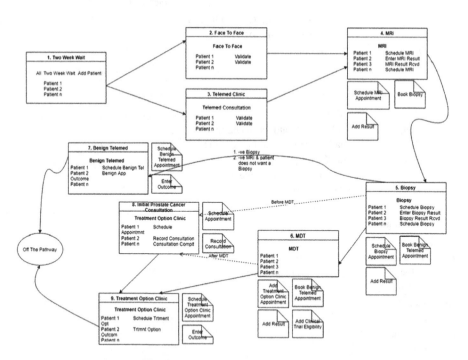

**Fig. 1.** Preliminary process workflow

### 3.3  Patient Process Gates

Process maps have been advanced from a patient perspective. This includes the process workflow, patient experience/activities and the associated pathway (see Appendix 1).

### 3.4  Key Process Gates

The emerging technology should focus on those process gates where (1) there is a direct interface with the patient/family and (2) patient preferences and quality of life issues should be considered. This includes:

- Patient consultation
- MDT Meeting & Diagnosis
- Treatment meeting

### 3.5  Patient and Clinical Team States

States have been defined for both clinical teams and patients (see Appendix 2: Table 5).

### 3.6  Patient Data Map, Processes and Stakeholders

A high-level data map has been advanced which depicts different types of patient information which is captured as the patient moves through the pathway. As indicated in Fig. 2, the categories include: (1) patient personal details, (2) process information, (3) appointments information, (4) clinical information (this pathway), (5) clinical information (other pathways/processes), (6) process stage/consultant specific information (linking to key clinical areas of focus), and (7) administrative information.

### 3.7  Extending Existing Electronic Health Record

The intelligent Electronic Health Record (EHR) should reflect a holistic view of the person – capturing information about (1) their needs and ability, (2) their health and (3) associated communications across the continuum of the cancer care process. The clinical areas of focus should underpin all enhancements to the EHR. Accordingly, human factors principles associated with these areas of focus can be translated into goals for the emerging technology. The new technology should promote key states for (1) the patient and family, along with (2) the clinical team – as defined previously in Tables 2 and 3.

### 3.8  Important Role of Cancer Nurse Specialist (CNS)

Preliminary research indicates the key role played by the Cancer Nurse Specialist (CNS) in terms of (1) advocating for the patient (i.e. consideration of patient need, context and preferences at the MDT), (2) providing emotional support to the patient (for example, treatment meeting with patient), (3) ensuring the patient gets the appropriate care, and (3) linking up the patient with psychosocial supports, including supports in the community. Overall, this technology should support the task activities of the CNS.

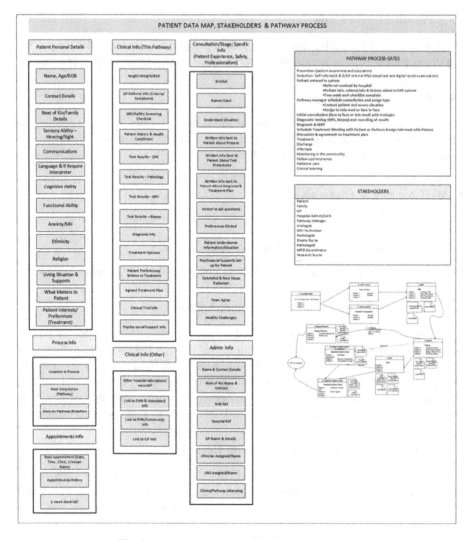

**Fig. 2.** Patient data map, stakeholders & pathway

## 4   Emerging Concept and Initial Validation

### 4.1   Emerging Concepts

Several early stage technology concepts and associated user interface prototypes have been advanced. Figure 3 below depicts an early stage prototype for MDT & Diagnosis. This initial prototype (Fig. 3) requires optimisation in relation to a horizontal projetor layout. In addition, different information views may be required (with/without MDT report information).

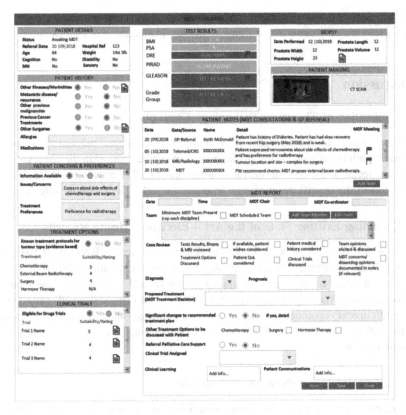

**Fig. 3.** Example prototype: MDT & diagnosis

## 4.2   Initial Validation

The digital transformation of oncology pathways will enable systems to be designed to support the treatment of patients and the communication and coordination needs of the multi-professional care team members. Preliminary feedback indicates that this technology will yield many benefits from both a patient experience and patient safety perspective. Potential benefits include:

- Build trust between clinical team and patients
- Focus attention on patient and family involvement
- Promote patient briefing and debriefing – embed in workflow for any consultation with patient
- Promote patient participation and listening to the patient – embed questions concerning patient questions, interests and concerns
- Promote compassion and respect (embed questions – how you are feeling)
- Improve team situation awareness and decision making
- Reduce errors
- Support compliance
- Promote a safe environment where team members can raise concerns

- Reduce delays in diagnosis and treatment and unnecessary treatment
- Consideration of patient interest and wellbeing in treatment decisions

## 5    Discussion

### 5.1    Application of Theory to Technology Concepts

The above research demonstrates how theoretical concepts pertaining to patient experience, patient safety and staff professionalism can be utilized in the context of new cancer care technology. As demonstrated in relation to MDT & Diagnosis (see Fig. 2), this had led to the specification of new information fields in workflow screens.

### 5.2    Extending Existing State of the Art – Electronic Health Records

Further, it illustrates a new approach to Electronic Health Records (EHR). The emerging EHR combines information about (1) patient identity, ability and need, (2) patient/clinician communications and (3) heath related information. The inclusion of information pertaining to (1) patient identity, ability and need reflects and (2) patient/clinical communications represents a paradigm shift in relation to existing implementations of EHR. Specifically, it reflects a relationship centered approach to the design of EHR's.

### 5.3    Staff Training and Person-Centered Care

Staff training is a key focus of the implementation plan. As noted previously, clinicians observed that this new technology should enhance person centered care and not hamper interpersonal communications. It is anticipated that best practices will be established as part of the implementation program. That is, staff will provide feedback as to how this is working in practice, and work together in relation to establishing usage protocols. Further, it is anticipated that this may also yield user interface design recommendations for specific interface screens.

### 5.4    Study Limits, Areas for Further Research and Next Steps

Research is also underway in relation to the application of voice interaction and other multimodal inputs types, for clinician workflows. It is anticipated that this may simplify data entry and result in time savings. Further, this may impact on the acceptability of the proposed system.

The emerging prototypes will be further specified as part of co-design/validation activities with relevant stakeholders. Further feedback will be elucidated during a pilot implementation of the proposed software with at the hospital.

Follow up human factors research will be undertaken to assess the lessons learned from the initial implementation. It is anticipated that this will provide insight as to what is acceptable to end users, how the technology is used in real operations, and usability issues. Further, it will provide information regarding challenges at an organizational level (including process change, resourcing and capacity and cultural issues) and technical challenges. This feedback is necessary to validate the proposed solution.

# 6 Conclusions

The provision of a patient centered service, underpinned by (1) strong teamwork and attention to professionalism, and (2) appropriate information technology (i.e. accurate and up to date medical information about the patient shared fully between all stakeholders, at the point of care), is a key goal for the NHS. Overall, the proposed technology attempts to address this goal, and establish an appropriate balance between focusing on (1) cure/cancer treatment outcomes and (2) quality of life.

The initial stakeholder feedback indicates that this technology provides an opportunity to influence the behavior and actions of clinicians, enhancing professionalism and impacting on patient experience and patient safety.

The digital transformation of oncology pathways will enable systems to be designed to support the treatment of patients and the communication and coordination needs of the multi-professional care team members. In principle, this will yield benefits at a patient and staff level.

The innovative fusion of oncology workflows with existing Electronic Health Records technology is applicable to other cancer care pathways.

# Appendix 1: Patient Process and Experience

See Table 4.

**Table 4.** Process gates for patient & patient experience & high-level pathway

| # | Classification | High level process | Sub process | Pathway |
|---|---|---|---|---|
| 1 | Prevention | Patient awareness and education | Education | Community |
| | | | Self-management of health | |
| 2 | Detection | Patient experiences symptoms | Patient experiencing symptoms (or not) | Community |
| | | | Patient awareness of symptoms (or not) | |
| | | | Patient concern over symptoms/patient avoidance of systems (or not) | |
| | | | Doubts and worries | |

(*continued*)

**Table 4.** (*continued*)

| # | Classification | High level process | Sub process | Pathway |
|---|---|---|---|---|
| | | | Communication with family/friends re symptoms (or not) | |
| | | | Decision to follow up on symptoms (schedule appointment with GP or pending severity/symptoms, presentation to A & E) | |
| | | Initial health check with GP (or A & E Dr) | Review of symptoms | Community – GP service |
| | | | Tests (PSA blood test and digital rectal examination) | |
| | | | Feedback about tests | |
| | | GP follow up & patient referral | Pending outcome, patient receives referral to hospital | Community – GP service |
| | | | Patient receives initial education information | |
| | | | GP set expectations re next steps | |
| 3 | Initial consultation/ appointment | Telephone call with pathway manager | Confirmation of hospital appointment (tele-med or face to face) and process | Hospital/prostate cancer pathway |
| | | Initial consultation with urologist/clinician and team (face to face or tele-med) | Review symptoms Set expectations re process and nature of tests Obtain education information (or not) Confirm MRI | |
| 4 | Diagnosis | Patient attends hospital for diagnostic testing (MRI) and undergoes MRI | | Hospital/prostate cancer pathway |
| | | Patient attends hospital for biopsy and undergoes test | | |
| | | Patient obtains feedback about tests & talks to CNS for first time | | |
| | | Patient finds out that needs to meet consultant and to bring person with them or Patient finds out that not | | |

(*continued*)

**Table 4.** (*continued*)

| # | Classification | High level process | Sub process | Pathway |
|---|---|---|---|---|
| | | have cancer but symptoms to be monitored | | |
| 5 | Treatment meeting | Patient prepares for treatment meeting | Patient prepares for meeting with Consultant Patient concern over test results Patient suspects cancer prognosis Patient read available literature Living with uncertainty Waiting | Hospital/prostate cancer Pathway |
| | | Patient and family meet with Consultant & CNS to obtain test results, prognosis and discuss treatment plan | Patient finds out have cancer Discussion of prognosis and treatment options Agreement on treatment plan or postpone decision Obtain education information (or not) Obtain info about psychosocial supports (or not) Assignment to clinical trial | |
| 6 | Treatment | Patient digests prognosis & prepares for treatment | Taking it all in/acceptance Support – family/friends Hormone treatment Patient obtains psychosocial supports (or not) Contact with CNS (or not) Self-education (or not) | Hospital/prostate cancer pathway Community |
| | | Treatment in hospital/outpatient | Admissions Meets treatment team Undergoing treatment (surgery, radiotherapy, chemotherapy) Life in hospital/as outpatient Coping with treatment Living with uncertainty Supports | |

(*continued*)

**Table 4.** (*continued*)

| # | Classification | High level process | Sub process | Pathway |
|---|---|---|---|---|
| | | | Contacts with CNS | |
| | | Feedback about treatment | | |
| 7 | Discharge | Treatment ends/discharge from hospital | | Hospital/prostate cancer pathway Community |
| 8 | Aftercare | Aftercare (at home) and dealing with initial side effects of treatment | | Community |
| | | Returning to 'normal life' and managing treatment side effects (mid and long term) | | |
| 9 | Survivorship | Survivorship & monitoring of symptoms (GP, PHN) | | Community |
| 10 | Recurrence | | | Hospital/prostate cancer pathway Community |
| 11 | Palliative care | | | Hospital/prostate cancer pathway Community |

# Appendix 2: States to Be Achieved (Patient Experience and Safety)

**Table 5.** States to be achieved (patient experience & safety)

| States to promote/support | States to manage/mitigate & reduce | States to avoid |
|---|---|---|
| Calm - although, dealing with uncertainty - living in the unknown - living in an indeterminate state | Anxiety and fear | Being treated like a set of symptoms - objectification of patient |
| Coping - dealing with the intensity of a life altering experience of being diagnosed with cancer | Loss of independence | Loss of independence |
| Living in the present | Stress | Loss of control/sense of powerlessness |
| Independence | Feeling lost | Psychosocial and emotional stress |
| Understanding situation - knowing situation | Uncertainty | Feeling lost |

(*continued*)

**Table 5.** (*continued*)

| States to promote/support | States to manage/mitigate & reduce | States to avoid |
|---|---|---|
| Have an identity that matters - who they are and how they are feeling matters - being understood - you are more than an illness, you have a name, you have a family situation, you have a work situation, you are at a point in the treatment, you have gone through X, Y & Z | Loss of control/sense of powerlessness | Loss of confidence in clinical team (misinformation, error in diagnosis, inappropriate expectations set) |
| Being treated like a human being - not set of symptoms | Discomfort and pain | Loss of trust in clinical team (misinformation, error in diagnosis, inappropriate expectations set) |
| Feeling of being in control - not powerless | Negative side-effects from treatment | Anxiety and fear |
| Feeling of being safe | Difficulty understanding information | Patient being misinformed |
| Trust in clinical team (on your side, understand you, getting the best treatment, not with-holding information) | Patient misinformed | Confusion |
| Confidence in clinical team | Loss of identity | Late presentation to Dr |
| Listened too - preferences, concerns, interests | Disempowerment | Isolation during treatment |
| Patient time not being wasted or under allude - efficient process - waiting times, avoidance of delays getting blood tests and x-rays, clinical team have right information about patient situation | Fear | Isolation after treatment |
| Patient's family/friends are involved - social supports | Reduced social connection - involvement of family/friends | Reduced social connection - involvement of family/friends |
| Wellness | Physical discomfort | Self-neglect |
| Active partner in process (with team) | Patient unease/embarrassment | Lack of participation/engagement - not showing up for consultations, treatment |
| | Communication difficulties | Reduction in human contact - team |

(*continued*)

**Table 5.** (*continued*)

| States to promote/support | States to manage/mitigate & reduce | States to avoid |
|---|---|---|
| Team know who you are, specific situation and what matters | | |
| Patient being informed | Boredom | Infantilization |
| Positive patient experience (out-patient) | Sense of powerlessness | Uncertainty |
| Positive patient experience (in-patient) | Stress | Loss of identity |
| Quality of life | Frustration | Feeling unsafe |
| Appropriate expectations of care process | Confusion | |
| Understanding of treatment options and risks/benefits | Negative thinking | |
| Understanding of situation/prognosis | Depression | |
| Positive communication with clinicians | Self-neglect | |
| Access to supports/services | Lack of participation/engagement - not showing up for consultations, treatment | |
| Communication with family/friends | Feeling unsafe | |
| Awareness | | |
| Empowering person | | |
| Dignity/respect | | |
| Acceptance | | |
| Resilience/coping | | |
| Regular interaction with team | | |
| Get support/help if need it (psychosocial support services, financial support) | | |
| Patient education - understanding health impact/physical impact - general sickness, loss of appetite, low load capacity | | |
| Patient education - understanding work impact - professional limitations | | |
| Patient education - understanding social impact - | | |

(*continued*)

**Table 5.** (*continued*)

| States to promote/support | States to manage/mitigate & reduce | States to avoid |
|---|---|---|
| family life and leisure activities | | |
| Patient education - understanding emotional/psychological impact - loneliness, fear, feeling cut off from normal routine, loss of control | | |
| Patient privacy and dignity upheld | | |
| Patient is comfortable in treatment environment - privacy, space, noise, lighting, food, access to entertainment, own room, comfortable room, comfortable chair for chemo | | |
| Patient is safe in treatment environment - germs, access to nurses, avoidance of harm, avoidance of error | | |
| Patient has equal access to best treatment | | |
| Patient has access to specialist cancer nurse | | |
| Patient has access to clinical trials (if match criteria) | | |
| Patient is self-managing (at home/in the community) | | |
| Patient is vigilant and actively tracking symptoms (at home/in the community) | | |

# References

1. Siegel, R., Ma, J., Zou, Z., Jemal, A.: CA cancer. J. Clin. **64**(1), 9–29 (2014). https://doi.org/10.3322/caac.21208
2. Thompson, I., et al.: Guideline for the management of clinically localized prostate cancer: 2007 update. J. Urol. **177**(6), 2106–2131 (2007)
3. Institute of Medicine: Crossing the Quality Chasm: A New Health System for the 21st Century, vol. 6. National Academy Press, Washington, DC (2001)
4. Starfield, B.: Is patient-centered care the same as person-focused care? Perm. J. **15**(2), 63–69 (2011)

5. Kitwood, T.: Dementia Reconsidered: The Person Comes First. Open University Press, Buckingham (1997)
6. Nolan, M.: Relationship-centred care: towards a new model of rehabilitation. Br. Int. J. Ther. Rehabil. **9**, 472–477 (2002)
7. Soklaridis, S., Ravitz, P., Adler, G., Nevo, A., Lieff, S.: Relationship-centered care in health: a 20-year scoping review. Patient Exp. J. **3**(1), 130–145 (2016)
8. Beach, M.C., Inui, T., Relationship-cantered care research network: relationship-centered care: a constructive reframing. J. Gen. Intern. Med. **21**(Suppl 1), S3–S8 (2006)
9. Wolf, J., Niederhauser, V., Marshburn, D., LaVela, S.: Defining patient experience. Patient Exp. J. **1**(1), Article no, 3 (2014)
10. Hewitson, P., Skew, A., Graham, C., Jenkinson, C., Coulter, A.: People with limiting long-term conditions report poorer experiences and more problems with hospital care. BMC Health Serv. Res. **14**, 33 (2014)
11. NHS Long term plan. https://www.longtermplan.nhs.uk/online-version/. Accessed 24 Jan 2019
12. National Cancer Patient Experience Survey 2017: National Results Summary (2017)
13. Taylor, C., Shewbridge, A., Harris, J., Green, J.: Benefits of multidisciplinary teamwork in the management of breast cancer. Breast Cancer: Targets Ther. **5**, 79–85 (2013)
14. Public Health England: Surveillance of surgical site infections in NHS hospitals in England: April 2016 to March 2017, December 2017. https://assets.publishing.service.gov.uk/government/uploads/system/uploads/attachment_data/file/666465/SSI_annual_report_NHS_hospitals_2016-17.pdf. Accessed 24 Jan 2019
15. Madden, D.: Building a culture of patient safety: report of the commission on patient safety and quality assurance. Department of Health, Ireland (2008)
16. Dixon-Woods, M., Pronovost, P.J.: Patient safety and the problem of many hands. BMJ Qual. Saf. **25**, 485–488 (2016)
17. JCP Editors: Research in review - integrating electronic health records into clinical pathways for radiation oncology reduces waiting times. J. Clin. Pathways **2**(2), 12–15 (2016)
18. Cousins, J.B., Whitmore, E., Shulha, L.: Arguments for a common set of principles for collaborative inquiry in evaluation. Am. J. Eval. **34**(1), 7–22 (2013)
19. Van Maanen, J.: Tales of the Field: On Writing Ethnography. University of Chicago Press, Chicago (1988)
20. Hammersley, M., Atkinson, P.: Ethnography: Principles in Practice, 3rd edn. Routledge, London (2007)
21. Pruitt, J., Grudin, J.: Personas: practice and theory. In: Proceedings of the 2003 Conference on Designing for User Experiences (DUX 2003), pp. 1–15. ACM, New York (2003). http://dx.doi.org/10.1145/997078.997089
22. Bødker, S., Burr, J.: The design collaboratorium. A place for usability design. ACM Trans. Comput. Hum. Interact. **9**(2), 152–169 (2002)

# Usability Testing of a Mobile Application for Alleviating Postpartum Emotional Disorders: A Case of We'll

Wen-Ko Chiou[1], Shih-Chen Lai[2], and Ding-Hau Huang[3(✉)]

[1] Chang Gung University, Taoyuan, Taiwan
[2] Ming Chi University of Technology, New Taipei City, Taiwan
[3] National Taipei University of Business, Taoyuan, Taiwan
hauhuang@ntub.edu.tw

**Abstract.** Postpartum emotional disorders depending on the severity of symptoms can be divided into postpartum blues, postpartum depression, and postpartum psychosis. Those who develop severe symptoms may intend to commit suicide or harm the newborn. Therefore, these women need professional medical assistance and care services. A previous study (Kao 2017) used social support as the basis to develop a simulation trial version of a mobile application (App), We'll, which helps women suffering from postpartum emotional disorders relieve depression via its function of interaction. The We'll app for the present study is a trial simulation version. The official version of Android We'll system hasn't been evaluated its usability yet. The purpose of the study is for the usability evaluation of Android We'll system. The researchers indicated users' usability, satisfaction, and feedback regarding the interface and functional frameworks of the current app version. This study recruited 30 participants with the inclusion criteria of Taiwanese women aged 20 to 40 years who had experience in giving birth. Task testing comprised 12 items covering all functions provide by the app. All of the participants completed all tasks. The participants were asked to perform thinking aloud during the task testing period. On the basis of the feedback to the thinking aloud process during the test, interface operation issues were categorized into three types of errors, namely, navigation error, presentation error, and control error by the nature of errors and severity regarding how the errors influenced task completion. The overall average score of the SUS was 70.5, higher than the designated standard average of the SUS. Therefore, the satisfaction toward We'll met the standard level. After the aforementioned procedure, usability task testing results were organized to determine the following problems that need to be solved. (a) Redesign the house icons of friends, family, and hospital on the home page (b) Enlarge the click area of friend and family rows (c) Improve the presentation of the EDPS test results, change the histogram into numeral score feedback, and add suggestions and reminders (d) Establish a dynamic tutorial for first-time login users.

**Keywords:** Postpartum emotional disorder · Postpartum blues · Postpartum depression · Usability test · Mobile application

© Springer Nature Switzerland AG 2019
V. G. Duffy (Ed.): HCII 2019, LNCS 11582, pp. 23–40, 2019.
https://doi.org/10.1007/978-3-030-22219-2_2

## 1 Introduction

Nowadays, technology development changes rapidly. Due to the advance of technology and medicine, we are able to cure and control many diseases. However, the flourishing modern development also brings modern plague, depression, which is difficult to be solved. The advanced and ever-changing modern development drives convenience and quality in our life but brings invisible and heavy burden to people in three aspects- physiology, psychology, and society. As a result, depression is gradually developed without being noticed. Currently, there are around 4% of total populations in the world suffering from depression and it has become one of the most common and most difficult to prevent mental diseases all over the world. In addition, the impact comes along with depression is more than what we generally recognize as feeling down in spirits or more seriously, the intention of undervaluing their own lives and committing suicide. It will invade our daily life and slowly cause sufferers losing ability and vitality in life and further lead to the status of unable to work or unable to take care of themselves in daily life. Other than corroding sufferers' psychological and physical functions, the productivity and operation in social and economic levels are reduced due to the growth of depression on a large scale. It makes depression be regarded as one of the most urgent issues that needs to be overcome.

In terms of gender, the percentage of female suffering from depression is twice than male. Pregnant or postpartum women are one of the groups with high-possibility depression suffering because most women experience drastic hormone changes during menstrual period, pregnancy and prenatal period and menopause; it will further affect emotional response. Among them, it is often seen the women at pregnancy and prenatal period suffer from postpartum emotionally handicapped. The most common symptom for postpartum emotionally handicapped is postpartum blues (baby blues) and postpartum depression (PPD). Around 50% to 80% parturient women suffer from emotional instability or temporary postpartum depression, and most parturient women who encounter the symptom will be able to improve in the short time with proper social support (including husband, family, and friends) and sufficient assistance. If the symptom of depression in low spirits lasts more than two weeks, it might cause postpartum depression. Its prevalence rate is around 10–15% (Cox et al. 1993; Darcy et al. 2011; Gavin et al. 2005).

Due to the rapid development of technology, E-mental health (EMH) service has become the application trend for current non-medication treatment. Professional functions and effective information are provided through online social media to allow users improving their mental health problems. The prevalent smart phones and tablet devices contribute to the transformation of EMH into the mode of mobile health (mHealth) service. Combining EMH with social support is one of the important links to effectively improve and reduce the risk of parturient women suffering from postpartum depression. Previous research (Kao 2015) had established an EMH system in the form of APP- We'll, Wishing Well. The system focuses on boosting parturient users' social support and self-esteem (Shaw and Gant 2002) and provides the service of self-check with Edinburgh Postnatal Depression Scale (EPDS) (Shen et al. 2015) in order to further relieve and prevent postpartum emotionally handicapped and depression problems.

The symptom of postpartum emotionally handicapped will usually disappear automatically in several days after delivery. Few serious cases might be involved with postpartum depression (prevalence rate is around 10–15%) and parturient women might have the intention to commit suicide and the risk of injuring the newborn. However, the symptom usually gets worse and worse because parturient women may not able to be aware of the symptom or are ignored by family, relatives, and friends so that they fail to offer timely proper assistance and support.

Based on the principle of "an ounce of prevention is worth a pound of cure", the early the status of postpartum emotionally handicapped can be found, the better the effectiveness of intervention will be. Previous research (Kao 2017) had developed APP system to support postpartum emotionally handicapped according to the theories and concepts of postpartum emotionally handicapped. A mobile application program structure, "We'll, Wishing Well", has been established and the system uses the interaction mode of "making a wish" as the main activity for users to making a wish to Wishing Well with an expecting and positive attitude. The wishes are solved and fulfilled through the efforts of the online APP users to enhance users' mental status and quality. We'll get you well; therefore, the APP is named as "We'll, Wishing Well" (Fig. 1).

**Fig. 1.** The homepage of APP "We'll"

The system of the previous research is a version of simulation testing. Therefore, the research evaluates three performance evaluation of effectiveness, efficiency, and satisfaction through usability testing based on the current framework of We'll. The problems related to APP operation or interface are improved and modified through the results of usability testing and further advance its effectiveness, efficiency, and satisfaction.

## 2  Literature Review

### 2.1  Postpartum Emotionally Handicapped

Women at pregnancy and prenatal period might have drastic hormone changes before and after delivery and cause the symptom of postpartum emotionally handicapped; its prevalence rate is around 40%–80% (Evins and Theofrastous 1997). Other than the impact from physiological conditions, parturient mental status might also be affected by external pressure, such as pressure of childcare, marital relationship, work and family (Stowe and Nemeroff 1995). These lead to the extension of postpartum emotionally handicapped symptom.

Postpartum emotionally handicapped is the most common issue on women at postpartum period and it can be divided into three stages according to the duration of the illness and the seriousness of the illness. They are postpartum blues (maternity blue or baby blues), postpartum depression (PPD) and postpartum psychosis respectively (Robertson et al. 2004).

Postpartum blues is the most common situation of postpartum emotionally handicapped and its incidence rate is around 30%–75% (O'hara et al. 1984). It usually occurs in a few days after delivery and the symptom includes emotional instability, easy to lose temper, sleep disorder and depraved appetite. Relevant emotional and physiological disorder symptoms are usually minor and they will be self-healed gradually in a couple of days; no medication or other treatment will be required (Kennerley and Gath 1989; Pitt 1973). If the symptom lasts for more than two weeks but is not getting better, it is likely to trigger postpartum depression. It is the major depression under non-psychosis with the prevalence rate of 10%–15% (Cox et al. 1993; O'hara et al. 1991; Wisner et al. 2002). Its symptom is slightly similar to maternity blues and parturient women might feel valueless, lose interests towards life or got bored of life. The cycle of the symptom usually lasts for more than two weeks or several months and the sufferers might have the intention of committing suicide or the risk of injuring the newborn if the level of the illness is serious. There are around 20% parturient women ending their lives by committing suicide due to the postpartum depression (Lindahl et al. 2005), and it requires medical assistance and care. Postpartum psychosis is the most serious and rare illness among the postpartum emotionally handicapped symptom and the probability is one to two in one thousand (around 0.1% to 0.2%) (O'hara et al. 1984). It might cause significant emotional instability on parturient women and even involve with the symptom of reality deviation, including illusion or delusion (Brockington et al. 1981). Therefore, it usually requires medical assistance and hospitalized for observation and treatment.

### 2.2  Current Status and Development of Mobile Health and E-Mental Health

The original concept of mobile health (mHealth) is to use mobile medical instrument or equipment in the medical clinic to provide patients more convenient medical behaviors of inquiry and health examination. The development until now is that the mobile health has used information and communication technology, such as computer, mobile phone, and communications satellite, to provide broader medical services and information. The current scope of mobile health includes (1) mobile medical equipment installation and medical services in the hospital and (2) distance medical care and health care outside the hospital.

E-mental health (EMH) is the trend of current mental medical care service. It provides professional functions to solve the problems of mental health. Following four types of medical services are provided through internet via the media of social media, chat room, forum, bulletin board system, and blog: (1) information related to medical care (Lambousis et al. 2002; Santor et al. 2007), (2) illness screening, evaluation, and monitoring (Becker et al. 2008; Chinman et al. 2007; Diamond et al. 2010; Donker et al. 2009; Gringras et al. 2006; Gualtieri 2007; Heron and Smyth 2010; Khazaal et al. 2009), (3) medical intervention (Bergström et al. 2010; Khanna and Kendall 2010; Lindahl et al. 2005), and (4) social support (Scharer 2005).

With the advance of technology and the popularity of smart phone, the service format of e-Health is pushed towards to the service format of mobile health APP. Doctors and patients can carry out self-health management or remote patient information control through relevant application programs in the mobile phone. According to the survey of current mobile medical APP done by WHO, the search of depression is ranked the second, only after diabetes (Martínez-Pérez et al. 2013). Therefore, it will definitely be able to increase the intention of APP use and satisfaction of APP if the functions of mobile medical APP, We'll, Wishing Well, can be effectively integrated as well as the usability of application programs can be advanced.

## 2.3 Usability Evaluation of Interactive System

ISO 9241 defines usability as a product or service that can be used by specific users efficiently and effectively to achieve a specific target or complete the task. Usability also means the method used during the process of design to advance the level of easy-to-use for products or services.

Nielsen (1994) proposed usability is mainly to explore how to communicate with users, observe users' working environment and conduct scenario analysis in order to find out problems related to product usability. Usability is to allow representative users to operate products or experience services as well as execute a series of tasks in order to test the system. When conducting usability testing, it should follow three indicators of effectiveness, efficiency, and satisfaction as the standards for practical evaluation. Usability evaluation can be divided into the following five elements (Nielsen 1994; Shneiderman and Plaisant 2005): (1) learnability, (2) efficiency, (3) memorability, (4) errors and (5) satisfaction.

Usability scenario testing has been widely applied to the processes of product evaluation and system development. Usability evaluation for system interface must find out the characteristics of the system first before following the characteristics to determine the attributes (such as learnability, errors, and efficiency) and functions that are to be evaluated.

The measurement standard used to execute usability testing can be classified into the following indicators (Albert and Tullis 2013; Sauro and Lewis 2016). Task success: whether users complete the task; task time: the time users spend to complete the task;

error: unexpected errors when users execute the task, such as missing or pressing the wrong button, and errors sometimes delay the execute time or even lead to the failure of the task; efficiency: the dimension for efficiency evaluation is wide and it can be defined as the possession of higher efficiency if the product allows users to complete the task in the shorter time with lower occurrence of error; learnability: beginners knowledge towards products from unfamiliar to professional is the learning process of the user's. The level of difficulty and the speed of familiarity of the process are regarded as learnability.

The evaluation elements for usability mentioned above and the indicators for usability testing vary according to using status of different products or services, content of testing, or target users of the final purpose to make choices of testing standards in order to enhance the effectiveness of usability testing.

## 2.4   Relevant Research for APP Usability Evaluation

From above, usability testing evaluation can set up the evaluation indicators according to different product demands and the three indicators of effectiveness, efficiency, and satisfaction mentioned in ISO 9241-11 are used as the standards for practical evaluation (Gunter et al. 2016; O'Malley et al. 2014; Mirkovic et al. 2014). According to Gunter's research (2016) on usability evaluation and development of APP: WoundCheck that provides patients after surgery the service of monitoring wound after surgery, main function of the APP is to provide users photo records. The final target for the design is to monitor wounds after users being discharged from hospital and during return visits. The evaluation of usability done in this study is to use user's operation on six tasks and system usability scale (SUS) as standards for satisfaction evaluation. It is conducted in two stages; the functional problems found after the first stage test will be slightly adjusted and the version of the revised function will be tested the usability evaluation in the second stage. The APP version after improvement in the second stage is with better using efficiency and task completion rate than the version in the first stage. Therefore, it approves an APP that combines mobile phone application program with wound monitoring after surgery is the design that meets effectiveness of usability and the expectation from users.

Mirkovic et al. (2014) conducted a research of usability evaluation on APP: Connect Mobile, that implements disease management on patients with cancer. It tests usability evaluation on general smart phone and tablet device to compare APP usability and difference between the two devices. After completing usability task testing and semi-structured interview, the research reveals the difference of usability test on smart phone and tablet device. Users' effectiveness and efficiency in completing the task will be affected by different devices used. Therefore, the research suggests different APP system versions should be designed for different devices.

Lim et al. (2015) aimed to develop a mobile phone APP that is to be used for medical work at the areas with insufficient medical resources for immediate toxemia of pregnancy on the parturient women in the area. The study is a usability evaluation test done in two stages, and it is assessed with scenario testing, think aloud, and questionnaire survey. In order to classify the usability errors found during the testing, the study defines errors at usability evaluation testing as (1) navigation errors,

(2) presentation errors, and (3) control usage errors. The order of priority usability problem-handling will be determined by the frequency and seriousness of the error occurred.

English et al. (2016) investigated APP development for child care at areas with limited medical resources in order to reduce child mortality and implemented usability testing on the APP system. The users of the system are set medical practitioners with different education background as default. The testing process is divided into two stages and time and number of errors to complete the task by respondents are collected during the testing. In order to define the reason of error and improve usability problems effectively, The study classifies the error of the task into three types: (1) navigation errors, (2) control usage errors, and (3) outcome errors. The levels of seriousness according to the impact on the task are (1) low severity: it won't affect users completing the task but will affect the using efficiency and satisfaction; (2) medium severity: users have problems of operation when executing the task and it will affect effectiveness, efficiency, and satisfaction, and high severity: users will fail to complete the task. The study defines and classifies the type of error in order to provide assistance to subsequent improvement and optimization on the APP system.

Currently, a lot of APP systems use usability testing to evaluate its system and verify system effectiveness, efficiency, and satisfaction through the combination of task evaluation and questionnaire. From literature review, it is found defining the characteristics of operational errors and the seriousness will be able to effectively contribute to the subsequent functional improvement on the system. Therefore, evaluation methods mentioned on above literatures will be referred for the usability evaluation on our research.

# 3   Methods

## 3.1   Experimental Design

The research uses usability task testing to provide respondents user experience of participating in real situation. Through data of usability testing and respondents' feedback on the interface and usability problems of the current We'll APP version, they are used as the basis of subsequent modification on APP in the future.

In order to meet the standardization of the equipment used, the usability testing uses unified ASUS ZenPad 8.0 Tablet for testing. Canon 760D single lens reflex camera and Lumix LF-7 bridge camera are used for behind-the-scenes footage during usability testing and recording interface process of operational scenario tasks. The research is divided into four stages. The first stage is research introduction to explain the procedure and purpose of usability testing, basic operation of the interface, and scenario task as well as allows respondents to get familiar with the operation of ASUS ZenPad 8.0 Tablet. The second stage is the usability scenario test done by respondents and respondents are asked to think aloud during the process in order to encourage respondents to express their thinking process during the testing. In the third stage, satisfaction evaluation questionnaire will be carried out after completing scenario testing, including demographic questionnaire to record the respondent's basic information and system usability scale (SUS) to evaluate the usability satisfaction on APP. In the final stage, an interview with five post-testing qualitative questions will be done on respondents.

Process of usability testing includes the following four stages: (1) respondent recruitment, (2) usability task testing, (3) satisfaction questionnaire survey, and (4) post-testing qualitative interview; as shown on Fig. 2.

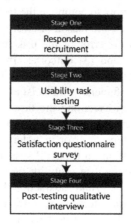

**Fig. 2.** Usability testing flow chart

The target of usability testing is (1) to test under the condition of scenario task to understand the common operational errors during the process; (2) to find out satisfaction on APP through the questionnaire survey; (3) to guide respondents providing feedback on usability and satisfaction on the APP during interview. The problems on operational process or interface of the APP that are found through the data and feedback collected from respondents during the testing will be modified and improved immediately.

During the implementation of the scenario task, the number of times that respondents need to be reminded and the type of error during the task implementation will be classified and recorded. The reminding standards and definition of each type of error are explained as below:

(1) Remind: The delay of operational process caused by the same step operated by the respondent for more than two times during the testing or the assistance requested by the respondent actively will generate the action of reminding; the reminded operational problems and types should be recorded.
(2) Navigation error: The function provided by the interface that fails to guide the respondent to achieve the function or feedback pre-set during the implementation of the scenario task and causes time delay of implementation will be classified as navigation error.

(3) Presentation error: The icon problems on the interface that cause the respondent fails to judge the function or makes wrong judgment and further delay the task will be classified as presentation error.

(4) Control usage error: If the time delay is caused by respondent being not able to enter the demand message during the testing or executing wrong functions and might further affect the completion of the task, it will be defined as control usage error.

## 3.2  Respondent

The research recruits 30 respondents for the experiment. The recruitment conditions are (1) women that have pregnant and delivery experience and have children, (2) women with age between 18 and 45 years who are still planning for pregnancy or have opportunities to give birth, and (3) women who have smart phone and experience of using it for more than four years as well as the habit of using tablet device in the daily life.

Exclusion criteria on the respondent includes (1) women with age more than 45 years old, (2) women who have pregnant experience but without delivery experience, and (3) pregnant women with foreign nationality or who cannot read Chinese due to the current system and scale are all presented in Chinese.

## 3.3  Introduction of Usability Scenario Task Testing

In order to test the usability and effectiveness of We'll, Wishing Well, respondents are recruited for scenario task testing. Respondents must complete 12 preset tasks during the test, and the content of the tasks covers all of the functions provided by APPP. The step and content of the scenario tasks are as shown on Table 1.

## 3.4  System Usability Scale (SUS)

The study uses system usability scale (SUS) developed by John Brooke in 1986 to measure the respondent's subjective perception on operational interface and usability.

# 4  Results and Discussion

## 4.1  Analysis of the Respondents

The study recruited 30 respondents in total, and case enrollment was from April 30th, 2018 to September 11th, 2018. 90% of the respondents were primipara, 60% of them used aided APP during pregnancy, and all of the respondents had the experience of using smart phone for more than 4 years.

## 4.2  Analysis of Scenario Task Testing

Table 2 shows the number of times of reminding when executing the task and the number of total errors of each task during the usability testing of APP- We'll, Wishing

**Table 1.** Content of usability scenario task

| Variable | Content of the task |
|---|---|
| Task 1 | Log in APP with FB account and enter personal details |
| Task 2 | Take a screenshot of the first emotional state test result done on APP (Edinburgh questionnaire) |
| Task 3 | Click houses of friends' and search friends from the left column to add one good friend |
| Task 4 | Click your house and search family members from the left column to add one family member |
| Task 5 | Throw a gold coin to the wishing well, make a wish for action assistance, and choose to open to the public |
| Task 6 | Throw a gold coin to the wishing well, make a wish for expressing emotion, and choose not to open to the public. (Choose to make the wish to either family member or friend) |
| Task 7 | Click houses of friends' and search friends from the left column and select to deliver the gold coin to the friend in the first priority |
| Task 8 | Click houses of friends' and search friends from the left column. Select the friend in the first priority and select the function of visiting good friends to reply his/her wish |
| Task 9 | Clink your house and search family members from the left column. Select the family member in the first priority to enter setup to remove family relationship |
| Task 10 | Click knowledge of health education in the hospital, select notice of postpartum care center, answer questions after reading the notice to obtain the gold coin, and take a screenshot |
| Task 11 | Throw a gold coin to the wishing well, make a wish for specific experience and knowledge, and choose to make it public. Upload the screenshot from task 2 and task 10 |
| Task 12 | Log out App |

Well. The 30 respondents recruited at the stage all completed the entire scenario task testing during the tested period, and the final statistics revealed 93 times of task reminding were executed as well as 8 times of navigation error, 50 times of presentation error, and 6 times of control error were accumulated.

The reminding standard used for the usability testing in the research was the action of reminding would be done when the delay of the operational process was caused by the respondent operating the same step for more than two times or respondent requesting assistant actively during the task testing. During the testing, most of the respondents were not able to distinguish the houses of friends' and their own smoothly and it caused the delay of the task execution while some respondents said they forgot which icon of house on EDPS questionnaire should be clicked to guide the function. Through the observation during the testing, it revealed one of the key reasons that respondents need reminding is the difficulty in identifying the icon of house function.

Presentation error was the more frequent type of error occurred during the testing, and it could be imputed to task (3) click houses of friends' and search friends from the left column to add one good friend and task (4) click your house and search family

**Table 2.** Record of times of each type of error

| Task | Remind | Navigation error | Presentation error | Control error |
|------|--------|------------------|--------------------|---------------|
| 1 | 10 | 0 | 2 | 3 |
| 2 | 11 | 0 | 7 | 0 |
| 3 | 18 | 3 | 15 | 0 |
| 4 | 15 | 0 | 9 | 0 |
| 5 | 10 | 2 | 4 | 1 |
| 6 | 0 | 0 | 0 | 0 |
| 7 | 4 | 1 | 1 | 0 |
| 8 | 7 | 0 | 5 | 0 |
| 9 | 4 | 0 | 0 | 1 |
| 10 | 2 | 0 | 4 | 0 |
| 11 | 11 | 2 | 3 | 1 |
| 12 | 1 | 0 | 0 | 0 |
| Total | 93 | 8 | 50 | 6 |

members from the left column to add one family member. There were 18 respondents reflected the houses of friends and their own on the homepage of APP were with very low identifiability when executing the two tasks. It caused confusion and led to mis-judgment during task execution. Homepage of We'll, Wishing Well is as Fig. 3.

**Fig. 3.** Homepage of We'll APP (the first one on the left is user's own house, middle one is hospital, and the first one on the right is friend's house)

There were 8 times of navigation error in the testing. Respondents expressed the design for menu clicking among friends and family members were not intuitive enough at task (3) click houses of friends' and search friends from the left column to add one good friend. The design on APP was to click the name of the friend or family member to show the window of functional option, but respondents repeat-clicked the icon of friends or family members with intuition during the operation. Therefore, APP system was not able to show the window of functional option. The interface of friend list on We'll, Wishing Well is as shown on Fig. 4.

**Fig. 4.** Interface of friends on We'll APP (the left column is the list of friends)

There were 6 times of control error, including 4 of the respondents were students but there was no option of student on the menu design for occupation on APP when they first logged in and required to enter the personal details. As a result, they used service industry as an alternative and it was classified as control error because the correct information was not able to be entered. In addition, many respondents reflected after completing Edinburgh Questionnaire (EDPS) for task (2) that the test result used bar chart and color for identification (green: low severity; yellow: medium severity; red: high severity) and they were not able to precisely interpret the testing results and reminding of the questionnaire; as shown on Fig. 5.

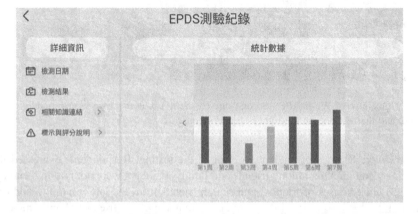

**Fig. 5.** Interface of post-testing records for Edinburgh Questionnaire (EDPS) on We'll APP (Color figure online)

### 4.3   Analysis of Scenario Task Execution Time

Average time used to complete each task is shown on Table 3.

**Table 3.** Table showing time used for each scenario task

| Task | Mean | SD | Min | Max |
|------|------|------|-----|-----|
| 1 | 123.83 | 47.36 | 66 | 280 |
| 2 | 64.9 | 18.95 | 36 | 129 |
| 3 | 51.33 | 17.81 | 30 | 103 |
| 4 | 35.17 | 12.99 | 15 | 78 |
| 5 | 44.57 | 13.23 | 26 | 75 |
| 6 | 39.23 | 10.57 | 16 | 56 |
| 7 | 34.17 | 18.44 | 9 | 118 |
| 8 | 42.23 | 27.83 | 16 | 121 |
| 9 | 29.6 | 10.55 | 13 | 53 |
| 10 | 50.6 | 14.09 | 23 | 82 |
| 11 | 51.53 | 15.72 | 32 | 87 |
| 12 | 21.93 | 12.43 | 6 | 58 |
| Total | 49.09 | 10.31 | 6 | 280 |
| | | | | Time (sec) |

### 4.4   Analysis of Satisfaction on System Usability

The average point of the system usability scale (SUS) questionnaire done by the 30 respondents in the study is 70.5 and it is greater than the average SUS point of 68, which shows the satisfaction on We'll meets the standard. The simulation testing version of SUS questionnaire points on the previous research is 78.54. The points for both simulation version and the Android version used for the study fall in the interval of level C. Therefore, there is no significant difference of usability evaluation between the two systems and they both achieve the point better than average, which represent the system is affirmed and recognized by users.

### 4.5   Discussion

The study conducts usability evaluation on We'll mobile APP version to verify the usability of its APP version and find out the operational problems on the interface or functions. According to the data of the testing results, the problems to be improved on We'll are analyzed and summarized as well as correction proposals are proposed and executed in order to achieve the target of APP interface and functional design optimization.

The previous developed We'll system framework according to social support and established the version of simulator. The research only tested usability testing on scenario task on the three functions provided: (1) real-time testing: providing Edinburgh questionnaire testing, (2) formal support: providing professional health education knowledge, such as notice for maternal women, and (3) non-formal support: providing the function of wishing well to advance social support through making wishes. The research focuses on more details and designs 12 tasks for usability scenario testing in terms of the main functions provided by APP, including basic information, navigation function, interface operation, and We'll. A lot of usability data and interface operational problems that are not known from the previous research are found out through scenario task test.

Depression issues and social impact are emphasized more and more in recent academic research. "Depression Monitor" APP established by Nasser (2012) has completed the development and can be downloaded free of charge on APP store provided by Apple; as shown on Fig. 6. Depression Monitor APP provides depression evaluation scale (Patient Health Questionnaire-9, PHQ-9) to allow users using PHQ-9 to test their depression status through APP. Furthermore, the previous research on depression issues focused on postpartum depression women and developed We'll APP to introduce the most common Edinburgh postnatal depression scale to screen out postnatal women's mental state. Both Depression Monitor and We'll APP provide scale screening tool for the area but Depression Monitor only provides scale screening, integration, and transmission through one-way information (that is, users fill out the scale and submit it to the system for system to provide the feedback to users). However, We'll establishes an interactive social media platform between puerperal and supporters based on social support framework. It presents interactive interface of making wishes through play as well as provides professional child-rearing health education knowledge to puerperal so that they can obtain evaluation screening, professional information and emotional support through We'll.

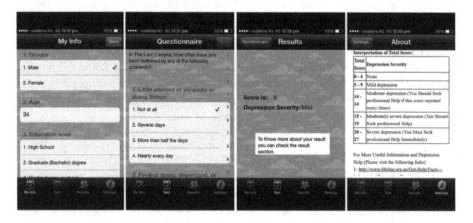

**Fig. 6.** "Depression Monitor" APP (BinDhim et al. 2014)

Overall, respondents completed all the scenario tasks without any major error and it revealed the competence of technology on the current systematic framework of We'll meets the standard (O'Malley et al. 2014). The mutual verification by the number of times of reminding and the type of errors during task execution found out the usability problems of the interface (Hong et al. 2014; Lim et al. 2015; Gunter et al. 2016) while the operational problems defined by navigation error, presentation error, and control error during task execution were effective for the subsequent modification proposals proposed (Mirkovic et al. 2014; Hong et al. 2014; English et al. 2016). Besides, the overall average point of system usability scale (SUS) is 70.5 and it is clearly higher than the average point of the scale (Brooke 1996), showing a certain level of satisfaction on the usability of We'll from respondents.

Other than the discussion above, respondents also provided suggestions and feedback to We'll through post-test qualitative interview, such as (1) proactive dynamic interface-using teaching can be established for the first-time logging in to strengthen users' familiarity towards interface; (2) adding pregnancy records to the function of hospital icon, including baby's ultrasonography images and records of prenatal visit; (3) establishing online professional counseling for obstetrics & gynecology to solve puerpera's questions in real time on line; (4) producing dynamic feedback when delivering the gold coin to friend or family member in order to strengthen the link between the user and friend or family member; (5) designing the linking function for dad so that both puerperal users and their husband can link to the function of reminding with the APP account for husbands to be reminded the using status (making a wish, the point after emotional state test, and its evaluation) after completion; (6) function of wishes made can be added to the function of wishing well to allow users to review the status and record of the wishes in the past.

The next stage of the research will conduct modification on We'll based on the usability testing result this time as well evaluate users suggestions to add new functions in order to enhance the usability and effectiveness of We'll so that the target users in the future will have higher evaluation and satisfaction towards We'll.

## 5  Conclusions and Suggestions

The research verifies whether the design of interface and function meet usability and satisfaction through the data of effectiveness and satisfaction collected during usability testing execution, and the testing data collected and respondents' feedback will be used as the reference to optimize APP function and interface. 30 respondents all successfully completed 12 tasks during scenario testing and the problems occurred during operation were smoothly solved after task reminding. Therefore, it can be seen that the usability and effectiveness of APP functional framework has achieved a certain level of use. The result measured by system usability scale (SUS) also revealed the respondents' satisfaction towards current version also meets the standard of system satisfaction. The usability testing for this stage has been completed and the testing data & suggestions provided by respondents during testing will be applied for problem modification and function optimization on the current version. A revised version will be launched to enhance APP usability and satisfaction from target users.

The results of usability task testing show the problems of We'll APP interface or functions, and it is suggested to make the following improvement and modification for subsequent research:

1. Re-designing the appearance of house icon for friends, family member, and the hospital on the home page to strengthen user's identifiability and effectively enhance user's recognition towards icon function.
2. Expanding reflection area on the list of friends and the list of family members to make sure the window of functional option will be shown when users click the icon or name of their friends' or family members'.
3. Improving the presentation of EDPS testing result to change the bar chart to actual points as well as add suggestion reminding in order to strengthen users' emotional states and understanding towards questionnaire feedback.
4. Establishing dynamic interface functional using teaching when users log in for the first time to strengthen users' connection and functional familiarity towards the APP.

# References

Albert, W., Tullis, T.: Measuring the User Experience: Collecting, Analyzing, and Presenting Usability Metrics. Newnes, Oxford (2013)

Becker, J., et al.: Functioning and validity of a computerized adaptive test to measure anxiety (A-CAT). Depress. Anxiety 25(12), E182–E194 (2008)

Bergström, J., et al.: Internet-versus group-administered cognitive behaviour therapy for panic disorder in a psychiatric setting: a randomised trial. BMC Psychiatry 10(1), 54 (2010)

BinDhim, N.F., Shaman, A.M., Trevena, L., Basyouni, M.H., Pont, L.G., Alhawassi, T.M.: Depression screening via a smartphone app: cross-country user characteristics and feasibility. J. Am. Med. Inform. Assoc. 22(1), 29–34 (2014)

Brockington, I.F., Cernik, K.F., Schofield, E.M., Downing, A.R., Francis, A.F., Keelan, C.: Puerperal psychosis: phenomena and diagnosis. Arch. Gen. Psychiatry 38(7), 829–833 (1981)

Brooke, J.: SUS-A quick and dirty usability scale. Usability Eval. Ind. 189(194), 4–7 (1996)

Chinman, M., Hassell, J., Magnabosco, J., Nowlin-Finch, N., Marusak, S., Young, A.S.: The feasibility of computerized patient self-assessment at mental health clinics. Adm. Policy Ment. Health Ment. Health Serv. Res. 34(4), 401–409 (2007)

Cox, J.L., Murray, D., Chapman, G.: A controlled study of the onset, duration and prevalence of postnatal depression. Br. J. Psychiatry 163(1), 27–31 (1993)

Darcy, J.M., Grzywacz, J.G., Stephens, R.L., Leng, I., Clinch, C.R., Arcury, T.A.: Maternal depressive symptomatology: 16-month follow-up of infant and maternal health-related quality of life. J. Am. Board Fam. Med. 24(3), 249–257 (2011)

Diamond, G., et al.: Development, validation, and utility of internet-based, behavioral health screen for adolescents. Pediatrics (2009)

Donker, T., van Straten, A., Marks, I., Cuijpers, P.: A brief Web-based screening questionnaire for common mental disorders: development and validation. J. Med. Internet Res. 11(3), e19 (2009)

English, L.L., et al.: The paediatric risk assessment (PARA) mobile app to reduce postdischarge child mortality: design, usability, and feasibility for health care workers in Uganda. JMIR mHealth uHealth 4(1), e16 (2016)

Evins, G.G., Theofrastous, J.P.: Postpartum depression: a review of postpartum screening. Prim. Care Update Ob/Gyns 4(6), 241–246 (1997)

Gavin, N.I., Gaynes, B.N., Lohr, K.N., Meltzer-Brody, S., Gartlehner, G., Swinson, T.: Perinatal depression: a systematic review of prevalence and incidence. Obstertrics Gynecol. **106**(5, part 1), 1071–1083 (2005)

Gringras, P., Santosh, P., Baird, G.: Development of an Internet-based real-time system for monitoring pharmacological interventions in children with neurodevelopmental and neuropsychiatric disorders. Child Care Health Dev. **32**(5), 591–600 (2006)

Gualtieri, C.T.: An internet-based symptom questionnaire that is reliable, valid, and available to psychiatrists, neurologists, and psychologists. Medscape Gen. Med. **9**(4), 3 (2007)

Gunter, R., et al.: Evaluating patient usability of an image-based mobile health platform for postoperative wound monitoring. JMIR mHealth uHealth **4**(3), e113 (2016)

Heron, K.E., Smyth, J.M.: Ecological momentary interventions: incorporating mobile technology into psychosocial and health behaviour treatments. Br. J. Health. Psychol. **15**(1), 1–39 (2010)

Hong, Y.: Testing usability and acceptability of a web application to promote physical activity (iCanFit) among older adults. JMIR Hum. Factors **1**(1), e2 (2014)

Kennerley, H., Gath, D.: Maternity blues: I detection and measurement by questionnaire. Br. J. Psychiatry **155**(3), 356–362 (1989)

Khanna, M.S., Kendall, P.C.: Computer-assisted CBT for child anxiety: the coping cat CD-ROM. Cogn. Behav. Pract. **15**(2), 159–165 (2008)

Khanna, M.S., Kendall, P.C.: Computer-assisted cognitive behavioral therapy for child anxiety: results of a randomized clinical trial. J. Consult. Clin. Psychol. **78**(5), 737 (2010)

Khazaal, Y., et al.: Brief DISCERN, six questions for the evaluation of evidence-based content of health-related websites. Patient Educ. Couns. **77**(1), 33–37 (2009)

Lambousis, E., Politis, A., Markidis, M., Christodoulou, G.N.: Development and use of online mental health services in Greece. J. Telemed. Telecare **8**(2_suppl), 51–52 (2002)

Lim, J., et al.: Usability and feasibility of PIERS on the Move: an mHealth app for pre-eclampsia triage. JMIR mHealth uHealth **3**(2), e37 (2015)

Lindahl, V., Pearson, J.L., Colpe, L.: Prevalence of suicidality during pregnancy and the postpartum. Arch. Women's Ment. Health **8**(2), 77–87 (2005)

Martínez-Pérez, B., De La Torre-Díez, I., López-Coronado, M.: Mobile health applications for the most prevalent conditions by the World Health Organization: review and analysis. J. Med. Internet Res. **15**(6), e120 (2013)

Mirkovic, J., Kaufman, D.R., Ruland, C.M.: Supporting cancer patients in illness management: usability evaluation of a mobile app. JMIR mHealth uHealth **2**(3), e33 (2014)

Nasser, F.B.: Health Monitor Project. Smart Health Project (2012)

Nielsen, J.: Usability Engineering. Elsevier, Amsterdam (1994)

O'hara, M.W., Neunaber, D.J., Zekoski, E.M.: Prospective study of postpartum depression: prevalence, course, and predictive factors. J. Abnorm. Psychol. **93**(2), 158 (1984)

O'hara, M.W., Schlechte, J.A., Lewis, D.A., Varner, M.W.: Controlled prospective study of postpartum mood disorders: psychological, environmental, and hormonal variables. J. Abnorm. Psychol. **100**(1), 63 (1991)

O'Malley, G., Dowdall, G., Burls, A., Perry, I.J., Curran, N.: Exploring the usability of a mobile app for adolescent obesity management. JMIR mHealth uHealth **2**(2), e29 (2014)

Robertson, E., Grace, S., Wallington, T., Stewart, D.E.: Antenatal risk factors for postpartum depression: a synthesis of recent literature. Gen. Hosp. Psychiatry **26**(4), 289–295 (2004)

Santor, D.A., Poulin, C., LeBlanc, J.C., Kusumakar, V.: Online health promotion, early identification of difficulties, and help seeking in young people. J. Am. Acad. Child Adolesc. Psychiatry **46**(1), 50–59 (2007)

Sauro, J., Lewis, J.R.: Quantifying the User Experience: Practical Statistics for User Research. Morgan Kaufmann, Burlington (2016)

Scharer, K.: An Internet discussion board for parents of mentally ill young children. J. Child Adolesc. Psychiatr. Nurs. **18**(1), 17–25 (2005)

Shaw, L.H., Gant, L.M.: In defense of the internet: the relationship between Internet communication and depression, loneliness, self-esteem, and perceived social support. CyberPsychology Behav. **5**(2), 157–171 (2002)

Shen, N., et al.: Finding a depression app: a review and content analysis of the depression app marketplace. JMIR mHealth uHealth **3**(1), e16 (2015)

Shneiderman, B., Plaisant, C.: Designing the User Interface: Strategies for Effective Human-Computer Interaction. Pearson Education Inc., Upper Saddle River (2005)

Stowe, Z.N., Nemeroff, C.B.: Women at risk for postpartum-onset major depression. Am. J. Obstet. Gynecol. **173**(2), 639–645 (1995)

Wisner, K.L., Parry, B.L., Piontek, C.M.: Postpartum depression. N. Engl. J. Med. **347**(3), 194–199 (2002)

高鈞瑩: 以社會支持發展產後憂鬱症及產後情緒低落輔助APP之研究與設計 (未出版之碩士論文) 長庚大學,桃園市 (2017)

# A Lightweight and Affordable Sleep Quality Monitoring and Visualization System with a GSR Sensor for Users in Rural Areas to Facilitate Tele-Health

Yang Du, Qiming Sun, Kou Wang, and Tiffany Y. Tang[✉]

Media Lab, Department of Computer Science, Wenzhou-Kean University,
Wenzhou, China
{duya, sunq, wangkou, yatang}@kean.edu

**Abstract.** Having quality sleeping is very critical for individuals to maintain a healthy life. Over the years, thanks to the big advances in wearable and sensing technologies, a wide variety of wearable devices had been pushed to the market. However, for rural users including those in China, these devices are still largely inaccessible. In this paper, we describe the development of a lightweight and affordable real-time sleep monitoring system to serve such purpose. To significantly reduce its cost, a galvanic skin response sensor (GSR) was adopted. GSR sensor can be used to measure the conductivity of the skin and has been widely adopted in physiological assessment. In order to study the feasibility of our system, we performed two small pilot tests and obtained promising results.

The lightweight system is especially valuable in providing affordable solutions to Chinese users in rural areas where the higher-end wearable devices are not accessible. Meanwhile, the data could be automatically generated and sent to doctors in a remote site for further medical analysis as well.

**Keywords:** Sleep quality · Galvanic skin response (GSR) · Monitoring · Visualization · Tele-health

## 1 Introduction

Are you always awake in the middle of night, staring at the ceiling stunned and desperate to have a good sleep? Or maybe you are hard to stay a constant asleep which indicates that you wake up multiple times during sleep. Nowadays, more and more people are puzzled by these different kinds of low sleeping quality and demand an efficient way to obtain information on the quality of their sleep. Meanwhile, lack of quality sleep is also associated with obesity, diabetics [4, 12], mental problems and even accidents [19]. A sleep monitoring system would benefit the individuals as well as medical professionals.

Motivated by these previous works, in this paper, we present a lightweight integrated system consisting of a Galvanic Skin Response sensor (GSR) [5] and a laptop which receives and visualize the data obtained from the sensor. The moving patterns of the GSR value which is widely used to assess automatic activity, could then be

© Springer Nature Switzerland AG 2019
V. G. Duffy (Ed.): HCII 2019, LNCS 11582, pp. 41–49, 2019.
https://doi.org/10.1007/978-3-030-22219-2_3

examined by users and doctors (including those in a remote site to facilitate tele-health).

Two feasibility studies had been performed and described here to demonstrate the high potential of such systems, especially for rural users who do not have access to quality devices and medical services.

The organization of this paper is as follows. In Sect. 2, we present some earlier works on sleep monitoring via GSR and establish the motivation of our study by describing the link between GSR and sleep quality monitoring, GSR and GSR and pressure level in education settings. In Sect. 3, we show the key functions of system, followed by two small-scale pilot studies in Sects. 4 and 5. We conclude this paper and discuss our future work in Sect. 6.

## 2 Related Works

### 2.1 Sleep Quality Monitoring via GSR

Lack of quality sleep is also associated with obesity, diabetics [4, 12], mental problems and even accidents [19]. A sleep monitoring system would benefit the individuals as well as medical professionals.

With the advances of such technologies as sensing and wearable technologies, there are a number of commercial- as well as research-grade wearable devices for sleep monitoring [13, 21], among them, the pricey AMI MotionLongger (USD 795; excluding software), Microsoft Band 2 (USD 224, discontinued), to more affordable ones including Jawbone UP (USD 34, discontinued), Fitbit Alta (USD 130), etc. (See [8] for a review of home-use sleep monitoring system). However, most of these are not accessible to the large number of rural users including those in China, which motivates our study. In particular, in this paper, we present a lightweight and affordable sleep monitoring system consisting of a GSR sensor and a computer which receives and visualize the obtained data. Before we describe our system architecture, we will briefly discuss the link between GSR value and sleep quality.

### 2.2 The Link Between GSR and Sleep Quality Monitoring

Galvanic skin response (GSR) is often adopted as indicators of automatic activity; therefore, it has been widely applied in physiological investigations [15, 20].

A large number of previous works had linked GSR value to sleep quality measurement [3, 10, 16], mainly due to its association with the sympathetic nerve [6, 15].

Following these previous works and drawn from previous results, in our current system, we adopt GSR values to measure users' automatic activity during typical sleeping position (on bed). No specific postures had been considered.

### 2.3 The Link Between GSR and Pressure Level in Education Settings

GSR has often been adopted as indicators of pressure and/or anxiety levels; and widely applied in physiological investigations [15, 20]; with its high portability and open-source quite prototyping platform Arduino, it also has gained attention in the learning community to examine and assess learners' anxiety and pressure level to name a few, [2, 11, 14], since learners' emotional states have significant effects on learning activities [1, 18] and learning outcome [22]. However, most of the studies directly record and monitor learners' GSR values during various learning activities in order to measure their anxiety level [2, 11], instead of measuring their sleep quality, which differentiates our study from these earlier ones.

## 3 System Overview

### 3.1 Connecting the GSR Sensor via the USB Interface

The GSR sensor is collected to our main monitoring system via the typical USB. The major design rationale is to simplify the system setup particularly for those rural users who are not familiar with computer hardware.

### 3.2 GSR Data Collection

In order to find the relationships between sleep quality and the GSR data, we obtain the GSR data from users during their sleep, similar to the testing environment in [7, 9, 16], the GSR senor receives the GSR data and sends it back to the system (see Fig. 1 for our system user interface). The system automatically extracts the GSR data in every 3 s; the new value will be updated and shown in the system's user interface accordingly.

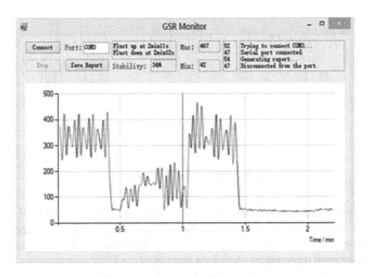

**Fig. 1.** The interface of the GSR data monitor

Besides, the maximum and the minimum value will be shown per unit time on the interface. In this way, users can directly observe whether or not there is a sharp change of the GSR value in a short period of time.

In the implementation part, we adopted the multi-threading strategy so that the system can run continuously without any conflicts and affecting the front-end applications.

### 3.3 Visualizing and Summarizing the Test Results

Our system can generate and visualize the GSR data at the user's request (see Fig. 2 for a sample of such graph). Refer to Fig. 2, the value on the X axis stands for the processing time and the value on the Y axis stands for the GSR value. Besides, the visualization offers to advantages to allow users and medical doctors (especially those at a remote site to support tele-health [17]) to directly and clearly observe the moving trend of the GSR value, which is in turn linked to their activities during sleep. Two functions had been built into our system to facilitate such process. The first is to dynamically update the data and users can check out the GSR values when they have time. At the end of test, the system will generate a text document which will show the result as shown in Fig. 4. This text directly provides the useful information for the user. In the text, the time when the curve fluctuates up and fluctuates down are shown.

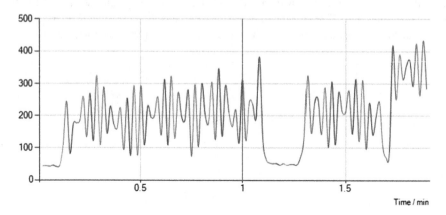

**Fig. 2.** A sample of the moving GSR data

The second function is to allow users to take a closer examination of their own data; to achieve it, the user only needs to move their mouse to the user interface and click the left button on the mouse. Then they need to press the button continuously and move it in the bottom right direction as shown on the Fig. 2.

Figure 2 can be compared with Fig. 3 to notice the variations. Also, if users can press the button on the top right corner to go back to the original display mode. The ease of use of our system offers rural users who might not have higher education better advantages.

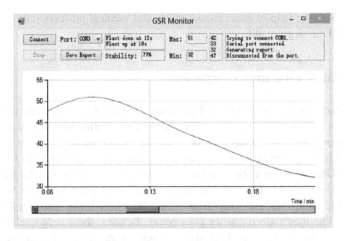

**Fig. 3.** The closer look at the GSR data in the user interface

### 3.4 Autogenerating the Data and Store It as a File for Remote Medical Analysis

The test results are considerably vital for users to analyze their sleep quality, so it is very important to store the result securely and reliably. In our system, the textual summarized results are autogenerated which can save unnecessary operation time for analysis (see Fig. 4).

```
GSR Analysis Report 2018/3/12 16:09
Total Time Spent: 1min54s
Maximum GSR Value: 434 at 1min53s
Minimum GSR Value: 42 at 5s
Total Fluctuation Times: 96
Percent of stable time: 15%
Average Fluctuation Interval: 1
Details:
Fluct up at 7s
Fluct up at 8s
Fluct down at 9s
Fluct up at 10s
Fluct up at 12s
Fluct up at 13s
Fluct down at 14s
Fluct up at 15s
Fluct down at 16s
Fluct up at 17s
Fluct down at 18s
Fluct up at 19s
Fluct down at 20s
Fluct up at 21s
Fluct down at 22s
Fluct up at 23s
Fluct up at 24s
Fluct down at 25s
Fluct up at 26s
```

**Fig. 4.** System generated summarizing report

The generated result file includes several important factors, such as the total time spent, maximum and minimum GSR value, the total fluctuation time, and the average fluctuation. With the help of these factors, users and medical professionals can have an overview of their sleep quality.

## 4 Pilot Study One and Discussion

In order to study the feasibility of our design, we conducted a preliminary study on one subject who is a college student and collect GSR values during his sleep at night. After collecting the research data, analyzing the result and obtaining the variation tendency of GSR value, his sleep quality is assessed and visualized. As shown in Fig. 5, each point stands for a GSR value and the distribution of these points indicates the trend of the GSR value development. The red line in Fig. 5 stands for the variation value's tendency. As the time increases, the GSR value becomes lower and constant which indicates that the user's sleep quality goes better. Besides, there is few relatively high GSR values existing at the latter half of test. Then compared with the first half of test, the GSR values changes stupendously and more frequently. The points in this area distribute irregularly which indicates that the user doesn't fall asleep during this period of time. After analyzing, the conclusion of the user's sleep quality comes out. This user didn't spend too much time falling asleep and his sleep relatively stay continuous so his sleep quality is satisficing.

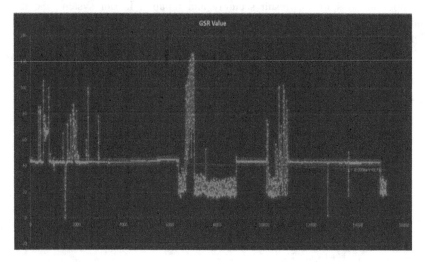

**Fig. 5.** The data analysis of collected GSR value in the pilot study (Color figure online)

### 4.1 Discussion

After accomplishing the resulting analysis, users can obtain the information that the tendency of the GSR values changes. They can directly judge the sleep quality by observing the number of percentages of stable time shown in Fig. 4. If this value is high, it indicates that the user's sleep quality is high Compared with other previous works, our system is more sensitive to the slight movements of users during sleep and the visualization can be shown in a real-time mode. When the users' GSR values changes, it immediately responses to the shifty curve. Besides, users can also observe the exact measurement number in the stored text result. Some systems depend on the user's movement to know the sleep quality and it comes to some problems. If the user is used to turn over body during sleep, will the system distinguish this action? Another problem is that when user keep static, they may sit in quietness without any movements. In this situation, these systems always assume that users are sleeping, which is the significant weaknesses. After the comparisons with these previous works, the galvanic skin response is more suitable for measure the sleep quality: the user's body causes the constant electrical characteristics changes on the user's skin. When users sleep, their GSR values stay in a relative constant level and the values are lower than when they are active. This feature offers a guarantee on detecting the quality of the user's sleep.

In order to examine the sensitive of the data collector in order to distinguish a user's emotion, we conducted a second pilot study. Details are shown in the following section.

## 5   Pilot Study Two and Results

The sleep quality monitor system is a quick, efficient and accurate way to examine people's sleep quality in different situations. In most cases, the changes of the GSR value measured by the GSR sensor will indicates the percent of stable time when testers are sleeping. If the percent of stable time is higher, the tester's sleep quality is better. We conducted a second study on a male college subject to examine his sleep quality before he was going to take an exam. Figure 6 shows the GSR data on the eve of this examination. According to the graph, we found the volatility of the GSR value. The volatility is very large which indicates that the subject's GSR value is not stable when he was sleeping. This result indicates that his sleep quality is not good which may be resulted from the coming exam, which might occur due to his anxiety.

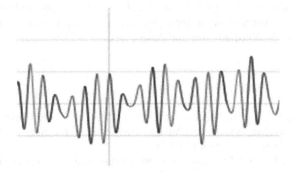

**Fig. 6.** The GSR value volatility of the subject's sleep on the examination day

To further examine whether there exists some differences of GSR value between his sleep on a normal day and the sleep on the coming test day, we compare the GSR value in these two situations. We found that the GSR value is more stable during the normal day sleep which is align with our expectation (Fig. 7).

Those said, we might be able to conclude that the pressure of examinations will influence student's sleep quality which can then be directly examined from the GSR value.

One immediate application of such findings is to allow users to self-regulate and self-manage their pressure level through monitoring their daily sleep quality, which might also offer remote therapists enough data to offer medical or physiological helps, if needed. Although such applications are commercially available, they are rarely adopted in rural areas.

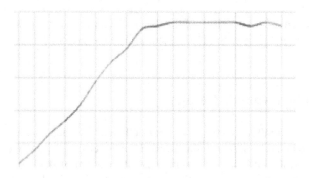

**Fig. 7.** The GSR value volatility of the subject's sleep on a normal day

## 6   Concluding Remarks and Future Works

Our sleep quality monitoring system is a quick, lightweight, efficient device with satisfying results to offer users to examine their own sleep quality; meanwhile, the collected data can also facilitate intelligent tele-health, which is a future path we are seeking in the future. of using GSR to test the sleep quality is still in its infancy at this point especially for users in rural areas. Hence, it is very urgent for researchers to greatly develop such affordable one for these users.

## References

1. Allen, B., Carifio, J.: Methodology for the analysis of emotion experiences during mathematical problem solving. In: Annual Conference of the New England Education Research Organization, Portsmouth (1995)
2. Apostolidis, H., Tsiatsos, T.: Using sensors to detect student's emotion in adaptive learning environment. In: Proceedings of the Second International Conference on Innovative Developments in ICT, pp. 60–65 (2011)

3. Asahina, K., Omura, K.: Phenomenological study of paradoxical phase and reverse of sleep. Jpn. J. Physiol. **14**, 365–372 (1964)
4. Foley, D., Ancoli-Israel, S., Britz, P., Walsh, J.: Sleep disturbances and chronic disease in older adults: results of the 2003 national sleep foundation sleep in America survey. J. Psychosom. Res. **56**(5), 497–502 (2004)
5. Galvanic Skin Response (GSR): Encyclopedia of Pain, p. 1351 (2013)
6. Gutrecht, J.A.: Sympathetic skin response. J. Clin. Neurophysiol. **11**(5), 519–524 (1994)
7. Hao, T., Xing, G., Zhou, G.: iSleep: unobtrusive sleep quality monitoring using smartphones. In: Proceedings of ACM SenSys 2013, Article No. 4 (2013)
8. Kelly, J.M., Strecker, R.E., Bianchi, M.T.: Recent developments in home sleep-monitoring devices. ISRN Neurol. **2012**, 768–794 (2012)
9. Kwasnicki, R.M., et al.: A lightweight sensing platform for monitoring sleep quality and posture: a simulated validation study. Eur. J. Med. Res. **23**, 28 (2018)
10. Lester, B.K., Burch, N.R., Dossett, R.C.: Nocturnal EEG-GSR profiles: the influence of presleep states. Psychophysiology **3**(3), 238–248 (1967)
11. Moukayed, F., Yun, H., Bisson, T., Fortenbacher, A.: Detecting academic emotions from learners' skin conductance and heart rate: a data-driven approach using fuzzy logic. In: Proceedings of DeLFI Workshops 2018 co-located with 16th e-Learning Conference of the German Computer Society (DeLFI 2018) Frankfurt, Germany (2018)
12. Parish, J.: Sleep-related problems in common medical conditions. Chest J. **135**(2), 563–572 (2009)
13. Sano, A., Picard, R.W., Stickgold, R.: Quantitative analysis of wrist electrodermal activity during sleep. Int. J. Psychophysiol. **94**, 382–389 (2014)
14. Santoso, H., Yjima, K., Shusaku, N., Ogawa, N.: Evaluation of student's physiological response towards e-learning courses material by using GSR sensor. In: 9th IEEE/ACIS International Conference on Computer and Information Science, IEEE/ACIS ICIS 2010, Yamagata, Japan, 18–20 August 2010, pp. 805–810 (2010)
15. Shi, Y., Ruiz, N., Taib, R., Choi, E., Chen, F.: Galvanic skin response (GSR) as an index of cognitive load. In: Extended Abstracts on Human Factors in Computing Systems, CHI 2007, New York, NY, USA, pp. 2651–2656 (2007)
16. Shiihara, Y., Umezawa, A., Sakai, Y., Kamitamari, N., Kodama, M.: Continuous recordings of skin conductance change during sleep. Psychiatry Clin. Neurosci. **54**, 268–269 (2000)
17. Spaulding, R., Stevens, D., Velasquez, S.E.: Experience with telehealth for sleep monitoring and sleep laboratory management. J. Telemed. Telecare **17**(7), 346–349 (2011)
18. Spering, M., Wagener, D., Funke, J.: The role of emotions in complex problem–solving. Cogn. Emot. **19**, 1252–1261 (2005)
19. Surantha, N., Kusuma, G.P., Isa, S.M.: Internet of things for sleep quality monitoring system: a survey. In: 2016 11th International Conference on Knowledge, Information and Creativity Support Systems (KICSS), pp. 1–60. IEEE (2016)
20. Westeyn, T., Presti, P., Starner, T.: ActionGSR: a combination galvanic skin response-accelerometer for physiological measurements in active environments. In: Proceedings of 2006 10th IEEE International Symposium on Wearable Computers, pp. 129–130 (2006)
21. Yoon, J.: Comparing 10 Sleep Trackers How well do they track your sleep? A 9-day minute-by-minute comparison (2017). http://sleep.cs.brown.edu/comparison/. Accessed 25 Oct
22. Zeidner, M.: Test anxiety in educational contexts: what I have learned so far. In: Schutz, P. A., Pekrun, R. (eds.) Emotion in Education, pp. 165–184. Academic Press, San Diego (2007)

# ECG Identification Based on PCA and Adaboost Algorithm

Qi Liu[1], Yujuan Si[1,2]([✉]), Liangliang Li[1], and Di Wang[1]

[1] College of Communication Engineering,
Jilin University, Changchun 130012, China
1508009282@qq.com, siyj@jlu.edu.cn
[2] Zhuhai College of Jilin University, Zhuhai 519041, China

**Abstract.** Electrocardiogram (ECG) is a weak electrical signal that reflects the process of heart activity, and has multiple excellent features such as uniqueness, stability, versatility, non-repeatability, easy collection and so on. As a new type of biometric authentication technology, the feature extraction and classification of ECG have become a hot research topic. However, there still exists some problems such as poor timeliness and low recognition accuracy. In order to solve these problems, in this paper, we propose an identification method based on Principal Component Analysis (PCA) and Adaboost algorithm. In this method, firstly, we remove the noise from the ECG signal and segment the ECG signal into multiple single heart beats based on detected R points. Then, PCA is used to process heart beat data to reduce feature dimension. Finally, the Adaboost algorithm is used to ensemble weak classifiers to construct a stronger classifier with higher accuracy. In order to validate the effectiveness of the proposed method, we tested our algorithm on 89 healthy subjects of the ECG-ID database. Experimental results show that the proposed method can achieve accuracy rate of 98.88% within 7 s, which demonstrates that the proposed method can provide an effective and practical way for ECG identification.

**Keywords:** ECG · Identification · PCA · Feature extraction · Adaboost

## 1 Introduction

Electrocardiogram (ECG) is a kind of weak electrical signal that reflects the beating law of the heart. As a common physiological signal in human body, ECG signals contain measurable characteristic discrepancies among different individuals. Generally, ECG signals are periodic and composed of the similar P-QRS-T waves. However, for different individuals, the position, period and amplitude of each characteristic point are different, which is the basis for ECG signals to be used in personal identification [1]. ECG signals include the following advantages: universality, uniqueness, stability and measurability, which are the necessary conditions of biometrics. In addition, ECG, as a biological feature of human body, is not easy to be stolen, and its safety is relatively higher. Meanwhile, since the ECG signal is one-dimensional, there is low computational complexity in preprocessing and feature processing.

V. G. Duffy (Ed.): HCII 2019, LNCS 11582, pp. 50–62, 2019.
https://doi.org/10.1007/978-3-030-22219-2_4

At present, the research on ECG identification algorithm can be divided into two categories [2]: feature extraction algorithm based on reference point detection and feature extraction algorithm based on non-reference point detection. The feature extraction algorithm based on reference point detection mainly extracts the amplitude, interval, slope, area, angle and other geometric features of ECG signals for identification. Chen et al. [3] extracted five features of Q wave position, S wave position, QRS interval, RQ amplitude difference and RS amplitude difference, this method used Support Vector Machine (SVM) to classify and recognize; Palaniappan et al. [4] intercepted the QRS segments of ECG signals, and extracted five feature points and one morphological coefficient of the segment, this method used the Back-Propagation neural network (BP) to classify and recognize. The feature extraction algorithm based on non-reference point detection is mainly based on transform features, such as time-frequency transform, wavelet transform and sparse coding. Zhao et al. [5] used Fast Fourier's matching tracking method and sparse decomposition of characteristic coefficients to classify and recognize by SVM; Chen et al. [6] used the singular value and dissimilarity distance of the wavelet transform matrix of ECG as the characteristic parameters, SVM was used to classify and 40 samples were identified, the recognition accuracy was 97.82%.

In the above literature, the feature extraction use the reference points overly relies on the positioning accuracy of the reference points, it only focuses on the local information and ignore the overall characteristics of the signal. The feature extraction algorithm based on non-reference point use all the information of the signal, so that this algorithm contains a large amount of redundant information, and the computation complexity is increased by feature transformation. For the common classification models, k-Nearest-Neighbor (KNN) is not regularized for identification, and class deviation is easy to occur in case of sample imbalance. Although SVM performs well, it is sensitive to missing data and the kernel functions should be selected carefully. The learning speed of neural network is slow, and it is easy to fall into local minimum.

Based on the above problems, the feature point location, feature redundancy and classification model selection are analyzed. An ECG identification algorithm based on PCA and Adaboost classifier is proposed in this paper. We extracted complete heart beats through R points, then the PCA was used to process the multidimensional features, removed inter correlation and redundant information, the PCA method can reduce the high-dimensional features to low dimensional features. Finally, Adaboost algorithm was used to construct strong classifier for classification and match. Adaboost algorithm has been successfully applied to face recognition [7], license plate recognition [8], disease diagnosis [9] and other fields because of its simple flow and ideal classification effect. The strategy of "reassigning weights" is adopted to combine weak classifiers weighted into strong classifiers with higher accuracy, which can improve the accuracy of ECG identification. In this paper, the simulation experiment based on ECG-ID database shows that the recognition accuracy and timeliness of the proposed algorithm are improved, which proves that the algorithm has a better performance.

# 2 ECG Signal Preprocessing and R Point Location

## 2.1 Denoising

ECG signal is a kind of weak electrical signal. It is easy to be disturbed by noise when collecting, which will affect the accuracy of identification. So the ECG signal needs to be denoised. The noises in the ECG signal mainly include baseline drift (<1 Hz), power frequency interference (50 Hz or 60 Hz), electromyographical interference (30–300 Hz). According to the frequency distribution of noise and ECG signal, we adopt the adaptive wavelet soft threshold method [10] for denoising. The sampling frequency of the signal in the ECG-ID database is 500 Hz. According to the Nyquist sampling theorem, we can know that the frequency of ECG signal is 0–250 Hz, the db4 wavelet is used to decompose the signal with 9 layers. The frequency distribution is shown in Table 1. The frequency of ECG signal mainly distributes in 0.05–100 Hz, of which QRS frequency is 3–40 Hz and S-T frequency is 0.7–10 Hz. So we use 9-layer db4 wavelet to decompose and reconstruct. According to the frequency distribution in the Table 1, the wavelet coefficients of the high frequency component in first layer can be directly set to zero, and the wavelet coefficients of the low frequency component in ninth layer can be set to zero. Then the soft threshold method is used to remove the noise which frequency is mixed with ECG signal.

**Table 1.** The 9 layer decomposition of ECG signal

| Decomposition level | Low-frequency component (Hz) | High-frequency component (Hz) |
|---|---|---|
| 1 | 0–125 | 125–250 |
| 2 | 0–62.5 | 62.5–125 |
| 3 | 0–31.2 | 31.2–62.5 |
| 4 | 0–15.6 | 15.6–31.2 |
| 5 | 0–7.8 | 7.8–15.6 |
| 6 | 0–3.9 | 39–7.8 |
| 7 | 0–2.0 | 2.0–3.9 |
| 8 | 0–1.0 | 1–2.0 |
| 9 | 0–0.5 | 0.5–1 |

First, the threshold of the high-frequency coefficients of each layer is determined, the formula is defined as follows:

$$thr = \alpha_k \times \sqrt{2\log(n)} \times \sigma \tag{1}$$

Where $n$ is the signal length of the threshold processing. $a_k$ is the weighted threshold coefficient of the decomposition of each layer, and $\sigma$ is defined as follows:

$$\sigma = \frac{median(|d(k)|)}{0.6745} \tag{2}$$

Where $d(k)$ is the wavelet coefficients of each scale. $k$ is the number of layers being processed.

In order to adapt to the wavelet decomposition thresholds of different layers, the weighted threshold method is adopted and the weight is designed, the formula is defined as follows:

$$\alpha_k = \begin{cases} 0.25 & f \leq 30\,\text{Hz} \\ 0.5 & 30\,\text{Hz} < f < 125\,\text{Hz} \\ 0 & f \geq 125\,\text{Hz} \end{cases} \tag{3}$$

Finally, the processed coefficients of the filtered coefficients are reconstructed, and the denoising results of individuals 3 and 9 are shown in Fig. 1. From the graph, we can see that the noise is basically removed, which can meet the needs of identification.

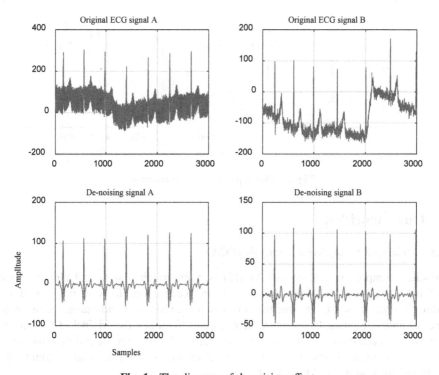

**Fig. 1.** The diagram of de-noising effect

## 2.2    R Point Location

The peak value of R wave is the largest in ECG signal, and its location is the simplest. In this paper, the second order difference threshold method [11] is used to locate the peak value of R wave. Figure 2 is the R point detection chart.

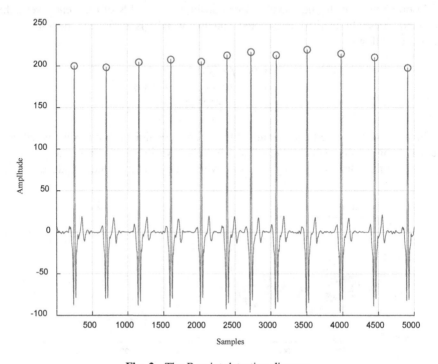

**Fig. 2.** The R point detection diagram

# 3    Our Algorithm

## 3.1    Principal Component Analysis (PCA)

Principal component analysis (PCA) [12] is a multivariate statistical algorithm for optimal orthogonal transformation in pattern recognition. It is mainly based on orthogonal projection to remove the correlation between data and maximize the variance of projection data. Using a few main features to replace the original ECG data can remove the correlation of ECG waveform characteristics. This algorithm reduces the data dimension and highlights the main characteristics of the data while retaining the main information of the ECG signal.

The process of principal component analysis is as follows:

(1) Suppose the sample set $X = (x^1, x^2, \ldots, x^m)$ is composed of $m$ heart beat samples, the dimension of each sample is $n$. Take the sample set to remove the mean:

$$x_{ij}^* = x_{ij} - \bar{x}_i \quad (i = 1, 2, \ldots, n; \ j = 1, 2, \ldots, m) \tag{4}$$

(2) Calculate the covariance matrix:

$$\Sigma = \frac{1}{m} X X^T \tag{5}$$

(3) Calculate the eigenvalue $(\lambda^1 \geq \lambda^2 \geq, \ldots, \geq \lambda^n)$ of the $\Sigma$ and its corresponding eigenvector $(\omega^1 \geq \omega^2 \geq, \ldots, \geq \omega^n)$.

(4) Determine the required low dimension $d'$ according to contribution rate

$$\varphi = \frac{\sum_{i=1}^{d'} \lambda_i}{\sum_{i=1}^{n} \lambda_i} \tag{6}$$

Where $d'$ is determined according to the demand of principal component contribution rate $\varphi$.

(5) Transform n-dimensional sample set X into $d'$ dimension space:

$$Z = W^T X \tag{7}$$

$$W = (\omega_1, \omega_2, \ldots, \omega_{d'}) \tag{8}$$

## 3.2  Adaboost Algorithm

Adaboost algorithm was proposed and developed by Freund [13] in 1996. The Adaboost algorithm adopts the strategy of "reassigning weights" to train the weak classifiers for several rounds, and automatically improve the weights of the wrong samples in the previous training. The weights of weak classifiers with low misclassification rate are added, and the weight of every weak classifier is combined to the weight of the final strong classifier. Adaboost algorithm is often used in the study of binary classification problems, and ECG identification is a multi-classification problem, so the traditional Adaboost algorithm needs to be improved. Zhu et al. [14] proposed an improved algorithm called Stagewise Additive Modeling using a Multi-class Exponential loss function (SAMME). It extends the Adaboost algorithm directly to multiple types of problems. The SAMME algorithm reduces the requirement for the correct class rate of the weak classifier from 1/2 to 1/k, which means that in the multi-classification problem, the performance of the weak classifier can be accepted as long as it is better than random guess.

The steps of this algorithm are as follows:

The sample set is given: $\{(x_1, y_1), (x_2, y_2), \ldots, (x_m, y_m)\}$ which $x_i$ represent the ECG signal eigenvector, $y_i$ represent the category label of $x_i$, and $y_i \in Y = (1, 2, \ldots, K)$.

Step 1: Initialize the weight of training samples:

$$w_1 = \frac{1}{m}(i = 1, 2, \ldots, m) \tag{9}$$

Step 2: For $t = 1, 2, \ldots, T$ ($T$ is the number of iterations):
(1) Train the weak classifier $h_t$ according to the sample distribution $\omega_t$.
(2) Calculate the Prediction Error of Weak Classifier $h_t$:

$$e_t = \sum_{i=1}^{N} \omega_1(i) \bullet 1[y_i \neq h_t(x_i)] \tag{10}$$

Where $1[*]$ means that when $[*]$ is established, it equals 1, otherwise it equals 0.
(3) Calculate the weight of weak classifier $\alpha_t$ based on prediction error $e_t$:

$$a_t = \frac{1}{2}\ln(\frac{1 - e_t}{e_t}) + \log(K - 1) \tag{11}$$

Where K is the number of categories.
(4) Reassign the next training sample according to the weight $a_t$:

$$\omega_{t+1}(i) = \frac{\omega_t(i)}{B_T} * \begin{cases} e^{-a_t}, & if \quad y_i = h_t(x_i) \\ e^{a_t}, & if \quad y_i = h_t(x_i) \end{cases} \tag{12}$$

Where $B_T$ is a normalization factor that normalizes $\omega_t^{t+1}$.
Step 3: Built final strong classifier:

$$H(x) = \arg\max_{y \in Y} \sum_{t=1}^{T} a_t \bullet 1[h_t(x_i) = y_i] \tag{13}$$

### 3.3    The Flow of PCA_Adaboost Algorithm

Based on the simple and efficient Adaboost algorithm, a strong classifier is formed by combining PCA and Adaboost. It improves the timeliness and accuracy of ECG recognition, and has a good feasibility and practical significance. The flow chart is shown in Fig. 3.

## 4    Experiments and Results

### 4.1    Experimental Environment and Database

The experimental environment in this paper is the personal PC of the Windows10 operating system, the processor is Intel (R) Core (TM) i5-7500, the memory is 4 GB, and the compilation environments are Matlab2017b and Python3.6.

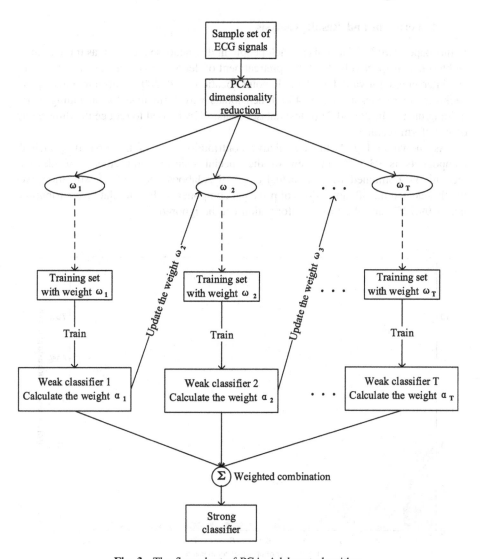

**Fig. 3.** The flow chart of PCA_Adaboost algorithm

This data is derived from the ECG-ID database [15] in Physionet, which contains ECG signals from 90 people. The signal acquisition frequency is 500 Hz and the resolution is 12bit, of which the seventy-fourth individual only collect one signal, and the remaining 89 people have at least two ECG signals collected at different times. Since only one signal was collected, the seventy-fourth individuals does not satisfy the experimental conditions of identification in this paper, we will eliminate the number seventy-fourth individual. This paper will use the remaining ECG signals from 89 people to carry out the identification experiment.

## 4.2    Experiment and Result Analysis

In this paper, two ECG signals of each people in the database are taken as training data and test data respectively. First, the pretreatment of denoising is used. Then, 150 points are intercepted forward based on R-point location, and 300 points are intercepted backward to extract a total of 450-dimensionals waveform features, including 2116 training dataset beats and 2110 test dataset beats. PCA is used to reduce the dimension of waveform features.

As shown in Fig. 4, the cumulative contribution rate of the first 10 principal components is 93.56%. In view of the special security requirements of identity recognition, combined with the actual effect of Adaboost classifier classification, we finally selected the 30 dimensions of principal components, the cumulative contribution rate is 99.72%, and the loss of information can be ignored.

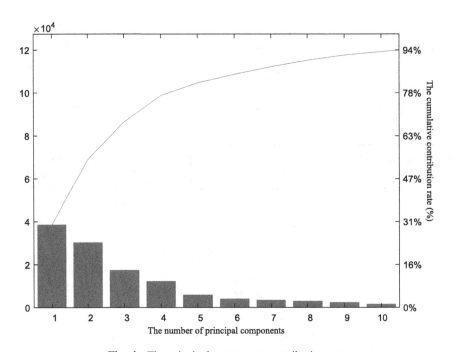

**Fig. 4.** The principal component contribution rate

Figure 5 is a comparison map of waveform characteristics and PCA dimension reduction characteristics. From the graph, we can see that the heart beat waveform of individual A is relatively close at different times, but it is quite different from individual B and individual C. For PCA dimensionality reduction features, it can be seen that the characteristics of the same individual are closer, and different individuals have more obvious differences. PCA dimensionality reduction highlights the main features of ECG data, reduces the dimensionality of ECG data, and reduces the correlation between ECG signals and the redundant information that interferes with the recognition accuracy. This algorithm improves the recognition efficiency and recognition accuracy.

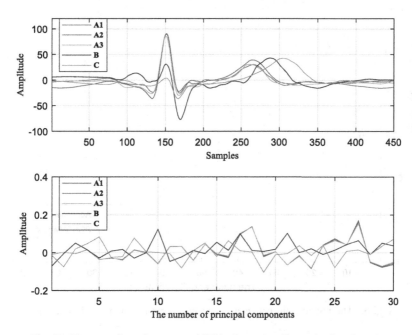

**Fig. 5.** The waveform features and PCA dimensionality reduction features

Under the same experimental standard, the decision tree is used as the base classifier. And we compared the recognition accuracy of Adaboost algorithm with PCA feature dimension reduction and without PCA feature dimension reduction at different iterations, as shown in Fig. 6.

It can be seen from the Fig. 6 that the recognition accuracy is positively correlated with the different number of iterations. The recognition accuracy is basically stable when the number of iterations is 40 without PCA feature reduction. The recognition accuracy is basically stable when the number of iterations is 30 with PCA feature reduction, and the recognition time is increased with the number of iterations. In this paper, 40 iterations were used to construct the recognition model.

In the same data set the algorithm proposed in this paper was compared with KNN, SVM, BP. And the accuracy rate and average time consuming is shown in Table 2. Among them, KNN classifier parameter K = 5; SVM classifier uses linear kernel function; BP neural network adopts 30-20-89 network [16], the transfer function is "tansig", the minimum gradient is 1.0−e7, and the upper limit of iteration is 500.

In this section, we defined the PCA and KNN recognition method is PCA_KNN, PCA and SVM recognition method is PCA_SVM, PCA and BP recognition method is PCA_BP. This algorithms were compared with KNN, SVM, BP, and Adaboost algorithms. And as shown in the Table 2, the methods combined with the PCA feature dimensionality reduction can improve the recognition accuracy and recognition

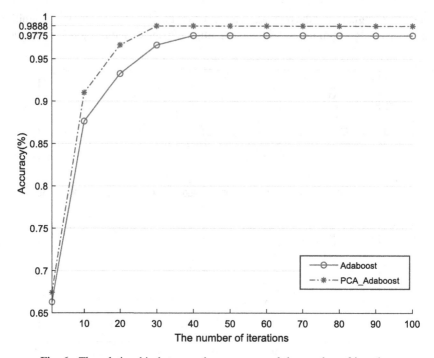

**Fig. 6.** The relationship between the accuracy and the number of iterations

**Table 2.** Comparison of different classifier recognition results

| Algorithm | Accuracy rate (%) | Average time consuming (s) |
| --- | --- | --- |
| KNN | 89.89 | 24.00 |
| BP | 95.51 | 240.00 |
| SVM | 95.51 | 320.00 |
| Adaboost | 97.75 | 110.00 |
| PCA_KNN | 92.13 | 5.00 |
| PCA_BP | 96.63 | 12.00 |
| PCA_SVM | 96.63 | 20.00 |
| PCA_Adaboost | 98.88 | 7.00 |

timeliness. Among them, the accuracy of PCA_KNN algorithm is 92.13%, the accuracy of PCA_BP algorithm is 96.63%, the accuracy of PCA_SVM algorithm is 96.63%, and the accuracy of PCA_Adaboost algorithm can reach 98.88%. In view of the time-consuming of recognition, the PCA feature dimension reduction greatly reduces the time recognition required, while the average time consuming is basically reduced by one order of magnitude, and the timeliness of recognition is improved. Compared with the PCA_KNN algorithm, PCA _SVM algorithm PCA_BP method, the recognition time of the proposed algorithm is less than PCA_BP and PCA_SVM. Although it takes much more time than the PCA_KNN algorithm, the recognition accuracy is much higher than PCA_KNN algorithm. Experiments show that PCA algorithm extracts the principal components of ECG signals instead of the original ECG waveform features, and removes the correlation between ECG signals and redundant information interfering the recognition accuracy. The PCA algorithm improves the recognition accuracy, reduces the data dimension of ECG signals, reduces the computational complexity of the algorithm, and improves the recognition efficiency. The Adaboost algorithm adopts the strategy of "weight assignment", to trains the training samples of ECG signals through weak classifiers, it also improves the weight of the wrong samples of the previous ECG signals, reduces the weights of the correct samples of the ECG signals, and increases the weights of the classifiers with small error rates, and reduces the weight of the classifier with large error rates. Several rounds of training and automatic adjustment are combined into a strong classifier with high recognition accuracy.

# 5  Conclusions

In order to improve the timeliness and accuracy of ECG identification, an ECG identity recognition method based on PCA and Adaboost algorithm was proposed in this paper. This paper mainly studies the dimensionality reduction and classification using waveform characteristics. Firstly, we extracted the single beat based on R point positioning, and PCA was used to reduce the dimension of this feature. Since PCA can remove the correlation and redundant information in original waveform features, the computation complexity of ECG identification using PCA features will be reduced. As a result, not only the running time of the algorithm can be decreased significantly, but also the need for timeliness of algorithm can be well satisfied. Then the Adaboost algorithm was applied to PCA features for model training. Specially, the "reassigning weights" strategy was adopted to combine multiple weak classifiers into one strong classifier for better classification effect. In our experiments, the algorithm was evaluated on ECG-ID database and accuracy of 98.88% could be achieved within 7 s. The experimental results show that our method has good performance on both identification accuracy and timeliness. The next step is to verify the reliability of the algorithm for the ECG signal data collected by ourselves.

**Acknowledgments.** This work was supported by the Science and Technology Development Plan Project of Jilin Province under Grant Nos. 20170414017GH and 20190302035GX; the Natural Science Foundation of Guangdong Province under Grant No. 2016A030313658; the Innovation and Strengthening School Project (provincial key platform and major scientific research project) supported by Guangdong Government under Grant No. 2015KTSCX175; the Premier-Discipline Enhancement Scheme Supported by Zhuhai Government under Grant No. 2015YXXK02-2; the Premier Key-Discipline Enhancement Scheme Supported by Guangdong Government Funds under Grant No. 2016GDYSZDXK036.

# References

1. Biel, L., Pettersson, O., Philipson, L., et al.: ECG analysis: a new approach in human identification. IEEE Trans. Instrum. Meas. **50**(3), 808–812 (2002)
2. Babak, M.A., Sharafat, A.R., Setarehdan, S.K.: An adaptive backpropagation neural network for arrhythmia classification using R-R interval signal. Neural Netw. World **22**(6), 535–548 (2012)
3. Chen, X., Chen, G., Shen, H.: ECG sensor signal identification method based on SVM. Transducer Microsyst. Technol. **33**(10), 40–42 (2014)
4. Palaniappan, R., Krishnan, S.M.: Identifying individuals using ECG beats. In: International Conference on Signal Processing & Communications. IEEE (2005)
5. Zhao, Z., Yang, L., Chen, D.: Research of ECG identification based on FFT-matching pursuit algorithm. Chin. J. Sens. Actuators **26**(3), 307–314 (2013)
6. Chen, D., Zhao, Z.: Identification method of ECG signal based on SVD and dissimilarity analysis. Comput. Simul. **33**(2), 427–432 (2016)
7. Jammoussi, A.Y., Ghribi, S.F., Masmoudi, D.S.: Adaboost face detector based on joint integral histogram and genetic algorithms for feature extraction process. SpringerPlus **3**(1), 355 (2014)
8. Song, M.K., Sarker, M.M.K.: Modeling and implementing two-stage AdaBoost for real-time vehicle license plate detection. J. Appl. Math. **2014**, 1–8 (2014)
9. Ahmed, W., Khalid, S.: ECG signal processing for recognition of cardiovascular diseases: a survey. In: Sixth International Conference on Innovative Computing Technology. IEEE (2017)
10. Bin, H., Bai, Y., Zhang, Y.: Wavelet soft threshold ECG denoising based on different empirical mode decomposition. Math. Pract. Theory **46**(6), 136–144 (2016)
11. Yang, Z.: Real-time detection of ECG waveform based on differential algorithm. J. Mudanjiang Normal Univ. (Nat. Sci. Ed.) (4), 23–25 (2015)
12. Martinez, A.M., Kak, A.C.: PCA versus LDA. IEEE Trans. Pattern Anal. Mach. Intell. **23**(2), 228–233 (2002)
13. Freund, Y., Schapire, R.E.: A decision-theoretic generalization of on-line learning and an application to boosting. J. Comput. Syst. Sci. **55**(1), 119–139 (1997)
14. Zhu, J., Zou, H., Rosset, S., et al.: Multi-class AdaBoost. Stat. Interface **2**(3), 349–360 (2009)
15. Lugovaya, T.S.: Biometric human identification based on electrocardiogram. [Master's thesis] Faculty of Computing Technologies and Informatics, Electrotechnical University "LETI", Saint-Petersburg, Russian Federation (2005)
16. Yu, J., Si, Y., Liu, X., Wen, D., Luo, T., Lang, L.: ECG identification based on PCA-RPROP. In: Duffy, V.G. (ed.) DHM 2017. LNCS, vol. 10287, pp. 419–432. Springer, Cham (2017). https://doi.org/10.1007/978-3-319-58466-9_37

# Increasing Availability Control of Human Biological Samples Using a Mobile Management System

Leonardo Lima Marinho[1], Isabel Cristina P. da Nóbrega[2],
Nayat Sanchez Pi[1,2], Rosa Maria E. Moreira da Costa[1,2(✉)],
and Vera Maria B. Werneck[1,2]

[1] Computational Sciences Graduation Program, Universidade do Estado do Rio de Janeiro – UERJ, Rio de Janeiro, RJ, Brazil
leonardomarinho_10@hotmail.com,
{nayat,rcosta,vera}@ime.uerj.br
[2] Telehealth and Telemedicine Graduation Program, Universidade do Estado do Rio de Janeiro – UERJ, Rio de Janeiro, RJ, Brazil
isacris.pacheco@gmail.com

**Abstract.** Biobanks and biorepositories present major challenges in managing, storing and making available large amounts of samples and associated information. The ability to share these samples is an important issue to improve research using human biological samples. A systematic review of the literature on information management of biobanks and biorepositories provided a wealth of knowledge and stimulated a proposal for a system to support its management process. The SIGIBio (Biobank and Biorepository Information Management Support System) was defined and developed to manage these samples considering the complex treatment of these data, in a mobile system. It features open up possibilities for organizations and researchers to access and share biobank and bio-repositories samples. The SIGIBio system was described in terms of requirements, stages of development, scenarios and technical aspects. The first version of SIGIBio was presented to researchers and a usability test was performed to confirm its applicability and interface aspects. In the future, SIGIBio will be an open and free system that can be adopted by different researchers and organizations.

**Keywords:** Mobile management system · Biobank · Biorepository

## 1 Introduction

In the last decades new challenges in the Healthcare area have appear which increasingly require the support of new technologies of communication and collaboration. Advances in the process of knowledge construction, especially in the areas of genetics, cell therapy, molecular biology and bioinformatics have changed the basic, clinical and translational research course, generating a growing need for storage of biological materials and associated information [1].

© Springer Nature Switzerland AG 2019
V. G. Duffy (Ed.): HCII 2019, LNCS 11582, pp. 63–74, 2019.
https://doi.org/10.1007/978-3-030-22219-2_5

In addition, there is a demand from research institutions for sharing information about stored human biological samples. Nowadays, researchers face difficulties in finding out which organizations have biobanks that contain samples needed for their research projects. This demand can be achieved through the creation of a network of biobanks and biorepositories.

In this context, the objective of this paper is to present the development process of a mobile system (SIBIBio - Biobanking and Biorepository Information Management Support System), which was created to manage relevant information on control of the storage and donation of biological materials for research. Due to the different professional profiles that manage and use biobanks and biorepositories samples, it is very important that the system interfaces are intuitive and have good levels of usability, provide mobility and also have security guarantees for everyone involved in the research.

SIGIBio requirements were defined based in a systematic literature review of the information management of biobanks and biorepositories, which considered papers between 2010 and 2017 [2].

This work is divided into five sections, including this introduction. Section 2 presents the general concepts of biobanks and biorepositories and management systems in this area. In Sect. 3, SIGIBio is described in terms of requirements, stages of development, scenarios and technical aspects. Section 4 reports the usability tests of the SIGIBio. Finally, the conclusions and future works are in the last section.

## 2   Biobanks and Biorepositories

Both biobanks and biorepositories store human biological samples, but they have some differences between them. Biobanks are under the responsibility of an institution, operating without a predetermined deadline. Their stored samples can be requested by researchers for use in many searches. Whereas, biorepositories are under the responsibility of a researcher, existing only while one or more specific researches are being carried out [4].

In Nóbrega's research [2], 51 papers were selected: 21 of these works reported on procedures for managing biobanks and biorepositories and 14 described some biobanks and biorepositories software requirements. These papers stressed the importance of laboratory information management systems or sample management systems, which must be web-based and interoperable. Also, the systems must have security, robustness, audibility and the ability to manage the information contained in modern biobank and biorepository models. In addition, they should follow the ethical aspects of not exposing confidential information from donors or researchers and provide intelligent sample search to increase their use among relevant researches.

Brazil does not have a good public technological structure for the control of storage and loan of biological samples. Therefore, the importance of creating an architecture that facilitates access to the information contained in each biobank and biorepository is highlighted, to reduce the fragmentation of the databases used in research projects and to speed up them [5].

Some systems [6–9] that propose to manage biobanks were analyzed through information available on their own websites. All of these are proprietary software which cost between U$ 75.00 and U$ 245.00 in their most basic monthly plans, as can be seen in Table 1. In addition, none of them supports a network of connected biobanks, as they are not accessible to be used openly by various organizations.

**Table 1.** Comparison of biobank and biorepository management systems

| System name | Main differentials | Monthly cost (basic plan) |
| --- | --- | --- |
| LABA [6] | The request of custom functionality is available; maintains a history of laboratory activities | U$ 195.00 |
| LabCollector LIMS [7] | Enables the use of user groups with different permissions; manages diagrams with the workflows performed in the laboratory | U$ 245.00 |
| Freezer PRO [8] | It has configurable alerts of low number of samples and expiry date, among others; allows us to configure the freezers exactly as they are arranged in the laboratory | U$ 79.00 |
| CloudLIMS [9] | Allows the management of samples batches transferred; manages studies on the samples | U$ 75.00 |

# 3 SIGIBio

SIGIBio was created with the purpose of being a generic system for the control and management of a biobank or biorepository in any organization of any size. SIGIBio main objectives are: generality, to be able to be used in different organizations; mobility, so that it can be accessed in various devices; and availability so that it is possible to perform an optimization of the processes involving the management of biological samples.

Next, the list of requirements is described, enhancing aspects presented in the review, followed by development steps, usage scenarios and technical aspects.

## 3.1 Requirements

The initial requirements of the system were defined based on a review of the requirements analysis proposed by Nóbrega [2]. Thereby, it was decided that the scenario of quality management in the laboratory, although important for the proper functioning of a biobank or biorepository, would be outside the scope of the first system version.

After this review, it was defined that the system should be able to manage: (i) users, access and permissions, (ii) data from institutions and projects, (iii) data from research participants and their collected materials, (iv) biological samples, methodologies and results, and (v) requests and shipments of samples.

In addition, the system should meet the following non-functional requirements: (i) security, so that only authorized users are able to view and change data on the system, using permission levels; (ii) good usability, so that users feel satisfied when using it; (iii) efficiency, with a satisfactory response time; (iv) maintainability, allowing its source code to be easily adaptable for specific cases, or if new requirements or changes to existing requirements arise; (v) mobility and ease of access, when it is possible to access it through the Internet; (vi) use the ICD-10 (International Classification of Diseases) list when referring to diseases.

## 3.2 Development Stages

After defining the list of initial requirements, it was verified that the client-server architecture would be the most adequate for the implementation of the proposed system in this early stage, for being simpler than others. Thus, the data manipulated by it could be stored on a single server, while different clients could access it over the internet. These clients, communicating with the server through an API (Application Programming Interface), can use different platforms, such as mobile or desktop. For the initially proposed scope, it was decided that creating a single responsive website (suited to different sizes and screen resolutions, working well on different devices such as tablets, smartphones and desktops) would be enough as a client.

In these steps, the same development process was applied: (i) modeling and creation of database schemas; (ii) programming the server application; (iii) programming the client application; (iv) visual and usability improvements in the client application; (v) manual tests and corrections of specific problems.

Recent and well-known technologies were considered to facilitate the system development and upgrades. Having the technologies and requirements defined the modules of users' management as access, permissions and management of institutions and projects were implemented.

Finally, with the system running in a simulated environment, a usability test was performed with five experts. They were asked to evaluate the system, and the results of these tests are presented in Sect. 4.

## 3.3 Usage Scenarios

In the current version of the system, there are five modules: (i) management of users, access and permissions, (ii) management of institutions and projects, (iii) management of research participants and collected materials, (iv) management of samples, methodologies and results, and (v) management of samples batches. Figure 1 shows the start screen of the system.

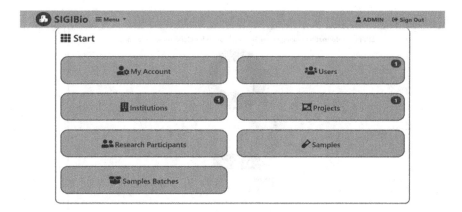

**Fig. 1.** Start screen – SIGIBio

## Management of Users, Access and Permission

Because secrecy is critical to some of the system information, especially to those related to research participants, this module is essential for the correct functioning of all others. No action (except registering or authenticating) can be performed on the system unless the user is authenticated.

The access control is done through a username and a password, defined during the registration of the user. Permissions control is based on three types of permissions: administrator, internal user and external user.

The administrator can perform any action on the system. It is responsible for approving users, projects, institutions and requested samples batches. In the case of a biobank, it is an employee of the biobank managing institution, being a level above the internal users. On the other hand, in a biorepository, the researcher is responsible for it.

The internal user is responsible for the management of samples, methodologies and results, and is also an employee of the managing institution. He can dispatch new samples batches and receive the returned ones. In addition, in the case of a biobank, it manages the participants who donate samples directly to it, not to a specific project, also managing the materials collected from them.

Finally, the external user can manage or be part of one or more institutions, as well as manage or be part of projects. He can manage participants of his projects, as well as the materials collected from them. Also, he can request samples batches for his projects.

Any user, when registering in the system, must indicate what permission he wishes to have. After registering, an administrator user will evaluate his data and approve or reject his registration. If the new user is approved, he will be able to use all the system features allowed for his permission level (Fig. 2).

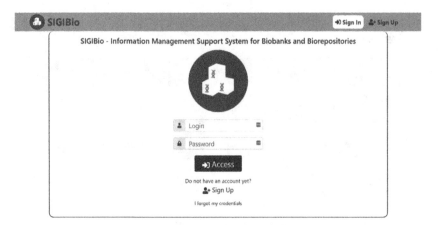

**Fig. 2.** Access screen – SIGIBio

## Management of Institutions and Projects

An external user can register an institution and manage it. Users can be associated with an institution as their professionals. An institution may have registered projects.

Similarly, an external user can register their projects, associate them with one or more institutions, and manage them. Users can be associated with a project as their professionals. A project can have registered research participants. It may also be in possession of one or more samples batches.

In both cases, the registration is started as pending, and only becomes valid and visible from the moment it is approved by an administrator (Fig. 3).

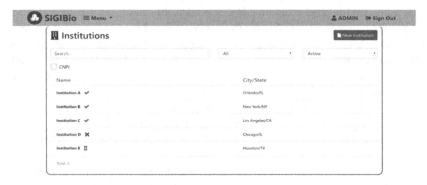

**Fig. 3.** Institutions list screen – SIGIBio

## Management of Research Participants and Collected Materials

Research participants may be associated to a specific project, being registered by external users, or not associated with any project, donating material directly to the managing institution of the biobank. In this case, an internal user is responsible for registering him.

When registering a participant, a file with his signed ICF (Informed Consent Form) must be attached, as it is the document that proves the participant is aware of the donation and its consequences.

A research participant can donate one or more materials, called collected materials. These will then be processed by an internal user to be transformed into samples that can be used in researches. Figure 4 details some aspects involved is this stage.

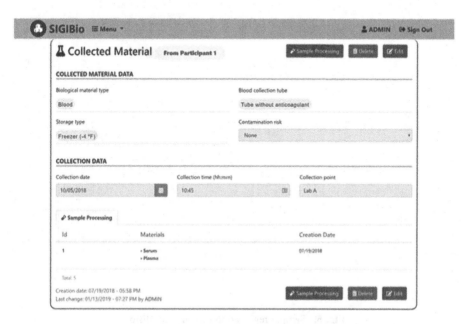

**Fig. 4.** Collected material registration screen – SIGIBio

## Management of Samples, Methodologies and Results

This is the central module of SIGIBio with the main functionalities. Internal users can manage sample boxes by having a view of their free positions. External users can view available samples to request.

Internal users can register samples from a material collected from a research participant. It should be allocated in a free box position (Fig. 5). They can also manage all sample data, as well as their methodologies and results.

External users may manage methodologies and results of samples that are in a batch intended for a project of this user, in addition to viewing and requesting samples for research.

**Fig. 5.** Sample registration screen – SIGIBio

## Management of Samples Batches

External users can request a group of samples for their research projects. The responsible for the lot is the person who requested the sample being one of the professionals assigned to the project. The operation of this module is described in Fig. 6.

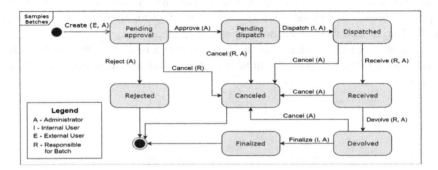

**Fig. 6.** State transition diagram - samples batch

### 3.4    Technical Aspects

Various programming standards have been used to make the development of the system simpler and to make it easier to maintain. Reuse of code through inheritance and auxiliary classes, well-defined names, modularization, separation of layers by responsibility, standardized formatting and small and objective functions were some of the techniques used.

The communication between client and server was implemented using the Hypertext Transfer Protocol (HTTP). Thus, the server provides an API from which the client can access and manage the system data. The server was implemented to offer a RESTful web service, name given to web services that follow the REST (Representational State Transfer) principles. REST is, in short, an architectural style to be used in the World Wide Web that focuses on the components, connectors and data of a system [10].

The database management system was MySQL [11]. It was chosen for being free, open source, widely used in the market and easy to learn and use, among others.

The implementation of the server was done with the platform Node.js [12], which allowed both client and server to be written in the same programming language: TypeScript [13]. This is an open source language developed by Microsoft that provides the necessary features of the latest version of JavaScript and adds features such as better support for data typing and objects orientation. In addition, the Express framework [14] supports web development with Node.js.

The implementation of the client was done in TypeScript with Angular [15], a proper framework for the creation of SPAs (Single Page Applications, which behave like smartphone applications, without complete screen transitions, having only part of the content reloaded) [16]. Using Bootstrap [17], the website is responsive, aiming to bring good usability in both smartphones and desktop computers.

## 4    Usability Tests

After completing the development of the SIGIBio first version, five health research professionals were invited to perform a usability test on the system. According to Nielsen [18], a research on system usability with at least five participants with similar profiles already demonstrates trends that can be significant.

The evaluation methodology used was the SUS (System Usability Scale) [19]. According to Brooke, its creator, usability is somewhat difficult to measure quantitatively. However, there are some points that must be addressed when attempting to measure this property: effectiveness, the ability of users to complete tasks using the system; efficiency, the amount of resources consumed when performing tasks in the system; and satisfaction, the subjective reactions of users when using the system.

And SUS assesses these points quickly and reliably, having been selected for the SIGIBio evaluation for these reasons. Ten statements are made, and the evaluators are instructed to answer each one with scores ranging from 1 to 5, where 1 means completely disagree and 5 means completely agree.

To carry out the usability tests of SIGIBio, the professionals were asked to test all the main functionalities of the following areas of the system: (i) access and users,

(ii) research participants, (iii) collected materials, (iv) samples boxes, (v) samples and (vi) methodologies and results.

After using the system, they were asked to evaluate the system using SUS. Figure 7 shows the statements of the SUS and the answers provided by all participants of the evaluation.

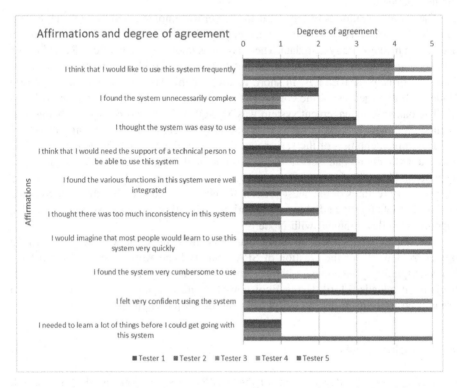

**Fig. 7.** Affirmations of the SUS and degrees of agreement of the invited participants

According to Brooke [19], after collecting these notes, the SUS score of a single participant should be calculated as follows: for each statement of odd index, subtract the value 1 from the given note; for each even index statement, subtract the given note from the value 5; add all new notes and multiply by 2.5. At the end, simply calculate the arithmetic mean between the final scores of each participant. Thus, we arrive at the result shown in Fig. 8.

According to Bangor, Kortum and Miller [20], who carried out an empirical evaluation of this methodology, the SUS applied in web interfaces has the value of 68 points as average grade. As can be seen, the average score of the participants who evaluated SIGIBio is 80 points. Still according to them, this value is between good and excellent.

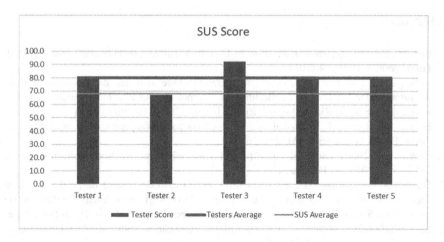

**Fig. 8.** Score of each tester

## 5 Conclusion

The work carried out by Nóbrega [2] justified the need for a system like SIGIBio for institutions that manage biobanks or biorepositories. Thus, it was developed as a tool to facilitate the conduction of researches with biological samples and their management. Professionals who use it spend less time on routine activities related to the handling of biological samples and can make better use of this time on other tasks.

Based on a literature review [2] on what would be important to implement, using modern technologies and development techniques geared towards source code quality and graphical user interfaces, this first version of SIGIBio was developed considering future changes and improvements. In addition, the usability tests showed a good acceptance by the health professionals who evaluated it. There are still several aspects that can be considered to expand and improve the functionality of SIGIBio. Some modules are already planned to be implemented in future releases. The quality management module in the laboratory, as suggested by Nóbrega [2], should have the capacity to manage data related to the management of research laboratories. The statistics module will be able to generate and display reports on the use of SIGIBio, such as which sample types are most requested for searches. Researchers can use the information available in their projects. In addition, managerial decision making will be easier for the administrators of the biobank or the biorepository managed by the system.

In addition to these, there will be the integration module. From it, it is expected that SIGIBio will become the basis for a network of connected biobanks and biorepositories, as suggested by Eder, Gottweis and Zatloukal [3], by disseminating information between institutions and between researchers in a simple and effective way.

Finally, it is important to stress that any tools that facilitate and accelerate the work of researchers help directly in the development of the whole society, since only the research and the dissemination of knowledge are capable of this.

# References

1. List, M., Schmidt, S., Trojnar, J., Thomas, J., et al.: Efficient sample tracking with OpenLab Framework. Sci. Rep. **4** (2014)
2. Nóbrega, I.C.: Revisão sistemática de literatura sobre sistemas de biobancos e biorrepositórios. Dissertation of Telehealth, and Telemedicine Graduation Program - Universidade do Estado do Rio de Janeiro, Rio de Janeiro (2017). (in Portuguese)
3. Eder, J., Gottweis, H., Zatloukal, K.: IT solutions for privacy protection in biobanking. Public Health Genomics **15**(5), 254–262 (2012)
4. Biobancos e Biorrepositórios. https://portal.fiocruz.br/biobancos-e-biorrepositorios. Accessed 22 July 2018. (in Portuguese)
5. Gonçalves, A.A., Pitassi, C., de Assis Jr., V.M.: O caso do sistema de gestão do banco nacional de tumores do inca no brasil. In: CONTECSI-International Conference on Information Systems and Technology Management, pp. 1520–1535 (2012). (in Portuguese)
6. LABA-Laboratory Assistant and Biobanking Application. https://biobanking.software/#biobanking. Accessed 22 July 2018
7. LABCOLLECTO - LIMS for BioBanking. http://labcollector.com/solutions/applications/biobanking/. Accessed 22 July 2018
8. FREEZERPRO. https://www.freezerpro.com/. Accessed 22 July 2018
9. CLOUDLIMS. https://cloudlims.com/industries/biobank-lims-software.html. Accessed 22 July 2018
10. Fielding, R.T.: REST: architectural styles and the design of network-based software architectures. Doctoral dissertation, University of California (2000)
11. MYSQL. https://www.mysql.com/. Accessed 22 July 2018
12. NODE.JS. http://nodejs.org/en/about/. Accessed 22 July 2018
13. TYPESCRIPT. https://www.typescriptlang.org. Accessed 22 July 2018
14. EXPRESS. http://expressjs.com/pt-br/. Accessed 22 July 2018
15. ANGULAR. http://angular.io. Accessed 22 July 2018
16. O que é single page application?. http://blog.locaweb.com.br/artigos/desenvolvimento-artigos/o-que-e-single-page-application/. Accessed 22 July 2018
17. BOOTSTRAP. Disponível em. https://getbootstrap.com/. Accessed 22 July 2018
18. Nielsen, J.: Why You Only Need to Test With 5 Users. Jakob Nielsen's Alertbox (2000). http://www.useit.com/alertbox/20000319.html. Accessed 28 Sept 2018
19. Brooke, J., et al.: SUS-A quick and dirty usability scale. Usability Eval. Ind. **189**(194), 4–7 (1996)
20. Bangor, A., Kortum, P.T., Miller, J.T.: An empirical evaluation of the system usability scale. Int. J. Hum.-Comput. Interact. **24**(6), 574–594 (2008)

# Using Computer Simulation for Reducing the Appointment Lead-Time in a Public Pediatric Outpatient Department

Miguel Ortiz-Barrios[1]([✉]), Genett Jiménez-Delgado[2], Sally McClean[3], and Giselle Polifroni-Avendaño[4]

[1] Department of Industrial Management, Agroindustry and Operations, Universidad de La Costa CUC, Barranquilla, Colombia
mortiz1@cuc.edu.co
[2] Department of Engineering in Industrial Process Engineering, Institución Universitaria ITSA, Barranquilla, Colombia
gjimenez@itsa.edu.co
[3] School of Computing, University of Ulster, Coleraine, Co., Londonderry BT52 1SA, UK
si.mcclean@ulster.ac.uk
[4] Department of General Management, Sofast Ingeniería S.A.S., Barranquilla, Colombia
gisele2127@gmail.com

**Abstract.** Pediatric outpatient departments aim to provide a pleasant, effective and continuing care to children. However, a problem in these units is the long waiting time for children to receive an appointment. Prolonged appointment lead-time remains a global challenge since it results in delayed diagnosis and treatment causing increased morbidity and dissatisfaction. Additionally, it leads to an increased number of hospitalization and emergency department visits which augments the financial burden faced by healthcare systems. Despite these considerations, the studies directly concentrating on the reduction of appointment lead-time in these departments are largely limited. Therefore, this paper proposes the application of Discrete-event Simulation (DES) approach to evaluate potential improvement strategies aiming at reducing average appointment lead-time. Initially, the outpatient department is characterized to effectively identify the main activities, process variables, interactions, and system constraints. After data collection, input analysis is conducted through intra-variable independence, homogeneity and goodness-of-fit tests followed by the creation of a simulation model representing the real pediatric outpatient department. Then, Mann-Whitney tests are used to prove whether the model was statistically comparable with the real-world system. After this, the outpatient department performance is assessed in terms of average appointment lead-time and resource utilization. Finally, three improvement scenarios are assessed technically and financially, to determine if they are viable for implementation. A case study of a mixed-patient type environment in a public pediatric outpatient department has been explored to validate the proposed methodology. Statistical tests demonstrate that appointment lead-time in pediatric outpatient departments may be meaningfully minimized using this approach.

© Springer Nature Switzerland AG 2019
V. G. Duffy (Ed.): HCII 2019, LNCS 11582, pp. 75–86, 2019.
https://doi.org/10.1007/978-3-030-22219-2_6

**Keywords:** Discrete-event simulation (DES) · Healthcare · Appointment lead-time · Pediatric · Outpatient care

# 1  Introduction

Patient waiting time is an important indicator of healthcare quality of service. Patients perceive long waiting times as a barrier to obtaining services, while they can also be stressful for both patients and healthcare professionals [1]. Waiting time reduction is a multi-faceted problem, encompassing diagnosis, prioritization, and triage of patients, monitoring and management of wait times, provision of adequate physical resources, and appropriate provision staff human resources and equipment [2]. In particular, prolonged appointment lead-time remains a global challenge across many medical specialties leading to delayed diagnosis and treatment as well as increased morbidity and dissatisfaction. Also, for most specialties, lengthy waits can lead to increased hospitalization and emergency department visits which exacerbate the overall problems for healthcare systems.

Despite attempts to ensure that pediatric outpatient departments provide a pleasant, effective and continuing care to children, there have frequently been problems with long waiting time for children to receive an appointment. In addition to the known consequences of prolonged wait times for adults, including further suffering, emotional distress and economic hardship, young patients particularly vulnerable as "children often require treatment at critical times to ensure appropriate development" [2]. Also, pediatric care, often involves many confounding factors, such as the degree of parental anxiety, the urgency of the illness and availability of appropriate services [3].

Discrete Event Simulation (DES) has been widely used systems for many years to model health-care and some previous work has used this approach to provide waiting time improvement strategies in general, and also specifically for outpatients [4]. For example, a simulation model was described to improve the performance of a healthcare facility by providing a simulation model for reducing outpatient waiting time by focusing on schedules of the healthcare providers [5]. A recent example is provided by [6] who analyzed the appointment scheduling system in an Obstetrics-Gynecology Department as the basis of a simulation-based decision support system for the evaluation and optimization of scheduling rules and waiting time. This system was used to identify a number of critical factors that influenced patient waiting times and proposed strategies to reschedule outpatient appointments and significantly improve patient waiting times. In general, such simulation and analysis of patient flows can contribute to the efficient functioning of a healthcare system as discussed by a recent paper which provides a number of examples and also some exploratory simulation tools [7].

In spite of such previous work, the number of earlier studies that focused on the reduction of appointment lead-time in pediatric outpatient departments is limited. As such, this paper proposes the application of Discrete-event Simulation (DES) approach to evaluate potential improvement strategies aiming at reducing average appointment lead-time for pediatric patients. The main activities process variables, interactions, and system constraints are identified and used to create a simulation model representing the pediatric outpatient department. Following validation, three improvement scenarios are considered, namely improving appointment scheduling policy, improving capacity and decreasing consultation time through eliminating non-value activities.

The remainder of this paper is organized as follows: In Sect. 2 the legal framework that motivates this intervention is presented whereas the proposed methodology is explained in Sect. 3. In Sect. 4, a case study in an outpatient pediatric department from Colombia is described. Finally, Sect. 5 illustrates the conclusions and future work.

## 2 The Legal Framework

Healthcare has been considered in the Colombian Political Constitution, as an essential public service that is in charge of the Government and should be therefore provided under its very strict regulation, monitoring, and control [10]. It was initially conceived as a right of a pragmatic nature, however, it has been recognized, by the constitutional jurisprudence, as a fundamental right that "comprises the prompt, efficacious, and high-quality access to healthcare services for preserving, improving and promoting the health" [11]. The Colombian Constitution of 1991 enshrines the right to health as a fundamental guarantee of children, by establishing the prevalence of their rights over the rights of other groups; this is due to the special protection provided by the Government. Law No. 1751 (2015) stipulates that healthcare given to groups object of special protection, including the adolescent population, "will not be limited by any type of administrative or economic restraint"; however, having regard to the principle of progressivity, the Government must adopt policies that aim towards expanding access to healthcare services and improving its delivery [11] as needed in the outpatient pediatric department that will be studied in Sect. 4.

In view of the foregoing, the Ministry of Health and Social Protection, by the Resolution 429 (2016), adopted a Comprehensive Healthcare Policy (CHP) whose operational framework corresponds to the Comprehensive Model for Healthcare which comprises, as one of its factors, the regulation of Integral Routes of Healthcare (IRH) [12]. The IRH contains, among other components, the Integral Route for the promotion and maintenance of health and wellness. Such route covers the sectorial and inter-sectorial actions directed towards the health promotion and disease prevention through the comprehensive assessment of health and the early detection of impairments. For the IRH design and implementation, the members of healthcare sector must use the methodological manual adopted by the Resolution No. 3202 (2016) providing the life course approach as a transverse approximation supporting the continuous monitoring of individuals' health. One of the life stages contained in this approach is the Early Childhood which covers the period from pregnancy up to the first five years of life and is the essential cycle for the further development of human being. Another life stage is Childhood referring to the time between the ages of 6 and 11 years old. In such a period, the healthcare sector must be a guarantor of the integral development of children. This has to be also extended to the Adolescence (from 12 to 17 years), a period in which the individual's socialization process is defined [13].

## 3   Proposed Methodology

For providing a good representation of outpatient pediatric departments, it is necessary to take into account the child heterogeneity, multiple care options and the existing interactions with other healthcare services (i.e. surgery, hospitalization, and emergency). In this regard, it is very important to ensure that the simulated model is statistically comparable with the real-world department in terms of assumptions, architecture, and performance [8, 9]. Integrated decision support systems should be then incorporated by health service managers to address the complexity of outpatient departments and the need for improving their performance under restricted resources. Such systems must be underpinned by robust methodological approaches that allow decision makers to identify and tackle process drawbacks. An example of these approaches can be seen in Fig. 1. This framework has the potential to support performance analysis and operational evaluation of potential improvement interventions across the outpatient pediatric systems.

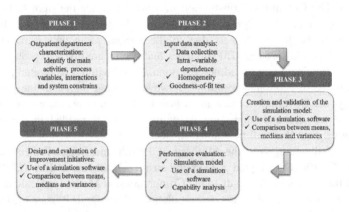

**Fig. 1.** The proposed framework for modelling outpatient pediatric departments and designing cost-effective initiatives

- **Phase 1** *"Outpatient department characterization"*: In this phase, the health service managers, doctors, nurses and administrative staff are asked to give information that helps to elicit the different stages (e.g. Scheduling, Billing, and Outpatient Care), system restrictions and assumptions within the outpatient pediatric department. A conceptual model is then developed (using flow diagrams) to be later incorporated into a DES. The exogenous/endogenous variables and costs associated with the outpatient care journey are also identified to fully represent the performance and uncertainty of the department under study.
- **Phase 2** *"Input data analysis"*: In this step, the data corresponding to the variables and parameters identified in Phase 1, are gathered from the information sources of the outpatient pediatric department under analysis. Such information must be properly filtered and assessed to avoid the inclusion of low-quality data into the DES model. The use of suitable data is important to ensure the equivalence between

the simulated model and the real-world outpatient department. The next step is to undertake an intra-variable independence test (i.e. statistical auto-correlation test) to determine whether the data follow a probability distribution or depends on other variables. A heterogeneity analysis is later carried out to detect (if possible) sub-groups of data in each variable. Statistical tests such as Kruskal-Wallis and log-rank can be applied to this particular aim. If the data are not found to be homogeneous, a probability distribution must be used to represent each sub-group; otherwise, one probability distribution is enough to model the whole dataset. Finally, a goodness-of-fit technique is performed to verify whether a statistical distribution function suitably fits the data and consequently calculate the distribution parameters that will be introduced into the simulated model.

- **Phase 3** *"Creation and validation of the simulation model"*: In this phase, a simulation software (Arena 14.5 ®) is employed to give a virtual illustration of the real outpatient pediatric department. This promotes effective user engagement by animating the patient flows, clinical settings, and resources linked to the patient journey within the department. The conceptual model described in Phase 1 and the results of input data analysis (see Phase 2) are jointly incorporated in the software for transparency validation and further process analysis. To ensure the suitability and robustness of the results provided by the simulation software, it is necessary to rigorously examine the model transparency and conduct validation tests. To do these, key performance indicators and simulation run length need to be outlined. In this regard, 10 runs should be initially performed to estimate the sample size (number of runs) that will be used to conclude whether the simulated model is statistically equivalent to the outpatient pediatric department under study. To validate this hypothesis, a comparison between means/medians can be carried out. If the resulting p-value is greater than the alpha level ($\alpha = 0.05$), the model is considered to be a good representation of the real version and it is, therefore, useful for analysis and prediction. Alternatively, it should be examined and improved to guarantee high accuracy and applicability.

- **Phase 4** *"Performance evaluation"*: After cross-checking the simulation results with the outcomes derived from the real outpatient department, the health service managers can proceed with the performance assessment and analysis. In this phase, the *appointment lead-time (ALT)* has been selected as the main performance indicator. The current ALT should be compared to the target (Upper specification limit – USL = 8 days) in order to determine how well the process meets the standard established by the Ministry of Health [14]. In this phase, process capability indicators Pp, Ppk, DPMO and sigma level are calculated to conclude on the current process behavior.

- **Phase 5** *"Design and evaluation of improvement initiatives"*: Health service managers are also interested in evaluating and comparing different initiatives with a view to improving the ALT in outpatient pediatric departments. The interventions should be designed with the aid of the managers and medical staff to guarantee that they are realistic and can be executed without violating preexisting conditions. Such interventions are later modeled and initially run 10 times in Arena 14.5 ® software. After this, the final sample size is achieved and the scenario is run again according to the calculated simulation length. The results, in terms of ALT, are then statistically compared to the current performance using a test between means or medians. In this case, if the p-value is less than the alpha level (0.05), the proposed intervention is deemed cost-effective and may result in a reduced ALT. Otherwise, it is not considered as satisfying and should not be then implemented in the real outpatient pediatric department.

## 4   An Illustrative Example: Modeling an Outpatient Pediatric Department from the Public Sector

### 4.1   Outpatient Department Characterization

A conceptual model was provided to analyze the patient journey within an outpatient pediatric department from the public sector. In detail, three autonomous stages (Scheduling, Billing and Outpatient Care) and two appointment types (First-time and monitoring) were identified (refer to Fig. 2). Our model was underpinned by a 1-year prospective dataset obtained from the User Information System (UIS) and consisting of all the pediatric appointments scheduled between 24 December and 31 December (n = 8309 appointments). In this period, 4011 (48.27%) requests were first-time appointments and the rest (4298) were asked for monitoring purposes. The patients are children between the ages of 1 and 10 years old.

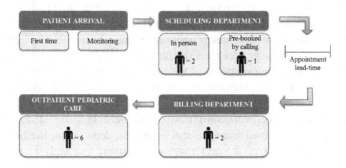

**Fig. 2.** The conceptual model for the outpatient pediatric department

The pediatric appointments are initially booked in the Scheduling department by two servers ($SD_1$, $SD_2$) who operate according to the shifts $S_1$ (8:00 am–12:00 pm; 2:00 pm–5:00 pm) and $S_2$ (8:00 am–1:00 pm; 3:00 pm – 5:00 pm) respectively. The appointments can be also telephonically programmed with the aid of the server $SD_3$ whose shift work is $S_1$. The scheduling policy consists of booking in accordance with the availability of pediatricians, consultation rooms and type of appointment. However, this process is currently affected by the arrival of new urgent patients, cancellations of medical agenda and equipment breakdowns. These factors increase the complexity of the scheduling problem and new approaches can be therefore needed for addressing the dynamic scenario here described. The patients are asked to arrive 1 h before the appointment time in order to deliver the service authorization to one of the servers (SB$_1$, SB$_2$) who operate in the Billing department during the S$_1$ and S$_2$ shifts respectively. This unit verifies whether the patients are already registered in the UIS and if their corresponding data are complete. If the aforementioned conditions are fully satisfied, the servers proceed with generating the invoice and service order. Afterwards, the patients go into the waiting room and stay there until they are seen by a pediatrician. In this department, there are six pediatricians who serve according to the shifts depicted in Table 1. On the other hand, it was detected that all the pediatricians arrive late every day. In addition, they tend to cancel their medical agenda every three weeks.

**Table 1.** Work shifts of pediatricians

| Pediatrician code | Monday | Tuesday | Wednesday | Thursday | Friday |
|---|---|---|---|---|---|
| 001 | 8:00 am–12 pm | 8:00 am–12 pm | X | 8:00 am–12 pm | X |
| 002 | X | X | X | 8:00 am–12 pm | X |
| 003 | X | X | 8:00 am–12 pm | X | X |
| 004 | X | 8:00 am–12 pm | X | 8:00 am–12 pm | 8:00 am–12 pm |
| 005 | X | 1:00 pm–5:00 pm | X | 1:00 pm–5:00 pm | 1:00 pm–5:00 pm |
| 006 | 8:00 am–12 pm | X | X | X | X |

With these considerations in mind, we defined six process variables: (1) time between arrivals for first-time appointments, (2) time between arrivals for monitoring appointments, (3) service time in Scheduling department (in-person attention), (4) service time in Scheduling department (by phone calls), (5) service time in Billing department, and (6) service time in outpatient pediatric care.

## 4.2 Input Data Analysis

After gathering the data corresponding to the identified process variables, an independence test was conducted to validate the randomness assumption. The results are detailed in Table 2. In this case, all the variables were found to be random since the p-values were greater than the alpha level (0.05). Once the independence was verified, a heterogeneity analysis was conducted for each dataset in order to discriminate pipelines (refer to Table 3). In this respect, an Analysis of Variance (ANOVA) concluded that the *time between arrivals* should be modeled separately based on the pediatric appointment type. This is because the p-value (0) was found to be less than the established error level (0.05). In contrast, *service time in Scheduling department, service time in the Billing department,* and *service time in outpatient pediatric care* were concluded to be homogeneous since the resulting p-values (0.8114, >0.15, >0.15) provided enough support to accept the null hypothesis (homogeneity).

**Table 2.** P-values emanating from the independence tests

| Process variable | P-value |
|---|---|
| Time between arrivals (first-time appointments) | 1.0 |
| Time between arrivals (monitoring appointments) | 1.0 |
| Service time in the Scheduling department (in-person attention) | 0.537813 |
| Service time in the Scheduling department (by phone calls) | 0.453305 |
| Service time in the Billing department | <0.05 |
| Service time in outpatient pediatric care | <0.05 |

**Table 3.** ANOVA outcomes

| Process variable | P-value |
|---|---|
| Time between arrivals | 0 |
| Service time in the Scheduling department | 0.8114 |
| Service time in the Billing department | >0.15 |
| Service time in outpatient pediatric care | >0.15 |

After validating the independence assumption and data homogeneity, the probability distributions representing the process variables were identified using Goodness-of-fit tests. For instance, the chi-squared test ($\chi^2 = 2.46$, d. f. = 1, p-value = 0.126) validated the Weibull assumption of *time between arrivals (monitoring appointments)*. The rest of the probability distributions and parameters are presented in Table 4.

**Table 4.** Probability distributions of process variables

| Process variable | Probability distribution |
|---|---|
| Time between arrivals (first-time appointments) | EXPO (45.5) min. |
| Time between arrivals (monitoring appointments) | 2.13 + WEIB (1.42, 4) days |
| Service time in the Scheduling department | NORM (3.70; 1.77) min/appointment |
| Service time in the Billing department | UNIF (2.4; 5.7) min/appointment |
| Service time in outpatient pediatric care | NORM (35; 5.7) min/appointment |

### 4.3    Creation and Validation of the Simulation Model

A simulation model was created to offer a virtual illustration of the outpatient pediatric department under study (refer to Fig. 3). To guarantee the robustness and reliability of the simulation results, we ran the virtual model for a time period of 372 days with 9 h per day (opening period). After initial analysis, we concluded that 100 of these days were needed as a warm-up period. Such period helps the model to reach a steady condition and offer reliable and realistic outcomes. Furthermore, a pre-sample (10 replications) was conducted to calculate the required sample size for suitably representing the process uncertainty. In this case, 40 replications were concluded to be enough for this particular aim. Afterwards, the results in terms of the *average appointment lead-time* per replication were gathered and processed to evaluate the hypothesis ($H_o$: $\mu = 7.66$ *days/appointment*|$H_a$: $\mu \neq 7.66$ *days/appointment*). To do this, a 1-sample t test (Confidence level = 95%) was carried out using Minitab 17 ® software. The p-value (0.638) and t-statistic (0.47) evidenced that the simulation model is statistically equivalent to the real outpatient pediatric department. Hence, it can be employed for performance evaluation and analysis of potential interventions.

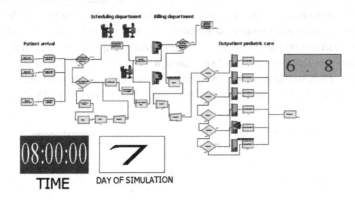

**Fig. 3.** DES model for the outpatient pediatric department

### 4.4    Performance Evaluation

Once the validation process was finished, the next step was to assess the capability of the outpatient pediatric department to meet the standard established by the local Ministry of Health (Upper specification limit = 8 days/appointment). After performing this analysis, the *average appointment lead time* was found to be 7.66 days/appointment with a standard deviation of 4.98 days/appointment. According to the capability analysis, 366959 out of 1 million of appointments will have an ALT > 8 days. In addition, the Ppu (0.05), Ppk (0.05) and sigma level (1.84) indicate that the process is not satisfactory and requires immediate intervention. It is thus necessary to create and pretest initiatives addressing the long appointment lead time (Fig. 4).

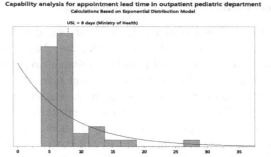

**Fig. 4.** Capability analysis in terms of appointment lead time

## 4.5 Definition and Evaluation of Improvement Initiatives

The simulation models give an opportunity to pretest improvement scenarios in outpatient departments in a satisfactory and safe manner. Despite this consideration, little evidence has been reported regarding the use of DES for this particular target [15]. The present research then attempts to fill this gap in the literature. Specifically, three initiatives were proposed by the health service managers to address the long ALT problem: (1) *Changes to appointment scheduling policy* (2) *Increase installed capacity* and (3) *Diminish the consultation time through eliminating non-value activities*. These interventions were then modeled and simulated with the aid of Arena 14.5 ® software. The results of each scenario were contrasted with the current performance in terms of ALT using the comparison test between medians (confidence level: 95%).

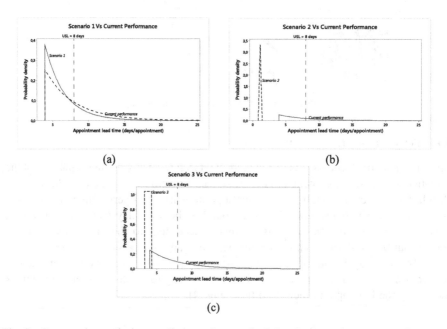

**Fig. 5.** Comparative analysis regarding appointment lead time between the current performance and (a) Scenario 1 (b) Scenario 2 (c) Scenario 3

Scenario 1 proposes that pediatricians 002 and 003 adopt the work shift of doctor 001. After simulation and analysis (Mann-Whitney test; CL = 95%), the ALT was found to be statistically equivalent (refer to Fig. 5a) in comparison with the current performance (p-value = 0.097; W = 565). On the other hand, Scenario 2 (refer to Fig. 5b) suggests the addition of 1 pediatrician with the same work shift established for pediatrician 006. In this case, the results evidenced that ALT can be meaningfully reduced (p-value = 0; W = 55). Ultimately, Scenario 3 (refer to Fig. 5c) considers the elimination of the time lost in interrogation. Such inefficiency is a consequence of outdated patients' medical records. After pretest and statistical examination, it was proved that the resulting ALT is meaningfully lower contrasted with the real-world department.

## 5   Conclusions and Future Work

Modelling outpatient pediatric departments has become a challenge for researchers and practitioners due to the presence of multiple pathways and interactions. It is hence fundamental that modelers receive support from the health service managers and medical staff to guarantee that the simulation models are robust and reliable. To this end, the collected data must be filtered and suitably processed so that high-quality information can be incorporated into the models. The acquisition of such information strongly depends on the engagement from the outpatient departments and their continuous assistance along the intervention.

Our proposed methodology develops integrated models for outpatient pediatric services and provides effective decision-making support for resource planning and process management. Nonetheless, this approach can be extended to cover interrelations with emergency care, radiology, laboratory diagnosis, and other health services so that more complex and informative scenarios can be assessed. Moreover, we plan in future work to combine this framework with cost models in order to also evaluate improvement scenarios financially.

The case study here presented evidences the functionality of simulation models when diagnosing outpatient pediatric services and pretesting improvement scenarios. In particular, it was concluded that the process is not capable to meet the standard set by the Ministry of Health regarding the appointment lead time. In addition, the results proved that Scenario 2 and Scenario 3 are beneficial for improving the performance of the department under analysis; however, both strategies should be financially evaluated before deciding on their implementation.

## References

1. Oche, M.O., Adamu, H.: Determinants of patient waiting time in the general outpatient department of a tertiary health institution in north Western Nigeria. Ann. Med. Health Sci. Res. **3**(4), 588–592 (2013)
2. Wright, J.G., et al.: Development of pediatric wait time access targets. Can. J. Surg. **54**(2), 107 (2011)

3. Tan, J.H.T., et al.: A quality improvement project to reduce waiting time for pediatric outpatient referral clinics in Singapore. Proc. Singap. Healthcare **26**(4), 224–229 (2017)
4. Günal, M.M., Pidd, M.: Discrete event simulation for performance modelling in health care: a review of the literature. J. Simul. **4**(1), 42–51 (2010)
5. Aeenparast, A., Tabibi, S.J., Shahanaghi, K., Aryanejhad, M.B.: Reducing outpatient waiting time: a simulation modeling approach. Iran. Red Crescent Med. J. **15**(9), 865 (2013)
6. Jamjoom, A., Abdullah, M., Abulkhair, M., Alghamdi, T., Mogbil, A.: Improving outpatient waiting time using simulation approach. In: 2014 European Modelling Symposium, pp. 117–125. IEEE, October 2014
7. Bean, D.M., Taylor, P., Dobson, R.J.: A patient flow simulator for healthcare management education. BMJ Simul. Technol. Enhanc. Learn. **5**(1), 46–48 (2019)
8. Ortiz, M.A., López-Meza, P.: Using computer simulation to improve patient flow at an outpatient internal medicine department. In: García, C.R., Caballero-Gil, P., Burmester, M., Quesada-Arencibia, A. (eds.) UCAmI 2016. LNCS, vol. 10069, pp. 294–299. Springer, Cham (2016). https://doi.org/10.1007/978-3-319-48746-5_30
9. Ortiz, M.A., McClean, S., Nugent, C.D., Castillo, A.: Reducing appointment lead-time in an outpatient department of gynecology and obstetrics through discrete-event simulation: a case study. In: García, C.R., Caballero-Gil, P., Burmester, M., Quesada-Arencibia, A. (eds.) UCAmI 2016. LNCS, vol. 10069, pp. 274–285. Springer, Cham (2016). https://doi.org/10.1007/978-3-319-48746-5_28
10. Constitución Política de Colombia (1991). http://www.secretariasenado.gov.co/index.php/constitucion-politica
11. Congreso de la República de Colombia: Ley 1751 de 2015. Por medio de la cual se regula el derecho fundamental a la salud y se dictan otras disposiciones, 16 February 2015. http://www.secretariasenado.gov.co/senado/basedoc/ley_1751_2015.html#26
12. Ministerio de Salud y Protección Social: Resolución 429 de 2016. Por medio de la cual se adopta la Política de Atención Integral en Salud, 17 February 2016. https://www.minsalud.gov.co/Normatividad_Nuevo/Resoluci%C3%B3n%200429%20de%202016.pdf
13. Ministerio de Salud y Protección Social: Resolución 3202 de 2016. Por la cual se adopta el Manual Metodológico para la elaboración e implementación de las Rutas Integrales de Atención en Salud — RIAS, se adopta un grupo de Rutas Integrales de Atención en Salud desarrolladas por el Ministerio de Salud y Protección Social dentro de la política de Atención Integral en Salud —PAIS y se dictan otras disposiciones, 25 July 2016. https://www.minsalud.gov.co/Normatividad_Nuevo/Reluci%C3%B3n%203202%20de%202016.pdf
14. Izquierdo, N.V., Viloria, A., Lezama, O.B.P., Gaitán-Angulo, M., Herrera, H.H.: Performance evaluation by means of fuzzy mathematics. The case of a clinical laboratory. J. Control Theory Appl. (2016). ISSN 0974–5572
15. Mohiuddin, S., et al.: Patient flow within UK emergency departments: a systematic review of the use of computer simulation modelling methods. BMJ Open **7**(5), e015007 (2017)

# Applying Multi-phase DES Approach for Modelling the Patient Journey Through Accident and Emergency Departments

Miguel Ortiz-Barrios[1(✉)], Pablo Pancardo[2],
Genett Jiménez-Delgado[3], and Jeferson De Ávila-Villalobos[1]

[1] Department of Industrial Management, Agroindustry and Operations,
Universidad de La Costa CUC, Barranquilla, Colombia
{mortiz1, jdeavila8}@cuc.edu.co
[2] Academic Division of Informatics and Systems,
Juarez Autonomous University of Tabasco, 86690 Cunduacan,
Tabasco, Mexico
pablo.pancardo@ujat.mx
[3] Department of Industrial Engineering,
Corporación Universitaria Reformada CUR, Barranquilla, Colombia
g.jimenez@unireformada.edu.co

**Abstract.** Accident and Emergency departments (A&ED) are in charge of providing access to patients requiring urgent acute care. A&ED are difficult to model due to the presence of interactions, different pathways and the multiple outcomes that patients may undertake depending on their health status. In addition, public concern has focused on the presence of overcrowding, long waiting times, patient dissatisfaction and cost overruns associated with A&ED. There is then a need for tackling these problems through developing integrated and explicit models supporting healthcare planning. However, the studies directly concentrating on modelling the A&EDs are largely limited. Therefore, this paper presents the use of a multi-phase DES framework for modelling the A&ED and facilitating the assessment of potential improvement strategies. Initially, the main components, critical variables and different states of the A&ED are identified to correctly model the entire patient journey. In this step, it is also necessary to characterize the demand in order to categorize the patients into pipelines. After this, a discrete-event simulation (DES) model is developed. Then, validation is conducted through the 2-sample t test to demonstrate whether the model is statistically comparable with the real-world A&ED department. This is followed by the use of Markov phase-type models for calculating the total costs of the whole system. Finally, various scenarios are explored to assess their potential impact on multiple outcomes of interest. A case study of a mixed-patient environment in a private A&E department is provided to validate the effectiveness of the multi-phase DES approach.

**Keywords:** Discrete-event simulation (DES) · Healthcare modelling · Accident and emergency department (A&ED) · Phase-type models

© Springer Nature Switzerland AG 2019
V. G. Duffy (Ed.): HCII 2019, LNCS 11582, pp. 87–100, 2019.
https://doi.org/10.1007/978-3-030-22219-2_7

# 1  Introduction

Accident and emergency department is a 24-h health area with prompt and appropriate service to care for those ill and injured patients in urgent need. A&E departments include resuscitation facilities and designated accommodation. Emergency services' objective is to avoid complications that could lead to even early death, considering that future quality of life and long-term mortality may be influenced by the early measures implemented in the A&E department. Competent services include access and availability to equipped facilities, specialized and trained professionals, and supporting services; all in an effective way [1].

But, A&E departments must face some difficulties as they are: overcrowding, long waiting times, patient dissatisfaction and high cost. That is why, in the last decade, some reforms and an increasing number of tools have been applied to A&E services to ensure that patients are seen, treated, admitted, and discharged appropriately [2].

A&E department crowding is an important and common international problem, so, researchers have an increasing interest in this field. Even in some countries, standards have been defined to monitor the maximum time in which a patient must be treated in these centers [3]. In the UK, the government set an operational standard that 95% of patients should wait <4 h in A&EDs [4]. In A&E departments, patient waiting time is another important factor in assessing the quality of health services and patient satisfaction. Several studies show that waiting time is a determining factor in patient satisfaction [5, 6].

One option to study, analyze and solve the problem is modeling and simulation. Modeling is usually used by healthcare professionals to represent all variables and scenarios involved in a real system and to understand its behavior. After building a model from observation or knowledge of a real system, it can be simulated [7]. Simulation is a methodology widely used to solve real-world problems, which mimics the operation of a real-world process or system, over time. It comprises the generation and observation of an artificial history of a system in order to produce inferences concerning the operating characteristics of the system under analysis. Simulation is used to describe and analyze the behavior of both existing and conceptual systems, perform diagnosis, and support the design of real systems [8].

Because of the complexity of providing quality services to health clinic users, Discrete Event Simulation (DES) has been used for at least two decades as an effective tool for allocating scarce resources and improving patient flow, while minimizing health service delivery costs and increasing customer satisfaction [9]. DES is a common stochastic analysis tool to perform experiments via computer modeling and test the likely effectiveness of different scenarios before their implementation.

An important advantage of DES is the possibility to represent the system-state description, which includes probability distribution of entity arrival, event duration, event status, and resources needed. Modeling and Simulation are key enablers to improve services in complex healthcare systems and propel major improvements in decision making, efficiency, and quality [7].

Our proposal is a conjunction of DES and the modeling of health processes in a multiphase approach. This approach consists of the representation of the real system through the simulation of discrete events together with the modeling of A&E stage throughout the patient journey. We here use DES in order to (i) better analyze the resource utilization under system restrictions, (ii) identify non-value activities, (iii) effectively administer interactions (iv) evaluate potential interventions to improve the patient experience along the A&ED journey and (v) facilitate engagement with the health service managers through animation.

On a different tack, a complexity is modeling the processes and interactions among different areas. Areas can be, for example, radiology, laboratory, intensive care unit, hospitalization, pharmacology, morgue, etc. Given the nature of this A&E system, Markov chains, supporting the multi-phase framework, are used to reflect the probabilities of being transferred from one service to another. Thereby, the relationships between services can be modeled with high accuracy and robustness.

The proposed approach enables sector managers to simulate scenarios or improvement strategies on the virtual model and the results of a possible implementation can be assessed both operationally and economically. In addition, it facilitates the evaluation and applications of joint strategies in the wild including A&E and other healthcare departments.

The remainder of this paper is organized as follows: In Sect. 2, a review on the related studies is presented whereas the suggested framework is explained in Sect. 3. In Sect. 4, a case study of an A&E department from a Southamerican clinic is described. Finally, Sect. 5 presents conclusions and future work.

## 2 Related Studies

There is a lot of research using modeling and simulation to study different scenarios in A&E departments. We analyzed some papers published in the last ten years. For instance, some strategies were proposed to address the ambulance diversion and overcrowding. The authors aimed to develop a tool for evaluating the effectiveness of various ambulance diversion strategies [10].

An interesting review is presented in [11] about comparing statistical modeling approaches to describe and predict emergency department patient load and crowding. Regression models, mathematical equations, time-series analyses, queuing theory based models, and discrete event simulation models were contrasted.

In particular, DES has been used to study and provide solutions to problems in A&E departments. In [12], a DES model was developed to forecast near-future operating conditions and validate those predictions in several scenarios of crowding. In [13], the authors developed a DES model to determine the proper ICU bed capacity that balances between service level and cost-effectiveness. The objective was to increase the bed availability so that ambulance diversion and surgery cancellation can be avoided.

In [14], a quality improvement department used a DES to predict and test patient flow, staffing policy, and other process-level changes. Different methodologies and tools from the industrial area have also been used to redesign processes and improve the efficiency of systems. Such case is illustrated in [15] where Six Sigma was used to develop a classification and selection process for an emergency department. Some key performance measures as length of stay and waiting time were considered. The results indicated a certain improvement in both parameters after DES implementation.

Discrete-event simulation models were implemented using SIMIO package. The study aimed at estimating the required number of doctors and examination rooms to achieve a service level of over 90%, at reasonable costs. The findings showed that modifying treatment processes and enabling more flexible staff hierarchy could enhance such service level [16].

On a different tack, phase-type models, used for describing flows with multiple outcomes and states, have gained increased prominence in healthcare applications [17]. For instance, in [18], a phase-type model was developed to describe the flow of each patient cluster based on the length of stay. The framework was also useful to provide predictions on bed occupancy. Another application can be evidenced in [19] where the authors used this approach to cost the stroke patient care from admission to discharge. In this case, the proposed methodology was used to underpin integrated planning, encompassing hospital and community services. However, in spite of these studies, the use of phase-type models is largely limited when addressing interactions with other healthcare services. Therefore, the novelty of our proposal is based on the combination of DES and Markov phase-type models to analyze interrelations and feedback between A&E departments and other healthcare settings (i.e. intensive care unit, hospitalization, and surgery) within hospitals so that holistic solutions can be provided to better assist health service managers in decision making (Fig. 1).

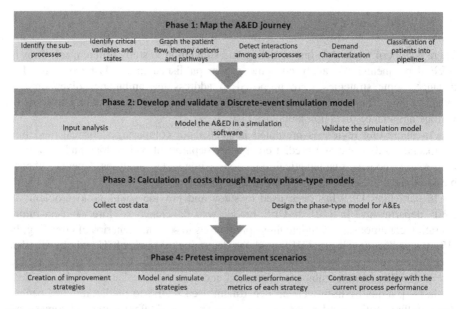

**Fig. 1.** The proposed framework for modelling and assessing operational changes in A&E departments and interactions.

# 3 The Proposed Framework

*Phase 1 "Map the A&ED Journey":* In this phase, it is necessary to identify the patient pathways, states (i.e. diagnosis and treatment), sub-processes (i.e. lab testing, radiology), key parameters and associated process variables that characterize the patient journey within the A&E department under analysis. It is also required to characterize the demand of each triage level so that DES phase-type models can be more detailed and informative. Thereby, health service managers are able to predict the waiting time, profile patient cohorts, improve resource management and make better decisions. The process information is later summarized in a conceptual model where all the process details, assumptions and components can be fully identified. In order to ensure a high accuracy and robustness of the model, the modelers should work closely to the clinicians and healthcare managers since they can provide information on the procedures and protocols attached to the patient journey as well as the existing interrelations with other healthcare services (i.e. hospitalization, intensive care unit, and surgery).

*Phase 2 "Develop and Validate a Discrete-Event Simulation Model":* A virtual model of the whole A&E department needs to be developed in order to obtain the current process behavior in terms of waiting time. To do this, modelers should collect appropriate data that represent the variables and parameters identified in Phase 1. In this regard, it is highly recommended to perform outlier analysis in order to detect special patterns and eliminate noise from datasets. This contributes to increasing the accuracy and reliability of the model as well as assessing the quality of measurement systems. Once the data are filtered, three statistical techniques are conducted to determine the correct manner of representing each process variable in the simulation model. Initially, an intra-variable dependence test is carried out to detect auto-correlations within a specific dataset. A homogeneity test is then carried out to categorize data into classes in accordance with similar profiles. The Kruskal-Wallis and log-rank tests can be employed for validating the heterogeneity assumption. If several classes are identified, a probability expression is then required for each class; otherwise, one distribution is enough to model the entire dataset. After this, the input analyzer feature of simulation packages is used to determine the probability expression (including parameter values) that better fits the data in case of randomness; alternatively, the modeler needs to find the formulae incorporating the dependency between the process variable and its (their) predictor (s). Once the statistical tests are complete, the resulting information is incorporated into the model. Such a model is suggested to be run 10 times in order to calculate the required number of replications that are necessary to represent the system uncertainty. After collecting the key variable value in each replication, a 1-sample t test is carried out to verify whether the virtual representation is realistic. If the resulting p-value is higher than the alpha level (0.05), then the model is concluded to be equivalent with the real A&E department; otherwise, it should be revised and improved until satisfying this condition. Finally, a capability analysis is performed to establish the current performance of the A&E department.

*Phase 3 "Calculation of Costs Through Markov Phase-Type Models":* Phase-type models have been proposed in this study to better modelling and analysis of specific cost measures in a queuing setting. They also serve as a base for evaluating whether certain scenarios are cost-effective for the A&E department. In this respect, the cost parameters to be employed in this intervention should be extracted from a reliable Financial Information System (FIS) so that real economic evaluation can be effectively performed. In this phase, homogeneity results from Phase 2 are considered to optimally stratify patients according to their triage level. After this, the length of stay (LOS) distribution of each group is modeled employing phase-type models. Such models also take into account the inter-arrival process of each patient class whose probability distribution can be also derived from Phase 2 through the Goodness-of-fit test. As a next step, transition rates for the phase-type models are calculated employing maximum probability estimation. Finally, the costs for the whole patient journey within the A&E department are estimated by implementing Markov classes.

*Phase 4 "Pretesting Improvement Scenarios":* Different improvement strategies can be suggested by health service managers for reducing the waiting time in the A&E departments. The proposed approach presented in this paper enables policymakers to evaluate the potential impact of such strategies before implementation. The strategies are then run by the modeler and the resulting waiting times are collected. After this, the simulated performance is statistically compared to the real behavior using a 2-sample t (if the data are normally distributed) or Kruskal-Wallis (if the data follow a non-normal probability distribution). If the resulting p-value is significant ($<0.05$), the strategy is recommended to be executed in the A&E department since it may reduce the waiting time (C. L. = 0.95). If not, it should not be considered.

# 4 An Illustrative Example: Modeling an Accident and Emergency Department of a Clinic

## 4.1 Map the A&ED Journey

The patient journey of an A&ED from a private clinic was mapped (refer to Fig. 2) to provide a wide understanding of the interactions with other healthcare services and performance in terms of waiting time. Specifically, interrelations with six sub-processes (Hospitalization, Surgery, Intensive Care unit, Morgue, Laboratory, and Radiology) were identified. Our model was underpinned by a 1-year dataset extracted from the Patient Data Management System (PDMS) and consisting of all the admission registered between 1 January and 31 December (n = 2506 admissions). The journey starts with two types of arrivals: walk-in and ambulance. Here, the watchman registers the arrival time and type of arrival. Then, the patients enter the A&ED and some assistants proceed with collecting personal data, type of emergency, and the health promotion organization. However, some patients have to stay in the waiting room until the initial assessment due to bed and doctor availability. During emergency care, the doctor decides which treatment should be applied and which lab and radiology tests must be conducted to establish a correct diagnosis and intervention. Depending on the patient evolution, a transfer to other healthcare services may occur. In accordance with the data recorded by the PDMS, the discharges were the following: 46.4% (Home), 20% (Hospitalization), 18.1% (Surgery), 15.3% (Intensive care), and 0.2% (Morgue).

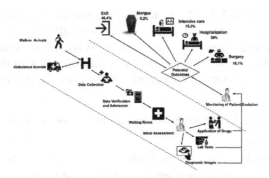

**Fig. 2.** Illustrative model for the A&E department

In the A&E department, there are 10 doctors who work in accordance with the schedule depicted in Table 1. Finally, four key variables were identified: (a) inter-arrival times for emergency patients, (b) initial assessment time (patients with chronic conditions), (c) initial assessment time (patients with minor complications) and (d) length of stay (LOS).

**Table 1.** Agenda of ED doctors

| Doctor code | Monday | Tuesday | Wednesday | Thursday | Friday | Saturday |
|---|---|---|---|---|---|---|
| 001 | 7 am–7 pm | 7 am–7 pm | 7 pm–12 am | 12 am–7 am 7 pm–12 am | 12 am–7 am | X |
| 002 | 7 am–7 pm | 7 am–7 pm | 7 pm–12 am | 12 am–7 am 7 pm–12 am | 12 am–7 am | X |
| 003 | 7 am–7 pm | 7 am–7 pm | 7 pm–12 am | 12 am–7 am 7 pm–12 am | 12 am–7 am | X |
| 004 | 8 am–10 am 3 pm–5 pm | 8 am–10 am 3 pm–5 pm | 8 am–10 am 3 pm–12 am | 12 am–5 am | X | X |
| 005 | 7 pm–12 am | 12 am–7 am 7 pm–12 am | 12 am–7 am | X | 7 am–7 pm | 7 am–7 pm |
| 006 | 7 pm–12 am | 12 am–7 am 7 pm–12 am | 12 am–7 am | X | 7 am–7 pm | 7 am–7 pm |
| 007 | 7 pm–12 am | 12 am–7 am 7 pm–12 am | 12 am–7 am | X | 7 am–7 pm | 7 am–7 pm |
| 008 | 12 am–7 am | X | 7 am–7 pm | 7 am–7 pm | 7 pm–12 am | 12 am–7 am 7 pm–12 am |
| 009 | 12 am–7 am | X | 7 am–7 pm | 7 am–7 pm | 7 pm–12 am | 12 am–7 am 7 pm–12 am |
| 010 | 12 am–7 am | X | 7 am–7 pm | 7 am–7 pm | 7 pm–12 am | 12 am–7 am 7 pm–12 am |

## 4.2 Develop and Validate a Discrete-Event Simulation Model

Once the data gathering regarding the three process variables is complete, an intra-variable dependence analysis was undertaken to verify the randomness assumptions.

The results are detailed in Table 2. The results demonstrated that all the variables were found to be random since the p-values were lower than 0.05. After this, a homogeneity test was carried through Analysis of Variance (ANOVA) in order to detect sub-groups of data in each variable (refer to Table 3). It was concluded that all the variables were homogeneous and can be therefore modeled without considering pipelines.

**Table 2.** The results of intra-variable dependence tests

| Key variable | P-value |
|---|---|
| Inter-arrival time for emergency patients | 0.569 |
| Initial assessment time (patients with chronic conditions) | >0.15 |
| Initial assessment time (patients with minor complications) | >0.15 |
| Length of stay (LOS) | 1 |

**Table 3.** The results of homogeneity tests

| Key variable | P-value |
|---|---|
| Inter-arrival time for emergency patients | >0.15 |
| Initial assessment time | <0.0005 |
| Length of stay (LOS) | 0.363 |

After completing the intra-variable dependence and homogeneity tests, the input analyzer feature of Arena 14.5 ® was employed to determine the probability expressions of each variable (refer to Table 4). For instance, the Kolmogorov-Smirnov test (p-value = 0.718) provided a good fit for the Weibull distribution of *length of stay (LOS)*.

**Table 4.** Probability expressions of each key variable

| Key variable | Probability expression |
|---|---|
| Inter-arrival time for emergency patients | EXPO (18.8) min; Entities per arrival: DISC (0.9223, 1, 0.9917, 2, 0.9986, 3, 1, 4) |
| Initial assessment time (patients with chronic conditions) | UNIF (10, 45) min/patient |
| Initial assessment time (patients with minor complications) | UNIF (10, 15) min/patient |
| Length of stay (LOS) | WEIB (2.22, 202.58) min/patient |

All the information derived from the input data analysis was included in the simulation model. Such a model was initially run 10 times in order to calculate the required number of replications that are required to represent the system variability. In this case, 91 runs were estimated as necessary for this particular aim. After collecting the resulting waiting times in each replication, a 1-sample t test was conducted for model

validation. Considering a p-value = 0.095 and T-value = $-1.69$, the model is concluded to be comparable with the real A&E department and can be therefore used for
capability analysis and exploration of improvement scenarios. After this, a capability
analysis (refer to Fig. 3) was conducted with the aid of Minitab 17®. In this regard,
A&E departments are called to meet the standard set by the National Health Institution
(Maximum waiting time = 30 min/patients). The analysis revealed that the average
waiting time is 34.69 min/patient with a shape of 2.36 min/patient and a scale of
39.13 min/patient. Furthermore, it was estimated that 624650 out of 1 million
admissions will have a waiting time >30 min. Complementary to these measures, the
Ppu ($-0.07$), Ppk ($-0.07$) and sigma level (1.28) evidence that the performance of the
A&E department under study is low satisfactory and then requires deep interventions.
These outcomes were presented to the general managers in order to explore various
scenarios of improvement.

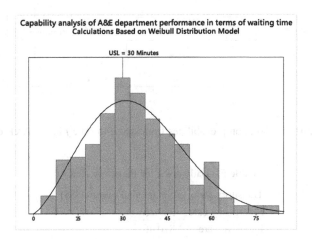

**Fig. 3.** Capability analysis to evaluate the performance of the A&E department under study

### 4.3 Calculation of Costs Through Markov Phase-Type Models

The healthcare costs used within the simulation were derived from the Financial
Information System (FIS) of the A&E department under analysis. The parameters of
the phase-type model were extracted from the Patient Data Management System
(PDMS). In particular, the phase-type model has two absorbing states and four transitory stages (refer to Fig. 4). It will be also assumed that these probabilities do not vary
over time in order to confirm the Markovian assumption.

The states will be labeled as presented below:

**0:** A&E department (Emergency care)
**1:** Intensive care
**2:** Surgery
**3:** Hospitalization

**4:** Discharge (Home)
**5:** Death

The phase-type model here described can be considered as an absorbing Markov chain where the long-term probability of both discharge and death states can be estimated. In addition, if the costs of each stage are fully known, it is then possible to calculate the average value-added cost per admission. The cost of each transitory state is enlisted in Table 5. With these considerations in mind, the matrix comprising of the long-term probabilities is finally derived (refer to Fig. 4).

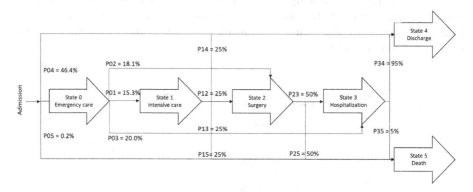

**Fig. 4.** Long-term absorption probabilities from state *i* to state *j* in the A&E department

**Table 5.** Daily costs for transitory states

| Transitory state | Average daily cost (US$) |
| --- | --- |
| Emergency care | 309.85 |
| Intensive care | 870.46 |
| Surgery | 1410.43 |
| Hospitalization | 516.44 |

According to Fig. 4, it can be determined that a patient who is in the Hospitalization department (stage 3) has 95.0% of likelihood to survive (discharge-state 4) and die with 5%. As a next step, the fundamental matrix is achieved (refer to Table 6).

**Table 6.** Fundamental matrix for the A&E department

| State *i* | State *j* | | | |
| --- | --- | --- | --- | --- |
| | 0 | 1 | 2 | 3 |
| 0 | 1.90 | 9.30 | 0.8 | 14.6 |
| 1 | 0 | 11.10 | 1.5 | 17.2 |
| 2 | 0 | 0 | 0.8 | 12.3 |
| 3 | 0 | 0 | 0 | 13.2 |

The fundamental matrix evidences the time (measured in days) that a patient spends in each transitory state of the A&E department. If a patient is in this area, the average stay will be 1.9 days and 9.3 days in intensive care. Furthermore, the admitted patient will spend 14.6 days (on average) in Hospitalization department. Considering the daily costs of each transitory state (refer to Table 5), it can be deduced that the average cost of a patient that is admitted in the A&E department and is later transferred to Hospitalization is US$8218.73.

### 4.4  Pretesting Improvement Scenarios

Computer simulation enables health service managers to assess the impact of certain changes in the A&E department before their implementation. This is highly recommended to avoid errors, diminish cost overruns, and identify cost-effective scenarios. In spite of these advantages, only a few studies have been reported in the literature regarding the use of computer simulation for the assessment and comparison of various scenarios in healthcare delivery. Motivated by the need for bridging this gap and minimizing the waiting time, the modelers and emergency managers agreed to evaluate three possible scenarios: (a) Implement a doctor who filters the admissions by identifying which ones are real urgencies [20], (b) Add a doctor who works according to the shift established for 008, 009, 010 and (c) Classify patients through a triage system. These scenarios were later modeled using Arena 14.5 ® software. The performance of each scenario was statistically analyzed through 2-sample t tests (C.L. = 95%) [21–23].

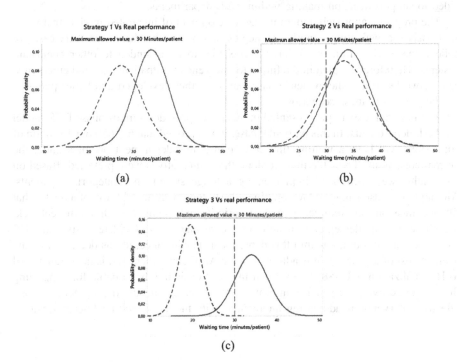

**Fig. 5.** The comparative analysis between the real behavior and (a) Strategy 1 (b) Strategy 2 (c) Strategy 3

Strategy #1 (refer to Fig. 5a) proposes to avoid the admission of non-urgent visits which can be instead redirected to priority outpatient care. In this case, the 2-sample t test revealed that the waiting time resulting from this scenario is lower than the current performance (p-value = 0; T = 13.15). On a different tack, Strategy #2 (refer to Fig. 5b) suggests augmenting the installed capacity by 48 h. However, no significant difference was detected between the actual performance and the proposed scenario (p-value = 0.095; T = −1.69). Finally, Strategy #3 (refer to Fig. 5c) proposes to implement the triage system which classifies patients into two groups: Triage 1–2 and Triage 3–5. In addition, it is necessary to aggregate 9 triage doctors who will be in charge of the classification process. In this scenario, the waiting time was concluded to be substantially minor in relation to the target and real A&E behavior (p-value = 0; T = 26.25).

## 5  Conclusions and Future Work

A&E departments are very difficult to model considering the multiple states, sub-processes, and interactions with other healthcare services. To correctly represent the real performance of these departments, it is necessary that modelers work alongside the health service managers so that the base structure, key variables, and parameters can be fully incorporated into the simulated version. The collection of appropriate data plays a relevant role in this aim. Thereby, more informative and detailed models can be provided to support decision making within A&E departments.

The proposed approach underpins the development of integrated models that serve as a basis for evaluating complex strategies involving other healthcare services. We believe that such a framework has the potential to be extended to other healthcare systems. Therefore, we plan in the future to intervene in outpatient care and emergency care networks so that the evidence base can be further developed and better planning can be granted in these scenarios.

The illustrative example presented in this paper provides a multi-phase DES model for A&E departments. In this particular case, it was proved that 624650 out 1 million of admissions will have a waiting time > 30 min if this department operates under the current conditions. To tackle this problem, three alternatives were pretested. Based on the results, we recommend implementing a triage system that categorizes patients. Although, it is also suggested to combine this strategy with the addition of a doctor that filters admissions and redirects patients to priority outpatient care. On a different tack, the phase-type model enabled health service managers to elucidate costs and LOS along the patient journey within this department. For instance, it was detected that the average cost of a patient that is admitted in the A&E department and is later transferred to Hospitalization is US$8218.73. Such information is highly valuable for supporting the economic evaluation of the improvement strategies and the deployment of cost-effective interventions addressing interactions with the associated healthcare services.

# References

1. West, R.: Objective standards for the emergency services: emergency admission to hospital. J. R. Soc. Med. **94**(Suppl. 39), 4 (2001)
2. Dolan, B., Holt, L. (eds.): Accident & Emergency: Theory into Practice. Elsevier Health Sciences (2013)
3. Higginson, I.: Emergency department crowding. Emerg. Med. J. **29**(6), 437–443 (2012)
4. Woodcock, T., Poots, A.J., Bell, D.: The impact of changing the 4 h emergency access standard on patient waiting times in emergency departments in England. Emerg. Med. J. **30** (3), e22 (2013)
5. Ajami, S., Ketabi, S., Yarmohammadian, M.H., Bagherian, H.: Wait time in emergency department (ED) processes. Med. Arch. **66**(1), 53 (2012)
6. Konrad, R., et al.: Modeling the impact of changing patient flow processes in an emergency department: Insights from a computer simulation study. Oper. Res. Health Care **2**(4), 66–74 (2013)
7. Dong, Y., Chbat, N.W., Gupta, A., Hadzikadic, M., Gajic, O.: Systems modeling and simulation applications for critical care medicine. Ann. Intensive Care **2**(1), 18 (2012)
8. Katsaliaki, K., Mustafee, N.: Applications of simulation within the healthcare context. J. Oper. Res. Soc. **62**(8), 1431–1451 (2011)
9. Günal, M.M., Pidd, M.: Discrete event simulation for performance modelling in health care: a review of the literature. J. Simul. **4**(1), 42–51 (2010)
10. Lin, C.H., Kao, C.Y., Huang, C.Y.: Managing emergency department overcrowding via ambulance diversion: a discrete event simulation model. J. Formos. Med. Assoc. **114**(1), 64–71 (2015)
11. Wiler, J.L., Griffey, R.T., Olsen, T.: Review of modeling approaches for emergency department patient flow and crowding research. Acad. Emerg. Med. **18**(12), 1371–1379 (2011)
12. Hoot, N.R., et al.: Forecasting emergency department crowding: a discrete event simulation. Ann. Emerg. Med. **52**(2), 116–125 (2008)
13. Zhu, Z., Hoon Hen, B., Liang Teow, K.: Estimating ICU bed capacity using discrete event simulation. Int. J. Health Care Qual. Assur. **25**(2), 134–144 (2012)
14. Rutberg, M.H., Wenczel, S., Devaney, J., Goldlust, E.J., Day, T.E.: Incorporating discrete event simulation into quality improvement efforts in health care systems. Am. J. Med. Qual. **30**(1), 31–35 (2015)
15. Mandahawi, N., Al-Shihabi, S., Abdallah, A.A., Alfarah, Y.M.: Reducing waiting time at an emergency department using design for Six Sigma and discrete event simulation. Int. J. Six Sigma Compet. Adv. **6**(1–2), 91–104 (2010)
16. Nahhas, A., Awaldi, A., Reggelin, T.: Simulation and the emergency department overcrowding problem. Procedia Eng. **178**, 368–376 (2017)
17. Fackrell, M.: Modelling healthcare systems with phase-type distributions. Health Care Manag. Sci. **12**(1), 11 (2009)
18. McClean, S., Barton, M., Garg, L., Fullerton, K.: A modeling framework that combines markov models and discrete-event simulation for stroke patient care. ACM Trans. Model. Comput. Simul. (TOMACS) **21**(4), 25 (2011)
19. McClean, S., Gillespie, J., Garg, L., Barton, M., Scotney, B., Kullerton, K.: Using phase-type models to cost stroke patient care across health, social and community services. Eur. J. Oper. Res. **236**(1), 190–199 (2014)
20. Hsia, R.Y., Friedman, A.B., Niedzwiecki, M.: Urgent care needs among nonurgent visits to the emergency department. JAMA Int. Med. **176**(6), 852–854 (2016)

21. Ortiz, M.A., López-Meza, P.: Using computer simulation to improve patient flow at an outpatient internal medicine department. In: García, C.R., Caballero-Gil, P., Burmester, M., Quesada-Arencibia, A. (eds.) UCAmI 2016. LNCS, vol. 10069, pp. 294–299. Springer, Cham (2016). https://doi.org/10.1007/978-3-319-48746-5_30

22. Ortiz, M.A., McClean, S., Nugent, C.D., Castillo, A.: Reducing appointment lead-time in an outpatient department of gynecology and obstetrics through discrete-event simulation: a case study. In: García, C.R., Caballero-Gil, P., Burmester, M., Quesada-Arencibia, A. (eds.) UCAmI 2016. LNCS, vol. 10069, pp. 274–285. Springer, Cham (2016). https://doi.org/10.1007/978-3-319-48746-5_28

23. Nuñez-Perez, N., Ortíz-Barrios, M., McClean, S., Salas-Navarro, K., Jimenez-Delgado, G., Castillo-Zea, A.: Discrete-event simulation to reduce waiting time in accident and emergency departments: a case study in a district general clinic. In: Ochoa, Sergio F., Singh, P., Bravo, J. (eds.) UCAmI 2017. LNCS, vol. 10586, pp. 352–363. Springer, Cham (2017). https://doi.org/10.1007/978-3-319-67585-5_37

# Discrete-Event Simulation for Performance Evaluation and Improvement of Gynecology Outpatient Departments: A Case Study in the Public Sector

Miguel Ortiz-Barrios[1]([⊠]), Pedro Lopez-Meza[2], Sally McClean[3], and Giselle Polifroni-Avendaño[4]

[1] Department of Industrial Management, Agroindustry and Operations, Universidad de La Costa CUC, Barranquilla, Colombia
mortizl@cuc.edu.co
[2] Department of Industrial Process Engineering, Institución Universitaria ITSA, Barranquilla, Colombia
plopezmeza@itsa.edu.co
[3] School of Computing, University of Ulster, Coleraine, Co., Londonderry BT52 1SA, UK
si.mcclean@ulster.ac.uk
[4] Department of General Management, Sofast Ingeniería S.A.S., Barranquilla, Colombia
gisele2127@gmail.com

**Abstract.** Gynecology outpatient units are in charge of treating different gynecological diseases such as tumorous, cancer, urinary incontinence, gynecological pain, and abnormal discharge. On-time attention is thus needed to avoid severe complications, patient dissatisfaction, and elevated healthcare costs. There is then an urgent need for assessing whether the gynecology outpatient departments are cost-effective and what interventions are required for improving clinical outcomes. Despite this context, the studies directly concentrating on diagnosis and improvement of these departments are widely limited. To address these concerns, this paper aims to provide a Discrete-event Simulation (DES) modelling framework to help healthcare managers gain a better understanding of the gynecology outpatient services and evaluate improvement strategies. First, the patient journey through the gynecology outpatient service is mapped. To correctly represent the system uncertainty, collected data is then processed through input analysis. Third, the data is used to model and simulate the real gynecology outpatient unit. This model is later validated to determine whether it is statistically equivalent to the real system. After this, using performance metrics derived from the simulation model, the gynecology outpatient department is analyzed to identify potential improvements. We finally pretest potential interventions to define their viability during implementation. A case study of a mixed-patient type environment in a public gynecology outpatient unit is presented to verify the applicability of the proposed methodology. The results evidenced that appointment lead times could be efficiently reduced using this approach.

© Springer Nature Switzerland AG 2019
V. G. Duffy (Ed.): HCII 2019, LNCS 11582, pp. 101–112, 2019.
https://doi.org/10.1007/978-3-030-22219-2_8

**Keywords:** Discrete-event simulation (DES) · Healthcare ·
Appointment lead-time · Gynecology · Outpatient care

# 1    Introduction

Gynecology outpatient units are responsible for treating many different and diverse conditions and chronic diseases such as such as cancers, urinary incontinence, gynecological pain, and abnormal discharge. Timely attention is thus needed to avoid severe complications, patient dissatisfaction, higher mortality, and increased healthcare costs. However, public healthcare systems are increasingly lacking in necessary resources and therefore need to manage scarce resources in an optimal manner. As such, there is an urgent need to monitor and evaluate the cost-effectiveness of gynecology outpatient departments as well as developing and assessing possible interventions which could alleviate such problems, with the aim of improving the efficiency of services as well as clinical outcomes.

With these considerations in mind, this paper aims to provide a Discrete-event Simulation (DES) modelling framework to help healthcare managers gain a better understanding of the gynecology outpatient services as well as facilitating the evaluation of improvement strategies. We initially focus on the entire patient pathway through the gynecology outpatient service and characterize the different phases of care, resource limitations, critical variables, and their interrelations. Following this, improvement strategies are identified and evaluated.

Despite the problems we have outlined, research directly concentrating on performance assessment and improvement of gynecology outpatient units has been severely limited [1]. In the current paper, we focus on developing a DES model for such units particularly in view of the fact that the animation features commonly found in simulation packages facilitate engagement with healthcare managers, thus enabling development of realistic and accurate models. Easy visualization of key relationships in the models is also an important aspect [2].

Such an approach has been used previously, to a limited extent, to help improve provision across a number of healthcare specialties. For example, a simulation model to characterize appointment-based hospitals facilities, with a particular focus on capacity deficiencies [3]; a similar approach was adopted by [4], who were concerned with improving appointment scheduling. In [5], the authors likewise focused on reducing patient waiting times and improving resource utilization. On a different tack, a simulation analysis was performed for reducing queues in a mixed-patient outpatient department [6]. In this case, two improvement scenarios were designed and assessed with regard to the simultaneous impact of operations, scheduling, resource allocation on patient waiting time, clinic overtime and resource utilization in general. As a result, an improvement proposal achieved a reduction of up to 70% in patient waiting times and 25% in physical space requirements. On a similar note, a framework using discrete-event simulation was provided to model stroke care and evaluate the impact of discharge queues and patient-centered care [7]. However, on a cautionary note, they also stressed that the availability of suitable data could prove to be a limitation on modeling healthcare services. Also, on a related theme to the current one, some previous work has been carried out using DES to improve Gynecology and Obstetrics departments with respect to reducing appointment lead times which are associated with poor patient satisfaction, variable and diverse healthcare services, and the development of long-term and severe complications with corresponding increases in fetal, infant and maternal mortality [8].

More generally, the current paper aims to define and evaluate novel improvement strategies through the use of discrete-event simulation for performance evaluation and improvement of Gynecology Outpatient Departments in the Public Sector. In particular, we evaluate three possible interventions: (i) establishing collaborative scenarios with similar departments, (ii) varying installed capacity and (iii) using local search algorithms to determine optimal schedules A case study of a mixed-patient type environment in a public gynecology outpatient unit is presented to validate the applicability of the proposed approach.

The remainder of this paper is organized as follows: In Sect. 2 the legal framework that motivates this study is shown whereas the proposed approach is explained in Sect. 3. In Sect. 4, a case study in an outpatient gynecology department from a Colombian maternal-child hospital is described. Ultimately, Sect. 5 presents the conclusions and future work.

## 2   The Legal Framework

The right to health has been recognized by the Colombian Institutional Court, in the XXI century, as an institutional, fundamental, autonomous, and irrevocable guarantee since it allows the full enjoyment of the other rights. In accordance with Statutory Law 1751 (2015), the right to health *"includes the timely, efficacious and access to high-quality healthcare services for the preservation, improvement, and promotion of health"* [9]. Given its connotation of mandatory essential public service, the government must manage, regulate and supervise its provision [10]. Additionally, due to its assistance-oriented nature of this right, the government must adopt public policies directed towards the expansion of coverage and the continuous improvement of service quality so that integral, effective and timely access can be granted [9].

In this sense, Law 100 (1993) and Law 1751 (2015) establish the principles of efficiency, quality, and opportunity as pillars determining healthcare as a substantial public service and fundamental right [9, 11]. Based on these laws, the Information System for Quality (ISQ) serves as a tool for monitoring the quality of service and assisting users in the selection of a healthcare provider [12]. Thereby, by means of the Resolution 256 (2016), the Ministry of Health and Social Protection enacted regulations on ISQ and established the gynecology appointment lead-time as an indicator for monitoring the quality of service provided to women. Such regulations apply to Department, District, and Municipal healthcare entities, among other members of this sector [13]. These considerations have motivated the design and evaluation of initiatives aiming at reducing the gynecology appointment lead time as those described within this paper.

## 3  Proposed Approach

*Step 1 "System Characterization":* To suitably model the outpatient gynecology department, it is required to identify their main components (sub-processes) and the associated process data (variables and parameters). This information is then consolidated in a flow diagram through which the modelers will be able to elicit the patient journey, detect interrelations and identify system constraints. The system details should be provided by health service managers, administrative staff, healthcare professionals, and other stakeholders involved in the outpatient unit. Such stakeholders should be highly committed to work closely to the modelers to ensure that the resulting simulation models are realistic and robust (Fig. 1).

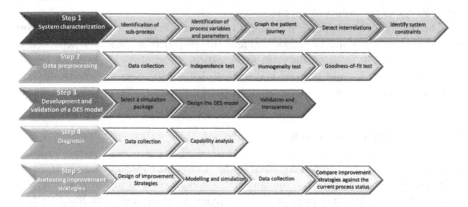

**Fig. 1.** The proposed approach for modelling outpatient gynecology departments and pretesting improvement interventions

*Step 2 "Data Preprocessing":* To ensure the robustness of the simulation model, it is necessary to incorporate high-quality data that provide a good representation of the real-world system. The data referring to the process variables and parameters should be collected from reliable information sources linked to the functioning of the outpatient gynecology department under study. The acquisition of such data enables modelers to develop more informative and detailed models which is more beneficial for health service managers when creating multidimensional interventions. If these data are not properly preprocessed, some bias can be introduced into the simulation model. To tackle this problem, three statistical tests are needed. First, a runs test is performed to establish whether a specific variable follows a random behavior or is correlated with other input variables. A homogeneity analysis is later performed to classify data into groups based on their similarity. The Kolgomorov-Smirnov and Kruskal-Wallis tests can be used for underpinning this approach. If the data are not consistent with the homogeneity hypothesis, each group is categorized in accordance with a probability function; alternatively, one probability expression is sufficient to model the variable behavior. The goodness-of-fit is finally assessed through a Chi-square test to determine whether a statistical model provides a good fit for the data. After this, the corresponding parameters are estimated to be incorporated into the simulation model.

*Step 3 "Development and Validation of a DES Model":* The problem under analysis requires the use of DES models in consideration of their capability to record individual entity (patients) experience, compare various improvement scenarios and analyze performance under restriction [14]. To create a DES application, the modeler should select a simulation package (i.e. Arena and Promodel) with animation features that facilitate user engagement. Then, the results derived from Steps 1 and 2 are fully incorporated into the DES model. Once finished, the modeler has to perform rigorous model transparency and validation in order to demonstrate its equivalence with the real outpatient gynecology department. To this end, it is first necessary to outline the performance metrics and simulation run length per replication. It is proposed to run the simulation for a warm-up period and then 10 times to calculate the final sample size (number of runs) that will be employed to verify whether the simulated model is significantly comparable to the real system. The validation is achieved by conducting a comparative test between means (if the data are normally distributed) or medians (if the data follow a non-normal probability function). If the p-value is higher than the alpha level ($\alpha = 0.05$), the null hypothesis cannot be rejected and the model can be hence deemed a good illustration of the real department. Otherwise, the model should be thoroughly revised and corrected by the modelers and service health managers until achieving an acceptable level of equivalence with the system under analysis. Reliable DES applications provide valuable support for understanding the performance of outpatient gynecology departments and identifying sources of inefficiency in healthcare provision.

*Step 4 "Diagnosis":* The use of DES for performance diagnosis of healthcare systems has gained increased prominence recently due to its capacity for measuring and storing system metrics per replication. Such metrics are an important output for conducting a deep analysis of the performance of outpatient gynecology departments and the detection of potential barriers [15, 16]. A crucial component of this step is the capability study which reveals how well the department satisfies the specifications established by the National Institute of Health. In this case, the key parameter is *appointment lead-time (ALT)* which is intended to be at 8 days as a maximum. In this step, capability indices like sigma level, Pp, Ppk, and DPMO are estimated to determine the gap between the process status and the desired performance.

*Step 5 "Pretesting Improvement Strategies":* DES provides a means to pretest improvement scenarios in a safe and effective manner. This is highly beneficial for policymakers who often address the need for optimally allocating resources to improve outpatient gynecology care. Such scenarios should then secure positive change and oriented to a well-defined problem as stated in Step 4. In this context, it is essential to count on the participation of health service managers and clinicians who can develop more solid and realistic initiatives that take into account the multidimensional nature of healthcare. The scenarios are later simulated by the modeler and firstly run 10 times. Afterwards, the final sample size is obtained and the scenarios are simulated again in accordance with the established run length. The resulting ALT is statistically contrasted with the real behavior by implementing a test for differences between means (if the data is normally distributed) or medians (if the data follow a non-normal probability distribution). If the derived p-value is significant (<0.05), the scenario is suggested to be implemented in the real-world since it may reduce the ALT (Confidence level = 95%). Otherwise, it should be discarded.

# 4   An Illustrative Example: Modeling an Outpatient Gynecology Department from a Maternal-Child Hospital

## 4.1   System Characterization

A flow diagram was designed to give an overview of the patient journey within an outpatient gynecology department from a maternal-child hospital. In particular, three sub-processes (Scheduling, Billing, and Outpatient Gynecology Care) and three appointment types (First-time, control, and priority) were distinguished (refer to Fig. 2). Our model was supported by a 1-year dataset gleaned from the User Information System (UIS) and comprising all the gynecology appointments booked between 1 January and 31 December (n = 13001 appointments). In this period, 1766 (13.6%) requests were priority appointments, 5717 (43.9%) corresponded to first-time consultations and the rest (5518) were asked for control purposes. The patients are women between the ages of 16 and 43 years old.

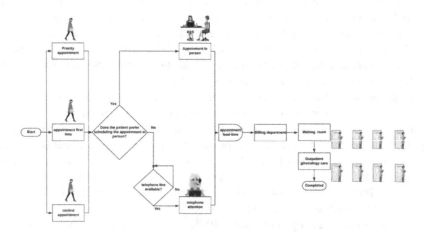

**Fig. 2.** The flow diagram for the outpatient gynecology department

The gynecology appointments are requested through the Scheduling unit where two assistants ($AS_1$, $AS_2$) serve in accordance with the work shifts $WS_1$ (8:00–12:00; 14:00–17:00) and $WS_2$ (8:00–13:00; 15:00–17:00) correspondingly. The appointments can be also scheduled by a phone call with the aid of the contact center agent $AS_3$ who operates according to $WS_1$. The appointments are booked based on the availability of gynecologists, consultation rooms and consultation type. Nonetheless, this process is influenced by the late arrival of gynecologists, cancellations of medical agenda (every three weeks) and equipment damage. These failures augment the complexity of the scheduling process and new methodologies can be hence required for responding to the context here presented. The patients are invited to arrive at the hospital 2 h prior to the consultation time in order to obtain the consultation order and invoice from one of the agents ($BA_1$, $BA_2$) who work in the Billing department conformed to $WS_1$ and $WS_2$ correspondingly. The patients then stay at the waiting room up to the consultation time.

In Outpatient Gynecology Care, there are six gynecologists who work in accordance with the agenda presented in Table 1.

**Table 1.** Agenda of gynecologists

| Gynecologist code | Monday | Tuesday | Wednesday | Thursday | Friday |
|---|---|---|---|---|---|
| 001 | 8:00–12:00 | 8:00–12:00 | X | 8:00–12:00 | X |
| 002 | X | X | X | 8.00–12:00 | X |
| 003 | X | X | 8:00–12:00 | X | X |
| 004 | X | 8:00–12:00 | X | 8:00–12:00 | 8:00–12:00 |
| 005 | X | 13:00–17:00 | X | 13:00–17:00 | 13:00–17:00 |
| 006 | 8:00–12:00 | X | X | X | X |

Ultimately, seven process variables were outlined: (i) time between arrivals for first-time appointments, (ii) time between arrivals for control appointments, (iii) time between arrivals for priority consultation (iv) service time in Scheduling division (in-person attention), (v) service time in Scheduling division (call center), (vi) service time in Billing division, and (vii) service time in outpatient gynecology care.

## 4.2 Data Preprocessing

Once the data collection referring to the seven process variables is finished, a runs test was undertaken to evaluate the independence hypothesis. The outcomes are described in Table 2. The evidence revealed that all the variables were concluded to be independent since the p-values were significant at an error level of 0.05. After validating this assumption, an Analysis of Variance (ANOVA) was performed for each variable in order to distinguish the sub-groups of data (refer to Table 3). It was concluded that the *time between arrivals* should be modeled independently considering the consultation type (p-value = 0). In turn, *service time in the Scheduling division, service time in the Billing division,* and *service time in outpatient gynecology care* were found to be homogeneous since the derived p-values provided enough evidence to accept the homogeneity assumption.

**Table 2.** P-values derived from the runs tests

| Process variable | P-value |
|---|---|
| Time between arrivals (first-time appointments) | 1.0 |
| Time between arrivals (control appointments) | 0.939 |
| Time between arrivals (priority consultation) | 1.0 |
| Service time in the Scheduling division (in-person attention) | 0.53 |
| Service time in the Scheduling division (call center) | 0.45 |
| Service time in the Billing division | <0.05 |
| Service time in outpatient gynecology care | <0.05 |

**Table 3.** ANOVA results

| Process variable | P-value |
|---|---|
| Time between arrivals | 0 |
| Service time in the Scheduling division | 0.82 |
| Service time in the Billing division | >0.15 |
| Service time in outpatient pediatric care | >0.15 |

Once the independence and homogeneity analysis are complete, the modelers have to specify the probability expressions that will represent each process variable from Table 3. To this aim, Goodness-of-fit tests were conducted at an error level of 0.05. For example, the Kolmogorov-Smirnov test (KS = 0.162, p-value > 0.15) provided good support for the Triangular assumption of *time between arrivals (control appointments)*. The final results of these tests are detailed in Table 4.

**Table 4.** Results of Goodness-of-fit tests

| Process variable | Probability expression |
|---|---|
| Time between arrivals (first-time appointments) | EXPO (45.5) days |
| Time between arrivals (monitoring appointments) | 2.13 + WEIB (1.42, 4) days |
| Time between arrivals (Priority consultation) | TRIA (2, 3.75, 5) days |
| Service time in the Scheduling division | NORM (3.70; 1.77) min/appointment |
| Service time in the Billing division | UNIF (2.4; 5.7) min/appointment |
| Service time in outpatient gynecology care | NORM (35; 5.7) min/appointment |

### 4.3  Development and Validation of a DES Model

A DES model was developed to provide a virtual representation of the outpatient gynecology department under analysis (refer to Fig. 3). To ensure the accuracy and robustness of the DES outcomes, we ran the simulation for 372 days with 9 h per shift-day. After the initial exploration, we found that 100 days can be assumed as a warm-up period. In addition, a pre-sample of 10 runs was undertaken to estimate the required sample size for properly representing the ALT variability. In this project, 35 replications were found to be statistically sufficient for explaining department performance. Next, the ALT values, recorded by Arena 14.5 ® in each replication, were processed to validate the model ($H_o$: $\mu = 7.76$ *days/consultation*|$H_a$: $\mu \neq 7.76$ *days/consultation*). To this aim, a 1-sample t-test (C.L. = 0.95) was conducted using Minitab 17 ® software. The resulting p-value (0.86) and t-statistic (−0.18) revealed that the virtual model is statistically compared with the real outpatient gynecology department. Therefore, it can be further used for the diagnosis and evaluation of improvement scenarios.

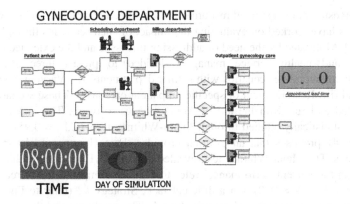

**Fig. 3.** The simulation model for the outpatient gynecology department

### 4.4 Diagnosis

After verifying the suitability of the DES model, the next stage was to determine how capable the outpatient gynecology department is to meet the target set by the National Health Institution (U.S.L. = 8 days/consultation). The capability study revealed that the average ALT is 7.7 days/consultation with a shape of 7.91 days/consultation and a scale of 0.96 days/consultation. Additionally, it was found that 404597 out of 1 million of consultations will have an ALT > 8 days. Complementary to these indices, the Ppu (0.06), Ppk (0.06) and sigma process level (1.74) argue that the performance is poor and then demands profound changes. These results were presented to the health service managers in order to design potential interventions that tackle the problem here described (Fig. 4).

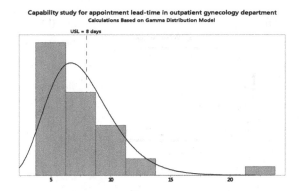

**Fig. 4.** Capability study of the outpatient gynecology department

### 4.5 Pretesting Improvement Scenarios

Discrete-event simulation allows modelers to evaluate changes in outpatient care delivery before implementation in a safe and effective manner [17–19]. This is useful to avoid the investment of restricted resources on low effective strategies. However, only a few studies have worked on evaluating the impact of such scenarios through the use of DES [20]. Motivated by the need of addressing this issue and the extended ALT, the researchers and health service managers decided to pretest three alternatives: (i) Establish collaborative scenarios with similar departments, (ii) Varying the installed capacity and (iii) Reassignment of specific outpatient care tasks. These scenarios were then modeled and run with the aid of Arena 14.5 ® software. The impact of each change was statistically studied through Mann-Whitney tests (C.L. = 0.95).

Strategy #1 proposes that an external provider shares 1 gynecologist in case of demand peaks. The Mann-Whitney test revealed that the ALT provided in this scenario is lower than the current performance (refer to Fig. 5a) compared to the real waiting time (p-value = 0; W = 980). On a different tack, Strategy #2 (refer to Fig. 5b) recommends increasing the installed capacity by 8 h. The results proved that ALT can be substantially minimized (p-value = 0; W = 980). Lately, the strategy #3 (refer to Fig. 5c) proposes to assign some activities of outpatient gynecology care to nurse practitioners (i.e. blood pressure measurement, calculate the patient's weight, fill out the paperwork). In this scenario, the ALT was found to be significantly lower with respect to the standard and current process behavior (p-value = 0; W = 980).

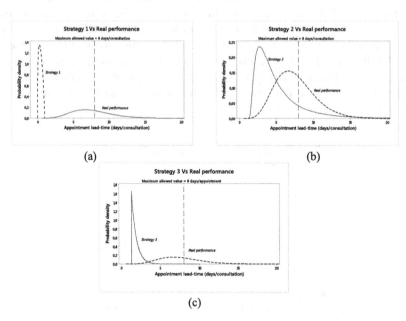

(a)          (b)

(c)

**Fig. 5.** The comparative study between the real performance and (a) Strategy 1 (b) Strategy 2 (c) Strategy 3

## 5 Conclusions and Future Work

In this article, we have verified the applicability of discrete-event simulation to reduce the appointment lead-time in outpatient gynecology departments. In particular, the capability analysis foresees that 40.46% of the consultations requests in this unit will have an ALT higher than the maximum allowable limit. To address this problem, three strategies were modeled and simulated with the assistance of health service managers and specialized software. In this project, all the strategies were concluded to be effective since they minimize the appointment lead-time indicator. Through these interventions, severe complications, patient dissatisfaction, higher mortality, and increased healthcare costs can be substantially avoided.

On a different tack, with the use of DES, health service managers and policymakers are able to evaluate the impact of potential improvement strategies before implementation. This is valuable to determine their viability, minimize errors during execution, allocate scant resources better and avoid extra charges. To this end, it is relevant to provide high-quality data and work closely with the modelers so that high accuracy and robustness of these models can be granted.

Our study contributes to the small reported evidence regarding the use of DES models for pretesting improvement scenarios and support viability evaluation. Nevertheless, we aim in future work to incorporate economic evaluation and develop cost-effectiveness indicators that offer a wider overview of the implementation in terms of investment returns and performance improvement. We also plan to consider interactions with other healthcare units (i.e. emergency departments, intensive care units, hospitalization divisions) to underpin integrated planning and resource management within maternal hospitals.

## References

1. Zhang, X.: Application of discrete event simulation in health care: a systematic review. BMC Health Serv. Res. **18**(1), 687 (2018)
2. Brailsford, S.C., Harper, P.R., Patel, B., Pitt, M.: An analysis of the academic literature on simulation and modelling in health care. J. Simul. **3**(3), 130–140 (2009)
3. Elkhuizen, S.G., Das, S.F., Bakker, P.J.M., Hontelez, J.A.M.: Using computer simulation to reduce access time for outpatient departments. BMJ Qual. Saf. **16**(5), 382–386 (2007)
4. Harper, P.R., Gamlin, H.M.: Reduced outpatient waiting times with improved appointment scheduling: a simulation modelling approach. OR Spectr. **25**(2), 207–222 (2003)
5. Santibáñez, P., Chow, V.S., French, J., Puterman, M.L., Tyldesley, S.: Reducing patient wait times and improving resource utilization at British Columbia Cancer Agency's ambulatory care unit through simulation. Health Care Manag. Sci. **12**(4), 392 (2009)
6. Wijewickrama, A.K.A.: Simulation analysis for reducing queues in mixed-patients' outpatient department. Int. J. Simul. Model. **5**(2), 56–68 (2006)
7. Gillespie, J., McClean, S., Garg, L., Barton, M., Scotney, B., Fullerton, K.: A multi-phase DES modelling framework for patient-centred care. J. Oper. Res. Soc. **67**(10), 1239–1249 (2016)

8. Ortiz, M.A., McClean, S., Nugent, C.D., Castillo, A.: Reducing appointment lead-time in an outpatient department of gynecology and obstetrics through discrete-event simulation: a case study. In: García, C.R., Caballero-Gil, P., Burmester, M., Quesada-Arencibia, A. (eds.) UCAmI 2016. LNCS, vol. 10069, pp. 274–285. Springer, Cham (2016). https://doi.org/10.1007/978-3-319-48746-5_28

9. Congreso de la República de Colombia: Law 1751 (2015). Por medio de la cual se regula el derecho fundamental a la salud y se dictan otras disposiciones, 16 February 2015. http://www.secretariasenado.gov.co/senado/basedoc/ley_1751_2015.html#26

10. Constitución Política de Colombia (1991). http://www.secretariasenado.gov.co/index.php/constitucion-politica

11. Congreso de la República de Colombia: Law 100 (1993). Por la cual se crea el sistema de seguridad social integral y se dictan otras disposiciones, 23 December 1993. http://www.secretariasenado.gov.co/senado/basedoc/ley_0100_1993.html#T%C3%8DTULO%20PREL IMIN

12. Ministerio de Salud y Protección Social: Decree 780 (2016). Por medio del cual se expide el Decreto Único Reglamentario del Sector Salud y Protección Social, 6 May 2016. https://www.minsalud.gov.co/Normatividad_Nuevo/Decreto%200780%20de%202016.pdf

13. Ministerio de Salud y Protección Social: Resolution 256 (2016). Por la cual se dictan disposiciones en relación con el Sistema de Información para la Calidad y se establecen los indicadores para el monitoreo de la calidad en salud, 5 February 2016. http://www.acreditacionensalud.org.co/sua/Documents/Resoluci%C3%B3n%200256%20de%20201620 SinfCalidad.pdf

14. Karnon, J., Stahl, J., Brennan, A., Caro, J.J., Mar, J., Möller, J.: Modeling using discrete event simulation: a report of the ISPOR-SMDM modeling good research practices task force–4. Med. Decis. Making 32(5), 701–711 (2012)

15. Izquierdo, N.V., Lezama, O.B.P., Dorta, R.G., Viloria, A., Deras, I., Hernández-Fernández, L.: Fuzzy logic applied to the performance evaluation. Honduran coffee sector case. In: Tan, Y., Shi, Y., Tang, Q. (eds.) ICSI 2018. LNCS, vol. 10942, pp. 164–173. Springer, Cham (2018). https://doi.org/10.1007/978-3-319-93818-9_16

16. Günal, M.M., Pidd, M.: Discrete event simulation for performance modelling in health care: a review of the literature. J. Simul. 4(1), 42–51 (2010)

17. Ortiz Barrios, M., Felizzola Jiménez, H., Nieto Isaza, S.: Comparative analysis between ANP and ANP- DEMATEL for six sigma project selection process in a healthcare provider. In: Pecchia, L., Chen, L.L., Nugent, C., Bravo, J. (eds.) IWAAL 2014. LNCS, vol. 8868, pp. 413–416. Springer, Cham (2014). https://doi.org/10.1007/978-3-319-13105-4_62

18. Ortiz, M.A., López-Meza, P.: Using computer simulation to improve patient flow at an outpatient internal medicine department. In: García, C.R., Caballero-Gil, P., Burmester, M., Quesada-Arencibia, A. (eds.) UCAmI 2016. LNCS, vol. 10069, pp. 294–299. Springer, Cham (2016). https://doi.org/10.1007/978-3-319-48746-5_30

19. Ortíz-Barrios, M., Jimenez-Delgado, G., De Avila-Villalobos, J.: A computer simulation approach to reduce appointment lead-time in outpatient perinatology departments: a case study in a maternal-child hospital. In: Siuly, S., et al. (eds.) HIS 2017. LNCS, vol. 10594, pp. 32–39. Springer, Cham (2017). https://doi.org/10.1007/978-3-319-69182-4_4

20. Mohiuddin, S., et al.: Patient flow within UK emergency departments: a systematic review of the use of computer simulation modelling methods. BMJ Open 7(5), e015007 (2017)

# Ambient Intelligence Model for Monitoring, Alerting and Adaptively Recommending Patient's Health-Care Agenda Based on User Profile

Manuel F. J. Patiño$^{(\boxtimes)}$ and Demetrio A. Ovalle$^{(\boxtimes)}$

Universidad Nacional de Colombia, Sede Medellín, Colombia
{mjpatinoc, dovalle}@unal.edu.co

**Abstract.** Currently, healthcare is a crucial issue for the entire population, especially for individuals who suffer from a chronic disease such as hypertension or diabetes. However, this care is carried out in medical centers, limiting the scope of health professionals. In fact, some monitoring, early warning processes, and health supporting that are not presently performed, could be carried out at the patient's location. The aim of this paper is to integrate WSN, ambient intelligence, multi-agent systems, and ontologies, in order to develop an ambient intelligence model that provides alerts, personalized recommendations, and adaptive health-care agendas. Personalized agendas based on chronic patient profiles offer appropriate physical activity, personalized food diet, and specific activities in order to control stress levels. For the validation of the proposed model, a prototype was constructed and applied to a case study considering several chronic patients. The results demonstrate the effectiveness of the proposed health-care ambient intelligence multi-agent model.

**Keywords:** Ambient intelligence · Healthcare · Multi-agent systems · Adaptive systems · Ontologies · Wireless sensor networks

## 1 Introduction

In recent years, there has been a lot of research and development using information technology (IT) in the field of medicine and health. Applying such technologies leads to the improvement of quality, safety and efficiency in medical care [1]. Technologies such as Mobile Health (m-Health) allow the interaction between health professionals and their patients, where mobile devices are used ubiquitously. This allows for noticeably improved medical care and diagnostic decision-making in health centers and at home [2, 3].

In addition, there are wireless sensor networks (WSN) in order to monitor all types of variables. In particular, in human health monitoring there are functional devices that alert when levels are out of the acceptable limits [4, 5]. However, if we strive for an autonomous and immediate reaction system to safeguard the life and well-being of patients, monitoring and alerting alone is not enough.

© Springer Nature Switzerland AG 2019
V. G. Duffy (Ed.): HCII 2019, LNCS 11582, pp. 113–124, 2019.
https://doi.org/10.1007/978-3-030-22219-2_9

Therefore, it is necessary to develop a system that complements the existing systems by implementing technologies such as ambient intelligence, multi-agent systems, ontologies, and recommendation systems. It is required to develop a context-aware adaptive ambient intelligence system that by itself can adapt its behavior to the context that is monitoring. In addition, it is required that the patient can visualize the sampled data through a human-computer interface, and that the system is able to suggest, recommend, and provide feedback to the user about the actions to adopt in order to obtain the desired result.

The aim of this paper is to propose an ambient intelligence model that integrates technologies such as WSN, multi-agent systems, ambient intelligence, ontologies, in order to provide adaptive health-care functions to chronic patients. We develop a prototype that consists of several modules that allow the deployment of adaptive functions on a human-computer interface. The system allows monitoring, alerting and offering recommendations, and healthy agendas to patients who do not have health professionals during their daily life. In addition, the system makes it possible for a health professional to visualize all the patient information.

The rest of the paper is organized as follows: Sect. 2 presents the conceptual framework of this research. Section 3 reviews some related works concerning AmI systems for healthcare. Section 4 describes the proposed model. Section 5 offers the model implementation and validation of the proposed model. Finally, the main conclusions and future research directions are presented in Sect. 6.

## 2   Conceptual Framework

This section provides main definitions used in this research work such as ambient intelligence, wireless sensor networks, ontologies, multi-agent systems, healthcare, among others.

### 2.1   Ambient Intelligence

Ambient Intelligence (AmI)) [6] is a concept raised by the ISTAG (Information Society Technologies Advisory Group) through a report [7] that was presented to the General Directory of INFSO (Information Society) of the European Commission. In this report, AmI consists of the creation of habitable spaces where the users interact in a natural and intuitive way through computational services in order to assist the accomplishment of their daily tasks. Among the main features of an AmI system are the following:

- The AmI environment must be context-aware, that is, it must be able to adapt its behavior based on the previously monitored variables.
- Information, communication, and services are offered to users in a ubiquitous, wireless, and transparent manner.
- Human-machine interaction is accomplished naturally and not intrusively.

According to Marzano [8], the five main characteristics of the AmI are the following:

- Embedded: many networked devices integrate and operate into the environment.
- Context-aware: these devices can recognize people and their contextual situation at any specific time.
- Personalized: AmI devices can adapt their behavior to the people's needs.
- Adaptive: AmI devices can autonomously change in response to people and their environment.
- Anticipatory: AmI devices can anticipate user needs and desires without a conscious mediation.

Consequently, an environment will be intelligent when it is unnoticeable, unobtrusive, and the different technologies that surround it complement each other to provide useful services to people. Thus, AmI environments could be implemented within different scenarios where the user lives, for example, domestic, mobile, public, and private environments [9].

## 2.2    Wireless Sensor Networks

Wireless sensor networks (WSN) are networks made up of several autonomous devices that have sensors, through which a monitoring and data acquisition system of the environment can be created. The WSN is a subfield of embedded systems that attempts to improve well-being and quality of life through home automation and health AmI environments. In addition, many companies and public organizations currently build WSN-based large-scale applications such as monitoring systems to provide early alerts to natural disasters, monitoring in the agricultural sector, industrial control, and transport. In a WSN, each device is autonomous and has the capacity of processing, storage, and sampling through its sensors [9].

## 2.3    Ontologies

Ontologies can be defined as a formal representation of a particular domain using a well-defined methodology that allows for the representation of the domain entities and the relationships existing among them [10]. Based on this, it is important to generate a formal representation of the adaptive learning course structure, in order to make inferences and generate recommendations for improving the learning process. Similarly, designing formal representations of a specific domain allows for readable and reusable information for computers and intelligent systems [11].

## 2.4    Multi-agent Systems

Multi-agent systems (SMA) issued from distributed artificial intelligence, are complex systems that are made up of autonomous agents. Each has the knowledge of a specific domain and the ability to interact with other agents to achieve a common goal [12]. In addition, agents are entities that have enough autonomy and intelligence to accomplish specific tasks with little or no supervision [13].

## 2.5    Healthcare

Chronic cardiovascular diseases (CVD) are a group of heart disorders and are the main cause of death in the world. Arterial hypertension (the most important preventable cause of CVD) is a disorder in which the force exerted by the blood on the walls of the arteries is higher than normal. The higher the tension, the more effort the heart has to exert to pump blood, increasing the risk of damage to the heart and blood vessels of major organs [14].

Diabetes is a chronic disease that occurs when an organism does not efficiently use the insulin it produces, or does not produce enough insulin. Insulin is the hormone responsible for regulating blood sugar. Hyperglycemia (blood sugar level higher than normal) degrades many organs and systems overtime, especially blood vessels and nerves [15].

Finally, for both diseases, monitoring, alerts, recommendations, and a healthy agenda, allows patients (if they are rigorous) to maintain stable blood pressure and/or suitable blood sugar levels, thus minimizing the chances of premature death and increasing healthy life habits.

## 3    Related Works

This section examines some related research that focuses on fields including ambient intelligence, ontologies, multi-agent systems and WSN. We will consider the advantages and disadvantages of various models and prototypes.

Corchado et al. [16] propose an autonomous intelligent agent developed for the control of healthcare of patients with Alzheimer in geriatric residences. The agent operates in wireless devices and integrates with complementary agents within an ambient intelligence multi-agent system, called ALZ-MAS (ALZheimer Multi-Agent-System) that interacts with the environment. An agent called AGALZ (Autonomous aGent for monitoring ALZheimer patients) was developed, with the objective of providing efficient work schedules, in real time, to the geriatric staff of the residences and therefore improving the quality of healthcare and supervision of patients in nursing homes. Each of the AGALZ agents is assigned to a nurse or doctor of a residence and additionally provides information on patient locations, historical data, and alarms. While staff members are carrying out their functions (following the plan envisaged by the agent), the plan may need to be modified due to delays or alarms. In this case, the agent is able to re-plan the initial proposed plan in real time.

Agreda et al. [17] analyze a possible solution to the problem of autonomy and independence of the elderly, which is mainly caused by the physical and physiological changes and the total or partial abandonment experienced by these people. In addition, authors attempt to solve this problem by analyzing and designing a model to provide the control of an intelligent environment that supplies aid and support to these people. The AmI environment attempts to help them in their daily lives by automating household processes, and by using all the information produced by the daily activity recorded to provide feedback to an intelligent model. This model serves as an information base to make decisions based on their behavior patterns and thus perform preventive actions to many of the typical problems of age with the appropriate alerts and additional procedures.

Restrepo et al. [18] propose an intelligent laboratory (SmartLab) located in a university environment. The authors use a meta-model to abstract the environment and its users, using WSN to acquire the contextual characteristics of the environment. It also uses intelligent agents to provide the required adaptation to offer personalized services according to the user's environment. The architecture of the SmartLab comprises a physical layer, an agent layer, an application domain, and a service layer. The physical layer is composed of WSN which senses environmental physical variables (temperature and luminosity) and monitors the users. The agent layer implements the context, user, and adaptation models by using several intelligent agents. The application domain layer formalizes and transfers the knowledge acquired by the system in a language that is understandable to intelligent agents. Finally, the service layer uses software to implement the AmI services provided to the users.

Roda et al. [19] develop a multi-agent architecture for environmental intelligence systems in health, which contributes to the treatment of people with brain injuries (ABI). It uses specific devices to control the movements of the patient taking into consideration physiological responses, such as the variation of heart rate, during their rehabilitation process. In addition, author describes the manner in which this system designs and executes therapies for people with ABI. Its design offers a meta-model to define the rehabilitation environment. Finally, the AmI uses fuzzy inference systems that allow the system to adapt the therapies and make decisions about the order of activities, tasks to be performed, and steps to follow in real time.

Su and Peng [20] deal with ontological and epistemological problems, developing a rehabilitation information service based on an ontology called as OntoRis, and using the agent technology to explore external ontologies for its integration with the OntoRis foundation. The AmI environment offers a rehabilitation service based on OntoRis ontology to help patients acquire prescribed practical knowledge about their rehabilitation. The rehabilitation service also accelerates recovery through suggestions and advice provided by evidence-based medicine. In addition, OntoRis can also serve as an interactive learning platform for people who are interested in rehabilitation medicine.

From the previously reviewed research works, we can conclude that some works still present shortcomings such as the following: (1) they do not use ontologies for knowledge representation; (2) they do not define user profiles to offer personalized services; (3) some of them do not integrate WSN for contextual monitoring; (4) they do not offer user adaptive recommendations including a healthy personalized agenda. The aim of this paper is to face these shortcomings and to provide a comprehensive solution concerning the use of adaptive systems and patient profiles for monitoring, alerting and adaptively recommending patient's health-care agenda.

## 4   Model Proposed

Figure 1 shows the architecture of the AmI model which is composed of six components as follows:

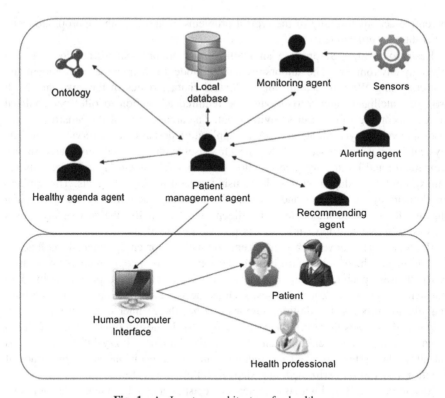

**Fig. 1.** AmI system architecture for healthcare

- Ontology: in this component the knowledge representation used by system is defined.
- Sensors: this component contains the WSN that monitors blood pressure and blood glucose in patients. This network integrates technologies that allow monitoring, storage, and real-time transmission (minute-by-minute) of the monitored variables.
- Database: this component stores all the information about the patient. This information contains not only the medical history of the patient but also its alerts, recommendations, and healthy agendas offered by the system.
- Human-computer interface: this component represents the interface through which the system interacts with the user. This interaction is bi-directional, that is, both user and system are always ready to provide information to each other.
- Users: this component represents the people who will use the system, in this case, patients and health professionals.
- Multi-agent system: this component is composed of five agents that will be described below.

Figure 2 shows the ontological structure designed for the healthcare based system. Within the development of the ontological structure, the following three stages have been considered: the first examines the characterization of user profiles, the second is related to a healthy agenda, and the third concerns alerts and recommendations. The patient profile is composed of personal information (full name, identification, etc.), as well as features of the medical condition (medical history, diseases, etc.). The structure of the healthy agenda in turn, comprises information about scheduling tasks that the patient has to perform. The structure of the third component is divided into three fields: monitoring, alerts, and recommendations. Those fields correspond to a specific patient profile. The aim is to store all of the health information concerning a given patient.

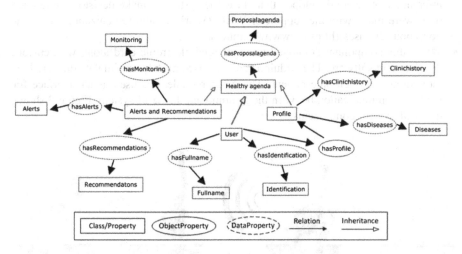

**Fig. 2.** Ontological structure

The multi-agent system consists of five software agents as follows:

- Patient management agent: this agent is responsible for handling and supervising all the components of the system. Its functions include communication with all other agents, storage in databases, ontology implementation, and human-computer interface execution.
- Monitoring agent: this agent is responsible for managing the communication with the sensors, receiving the monitoring information that sensors perform. In addition, it sends the gathered information to the patient's management agent.
- Alert agent: this agent is responsible for constantly monitoring the information gathered by the monitoring agent. Continuous supervision is performed in order to immediately alert the patient in case of some of the monitored values are outside of the normal range.
- Recommendation agent: this agent is responsible for analyzing the alerts issued by the alert agent. This allows it to recommend actions that should be taken as soon as possible to stabilize the levels of the monitored variables.
- Healthy agenda agent: this agent is responsible for analyzing the responses given by the patient through the questionnaire. The user profile and the analysis of the patient's responses allow to create an agenda of tasks that must be executed by him. These tasks help the diabetes and hypertension patients to maintain healthy lives.

## 5   Implementation and Validation

The prototype was implemented using various technologies depending on the particular system component. Next, we describe how each component was addressed and the technology used:

- Ontology: this component was developed using the Protégé tool V5.2.0. In addition, inference rules were developed that allow the system to make decisions. Inference rules were made with the support of WHO (World Health Organization) information about diseases (https://www.who.int/es).
- WSN: this component employed a commercial electronic card along with custom development software. The Arduino card was used in order to simulate the variables monitored to the chronic patient. The Xbee module was used as an interface for wireless communication between the Arduino and the AmI system. Figure 3 shows the AmI system components.

**Fig. 3.** AmI system components. From left to right: patient, Arduino-based wireless monitoring system, Xbee receiver module, computer.

- Database: this component developed in MySQL stores the patient's information as well as the relevant information offered by the system to the patient.
- Human-computer interface: this component was developed using NetBeans, a platform of modular components used to develop Java desktop applications.
- Users: this component was implemented, simulating five patient profiles considering several possible cases. It is considered for example how advanced the disease is and if the patient has both diabetes and hypertension at the same time.
- SMA: this component was implemented, using JADE as a platform for agent development. Figure 4 shows the communication performed between agents.

The AmI system autonomously performs alerts and recommendations in the presence of abnormal values of blood pressure or blood glucose.

In addition, the AmI system offers a healthy personalized weekly agenda adapted to the patient's health conditions. To do so, the system takes into account four inputs namely: (1) the information from the sensors that generate alerts; (2) the information provided by the patient through a questionnaire (see Fig. 5); (3) information from the previous healthy agenda, and finally, (4) information from the patient's medical history. Figure 6 presents the results of an alert and a recommendation provided by the system

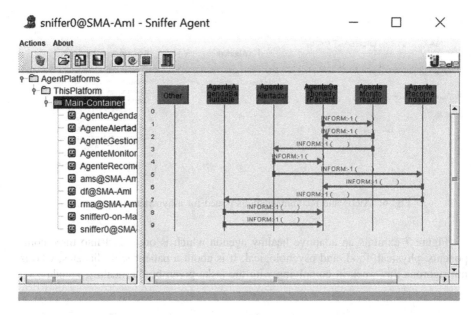

**Fig. 4.** Communication performed between agents using the JADE platform.

to a patient with arterial hypertension. In this case, the pressure reaches the value of 183/145 mmHg and therefore the system reacts, sending alerts and recommendations to the patient. An email is also sent to the health professional in charge of this patient.

**Cuestionario Semanal**

¿Cuánto pesa en kilogramos?  85

¿Consume cigarrillo?  ☑ Nunca     ☐ Ocasionalmente     ☐ Siempre

¿Cuántas horas de ejercicio realiza por semana?     ☑ menos de 1 hora   ☐ 1-2 horas   ☐ más de 2 horas

¿Cuántas horas de actividad social positiva realiza por semana?     ☐ menos de 1 hora     ☐ 1-2 horas     ☑ más de 2 horas

¿Cuánto es su nivel de estrés?    ☐ Bajo  ☑ Medio  ☐ Alto

¿Cuántos vasos de bebida azucarada bebe por semana?  ☐ menos de 1 vaso   ☑ 1-3 vasos   ☐ más de 3 vasos

¿Consume alcohol?  ☐ Nunca   ☑ Ocasionalmente   ☐ Siempre

¿Cuántas veces a la semana consume grasas saturadas?  ☐ menos de 1 vez     ☑ 1-3 veces   ☐ más de 3 veces

(Comidas rapidas, alimentos fritos, etc)

¿Cuántas veces a la semana consume alimentos con alto contenido de sal?  ☐ menos de 1 vez   ☐ 1-3 veces ☑ más de 3 veces

(Mecato salado, mango con sal, etc)

¿Cuán riguroso ha sido con la ingesta de medicamentos?    ☐ Nada riguroso   ☑ Medianamente riguroso   ☐ Muy riguroso

¿Presenta problemas podológicos? ☐ Si  ☑ No

(Dolencias en pie o tobillo)                                                                    Enviar

**Fig. 5.** Questionnaire used as input to generate a healthy agenda.

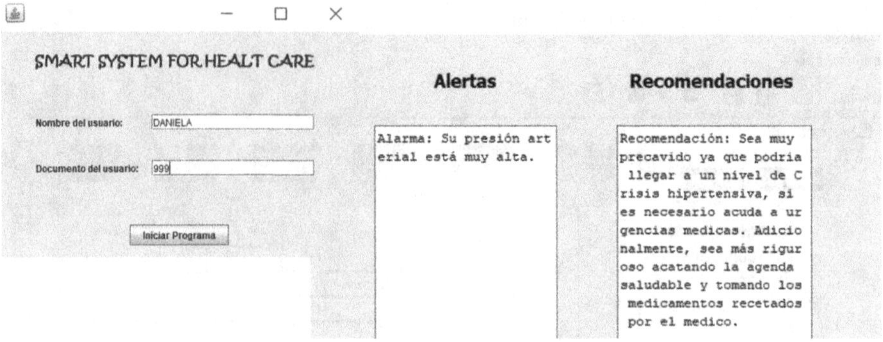

**Fig. 6.** Alerts and recommendations issued for a hypertension patient.

Figure 7 exhibits an adaptive healthy agenda which is organized into three components: physical, food, and psychological. It is about a patient with diabetes, who is not rigorous this week in complying with the tasks given by the healthy agenda.

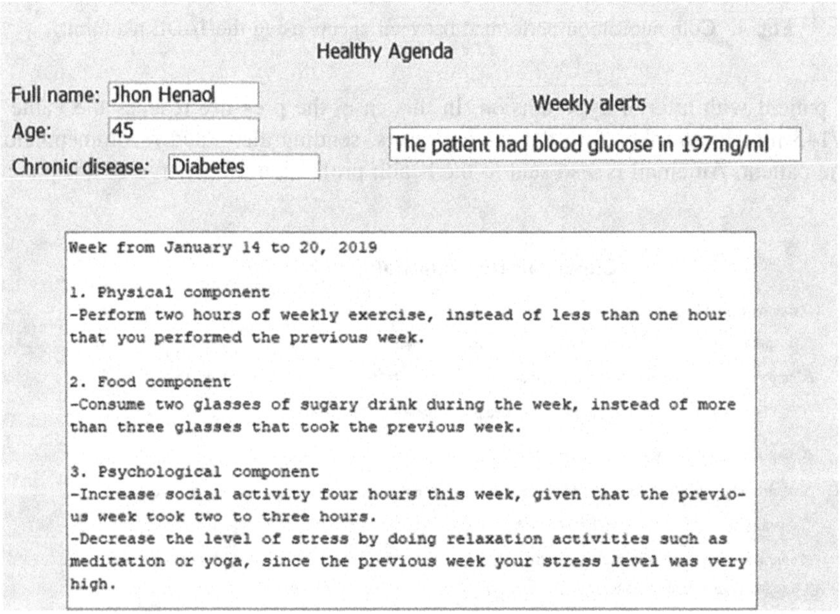

**Fig. 7.** Weekly scheduled tasks composing an adaptive healthy agenda.

In addition, the patient had an episode of very high level of blood glucose, during the previous week. Therefore, the new healthy personalized agenda issued from the AmI system brings new tasks and reminds him that he had a worrying event.

To validate the prototype model, several simulated chronic patient profiles are considered and their medical history is charged to the system database. The system takes into account the information of diseases, alerts, recommendations, and healthy agendas according to the patient's user profile. Later, a health professional can consult all the medical history of monitored data, and the information that the system has given to the patient.

Another case study for the prototype is when the system detects inconsistencies between the healthy agenda of the previous week and the answers obtained in the questionnaire by the patient. The above means that the patient is not complying with the proposed healthy agenda. In this case, the system generates a warning call that will appear in the adapted healthy agenda that the system is currently generating.

We can see that the AmI system reacts adequately to different alert events and takes into account whether or not the patient complied with the previous healthy agendas. Otherwise the system generates a new adaptive healthy week's agenda.

## 6 Conclusion and Future Work

From results obtained by the test of the prototype, we can conclude that the proposed AmI model fulfills the goals by providing integration among WSN, ontology, and multi-agent systems. In addition, the proposed model has the capacity to provide alerts, recommendations, and adaptive personalized healthy agendas according to the medical history, complying questionnaire, and previous healthy agenda of chronic patients.

Finally, as future work, it is proposed to complement the research using real patients along with commercial sensors in order to monitor health. Using the information of healthy agendas of other patients with similar profiles and applying a collaborative filtering technique could also be advantageous in order to improve the results obtained by the AmI system.

**Acknowledgments.** This research was developed by GIDIA (Artificial Intelligence Development Research Group) of the National University of Colombia, Medellin branch.

## References

1. Burney, S., Mahmood, N., Abbas, Z.: Information and communication technology in healthcare management systems: prospects for developing countries. Int. J. Comput. Appl. **4**(2), 27–32 (2010). https://doi.org/10.5120/801-1138
2. Oliveira, R., Frutuoso, S., Machado, J., Santos, M., Portela, F., Abelha, A.: Step towards m-Health in pediatrics. Proc. Technol. **9**, 1192–1200 (2013). https://doi.org/10.1016/j.protcy.2013.12.133
3. Silva, B., Rodrigues, J.: A novel cooperation strategy for mobile health applications. IEEE J. Sel. Areas Commun. **31**(9), 28–36 (2013). https://doi.org/10.1109/JSAC.2013.SUP.0513003
4. Free, C., Phillips, G., Watson, L., et al.: The effectiveness of mobile-health technologies to improve health care service delivery processes: a systematic review and meta-analysis. PLoS Med. **10**(1) (2013). https://doi.org/10.1371/journal.pmed.1001363

5. Pereira, A., Marinsa, F., Rodrigues, B., et al.: Improving quality of medical service with mobile health software. Proc. Comput. Sci. **63**, 292–299 (2015). https://doi.org/10.1016/j. procs.2015.08.346
6. Haya, P., Montoso, G., Alamán., X.: Un mecanismo de resolución de conflictos en entornos de inteligencia ambiental. In: Actas del Simposio de Computación Ubicua e Inteligencia Ambiental, UCAmI, pp. 11–18 (2005)
7. Venturini, V.: Sistema Multi-Agente basado en Contexto, Localización y Reputación para dominios de inteligencia Ambiental. Tesis de Doctorado en Ciencia y Tecnología Informática, Universidad Carlos III de Madrid – Escuela Politécnica Superior (2012)
8. Aarts, E., Marzano, S. (eds.): The New Everyday: Views on Ambient Intelligence. 010 Publishers, Rotterdam (2003)
9. Restrepo, S.: Modelo de Inteligencia Ambiental basado en la integración de Redes de Sensores Inalámbricas y Agentes Inteligentes. Tesis de maestría, Universidad Nacional de Colombia - Sede Medellín (2012)
10. Tramullas, J., Sánchez-Casabón, A.-I., Garrido-Picazo, P.: An evaluation based on the digital library user: an experience with greenstone software. Proc. - Soc. Behav. Sci. **73**, 167–174 (2013). https://doi.org/10.1016/j.sbspro.2013.02.037
11. Gaeta, M., Orciuoli, F., Paolozzi, S., Salerno, S.: Ontology extraction for knowledge reuse: the e-learning perspective. IEEE Trans. Syst. Man Cybern. - Part A: Syst. Hum. **41**(4), 798–809 (2011)
12. Mas, A.: Agentes Software y Sistemas MultiAgente: Conceptos, Arquitecturas y Aplicaciones. Pearson-Prentice-Hall (2004)
13. Wooldridge, M.: An Introduction to MultiAgent Systems (2009). http://books.google.com.br/ books/about/An_Introduction_to_MultiAgent_Systems.html?id=X3ZQ7yeDn2IC&pgis=1
14. OMS: Información general sobre la hipertensión en el mundo, una enfermedad que mata en silencio, una crisis de salud pública mundial. Organización mundial de la salud (2013)
15. Sarmar, N., Gao, P., Seshasai., S., et al.: Diabetes mellitus, fasting blood glucose concentration, and risk of vascular diseade: a collaborative meta-analysis of 102 prospective studies, Emerging Risk Factors Colladoration. The lancet (2010)
16. Corchado, J.M., Bajo, J., de Paz, Y., Tapia, D.I.: Intelligent environment for monitoring Alzheimer patients, agent technology for healthcare. Decis. Supp. Syst. **44**(2), 382–396 (2008). https://doi.org/10.1016/j.dss.2007.04.008
17. Agreda, J.A., Gonzalez, E.: Ambient intelligence based multi-agent system for attend elderly people. In: Proceedings of the 9th Computing Colombian Conference (9CCC) IEEE Conferences (2014)
18. Restrepo, S.E., Pezoa, J.E., Ovalle, D.A.: An Adaptive architecture for ambient intelligence based on meta-modeling, smart agents, and wireless sensor networks. IEEE Latin Am. Trans. **12**(8), 1508–1514 (2014)
19. Roda, C., Rodríguez, A., Lopez-Jaquero, V., Navarro, E., González, P.: A multi-agent system for acquired brain injury rehabilitation in ambient intelligence environments. Neurocomputing **231**, 11–18 (2017). https://doi.org/10.1016/j.neucom.2016.04.066
20. Su, C., Peng, C.: Multi-agent ontology-based Web 2.0 platform for medical rehabilitation. Expert Syst. Appl. **39**, 10311–10323 (2012)

# A Human-in-The-Loop Context-Aware System Allowing the Application of Case-Based Reasoning for Asthma Management

Mario Quinde[1,2(✉)], Nawaz Khan[1], Juan Carlos Augusto[1],
and Aléchia van Wyk[3]

[1] Research Group on Development of Intelligent Environments,
Middlesex University, London, UK
MQ093@live.mdx.ac.uk, N.X.Khan@mdx.ac.uk, J.Augusto@mdx.ac.uk
[2] Departamento de Ingeniería Industrial y de Sistemas,
Universidad de Piura, Piura, Peru
Mario.Quinde@udep.pe
[3] Department of Natural Sciences, Middlesex University, London, UK
A.VanWyk@mdx.ac.uk

**Abstract.** Determining the asthma health status of a person is a relevant task in the application of context-awareness and case-based reasoning for asthma management. As there are no devices that can track the asthma health status of a person constantly, it is necessary to use a Human-in-The-Loop (HiTL) approach for creating a solution able to associate their health status with context-related data. This research work proposes a system that implements the Asthma Control Questionnaire (ACQ) for determining the asthma health status of a person. The system links this health status to context-related data the person is exposed, and creates the cases to be used by the CBR component of the system. The system is then evaluated by users from a usability perspective through the Health IT Usability Evaluation Model (Health-ITUEM).

**Keywords:** Context-awareness · Case-based reasoning ·
Asthma management · Personalisation · Mobile health

## 1 Introduction

People with asthma suffer from an airway inflammation causing expiratory airflow limitation and respiratory symptoms such as wheeze, shortness of breath, chest tightness and cough that vary over time and intensity [5]. There is no cure for asthma but it can be treated based on a self-management approach [4,31,32]. Context-awareness (C-AR) can support the personalisation of asthma management plans, which is required to address the high heterogeneity level of asthma that makes people to have different triggers and symptoms [29,30].

© Springer Nature Switzerland AG 2019
V. G. Duffy (Ed.): HCII 2019, LNCS 11582, pp. 125–140, 2019.
https://doi.org/10.1007/978-3-030-22219-2_10

Context can be defined as *"the information which is directly relevant to characterise a situation of interest to the stakeholders of a system"*. C-AR is then defined as *"the ability of a system to use contextual information in order to tailor its services so that they are more useful to the stakeholders because they directly relate to their preferences and needs"*. Unlike Dey's definitions of context and C-AR [2,16] that go from the system to the user, these are more linked to a person-centric approach that goes from the user to the system.

Case-based reasoning (CBR) is a branch of artificial intelligence [1] that has already been applied in health sciences showing promising results [10,12]. CBR replicates *"the use of old experiences to understand and solve new problems"* [23]. It has been shown that CBR can be used together with C-AR to solve problems involving multidimensional context-related data [22]. Moreover, CBR is able to support the personalisation of local/personal restrictions by adapting medical knowledge and reasoning strategies based on contextual information [24].

Asthma can benefit from the synergy between CBR and C-AR because its heterogeneity requires patients to adapt their lifestyle to the constraints defining their asthma. They need to discover the triggers provoking their exacerbations and the symptoms shown when it occurs. They also need to adapt their management plans because the characteristics of their condition may change over time, or they may be exposed to environments with triggers they have not experienced before. Nevertheless, there are challenges to tackle before being able to exploit the synergy between CBR and C-AR for personalised asthma management.

This research work addresses an issue of using CBR/C-AR for asthma, which is how to determine the asthma health status of a person. This is important because the health status is highly relevant to define the context of a person with asthma and to complete the CBR cycle aiding their asthma management process. As there are no devices able to monitor the health status of a person constantly [30], a Human-in-The-Loop (HiTL) approach shall be used to create a solution able to determine and store the asthma health status of a person.

The main contribution of the research is a solution allowing people to determine their asthma health status through a system implementing the Asthma Control Questionnaire (ACQ) [18–21]. It is a mobile application using the ACQ to complete and store context-related data in form of cases to be used by the CBR component of the system. The design of the mobile application as a system showing explicit information [28] is described and then evaluated from a usability perspective.

The paper is divided as follows. Section 2 presents the state-of-the-art on the subject, Sect. 3 describes the methodology used in the research, Sect. 4 explains the benefits of using CBR and C-AR together for asthma management, and the challenge of determining the health status of a person. Then, the system to determine the health status and its validation are described in Sect. 5. The discussion of the outcomes and conclusions are presented in Sects. 6 and 7.

## 2    State-of-the-Art

C-AR is important for pervasive/ubiquitous computing [7,27] as it aids to personalising services based on contextual and situational information [3,9]. C-AR as part of Intelligent Environments has been applied to Transportation, Education, Production places, Smart offices, Intelligent supermarkets, Energy conservation, Entertainment, and Health [7]. In the health area, C-AR can aid people suffering from chronic conditions requiring lifestyle management [17]. C-AR solutions have been developed to support people suffering from high blood pressure [33], diabetes [14], cardiovascular conditions [15], among others.

A survey on C-AR for asthma condition management shows a lack of solutions allowing the personalisation of management plans [30]. This is important to highlight because personalisation is the key to implement effective asthma management plans given the high heterogeneity of the condition [31,32]. An approach to develop C-AR solutions allowing personalised asthma management is proposed as an attempt to close this gap [29]. It proposes to use three types of indicators in order to facilitate the description of patients' contexts and provide a more comprehensive support for complex decision-making processes like CBR.

CBR solves a new problem by reusing knowledge from previously solved problems that are similar to the new one [1]. This problem-solving paradigm can handle issues related to health sciences better than other techniques [11,12] and has already been used in several tasks including treatment planning, knowledge acquisition/management, among others [10]. CBR can be used together with C-AR in order to solve problems that are not completely understood, like adapting to evolving context adaptation [22] and personal constraints [24]. An example of the benefits from using CBR and C-AR together is shown in [26].

Monitoring the asthma health status of a person is an issue to tackle for allowing the application of CBR/C-AR in asthma management. This is challenging as there are no devices that can monitor the asthma health status of a person constantly [30]. Addressing this issue is important because it is needed to associate the context the person is exposed to their health status. Otherwise, it will not be possible to know whether a situation is dangerous or not, nor to determine what situations led to a health deterioration in the past for using them in the prediction of current and future risky situations.

This research work proposes to use a HiTL approach for implementing a C-AR system that determines the asthma health status of a person, relates it with the context the person is exposed, and creates/stores cases that can be used to apply CBR in asthma management. The system is a mHealth application whose HCI components gathering the asthma health status of a person is built based on the ACQ [18]. The HiTL approach takes human interaction into consideration, and makes humans a key part of the system [25].

## 3    Methodology

The research is led by the User-Centric Intelligent Environment Development Process, whose aim is to ensure the acceptance of technology by involving stake-

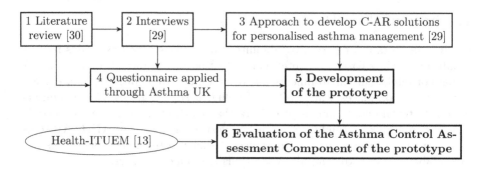

**Fig. 1.** Methodology

holders in all the stages. It has been used to develop technology helping people with special needs [6,8]. Figure 1 summarises the methodology process.

The *1. Literature review* showed a lack of C-AR solutions supporting personalised asthma management. Then, *2. Interviews* were held for having a better understanding about the necessities of people affected by asthma. From the outcomes of steps 1 and 2, an initial approach to develop C-AR solutions supporting personalised asthma management was proposed [29], and a questionnaire for defining more specific C-AR features of solutions supporting asthma management was developed. A partnership with Asthma UK [5] was formed, and they helped to spread the questionnaire among their representative sample of volunteers including patients and carers, gathering 42 responses.

A prototype was then developed considering the approach proposed in step 3 and the results of step 4. It includes an Asthma Control Assessment Component that aids to determining the asthma health status of a person. This component was evaluated by 5 people with asthma and 4 carers of people with asthma that interacted with the prototype. They were asked to answer a questionnaire based on the Health IT Usability Evaluation Model (Health-ITUEM) [13].

This research work mainly reports on steps 5 and 6 of the methodology described above. However, it also shows the results of the HCI-related questions that were included in the questionnaire spread in step 4 (Sect. 3.1).

### 3.1   Results of the Questionnaire Spread by Asthma UK

This section shows the results of the HCI-related questions that were included in the questionnaire spread by Asthma UK. Figures 2 and 3 show the assessment done by the respondents to some C-AR features of solutions supporting asthma management. Most of them assessed the features with 4 and 5: providing instructions in case of emergency (71.4%), showing a map highlighting near emergency centres (71.4%), reminding users about their medication intake (64.3%), and notifying patients' next of kin in case of emergency (69.0%). They were also asked to suggest other features, pointing out the following keywords covering their suggestions: asthma plan management (6 related-responses), medication

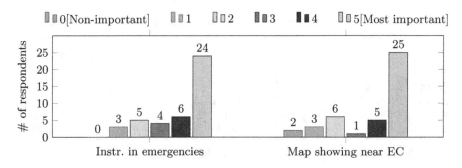

**Fig. 2.** Assessment of features of C-AR solutions (a)

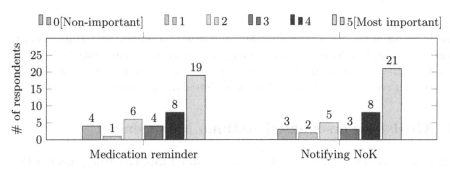

**Fig. 3.** Assessment of features of C-AR solutions (b)

management (5), notifying others when there is an emergency (2), nutrition management (1), and notifying when there is good weather (1).

Figure 4 summarises the stakeholders the respondents would like to contact in case of emergency, and how they would like to contact them. The axis *No* in Fig. 4 shows how many respondents do not want to contact each of the stakeholders listed. It suggests that the person to contact should be personalised depending on the scenario of the person with asthma. This statement is supported by respondents recommending different stakeholders to be notified when they were asked to suggest stakeholders that were not part of the response options. Among others, they suggested to notify the emergency department, general practitioners, doctors, work colleagues, and siblings, depending on their circumstances.

Figure 4 shows the preferred ways to contact the stakeholders in case of emergency. Showing a notification (alert) on the stakeholder's smartphone (47) is more preferred way to contact over using SMS (40), other messaging service (32) - like WhatsApp, Facebook Messenger, or Telegram, or other ways to contact them (8). The respondents could choose choosing more than one way of contacting each stakeholder. This means that a respondent could have chosen to contact their parents using a notification, SMS and Other MS all together.

Respondents were also asked about the information that should be send in case of emergency. 88.0% of them consider that the details of the emergency and

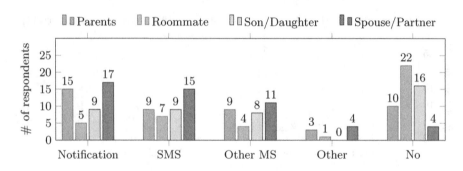

**Fig. 4.** How to contact in case of emergency?

the location of the person having the emergency are important information to send to the stakeholders when an emergency situation occurs. 66.67% of them consider that contact details is another important information to send. Finally, one person recommended to send Information about allergies.

## 4    CBR for Personalised Asthma Management

Figure 5 describes the CBR cycle for personalised asthma management, which has been adapted from the CBR cycle proposed by Aamodt and Plaza [1]. A *New problem* is a new case ($C_x$) to be analysed, which includes the context to which the person with asthma is or has been exposed. This context is made of the patient's, indoor and outdoor environmental indicators [29]. $C_x$ goes then to the *retrieval* stage, which is the first stage of CBR whose aim is finding the most similar case to $C_x$ ($C_s$) that is stored in the database of *previous cases*.

$C_s$ is the basis of the *reuse* stage that attempts predicting the possible outcome of $C_x$, considering the real outcome of $C_s$. The predicted and real outcome of a case is the predicted and real health status of the person with asthma when they are exposed to the context represented by that case. The health status is *normal* when the context does not affect them, and *deterioration* when the context negatively affects them. The predicted health status is defined in the *reuse* stage of the CBR, and the real health status is defined later in the *revise* stage by assessing the health status of the person with asthma.

The final stage is the *retain* stage in which the completely defined $C_x$ - that is represented by $\underline{C_x}$- is stored in the database of *previous cases* to be used in the future to assess other cases. Hence, CBR predicts the health status of a person that is exposed to a specific context by using the real health status the person experienced when they were exposed to a similar context in the past. Then, CBR confirms the real health status of the person for knowing the accuracy of its prediction and storing the new case to be used in future predictions.

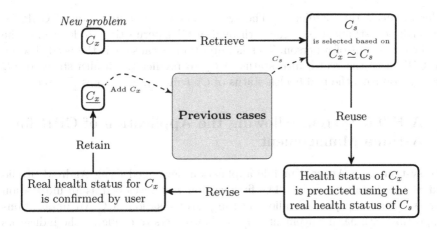

**Fig. 5.** CBR cycle adapted for personalised asthma management

## 4.1   The Challenge of Determining the Real Asthma Health Status

One of the issues of applying CBR for asthma management is defining the real health status of a person when is exposed to a specific context. It specially challenging as there are no commercial devices that can monitor the asthma health status of a person constantly [30]. This process is highly relevant because the real health status is needed to complete the case to store (*retain stage*), and to be used to predict the outcomes of future cases (*reuse stage*). Hence, if the *revision* is not completed, the accuracy of the prediction cannot be determined, and it will not be possible to use the knowledge of that case for future predictions.

This research work addresses the challenge of determining the asthma health status of a person by proposing a system that is based on the diary version of the ACQ [18–21]. The ACQ is made of questions that are answered using a scale of 7 (from 0 to 6). The average of the responses is used to assess if the asthma of the person is 'well-controlled' or 'not well-controlled' [19]. Four versions of the ACQ have been proposed and evaluated, concluding that the measurement properties of all four are almost identical [21]. The system implements the four versions: (1) assessing patient's symptoms, Peak Expiratory Flow (PEF) and rescue bronchodilator usage, (2) assessing patient's symptoms and rescue bronchodilator usage, (3) assessing patient's symptoms and PEF, and (4) assessing only patient's symptoms. Initially, the ACQ encourages to use the Forced Expiratory Volume in one second ($FEV_1$), however it is suggested to use the PEF for the diary version as it is more accessible for people [19].

The proposal is a HiTL system presenting explicit information about the new or updated context to the user, who then defines their health status and makes a decision considering this context [28]. Thus, the system will ask the user to assess their health status when they wake up, before going to sleep and whenever the user feels like in order to create new cases for the databases of *previous cases*, and when the CBR detects a potentially threatening context in order to *revise* this prediction. The system allows the application of CBR for personalised asthma management through a GUI permitting to determine the real health status of a person. This is important because it is the needed when the CBR uses the real health status of $C_s$ to predict the health status of $C_x$ (*reuse*), confirms the real health status of $C_x$ (*revise*), and stores $C_x$ (*retain*).

## 5    A HiTL System Allowing the Application of CBR for Asthma Management

The system is an Android mobile application developed using Android Studio and SQLite database engine. The first version was developed as an illustration of how to use an approach allowing the personalisation of C-AR applications supporting asthma management [29]. It allows users to configure the indicators to track and the features they need according to the specific characteristics of their asthma management plans. This research work adds a feature to this system, which is based on the explanation provided in Sect. 4.

### 5.1    System Architecture

The system architecture is shown in Fig. 6. The *Personalisation module* allows users to personalise the indicators to monitor, and some features like who to notify and how to notify them in emergencies. The *Report Generator* shows reports considering the personalisation done by the user [29]. The behaviour of the system for when it analyses context-related data is shown in Fig. 7, where the interaction between the *Case-Based Reasoner (CB)* and the *Context-Aware Reasoner (CA)* is illustrated. This behaviour occurs when the user configures the system for analysing context using the *CB* to discover potentially risky situations they are not aware of. If they do not activate this option, then the system will use the *CA* only, and not the *CB*, to analyse the context to which they are exposed.

The push approach in Fig. 7 shows how the system behaves when it analyses data in the background and discovers that the user is exposed to a potentially risky context. For this, the *Data Collectors* send data to the *Data Handler* (1.1), which interacts with the Database. The *Data Handler* stores this data and activates (1.2) the *CA* for it to assess the data that has been gathered. The *CA* gets the require data for the analysis (1.3, 1.4), and activates the *CB* (1.5) that assesses the new case (1.6) and sends the results back to the *CA* (1.7). The *CA* also analyses the context-related data considering the rules set up by the user (1.8), and activates the *Notification Engine* (1.9) that sends a notification to the user through the GUI (1.10, 1.11) asking them to assess their real health status in order to confirm whether there is a deterioration or not (1.12). The *CA* gets this response (1.13), stores it in the Database (1.14, 1.15), and activates the *Notification Engine* (1.16) that ask the GUI to show the user the outcome of their health assessment (1.17, 1.18). After this, the user can choose what to do. For instance, they may decide just to take their medication, or to use the system to deploy the emergency notification protocol that is explained in [29].

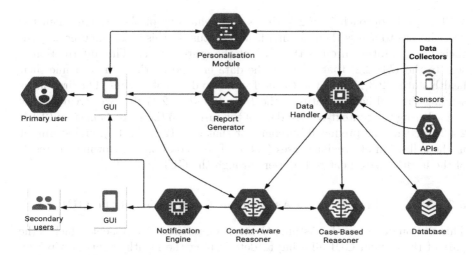

**Fig. 6.** System architecture with C-AR and CBR components

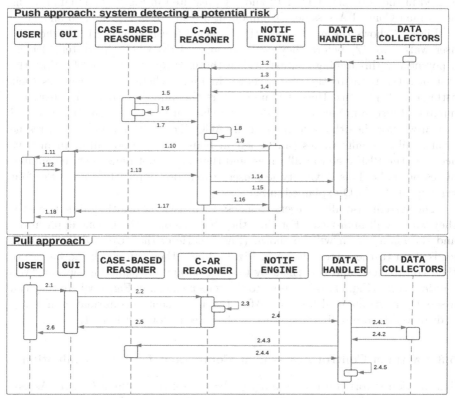

**Fig. 7.** Sequence diagram: push and pull approaches

The pull approach in Fig. 7 shows the behaviour of the system when the user chooses to assess their asthma health status. In this case, the user assesses their health status through the GUI of the system (2.1). This information is sent to the *CA* (2.2) that analyses the data entered by the user to define their health status (2.3). Then, the *CA* performs two different actions. The first one is sending the real health status to the *Data Handler* (2.4) that will create a case by gathering the context-related data of the case from the *Data Collectors* (2.4.1, 2.4.2), getting the predicted outcome for that case (2.4.3, 2.4.4), and storing it in the collection of previous cases (2.4.5). The second one is showing the result of the health assessment to the user through the GUI (2.5, 2.6).

## 5.2    The Asthma Control Assessment Component of the GUI

This section describes the Asthma Control Assessment Component, which is the part of the system GUI allowing to determining the health status of a person with asthma. This component is based on the ACQ explained in Sect. 4.1, and is used in the activities 1.11, 1.12 and 2.1 presented in Fig. 7. The main screens of Asthma Control Assessment Component are shown in Fig. 8, 9, 10 and 11.

Figure 8 shows the notification that appears (push approach) (1) when the user wakes up, (2) before they go to sleep, and (3) when the system detects a potentially threatening context. When the user taps on the notification, the system takes them to the screen shown in Fig. 9 where they can assess their asthma health status. Here, the user enters the value for their PEF test, the number of rescue bronchodilator puffs they have used in the past 24 hours, and the answer for the other questions of the ACQ. The PEF and number of rescue bronchodilator puffs values can be left in blank because not all of them have access to the PEF meter at all times, and they might not remember the number of rescue puffs. This flexibility lets users to choose implicitly among the four versions of the ACQ explained in Sect. 4.1.

The system also allows users to assess their asthma health status whenever they want (pull approach). For this, they have to open the mobile application, and the main screen will be shown (Fig. 10). Here, the *"Control test"* option leads them to the screen shown in Fig. 11 where they can check the history of their control test, and edit them by tapping on any of them. The option *"New Control Test"* (Fig. 11) takes users to the screen shown in Fig. 9, where they can assess their asthma health status. After the assessment, a confirmation message is displayed before redirecting users to the screen shown in Fig. 11.

## 5.3    Asthma Control Assessment Component Usability Evaluation

This section reports on the usability evaluation of the Asthma Control Assessment Component described in Sect. 5.2. The evaluation was based on the Health-ITUEM, which assesses nine usability-related concepts in order to evaluate the usability of health information technology [13]. The Health-ITUEM have been used to evaluate mobile health technology [13,30].

**Fig. 8.** Notification

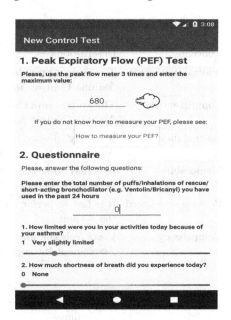

**Fig. 9.** New control test

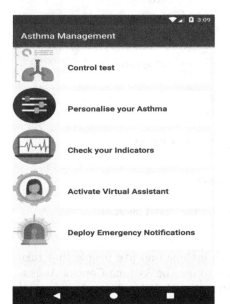

**Fig. 10.** Main screen

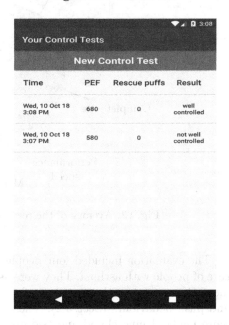

**Fig. 11.** Screen showing historical data

**Table 1.** Scenario mapping the Health-ITUEM concepts for the evaluation

| Concept | Description |
| --- | --- |
| Information needs | The system provides enough information to complete the Asthma Control Assessment |
| Completeness | The system provides enough information to know that the Asthma Control Assessment was completed |
| Learnability | It is easy to learn how to perform the Asthma Control Assessment through the system |
| Memorability | It is easy to remember how to perform the Asthma Control Assessment through the system |
| Performance speed | It is fast to perform the Asthma Control Assessment through the system |
| Competency | Users feels confident when they perform the Asthma Control Assessment through the system |

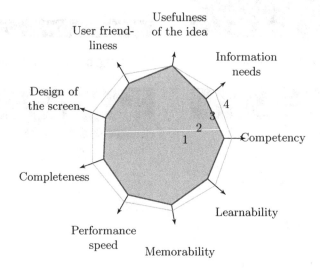

**Fig. 12.** Average of the responses for the closed questions

The evaluation included four people with asthma and five people that take care of people with asthma. They were asked to use the Asthma Control Assessment Component of the system, and to interact with it by simulating the pull and push behaviours (Sect. 5.2). Then, they were asked to answer a questionnaire made of nine closed and two open questions. One closed question asked about how useful the respondents perceive the idea of using previous risky situations for predicting future risky scenarios. Two closed questions assessed the overall GUI design and user-friendliness. The other six closed questions assessed six Health-ITUEM concepts. The open questions asked about the frequency the system should ask users to complete their asthma control assessment, and about the improvements the respondents would do to the system.

The scenario mapping the Health-ITUEM concepts for the evaluation of the Asthma Control Assessment Component (Table 1) was used to write the Health-ITUEM-related questions. The questionnaire did not include two Health-ITUEM concepts because the Asthma Control Assessment Component of the system was considered simple enough to avoid assessing its Flexibility and Error prevention. A Likert scale going from 0 (very low) to 4 (very high) was used for the closed questions. Figure 12 shows the average of the responses for these questions.

The analysis of the open questions shows that personalisation is highly important to define the frequency of showing the notification reminding to perform the Asthma Control Assessment. Six of them (66.67%) explicitly suggested that the frequency of the notifications should be defined considering the characteristics of the person with asthma. The other three suggested to show the notification two times a day, three times a day, and every 10–12 h.

The proposed improvements are mostly about enhancing the GUI. It was suggested to make the GUI more intuitive (2 respondents), and instructive about how to do the PEF test (1) and what to do if the outcome of the test is "not-well-controlled" (1). Two of them recommended using colours to differentiate the outcomes of the previous tests shown on Fig. 11. One suggestion was about providing an alternative version with simpler instructions for children (1). One respondent proposed to allow users to input data about previous risky situations in order to provide the system with a baseline for future predictions. Another one recommended to integrate the system with activity monitoring devices (e.g. smart watches) for gathering more data about the person's state.

## 6   Discussion

Figure 12 shows that the average of the responses for the quantitative questions are between 3 and 4, which are the two highest possible responses in the Likert scale that was used. It is also important to point out that all respondents assessed the idea of using previous risky situations for predicting future risky ones with 4 points, the highest possible response. This supports the idea of using CBR in personalised C-AR solutions supporting asthma management.

The number of positive, neutral and negative responses for the closed questions is another interesting outcome. A negative response has a value of 0 (very bad) or 1 (bad), a neutral one has a value of 2, and a positive one has a value of 3 (good) or 4 (very good). Memorability and Performance got only positive responses. Information needs, User-friendliness and Learnability got 8 positive and 1 negative responses. Competency got 8 positive and 1 neutral responses. Design of the screen and Completeness got 7 positive and 2 neutral responses.

The responses associated with the frequency of showing the notification asking users to assess their asthma control level differs in terms of absolute values. The difference among these responses could be related to their specific contexts but this should be further investigated. Nevertheless, there is evidence suggesting there is no unique frequency that can satisfy the requirements of the users.

Hence, another valuable outcome is the need for allowing users to set up the frequency of these notifications according to their specific situations.

## 7 Conclusions

This research works describes the HCI components of a solution implementing the ACQ in order to determine the asthma health status of a person. The interaction between the HCI and the CBR components of the solution is also explained. The benefits of this interaction are presented as a way of addressing an issue of using CBR for asthma management, which is linking the asthma health status to specific context-related data for creating the cases for the CBR. The solution was evaluated by users from a usability perspective showing positive results and pointing out some key points of improvement.

**Acknowledgement.** We thank Asthma UK for spreading the questionnaire (Section 3.1), among their representative network of people with asthma and carers. The Context and Context-awareness definitions in Section 1were provided by J.C. Augusto.

## References

1. Aamodt, A., Plaza, E.: Case-based reasoning: foundational issues, methodological variations, and system approaches. AI Commun. **7**(1), 39–59 (1994). https://doi.org/10.3233/AIC-1994-7104
2. Abowd, G.D., Dey, A.K., Brown, P.J., Davies, N., Smith, M., Steggles, P.: Towards a better understanding of context and context-awareness. In: Gellersen, H.-W. (ed.) HUC 1999. LNCS, vol. 1707, pp. 304–307. Springer, Heidelberg (1999). https://doi.org/10.1007/3-540-48157-5_29
3. Acampora, G., Cook, D.J., Rashidi, P., Vasilakos, A.V.: A survey on ambient intelligence in healthcare. Proc. IEEE **101**(12), 2470–2494 (2013). https://doi.org/10.1109/JPROC.2013.2262913
4. Asthma Australia: An Asthma Australia Site (2016). http://www.asthmaaustralia.org.au
5. Asthma UK: Asthma UK (2016). http://www.asthma.org.uk
6. Augusto, J., Kramer, D., Alegre, U., Covaci, A., Santokhee, A.: The user-centred intelligent environments development process as a guide toco-create smart technology for people with special needs. Univ. Access Inf. Soc. **17**(1), 115–130 (2018). https://doi.org/10.1007/s10209-016-0514-8
7. Augusto, J.C., Callaghan, V., Cook, D., Kameas, A., Satoh, I.: Intelligent environments: a manifesto. Hum.-Centric Comput. Inf. Sci. **3**(1), 12 (2013). https://doi.org/10.1186/2192-1962-3-12
8. Augusto, J.C., et al.: Personalized smart environments to increase inclusion of people with down's syndrome. In: Augusto, J.C., Wichert, R., Collier, R., Keyson, D., Salah, A.A., Tan, A.-H. (eds.) AmI 2013. LNCS, vol. 8309, pp. 223–228. Springer, Cham (2013). https://doi.org/10.1007/978-3-319-03647-2_16
9. Augusto, J.C., et al.: Handbook of Ambient Assisted Living, Ambient Intelligence and Smart Environments, vol. 11. IOS Press, Amsterdam (2012)

10. Begum, S., Ahmed, M.U., Funk, P., Xiong, N., Folke, M.: Case-based reasoning systems in the health sciences: a survey of recent trends and developments. IEEE Trans. Syst. Man Cybern. Part C (Appl. Rev.) **41**(4), 421–434 (2011). https://doi.org/10.1109/TSMCC.2010.2071862

11. Bichindaritz, I.: Case-based reasoning in the health sciences: why it matters for the health sciences and for CBR. In: Althoff, K.-D., Bergmann, R., Minor, M., Hanft, A. (eds.) ECCBR 2008. LNCS (LNAI), vol. 5239, pp. 1–17. Springer, Heidelberg (2008). https://doi.org/10.1007/978-3-540-85502-6_1

12. Bichindaritz, I., Montani, S.: Advances in case-based reasoning in the health sciences. Artif. Intell. Med. **51**(2), 75–79 (2011)

13. Brown, W., Yen, P.Y., Rojas, M., Schnall, R.: Assessment of the health IT usability evaluation model (health-ITUEM) for evaluating mobile health (mHealth) technology. J. Biomed. Inform. **46**(6), 1080–1087 (2013). https://doi.org/10.1016/j.jbi.2013.08.001

14. Chang, S., Chiang, R., Wu, S., Chang, W.: A context-aware, interactive m-health system for diabetics. IT Prof. **18**(3), 14–22 (2016). https://doi.org/10.1109/MITP.2016.48

15. Chatzitofis, A., et al.: Hearthealth: a cardiovascular disease home-based rehabilitation system. Proc. Comput. Sci. **63**, 340–347 (2015). https://doi.org/10.1016/j.procs.2015.08.352

16. Dey, A.K.: Understanding and using context. Pers. Ubiquit. Comput. **5**(1), 4–7 (2001). https://doi.org/10.1007/s007790170019

17. Isakovic, M., Cijan, J., Sedlar, U., Volk, M., Bester, J.: The role of mHealth applications in societal and social challenges of the future. In: 2015 12th International Conference on Information Technology - New Generations, pp. 561–566 (2015). https://doi.org/10.1109/ITNG.2015.94

18. Juniper, E., O'Byrne, P., Guyatt, G., Ferrie, P., King, D.: Development and validation of a questionnaire to measure asthma control. Eur. Respir. J. **14**(4), 902–907 (1999). http://erj.ersjournals.com/content/14/4/902

19. Juniper, E.F., Bousquet, J., Abetz, L., Bateman, E.D.: Identifying 'well-controlled' and 'not well-controlled' asthma using the asthma control questionnaire. Respir. Med. **100**(4), 616–621 (2006). https://doi.org/10.1016/j.rmed.2005.08.012

20. Juniper, E.F., O'Byrbe, P., Ferrie, P.J., King, D.R., Roberts, J.: Measuring asthma control. Clinic questionnaire or daily diary? Am. J. Respir. Crit. Care Med. **162**(4), 1330–1334 (2000). https://doi.org/10.1164/ajrccm.162.4.9912138

21. Juniper, E.F., Svensson, K., Mörk, A.C., Ståhl, E.: Measurement properties and interpretation of three shortened versions of the asthma control questionnaire. Respir. Med. **99**(5), 553–558 (2005). https://doi.org/10.1016/j.rmed.2004.10.008

22. Khan, N., Alegre, U., Kramer, D., Augusto, J.C.: Is 'Context-Aware Reasoning = Case-Based Reasoning'? In: Brézillon, P., Turner, R., Penco, C. (eds.) CONTEXT 2017. LNCS (LNAI), vol. 10257, pp. 418–431. Springer, Cham (2017). https://doi.org/10.1007/978-3-319-57837-8_35

23. Kolodner, J.L.: An introduction to case-based reasoning. Artif. Intell. Rev. **6**(1), 3–34 (1992). https://doi.org/10.1007/BF00155578

24. Montani, S.: How to use contextual knowledge in medical case-based reasoning systems: a survey on very recent trends. Artif. Intell. Med. **51**(2), 125–131 (2011). https://doi.org/10.1016/j.artmed.2010.09.004

25. Nunes, D.S., Zhang, P., Silva, J.S.: A survey on human-in-the-loop applications towards an internet of all. IEEE Commun. Surv. Tutor. **17**(2), 944–965 (2015). https://doi.org/10.1109/COMST.2015.2398816

26. Ospan, B., Khan, N., Augusto, J., Quinde, M., Nurgaliyev, K.: Context aware virtual assistant with case-based conflict resolution in multi-user smart home environment. In: 2018 International Conference on Computing and Network Communications (CoCoNet), pp. 36–44 (2018). https://doi.org/10.1109/CoCoNet.2018. 8476898

27. Perera, C., Zaslavsky, A., Christen, P., Georgakopoulos, D.: Context aware computing for the internet of things: a survey. IEEE Commun. Surv. Tutor. **16**(1), 414–454 (2014). https://doi.org/10.1109/SURV.2013.042313.00197

28. Qin, X., Tan, C.-W., Clemmensen, T.: Context-awareness and mobile HCI: implications, challenges and opportunities. In: Nah, F.F.-H., Tan, C.-H. (eds.) HCIBGO 2017. LNCS, vol. 10293, pp. 112–127. Springer, Cham (2017). https://doi.org/10. 1007/978-3-319-58481-2_10

29. Quinde, M., Khan, N., Augusto, J.C.: Personalisation of context-aware solutions supporting Asthma management. In: Miesenberger, K., Kouroupetroglou, G. (eds.) ICCHP 2018. LNCS, vol. 10897, pp. 510–519. Springer, Cham (2018). https://doi. org/10.1007/978-3-319-94274-2_75

30. Quinde, M., Khan, N., Augusto, J.C., van Wyk, A., Stewart, J.: Context-aware solutions for asthma condition management: a survey. Univ. Access Inf. Soc. (2018). https://doi.org/10.1007/s10209-018-0641-5

31. The British Thoracic Society: British guideline on the management of asthma: a national clinical guideline. Technical report (2016). http://www.brit-thoracic. org.uk

32. The Global Initiative for Asthma: Global strategy for asthma management and prevention. Technical report (2018). http://www.ginasthma.org

33. Wagner, S., Toftegaard, T., Bertelsen, O.: Increased data quality in home blood pressure monitoring through context awareness. IEEE (2012). https://doi.org/10. 4108/icst.pervasivehealth.2011.245968

# Experimental Web Service and Eye-Tracking Setup for Unilateral Spatial Neglect Assessment

Timothé Rossa[1,2,5], Pierre Pompidor[3], Nancy Rodriguez[3(✉)] ⓘ,
Arnaud Sallaberry[3,4], Pascal Poncelet[3], Marika Urbanski[5],
Clémence Bourlon[5], Antoine Seilles[6], and Guillaume Tallon[6]

[1] Université Lumière Lyon 2, Lyon, France
[2] ICM, Paris, France
[3] LIRMM, Université Montpellier, CNRS, Montpellier, France
{pierre.pompidor,nancy.rodriguez,arnaud.salaberry,
pascal.poncelet}@lirmm.fr
[4] Université Paul-Valéry Montpellier 3, Montpellier, France
[5] Hôpitaux de Saint Maurice, Saint Maurice, France
{timothe.rossa,marika.urbanski,
clemence.bourlon}@ght94n.fr
[6] NaturalPad, Montpellier, France
{antoine.seilles,guillaume.tallon}@naturalpad.fr

**Abstract.** Unilateral Spatial Neglect is a cognitive impairment commonly observed in patients after right hemispheric lesions. A patient with this condition will show a lack of attention or response to visual stimuli presented to the left space.

In order to assess visual neglect, several "paper and pencil" tests are traditionally used, like the Albert's Test or the Bells Test. Computer supported tests have been also proposed like Visual Spatial Search Task (VISSTA) or Starry Night Test (SNT). In this kind of tests, the patient is asked to detect all occurrences of a target among distractors ("cancellation task"). However, it has been noticed that these tests are not able to identify subtle but relevant NSU, especially in the chronic stage. In addition, compensatory attentional strategies can be developed by the patients in order to pass a test in which they have unlimited time. It is then important to measure reaction time and to adapt tests to increase diagnostic accuracy.

This abstract presents READAPT an application supporting the Bells Test, with the aim of overcoming the limits of existing static paper-and-pencil diagnostic tools and to facilitate recording and analysis of patient's visual scanning.

**Keywords:** Unilateral spatial neglect · IT diagnostic aid · Visual variables · Eye-tracking · Web visualization

## 1 Introduction

Unilateral spatial neglect (USN) is a syndrome commonly observed after a right brain damage [1]. Spatial neglect has been defined by Heilman [2] as «a failure to report, respond, or orient to contralateral stimuli that is not caused by an elemental

© Springer Nature Switzerland AG 2019
V. G. Duffy (Ed.): HCII 2019, LNCS 11582, pp. 141–155, 2019.
https://doi.org/10.1007/978-3-030-22219-2_11

sensorimotor deficit». Patients with USN do not orient or respond to visual stimuli on their left side [3, 4]. Although USN often reported with elementary sensory or motor neurological disorders, most researchers emphasize the role of impaired mechanisms of spatial attention [5] and non-spatially lateralized deficits of attention [6]. USN is a complex and heterogeneous syndrome, which could affect personal (e.g. patients can omit to shave/make up the left side of their face) peripersonal (e.g. patients cannot eat the left part of their dish) and/or extrapersonal spaces (e.g. patients can bump their wheelchair into left obstacles). This syndrome is one of the leading causes of handicap and long-term disability [7].

In order to assess visual neglect, several "paper and pencil" tests have been proposed like the Albert's Test [8] and the Bells Test [9]. Computer supported tests like VISSTA [10] or SNT [11] are also available. In this kind of tests, the patient is asked to detect all occurrences of a target among distractors. In the Bells Test, which is included in the French battery of USN [12], a 21.5 × 28 cm sheet is presented to the patient, 3 columns are on the left side of the sheet, one is in the middle and 3 on the right. The image contains different objects and a total of 35 bells (the target) distributed equally in the seven columns. The examiner notes by successive numbering the order of circling of bells. At the end of the task, the examiner can appreciate the spatial distribution of the omitted targets and evaluate the severity of the visual neglect. Indeed, the realization time, the number of omissions, and the analysis of the scanning strategy allow a quantitative and qualitative assessment of the unilateral spatial neglect. In addition, the test has a relatively weak learning effect.

However, it have been noticed that these tests are not able to identify subtle but relevant USN, especially in the chronic stage [13]. In addition, Pedroli [14] states that compensatory attentional strategies can be developed by the patients in order to pass a test in which they have unlimited time to identify static targets. The possibility to change the stimulus, the background and the time of presentation is useful to increase complexity and sensitivity of the test, even when only mild USN signs, and allowed for a better assessment of the deficit in spatial attention. On the other hand, one of the difficulties of detecting USN is that the patient's eyes are unimpaired, they can orient towards signals and the pupil can also react to signals.

In this study, we have created a computerized adaptation of the Bells Test called READAPT, which permit to manipulate different factors that could affect USN signs, and to realize eye tracking measures. Therefore, READAPT might overcome the limits of existing diagnostic tools and facilitate recording and analysis of patient's visual scanning.

The remainder of this paper is organized as follows. Section 2 discusses related work. Section 3 details READAPT application and how it implements the Bells Test. Section 4 presents eye-tracking functionality. The experimental protocol and results are presented in Sect. 5. Finally, Sect. 6 provides conclusions and directions for future work.

## 2  Related Work

On clinical trials, numerous paper and pencil tests are used to assess USN. Neglect signs can occur on bisection tasks (rightward deviation), copy tasks (omission of the left part of drawings) or visual search tasks (omission of targets on the left side). More than 60 standardized and non-standardized tools were identified to evaluate USN [15]. The variability of these assessments affected the reported rate of occurrence of USN. Visual cancellation tests are often used but such task can fail to detect mild [16]. Sensitivity results are different according batteries or tests used to assess USN [17]. Moreover, patterns of visual exploration are often lacking in such tests.

This has led to implement cancellation tests with a touchscreen interface [18], eye-tracking device [19, 20]. The importance of using dynamic task in the assessment of USN has been previously highlighted by Peskine et al. [21] and Deouell et al. [11] who showed that a computerized dynamic Starry Night Test (SNT) was more sensitive than paper and pencil tests. Computerized visual search task like Visual Spatial Search Task (VISSTA) has been also developed allowing to manipulate the number of distractors, the colour of the target, the exposure time of the stimuli presentation and the repetition of presentation over different periods of times [10].

Developing a digital diagnostic tool allows to:

- Ensure reproducibility under controlled experimental conditions (one of the limitations of current diagnostic tools is that conditions vary depending on the therapist and facility equipment).
- Simplify data entry and saving, and therefore monitor patient outcomes and compare these results with those of other clinical cases.
- Take additional information, impossible to follow without a numerical tool, during the execution of the task, such as the movements of patients eyes.
- Couple this diagnosis with rehabilitation exercises adapted to the results.

## 3  READAPT Web Application

Our application, READAPT, is a web application for USN assessment in the peripersonal space. It extends the traditional Bells tests by providing customizable scenes. The Bells test consists in finding specific graphical objects called targets, for instance bells, among many objects called distractors (apples, fishes...). Graphical objects differ from each other on shape and position, but are similar on other aspects, such as size, color... (Fig. 1). READAPT has been designed to provide a wider range of graphical aspects.

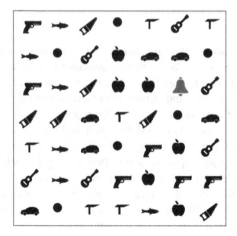

**Fig. 1.** A scene from READAPT application (Color figure online)

### 3.1 Design Study

In the following, "marks" denote graphical objects and "visual channels" are the variables controlling the aspects of these marks [22]. Since the raise of graphical semiology [23], and more recently data visualization [24, 25], we consider that a scene is composed by three kinds of marks: points, lines and areas. Visual channels controlling the appearance of these marks are position, shape, size, tilt, color (hue, luminance, saturation), and motion. In the early development of semiology, in particular when cartographic maps were made manually, texture was also considered as a visual channel, but it is not employed anymore since the raise of computers. Another channel, curvature, is also often mentioned in the literature. We do not include it in our list because it highly interferes with shape and thus is not relevant in our context.

In semiology and visualization, marks and channels are used to represent data. For instance, marks denote data elements and channels represent quantitative or qualitative attributes associated with these elements. This approach is not related for our work here. However, development in these fields pointed out interesting characteristics of visual channels (see [22, 24]). In particular, perception of visual channels differs in terms of effectiveness and expressiveness. Our assumption here is that, while variation on the different channels are not perceived equally, it is worth to explore further channels instead of just varying position and shape. That is why the application we propose here includes many parameters enabling to customize the different aspects of the marks as described in the next section. The purpose is to provide a more flexible tool, where the practitioner can adapt the level of difficulty according to her patient by using various visual channels. For instance, instead of using shape, or in addition to shape, targets can be rendered with specific color to make them more salient in a rehabilitation process context.

## 3.2  Tool Description

**Performing a Test.** READAPT is a Web application to test USN. The patient performing a test is asked to find a particular object, called target, on successive scenes. Each attempt is called a trial. Figure 1 shows such a scene, composed of 49 items: a target and 48 distractors. In the catch-trials (trials where the target is not present), the scene is composed of 49 distractors. In this example, the patient has to click on the red bell to success the trial. When she clicks on the screen, even if she does not succeed, a new trial is proposed. To launch the new trial, the patient is asked to click on a cross positioned at the center of the screen. Since the scene is divided as the original seven-column test, the order of appearance of the target in each column as well as the order of the trials, with and without a target, are randomized, in order to limit the learning effect. The result of each trial is recorded in a database.

**Customizing a Test.** In regard of the purpose defined above, before launching a test session, the practitioner has to set up the parameters listed in Table 1.

**Table 1.** Parameters

| | |
|---|---|
| Number of objects | Number of marks in a scene |
| Number of trials | Number of trials of the test |
| Timeout | Length of a trial in seconds (if the patient doesn't click on the scene before the end of the trial, the patient fails it and the following trial is proposed) |
| Disorder | If checked, the marks are randomly positioned without overlapping, else, the marks are positioned within the cells of a grid |
| Tilt | If checked, a random rotation is applied to each mark |
| Gradient | If checked, different number of marks on each line (according to several models) |
| Blurring | If checked, application of a cloaking mask |
| Size of distractors | Single choice among 5 values |
| Size of the target | Single choice among 5 values |
| Shape of the distractors | Multiple choices among predefined shapes |
| Shape of the target | Multiple choices among predefined shapes |
| Background color | Range for hue, saturation, luminance and opacity |
| Distractor color | Range for hue, saturation, luminance and opacity |
| Target colors | Range for hue, saturation, luminance and opacity |

Figure 2 shows the interface given to the practitioner. When several values are available for a visual channel, a random value is computed for each mark when the trials are rendered. For instance, if "Tilt" is checked, a random angle is computed and then applied to the mark. In the same way, when the practitioner selects a range for the hue, a random hue within this range is computed.

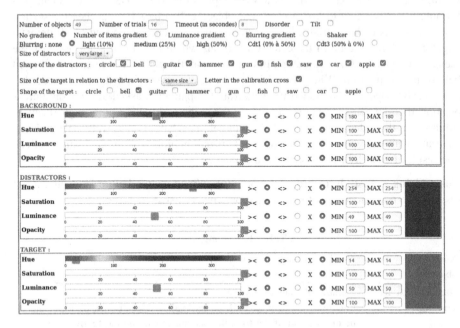

**Fig. 2.** READAPT user interface (Color figure online)

**Additional Functionalities.** When a practitioner access READAPT, she can select a patient or create a new one in the database. Each test session will be associated to this patient and the practitioner will have access to an interface showing his evolution over time. First a table shows the parameters of each session. Furthermore, the patient's response time, the distance from the click to the target (if present), and the relevance of his selection are recorded. A stacked bar chart is also provided. Each bar represents a session, and the portions of the bar represent the number of success (blue), nearby clicks, failures (red) and timeouts (orange).

### 3.3    Technical Aspects

This application consists of a set of programs written in PHP and JavaScript. PHP programs allow to configure via forms the different elements of the scenes composing a test session. The context of the sessions (non-nominal identifiers of medical agents and patients, dates, etc.) is recorded in a PHP database. The test results (identification of the presence or absence of a target by a left or right mouse click) are saved in tabular format.

The JavaScript language, which permits to modify dynamically the structure of the web pages displayed by the browser, and to record the Internet user's activity, was used to:

- create dual sliders selecting the different color components (hue, saturation, brightness and opacity) when configuring the tests;
- display in the browser, the different graphic elements of the scenes;
- record mouse usa and/or eye movements of patients.

Note that the d3.js JavaScript library is used to create sliders and display scene elements. This library allows to create graphical elements using the SVG (Scalable Vector Graphics) language, which produces vector graphics (all browsers host an SVG interpreter).

In addition, using the Node.js platform - a modular JavaScript interpreter running at the server level - we have also implemented JavaScript programs to record test settings and results, as well as the reconstruction of scenes as PNG images (again using SVG), on which the heat maps produced by the eye tracker are subsequently superimposed.

## 4    Eye-Tracking

READAPT is coupled with an eye-tracking recorder. We use the Eye Tribe eye tracker [26] for our experimental set-up. The eye movements of the patient are collected and then processed to build heat maps and gaze trajectory animation (Fig. 3). This data is superposed to trial's image in order to analyse the patient's visual search strategy. It has been shown that subjects presenting an attentional deficit will demonstrate a disorganized and chaotic scanning [9]. Therefore, following the gaze trajectory step by step will help examiners to detect a disturbed visual search.

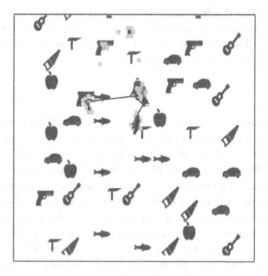

**Fig. 3.** Heat map (left) and trajectory for a trial

The eye-tracker is calibrated for each user. During the calibration, the user is asked to focus at several points on the screen. The device will then make a mapping between the point on the screen that the user looked at (gaze point) and the eye-tracker output.

To use the eye-tracker within the web navigator, the EyeTribe-WebSocket [27] has been used, a javascript based websocket application to wrap the EyeTribe SDK and transmit data. The d3.js library is used to display graphic elements. An application has been developed to accessing the eye-tracker data and information from READAPT in order to superpose the image generated for a trial and the gaze measures [28].

The heat map uses different shades of colour, here from yellow to red, to indicate the number of gaze positions of each zone (gaze positions are grouped into hexagons). Darker colours close to red indicate zones of high activity. An animation allows following the trajectory of the gaze. Once the animation is over, the positions are connected by lines representing the trajectory of the gaze [29].

## 5   Experiments

### 5.1   Participants

4 adults (1 man and 3 women) aged between 34 and 75 years old (m = 55,5 ± 17.02), suffering spatial neglect after right hemispherical stroke have been recruited for the study. Patients with neurological or degenerative disease prior the stroke, with major comprehension deficit, and/or refusing the consent form, have been excluded. Patients come from the medicine and rehabilitation department of the Saint-Maurice hospitals (Paris, France. Dr R. Péquignot) and the medicine and rehabilitation department of the Pitié-Salpetriere hospital (Paris, France. Dr P. Pradat-Diehl).

On the same basis, 8 control subjects (5 men /4 women) aged between 30 and 71 (m = 49.37 ± 12.97) have been included. The two groups do not present any differences concerning age (t test; t = −0.69, p = .500).

### 5.2   Task

Readapt software is based on the Bells Test evaluating spatial neglect in a peri-personal reference frame. This computerized version displays a visual scene made of 49 items: 1 target and 48 distractors. During the catch-trials (trial without target to test the attention AL involvement of the subject), the display is made of 49 distractors. On each trial, the subject have to indicate the presence or not of the target using respectively the left or right button of the mouse (thumb or index of the right hand). The visual scene is divided in 7 columns and lines. To reduce the learning effect, the target is presented randomly in every column and the trials/catch-trials are in a random order. Time in each trial is limited to 8 s while the time between trials depends on the action of the subject (click with the left button on the gray cross). Before each trial, a gray fixation cross is presented with a random letter on the middle of it. The subject has to read it out loud to ensure the experimenter that the visual attention is stick to the letter. This letter has a angular size of 0,5° to be sure that the reading of it is in foveal vision [30].

From this basic architecture, three versions were derived:

1. **Standard:** one block of 80 trials, including 10 catch-trials, during which the target appears 10 times in each column. No variation from the basic set-up is made here, to allow the strict comparison of the sensibility between the original test and ours.
2. **Items:** five blocks of 14 trials and 2 catch-trials corresponding to the 5 conditions of variation of the repartition of the distractors on the horizontal plan. This repartition evolves according to a gradient from the left to the right (in condition 1 and 2), from the right to the left (condition 4 and 5). The condition 5 is the control condition with no variation.
3. **Interference:** five blocks of 14 trials and 2 catch-trials corresponding to the 5 conditions of variation of the percentage of degradation of the scene on the horizontal plan. This degradation evolves according to a descending gradient from the left to the right (in condition 1 and 2), from the right to the left (condition 4 and 5). The condition 5 is the control condition with no degradation.

## 5.3   Procedure

All the participants have been tested in a quiet and isolated place, seating in front of the experimenter. Once the task has been explained, understood and that all the eventual interrogations have been cleared, the subject is tested with both the original Bells Test and the three versions of the task.

To evaluate the validity of our task, the subject is tested with the original Bells Test before the Readapt version, to allow the comparison between the results.

According to the set-up of [26], the subject is installed in front of the computer with the straightest position as possible at 60 cm of the screen with the eye in the axe of the center of the screen. The Eye-tracker is just under the screen at a distance between 30 to 45 cm of the participant.

The computerized version it-self is split in two stages. A first stage of training allows ensuring the comprehension of the task, to validate the posture and the comfort, and to calibrate the device. With the same instructions as for the experimental stage, the training is composed of one block of 16 trials including 2 catch-trials. Once the training completed, the subject can start the second stage.

This second stage is composed of 3 variations ("Standard", "Items", and "Interference") in a randomized order. Each trial is made of a fixation cross at the center of the screen in which a random letter appears that has to be named out loud. Then, the subject must click on the left button of the mouse controller to trigger the appearance of the scene. In this phase, the task is to indicate the presence or not of a target (a black bell) using respectively the left or right button of the mouse controller. This controller is placed under the right hand of the subject with a 90° rotation counter clockwise to avoid the stimulus-response compatibility effect, or "Simon Effect" [31]. Depending of the subject's fatigability, breaks can be taken anytime during the appearance of the fixation cross whose time duration is determined by the action of the subject only.

## 5.4   Results

All the analysis realized for the study have been done with the RStudio software (open-source) and Microsoft Excel 2016. A control subject has been removed from the analysis because of abnormal performances in the computerized test. Possibly resulting of a slight vision anomaly due to a retinal surgery.

**Original Bell Test.** The analysis of the performances is based on the following quantitative variables: total duration of the task (seconds), number of omissions (total, and per columns), and the position of the first target marked (starting column of visual search). The visual search strategy has been recorded as a qualitative variable. The average performances are presented below (Table 2).

**Table 2.** Average performance to Bells Test, paper and pencil version, for patient and control groups.

|         | Total duration (s) | Total omissions | Omissions col. 1,2,3 | Starting point (n° col.) |
|---------|--------------------|-----------------|----------------------|--------------------------|
| Patient | 203.25             | 1.75            | 0.75                 | 1.75                     |
| Control | 116.125            | 0.125           | 0                    | 1.25                     |

- Total duration. The data follow a normal distribution (Shapiro-Wilk; Patient: $W = 0.93$, $p = .63$; Control : $W = 0.95$, $p = .72$) and the homoscedasticity is not refuted (Fisher; $F = 1.91$, $p = .43$). The T-test confirm a significant difference between the 2 groups (Student; $t = -5.0115$, $p < .001$).
- Omissions. The comparison between omissions in the left half of the scene (col. 1,2,3) between groups reveals no significant difference (Mann-Whitney; $U = 20$, $p = .216$). However, the total number of omissions (in the 7 columns) is significantly different between patients and controls ($U = 31$, $p = .005$). Patients omit actually more target than the controls.
- Starting point of the visual search. Investigate by the first bell crossed, this variable do not reveal an inter-group difference ($U = 17$, $p = .911$).

**Readapt.** The quantitative variables used for the performance analysis of the 3 versions of the computerized test are: the reaction time, number and position (column number) of the omissions, false alarms. The reaction time used corresponds to the trials with target during which it was correctly detected.

*Standard Version.* Reaction time (RT) – The comparison of the RT in and between groups shows significant differences. The comparison has been done using non-parametric tests because of the distribution of the data (Shapiro-Wilk).
In-group: A significant difference is observed in the patient group regarding of the position of the target in the visual scene (Kruskal-Wallis; $H(6) = 37.594$, $p < .001$). The Wilcoxon tests for paired samples show differences between the columns 1 and 5 ($p = .001$), 1 and 6 ($p < .001$), 1 and 7 ($p < .001$). In the control group ($H(6) = 30.712$, $p < .001$), the differences concern the columns 1–3, 1–4, 1–5, 2–4, 2–5, and 4–7.
Between-groups (see Fig. 4): The Mann-Whitney test shows evidence for significant differences for the columns 1 ($p < .001$), 2 ($p < .001$), 3 ($p < .001$), 4 ($p < .001$) et 5 ($p = .001$).

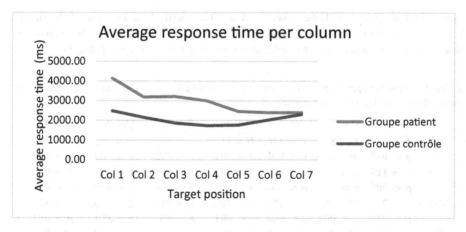

**Fig. 4.** Evolution of the average response time in milliseconds for each group against target position (column number between 1 and 7)

Omissions (see Fig. 5) – Mann-Whitney tests show between-groups significant differences for the number of omissions in the columns 1 (U = 31.5, p = .008), 2 (U = 28.5, p = .028), 3 (U = 24, p = .049) et 4 (U = 24, p = .049).

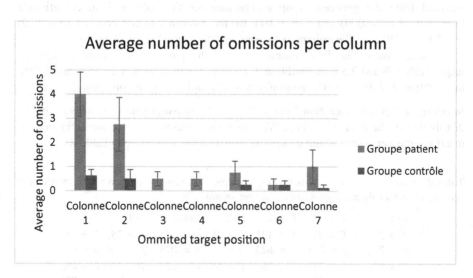

**Fig. 5.** Average number of omissions with related errors per group against target position in the standard version

False alarms – The false alarms rate for the patient and control groups are respectively 12,5% and 17,5%.

*Items Version.* Reaction Time – We used non-parametric tests because of the distribution of the data. The Mann-Whitney tests revealed evidence for differences of reaction time per columns and conditions between the two groups (Table 3).

**Table 3.** Mann-Whitney tests for in-group response time comparison for the Items version, for each column. Significant results are shown in bold.

|       | Col. 1 | Col. 2 | Col. 3 | Col. 4 | Col. 5 | Col. 6 | Col. 7 |
|-------|--------|--------|--------|--------|--------|--------|--------|
| Cdt 1 | $U = 80$, $p = .017$ | $U = 88$, $p = .033$ | $U = 126$, $p < .001$ | $U = 113$, $p = .001$ | $U = 86$, $p = .192$ | $U = 68$, $p = .451$ | $U = 89$, $p = .136$ |
| Cdt 2 | $U = 115$, $p < .001$ | $U = 117$, $p = .001$ | $U = 97$, $p = .046$ | $U = 103$, $p = .018$ | $U = 106$, $p = .008$ | $U = 98$, $p = .038$ | $U = 98$, $p = .038$ |
| Cdt 3 | $U = 71$, $p = .012$ | $U = 85$, $p = .004$ | $U = 111$, $p = .002$ | $U = 120$, $p < .001$ | $U = 91$, $p = .047$ | $U = 113$, $p = .001$ | $U = 83$, $p = .263$ |
| Cdt 4 | $U = 60$, $p = .004$ | $U = 77$, $p = .033$ | $U = 119$, $p < .001$ | $U = 90$, $p = .022$ | $U = 101$, $p = .025$ | $U = 104$, $p = .013$ | $U = 98$, $p = .038$ |
| Cdt 5 | $U = 104$, $p < .001$ | $U = 93$, $p < .001$ | $U = 87$, $p = .002$ | $U = 69$, $p = .403$ | $U = 93$, $p = .081$ | $U = 103$, $p = .016$ | $U = 88$, $p = .033$ |

__Omissions – Significant differences about the number of omissions per column emerged from the between group comparison for the column 1 in conditions 1 (p = .049), 3 (p = .009) and 4 (p = .01); for the column 2 in conditions 4 (p = .049) and 5 (p = .049); for the column 3 in condition 5 (p = .049) (cf. Annexe 7).

False alarms – The false alarms rates for the patient and control groups are respectively 0% and 2.5% in condition 1, 0% and 5% in condition 2, 2.5% and 8.75% in condition 3, 2.5% and 0% in condition 4, 5% and 1.25% in condition 5.

*Interference Version.* Reaction Time – We used non-parametric tests because of the distribution of the data. The Mann-Whitney tests revealed evidence for differences of reaction time per columns and conditions between the two groups (Table 4).

**Table 4.** Mann-Whitney tests for between-groups response time comparison for the Interference version, for each column. Significant results are shown in bold.

|         | Col. 1 | Col. 2 | Col. 3 | Col. 4 | Col. 5 | Col. 6 | Col. 7 |
|---------|--------|--------|--------|--------|--------|--------|--------|
| Cdt 1 | $U = 34$, $p = .203$ | $U = 97$, $p < .001$ | $U = 107$, $p = .022$ | $U = 48$, $p = 1$ | $U = 8$, $p = .075$ | $U = 25$, $p = .306$ | $U = 25$, $p = .665$ |
| Cdt 2 | $U = 61$, $p = .003$ | $U = 110$, $p = .004$ | $U = 86$, $p = .100$ | $U = 58$, $p = .724$ | $U = 67$, $p = .681$ | $U = 49$, $p = 1$ | $U = 69$, $p = .026$ |
| Cdt 3 | $U = 49$, $p = .006$ | $U = 68$, $p < .001$ | $U = 102$, $p = .019$ | $U = 74$, $p = .249$ | $U = 72$, $p = .185$ | $U = 96$, $p = .019$ | $U = 59$, $p = .870$ |
| Cdt 4 | $U = 41$, $p = .307$ | $U = 80$, $p = .02$ | $U = 62$, $p = .109$ | $U = 69$, $p = .787$ | $U = 51$, $p = .677$ | $U = 73$, $p = .610$ | $U = 69$, $p = .412$ |
| Cdt 5 | $U = 53$, $p = .313$ | $U = 82$, $p = .010$ | $U = 102$, $p = .019$ | $U = 79$, $p = .382$ | $U = 83.5$, $p = .137$ | $U = 73$, $p = .278$ | $U = 94$, $p = .070$ |

Omissions – Significant differences about the number of omissions per columns emerged from the between group comparison for the column 1 in conditions 1 (p = .01), 2 (p = .001), 4 (p = .041) and 5 (p = .009); for the column 2 in conditions 3 (p = .049) and 5 (p = .049); for the column 4 in condition 1 (p = .049); for the column 7 in condition 1 (p = .041) (cf. Annexe 8).

False alarms – The false alarms rates for the patient and control groups are respectively 0% and 2.5% in condition 1, 0% et 5% in condition 2, 2% et 1,25% in condition 3, 2.5% et 3,75% in condition 4, 2,5% et 5% in condition 5.

# 6   Conclusion

Spatial neglect is the difficulty in detecting, responding to or pointing to significant stimuli located on the opposite side of a brain injury, which cannot be attributed to a sensory or motor deficit. Patients often have weak spatial neglect and only capture a portion of the signals from the left side of the image. The traditional technique for assessing USN is the Bells Test, which consist in finding specific graphical objects (bells) called targets, among many objects called distractors. However, this kind of tests fails to identify subtle impairments and compensatory attentional strategies. It is then important to accurately measure reaction time and to help examiners to easily adapt tests to increase diagnostic accuracy.

Our application, READAPT, is a web application for USN assessment. It extends the traditional Bells tests by providing customizable scenes. The purpose is to provide a more flexible tool, where the practitioner can adapt the level of difficulty according to her patient by using various visual channels. For instance, instead of using shape, or in addition to shape, targets can be rendered with specific color to make them more salient in a rehabilitation process context. The application includes many parameters enabling to customize the different aspects of the marks: type (distractor or target), number, shape, size and colour of objects as well as the background colour and distribution of distractors and targets. A scene can also be created without targets. A session can be defined, regrouping several trials and a timeout.

Performances of several patients and control subjects were used to demonstrate the feasibility and the ability of the system to distinguish between normal and neglect subjects, based on reaction times and target omissions.

These results represent a proof of concept for our application and encourage us to continue its development. We hope that the new data acquired and the follow-up of patients will make it possible to better understand USN. In particular, we believe that there are many degrees of impairment and we hope that appropriate responses are possible depending on the different cases.

In addition to being usable with patients in a clinical evaluation context, the application allows for the construction of several personalized tests and therefore could be used for experiments concerning the evaluation of the relevance of visual variables in the HCI domain.

# References

1. Azouvi, P., et al.: Sensitivity of clinical and behavioural tests of spatial neglect after right hemisphere stroke. J. Neurol. Neurosurg. Psychiatry **73**, 160–166 (2002)
2. Heilman, K.M.: Neglect and Related Disorders. Oxford University Press, New York (1985)
3. Heilman, K.M., Valenstein, E.: Mechanisms underlying hemispatial neglect. Ann. Neurol. **5**, 166–170 (1979)
4. Heilman, K.M., Watson, R.T., Valenstein, E.: Neglect and related disorders. In: Heilman, K. M., Valenstein, E. (eds.) Clinical Neuropsychology, 2nd edn, pp. 279–336. Oxford University Press, New York (1985)
5. Urbanski, M., et al.: Unilateral spatial neglect: a dramatic but often neglected consequence of right brain damage. Revue Neurologique **162**, 1–18 (2007). (in French)
6. Husain, M., Rorden, C.: Non-spatially lateralized mechanisms in hemispatial neglect. Nat. Rev. Neurosci. **4**(1), 26–36 (2003)
7. Bartolomeo, P.: Attention Disorders After Right Brain Damage - Living in Halved Worlds. Springer, London (2004)
8. Albert, M.L.: A simple test of visual neglect. Neurology **23**, 658–664 (1973)
9. Gauthier, L., Dehaut, F., Joanette, Y.: The bells test: a quantitative and qualitative test for visual neglect. Int. J. Clin. Neuropsychol. **11**(2), 49–53 (1989)
10. Erez, A.B., Katz, N., Ring, H., Soroker, N.: Assessment of spatial neglect using computerised feature and conjunction visual search tasks. Neuropsychol. Rehabil. **19**(5), 677–695 (2009). https://doi.org/10.1080/09602010802711160
11. Deouell, L.Y., Sacher, Y., Soroker, N.: Assessment of spatial attention after brain damage with a dynamic reaction time test. J. Int. Neuropsychol. Soc. **11**(6), 697–707 (2005). https://doi.org/10.1017/S1355617705050824
12. Azouvi, P., Bartolomeo, P., Beis, J.-M., Perennou, D., Pradat-Diehl, P., Rousseaux, M.: A battery of tests for the quantitative assessment of unilateral neglect. Restor. Neurol. Neurosci. **24**, 273–285 (2006)
13. Rengachary, J., d'Avossa, G., Sapir, A., Shulman, G.L., Corbetta, M.: Is the posner reaction time test more accurate than clinical tests in detecting left neglect in acute and chronic stroke? Arch. Phys. Med. Rehabil. **90**, 2081–2088 (2009). https://doi.org/10.1016/j.apmr.2009.07.014
14. Pedroli, E., Serino, S., Cipresso, P., Pallavicini, F., Riva, G.: Assessment and rehabilitation of neglect using virtual reality: a systematic review. Front. Behav. Neurosci. **9** (2015). https://doi.org/10.3389/fnbeh.2015.00226
15. Menon, A., Korner-Bitensky, N.: Evaluating unilateral spatial neglect post stroke: working your way through the maze of assessment choices. Top. Stroke Rehabil. **11**(3), 41–66 (2004). https://doi.org/10.1310/KQWL-3HQL-4KNM-5F4U
16. Bowen, A., McKenna, K., Tallis, R.C.: Reasons for variability in the reported rate of occurrence of unilateral spatial neglect after stroke. Stroke **30**(6), 1196–1202 (1999)
17. Mizuno, K., Kato, K., Tsuji, T., Shindo, K., Kobayashi, Y., Liu, M.: Spatial and temporal dynamics of visual search tasks distinguish subtypes of unilateral spatial neglect: comparison of two cases with viewer-centered and stimulus-centered neglect. Neuropsychol. Rehabil. **26**(4), 610–634 (2016). https://doi.org/10.1080/09602011.2015.1051547
18. Rabuffetti, M., et al.: Spatio-temporal features of visual exploration in unilaterally brain-damaged subjects with or without neglect: results from a touchscreen test. PloS One **7**(2), e31511 (2012). https://doi.org/10.1371/journal.pone.0031511
19. Behrmann, M., Watt, S., Black, S.E., Barton, J.J.: Impaired visual search in patients with unilateral neglect: an oculographic analysis. Neuropsychologia **35**(11), 1445–1458 (1997)

20. Müri, R.M., Cazzoli, D., Nyffeler, T., Pflugshaupt, T.: Visual exploration pattern in hemineglect. Psychol. Res. **73**(2), 147–157 (2009). https://doi.org/10.1007/s00426-008-0204-0

21. Peskine, A., et al.: Virtual reality assessment for visuospatial neglect: importance of a dynamic task. J. Neurol. Neurosurg. Psychiatry **82**(12), 1407–1409 (2011). https://doi.org/10.1136/jnnp.2010.217513

22. Munzner, T.: Visualization Analysis & Design. AK Peters Visualization Series. CRC Press, Boca Raton (2014)

23. Bertin, J.: Semiology of Graphics: Diagrams, Networks, Maps. University of Wisconsin Press, Madison (1983)

24. Ware, C.: Information Visualization: Perception for Design. Morgan Kaufmann, Burlington (2000)

25. Ward, M., Grinstein, G., Keim, D.: Interactive Data Visualization: Foundations, Techniques, and Applications. A K Peters Ltd., Natick (2010)

26. Ooms, K., Dupont, L., Lapon L., Popelka S.: Evaluation of the accuracy and precision of a low-cost eye tracking device. J. Eye Mov. Res. **8**(1), 5, 1–24 (2015)

27. The Eye Tribe Web Socket. https://github.com/kzokm/eyetribe-websocket

28. Govin, C.: Development of the READAPT application – Eye-tracking & Web. Internship report. University of Montpellier (2018). (in French)

29. Beuret, M.: Analysis of visual characteristics using an eye-tracker. Internship report. University of Montpellier (2017). (in French)

30. Kristjánsson, A., Vuilleumier, P., Malhotra, P., Husain, M., Driver, J.: Priming of color and position during visual search in unilateral spatial neglect. J. Cogn. Neurosci. **17**(6), 859–873 (2005)

31. Simon, J.R., Rudell, A.P.: Auditory S-R compatibility: the effect of an irrelevant cue on information processing. J. Appl. Psychol. **51**, 300–304 (1967)

# Human-Robot Interaction
# in Health Care Automation

Sumona Sen[✉], Lisanne Kremer, and Hans Buxbaum

Robotics and Human Engineering Lab,
Niederrhein University of Applied Sciences,
Reinarzstr. 49, 47805 Krefeld, Germany
{sumona.sen,lisanne.kremer}@hsnr.de
http://www.hs-niederrhein.de

**Abstract.** Robot-based assistance systems are widely utilized in industrial production today. In the near future, the numbers of applications in private households as well as in health care are also expected to grow. Such systems need to act and react autonomously, to cooperate and to perform supportive functions. This paper starts with the description of a project of a specially developed humanoid care robot and focusses on the lessons learned from this project. Afterwards, concepts and ideas of industrial human-robot interaction will be presented and discussed with regard to the special requirements in health care automation, such as safety and human factors. Finally, a new full-scope simulation system will be introduced, which should allow experiments on Situation Awareness and usability with experiments with probands under constant environmental conditions.

**Keywords:** Health care automation · Human-robot interaction ·
Full-scope simulation · Situation Awareness

## 1 Introduction

Human-robot interaction (HRI) systems are novel applications in robotics. They were introduced in the last few years in the industrial sector and quickly applied there. In the course of Industry 4.0 campaigns, collaborative robot systems were developed that can be used without protective fences in direct interaction with humans. Suitable robot systems, procedures and new protection concepts are now available. A transfer to the requirements of health care automation seems possible in principle. This paper presents concepts and systems of collaboration between humans and robots and then focuses on the important issue of security in the man-machine interface. The current standards for the permissible operating modes are introduced and the various operating modes are examined for applicability in the field of health care automation. Finally, the concept of a full-scope simulator will be presented, which should allow investigations with probands.

© Springer Nature Switzerland AG 2019
V. G. Duffy (Ed.): HCII 2019, LNCS 11582, pp. 156–168, 2019.
https://doi.org/10.1007/978-3-030-22219-2_12

## 2  A Humanoid Robotics Approach for Health Care Automation

In the *Rhoni* project, a prototype of a humanoid robot has been developed in our laboratory in recent years [1]. The Rhoni project deals with the conception and the construction of a humanoid robot. The idea is to develop a human-shaped robot that can take over simple tasks in household and health care applications: helping to get up and getting dressed, tidying up or getting a part out off the kitchen shelf. Not the replacement of in-patient care by robots is in the focus, furthermore it is rather about relieving the staff by taking over supporting activities: bring away laundry bags, food or distribute medication, empty trash, transport files or get drinks. A chance for seniors and disabled people to stay longer in their own homes. The construction of a skeletal structure, modeled on man, should increase the acceptance of the machine. In addition, behavior-oriented social characteristics such as intelligence, autonomy and ability to learn should be achieved [2]. Figure 1 shows the prototype humanoid robot which has a size of 1.90 m and weights 80 kg with 54 joints and drives installed.

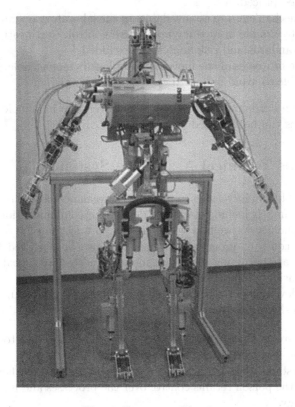

**Fig. 1.** Prototype Rhoni

Despite intensive work on the project, many goals have not yet been achieved. Lessons learned, however, were formulated as following theses [3]:

- The overall system of a humanoid robot is of enormous complexity, the training of operators and maintenance manpower is very difficult.
- The error rate is extremely high. The amount of maintenance and servicing work is correspondingly high.
- In particular, the user interface is problematic. The operators, already in the laboratory, are often overwhelmed, because checklists and switching sequences must be observed. People in need of health care would be overstrained with the user interface. The problem of man-machine communication is still unsolved for humanoid robots.
- Movements of the humanoid robot are hard-coded and not very sensory supported. There are no variants in the movement or autonomous movements that are not intended by the programmer.
- The humanoid robot can not make autonomous decisions. It is a mechanical engineering project and information technology procedures are therefore only rudimentary. Real autonomy requires powerful artificial intelligence and learning-based procedures.
- Protection mechanisms are not available. In the laboratory operation, security is provided by double occupancy and active control. Certification according to current standards and risk analysis is excluded.
- The dynamic processes of the movement are hardly manageable. A humanoid robot is unable to avoid unknown obstacles when walking.

According to the current state of the art, however, the humanoid concept for care applications can not be used.

## 3    Robots as Technical Assistance Systems

In many areas of life an increasing connection between people and technology can be observed. Examples include electronic devices for communication technology, such as smartphones, as well as technical support systems in the home and much more. A constant process of change can also be observed here: people and technology are becoming more and more connected, technical systems are becoming increasingly important in the human environment.

Along this development, the following two different types of support systems can be distinguished from each other:

- Technical systems that substitute one person and thus lead to relief. Here, the technique performs the task for humans.
- Technical systems that help people perform their tasks without replacing them. Here, the person retains control over the processes and is supported by the technology.

Robots in HRI systems can not be assigned to one or the other group [4]. These are systems that can and should relieve people of straining jobs or tasks causing negative effects on their health. However, they are not meant to completely substitute human, but to support him. The human being keeps control at all times. HRI is thus arranged exactly between the two described areas.

# 4 Human-Robot Interaction (HRI)

The human-robot interaction (HRI) was recently introduced in industrial contexts with the goal to keep people with their cognitive abilities as an active link in the production chain. Improving quality and productivity with a high number of variants through automation, while at the same time aging and dwindling specialist personnel, requires creating new conditions for direct collaboration of humans and robots.

## 4.1 Safety Requirements in HRI Systems

HRI systems have different safety requirements than those used previously for industrial robots. The main principle of the spatial separation of humans and robots is lifted. The safety-related implementation of HRI systems must therefore be fundamentally re-evaluated. The safety fences used very often in the safety technology of previous robot systems can find no further application in HRI systems for reasons of principle of collaboration. In contrast to the classic six-axis industrial robot, most HRI systems are equipped with more than six axes.

## 4.2 Taxonomies in HRI Systems

According to Fig. 2, three different forms of interactions between humans and robots are distinguished as follows [5]:

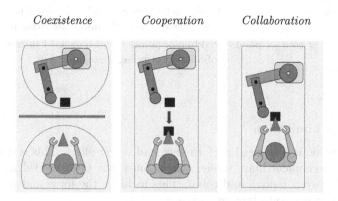

*Coexistence*        *Cooperation*        *Collaboration*

**Fig. 2.** Taxonomies in HRI systems

– *Coexistence*
Coexistence in this context means only an episodic encounter of robot and human, whereby the interaction partners do not have the same goal. The interaction is limited in time and space.
– *Cooperation*
Cooperation works towards a higher common goal. The actions are not directly linked and depend on a clearly defined and programmed division of tasks.
– *Collaboration*
Collaboration describes the interaction and direct collaboration between human and robot with common goals and sub-goals. The coordination of subtasks is ongoing and situational. Synergies should be used.

### 4.3  Harm Reduction

The aim of harm reduction is to reduce injury in the event of a collision to the smallest degree. Injuries while collaborating operation can occur for different reasons. Firstly, by direct contact, in a collision, on the other hand by the sharp edges of the tool, which is mounted on the robot. In addition, there is the danger that certain body regions can be pinched by a gripper. In all cases of conflict, it is important to keep the damage to a minimum. In order to minimize the risk of injury, safety-related design measures must be carried out on the robot. According to Table 1, this includes power limitation, compliance and damping at contact points.

**Table 1.** Injury reducing in HRI applications

| Design method | Effect |
| --- | --- |
| Power limitation | Reduced power and force effect, Bio-mechanical limit values |
| Compliance | Plastic deformation of robot components, Installation of predetermined breaking points |
| Damping at contact points | Padding of pointed, sharp or hard surfaces on robots and gripping system |

### 4.4  Power Limitation

Power limitation is a reduced performance and power effect. This is determined by the bio-mechanical limit values, which must not be exceeded in the case of contact between human and robot. This includes the force and pressure on humans, which is also to keep as low as possible.

Since the human being is in the immediate vicinity of the robot, the robot has to drive slower to limit the force effect. This can be achieved by permanent monitoring of the power consumption of the drives by the robot controller [6].

## 4.5   Compliance

Compliance refers to the plastic deformation of certain robot parts in the event of a collision. This can be achieved with special elastic materials used to construct or equip the arm members. In addition, elastic drives are proposed as a protection concept [6]. A robot equipped in this way can react elastically to collisions and injuries can be avoided.

Another approach to compliance is the installation of predetermined breaking points. In addition to the HRI robot itself, the tools attached to the robot can lead to injuries. For example, a gripper mounted on the flange can wound people due to any existing edges. Here, a break at the joint of the gripper would cause it to break off to prevent further injury. In this case, a collision would have to have a force acting on the person which exceeds the stipulated biomechanical limit values. The goal of breaking points is to increase safety and minimize injury risks.

## 4.6   Damping at Contact Points

Damping at contact points is understood to be the external covering of pointed, sharp or hard surfaces by means of an elastic sleeve. The robot is designed so that as few danger spots as possible can occur during a collision. The elastic sleeve, which is attached to the robot, serves to dissipate the stored kinetic energy in exposed areas of the robot. These locations can be, for example, areas in the vicinity of the axes, since there is a high risk of crushing. Sharp edges are concealed and securely padded.

# 5   HRI in Health Care

Can systems derived from industrial HRI provide an approach to assistance systems in health care? Are robots generally an option to relieve the nursing staff? What could the future bring and what has already arrived in everyday health care? What is done in other economies?

A look to Japan shows, that robotics can actually be used to relieve the nursing staff in health care. No other industrialized nation is aging so fast, so research on corresponding systems was started early in Japan. There are a number of prototypes in Japanese research institutes and pilot installations. In addition to collection and delivery services, Japanese research focuses on systems for lifting, carrying and supporting those in need of care. In Germany, there are also a number of research projects on the subject of care automation. Pickup and delivery services are also being automated here, but the focus is rather on supporting nursing staff. For example, autonomous care wagons should support the staff of inpatient care facilities by automatically providing care utensils [7].

For the development of assistance systems in health care automation, the use of the HRI robots described above in a care-specific system technology is also suitable. In contrast to previous research approaches, it is possible to use technically available, standardized and therefore also economically interesting automation systems. There is also considerable know-how in HRI, which would then also be available for new developments in other fields of application. The assistance functions that are so far in the focus of health care automation, such as fetching, providing, applying, and delivering, are furthermore familiar to applications in industrial handling technology and have been solved in a variety of forms. The endangerment of humans must be ruled out, the safety has unconditional priority. However, this is not only a dogma of caring automation. Safety is also guaranteed at all times for the HRI in its current areas of application. There are also a number of experiences, methods and last but not least regulations that describe exactly how operational safety is defined and measured. If these insights are extended by methods of human factor engineering and the man-machine interfaces are adapted to the new applications, then e.g. an application of a HRI robot arm on an autonomous trolley could be possible in the near future of health care.

## 6     HRI Simulation Involving Human Factors

Capturing of human expectations and information processing can be achieved based on human factors methods in HRI contexts by proband experiments, but the results suffer from changing environmental conditions and distractions caused by environmental influences. In our former works we predicted that the results would be more resilient, when measured under constant conditions in the experiment [8]. In addition to constant conditions, a special procedure in the development of appropriate applications is required for the HRI method. For this purpose, we introduced a combination of real test environment and simulator (HRI full-scope simulator) [9].

Of course, a large number of simulation methods already exist in the field of robotics. However, these are limited to the questions of kinematics (e.g. accessibility of gripping positions) or cycle times, depending on the type of simulation and application. At best, humans are included in these simulations as a kinematic model of an ergonomics simulation.

However, there are also a large number of occupational and psychological aspects in the HRI, which should be the subject of planning for the HRI facility. Conceivable investigations are, e.g.:

- How is the operator's attention focused on a particular situation?
- Is there a connection between perception and hazard potential that is relevant in the safety analysis?

Such and similar questions can not or not fully be answered with today's robotic simulation systems.

### 6.1     Full-Scope Simulation

So far, full-scope simulators have been used exclusively in power plant technology, especially in nuclear technology, where a full-scope simulator is defined as

" ... a simulator incorporating detailed modeling of systems of Unit One with which the operator interfaces with the control room environment. The control room operating consoles are included. Such a simulator demonstrates expected plant response to normal and abnormal conditions [10]."

Accordingly, a full-scope simulator is understood to be a simulator which simulates the behavior of the modeled reference system (here in the technical language of power plant engineering: Unit One) in order to investigate the operator's interactions with the system. The control elements of the reference system are part of the full-scope simulation. Such a simulator is used to train operators in dealing with the regular and irregular operating conditions. In power plant operation, a constant and effective training of the operators is required. The goal is to operate the power plants safely and efficiently. Many important parts of the training programs are carried out by such full-scope simulators. These training programs are designed to increase the operators' decision-making skills and analytical skills and to prepare them for problems that may arise when operating the actual system [11]. Full-scope simulators are recognized as an effective tool for operator training and are used in particular for nuclear power plants.

Through the use of a large number of different human-machine interfaces, people are directly involved in the simulation processes. Furthermore, there is a causal relationship between human actions and the resulting system states. In addition to improving operator performance through training programs, these simulators are also used to improve plant and personnel safety, reliability, and reduce operating costs. Full-scope simulators are also often used to train new employees, staff development and public relations. In addition, occupational science and psychological aspects (human factors) are part of full-scope simulations. These include surveys on perception, attention control and Situation Awareness.

## 6.2   Human Factors

The scientific discipline of human factors is defined as the understanding of interactions between humans and other system elements. Above all, these are methods, theories and principles that contribute to the optimization of human well-being and overall system performance [12]. The term human factors results from the psychic, cognitive and social factors influencing socio-technical systems. One focus is on the design of human-machine interfaces, especially on security issues and psychological aspects [13].

Due to the increasing degree of automation, human skills in the system have a different role, for example in the form of control activities. The question arises as to which human characteristics, for example in cooperation with robots, can and should be taken into account. Among other things, the topics of environment design, task assignment and responsibilities play an important role.

Perception is a conscious sensory experience (proximal stimulus followed by information processing) caused by a physical, distal stimulus, e.g., Seeing, hearing, tasting and smelling, touch and pain senses. The perception can then be, for example, an auditory or visual process, although other channels of perception may also be considered. For the perception of environmental stimuli they must meet a sense organ. The receptors of the sensory organ convert the stimuli into electrical signals, which are sent to the brain via nerve tracts. The signals generated by the receptors are analyzed and processed on the way to the brain and in the brain itself, until finally a conscious perception experience occurs. Sensitivity-influencing environmental factors that could play a role in full-scope simulation are, e.g., lighting, noise exposure and vibration.

A look at the human perception process shows that at the end of information processing ideally comprehensive mental models emerge, which allow situational perceptions. From the incoming stimuli of the outside world only those are picked up and then action-relevant, to which attention is paid from the abundance of incoming stimuli based on experience, expectation or attitudes [14]. The process of how individuals perceive and mentally represent a great deal of information in order to be able to act effectively in a given situation is called Situation Awareness.

### 6.3   Situation Awareness

Endsley defines Situation Awareness as " ... perception of the elements in the environment within a volume of time and space, the comprehension of their meaning and the projection of their status in the near future [15]". Situation Awareness is a construct consisting of three levels. Level 1 describes the perception of the elements of the environment. Due to inadequate presentation and cognitive abbreviations, this can lead to misperceptions and thus a wrong understanding of the situation. Level 2 describes the understanding of the situation and deals with errors in the correct integration of the information recording. A lack of mental models or blind trust can lead to wrong predictions and thus a wrong decision. Level 3 refers to the prediction of future events. This depends on the expert status of the persons [15].

There are various methods for recording Situation Awareness. A distinction is made between direct and indirect procedures. Direct procedures provide direct access to the product of Situation Awareness, while indirect procedures relate to the process of situational awareness or the outcome of awareness of the situation. To investigate Situation Awareness, various process measures can be used according to Endsley. These include verbal protocols (thinking aloud), psychophysiological measures (ECG, heart rate) or communication analysis. Such process measures, however, are seldom used, for example, in aviation, since these methods permit subjective interpretations or require very complex measurement techniques for detecting psychophysiological measures. In objective processes, the knowledge of the person about the current situation is queried and thus the measure of Situation Awareness is formed.

### 6.4   Assessment of Situation Awareness by Full-Scope Simulation

The Situation Awareness Global Assessment Technique (SAGAT) method is used to investigate and evaluate Situation Awareness. Prerequisite for such an investigation is a realistic simulation environment. This simulation is frozen at random times, which means that the simulation stops and all information sources are turned off. The probands are questioned by an operator about their actual perception of the situation. This is called freezing [16].

The full-scope simulator performs a freeze according to the SAGAT method automatically. For this purpose, the process stops unexpectedly for the proband. The lighting is changed to darken the workplace, so that the proband loses the workplace out of focus. Rehearsed noise from the audio system is also stopped. Instead, the proband is asked questions to query psychological aspects to Situation Awareness. After the questions are answered, the light switches back, the sound or noise comes back on and the frozen process continues automatically. The experiment is continued. The freeze can be carried out several times automatically, depending on the specification and planning of the experiment.

## 6.5   HRI Full-Scope Simulator

The HRI full-scope simulator is a modular, expandable small room system, build as a room-in-room concept. The dimensions of the small room system can vary depending on the simulation task. On the one hand, the HRI full-scope simulator is supposed to simulate spatially close cooperation between humans and robots. On the other hand, it makes sense to be able to adapt the available interior in the simulator to the respective HRI situation. The requirement of the changeover flexibility is therefore essential to be ready for changing configurations [9]. Figure 3 shows a sketch of this small room from outside.

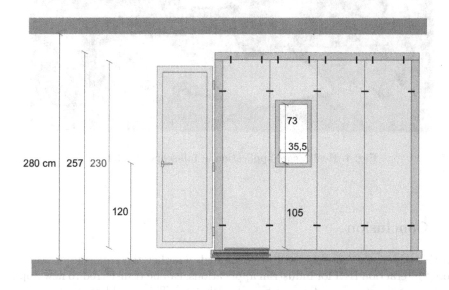

**Fig. 3.** Modular small room system as full-scope simulator

Inside the room, controllable environmental conditions prevail in order to study influences of light, noise and temperature or to exclude their influence.

The HRI full-scope simulator is used to set up the HRI system to be tested in order to perform proband experiments under specified conditions. The aim is to obtain statistically relevant statements on Situation Awareness, perceived safety and focused attention. Also distraction and error susceptibility can be examined. The basic dimensions are sufficient for a compact HRI workplace. Due to the modular design of the small room system, it is possible to enlarge or modify the space by mounting extension modules. The noise reduction of 44 dB is sufficient to minimize the typical outside noise of the room, such as, e.g., talking or computer ventilation, so that they are barely registerable in the inside, let alone lead to a loss of concentration.

Figure 4 shows the pilot HRI installation of a health care application. The proband is placed in the hospital bed. During the experiment the proband is served by an HRI robot with drinks and medicine.

**Fig. 4.** Health care application in full-scope simulation

## 7   Conclusion

In this paper, the question will be examined, whether the concepts of human-robot interaction HRI for industrial applications, can be transferred to new applications of assistance systems, e.g. in health care. This would open the opportunity to use technically available, standardized and economically interesting automation devices and to utilize available know-how.

Assistance functions such as fetching, providing, applying and bringing are solved in a variety of ways in industrial handling technology and could simply be transferred. A hazard to humans must be avoided in any case. In the previous areas of industrial application of the HRI, there are experiences, methods and regulations that determine what constitutes operational safety and how it is measured.

The question of how to obtain statistically relevant statements on human factors, e.g., Situation Awareness is being investigated. This is relevant to hazards, e.g., to avoid by distraction. These statements are to be obtained by means of a simulation method. Based on the concept of the full-scope simulation. well known in the field of energy technology, a simulation with real components and a man-in-the-loop approach is used.

The scientific background is the idea that in experiments with probands, comparable results can only be achieved, if uniform conditions prevail and the experimental procedures do not differ between the probands. The simulation concept for HRI has been specially developed to meet the requirements of ergonomics research and work psychology. With proband experiments under constant environmental conditions, studies on human factors, such as Situation Awareness, and later on, e.g., perceived safety and focused attention can be executed there.

# References

1. Fervers, A., Esper, M.: Dokumentation Humanoider Roboter RHONI. Projektbericht. University of Applied Sciences Niederrhein, Krefeld, Germany (2016)
2. Hoffmann, L.: That robot touch that means so much: on the psychological effects of human-robot touch. Ph.D.-Thesis, University of Duisburg-Essen, Germany (2017)
3. Buxbaum, H., Sen, S.: Kollaborierende Roboter in der Pflege – Sicherheit in der Mensch-Maschine-Schnittstelle. In: Bendel, O. (ed.) Pflegeroboter, pp. 1–22. Springer, Wiesbaden (2018). https://doi.org/10.1007/978-3-658-22698-5_1
4. Weidner, R., Redlich, T., Wulfsberg, J.P.: Technische Unterstützungssysteme. Springer, Heidelberg (2015). https://doi.org/10.1007/978-3-662-48383-1
5. Onnasch, L., Maier, X., Jürgensohn, T.: Mensch-Roboter-Interaktion - Eine Taxonomie für alle Anwendungsfälle. Bundesanstalt für Arbeitsschutz und Arbeitsmedizin (BAuA), Dortmund (2016)
6. Spillner, R.: Einsatz und Planung von Roboterassistenz zur Berücksichtigung von Leistungswandlungen in der Produktion. Herbert Utz Verlag München (2014)
7. Sorell, T., Draper, H.: Robot carers, ethics, and older people. Ethics Inf. Technol. **16**(3), 183–195 (2014)
8. Sen, S., Kunz, S.: Human Factor in der Mensch-Roboter-Zusammenarbeit. Bundesanstalt für Arbeitsschutz und Arbeitsmedizin (BAuA) - Posterpräsentation, Dortmund (2017)
9. Buxbaum, H., Kleutges, M., Sen, S.: Full-scope simulation of human-robot interaction in manufacturing systems. In: Proceedings of the 51st Winter Simulation Conference, Gothenburg, Sweden (2018)
10. Licence-Document-1093: Requirements for the full scope operator training simulator at Koeberg nuclear power station. National Nuclear Regulator (2006)
11. Tavira-Mondragon, J., Cruz-Cruz, R.: Development of power plant simulators and their application in an operators training center. In: Ao, S.I., Amouzegar, M., Rieger, B. (eds.) Intelligent Automation and Systems Engineering. LNCS, vol. 103, pp. 243–255. Springer, New York (2011). https://doi.org/10.1007/978-1-4614-0373-9_19

12. Czaja, S.J., Nair, S.N.: Human Factors Engineering and Systems Design. In: Salvendy, G. (ed.) Handbook of Human Factors and Ergonomics, 4th edn, pp. 38–56. Wiley, Hoboken (2012)
13. Badke-Schaub, P., Hofinger, G., Lauche, K.: Human Factors - Psychologie sicheren Handelns in Risikobranchen. Springer, Heidelberg (2012). https://doi.org/10.1007/978-3-642-19886-1
14. Wenninger, G.: Arbeitssicherheit und Gesundheit: Psychologisches Grundwissen für betriebliche Sicherheitsexperten und Führungskräfte. Asanger Verlag (1991)
15. Endsley, M.R.: Design and evaluation for situation awareness enhancement. In: Proceedings of the Human Factors Society 32nd Annual Meeting, vol. 32, pp. 97–101 (1988)
16. Endsley, M.R., Kiris, E.O.: Situation awareness global assessment technique (SAGAT) TRACON air traffic control version user's guide. Texas Tech University Press, Lubbock (1995)

# Uncovering User Affect Towards AI in Cancer Diagnostics

Stephanie Tom Tong$^{(\boxtimes)}$ (iD) and Pradeep Sopory

Wayne State University, Detroit, MI 48201, USA
{stephanie.tong, psopory}@wayne.edu

**Abstract.** Despite the rapid application of artificial intelligence (AI) to healthcare, we know comparatively little about how users perceive and evaluate these tools. Following "dual route" theories of information processing from decision science, we propose that because users lack the expertise to rationally understand AI through cognitive evaluation, they rely on their feelings or heuristic route processing to make judgments about AI systems and recommenders. Therefore, *affect* becomes an important component that influences people's willingness to adopt AI—and this may be especially true in a context like personal health, where affect is both explicit and heightened. Using the context of remote dermatological skin cancer screening, we examined people's affective perceptions of an autonomous AI algorithm capable of making recommendations about skin lesions (as either cancerous or benign). In a three-stage study ($n = 250$), we found that people do hold complex affective responses toward AI diagnostics, even without directly interacting with AI. Findings are relevant to designers of AI systems who might consider how users' *a priori* affect may make them more or less resistant to technological adoption. Additionally, the methodological approach validated in this study may be used by other scholars who wish to measure user affect in future research.

**Keywords:** Affect · Healthcare · Audience · Artificial intelligence

## 1 Introduction

> *Is it really possible to tell someone else what one feels?*
> *– Leo Tolstoy, Anna Karenina*

Although automated artificial intelligence (AI) technology has been applied to assist decision making across many domains of human life, one burgeoning area where AI systems have recently come into practice is modern-day healthcare. Automated algorithms facilitate everything from treatment decisions, communication among medical staff and their patients, and data retrieval and storage [25]. Such systems serve as an aid to patients and practitioners, with most systems requiring a human user to input commands and data.

However, recent gains in AI are dispensing with the need for human oversight: For example, in 2017, computer scientists at Stanford University [9] and the University of Heidelberg [11] developed a deep learning algorithm capable of detecting skin cancer by scanning thousands of images of patients' skin. The algorithm did so autonomously,

© Springer Nature Switzerland AG 2019
V. G. Duffy (Ed.): HCII 2019, LNCS 11582, pp. 169–177, 2019.
https://doi.org/10.1007/978-3-030-22219-2_13

gaining accuracy with practice, and validation tests have shown that it either matched or outperformed board-certified dermatologists at diagnostic classification of patients' skin photographs without any human supervision [9, 11].

Other types of AI technology are now being offered directly to patients through mobile applications. A recent study counted 40 different mobile dermatology applications across Android and Apple systems that allow patients to "upload and receive dermatologist or algorithm-based feedback about the malignancy potential of lesions" [1]. Although several researchers and developers have worked to refine these autonomous AI technologies, few of them have paused to question whether people will entrust it with something as important as their personal health. There have been many popular press stories touting the promise of new mobile apps, recommender systems, and AI tools designed to improve people's personal health, yet so many of these systems fail to reach their potential, instead meeting their demise after users fail to fully trust them [13]. Users' reluctance to adopt AI technologies has also led some academic researchers to similarly conclude that AI will never fully enter into the realm of personal health if the user interface design does not meet users' needs [14].

One component currently being overlooked in the development of many of these automated tools for personal health is *audience affect* toward these AI technologies. This is a critical oversight because how people feel about these systems may influence their decision to adopt them. Therefore, this study poses the question, "How do people perceive and evaluate AI technology in the context of their personal health?"

## 2  Background

Following "dual route" theories of decision making, we propose that when evaluating any kind of unfamiliar or new object (in this case, AI diagnostic technologies), people often rely on cognitive routes of rational logic and affective routes of feeling. However, the context of personal health is a very unfamiliar one—and in such a case, we argue that people are more likely to rely on affective routes for decision making, as opposed to cognitive routes. Affect has been shown to be important form of information during decision making when evaluating unfamiliar objects [18], particularly with regard to healthcare decisions [10]. In this study, we define *affect* as the "good" or "bad" feelings we experience—both consciously and unconsciously—and posit that these positive or negative feelings color our evaluations, decisions, and judgments [18, 22]. These positive and negative feelings comprise our *integral affect,* which is the form of affect that occurs as a product of the decision or during the decision making process itself [18, 24].

Most existing studies have focused on people's direct thoughts and cognitions about AI, which are often derived after some experience with a system. Examining only users' cognitive route processing excludes an entire route of affective heuristics that may influence users' perceptions and attitudes toward AI recommender systems. Interestingly, those who have explored users' integral affect have found it to be an important component of their acceptance of algorithmic recommender systems [6, 15]: For example, recent work in human-computer interaction reveals that affect plays an important role in audiences' perceptions of the AI algorithms found in popular social media systems like Facebook and Twitter [8].

Elsewhere, Katz and colleagues [14] examined the nature of user acceptance of systems designed to aid in the management of Type 1 diabetes. Their findings suggested that one factor contributing to low adoption rates of these mobile applications was a failure to meet users' emotional needs; instead user interface designs lacked emotional sensitivity, causing a strong negative emotional response for users that led to rejection of the technology. As these results suggest, failure to accurately assess and account for user affect can have negative consequences for technological adoption.

This brief review shows that although a more specific focus on user affect would be relevant to AI research, yet much existing work has not explicitly examined the affective component in user evaluation of AI. Thus, this study's main contributions are to carefully examine the affective element of the human decision making process and to develop and validate a methodology to measure it, so affect can be easily assessed and accounted for in future AI systems research.

## 2.1  The Importance of Affect in AI Acceptance

To summarize, we propose that if users cannot rely on cognitive route processing when evaluating AI in a familiar context like social media, they are even less likely to do so in a less familiar context like healthcare. In forgoing cognitive routes and logical evaluation, people will turn to their feelings to make judgments about AI, and whether or not they should accept them [23]. Thus, knowing whether people will accept or reject AI for their personal health requires knowing more about their affective response.

## 2.2  The Present Study

Building on our review of studies on social recommenders, product recommenders, and AI mobile health applications, we hypothesize that users will have a complex affective response to autonomous AI in the context of cancer screening as well. Importantly, we conceptualize a priori integral affect as separate from but related to other key constructs in the recommender systems literature such as users' post facto trust or confidence, which are often derived after receiving detailed explanations of the algorithm's functions or after direct observation or contact with the algorithm itself [4, 9, 14, 16]. In this study, we assert that users' affect toward AI can be formed without ever interacting with it or seeing it make a recommendation. In this sense, people's "first impression" of AI produces an affective response. It is this initial affective response that we predict will impact people's acceptance of unfamiliar AI technologies. We examine this *a priori* affective response is what we examine in the current study.

To investigate this line of thinking, we rely on the *affect heuristic* framework from decision science [23] to predict that people's affect towards AI will be consistent with their evaluations of its potential risks or benefits. In essence, we theorize that a user's evaluation of technology follows his or her feelings. Specifically, the affect heuristic predicts that people develop an "affect pool" containing multiple "tags" of both good and bad feelings associated with a specific object. When people are asked to evaluate how risky or beneficial that object or technology is, they consult those affect pools for information. When affect pools contain positive feelings about technology, they judge the technology's overall risks as low and potential benefits as high; but when they have negative affect towards technology, risks are evaluated as high and benefits as low.

The affect heuristic has been applied to understand people's affective response to many kinds of technologies—including nuclear power, pesticides, and food additives [see 23]. The current study extends its application into AI related affect. Therefore, the first step in understanding people's judgments regarding AI technology is to uncover people's affective response. Once audience affect is better understood, we can more accurately assess people's intent to accept or reject autonomous AI for personal health.

## 3 Method

This study investigated people's affective response to AI diagnostic technology using dermatology screening as the context. We created an illustrative scenario (Fig. 1) and then pretested it via a focus group of adults recruited from an urban university ($n = 12$, 4 male) that judged it as believable. After refining the scenario based on the focus group feedback, we executed the study in three stages: (1) affective item generation, (2) item refinement and scale creation, and (3) test of scale validation. We report on the results of all three stages of the study below.

You have had a mole on your arm for years. It has been there as long as you can remember—since you were young. But over the last month, you have noticed that the mole has begun to change in color, shape, and size. You are now concerned enough about the mole that you decide to have it examined for signs of skin cancer.

Recently, you have discovered a new form of skin cancer screening known as direct-to-patient dermatology. Direct-to-patient dermatology uses a computer algorithm to examine patients. The algorithm is a type of artificial intelligence technology. Instead of going to the dermatologist's office, patients can take photographs of their skin using their cell phones. The algorithm then evaluates patients' photographs looking for signs of skin cancer. Because the algorithm can screen for signs of skin cancer without any human help, it might make a doctor's appointment unnecessary.

**Fig. 1.** Experimental scenario text.

## 4 Results

### 4.1 Stage 1: Item Generation

In the first stage, the scenario in Fig. 1 describing AI dermatological screening with a deep learning algorithm was presented to another focus group of 25 participants (10 male). These focus group participants provided up to five words describing how they felt about AI algorithm described in the scenario. This procedure resulted in 43 unique affect-related words and phrases (e.g., surprising, worried, exciting, convenient, scary, too new, etc.). These words and phrases were used to "seed" the survey items developed for Stage 2 of the study.

## 4.2 Stage 2: Scale Refinement

In the second stage, the scenario was presented to a sample of participants recruited from Amazon Mechanical Turk (Mturk) ($n$ = 85 participants; 56 male). Due to the nature of the experimental context of skin cancer, we specifically sampled for individuals who have an elevated risk of developing skin cancer (e.g., people of Caucasian, non-Hispanic descent).

Mturk participants have been shown to successfully perform a range of experimental tasks [5], and often show great amounts of intrinsic motivation and demographic diversity [2, 3, 12]. As Mturk participants would also be somewhat familiar with computing technology, they were considered an ideal population for the current topic of investigation, AI.

After providing informed consent, participants answered basic demographic items (sex, age, race). They then indicated their familiarity with computer programming and computer algorithms using two items adapted from Lee and Baykal [17], "Which statement best describes your knowledge of computational programming (algorithms)?" followed by the response scale: 0 = "I have no knowledge at all", 1 = "a little knowledge", 2 = "some knowledge", 3 = "a lot of knowledge" ($r$ = .75). The sample had a moderate familiarity with computing technology, $M$ = 1.87, $SD$ = 0.79.

Participants read the scenario and then provided their responses to the question "Please indicate how you feel about the AI technology described in the above situation" for all 43 affective items from Stage 1, using a 5-point scale with 1 = "not at all" to 5 = "a great deal". These responses were examined using exploratory factor analysis with promax rotation that, after dropping non-loading and cross-loading items, revealed 7 items reflecting *positive affect toward AI* ($M$ = 3.44, $Mdn$ = 3.57, $SD$ = 0.88, $\alpha$ = .93) and 7 items reflecting *negative affect toward AI* ($M$ = 2.04, $Mdn$ = 1.85, $SD$ = 0.95, $\alpha$ = .82) that together accounted for 53% of the variance (see Table 1).

**Table 1.** Item labels and factor loadings from Stage 2.

| Item wording | Factor loadings |
| --- | --- |
| *Positive affect* | |
| Good | .71 |
| Convenient | .70 |
| Positive | .74 |
| Hopeful | .90 |
| Innovative | .76 |
| Intriguing | .87 |
| Interesting | .77 |
| *Negative affect* | |
| Negative | .69 |
| Nervous | .81 |
| Unsure | .79 |

(*continued*)

**Table 1.**  (*continued*)

| Item wording | Factor loadings |
|---|---|
| Hesitant | .83 |
| Concerning | .82 |
| Scary | .86 |
| Bad | .69 |

### 4.3  Stage 3: Scale Validation

In Stage 3, we assessed the final affect scales for construct validity by using a new sample of Mturk participants ($n$ = 140, 82 male). We also assessed more specific demographics for this final validation study sample that consisted of participants with a range on *educational background* (19 = high school, 50 = some college, 58 = college degree, 13 = graduate degree) and *annual household income* (reported in US dollars; 22 = less than $25,000, 52 = $25,000–$49,999, 35 = $50,000–$74,999, 15 = $75,000–$99,000, 16 = $100,000+). This sample also had a moderate level of familiarity with computer programming and algorithms, $M$ = 2.06, $SD$ = 0.81. As in Stage 2, we oversampled for individuals who have an elevated risk of developing skin cancer resulting in a final sample of: 116 = Caucasian/white, 7 = African-American/Black, 10 = Asian, 4 = Hispanic/Latino, 1 = Native American, 2 = other.

**Table 2.**  Correlations of AI positive and negative affect with Technology Readiness Index.

| Variable | 1 | 2 | 3 | 4 | 5 |
|---|---|---|---|---|---|
| 1. Negative affect | | | | | |
| 2. Positive affect | $-.15^*$ | | | | |
| 3. TRI innovation | $-.27^+$ | $.15^*$ | | | |
| 4. TRI optimism | $-.22^+$ | .09 | $.50^+$ | | |
| 5. TRI discomfort | $.23^+$ | .01 | $-.40^+$ | $-.51^+$ | |
| 6. TRI insecurity | $.31^+$ | $-.19^*$ | $-.26^+$ | $-.32^+$ | $.36^*$ |

$N$ = 140. $^*p < .05$; $^+p < .01$ (one-tailed).

After answering these demographic questions, participants answered the Technology Readiness Index (TRI), which assesses people's readiness to embrace new technologies across the four dimensions of *innovation, optimism, discomfort, and insecurity* [20]. Lastly, participants read the illustrative scenario in Fig. 1 and provided responses on the final set of affect scales.

Analyses revealed strong evidence of construct validity, with users' algorithmic affect scores correlating with the TRI across multiple dimensions in expected directions. Specifically, participants' overall positive AI affect toward the diagnostic algorithm was inversely associated with their scores on TRI insecurity and directly associated with feelings of innovation. Participants' negative AI affect scores were directly associated with their TRI insecurity and discomfort scores, and negatively associated with TRI innovation and optimism (see Table 2).

# 5 Discussion

Understanding user affective response to AI health systems is a necessary, but currently missing, piece of the HCI technology landscape. The results of this study suggest that people (a) have a complex affective response to algorithmic systems in the context of personal health and that (b) it is measureable.

These results shed new light on the role that integral affect plays in people's attitudes toward AI health technologies. Interestingly, this study demonstrates that people do have an affective response to AI technology and tools, even without ever interacting with it directly. This is similar to what some theorists have described as *dispositional trust* in machines, which—like the current study's measure of integral affect toward AI algorithms—is rooted in people's schema or heuristics regarding technology rather than in direct contact with it [19]. That people carry such affect into their decision making is an important consideration for scholars, medical professionals, and developers to consider.

Scholars who are working in the area of AI system adoption may consider how this pre-existing affect toward technology may be associated with users' likelihood to adopt those systems. Should other researchers wish to measure a priori user affect, this study provides a validated methodological approach and tool for assessing affect that can be easily applied to other contexts and forms of AI technology.

Medical professionals might consider that their patients' affective responses during decision making is driven not only by what they know, but also their feelings. Interestingly, medical professionals are often trained to balance patients' informational concerns regarding both "biomedical and psychosocial issues" [21] and ensuring that patients are well-informed by "communicating clinical evidence" and "presenting recommendations informed by clinical judgments" [7]. Common wisdom regarding patient decision making is that a well-informed patient will make wiser decisions [7]; however, the current results suggest that medical professionals ought to pay attention to their patients' emotion and affective responses as well as this is an equally important factor that may influence their decision making and behavior.

These findings are especially relevant to developers who are creating AI systems for application in contexts likely to be associated with high levels of affect, such as personal health. Designers might consider audiences' initial affective reactions to AI technologies, and the results of the present study can help them test audience response as they create the tools. Knowing ahead of time that they face high levels of *a priori* negative affect from their target audience may help designers address barriers to adoption up front, as opposed to during later stages of development or testing.

Though affective response to technology was shown to be multi-faceted, decisions about personal health often raises other strong feelings. When patients are asked to make decisions, they often weigh multiple factors such as medical technology, cost, technological efficacy, and side effects; each of these factors can create affect, thereby complicating the overall affective response. The current study focused specifically on medical decisions in the context of healthcare, but future studies might consider examining the affective response to AI technology in other decision making environment.

**Acknowledgements.** This work was supported by the National Science Foundation (Award No. NSF 1520723). The authors thank Rachelle Prince for her help with data collection.

# References

1. Brewer, A.C., et al.: Mobile applications in dermatology. JAMA Dermatol. **149**(11), 1300–1304 (2013). https://doi.org/10.1001/jamadermatol.2013.5517
2. Buhrmester, M., Kwang, T., Gosling, S.: Amazon's mechanical Turk: a new source of inexpensive, yet high-quality, data? Perspect. Psychol. Sci. **6**(1), 3–5 (2011)
3. Casler, K., Bickel, L., Hackett, E.: Separate but equal? A comparison of participants and data gathered via Amazon's MTurk, social media, and face-to-face behavioral testing. Comput. Hum. Behav. **29**, 2156–2160 (2013). https://doi.org/10.1016/j.chb.2013.05.009
4. Chang, S.F., Harper, M., Terveen, L.G.: Crowd-based personalized natural language explanations for recommendations. In: Proceedings of the 10th ACM Conference on Recommender Systems, RecSys 2016, pp. 175–182. ACM, New York (2016). https://doi.org/10.1145/2959100.2959153
5. Crump, M.J., McDonnell, J.V., Gureckis, T.M.: Evaluating Amazon's Mechanical Turk as a tool for experimental behavioral research. PLoS One **8**(3), e57410 (2013)
6. Dzindolet, M.T., Peterson, S.A., Pomranky, R.A., Pierce, L.G., Beck, H.P.: The role of trust in automation reliance. Int. J. Hum.-Comput. Stud. **58**(6), 697–718 (2003). https://doi.org/10.1177/1359105317693910
7. Epstein, R.M., Alper, B.S., Quill, T.: Communicating evidence for participatory decision making. JAMA **19**, 2359–2366 (2004). https://doi.org/10.1001/jama.291.19.2359
8. Eslami, M., et al.: First i "like" it, then i hide it: folk theories of social feeds. In: Proceedings SIGCHI Conference on Human Factors in Computing Systems (CHI 2016), pp. 2371–2382. ACM, New York (2016). https://doi.org/10.1145/2858036.2858494
9. Esteva, A., et al.: Dermatologist-level classification of skin cancer with deep neural networks. Nature **542**, 115 (2017). https://doi.org/10.1038/nature21056
10. Ferrer, R.A., Green, P.A., Barret, L.F.: Affective science perspectives on cancer control: Strategically crafting a mutually beneficial research agenda. Perspect. Psychol. Sci. **10**(3), 328–345 (2015). https://doi.org/10.1016/j.copsyc.2015.03.012
11. Haenssle, H., et al.: Man against machine: diagnostic performance of a deep learning convolutional neural network for dermoscopic melanoma recognition in comparison to 58 dermatologists. Ann. Oncol. (2018). https://doi.org/10.1093/annonc/mdy166
12. Hauser, D.J., Schwarz, N.: Attentive Turkers: MTurk participants perform better on online attention checks than do subject pool participants. Behav. Res. Methods **48**, 400–407 (2016). https://doi.org/10.3758/s13428-015-0578z
13. Johnson, C.Y.: The tech industry thinks it's about to disrupt health care. Don't count on it. https://www.washingtonpost.com/news/wonk/wp/2018/02/09/health-care-the-industry-thats-both-begging-for-disruption-and-virtually-disruption-proof/?utm_term=.c7b4312afdd7. Accessed 12 Dec 2018
14. Katz, D., Price, B.A., Holland, S., Dalton, N.S.: Data, data everywhere, and still too hard to link: Insights from user interactions with diabetes apps. In: Proceedings of 2018 CHI Conference on Human Factors in Computing Systems. ACM, New York (2018). https://doi.org/10.1145/3173574.3174077

15. Kouki, P., Schaffer, J., Pujara, J., O'Donovan, J., Getoor, L.: User preferences for hybrid explanations. In: Proceedings of the 11th ACM Conference on Recommender Systems (RecSys 2017), pp. 84–88. ACM, New York (2017). https://doi.org/10.1145/3109859.3109915

16. Lee, J., See, K.A.: Trust in automation: designing for appropriate reliance. Hum. Factors **46** (1), 50–80 (2004). https://doi.org/10.1518/hfes.46.1.50_30392

17. Lee, M., Baykal, S.: Algorithmic mediation in group decisions: fairness perceptions of algorithmically mediated vs. discussion-based social division. In: Proceedings of SIGCHI Conference on Computer Supported Cooperative Work (CSCW 2017), pp. 1035–1048. ACM, New York (2017). https://doi.org/10.1145/2998181.2998230

18. Loewenstein, G., Lerner, J.S.: The role of affect in decision making. In: Davidson, R.J., Scherer, K.R., Goldsmith, H.H. (eds.) Handbook of Affective Science, pp. 619–642. Oxford University Press, Oxford (2003)

19. Merritt, S.M., Ilgen, D.R.: Not all trust is created equal: dispositional and history-based trust in human-automation interactions. Hum. Factors **50**(2), 194–210 (2008). https://doi.org/10.1518/001872008X288574

20. Parasuraman, A.: Technology readiness index (TRI) a multiple-item scale to measure readiness to embrace new technologies. J. Serv. Res. **2**(4), 307–320 (2000). https://doi.org/10.1177/109467050024001

21. Roter, D.L., Stewart, M., Putnam, S.M., Lipkin Jr., M., Stiles, W., Inui, T.S.: Communication patterns of primary care physicians. JAMA **277**, 350–356 (1997). https://doi.org/10.1001/jama.1997.03540280088045

22. Schwarz, N.: Feelings-as-information theory. In: Van Lange, P., Kruglanski, A., Higgins, E. T. (eds.) Handbook of Theories of Social Psychology, pp. 289–308. Sage, Thousand Oaks (2011)

23. Slovic, P., Peters, E., Finucane, M.L., MacGregor, D.G.: Affect, risk, and decision making. Health Psychol. **24**(4S), S35–S40 (2005). https://doi.org/10.1037/0278-6133.24.4.S35

24. Västfjäll, D., et al.: The arithmetic of emotion: Integration of incidental and integral affect in judgments and decisions. Front. Psychol. **7**, 325 (2016). https://doi.org/10.3389/fpsyg.2016.00325

25. Ventola, C.L.: Mobile devices and apps for health care professionals: uses and benefits. Pharm. Ther. **39**(5), 356–364 (2014)

# Quality of Life Technologies

# Architecture-Neuroscience Cooperation: Project Recommendations to Therapeutic Gardens Design for the Non-pharmacological Treatment of Individuals with Alzheimer's Disease

Barbara Alves Cardoso de Faria[1](✉) 🆔 and Rachel Zuanon[2] 🆔

[1] Anhembi Morumbi University, São Paulo, Brazil
barbara.acff@gmail.com
[2] State University of Campinas [UNICAMP], Campinas, Brazil
rzuanon@unicamp.br

**Abstract.** The Neuroscience-Architecture cooperation indicates the potentiality of the built space in molding and shaping the structure of the brain and, consequentially, impacting and transforming the human behavior. Such potentiality is supported by the concept of neuroplasticity. Changes in the structure of the brain can also be verified in individuals with neurological degenerative diseases, such as Alzheimer's disease. Nowadays, the number of diagnostics of the disease is over 47 million cases all over the globe. Its treatment is based on pharmacological and non-pharmacological procedures. The pharmacological consists of medication administration to the patient whereas the non-pharmacological encompasses a set of cognitive, sensorimotor, and somatosensory stimuli directed to minimizing symptoms and postponing the advance of the disease. Considering the latter, the present research brings several contributions, discussing and proposing 45 project recommendations to the landscape design of therapeutic gardens, integrating the scope of non-pharmacological treatments of Alzheimer. From the analysis of two Brazilian clinics dedicated to the care of these patients, the research points out vulnerabilities and capacities of their respective projects, aiming at the promotion of a better life quality, wellness and conviviality for the residents of these spaces.

**Keywords:** Landscape design · Neuroscience · Alzheimer's disease ·
Therapeutic gardens · Guidelines on design

## 1 Introduction

Researches concerning the Architecture-Neuroscience cooperation [1–6] indicate potentialities of the built space to promote a significant set of stimuli on the human brain. Such a statement also discloses a new understanding, suggesting that such stimuli, coming from the environment where the individual is placed, are able to impact and influence the behavior. By being constantly stimulated, the brain reacts to those stimuli. And this set of neural reactions through time models and shapes the very

© Springer Nature Switzerland AG 2019
V. G. Duffy (Ed.): HCII 2019, LNCS 11582, pp. 181–199, 2019.
https://doi.org/10.1007/978-3-030-22219-2_14

structure of the brain, changing it. Thus, these changes are applied to human behavior and how one experiences the space and develops his or her activities [6].

The capacity of the brain to adapt and to be molded, both in its structure and the functions performed by the nervous system, is called "neuroplasticity" [2, 7, 8]. It happens all through the human being formation period and also through adult life. Those changes on the brain structure can also be verified in individuals with degenerative neurological diseases, such as the Alzheimer's disease.

Alzheimer is a neurological progressive disease, characterized by the gradual impairment of cognitive and motor functions. Nowadays, the number of diagnosed cases reaches 47 million people all over the world, being one million of them in Brazil. The treatment is based on pharmacological and non-pharmacological procedures. The pharmacological consists of medication administration to the patient whereas the non-pharmacological encompasses a set of cognitive, sensory-motor, and somatosensory stimuli directed to minimizing symptoms and postponing the advance of the disease. In this scope, the contributions of living and staying in green areas are noteworthy, especially when associated with walking, light physical exercises, among many other activities that provide positive experiences to the patient's emotional state and health.

The beneficial relations that individuals develop with nature are anchored to the concept of "biophilia", which indicates the connection between human beings and nature as intrinsic and perennial through all their existence. The human beings have their origins bonded to nature, and they need nature to survive. In other words, the individual is biologically prepared to feel safe and comfortable in natural environments and spaces projected with green areas [10].

Ulrich [10] proposes that human beings develop their aesthetic standards from their memories related to nature. These memories have an emotional character and are essential to the understanding of human behavior. Such memories, which refer individuals to their own subjective universe, are called "affective memories". They can be evoked by scents, flavors, sounds, textures, colors, landscapes, that is to say, through a whole range of mental images formed in the brain, which are associated with moments of high emotional value to the individual. The immediate result of these memories is temporary changes in the body state that can induce it to wellness [11].

In this context, and considering the scope of architecture, we can assess the fundamental role that the landscaping project plays in the configuration of green areas, especially in the project of therapeutic gardens dedicated to the care of patients with neurological degenerative diseases, such as Alzheimer. With the objective of bringing significant contributions to the progress of this investigation area, this paper proposes and discusses 45 recommendations to landscaping projects of therapeutic gardens in clinics for treatment of people with Alzheimer's disease. In this scope, we point out the vulnerabilities and potentialities of these projects, in order to provide better life quality, wellness and living to the residents of these places.

## 2   Methodology

Literature [3, 13–18] presents a series of recommendations concerning the consistent configuration of therapeutic facilities and care procedures to patients with Alzheimer. Taking these references as a starting point, this research conducts field investigations of the green areas of two clinics dedicated to the care of patients with Alzheimer's disease in Brazil. The first is located in the city of Campinas, and the second in the city of Catanduva, both in the interior of the State of Sao Paulo. In the picture below, the color green represents the amount of green area present in both clinics (Fig. 1).

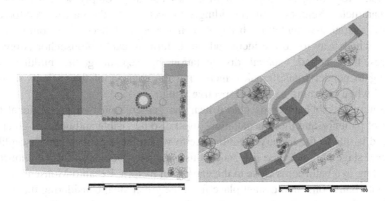

**Fig. 1.** Schematic Design of SeniorVit (left) and Recanto Monsenhor Albino (right). Source: Authors (Color figure online)

Investigations took place between August 2017 and December 2018. The collection of references from scientific literature along with the results obtained through field investigations configure the scope of project recommendations and parameters, through which the green areas of both clinics were evaluated. This frame of recommendations is structured by eight categories: (a) accesses; (b) specific activities; (c) pathways; (d) comfort; (e) spaces/stimuli; (f) planting/sensory stimulus; (g) safety and conservation; (h) uses.

## 3   Results and Discussions

From the studies of the facilities and the green areas present on both clinics, we further present the eight parameters applied in this analysis as well as the results and discussions. In the tables below, the green fields of the column "project recommendation" indicate contributions proposed by the authors of this paper whereas the white fields represent contributions coming from the literature:

**(a) Accesses**

Considering the element "Access", the clinic SeniorVit fully complies with five project recommendations and partially complies with one. The second clinic, Recanto Monsenhor Albino fully complies with four recommendations, and partially with two among the six comprising this category. In sequence, we discuss the respective results.

The "Number of doors allowing direct access to the garden" must be limited, considering that in the second stage of the Alzheimer's disease patients can be confused when more than one pathway is presented. The repetition of activities (such as visits to the garden) stimulates the patients' cognitive functions, and accessing these activities through a single pathway minimizes potential exhaustion due to spatial disorientation. Regarding this aspect, both clinics partially comply with the aforementioned parameter. SeniorVit, by providing two accesses to the garden, reinforces the residents' spatial disorientation, because their chances of becoming confused when deciding which way to go are increased. In its turn, Recanto Monsenhor Albino also reinforces the patients' spatial disorientation by separating the building wings according to gender (male/female), increasing the chances of the patients becoming confused when returning to their respective wing.

The number of "bathrooms placed near the garden" must be proportional to the number of patients, and these installations must also be visible and near the green area. This need is due to the urinary incontinence to which these patients are susceptible in the second stage of the disease [3]. As for this parameter, SeniorVit fully complies with it, providing two bathrooms close to the garden. In its turn, Recanto Monsenhor Albino places both bathrooms in a distant place from the green area; considering that this area comprises all the terrain of the clinic, such placement makes it impossible for residents to see the bathrooms when they develop activities there. It is recommended the placement of bathrooms on the green area for the patients and the clinic's staff.

The "freedom of access to the garden" is essential, especially in the first stage of the disease, as it stimulates the patients' autonomy, their cognitive functions, and slows the progress of short term memory loss. In contrast, patients with high cognitive impairment should not remain in the gardens without supervision of team members, so locking the doors is important to avoid situations whose may represent risks to these patients. Besides that, "ease of access to the garden" fosters the feeling of safety and helps patients with their spatial orientation. Both parameters are fully and accordingly accomplished by the two clinics. SeniorVit's garden can be seen through the living room and the annex building, and the green area is available to the patients and the care staff all through the day and sometimes at night. This usage availability promotes the presence and living in the garden. In the case of Recanto Monsenhor Albino, the green area surrounds all the buildings, allowing patients to have direct contact with the garden all over the area between sheds. Beyond promoting conviviality among patients in this area, the easy access to the garden also reinforces their biophilic connection with nature.

As for the "accessibility" parameter, not only it is demanded by law[1], but it is also indispensable to the patients' safe and comfortable mobility. Both clinics are in full

---

[1] Further information about NBR9050 available in: https://goo.gl/S7veFJ.

compliance with it, as they provide: sidebars on the walls to assist locomotion; non-slip flooring; proper terrain relief for waking; ramps with proper inclination; and absence of obstacles or steps impeding access to the green area (Table 1).

**Table 1.** Scope of recommendations in the category "Accesses". Source: Authors.

| Project Recommendation | SeniorVit Clinic | Recanto Monsenhor Albino |
|---|---|---|
| Number of doors allowing direct access to the garden | [Partially accomplished]. Two accesses to the Garden: living room and suite's hallway can cause spatial disorientation. | [Partially accomplished]. There is one exit per wing (male and female). Due to this separation, patients can feel confused when out of their wings. |
| Bathrooms placed near the garden | [Fully accomplished]. Two indoor bathrooms near the garden. | [Partially accomplished] Sheds offer bathrooms, but they are far from the green area. |
| Freedom of access to the Garden due to locked doors during the day | [Fully accomplished]. Doors are kept open during the day for patients in the first stage of the disease. | [Fully accomplished]. The doors of both wings are kept open during the day for patients in the first stage of the disease. |
| Ease of access to the Garden by patients | [Fully accomplished]. Accesses are kept open during the day under the supervision of nurses. | [Fully accomplished]. The configuration of the clinic allows easy access to the green area. |
| Accessibility | [Fully accomplished]. Ramps and handrails are available in the accesses. | [Fully accomplished]. Ramps and handrails are present in all the accesses. |
| Internal pathways leading to the garden | [Fully accomplished]. Hallway in the dorm area with direct access to the garden. | [Fully accomplished]. Every internal pathway has a connection to the garden, as the green area surrounds both wings. |

## (b) Specific Activities

Regarding the element "specific activities", SeniorVit Clinic fully complies with four project recommendations and partially complies with one of them, whereas Recanto Monsenhor Albino fully accomplishes one recommendation and partially with the remaining four. The respective results are shown below.

The "areas for manual activities" are extremely relevant to the patients' routine. The stimuli from these activities promote the increase of vitamin D production by the organism; strengthen the conviviality among patients and the care staff; and promote neuroplasticity and cognition through the somatosensory perception of different textures, scents and flavors during the recognition of species from the garden.

Regarding this issue, as SeniorVit provides a smaller green area, its usage potential for these activities is limited. In contrast, the extent of terrain used as green area in Recanto Monsenhor Albino, which is comparable to a farm, allows the planting of a wide range of species and manual activities.

As it is important for the residents to have an area to develop manual activities, it is also indispensable that they have the "opportunity to exercise in green areas". Walking, physiotherapy, stretching and other light physical activities allow the patients to keep their bodies active, preventing the risk of exhaustion related diseases. Besides that, they are closely related to the stimuli the body can provide to the brain, for example, the liberation of hormones such as endorphin, and the absorption of vitamin D by the contact with sunlight. Furthermore, being in open areas helps patients to acknowledge the different hours of the day, and to sense temperature, sounds, and the wind, which also aids the maintenance of their circadian rhythms. In SeniorVit, patients are encouraged to use the garden area and constantly develop light physical activities. In Recanto Monsenhor Albino, since the second half of 2018 patients can make use of a new small square with concrete floor and outdoor gym equipments, installed in front of the Friendship Square. However, this area has no roof, and in periods of high temperatures the iron-made equipments heat up, which can harm patients. Moreover, despite the wide green area of the clinic, patients have indoor physiotherapy sessions.

The "interaction with species and garden caring" and the "harvesting for use in manual activities" also strengthen conviviality among patients and between them and the care staff. But these activities also provide other results: they stimulate the sensorial motor system of the patients; and exercise cognition through the perception of colors, scents, flavors, and textures. Planting and harvesting, while involving patients in the life cycle of species, promote the memorization of seasons. SeniorVit, despite its reduced green area with a low diversity of fruit species, reinforces the patients' contact with the vegetable garden and encourages harvesting for manual activities. Recanto Monsenhor Albino, in its turn, has horticulture as part of its therapies along with the harvesting of species for decoration. However, these activities are performed only by patients on the first stage of the disease.

The "daily time for patients to interact in the green area" shows the importance of routine in the life of patients with recent and long term memory loss. Through repetitive activities performed always at a particular time, their cognition is exercised [19]. In its time schedule, SeniorVit considers visitations and a daily program of activities and conviviality at the garden, while Recanto Monsenhor Albino does not establish a routine for patients to enjoy the area of the gardens. Here, it was verified only the incentive for walking in the morning (Table 2).

**Table 2.** Scope of recommendations in the category "Specific activities". Source: Authors.

| Project Recommendation | SeniorVit Clinic | Recanto Monsenhor Albino |
|---|---|---|
| Areas for manual activities involving horticulture and soil managing | [Partially Accomplished]. There is a vegetable garden, but not an expressive amount of fruit species. Patients are encouraged to participate in the cultivation. | [Fully accomplished]. There is a huge vegetable garden for planting and internal consumption and a wide variety of vegetables and greenery, which are cultivated with the help of patients. |
| Suitable areas for physical activities, such as physiotherapy and walks | [Fully accomplished]. The garden arrangement is suited for the care staff to develop physical activities with the patients. | [Partially accomplished]. Square with gym equipments used by patients in the first stage of the disease. Physical therapy takes place indoors. |
| Patient interaction with species and garden caring | [Fully accomplished]. Patients have contact with the Garden on a daily basis and are encouraged to take care of the species. | [Partially accomplished]. Patients with light cognitive impairment help to take care of the garden, however, this activity is not part of a sensory therapy program. |
| Harvesting species for use in manual activities | [Fully accomplished]. Patients are encouraged to harvest species and perform manual activities with them, such as producing paintings, bouquets, and collages | [Partially accomplished]. Manual activities involving growing vegetable species comprehend horticulture and flower harvesting for indoor decoration, undertaken only by patients in the first stage of the disease. |
| Daily time for patients to interact in the green area | [Fully accomplished]. Patients interact with the green area on a daily basis, usually at the same time in the mornings and afternoons. They are also free to enjoy the area when not performing scheduled activities. | [Partially accomplished]. Mornings are the only period for using the green area, which occurs on walks, which have no specific time. |

## (c) Pathways

Considering the element "pathways", among the five project recommendations of this category, both clinics fully comply with two of them. In contrast, the remaining three are partially accomplished by Recanto Monsenhor Albino whereas SeniorVit partially accomplishes one of them, leaving the other two unaccomplished. The results are presented below.

The "route complexity" and the "route suggested by floor planning and design" are key characteristics for patients' autonomy. Less complex pathways provide more favorable conditions for patients to orient themselves on space. In this sense, "floor planning and design" should guide patients through the routes they have to take, minimizing their chances to get lost. Even in small areas, floor planning and design is essential. In both clinics, pathways are not fully defined. There is no route suggested by floor planning and design in the green area of SeniorVit. On the other hand, in Recanto

Monsenhor Albino, particularly in the wing connection area, there is a planned floor, handrails and roof, which indicate the path connecting the wings. Both clinics have elements on the landscape that serve as "marks for the orientation of the patients on their routes". SeniorVit has a water fountain in the middle of the garden, while Recanto Monsenhor Albino has huge species of palm trees, furniture disposed on the green area and a grotto with the image of Blessed Virgin Mary. This grotto is not only a hallmark of the garden's landscape but is also of extreme importance for almost every resident and staff member, since Catholicism is predominant in the region's culture. Therefore, habits involving the practice of faith, such as prayers and image contemplation, can be done at this grotto. These subjective practices evoke affective memories of patients, being closely connected to emotions and personal experiences of the individuals. According to Damásio [20], everything an individual experiences (feels) or manifests (expresses) through emotions has an affective character. Thus, personal memories of religious activities performed in other contexts than the clinics have the potential to bring positive feelings and emotions in the patients and also to connect them to their faith.

The "smooth topography" is crucial to the comfort and safety of patients. The smooth grounds ups and down can help strengthen the leg muscles, as well as the performance of aerobic exercise and breathing control. Both clinics are in full compliance with this project recommendation, as their green areas are set on a flat topography. In SeniorVit this area is completely flat, with just one access needing a ramp. Meanwhile, Recanto Monsenhor Albino has minor irregularities in its space, which do not impact the natural topography of the terrain at all.

The recommendation "pathways that protect patients from bad weather" comprehends the importance of protecting patients from hostile conditions. As individuals with Alzheimer progressively lose their motor abilities and sensibility, they also lose the capacity to distinguish between very high or low temperatures, becoming incapable of protecting themselves from harsh weather conditions. Because of that, green areas and outdoor places must provide protection to residents. SeniorVit has no cover on the garden area. Only the annex has it, but this building is actually located beside the green area. The pathways of Recanto Monsenhor Albino are protected with roofs made of polyvinyl chloride lining (better known as PVC). This material is widely used in linings because of its capacity to resist bad weather conditions and also due to its thermal insulation quality. With the aid of trees, the roofs produce effective shadows for the protection of patients along the pathways. However, in windy or rainy days, the roof is not quite effective, as the sides of the pathways are not protected (Table 3).

**Table 3.** Scope of recommendations in the category "Pathways". Source: Authors

| Project Recommendation | SeniorVit Clinic | Recanto Monsenhor Albino |
|---|---|---|
| Route complexity for patients | [Partially accomplished]. Open space with no defined route, no complexity at all. | [Partially accomplished]. Pathways are marked with different floor tiles; roof covers and handrails are only noted in the wings connection area. |
| Landscape marks and attention-grabbing elements on the patients' pathways | [Fully accomplished]. There is a water fountain in the middle of the garden. Three huge tree species configure distinctive marks. | [Fully accomplished]. Some marks are noted: a grotto with the image of Our Lady of Aparecida; tall vegetable species stand out in the area. |
| A route is suggested by floor planning and design | [Not accomplished]. There is no floor planning and design suggesting a particular route. | [Fully accomplished]. The entire route is specifically planned and designed. |
| Smooth topography for the patients' walks and permanence | [Fully accomplished]. Plain topography all over the garden area. | [Fully accomplished]. The terrain is plain enough to be comfortable for the patients. |
| Pathways that protect patients from bad weather | [Not accomplished]. The green area has no cover at all. | [Partially accomplished]. Pathways are protected by a roof cover, however, its dimension is not appropriate in cases of strong winds and rain. |

**(d) Comfort**

In what regards the parameter "comfort", Recanto Monsenhor Albino fully accomplishes six of the project recommendations, while one is not accomplished. SeniorVit fully accomplishes three recommendations, partially accomplishes another three, and does not accomplish one. The results are as follows:

The "presence of furniture for the resting of patients and their families", as well as "shadows after midday" are vital to the comfort and conviviality on the green area. Individuals with Alzheimer require such cares since their skin sensibility is intensified through their lives and, consequently, the risks of being exposed to high or low temperatures increase [3]. Regarding this topic, Recanto Monsenhor Albino is in compliance with such requirements, providing a square with furniture and a large area with shadows. SeniorVit, on the other hand, provides furniture in the annex, which functions as an extension of the garden, even though it is not located in the green area.

Both clinics have "indoor environments with a direct view of the garden". In SeniorVit, one can see the garden through the living room whereas in Recanto Monsenhor Albino the landscape can be seen through the windows of every wing. This view, which comprehends aspects of nature, is essential for the patient to have the perception and notion of time: if it is night or day, raining or not, if the garden is like the day before or if something has changed in it. This observation exercise stimulates the patients' brain and assists their cognitive processes [21]. Such a connection between indoor spaces and the gardens stimulates the connection that patients establish with the green area, which can be appreciated even in days or periods when actually staying on the garden is not possible. The link between built spaces and nature brings several benefits to human beings, bringing them close to a primitive, biophilic relation with nature. When added to a built space, nature elements can induce positive cognitive and emotional changes, reduce expressively the stress level of individuals, promote wellness and benefit their health [17].

The recommendation "orientations of predominant winds in the region" speaks of the condition of the clinics' territories and the relation of this placement with the comfort of the patient in open and outdoor areas. Besides that, the exchange of air in areas next to the gardens is necessary, because it provides better temperature conditions and promotes the hygiene of spaces through air renovation. SeniorVit has the configuration of a residence, with barriers against the strong winds of the region of Campinas (Sao Paulo), coming mainly from the southeast. But these barriers do not affect the exchange of air or the health conditions of the space where the annex building is. As for the territory of Recanto Monsenhor Albino, it is affected by slow speed winds coming mainly from the east. The clinic topography and its ranch configuration, so to speak, do not create barriers for the wind flow. However, winds are welcome in the area, as they reduce the heat sensation due to the high temperatures of the region of Catanduva (Sao Paulo).

The presence of the element "water" in the garden is quite desirable. Not only this element is necessary for the survival of all species, but it also improves the relative humidity in periods of dry weather, preserves more pleasant temperatures in hot days, and also becomes part of the environment natural landscape, acting as a somatosensory stimulus and promoting wellness and comfort for individuals making use of the space. SeniorVit has a water fountain at the center of the garden. It works during the day and the water sound integrates the therapeutic activities performed at the garden. Considering the great benefit that the presence of water brings to the space and patients, it should be used more frequently and with different installations, like a small lake or cascades, referring to more natural configurations and becoming more related to the flora of the space. However, making further use of this element requires caution so that it does not represent a danger for the patients. For example, deep lakes or lakes with no protection borders should be avoided, as patients can become wet, get hurt or even drown.

Recanto Monsenhor Albino does not have any part of its landscape where the element "water" is used. Its bucolic configuration, wide space, and climatic characteristics make it propitious for the green area project to make use of this element.

As for "sounds external to the clinic that can disturb interaction" it is important to consider that strange or loud noises can frighten, irritate, and even disorient the patients. Individuals who have lost neurological functions tend to have difficulties in associating sounds, a task performed by the primary auditory cortex [22]. In contrast, pleasant and familial sounds stimulate cognition and promote the patients' wellness. SeniorVit, being located in an urban area, with many vehicles and people, does not fulfill this recommendation, because external sounds can easily disturb patients' interaction at the garden. Recanto Monsenhor Albino, on the other hand, fully accomplishes this recommendation, as it is located in a quiet and rural-like area, far from the urban environment. There, it is possible to hear the sounds of different animals, the wind blowing through leaves, and people talking, that is, the landscape (what is seen) is in perfect harmony with the sounds it produces. This harmony is quite beneficial for the patients because the primitive connection that human beings have with nature predisposes them to this association among senses.

Regarding "pleasant ambient temperature", it involves avoiding thermal conditions that can represent risks for the health of patients with Alzheimer, considering their progressive sensibility towards high and low temperatures throughout the disease [3]. Therefore, particular devices should be employed in the project of the space in order to keep it with adequate temperatures for sensible patients. In this sense, SeniorVit makes use of elements such as a water fountain, grass designed floor, ceramic floor, and visible roof cover on the annex building. Recanto Monsenhor Albino, in its turn, has living areas with shadows; huge treetops, which help to stabilize the temperature; grass floor, which absorbs heat; and the ceiling height of the buildings is low, allowing better ventilation (Table 4).

**Table 4.** Scope of recommendation in the category "Comfort". Source: Authors.

| Project Recommendation | SeniorVit Clinic | Recanto Monsenhor Albino |
|---|---|---|
| Presence of furniture for the resting of patients. Layout suggesting places to stay | [Partially accomplished]. Furniture is present on the annex building and barbecue areas. No permanent furniture is present in the grass area. | [Fully accomplished]. There are permanent benches in the green area. |
| Sun Trajectory X Staying area layout | [Partially accomplished]. Seats are available only on the roof covered areas (annex building/barbecue area). | [Fully accomplished]. There is a square with plenty of shadows. Where sunlight is excessive, there is no staying layout. |
| Living room for patients with a direct view of the garden | [Fully accomplished]. The living room (indoor environment) offers a direct view of the garden. | [Fully accomplished]. The living room of both wings has openings for the green areas. |
| Orientation of predominant winds in the region | [Fully accomplished]. The wind comes, especially from the southeast. The clinic's building appropriately blocks strong winds without making the environment unhealthy. | [Fully accomplished]. Low-speed winds, predominantly from the east. The low speed of the winds allied with the topography of the region produces a pleasant climate for the patients. |
| Presence of the element "water" in the composition of the garden | [Partially accomplished]. There is a water fountain in the garden. | [Not accomplished]. There is no water in the green area. |
| Sounds external to the clinic that can disturb interaction | [Not accomplished]. The clinic is set on an urban area among residences and stores, close to the street. | [Fully accomplished]. The clinic is located in an area far from the city, so it has pleasant ambient sounds, as birds and animals. Loud noises or cars are not heard. |
| Pleasant environment temperature | [Fully accomplished]. The elements of the area favor a stable mild temperature. | [Fully accomplished]. The elements of the area favor a stable mild temperature. |

**(e) Spaces/Stimuli**

As for the element "spaces and stimuli", it is comprised of three project recommendations. SeniorVit fully accomplishes two and partially one of them. Recanto

Monsenhor Albino fully accomplishes one, partially another one, but does not accomplish a third one. The results are as follows.

For the "patient's brain to be constantly stimulated by the built space", there must be elements in it offering the patients recollections or at least bringing them something familiar. Therefore, architectonical elements have a powerful role in activating the individual's memory and cognition [2]. "Elements that establish a connection with the history and culture of patients" can also increase this contribution. By stimulating the recollection of affective memories and an immediate and intense identification of the individual with the space, these elements also reinforce the feelings of belonging and promote the appropriation of the place, which brings positive emotions on individuals with neurological dysfunctions [3]. In this category, SeniorVit presents consistent results, as its garden has vegetable species familiar to the patients, positively stimulating their brains and behaviors through the colors, forms, sizes and diverse textures of these vegetables. In contrast, the bucolic, almost tedious landscape of Recanto Monsenhor Albino does not offer diverse sensorial stimuli to its patients capable of activating their memories and bring recollections. In this scenario, only the grotto with the image of Blessed Virgin Mary establishes a relation with a cultural aspect of most of the patients (about 90% of them are Catholic).

The "form of architectural elements or the disposal of vegetable species in the garden can trigger hallucinations or patients' irritability". Such possibility directly influences the safety of individuals on the green areas, affecting their autonomy and confidence. That is, the projection of shapes and shadows can frighten or even traumatize them in severe cases. Regarding this issue, both clinics arrange their green areas favoring contemplation and a welcoming and safety feeling for their residents, with no information capable of negatively interfering in their experiences and interactions (Table 5).

**Table 5.** Scope of recommendations in the category "Spaces/Stimuli". Source: Authors.

| Project Recommendation | SeniorVit Clinic | Recanto Monsenhor Albino |
|---|---|---|
| Architectonic elements that stimulate the brain and positive behaviors | [Fully accomplished]. Presence of different and familiar vegetable species to the patients | [Not accomplished]. Few elements stimulate the brain. Monotonous landscape. |
| Elements composing the garden landscape relate to the cultural life history of patients | [Partially accomplished]. Besides the regular species of the region, already familiar to the patients, there are no other elements related to their culture or life history. | [Partially [accomplished]. Only the grotto with a religious image represents an important cultural element for the patients. |
| Avoiding plants, structures, shadows, statues and other architectural elements with forms that can trigger hallucinations or illusions | [Fully accomplished]. The structure of the garden is wide, without compromising shadows created by the covers or trees. | [Fully accomplished]. No elements work as trigger elements for irritability |

**(f) Planting/Sensorial Stimulus**

The element "planting and sensorial stimuli" comprises six project recommendations. Among these, SeniorVit fully accomplishes three, however, the other three are not applied. Recanto Monsenhor Albino fully accomplishes two, partially another two, and the remaining two are not accomplished. The results and discussions are as follows:

Just as the form and configuration of the built space can affect how patients stay in the green area, the vegetable species chosen for the landscaping project can also produce positive or negative effects on them. That is why it is crucial to avoid using "plants with shapes that can trigger irritability". Considering that, both clinics are in full compliance with what is recommended. Both gardens present traditional species from the Brazilian fauna, such as palm trees, bromeliads, trumpet trees, cerimans (*Monstera deliciosa*), pacovás (*Philonendrum martianum*), ferns, among others, which are familiar and from the local culture.

The planting of "species that evince seasonality" and "species with vibrant colors" are related and reflect the landscape's potential to be part of a patient's routine. For the individual with Alzheimer's disease, it is important to acknowledge the change of seasons and to feel different sensations caused by the alternation of the weather and temperatures. Such perception allows patients to understand the times of the year, be oriented within time and adjust their circadian rhythms [16]. In both clinics, plants show little or no seasonality at all, creating monotonous landscapes through most part of the year. Color vibrant species are seen in small amounts in Recanto Monsenhor Albino, nonetheless.

Concerning "popular species", they are expressive in both clinics and are the kind of plants that can be manipulated by patients, producing somatosensory stimuli, such as vegetable gardens, where patients with a higher level of cognitive preservation are encouraged to take part in planting and harvesting. Usually, individuals are willing to manipulate plants and flowers they already know. Besides that, handling familiar species helps patients to recollect affective memories. Species that were part of their lives or marked an important moment of their trajectories can evoke memories that bring positive emotions and feelings.

As for "plants and/or flowers with remarkable scents", researches about the potential of smell [23] show it as humans' most acute sense. In patients with reduced brain functions, stimulating this potential represents a significant form of delaying the loss of such functions. However, both clinics do not have plants and/or flowers that exhale remarkable scents. Species such as lavender (*Lavandula*), jasmine (*Jasminum*), gardenia (*Gardenia jasminoides*), "manacá-de-cheiro" (*Brunfelsia uniflora*), night-blooming jasmine (*Cestrum nocturnum*) could be incorporated to the landscaping project of the clinics, helping to promote the set of satisfactory somatosensory stimuli to patients (Table 6).

**Table 6.** Scope of recommendation in the category "Planting/Sensorial stimulus". Source: Authors.

| Project Recommendation | SeniorVit Clinic | Recanto Monsenhor Albino |
|---|---|---|
| Plants with shapes/scents that can trigger irritability | **[Fully accomplished].** There are no exotic species or with shapes or scents that might stress patients | **[Fully accomplished].** None of the plants can trigger irritability |
| Plants that evinces changes according to the change of seasons. Seasonal planting | **[Not accomplished].** Homogeneous planting, that does not value the seasonality of species and the reconfiguration of the garden they could provide | **[Not accomplished].** Homogeneous planting, that does not value the seasonality of species and the reconfiguration of the garden they could provide |
| Plants and flowers with vibrant colors | **[Not accomplished].** No species with vibrant colors | **[Partially accomplished].** The garden setting is predominantly green, with few colorful species |
| Popular species that remind plants used in residences | **[Fully accomplished].** There are popular species, recognized by the patients, such as palm trees, orchids, calliopsis, and edible vegetables. | **[Fully accomplished].** There are familiar species for the patients, such as bromeliads, orchids, ferns, and palm trees, not to mention the greenery and vegetables from the vegetable garden. |
| Species that can be assessed by the patients, stimulating their touch, smell and vision | **[Fully accomplished].** Every species can be accessed by the patients. | **[Fully accomplished].** Every species can be accessed by the patients. |
| Plant and / or flowers with remarkable scents | **[Not accomplished].** There are no plants or flowers with remarkable scents. | **[Not accomplished].** There are no plants or flowers with remarkable scents. |

### (g) Safety and Conservation

Regarding the element "safety and conservation", from the seven projects recommendation to green areas, SeniorVit fully accomplishes five and partially two. Recanto Monsenhor Albino fully accomplishes three of the recommendations, leaving another three partially applied, and one not accomplished.

The "presence of emergency doors" is essential for the garden security, and is required by law[2]. Emergency exits should be indicated by signs, but they should not stand out excessively in the landscape, as they can cause agitation and curiosity in patients with Alzheimer [13]. SeniorVit has one emergency exit in the back of the garden, while the rural Recanto Monsenhor Albino, being similar to a farm, has a vast outdoor area with no buildings and closed with gates, but there is no emergency exit in the green area.

The "visibility of the entire garden perimeter" is also related to patients' safety. Besides that, comprehending all the extension of an area promotes individual autonomy [17]. For Albright [24] the environment must favor visual perception, thus more defined "neural maps" can be formed in the brain. These maps are called "wayfinding",

---

[2] Further information about NBR9077 available in: https://goo.gl/Zku1dJ.

and are related to the analysis of the space performed by the individual who lives in it. This spatial organization assures the proper visual perception and, consequently, allows individuals to locate themselves and wander around with no obstacles. Due to its neuroplasticity - that is, the brain's capacity to change its own structure - it is possible to infer the crucial role that the built space and the stimuli generated by it play on the neural architecture of the individual living in this place. From that, it is possible to identify a straight connection between the spatial configuration of a clinic and the behavior of its residents. In other words, the "visibility of the entire garden perimeter" has the potential to inhibit or intensify negative or positive stimuli and, therefore, provide greater autonomy or complete dependence of the patient.

As already mentioned, Recanto Monsenhor Albino encompasses a wide field, making it impossible to grasp at once all its green area. SeniorVit, on the other hand, is organized like a residence, allowing the observation of the garden as a whole from the living room and some of the residents' rooms.

There are no "toxic plants" in the clinics. This condition permits patients to be free – as far as the stage of their disease allows – to handle species of the garden, smell their scents and even taste their flavor, since there is no risk of intoxication. Similarly, "plants with textures that can hurt patients" should be avoided, in order to prevent injuries, scratches or deep wounds that can occur because of species with big thorns. In both clinics, vegetable species with forms that can cause light damages in residents can be found.

The Brazilian norm which regulates accessibility, NBR9050, recommends the "presence of support handrails" in order to assure safety walks for individuals with limited motor functions, such as patients with Alzheimer. Both clinics have handrails on their facilities, however, they are not present outdoors, in the grass areas. This shortcoming prevents patients from walking around freely in such areas and also limits their possibilities of having tactile stimuli produced by walking barefoot feeling the ground [16].

The presence of a "straight connection between indoor environments and the garden" favors the patients' locomotion and autonomy. It also establishes an access routine and a straight path, which helps patients to reach the garden without getting lost. A simple access for a healthy brain may be very complex for a brain with Alzheimer's disease. The hippocampus, the place where mental maps are formed, is affected by the disease, which impacts negatively in the individual's reasoning ability [3]. Considering this topic, both clinics fully accomplish the recommendations, providing direct and simple accesses to the garden.

"Garden maintenance" is fundamental for this area to remain clean, well maintained and free of risks or danger for patients. Indeed, both clinics care for their green areas keeping them clean, considering that dry leaves, twigs, and thorns can hurt and patients might take them in the mouth (Table 7).

**Table 7.** Scope of recommendation in the category "Safety and Conservation". Source: Authors.

| Project Recommendation | SeniorVit Clinic | Recanto Monsenhor Albino |
|---|---|---|
| Presence of emergency doors | [Fully accomplished]. There is an emergency gate on the back of the garden. The access to it is visible and safe. | [Not accomplished]. No emergency exits or signs of it were identified. |
| Visibility of the entire garden perimeter | [Fully accomplished]. There's a wide view of the garden. | [Partially accomplished]. The landscape is quite wide and patients can find it difficult to grasp the entirety of the garden. |
| Existence of toxic plants | [Fully accomplished]. No toxic plants present. | [Fully accomplished]. No toxic plants present. |
| Existence of plant with textures that can hurt patients | [Partially accomplished]. There are some species such as the phoenix palm tree that can hurt the face or hands of the patients. | [Partially accomplished]. There are some species such as the phoenix palm tree and agaves that can hurt the face or hands of the patients. |
| Support handrails for walks on the green area | [Partially accomplished]. The entire access to the garden has handrails, however, there is no support for walks on the green area. | [Partially accomplished]. There are handrails on the path that leads to the green area, however, there is no support for walks on the grass area. |
| Straight connection between indoor environments and the garden | [Fully accomplished]. The main living room is connected to the garden. | [Fully accomplished]. The openings of the wings and shelters are connected to the green area. |
| Garden maintenance | [Fully accomplished]. Maintenance is daily kept by a gardener. Patients are encouraged to help him under the supervision of the care staff. | [Fully accomplished]. Maintenance is kept daily by a staff of gardeners |

## (h) Uses

The element "Uses" comprises six project recommendations. Regarding this last parameter, SeniorVit fully accomplishes four recommendations but does not comply with two. Recanto Monsenhor Albino fully accomplishes two, leaving two partially implemented and another two not implemented at all. The results are described below:

None of the clinics has "separate gardens" for different stages of Alzheimer. As the disease advances, the patient's brain is affected by changes in its structure, which cause the loss of certain cognitive and motor skills. Such losses, related to the different stages of this disease, require different approaches. Therefore, such recommendation aims to provide the patients with the best way for them to appropriate the space. In the first stage of the disease, pathways can still be more complex and topography can have more pronounced slopes. However, in the second stage, it is necessary to stimulate the patients' senses through scents, sounds, and a diverse landscape. Thus, the space should not have any type of obstacle or interference [13].

Regardless of the disease level, patients should be "encouraged to keep a relation of care with the garden", in order to create a routine and familiarity with the place [17]. This process, besides serving as a form of occupational therapy for patients, also evoke affective memories of those who usually performed such activities before the manifestation of the disease, such as: garden care, watering plants, harvesting fruits and cultivating vegetable gardens. SeniorVit has a vegetable garden and a drinking fountain for birds, and patients are encouraged to take care of these equipments along with the clinic's staff. Recanto Monsenhor Albino also has a vegetable garden, and patients with less cognitive impairments are encouraged to plant and harvest.

Both "the care staff and residents' families use the green area" of both clinics. These spaces are used as socialization and celebration areas, reinforcing the encounter of individual and nature [10].

The "nocturnal use of the garden" is only available for SeniorVit patients. The huge green area of Recanto Monsenhor Albino is not appropriate for a safe walk or visitation on evenings, since the patient can get lost, become afraid or irritated due to the absence of light [13].

The "flexibility of use" is also a crucial parameter for a therapeutic garden. SeniorVit uses the green area for therapies, walks and celebrations during the day, and sometimes during the evening. Recanto Monsenhor Albino, in contrast, conducts therapy and physiotherapy sessions indoors, despite having a huge garden suited for these activities (Table 8).

**Table 8.**  Scope of recommendations in the category "Uses"; Source: Authors.

| Project Recommendation | SeniorVit Clinic | Recanto Monsenhor Albino |
|---|---|---|
| Separate gardens for the different stages of the disease | [Not accomplished]. The garden is used by all the patients with no separation among disease stages. | [Not accomplished]. Every patient enjoys the same area of the Garden with no separation among disease stages. |
| Elements encouraging patients to help in the care of the garden | [Fully accomplished]. The vegetable garden and the drinking fountain for birds encourage patients to take part in the care routine of the garden. | [Partially accomplished]. Besides taking care of the vegetable garden, patients are not encouraged to care for other spaces of the green area. |
| Uses of the garden by the care staff | [Fully accomplished]. Care staff members use the garden to relax. | [Fully accomplished]. All the care staff declares to use the garden for resting, contemplation and socializing. |
| Uses of the garden by families of the patients | [Fully accomplished]. Families use the garden when visiting. | [Fully accomplished]. Families use the garden when visiting. |
| Nocturnal use of the garden | [Not accomplished]. Once a week patients – assisted by the care staff – take a walk on the garden for short periods of the evening, usually after dinner. | [Not accomplished]. The garden is not used during the evening. |
| Garden configuration for the practice of therapies, socialization and diverse activities with every patient | [Fully accomplished]. The annex building and the barbecue area work as extensions of the garden, where socialization and manual activities take place. | [Partially accomplished]. Even though the area is suited for these activities, they are performed indoors. |

# 4 Conclusion

Departing from studies about the brain and from an approach based on the cooperation between Architecture and Neuroscience, [1–6, 9] this research analyses and defends the strong potential of landscape projects for the promotion of wellness and life-quality of individuals with Alzheimer, considering such initiative as part of the set of non-pharmacological treatments for this disease. Both the analysis and the defense are structured: (1) on the concept of neuroplasticity, that indicates a clear co-evolution between the structure of the brain and the space someone inhabits. That is to say, the significant potential of the living environment of an individual to shape and mold the physical structure of the brain and, consequently, its behavior; as well as the expressive transformation of the physical space planned and executed by the human brain, activities encompassed by the fields of Architecture and Design; (2) on the concept of *biophilia*, that affirms the intrinsic and positive attachment between human being and nature. In other words, humans and nature are biologically connected, a lifelong deal with clear benefits for humankind; (3) on the concept of affective memory, which evinces how memories are modulated by emotions; and the contributions to the organism and wellness of humans, which derive from the stimuli (somatosensory, sensory-motor and cognitive) to evoke memories with positive emotional value.

The results obtained by the research indicate 45 project recommendations to the landscape project of clinics dedicated to the care of Alzheimer's disease patients. From these recommendations, 25 are derived from literature review [3, 11–16] and 20 come from field investigations undertaken on two clinics in the state of Sao Paulo, Brazil: SeniorVit (Campinas) and Recanto Monsenhor Albino (Catanduva).

At SeniorVit, 28 recommendations are fully accomplished, 9 partially accomplished and 8 not accomplished; at Recanto Monsenhor Albino, on the other hand, 23 recommendations are fully applied, 15 only partially, and 7 are not applied.

From the results obtained, it is possible to affirm that the absence of a landscape project specifically oriented towards the treatment of patients with Alzheimer and its use also by the care staff explains the deficiencies and the need of project improvements in both clinics. Such finding reaffirms the importance of landscaping in this type of space. Another point is that a directly proportional relation can be inferred between somatosensory, sensory-motor and cognitive benefits for the patients and the increase in the number of fully accomplished project recommendations.

It is important to stress the research gap in Brazilian literature concerning the contribution of landscaping projects to the non-pharmacological treatment of patients with Alzheimer. Therefore, the field investigations undertaken in this research are an important contribution. These investigations made it possible to increase the number of project recommendations for therapeutic gardens already available on international literature, while also adding new parameters of analysis stemming from the needs identified in the field. It is expected then that the set of parameters presented here can be used in further studies, and that it can also be expanded through new propositions generated by investigations performed either in Brazil or abroad. Such expansion strengthens the cooperation between Architecture, Design, and Neuroscience and promotes the wellness and life quality of patients with degenerative neurological diseases.

# References

1. Mallgrave, H.: The Architect's Brain. Wiley-Blackwell, UK (2010)
2. Pallasmaa, J., Mallgrave, H., Arbib, M.: Architecture and Neuroscience. TapioWirkkala Rut Bryk Foundation, Finland (2013)
3. Zeisel, J.: Inquiry by Design: Environment/Behavior/Neuroscience in Architecture, Interiors, Landscape, and Planning. W. W. Norton, New York (2006)
4. Zuanon, R., de Faria, B.A.C.: Landscape design and neuroscience cooperation: contributions to the non-pharmacological treatment of Alzheimer's disease. In: Duffy, V.G. (ed.) DHM 2018. LNCS, vol. 10917, pp. 353–374. Springer, Cham (2018). https://doi.org/10.1007/978-3-319-91397-1_29
5. Zuanon, R., Ramos da Silva Oliveira, M., Gallo, H., Lima Ferreira, C.: Drawing memories: intersections between the sites of memory and the memories of places. In: Duffy, V.G. (ed.) DHM 2018. LNCS, vol. 10917, pp. 375–391. Springer, Cham (2018). https://doi.org/10.1007/978-3-319-91397-1_30
6. Zuanon, R.: Design-neuroscience: interactions between the creative and cognitive processes of the brain and design. In: Kurosu, M. (ed.) HCI 2014. LNCS, vol. 8510, pp. 167–174. Springer, Cham (2014). https://doi.org/10.1007/978-3-319-07233-3_16
7. Lent, R.: Neurociência da Mente e do Comportamento Guanabara. Koogan, Rio de Janeiro (2008)
8. Lundy-Ekman, L.: Neurociência: fundamentos para reabilitação. Elsevier, Rio de Janeiro (2004)
9. Anthes, E.: Building around the mind. Sci. Am. Mind **20**(2), 52–59 (2009)
10. Ulrich, R.: How design impacts wellness. Healthcare Forum J. **30**, 20–25 (1992)
11. Damasio, A.R.: Em busca de Espinosa: prazer e dor na ciência dos sentimentos. Companhia das Letras, São Paulo (2004)
12. Gerlach-Springgs, N., Kaufman, R., Warner, S.: Restorative Gardens: The Healing Landscape. Yale University Press, New Haven (1998)
13. Zeisel, J., Hyde, J., Levkoff, S.: Best practices: an Environment Behavior (EB) model for Alzheimer special care units. Am. J. Alzheimer's Care Relat. Disord. Res. **9**, 4–21 (1994)
14. Zeisel, J., Raia, P.: Nonpharmacological treatment for Alzheimer's disease: a mind-brain approach. Am. J. Alzheimer's Dis. Other Dement. **15**, 331–340 (2000)
15. Zeisel, J.: Improving person-centered care through effective design. Gener.: J. Am. Soc. Aging **37**(3), 45–52 (2013)
16. Marcus, C., Sachs, A.: Therapeutic Landscapes: An Evidence-Based Approach to Designing Healing Gardens and Restorative Outdoor Spaces. Wiley, Hoboken (2013)
17. Pappas, A.: Exploring Therapeutic restoration theories of nature and their application for design recommendations for an Alzheimer's garden at Wesley Woods Hospital. Master thesis in Architecture, University Of Georgia, Athens (2006)
18. Hernandez, R.: Effects of therapeutic gardens in special care units for people with dementia. J. Hous. Elderly **21**(1–2), 117–152 (2007)
19. Garcia, J.M.: Clinica SeniorVit, Campinas. Presential interview held in August 2017 (2017)
20. Damasio, A.R.: O erro de Descartes: emoção, razão e o cérebro humano. Companhia das Letras, São Paulo (1996)
21. Chapman, J., Hazen, T., Noell-Waggoner, E.: Gardens for people with dementia. J. Hous. Elderly **2**(3–4), 249–263 (2007)
22. Smith, T.: Cérebro e sistema nervoso. Círculo de Leitores, Lisboa (1993)
23. Bushid, C., Magnasco, M.O., Vosshall, L.B., Keller, A.: Humans can discriminate more than 1 trillion olfactory stimuli. In: Science, American Association for the Advancement of Science (AAAS), vol. 343, no. 6177, pp 1370–1372 (2014)
24. Albright, T., Desimone, R., Gross, H.G.: Columnar organization of directionally selective cells in visual area MT of the macaque. J. Neurophysiol. **51**(1), 16–31 (1984)

# Design and Usability Evaluation of Interface of Mobile Application for Nutrition Tracking for People with Parkinson's Disease

Bojan Blažica$^{(\boxtimes)}$, Peter Novak, Franc Novak,
and Barbara Koroušić Seljak

Jozef Stefan Institute, Jamova Cesta 39, 1000 Ljubljana, Slovenia
bojan.blazica@ijs.si

**Abstract.** The importance of nutrition for Parkinson's disease patients has been acknowledged in many papers. On the other hand, the usability of tools supporting nutrition interventions is not well studied. This paper presents a case study on how to design a nutrition tracking mobile application for users with Parkinson's disease. We focus on the design choices made to accommodate users and findings from usability testing with users.

**Keywords:** Design for limited mobility users · Parkinson disease · UI design · Usability testing · Nutrition tracking

## 1 Introduction

Parkinson's disease (PD) is a long-term disorder of the central nervous system that mainly affects the motor system. It belongs to a group of conditions called motor system disorders, which are the result of the loss of dopamine-producing brain cells. The four primary symptoms of PD are tremor, or trembling in hands, arms, legs, jaw, and face; rigidity, or stiffness of the limbs and trunk; bradykinesia, or slowness of movement; and postural instability, or impaired balance and coordination. As these symptoms become more pronounced, patients may have difficulty walking, talking, or completing other simple tasks [1]. There are 10 million patients worldwide (1.2 million in the EU [2]). Their lives are dependent on others and there is no cure, we can only postpone the onset of symptoms or treat their severity. "The combined direct and indirect cost of Parkinson's, including treatment, social security payments and lost income from inability to work, is estimated to be nearly \$25 billion per year in the United States alone. Medication costs for an individual person with PD average \$2,500 a year, and therapeutic surgery can cost up to \$100,000 dollars per patient" [2].

Given the above, it is no surprise that several research projects have been funded to advance our knowledge of PD (Rempark1[1], Sense-Park[2], Cupid[3], Neurotremor[4]).

---

[1] http://www.rempark.eu/.

[2] http://www.sense-park.eu/.

[3] http://www.cupid-project.eu/.

[4] http://www.car.upm-csic.es/bioingenieria/neurotremor/.

© Springer Nature Switzerland AG 2019
V. G. Duffy (Ed.): HCII 2019, LNCS 11582, pp. 200–208, 2019.
https://doi.org/10.1007/978-3-030-22219-2_15

The work presented in this article was part of the PD_manager[5] project, which built and evaluated an innovative, mHealth, patient-centric ecosystem for Parkinson's disease management. More specifically the aim of PD_manager was to:

1. model the behaviors of intended users of PD_manager (patients, caregivers, neurologists and other health-care providers),
2. educate patients, caregivers and healthcare providers with the focus on occupational and speech therapies and
3. propose a set of unobtrusive, simple-in-use, cooperative, mobile devices that will be used for symptoms monitoring and collection of adherence data (smartphone, sensor insole, smart pillbox, wristband with sensors for acceleration, heart rate, etc.).

Many studies exist on ICT solutions to aid people with Parkinson's, from passive monitoring to tele-rehabilitation [3]. This paper focuses on the design and evaluation of a user interface of a mobile application for tracking nutrients and foods consumed by Parkinson's disease patients.

## 2  Design Decisions and Argumentation

The design started with a literature review, which includes interfaces for the elderly [4–7] and for people with Parkinson's [8–13], yet we were unable to find anything specific on designing nutrition tools for Parkinsonians (despite nutrition being recognized as important to manage the disease).

We designed an information structure that helps users understand the system and designing an interaction that makes it easy for them to finish a given task. Our goal was to design whole experience more user-friendly by designing the interface that enables users to quickly recognize the objects on the screen. With specifically designed visual language provides we helped patients to locate interactive elements on screen, pay attention to the most important information and differentiate between input text and instructions. Furthermore, it enabled users to understand which functions are available to them and stay aware of the current activity that they are participating in.

Design choices were made with patients in mind and were grounded in design principles of graphical user-interfaces and visual communications. We used color and shape in a way that utilizes selective and associative perception of the visual variable. We determined the same color for objects with the same functionality, which made it easy for users to recognize, locate and isolate them and group them into categories (e.g. static and interactive objects). We used the difference of shape to enable users to differentiate between subcategories, while preserving the perception of the main categories (e.g. icons of functions and input suggestions – both interactive objects). We designed a few instances of different brightness of information and increasing the difference between them to establish visual hierarchy and make it easier for users to process visual information. We also used semiotic principles to communicate different functions of buttons and provide the feedback of successfully completed tasks. We

---

[5] http://www.parkinson-manager.eu/.

unified visual language throughout the whole app to make the interface predictable and consequently allow users to quickly learn how to use the app.

Because of designing mainly for elder users the visual style differed from the ones usually found in mobile applications. It had more boldness, strong use contrast and the presence of clear, emphasized elements. Aesthetic value was compromised in some parts for making sure that the interface as evident as possible for the users from the focus group, which may have problems with their sight.

Designed visual language helps users to:

1. to see what they can tap on and what not by coloring all the interactive elements blue and all the static one's gray;
2. to focus on the most important parts of the screen by applying bigger contrast to them;
3. to recognize what activity, they are performing by assigning different background color to different tasks (meal input – black background, meal tagging – white background);
4. to know when they have completed the task;
5. differentiate which text is an input and which not with fonts (same typeface family – non-input: sans serif, input: serif) and which text is an instruction and which not with font styles (non-instructions: regular, instructions: italic);
6. to perceive which are the available functions by visualizing them with icons;

Designed structure enables users to:

1. to easily read what's written on the screen by avoiding sentences and using short words with big text size and bold font;
2. to process information by revealing it progressively;
3. to check and correct entered data by making it always visible on the screen with editing option to correct mistakes;
4. to perform tasks in an self-evident way by dividing the interface accordingly (upper part for meal input, lower part for meal tagging).

Designed interaction makes it possible for users:

1. to easily hit targets by making them high and full-width;
2. to predict where something appears on the screen with consistent placing;
3. to interact with the tool with minimal tapping;
4. to easily select values by providing input suggestions;
5. to find what they are searching for by grouping similar information together.

## 3   Usability Evaluation

The usability test focused on the usability features defined by the ISO 9241-11: Guidance on Usability [14]. In this standard, the usability is defined as the extent to which a product can be used by specified users to achieve specified goals with effectiveness, efficiency, and satisfaction in a specified context of use. In this regard,

- effectiveness denotes the accuracy and completeness with which the users achieve specified goals;
- efficiency measures the resources expended in relation to the accuracy and completeness with which users achieve their goals; and
- satisfaction designates the freedom from discomfort, and positive attitudes towards the use of the product.

In our case, the metrics of effectiveness was related to the amount of functionalities exemplified in the performed tasks, while the metrics of efficiency focused on the time used to perform the given tasks. Satisfaction was assessed by means of recorded remarks of the moderator and a post-test questionnaire.

**Fig. 1.** Login credentials and logout; testing with these screens revealed how troublesome can a basic interaction such as typing be for people with Parkinson's. They suggested to have the keyboard layout always in landscape so that keys are spaced more abundantly and to have the option to see the password when typing as typos are more frequent.

The usability test included think-aloud sessions with users performing the following tasks with an interactive prototype:

1. Login credentials and logout (Fig. 1),
   (Username input and password input, confirm button;
   menu selection, conform choice)
2. Recording current meal with a picture (Fig. 2),
   (Menu select, picture take, button confirm, review collection)

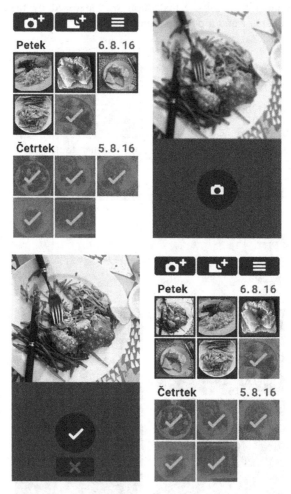

**Fig. 2.** Recording current meal with a picture was mostly well understood and accepted by the participants.

3. Editing previously entered meal (Fig. 3),
   (Food ingredient input, quantity input, confirm, repeat, confirm meal)

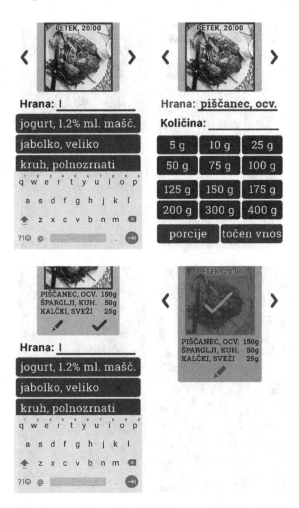

**Fig. 3.** Editing previously entered meal. Participants appreciated the fact that most input and editing can be done via buttons thus minimizing the amount of typing needed.

4. Recording meal without picture (Fig. 4),
    (day input, hour input, minutes input)

A post-test interview allowed the user to express his/her opinion and answer: what impression did you have using the app, were the elements in the app clear and readable, was it possible for you to normally press the elements, where they big enough, was the order of the screens understandable?

6 patients were recruited in the rehabilitation center Soča where the sessions were executed during scheduled visits. In general, users praised the application and accepted it well, however some issues emerged:

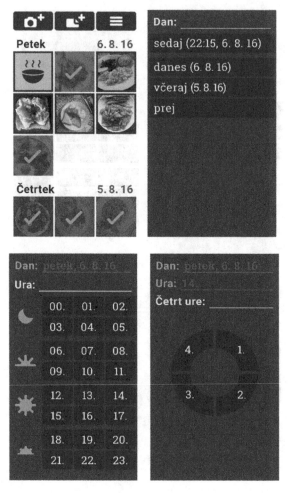

**Fig. 4.** Recording meal without picture. The problem that appeared here was selecting the 14:15 time as it lies between the first and second quarters on the pictogram. Correcting the target area sensible for touch solved the current problem, but special attention must be paid to such details.

1. Food input suggestion were not accurate as users would like (e.g. yoghurt 3.5% milk fat, suggested 1,2% milk fat from different brand).
2. Patients felt the need to additionally confirm their input (misusing the arrow which is actually used to confirm the whole meal not just the ingredient).
3. The meaning of the settings button (cog) was not clear.
4. A patient did not consider scrolling at all.
5. Entering time of meal - minutes was not intuitive.
6. Default keyboard use should be in landscape mode to allow for more space between keys.
7. The need to have a button making password visible during entering.

# 4 Conclusion

The work presented is a successful case-study of how to design interfaces for ICT solutions for a specific target group as people with Parkinson's disease. Although the principles used to design the application build on general HCI and more specific accessibility literature, the value of the presented work lies in its specificity for PD patients – a growing and underserved population. Although based on a limited number of participants, to the best of our knowledge, this study is the only documented work on designing a nutrition diet monitoring and planning application specific for Parkinson's patients.

# References

1. Parkinson's Disease Information Page. NINDS, 30 June 2016. http://www.ninds.nih.gov/disorders/parkinsons_disease/parkinsons_disease.htm
2. European Parkinson's disease association. http://www.pdf.org/en/parkinson_statistics. Accessed Aug 2016
3. Cikajlo, I., et al.: Can telerehabilitation games lead to functional improvement of upper extremities in individuals with Parkinson's disease?. Int. J. Rehabil. Res. (Internationale Zeitschrift fur Rehabilitationsforschung). Revue internationale de recherches de readaptation 41(3), 230 (2018)
4. Human Factors Approaches. Human Factors and Ageing Series, 2nd edn. CRC Press, New York
5. Moreno, L., Martínez, P.: A review of accessibility requirements in elderly users' interactions with web applications. In: Proceedings of the 13th International Conference on Interacción Persona-Ordenador (INTERACCION 2012), Article 47, 2 p. ACM, New York (2012). https://doi.org/10.1145/2379636.2379682
6. Silva, P., Holden, K., Jordan, P.: Towards a list of heuristics to evaluate smartphone apps targeted at older adults: a study with apps that aim at promoting health and well-being. In: 2015 48th Hawaii International Conference on System Sciences (HICSS), pp. 3237–3246 (2015). https://doi.org/10.1109/hicss.2015.390
7. Motti, L.G., Vigouroux, N., Gorce, P.: Interaction techniques for older adults using touchscreen devices: a literature review. In: Proceedings of the 25th Conference on l'Interaction Homme-Machine (IHM 2013), p. 125, 10 p. ACM, New York (2013). https://doi.org/10.1145/2534903.2534920
8. Nunes, F., Silva, P.A., Cevada, J., Correia, B.A., Teixeira, L.: User interface design guidelines for smartphone applications for people with Parkinson's disease. Univ. Access Inf. Soc. 15, 659–679 (2015). https://doi.org/10.1007/s10209-015-0440-1
9. Maziewski, P., Suchomski, P., Kostek, B., Czyzewski, A.: An intuitive graphical user interface for the Parkinson's Disease patients. In: 2009 4th International IEEE/EMBS Conference on Neural Engineering, Antalya, pp. 14–17 (2009). https://doi.org/10.1109/ner.2009.5109223
10. Barros, A.C., Cevada, J., Bayés, À., Alcaine, S., Mestre, B.: Design and evaluation of a medication application for people with Parkinson's disease. In: Mobile Computing, Applications, and Services: 5th International Conference, MobiCASE 2013, Paris, France, 7–8 November 2013, Revised Selected Papers, pp. 273–276 (2013). https://doi.org/10.1007/978-3-319-05452-0_22

11. McNaney, R., et al.: Designing for and with people with Parkinson's: a focus on exergaming. In: Proceedings of the 33rd Annual ACM Conference on Human Factors in Computing Systems (CHI 2015), pp. 501–510. ACM, New York (2015). https://doi.org/10.1145/2702123.2702310

12. Assad, O., et al.: Motion-based games for Parkinson's disease patients. In: Anacleto, J.C., Fels, S., Graham, N., Kapralos, B., Saif El-Nasr, M., Stanley, K. (eds.) ICEC 2011. LNCS, vol. 6972, pp. 47–58. Springer, Heidelberg (2011). https://doi.org/10.1007/978-3-642-24500-8_6

13. Barros, A.C., Cevada, J., Bayés, À., Alcaine, S., Mestre, B.: User-centred design of a mobile self-management solution for Parkinson's disease. In: Proceedings of the 12th International Conference on Mobile and Ubiquitous Multimedia (MUM 2013), Article 23, 10 p. ACM, New York (2013). https://doi.org/10.1145/2541831.2541839

14. ISO 9241-11: Ergonomic requirements for office work with visual display terminals (VDTs), Part 11: Guidance on usability (1998)

# Thermoregulating and Hydrating Microcapsules: Contributions of Textile Technology in the Design of Wearable Products for Wheelchair Dependents

Veridianna Cristina Teodoro Ferreira[1][✉] 🆔
and Agda Carvalho[2][✉] 🆔

[1] Graduate Program in Design, Anhembi Morumbi University, São Paulo, Brazil
veridiannaf@gmail.com
[2] Graduate Program in Design, Anhembi Morumbi University; and Graduate
Program in Arts, UNESP, São Paulo, Brazil
agdarcarvalho@gmail.com

**Abstract.** In this essay we present a number of functionalization methods for textiles through the use of microcapsules. For this purpose, the text explores the contributions of textile technology and reports on ways to obtain the functionalization of active components in textiles, as well as the possibilities of using encapsulation in everyday life. We also discuss the ways in which the microcapsules can be applied to fabrics and examine the durability of the properties with the everyday use. For a better understanding of the durability question, it is presented a research developed by the Minho University in 2011, which exposes the losses and damages of the microcapsules caused by daily maintenance. Though the possibilities of functionalization using this technique are manifold, in this essay we focus on the disabled body, specifically vis-à-vis wheelchair dependents who actively participate in the labor market, on account of the consequences that arise from remaining in the same position for hours. Thus, we present thermoregulating microcapsules that control the temperature of the skin, and moisturizing microcapsules that maintain the skin appropriately moisturized, with an aim to prevent pressure ulcers caused by excessive heat and friction. Through the use of microcapsules applied to the structure of textiles, we aim to provide greater comfort to the body of the wheelchair dependent, enabling the maintenance of adequate skin temperature and moisture levels, and thus preventing lesions caused by the lack of body movement.

**Keywords:** Product design · Textile technology ·
Thermoregulating and moisturizing microcapsules · Wheelchair dependents ·
Pressure ulcers

## 1 Introduction

Textile technology extends throughout different fields of activity, such as engineering, medicine and design, and provides a significant contribution for the performance of daily activities, seeing that the distinct procedures have potentiated the various uses and specificities of the products. The textile surface alters its characteristics after one or a

© Springer Nature Switzerland AG 2019
V. G. Duffy (Ed.): HCII 2019, LNCS 11582, pp. 209–221, 2019.
https://doi.org/10.1007/978-3-030-22219-2_16

few functionalizations are applied onto the fabric. According to Sánchez [1], the procedures for producing smart textiles center on microencapsulation, electronic and nanotechnology-based technologies. Each process adds qualities to the textiles and expands the possibilities for the user. This essay focuses on the use of microcapsules, and how this process can bring functional benefits to clothing and positively impact on the daily activities of physically disabled people, specifically vis-à-vis wheel-chair dependents.

"The word "disabled", when applied to people who suffer physical, sensorial or mental limitations, is the opposite in meaning to "able", and this very conception explains the difficulty of adapting built space, from housing to work environments, to the needs of the users with particular limitations and difficulties. Thus, many disabled people become incapable of performing everyday tasks, from the maintenance of their personal hygiene to their ability to work and engage in leisure activities, a situation that can result in the social exclusion of these people" [2].

The group of wheelchair dependents taken as a basis for this research relates particularly to those who actively participate in the labor market, seeing as we aim to analyze particular situations in which the disabled individual must remain in the same position for hours, resulting in the formation of skin lesions, also known as pressure ulcers. In this way, the focus of the present essay lies in the use of textile technology for optimizing the level of comfort of the wheelchair user's body. For this purpose, we must highlight the challenges faced by these individuals in performing their daily activities, and subsequently underscore the ways in which technology can exploit the potential of the design of textile surfaces, and consequently reinvent the functionalities of clothing.

"Between the people with physical disabilities and non-disabled people, there are evident differences in the living states. [...] people with limb disabilities have special needs for the aesthetic and functional structures of clothing, distinct from non-disabled people, and consequently their garments have specific design requirements" [3].

It is important to emphasize that the principles of exclusion of disabled persons from life in society inevitably influenced all peoples who were exposed to Greek culture, including Western society. For these peoples, physical beauty was often associated to character, which in turn rendered disabled individuals into objects of pity, who were the result of divine punishment, or else became a source of amusement for the majority of citizens, regarded by society as "normal" [4].

These individuals need special care to protect their skin from injuries caused by poor mobility, seeing that when the body remains in the same position for hours, it tends to heat up and sweat, forming lesions that can quickly be aggravated, compromising the individual's health. Hence, daily care is needed to provide comfort and well-being to the individual, including skin hydration, and which also meets their physiological needs.

The use of microcapsules can both enhance the qualities of textile surfaces. The applications produce long-lasting fragrances embedded in the textiles, or add insect repelling, sun protective and moisturizing functionalities. Moreover, it is possible to alter the color of the textile material according to the light intensity, and even regulate the user's skin temperature in relation to the outside environment, allowing the body to cool down when the physical surroundings are excessively hot, or warming up the body when the environment is very cold, which is made possible by way of thermoregulating capsules. These possibilities unlock the potential of a fabric and its function, enhance the quality of the material, and also improve the user's protection.

In what refers to body comfort based on physiological needs, it is also worth highlighting the use of microcapsules in clothing to facilitate a healthy rate of body transpiration, preventing or reducing the formation of body odor, and reducing discomfort caused by the accumulation of sweat and moisture in clothing.

These benefits can be applied to different textile materials, such as fabrics made of 100% cotton or even synthetic fibers, and thus the textile structure must be tested, as each type of fabric presents specifications and variations related to the level of absorption and to the deterioration or degradation of the functional components.

Seeing that the research study in question aims to contribute to the level of comfort and skin protection of disabled people, the microcapsules should, ideally, be applied to 100% cotton fabric, on account of its textile qualities: comfort, softness, durability and low cost, besides the material's great capacity for absorbing sweat [5].

There are numerous ways to achieve the functionalization of textiles through the use of microcapsules, and this technology is being tested and applied in different manners on a daily basis. Among the different segments that apply microcapsules, we can highlight its use in carbon paper, liquid crystal, adhesives, cosmetic products, insecticides, medical drugs and other medical uses, in food and in the textile industry [6–8].

In addition to bringing thermal and skin comfort to wheelchair users, it is also important to address the durability of these microcapsules, seeing as often the data relating to this factor are not explicit and confound the user with regard to the lifespan of the active components in the fabric.

For this purpose, this essay dwells on research developed by Cruz et al. [9], at Universidade do Minho, in Portugal, where durability tests are performed on the microcapsules, also demonstrating their behavior after being washed in domestic washing machines. Based on this study, we can observe the amount of microcapsules lost in every wash, which opens up new possibilities for the reapplication of the product, with a view to greater durability of the fabric with the active components.

The text emphasizes the importance of textile technology in the everyday life of the wheelchair dependent, and evidences the contribution and improvement of the use of encapsulation for moisturizing the skin during the performance of professional activities. It is also worth highlighting the need for improvement of the durability of the active components in the fabric, with an aim to increasing the number of washes without losing the article's required properties.

## 2  The Everyday Needs of Wheelchair Dependents Who Actively Participate in the Labor Market

The contributions afforded by microcapsules applied to textile articles are countless, as they enhance the functionality of the garment, fulfilling pre-established needs like the durability of the active components incorporated to the textile surface. The microcapsules break open according to the use of the clothing, and as a result of stimuli such as heat and light irradiation. Such properties reveal themselves as extremely useful for people with physical impairments, in light of the challenge of maintaining their skin appropriately moisturized.

There are also microcapsules that do not break open, but rather maintain the active components inside the shell, and alter their actual forms to provide comfort to the user in different situations, as for example thermoregulating capsules that regulate skin temperature. However, after successive washes, these microcapsules are eliminated from the fabric, and consequently must be reapplied, if necessary.

This type of thermoregulating microcapsule is extremely important when it comes to wheelchair users' clothing, particularly in garments worn from the waist down, seeing that these are often areas of the body with little or no sensibility in the case of wheelchair dependents. The active thermoregulator material controls the skin temperature, which provides both thermal comfort and the prevention of pressure ulcers caused by excess heat.

The application of active thermoregulating components in microcapsules eliminates the need for daily reapplication of the product, respecting the difficulties and limitations faced by people with physical disabilities, and thus facilitates the use of the actual wearable product.

Data obtained from the National Health Survey, conducted by the Brazilian Institute of Geography and Statistics - IBGE (2015), among a Brazilian population of 200.6 million people, reveal that 6.2% of people had at least one of the four impairments: intellectual, physical, hearing and visual. In Brazil, 0.8% or 1.6 million people live with intellectual disabilities, while 1.3%, or 2.6 million cope with physical disabilities. Hearing impairments, in turn, represents 1.1%, or 2.2 million people and visual impairments represents 3.6% or 7.2 million people [2].

This scenario demonstrates the relevance of this research in identifying, to start with, the contributions provided by textile technology for the everyday lives of these users, and also in discussing the possibilities of improvement in the development of products aimed at people with physical disabilities, with a view to ensuring their comfort, well-being, health and autonomy for performing their daily activities. The creation of products directed at disabled users requires an in-depth understanding of their needs and the difficulties faced on a daily basis. In Brazil, for example, there are no laws to differentiate the number of working hours of a wheelchair dependent and those of a person without a disability, where the number of hours generally varies from 6 to 10 consecutive hours. The 6-h working days includes a 15-min break, and the 10-h working day includes a 2-h interval for lunch or dinner.

In order to fulfill this number of hours of work, the wheelchair user must remain in the same position for long hours. The body heats up and transpires, besides having to cope with friction caused by small movements of the body against the chair. These characteristics induce the formation of skin lesions, also known as pressure ulcers.

To prevent these ulcers, the wheelchair dependent needs to change positions often, moisturize their skin a number of times a day, or even control their body temperature. These are some of the difficulties faced by the wheelchair user at the workplace, which evidences the relevance of textile technology-based solutions.

Among the different types of disabilities, people with physical impairments suffer more from pressure ulcers. The main cause for the formation of these lesions is the inadequate supply of blood and nutrients in a particular part of the body, due to external pressure exerted by an object against bony or cartilaginous prominences. Humidity and friction further aggravate the condition, as the sores appear in parts of the body that support its weight. For this reason, wheelchair dependents are more susceptible to developing pressure ulcers in the ischial region, which supports the weight of the body when a person is in a sitting position [10].

The first stage of development of pressure ulcers consists in a mild skin alteration, normally indicated by the appearance of a red spot on fair skin and a bluish or purple one on darker-colored skin. As the change is not abrupt, it frequently passes unnoticed, but there are other properties that indicate that they are pressure sores: the temperature of the skin being either hotter or colder; the skin's consistency or texture, which can be either firmer and thicker or lighter and softer; and for those with more sensitive skin, there can be physical pain or itching [11].

The second stage involves a decrease of the skin thickness (epidermis and/or dermis). The ulcer presents itself as a blister or small wound on the skin, though still superficial. The third stage is characterized by a significant loss of skin thickness with damage or necrosis of the subcutaneous tissue, almost reaching the underlying fascia. In the fourth stage, the tissue is extensively destroyed, presenting necrosis and even muscular and bone lesions, with or without loss of the whole thickness of the skin. In case the ulcer is not identified from the outset, it can evolve rapidly to the next stages, wherein the later stages are more difficult to treat.

The image below shows the depth of pressure ulcers in each of the four stages (Fig. 1):

## Stages of Pressure Sores

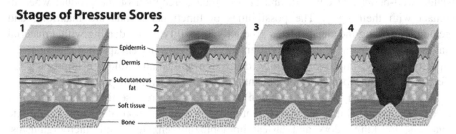

**Fig. 1.** Stages of pressure ulcer development (Source: https://mangarhealth.com/uk/news/new-mangar-health-websites-launched/)

In other words, with the use of these microcapsules, the microclimate between the seat surface and the user's body reaches an equilibrium state and ceases the production of sweat resulting from excessive heat, also preventing localized damage to the skin.

This functionalization provides greater thermal comfort for wheelchair dependents. At present, microcapsules are integrated into acrylic fibers and polyurethane foam, and used in various textile-related applications, such as ski garments, gloves, socks, nightwear, shoes, protection equipment, medical textile products, among others [11].

Another form of combating pressure ulcers is skin moisturizing, which minimizes lesions caused by friction between the skin and the wheelchair.

From this, we can infer that the concomitant application of microencapsulation of moisturizers and thermoregulation components can significantly prevent skin lesions in wheelchair users.

## 3 Possibilities for the Use of Microcapsules

Since the 1970s, author Papanek [12] has made appeals for designers to stop working within a culture of consumerism and superficiality, and start developing research projects that cater to the needs of all kinds of people, regardless of their social and economic circumstances.

In this sense, the range of different applications of textile technology point to important directions for future research in design. In the case of microcapsules, or active finishes, as they are known in the textile industry, offer many possibilities: scented lingerie, odor-absorbing kitchen aprons, pajamas that glow in the dark, t-shirts with antimicrobial compounds or ultraviolet protection, among other active finishes [13].

Microencapsulation consists in a technology of microparticles in the form of protective shells, whose casing material can be polymeric ceramic or gelatin, which enclose active ingredients. The active components can be solid, liquid or gaseous. This technology is mainly used for protection purposes and for controlled release of substances (that is, the product in the core can be gradually released as the product is being used).

The use of microcapsules as aimed at positively contributing to an individual's health, well-being and comfort, and also to their perception of the product when in contact with their body. The possibilities of functionalizations are manifold, and include: protecting the encapsulated product's instability, when dealing with a material that is sensitive to the outside environment; improving the encapsulated substance's capacity (namely, improve solubility, dispersion ability and fluidity); improving the lifespan of the encapsulated components, in such as way as to prevent degradation-based reactions (dehydration, oxidation); controlling the release time of the encapsulated substance; enabling the convenient and safe manipulation of encapsulated toxic materials; masking odors and tastes; immobilizing enzymes and microorganisms; controlling drug release and the manipulation of encapsulated liquids and solids; releasing the encapsulated components in a predictable manner; and ensuring thermal comfort [8].

Microcapsules are micron-sized capsules (>1 μm), generally ranging in diameter from 1 μm to 1000 μm. Particles smaller than 1 μm are called nanoparticles, and when larger than 1000 μm are called microgranules or microcapsules [14].

Microcapsules can have a spherical or irregular shape, and are composed of two parts: the core and the shell. The inner part is the core, which can be an active ingredient or contain one, and can be permanent or temporary. The outer shell, in its turn, protects the core. The image below represents the structure of a microcapsule, its outer shell and the active components contained in the core [15].

Microencapsulation has been know in the United States since 1968, when it was applied to a self-copying paper without the use of carbon for use in multiple-page commercial forms. Later on, in 1980, researches studies advanced, leading to the development of perfume-containing microcapsules. Regarded as the true form "olfactory communication," they were extensively explored in the advertising of perfumes, soaps, fabric softeners and detergents. In its turn, microencapsulation applied to textiles dates from early 1990 [1] (Fig. 2).

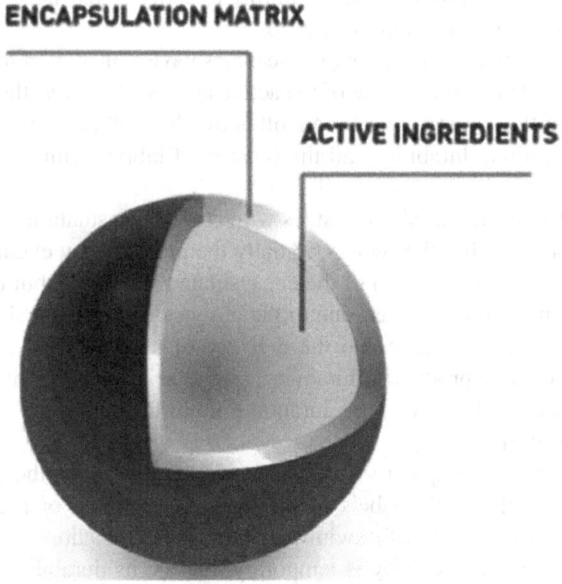

**ENCAPSULATION MATRIX**

**ACTIVE INGREDIENTS**

**Fig. 2.** Structure of a microcapsule (Source: https://capsularis.com/microencapsulation/?lang=en)

Even though they so small that they cannot be seen by the naked eye, microcapsules are able to cover a relatively large application area, and allow a relatively uniform and adequate liberation of the active components. By examining the contributions and possibilities of microencapsulation listed up to this point, we can conclude that the main objective of microencapsulation is to guarantee that the encapsulated material reaches the area of action without being adversely affected by the outside environment.

The encapsulated active components can be released by the rupture of the membrane; by slow and progressive dissolution of the polymer of the membrane; by friction; or biodegradation [1]; temperature-related degradation; pH-related acidity and alkalinity; solubility of the release medium, that is, rupture can occur through mechanical pressure or by friction [16]. It is important to highlight that the release mechanism of each type of microcapsule depends on the composition of the capsule shell material and its thickness. The shell protects the active components in the core, and influences the way in which the microcapsules will be broken. However, the ultimate purpose and benefits derived from their use are determined by the active components.

Microcapsules that do not break are developed with more resistant shells, with a view to embed themselves in the fabric for longer, thus achieving certain types of functionalization in ways where the active component does not leave the microcapsule. As an example, thermoregulating agents remain embedded the fabric, keeping the body warm when it loses body heat, or providing a cooling effect as the body heats up.

Microcapsules are used in the textile industry with the purpose of making people's daily lives easier and/or provide body comfort to individuals, in such a way as to respect their physical and physiological needs.

According to Cheng et al. [17], many researches have centered on the materials, the identification methods and the release of the active agents. However, those that focus of the performance of the active properties are often overlooked. In other words, studies to evaluate the application, durability and the finishes of fabrics with effectively embedded microcapsules.

This negligence results in microcapsules with "low encapsulation capacity and lack of mechanical stability". In other words, initially the product may eventually achieve a satisfactory degree of impregnation of the encapsulated substance, but the dynamics of its liberation becomes compromised due to the absence of mechanical stability, which adversely affects its performance and the delivery of its objectives [8]. This in turn impacts directly on the product's durability, as it arrives in the market with programmed obsolescence. However, the duration time of the substance's functionality is not explicit to the user.

Some manufacturers frequently make the information about the product and its functionalities available on the labels of the items of clothing, or present it through advertisement, as is the case with swimwear with sun protection. Nonetheless, they rarely clarify that this functionality is temporary, that is, its durability is linked to the number of washes. As these functionalities are achieved through the application of microcapsules, part of them are lost as the items of clothing are washed, and over time the remaining microcapsules tend to lose its properties and features.

From this perspective, the next section a durability test for thermoregulating microcapsules, applied to plain knit fabric (also known as jersey knit). By collecting microscopic samples, we aim to evidence the behavior of the microcapsules as a wearable product is used.

## 4  Durability of the Thermoregulating Effect Applied to the Fabric

The investigation and experiments conducted at the Textile Science and Technology Center at the Universidade do Minho, in Portugal, by Cruz et al. [9], together with Irmãos Araújo Ltd. [Araújo Brother's Ltd.], also from Portugal, include tests for durability and longevity of the thermoregulating microcapsules applied to jersey knit fabric. These microcapsules cater to the need of providing greater comfort to the user, based on their ability to absorb, store or release of heat energy depending on environmental and metabolic conditions.

This research is relevant for our investigation as the content addresses the durability of thermoregulating microcapsules, a feature of encapsulation that can greatly benefit wheelchair users. As referred to previously, the use of thermoregulation material contributes to the comfort of users in various different situations, especially to the body of people with physical disabilities that lead to poor mobility, such as wheelchair dependents. The wheelchair user often does not realize that a moderate degree of discomfort can lead to and even aggravate pressure ulcers.

Phase Change Materials (PCM) microcapsules are typically coated with a polymer membrane, generally polyurethane foam, containing paraffin liquid as a core component with phase change properties that are sensitive to small differences in temperature [9].

The durability test proposed by Cruz et al. [9] utilizes a 100% cotton jersey knit fabric, dyed with a reactive dye with medium reactivity and sustainability. After the dyeing process, the knit fabric is finalized with a thermoregulating finishing composed of PCM microcapsules. The finish is applied by impregnation in the process of bath exhaustion in industrial washing machines.

The impregnation method started being used in 1999, and is currently employed in the application of products like fragrances, vitamins, moisturizing crème and even insect repellant to textiles. Nelson [18] and Rodrigues et al. [19] use the dyeing processes for the impregnation of microcapsules in the fabric. According to Salem [20], normally the dyeing is carried out in an aqueous bath in either continuous or exhaustion processes.

In the case of continuous dyeing process, the impregnation bath remains stationary while the textile substrate is fed continuously through the padding bath. Next, the fabric is mechanically compressed and fixed by dry heat or vapor, or by prolonged repose. In the exhaustion process, in turn, the dye is displaced from the bath to the fiber, through direct and continuous contact obtained from the movement of one of them, or both [20].

Once the fabric is ready, the durability test is carried out. Twenty washes are performed at a temperature of 40°, and a drying cycle of approximately one hour, using domestic detergent. After every five washes, the durability of the finishing is evaluated using a high-resolution scanning electron microscope, equipped with field emission and integrated X-ray microanalysis system. For this purpose, 1 cm$^2$ samples are used [15].

Within this context, the distribution and behavior of the PCM microcapsules are evaluated according to the number of washes. The microscopic images below show the textile fibers at a magnification of 1000x, whereby it is possible to verify that after the fifth wash a significant reduction in the amount of microcapsules occurs [9].

After the 10th and the 15th wash, this amount is reduced even further, although no deformities were observed in the microcapsules (Fig. 3).

After the 20th wash, the microcapsules become scarce and present deformities. As the microcapsules become damaged, small eruptions on their surface appear. These damages or cracks in the shell walls result in a loss of the capacity for thermoregulation of the particles, since the inner liquid escapes encapsulation [9].

This level of damage can be verified and evaluated when viewed at a magnification of 15 000X. The Fig. 4 below summarizes the process of loss of textile's functionalization, as a result of successive washes.

In other words, with the loss of microcapsules after a number of washes, the thermoregulation potential of the textile is reduced.

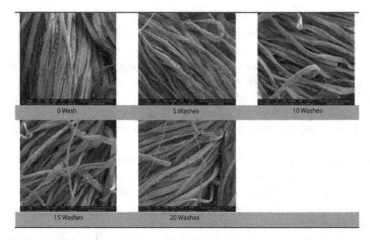

**Fig. 3.** Microscopic image at a magnification of 1000X. (Source: CRUZ et al. 2011)

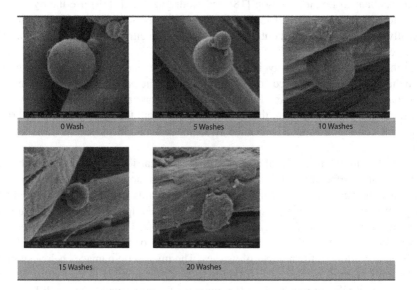

**Fig. 4.** Microscopic image at a magnification of 15 000X. (Source: CRUZ et al. 2011)

## 5   Main Discussions and Conclusions of the Study

Based on the data obtained, we have elected three main points for discussion: (1) environmental sustainability; (2) the financial sustainability of the wheelchair user; (3) the extension of longevity of textile surface functionalization. These aspects drive the advancement of the present study, with a view to investigate the contributions of the process of encapsulation of moisturizing and thermoregulating substances, capable of protecting the cutaneous tissue of wheelchair users.

Based on the tests performed by Cruz et al. [9], it is possible to infer that the successive home washes eliminate a large part of the thermoregulating and moisturizing microcapsules that constitute the functionalization of the textile, besides deforming the structure of the remaining microcapsules. This affects the original features of the product, compromising its efficiency, and also drastically reduces its lifespan. As a consequence, within a short period of time the product will be disposed of and the user will have to acquire a new one. In other words, in the case of users with reduced mobility, namely wheelchair dependents, who are the target audience of this study, the durability of the product does not cater to their daily needs for thermoregulation and skin moisturization for an indefinite period. Thus, we become conscious of two significant impacts: (1) on environmental sustainability and (2) on the financial sustainability of the wheelchair dependent, both ascribable to the rapid disposal of the product. As regards the first impact, it is worth emphasizing the constant and lasting negative effects of the textile industry on the environmental and social well-being of the planet. In addition to the serious problems caused by the acceleration of production and disposal of products, we must also account for the high levels of water consumption and for the massive contamination of the atmosphere due to the emission of carbon dioxide [21].

Concerning the second point, when the product loses its properties, its use is not feasible for the wheelchair dependent, since this exposes them to the development of new pressure ulcers. Faced with the impossibility of neglecting the protection of their skin, the user must resort to discarding the product and acquire a new one, thus corroborating to the unsustainable cycle described above.

In both cases, the role of Design/Designer entails a concern for ensuring a sustainable life cycle to the product, directed at extending its lifespan, increasing the possibilities of its reuse, and consequently, minimizing its chances of disposal. And herein lies the responsibility of the present research: identifying, proposing and developing procedures aimed at the extension of longevity of textile functionalization processes, specifically those relating to thermoregulation and moisturizing. In this sense, the possibilities of reapplication of the functionality by the wheelchair user themselves must be investigated. That is, a procedure that takes into account the motor difficulties of this public, and thus, enables the domestic reapplication of the microcapsules with the active components, in a manner that is practical and efficient for the user.

Thus the future developments of the research study point to experiments aimed at enhancing the resistance of shell walls of microcapsules, with a view to preserving their active properties in the textile structure for a longer period of time [22]. Also, assessing the viability of reapplication of these microcapsules by way of spray technology. In addition to these experiments, we must also investigate the use of cotton fibers, which are more adequate for sensitive skin, as the fibers minimize both the natural dehydration of the skin, and the friction between the textile surface and the cutaneous tissue [23].

Finally, from this perspective we must seek ways to collaborate with the sustainable cycle of product design, through processes focused on intelligent use and the consequent extension of a product's lifespan, the reduction of costs for users, and ultimately minimizing the negative impact on the environment; all of which must be achieved concomitantly to the comfort of wheelchair dependents in their everyday activities.

# References

1. Sánchez, J.C.: Têxteis inteligentes. Química Têxtil. **82**, 58–77 (2006)
2. Ferreira, V.C.T., Carvalho, A.: Inclusive design and textile technology in the everyday lives of wheelchair dependent. In: Duffy, V.G. (ed.) DHM 2018. LNCS, vol. 10917, pp. 295–307. Springer, Cham (2018). https://doi.org/10.1007/978-3-319-91397-1_25. http://hdl.handle.net/11449/171258. Acessed 20 Nov 2018
3. Chang, W.M., Zhao, Y.X., Guo, R.P., Wang, Q., Gu, X.D.: Design and study of clothing structure for people with limb disabilities. J. Fiber Bioeng. Inform. **2**(2), 61–66 (2009). https://doi.org/10.3993/jfbi06200910
4. Pezzolo, D.B.: Tecidos: história, tramas, tipos e usos. Editora SENAC, São Paulo (2007)
5. Qualharini, E.L., Anjos, F.C.: Ergonomia no espaço edificado para pessoas portadoras de deficiência (1998). http://www.abepro.org.br/biblioteca/ENEGEP1998_ART086.pdf. Accessed 15 Oct 2018
6. Madene, A., Jacquot, M., Scher, J., Desobry, S.: Flavour encapsulation and controlled release: a review. Int. J. Food Sci. Technol. **41**, 1–21 (2006). https://doi.org/10.1111/j.1365-2621.2005.00980.x. Accessed Dec 2018
7. Monllor, P., Bonet, M.A., Cases, F.: Characterization of the behaviour of flavour microcapsules in cotton fabrics. Eur. Polym. J. **43**, 2481–2490 (2007)
8. Peña, B., Panisello, C., Aresté, G., Garcia-Valls, R., Gumí, T.: Preparation and characterization of polysulfone microcapsules for perfume release. Chem. Eng. J. **179**, 394–403 (2012). www.elsevier.com/locate/cej. Accessed 17 Oct 2018
9. Cruz, J., Fangueiro, R., Araújo, P., Araújo, F.: Estudo da durabilidade do efeito de termoregulação em malhas com materiais de mudança de fase. In: International Conference on Engineering – UBI 2011, Portugal (2011)
10. Rocha, J.A., Miranda, M.J., Andrade, M.J.: Abordagem Terapêutica das Úlceras de Pressão: Intervenções Baseadas na Evidência. Acta Médica Portuguesa **19**, 29–38 (2006)
11. Dealey, C., Lindholm, C.: Pressure ulcer classification. In: Romanelli, M., Clark, M., Cherry, G.W., Colin, D., Defloor, T. (eds.) Science and Practice of Pressure Ulcer Management, pp. 37–41. Springer, London (2006). https://doi.org/10.1007/1-84628-134-2_5
12. Papanek, V.: Design for the Real World: Human Ecology and Social Change, 2nd edn. Thames & Hudson, London (1995)
13. CITEVE (Centro Tecnológico das Indústrias Têxtil e do Vestuário de Portugal). Vestuário com acabamentos Activos (2012). http://www.citeve.pt/bin-cache/XPQC1DD5C5476DF727 3C88ZKU.pdf. Acessed 20 Oct 2018
14. Ghosh, S.K.: Functional Coatings: By Polymer Microencapsulation. Wiley-VCH, Weinheim (2006)
15. Dubey, R., Shami, T.C., Rao, K.: Microencapsulation technology and applications. Def. Sci. J. **59**(1), 82–95 (2009)
16. Neves, J.: O estado da arte dos têxteis técnicos aplicações práticas de micro e nano camadas. In: Encontro de Design e Tecnologia Têxtil, Porto Alegre (2007). http://www.nds.ufrgs.br/Paper%20Porto%20Alegre%202%5B1%5D.pdf. Accessed 17 Oct 2018
17. Cheng, S.Y., Yuen, C.W.M., Kan, C.W., Cheuk, K.K.L.: Development of cosmetic textiles using microencapsulation technology. RJTA **12**(4), 41–51 (2008)
18. Nelson, G.: Application of microencapsulation in textiles. Int. J. Pharm. **242**, 55–62 (2002)

19. Rodrigues, S.N., et al.: Microencapsulated perfumes for textile application. Chem. Eng. J. **149**, 463–472 (2009). www.elsevier.com/locate/cej. Accessed Oct 2018
20. Salem, V.: Tingimento Têxtil: fibras, conceitos e tecnologias. Blucher, São Paulo (2010)
21. Salcedo, E.: Moda Ética Para Un Futuro Sostenible. Gustavo Gili, Barcelona (2014)
22. Rossi, W.S.: Estudo de Aplicações e Testes de Durabilidade de Microcápsulas em Tecidos. Dissertação De Mestrado Escola de Engenharia Faculdade De Arquitetura Programa De Pós-gradução em Design, Porto Alegre (2012)
23. Coelho, R.F.: Produção e Caracterização de Têxteis Com Propriedades Hidratantes. Faculdade De Engenharia Da Universidade do Porto/Centro de Nanotecnologia e Materiais Técnicos Funcionais e Inteligentes (2010)

# Estimating Age-Dependent Degradation Using Nonverbal Feature Analysis of Daily Conversation

Natsumi Kana[1], Yumi Wakita[1(✉)], and Yoshihisa Nakatoh[2]

[1] Osaka Institute of Technology, Osaka, Japan
yumi.wakita@oit.ac.com
[2] Kyushu Institute of Technology, Fukuoka, Japan

**Abstract.** In this paper, we study a system that estimates the degree of decline in the driving ability of elderly people using non-verbal information from daily conversations. It is necessary for us to find the factors that would affect the calculation of the degree of decline that has reached a problematic level for functioning daily life. We focus on the cases where elderly people cannot understand their partner's speech as their hearing and concentration abilities decrease with age. We analyze the relationship between the degree of understanding of the partner's speech and the non-verbal characteristic of the response scene. Based on the results of the acoustic analysis of each utterance, the fundamental frequency (F0) and acoustic power levels of when a person can understand their partner's speech tend to be higher than those when they cannot. The analysis of the synchronization of the head motions shows that brightness value of difference image when a person can understand their partner's speech is also higher than when they cannot. These results indicate that these non-verbal factors are effective in estimating the decline in the hearing and concentration abilities of the elderly.

**Keywords:** Degree of decline · Fundamental frequency · Synchronism of motion · Understanding level

## 1 Introduction

The number of traffic accident and death for elderly people is increasing every year, the main reason being "inappropriate driving". Although there is a drop in their driving ability, some elderly people don't have consciousness of their decline. They consider that it is the same as that of their youth. Several plans for dementia prevention and health maintenance measures have been proposed. However, such tools are not actively used for elderly people who have only a slight interest in health, thereby causing the sudden occurrence of serious accidents leading to death. Therefore, it is very important for a third party to notice the decline in driving ability of the elderly and to inform them of the decrease.

We are currently working on developing a system that can estimate the degree of decline. It depends on the age of an individual and informs them when the estimated result indicates a decline. We have already determined some acoustic features that are

© Springer Nature Switzerland AG 2019
V. G. Duffy (Ed.): HCII 2019, LNCS 11582, pp. 222–231, 2019.
https://doi.org/10.1007/978-3-030-22219-2_17

effective for evaluating this age-dependent degradation. The voice of a speaker over the age of 75 has some special characteristics [1]. For example, their laughter often becomes a voiceless sound, the value of F0 is unstable, and its distribution of F0 increases. As compared to speakers under the age of 75, these differences are observed to be significant when using a t-test. Several other papers have illustrated that the acoustic features of the human voice are effective in detecting the degradation as it ages [2–4]. For example, Tanaka et al. [5] reported the formant frequency shift in elderly speech.

However, these reports only describe age-dependent degradation. They do not estimate whether the degree of decline has reached a problematic level in daily life. This study aims to explore a system that can be used to evaluate the degree of decline in the driving ability of elderly people based on their daily conversations and inform them when the estimated result indicates a decline. To create this system, it is necessary to find the factors that could affect the evaluation of the degree of decline before it becomes an illness.

Davies HR et al. conducted a survey on approximately 15,000 people over the age of 50 and found that the risk of dementia in people with moderate loss of hearing is approximately 1.6 times more than those with normal hearing ability [6]. It is a known fact that a person's hearing and concentration ability declines with age. An older person is more likely to have difficulty understanding their partner's speech. If a system can distinguish an elderly's response in such a case, it can inform them that their hearing or concentration abilities are problematic. It may prove to be effective in minimizing the incidences of dementia and depression.

We have established that the F0 value for a person who can understand their partner's speech tends to be higher than those who cannot [7]. In this paper, we add to analyze acoustic power level and synchronism of the gestures of the speakers by using the free conversation database of elderly people. The result of this analysis enabled us to suggest a method that can automatically estimate the comprehension level of a person.

## 2   Conversation Analysis

### 2.1   Free Conversation Recording

We recorded eight sets of 3-min dyadic conversations. Figure 1 shows the location of these recordings. We used two microphones and a video camera for this purpose. Figure 2 is an example photo extracted from the video data. The conditions of the recordings are listed in Table 1. The participating speakers were previously acquainted, but we paired those people who had no prior contact with each other.

### 2.2   Acoustic Analysis Method

As a method of calculating F0, an algorithm called robust algorithm for pitch tracking (RAPT) was used. RAPT realizes F0 extraction with high accuracy by postprocessing using a dynamic programming method with multiple F0 candidates obtained using a

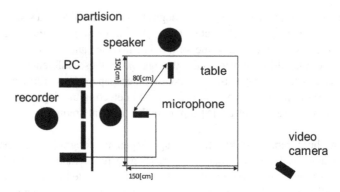

**Fig. 1.** Location of recording conversation

**Fig. 2.** Example photo extracted from the video data

**Table 1.** Conditions of conversation

| | |
|---|---|
| Number of speakers | 9 elderly speakers (5 males, 4 females) |
| Ages | 62–82 years old |
| Number of conversations | 8 conversations by 9 speakers |
| Conversation periods | Three minutes/conversation |
| Conversation condition | Free dyadic conversation |

correlation method. In RAPT, the time period to the peak of the normalized cross-correlation function shown by formula (1) taken as an F0 candidate [6]. x(n) means n-th speech signal.

$$\emptyset(m) = \frac{1}{\sqrt{e_1 e_m}} \sum_{n=1}^{N-1} x(n)w(n)x(n + |m|)w(n + |m|) \ |m| = 0, 1, \ldots, N-1 \quad (1)$$

$$e_j = \sum_{n=j}^{j+N-1} x(n)w(n) \tag{2}$$

As a method of calculating acoustic power level "$Lp$", we used the following formula (3)

$$L_p = 10 \log_{10} \left\{ \frac{1}{Tp_0^2} \int x(t)^2 dt \right\} \tag{3}$$

"$p0$" means minimum audible level, the value is 20[μPa]. "T" means the utterance period.

### 2.3    Response Motion Analysis Method

In this paper, we focus to analyze the synchronism of response motion (Ex. nodding, head swing etc.). After AD conversion, we used a frame difference method to analyze the area around head of each speaker. After extracting image sequences from the moving data, the difference images were calculated using the following formula (4). Here, $I_k$ indicates the value of the kth frame in the image sequences, $I_{k+1}$ indicates the value of the (k + 1)th frame, and the absolute difference image ID is defined as follows:

$$ID_{(K,K+1)} = |I_{K+1} - I_K| \tag{4}$$

After calculating the difference values between the frames, the difference image is converted to a grayscale image. The contributions of the three colors (red, blue, and green) were 29.9%, 11.4%, and 58.7%, respectively. Binary processing was performed on the brightness value of the difference image. A brightness value equal to or larger than the threshold value was set to 1 while that less than the threshold value was set to 0. One image dataset included two speakers. We used a mask file to separate the two speakers one by one. The sum of the brightness values of all pixels for each speaker was then calculated.

To analyzing the synchronism of the motion by each speaker, we calculate the multiplied values of the sum of brightness values for each speaker. Before calculating, we used a moving average method to the sum of brightness values of each speaker to decrease the influence of a slight time lag. The calculation values multiplied after a moving average process are used to evaluate the synchronism of the motion by each speaker.

## 3    F0 Analysis Experiments

### 3.1    Response Extraction

We listened to the recorded conversations and extracted only the responses using 8 conversations database spoken by 5 male persons. Table 2 shows the number of extracted response utterances. After extraction, we calculated the F0 of the extracted speech and excluded those whose F0 values could not be calculated.

**Table 2.** Number of extracted response utterances

|                      | "Ah" | "Uh" | "Eh" | "Oh" |
|----------------------|------|------|------|------|
| Number of utterance  | 77   | 96   | 9    | 5    |

We asked four persons to listen to the 30-second conversations, which included these response utterances, and judge the understanding level of the speakers. The judgment was performed in the following five steps: "5: He can understand the partner's speech", "4: He seems to be able to understand it", "3: I cannot say", "2: He does not seem to be able to understand it", "1: He cannot understand". We applied this 5-step evaluation to the extracted speech samples. The average value of the understanding level as the judgement results by four persons was defined as "Ave-UL".

### 3.2 Relationship Between F0 Value of Response Utterance and Understanding Level

We analyzed the F0 value of each response expression. Figure 3 shows the relation between the result of the 5-step evaluation and the average values of F0 of each utterance (Ave-F0). The F0 values are normalized by calculating the average of all F0 values of each speaker. The blue square points in Fig. 3 indicate the F0 values of the responses when the understanding level is under three, and the red round points indicate the F0 values when the understanding level is over three. The dotted line specifies the results of the regression analysis.

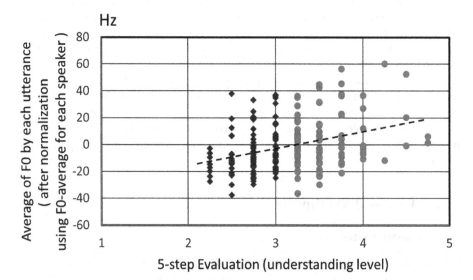

**Fig. 3.** Relationship between the Ave-F0 and the Ave-UL (Color figure online)

The results of the regression analysis indicate the Ave-F0 values when Ave-UL are low tend to be lower than those when the Ave-UL are high. But the tendency is modest.

### 3.3 Relationship Between F0 Values and Acoustic Power Levels

Figure 4 shows the relation between the "Ave-F0" and the average of acoustic power for each utterance (Ave-Power). Both of "Ave-F0" and "Ave-Power" values are already normalized by the average value for each speaker.

The response of which Ave-UL is under 2.5 was defined as **"Res-NUS"**. That means the response of the speaker when they could neither understand nor listen to the partner's speech. The response of which Ave-UL is over 3.5 was defined as **"Res-US"**. That means the response when the speaker could either understand or listen to the partner's speech.

The blue triangle points in Fig. 4 indicate the data of "Res-NUS" and the red round points indicate the data of "Res-US". The two black lines show the predicted interval calculated for the data of "Res-NUS", which has a confidence level of 95%.

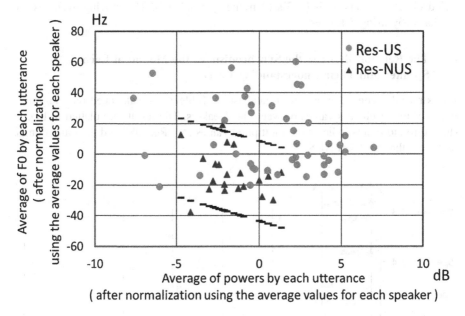

**Fig. 4.** Distribution of the Ave-F0 and the Ave-power of each speech utterance (Color figure online)

The results show the following:

- For almost of "Res-NUS", both of the "Ave-F0" and the "Ave-Power" values are under zero.

- In the case that both of "Ave-F0" and "Ave-Power" are over zero, all data are the case of "Res-US".
- The distribution when "Res-NUS" is narrower than that when "Res-US".
- Many data of "Res-US" were plotted outside of the prediction interval lines. These results illustrate the possibility that an elderly's understanding level of the partner's talk can estimate using F0 value and acoustic power level.

## 4  Brightness Analysis Experiments

### 4.1  Response Extraction

We extracted the 5 conversations from the database shown in Table 1. The extracted data included both response scenes of "Res-US" and "Res-NUS" in the same conversation. The total number of frames for "Res-US" and "Res-NUS" is 118 frames and 156 frames, respectively. These conversations were used to calculate the multiplied values of the sum of the brightness values between the two speakers. The sampling period of AD conversion is 0.33 s (3 frames per second). The moving averages are calculated by using 5 frames.

### 4.2  The Relation Between the Synchronism of the Motion of Each Speaker and Their Understanding Level

We extracted 5 conversations from database in Table 1 and calculated the multiplied values of the brightness values between the speakers. The results are platted in Fig. 5. The red round points indicate the multiplied values for "Res-US" and the blue triangle points are that for "Res-NUS".

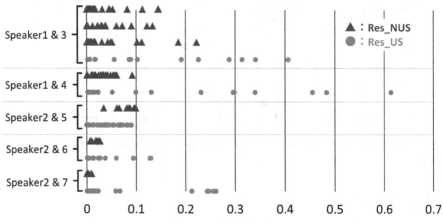

**Fig. 5.** Comparison of the synchronism degree between "Res-US" and "Res-NUS" (Color figure online)

The results are as follows:

- The multiplied values of "Res-US" tend to be greater than those of "Res-NUS".
- This tendency depends on the pair of speakers. In the case of only "Speaker2&5", the multiple values between for "Res-US" and for "Res-NUS" are almost same.
- The multiple values also depend on the pair of speakers.

To understand the reason behind the motion of a person who could not understand their partner's speech, we selected some response scenes in which the multiplied values are low and compared them to the brightness values by each speaker.

The Fig. 6(A) show the brightness values of two speakers in the case of "Res-NUS". The Fig. 6(B) show the multiplied values of the brightness values between the two speakers indicated in the Fig. 6(A). The two parts surrounded by dot lines in Fig. 6 (B) are examples that multiplied values are low. However, the brightness values of each speaker are not low (the parts surrounded by dot lines in Fig. 6(A)). This is due to the asynchronization of the motion between the two speakers when the duration for the moving average process is 5 frames.

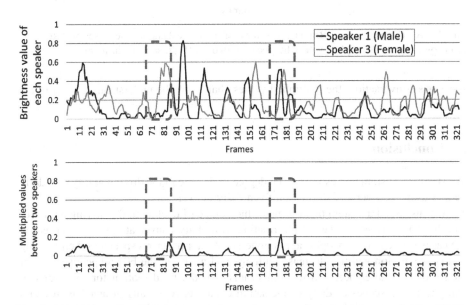

**Fig. 6.** (A) (Upper figure) Brightness values of two speakers in the case of "Res-NUS" (B) (Lower figure) Multiplied values between the two speakers, same as in figure (A).

The Fig. 7(A) show the brightness values of two speakers in the case of "Res-US". The Fig. 7(B) show the multiplied values of the brightness values between the two speakers indicated in the Fig. 7(A). Both of brightness values of each speaker are high and the multiplied values in Fig. 7(B) are also high. These are the cases which head motions are synchronized.

The conversation examples shown in Figs. 6 and 7 were spoken by the same speakers pair (speaker 1 and speaker 3). These figure suggest that even if the same

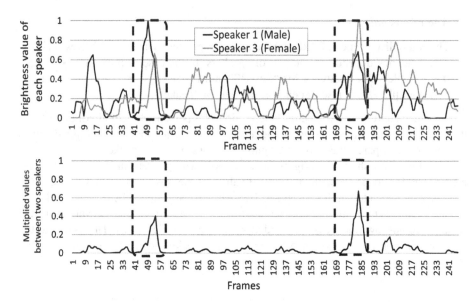

**Fig. 7.** (A) (Upper figure) Brightness values of two speakers in the case of "Res-US" (B) (Lower figure) Multiplied values between the two speakers, same as in figure (A)

speaker's conversation, the multiplied values change by the understanding level to the partner's talk.

## 5    Conclusion

We studied a system that estimates the degree of decline in the driving ability of elderly people using non-verbal information from daily conversations.

We discussed a system that estimates the degree of decline in the driving ability of elderly people using non-verbal information from daily conversations. We focused on the cases where elderly people cannot understand their partner's speech as their hearing and concentration abilities decrease with age and analyzed the F0 and acoustic power values of each utterance, and the synchronism of the head motion for each speaker using response scenes of daily conversation database. As results of analysis, it had a tendency that when understanding levels become low, both of the "Ave-F0" and "Ave-power" decreased and the synchronism of the head motion for each speaker also decrease. These results indicate that these non-verbal factors would be effective in estimating the decline in the hearing and concentration abilities of the elderly in daily life and suggest the probability of inform the degree of decline in the driving ability to elderly persons.

# References

1. Wakita, Y., Matsumoto, S.: Communication smoothness estimation using F0 information. In: 2016 Proceedings of the 4th IIAE International Conference on Intelligent Systems and Image Processing, September 2016
2. Nueller, P.B., Sweeney, R.J., Barbeau, L.J.: Acoustic and morphologic study of the senescent voice. Ear Noise Throat J. **63**, 71–75 (1985)
3. Sato, K., Sakaguchi, S., Hirano, M.: Histologic investigation of bowing of the aged vocal folds. Throat J. **8**, 11–14 (1996)
4. Nishio, M., Tanaka, Y., Niimi, S.: Analysis of age-related changes in the acoustic characteristics of the voice. Jpn. Soc. Logop. Phoniatr. **50**, 6–13 (2009)
5. Tanaka, Y., Igaue, H., Mizumachi, M., Nakatoh, Y.: Study of improvement of intelligibility for the elderly speech based on formant frequency shift. Int. J. Comput. Consum. Control (IJ3C) **3**(3), 57–65 (2014)
6. Talkin, D.: A robust algorithm for pitch tracking (RAPT). In: Kleijn, W.B., Pailwal, K.K. (eds.) Speech Coding & Synthesis, pp. 495–518. Elsevier, Amsterdam (1995)
7. Natsumi, K., Wakita, Y., Nakatoh, Y.: Changes in fundamental frequency and gesture of response corresponding to the understanding level of partner's talk. In: 2018 IEEE International Conference on Artificial Intelligence in Engineering and Technology, November 2018

# The Decision-Making System for Alzheimer's Patients by Understanding Ability Test from Physiological Signals

Peijia Liao[1], Fangmeng Zeng[1], Iwamoto Miyuki[2],
and Noriaki Kuwahara[1(✉)]

[1] Graduate School of Engineering and Science, Kyoto Institute of Technology,
Kyoto, Japan
nkuwahar@kit.ac.jp
[2] Department of Intelligence Science and Technology, Kyoto University,
Kyoto, Japan

**Abstract.** In recent years, end-of-life medical care and property allocation for Alzheimer's patients have received attention. Due to the declining birthrate and aging society, there will be more and more patients with Alzheimer's disease in the future. However, many patients with Alzheimer's disease are unable to make decisions as they wish, and people around them are also pressured to make decisions for them. Therefore, this study uses physiological signals to identify patients with Alzheimer's disease to judge understanding degree. At the same time, judge the emotional changes to help them better to express and live as they wish at the end of life. In this paper, we have improved the indistinctness of the unclear spectrogram of Brain Waves (EEG) used by the Short Time Fourier Transform (STFT), and improved the Wavelet Transform (WT) is better than STFT. We let the experimenter to solve the logical graphic questions in a specified time, collect the EEG of the experimenters and analyze it. Comparing the spectrogram of EEG when the experimenter gets the answer and judge the understood degree with CNN of Deep-learning.

**Keywords:** Alzheimer's patients · Decision making · Understanding degree · Brain waves

## 1 Introduction

### 1.1 Background

In 2017, the population of the world over 60 years old has reached 900 million. In Japan, the elderly population accounts for 27.6%, and in 2050 it may reach 2.1 billion. By then, Japanese aging population accounts will up to 37% of the total population [2]. At the same time, the cost of care for the elderly of country has also increased significantly. There will also be a large gap of health care resource and health care workers. According to statistics, 14% elderly people in 2017 suffered by Alzheimer's disease, but in less than 10 years, will increase to 20% elderly people with Alzheimer's disease. Because the cause of Alzheimer's disease is due to degenerative changes in the

V. G. Duffy (Ed.): HCII 2019, LNCS 11582, pp. 232–247, 2019.
https://doi.org/10.1007/978-3-030-22219-2_18

brain, patients with Alzheimer's disease can not be cured, and can only be prevented and maintained by medicine (Fig. 1).

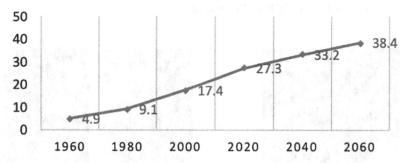

**Fig. 1.** The growth curve of the elderly people in Japan (Millions)

## 1.2 Stages of the Alzheimer's Disease

In the early stages of the Alzheimer's, and in the current situation that more and more elderly people living alone, the elderlies are not aware of their own changes by themselves. As a result, the patient does not leave medical decision and any property distribution documents when use as in accident. At the same time, the property distribution and medical choices often led to legal problems because of the failure to obtain the patient's thoughts. From a humanistic view, patients are unable to make decisions for themselves, so that in the last part of their lives, they can't live according to their own wishes [1, 3].

In the middle of the disease, because of aphasia and brain changes, they can't understand other people's words and can't express their needs through language. Therefore, at this time, did decision by the doctor and family members is the only way for the patient to solve the medical problem or the other one. However, this way is not fully meet the patient's intention usually. For example, the patient's problems how to do medical treatment or why they should be got a surgery or not etc. So that, because of they can't understand completely, when they are faced to do next decision, they will behavior negative emotions such as anxiety and fear.

## 2 Related Works

### 2.1 The Relationship Between Emotional Changes and Brain Waves

In the first year of the study, we found that emotional changes can be reflected by brain waves and heartbeats. This result consists of the signals of the central nervous system. The EEG and the heartbeat (ECG) of the autonomic nervous system. Sympathetic and parasympathetic nerves are also important components of emotions [5, 6]. We measure the EEG and ECG, and use the STFT method to extract the frequency domain features to obtain the spectrogram by python program, shows in Fig. 2(a). video pieces were labeled by per 15 s shows in Fig. 2(b). Using CNN in Deep-learning to analyze the changes of the spectrogram, CNN is used to classify the EEG changes [4]. The accuracy is 90%, the accuracy of the analyzed RRI spectrogram is 91%, and the accuracy of the EEG combined with RRI spectrogram is 93.3%. The accuracy curve for each network is as follows in Fig. 2(c) and (d).

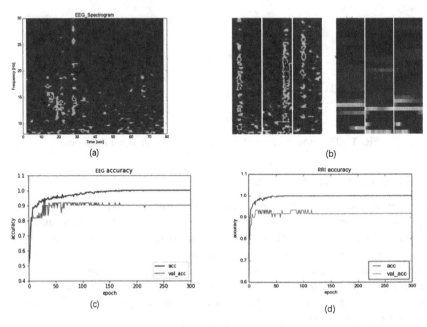

**Fig. 2.** (a) The Spectrogram of EEG data by SFTF. (b) Spectrograms of the High Arousal Class of EEG(L) and ECG(R). (c) Fig. 7. The Accuracy Curves of CNN1 for EEG Spectrograms. (d) The Accuracy Curves of CNN2 for RRI Spectrograms.

## 2.2    The Progress of Make a Decision with a Doctor

First of all, through the doctor's instructions, you must have a deep understanding of your own state with healthy and the information of a treatment plan. In order to ensure that patients have understanding ability, they need to restate their understanding through their own statements. After the doctor confirmed that they had understood it, asked them to say their opinions about their own treatment plans. The patients need the ability to compare options and have a deep understanding of the strengths and weaknesses in the treatment, and it is important that they should have a deep understanding of the risks. Finally, a comparison is made to make a decision and after compare with the doctor confirmed that they will, then the decision making will be judged [1, 3].

A medical choice is very rigorous and complex. Since some elderly people cannot explain their opinions or do not fully understand them, they will be judged as having no ability to make decisions. However, in real life, due to the doctor's explanation of the disease and treatment methods, the elderly is not fully aware of the self-state, or because the ugly and aphasia can not express their thoughts and can't explain the understanding of the problem. So an Alzheimer's elderly with the decision making ability or not are fully judged by who is talking with them. There is a large part of the unknown in the problem. It will also cause a large part of individual differences for personal reasons.

### 2.3 Uses Brain Waves to Test Human Understanding of Logical Problems

Sensual expressions such as emotions, stress can be measured by brain waves, but because of the measure difficulty in understanding problems of testing brain waves and brain activity, it's only a few data for brain waves with logic understanding. In the Nakagawa predecessor's research, although the accuracy of using the binary differentiation method is 60%, it is still proved that the measurement of the fMRI nuclear magnetic method verifies the understanding degree and the experimenter's memory, language with computer programs. Verifying the measured data in the program used by fMRI image thus to prove that the brain wave is integrated with brain activity, logical thinking, and understanding degree [7, 8].

In our study, based on physiological signals such as EEG and ECG, we successfully used deep learning methods to extract brain waves and heartbeats and analyze it. The EEG analysis consists mainly of four frequency bands: $\delta$ wave, $\theta$ wave, $\alpha$ wave, beta wave. Based on the feature extraction of ECG signals, heart rate variability (HRV) is determined by heart rate (HR) or RR interval and is calculated from R peak. The signal power in the low frequency (LF: 0.04–0.15 Hz) and high frequency (HF: 0.15–0.4 Hz) bands also seems to be closely related to emotion. The system enables the use of physiological signals to develop emotional prediction and understanding systems for Alzheimer's patients to support their interaction with caregivers and use the machine to determine the changes [9]. This is the position map of the machine when measuring the brain potential (Fig. 3).

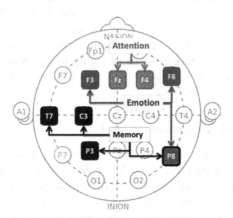

**Fig. 3.** The partial correlations of cortical functions with EEG channels.

## 2.4    Convolutional Neural Network

We use a spectrogram to first express the heartbeat interval RR transform and brain-wave transform. Colors are used to represent spectrograms with different frequencies. The convolutional neural network (CNN) is used here as a computer image recognition application. It has been proven very effective by computer vision and this is a widely used method as automatically capture the characteristics of the picture. So it can identify brainwave changes extract features efficiently [7, 8].

## 3    Experiments and Methods

### 3.1    Using the Logical Graphic Questions to Prove Logical Understanding-Ability

Logical graphic questions are often used in SPI comprehensive proficiency testing and North American IQ testing. The main ways to solve questions are to apply the rules of the graph and get answer [10–12]. Logical graphic questions include: use the rule as clockwise rotation and translation, object-centric rotation shows in Fig. 4(a), the symmetric flip, and the same element as (angle, number of corners, number of spaces, number of segments, etc.), and exclusive relation shows in Fig. 4(b), graphics addition and subtraction, the solid figure flattening shows in Fig. 4(c), the puzzle shows in Fig. 4(d). Therefore, the Logical graphic questions basically applies various logical thinking modes in the world, such as on-the-job training, admission, and other practical tests to test whether the tester has logical understanding-ability and sufficient IQ [13]. Therefore, the graphical reasoning can reflect a person's brain logical thinking activity as well as the degree of understanding.

### 3.2    The Experiment Design

The process is the first to understand the problem, the second analyze the problem, the third to express your own opinion, and finally to make choices [3]. Because the image reasoning problem can reflect a person's logical thinking ability and comprehension ability. So we focusing on thinking in a limited time, extract the brain waves in thinking process, and separate four kinds of "brain waves in don't understand (0%–25%)", "understand a little (25%–50%)", "don't fully understand (50%–75%)", "completely understand (over 75%)".

### 3.3    Participants and Experiment Protocol

Because of the difficulty of image reasoning problem, we invite healthy students to do experiment first, and use the proof of healthy brainwave as advancement [14].

We selected 12 college students with equivalent academic ability, aged 23–29, with logical thinking ability bachelors, masters and doctors as participants. The participants were five males and seven females from three countries in China, Japan and Korea. Let them to do graphical reasoning problems within five minutes.

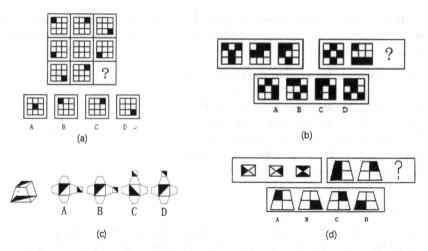

**Fig. 4.** (a) The Graphical Reasoning Question of object-centric rotation. (b) The Graphical Reasoning Question of exclusive relation. (c) The Graphical Reasoning Question of solid figure flattening. (d) The Graphical Reasoning Question of puzzle

- If participants don't understand what the mean is, the participants will be considered as giving up and extracting the brainwave of 'don't understand (0%–25%)'.
- If the participants don't give up and say the answer, if the answer is correct, it's will be considered as 'completely understand (over 75%)'.
- If the answer is incorrect, the recorder gives a hint and lets the experimenter think again. Then the participants can understand the prompt and get right answer, the brain wave at this time is used as 'don't fully understand (50%–75%)'.
- If participants still don't understand it very well after the prompt, participants need the recorder to fully explain the answer and then the participants can understand it. The brain wave at this time is used as 'understand a little (25%–50%)'.

The experiment requires the participants to say the answer immediately if he or she has the answer, but Rather than thinking over and over again [13, 15]. It is help the recorder to discover the brainwaves of the 'understood' moment. If participants can't understand anything within 2 min, the recorder will provide hints and continue the experiment, and record brainwaves until the participants understood.

### 3.4 Materials and Settings

The experiment was carried out in a laboratory environment with suitable conditions (T = 25 °C, RH = 5). The EEG and ECG signals are collected on the equipped recording PC (Dell Precision M3800. Picture reasoning was performed on a PC (HP Touch Smart). The subject sat about 50 cm away from the screen. The recorder sits opposite the subject and record all responses from the subject. At the beginning of brainwave recording, the title pictures are played and the timer is pressed. When the subject gives the answer or asks questions, the time is recorded immediately, which is convenient for the recorder to compare after the experiment. Though out the experiment, it was recorded with a video recorder, which was convenient for the recorder to compare in time after the experiment. [16–19]

- The recorder needs to record the following times:
- The time when the experiment starts;
- The time when the subject asks the question;
- The time when the subject gives the answer;
- The time when the subject gives the prompt;
- The time when the experimenter gives the answer;
- The subject r himself explained the time.

### 3.5  Experimental Device

Polymate II AP216 [24] is used to record both EEG and ECG signals. This is an integrated bio-signal recording device. Seven active electrodes are used to record the signals at a sampling rate of 1000 Hz.

The whole experiment of a subject, the brain wave of the experimenter (Right) and the time recorded by the recorder (Left) shows in Fig. 5.

**Fig. 5.**  The whole experiment of a subject

The recorder recodes the time of participant's behavior and display the monitoring instrument group: Polymate II AP216 Dell Precision M3800. It shows in Fig. 6.

Describes the electrode placement on the subject's body as a REF.E channel for the main electrode, for the acquisition of electrodes 1 and 2 for the ECG, and for the electrodes 3, 4, 5 for the EEG with two channels. (4,5 two dipole electrodes and 3 surfaces) shows in Fig. 7.

**Fig. 6.** Recodes the time and behavior of participant.

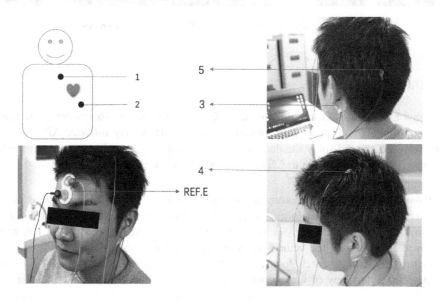

**Fig. 7.** The channel for participant.

- The data acquisition page on the measurement software AP Monitor [24] is explained. It can set the measurement conditions, main body information and monitor the waveform as the standard in the measurement process. It shows in Fig. 8.

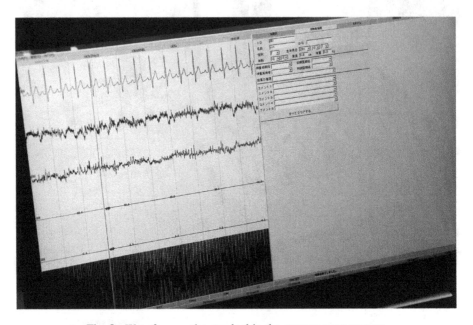

**Fig. 8.** Waveform as the standard in the measurement process.

## 4 Data Analysis

The raw ECG and EEG data measured by the Polymate II AP216 eliminates muscle tension, blinking and other small movements due to the display software AP Viewer. The software can redisplay the data waveform recorded by the instrument and export the specified part of the file to CSV format within a given period of time.

EEG Spectrogram

In the previous brain wave feature extraction, we used a short-term Fourier transform, and based on Fourier transform, we used 4-s interval and 1-s overlap in the small window for analysis. The analysis results is are clear that. The delta band (0–4 Hz) was removed to eliminate the remaining noise from pulses, neck movement, and eye blinking [25]. Our research focused on the alpha (8–14 Hz) and beta (14–30 Hz) frequencies. Frequency of various wavelengths.

### 4.1 Data Processing

Improvement of the processing method of brain wave image.

In the previous study, the short-time Fourier transform in the Fourier transform was used.

$$F(\omega) = \int_{-\infty}^{\infty} f(t)e^{-iwt}dt$$

Fourier transform in relatively non-stationary signals, the whole time-domain process is decomposed into several equal-length small spectrograms by adding panes. We use a pane every 4 s and overlap it for 3.9 s to convert the spectrogram. The converted images are shown below.

In the current study, since we need to clearly confirm the changes in the composition of the brainwaves of the experimenter, we need a clearer image. Therefore, the short-time Fourier transform is to add panes to the whole data, and then make FFT transform after narrowing. Because of the calculation method of overlapping panes, the point is calculated to be 0.1. The wavelet transform transforms the infinitely long sine and cosine functions into finite-length attenuated wavelets, which not only acquires the components of the frequency, but also accurately locates the time.

$$F(\omega) = \int_{-\infty}^{\infty} f(t)e^{-iwt}dt \qquad \Longrightarrow \qquad WT(\alpha, \tau) = \frac{1}{\sqrt{\alpha}} \int_{-\infty}^{\infty} f(t)\psi(\frac{t-\tau}{\alpha})dt$$

From the comparison of the formulas, we can see that the variables in Fourier transform are only w, and there are two variables in wavelet transform, poisoning $\alpha$ (scale) and variable $\tau$ (translation).

The sine and cosine waves of the wavelet transform (WT) are overlapped to obtain a larger value. Different from the Fourier transform, the wavelet transform not only knows which frequency components the signal has, but also knows which time domain these frequency components are embodied in. In the past, the brain waves analyzed by our analysis can clearly show the high frequency and dense frequency of the beta wave, but the performance is not very clear.

Now comparing the Fourier transform with the wavelet transform, we can find that the wavelet transform is more suitable for dealing with short-term, instantaneous sine wave changes, so the processed picture is clearer. It shows in Fig. 9 (Fre $= f * 10^3$ Hz).

In the new analysis, it is found that the wavelet transform is more suitable for processing EEG, and can suppress the concentrated noise of wave $\alpha$, and highlights the advantage of wave $\beta$, which is more obvious and effective for this experiment, and the subsequent deep learning CNN processing.

### 4.2 Experimental Results and Case Study

In this experiment, we collected brain waves of 12 people for 8 s hours. The number of data samples is 205. We conclude that wavelet transform is more suitable than Fourier

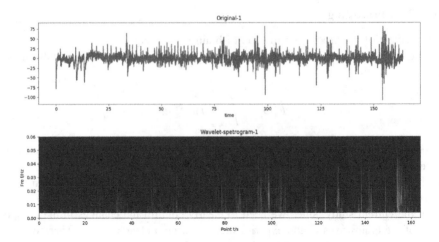

**Fig. 9.** The EEG spectrogram analyzed by WT.

transform for long-segment brain wave analysis. Wavelet transform can deal with noise, Eye, etc. more preferentially, and can clearly show the characteristics [24].

- Case A:

According to the response as the recorder and the video recording of experimenter A, we can find that when this experimenter did the first question, he did not understand the meaning correctly and could not answer the logicality of the questions, shows in Fig. 10. At this time, the brainwave α was obviously different from the wave β. When he feels stress and has an unknown problem than understood, the frequency of wave β is not particularly high, and the frequency of wave α is relatively average.

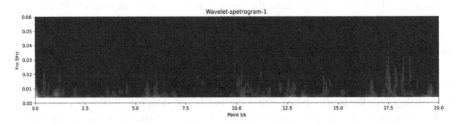

**Fig. 10.** The EEG of Experimenter A when he did the first question.

When he could solve the problems easily in the later period, and the frequency of the wave α was obviously different. The frequency of wave β is significantly higher when the experimenter solves the problem clearly.

From the Fig. 10 and the Fig. 11 a/b, we know when the experimenter couldn't understand how to solve the question, the EEG is not so clearly and will not behave with high frequency. But, when he can do it as an exercise after several questions, he can find the rule of it and understood it well with logical method (the understood EEG show in Fig. 11).

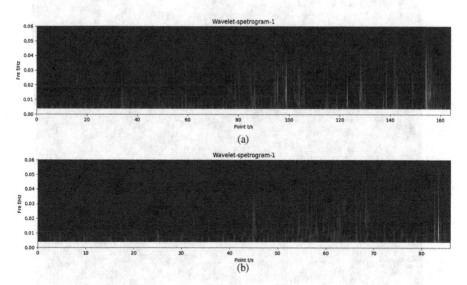

**Fig. 11.** (a) The EEG of Experiment A when he did the 2nd question. (b) The EEG of Experiment A when he did the 6th question.

Experimenter A enjoyed the experimental process and found it very interesting because he liked thinking [20, 22]. Although the first question presented a little failed, but he enjoyed the experiment process at the later stage. It was found that the experimenter's wave β was very obvious, and even wave α was close to zero.

• Case B:

In the experiment with experimenter B, she can't fully understand the structure of the question and the logic of the problem can not be correctly stated. The explanations of the experimenter B are not with completely logical. In this experiment, when the experimenter B is not fully understood by two hints provided by recorder, we can see that wave A always shows high frequency, while wave β rarely shows high frequency, shows in Fig. 12.

Experimenter B still didn't understand the logic of the questions until the 18th question and the 19th question, and could not put effective logical thinking and answers. In the 24th question and the 25th question, some β waves appeared slightly. Combine the observation and the experimenter B's answer comparison, the correct rate is only 32% in 25 questions, the explanation shows that there is low possibility to understand the logic of the question. The experimenter B's understand degree is only about 25%–35%.

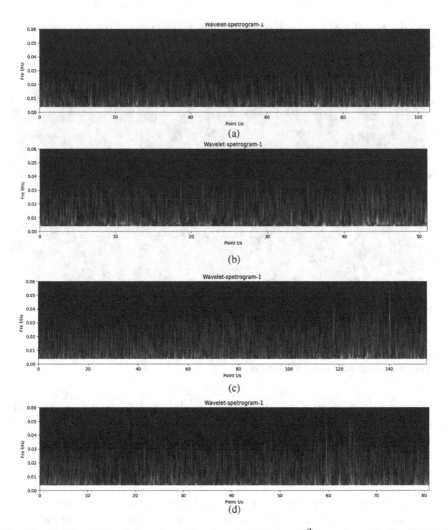

**Fig. 12.** (a) The EEG of Experiment B when he did the 18<sup>th</sup> question. (b) The EEG of Experiment B when he did the 19<sup>th</sup> question. (c) The EEG of Experiment B when he did the 24<sup>th</sup> question. (d) The EEG of Experiment B when he did the 25<sup>th</sup> question.

- Case C:

Because experimenter C was not voluntary to participate in the experiment, he felt more pressure in the whole experiment [21, 23]. Therefore, when he was passive and stressed, the frequency of wave $\alpha$ to $\beta$ transition was higher, shows in Fig. 13.

**Else Case.** Exclude a person because of personal habits, often shake the hair during the experimental so that records can not be clearly accepted, resulting in data can not be used, and the other data can be used as correct data.

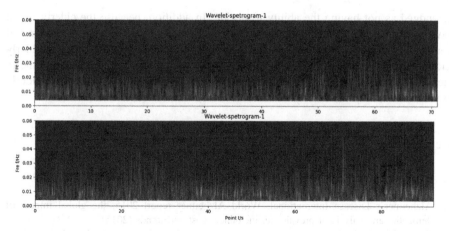

**Fig. 13.** When experimenter C feels pressure in 8$^{th}$ question.

**Result.** In this experiment, although the first few questions were not well understood, five of them could answer the following questions logically. Their brain wave characteristics were not obvious by wave B but accompanied by high-frequency wave A when the previous questions were used. In the latter questions, when we can understand the logic of the questions and answer them accurately, their high-frequency wave A decreases and high-frequency wave B appears, and the pressure is less than before.

Experiments have shown that brainwaves can capture the same person's brainwaves with clear thinking and logical thinking ability and feel pressure, which is not a particularly understandable difference between brainwaves.

When the experimenter has the ability to judge logical questions, although the brain waves are not clear when they did not understand in few questions of the forepart. But as the experiment progresses, they can make option comparisons by themselves, and the correct rate is above 80%, the understanding degree of the problem can reach 95%.

When the experimenter's own logic judgment ability and comparison ability are poor, in addition to the initial performance of the experimental pressure and can't fully understand even after given the answer. After passing the explanation of the recorder, they are still not correctly understood, and the understanding degree is about 55%, and it turns out that the correct rate of the question is 32%.

## 5 Work in the Future

We will analyses the relationship between ECG and understanding level, and use CNN for in-depth learning. Data results are also provided. Combining the same experimenter's understanding degree of different questions and the overall correct rate, Use supervised learning in deep learning to identify.

If the patient can make medical judgments through his own ideas, he or she needs a doctor to make an evaluation. At this time, it may be because the doctor's personal standards or the elderly are unable to explain because of nervousness, and then they are misjudged as not having the ability to decide. In addition, because the elderly might have problems of understanding and expression, resulting that elderly are lacking of treatment. Therefore, the machine can measure the emotional changes of the elderly and the understanding degree in that time is very important. And at the same time to measure their understanding ability, take simpler and easier explanations for the elderly to understand, help the elderly to make decisions that suit their own wishes.

# References

1. Narumoto, J.: Medical selection and decision support for persons with dementia, beginning of medical consent posposers **1**, 9–34 (2016)
2. Alzheimer's Disease International. World Alzheimer report 2015: the global impact of dementia: an analysis of prevalence, incidence, cost and trends (2015)
3. Kawasaki, Y.: Techniques for decision support assisted by nurses, nine skills and 30 techniques in decision support **2**, 22–41 (2017)
4. Hassett, J., Hisashi, H., Masahisa, K., Shoo, Y. (eds.): A Primer of Psychophysiology (1987)
5. Koyama, S., Hayashi, I.: Analysis of Kendo form from the viewpoint of respiratory phase. Res. J. Phys. Educ. Chukyo Univ. **18**(1), 57–64 (1978)
6. Inamori, Y.: Measurement and processing of heart rate, Kiyoshi Fujisawa, Shuji Kakinagi, Katsuo Yamazaki [compiled] Hiroshi Miyata [Auditorium] New and physiological psychology, vol. 1, pp. 158–171 (1998)
7. Badshah, A.M., Ahmad, J., Rahim, N., Baik, S.W.: Speech emotion recognition from spectrograms with deep convolutional neural network. In: 2017 International Conference on Platform Technology, February 2017
8. Nakagawa, T., Kamei, Y.: Quantifying programmers' mental workload during program comprehension based on cerebral blood flow measurement: a controlled experiment. In: ICSE Companion, pp. 448–451 (2014)
9. Soleymani, M., Lichtenauer, J., Pun, T., Pantic, M.: A multimodal database for affect recognition and implicit tagging. IEEE Trans. Biomed. Eng. (2012)
10. Acerbi, G., Rovini, E., Betti, S., Tirri, A., Rónai, J.F., Sirianni, A.: A wearable system for stress detection through physiological data analysis. Italian Forum Ambient Assist. Living **426**, 31–50 (2016)
11. Nakano, Y.: The insight problem solving in the puzzle game of Tangram. Bulletin of the Faculty of Education and Culture, Akita University—Educational Science, pp. 65–72 (2009)
12. Sakai, N.: Effects of chemical senses on easing mental stress induced by solving puzzles. Emot. Psychol. Res. **17**(2), 112–119 (2009)
13. Sakita, H., Takashi, H., Ito, Y., et al.: Effects of dynamic/static geometry on brain waves. Geogr. Res. **38**(Supplement1), 29–32 (2004)
14. Yamaguchi, Y., Yamaguchi, H.: Bio-informatic engineering study of fundamental learning problem solving process using electroencephalogram. Okayama University **2** (2002)
15. Tsutomu, M.: Toward the development of security evaluation method of hy-ometrics Biomedical Engineering **44** (1), 54–61 (2006)
16. Watanabe, S., Nagano, Y.: Examination of the influence on drawing subjects, heart rate and subjective feeling under observation by others. Bull. Bunkyo Gakuin Univ. Human Stud. Bull. **14**, 87–94 (2012)
17. Martin, O., Kotsia, I., Khosla, A., Kellnhofer, P., et al.: Eye tracking for everyone. IEEE (2016)

18. Saito, E., Jingu, H.: Possibilities of time-series affective evaluation to the effective design of circumstance. Trans. Jpn. Soc. Kansei Eng. **16**(1), 1–7 (2017)
19. Innami, Y., Kobayashi, T., Jung, J., et al.: An fMRI-MEG integrative method for dynamic imaging of multiple cortical activities. Trans. Jpn. Soc. Med. Biol. Eng. **44**, 777–784 (2005)
20. Nakao, Y., Tamura, T., Kodabashi, A., et al.: Orbitofrontal cortex contribution to working memory. N-back ERP study. Seitai Ikougaku **49**(6), 805–814 (2011)
21. Kiso, H., Kashiwasen, Kasamatsu, K., et al.: Changes in autonomic nervous activities before and after having an "awareness". In: The Conference Presentation of the Japan Human Engineering Society The 53rd Meeting of Japan Ergonomics Association, pp. 362–363. Institute Japan Ergonomics Association (2012)
22. Center for Educational Practice, Okayama University, **1**(1), 77–88 (2001)
23. Akira, O.: On the measurement of children's creative thinking power by graphic completion test. Nagasaki Univ. Educ. Faculty Educ. Sci. Res. Rep. **23**, 45–55 (1976)
24. Fujimoto, Y.: On the interpretation of logical thinking in mathematics and mathematics education. Bull. Faculty Educ. Ehime Univ.: Educ. 1ST **42**(2), 119–128 (1996)
25. Hadjidimitriou, S.K., Hadjileontiadis, L.J.: Toward an EEG-based recognition of music liking using time-frequency analysis. IEEE Trans. Biomed. Eng. (2012)

# Development of IoT Robotic Devices
# for Elderly Care to Measure Daily Activities

Yoshio Matsumoto[✉], Kunihiro Ogata, Isamu Kajitani,
Keiko Homma, and Yujin Wakita

Human Augmentation Research Center,
National Institute of Advanced Industrial Science and Technology (AIST),
6-2-3 Kashiwa-no-ha, Kashiwa, Chiba 277-0882, Japan
{yoshio.matsumoto,ogata.kunihiro,isamu.kajitani,
keiko.homma,wakita.y}@aist.go.jp
https://unit.aist.go.jp/harc/

**Abstract.** Various robotic devices for elderly care have been developed and commercialized in Japan. However, the introduction of such devices to the society has not been enough. One of the major reasons for this is that it is still not clear how we can best make use of them. In other words, we still do not have sufficient knowledge and evidences of such devices in the viewpoint of the benefit. Therefore, we started a project in which IoT (sensing and data communication) functions are embedded in the robotic devices to measure the activity of the users; how, when, where they are utilized by whom. It is also important to record the activities of caregivers. By utilizing developed devices, the activity data of elderly people in care facilities can be collected and analyzed in order to investigate the effective ways of device utilization. We are also using the receipt data of long-term care insurance to investigate the effect of welfare devices (including some of the robotic devices) covered by the insurance. Quantitative benefits of utilizing welfare devices in the viewpoint of the outcome in care will be shown.

**Keywords:** Evaluation · Robotic devices for nursing care · Big data ·
Outcome in care

## 1 Introduction

In Japan, more than 25% of the population is over the age of 65. The population of other advanced countries is also rapidly aging [1]. In order to solve such a social problem by improving the QoL (Quality of Life) of the elderly persons, and reducing the workload of the care givers, the robotic devices for elderly care have been intensively developed [2, 3]. However, these robotic devices have not become common in the care facilities yet. One of the major reasons is that the evaluation of the benefits insufficient and it is not clear how we can best use of the devices. To clarify the benefit of robotic devices, it is necessary to collect the usage data of devices and quantify its effect on the elderly care. Therefore, we started a project on "measurement, analysis

V. G. Duffy (Ed.): HCII 2019, LNCS 11582, pp. 248–263, 2019.
https://doi.org/10.1007/978-3-030-22219-2_19

and intervention technology of functioning of the elderly using care robots as probes" funded by NEDO (New Energy and Industrial Technology Development) in 2017.

## 2 Concept and Outline of the Project

### 2.1 Measurement of Daily Activities of the Elderly

In this project, IoT (sensing and data communication) functions are embedded in the robotic devices to measure the activity of the users [4]; how, when, where they are utilized by whom. This means that robotic devices work as assistive devices for elderly people and works as sensing probes for daily activities of the elderly people at the same time. The basic concept is shown in Figs. 1 and 2. We utilize off-the-shelf robotic devices for elderly care such as transfer aids, mobility aids which are commercialized from our previous project with companies. We additionally install sensing and data communication functions. Such as transfer aids, mobility aids in order for such devices to be able to collect activity data of daily living. The collected data can be analyzed and utilized for the feedback to realize better usage of the device for individuals, and to realize better function of the devices.

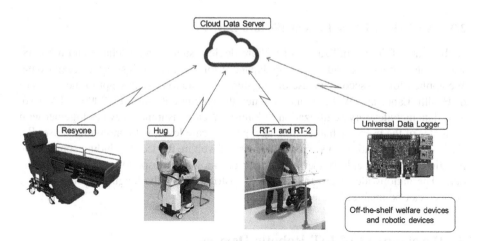

**Fig. 1.** IoT robotic devices for elderly care

### 2.2 Measurement of Care Activities of Care Staffs

It is also important to know what kind of care activities are given by care staffs. We thus developed a wearable-type sensing device to measure the care activities of the caregivers working at care facilities. An "e-skin" by made by Xenoma in which multiple strain sensors are embedded was utilized to measure many actions. Then the deep neural network was utilized to build a function to estimate various postures and actions.

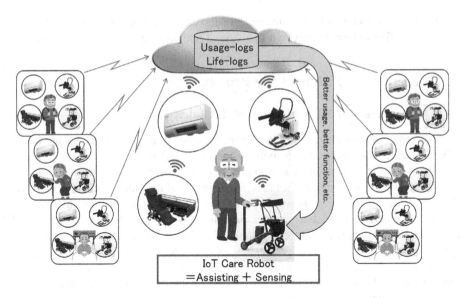

**Fig. 2.** Concept of IoT robotic device

### 2.3 Analysis of Usage Data of Welfare Devices

As big data of device utilization of welfare devices such as wheelchairs and rollators, we are also collecting and analyzing Japanese long-term care insurance receipt data. We applied for the secondary use of long-term care nationwide receipt to the Ministry of Health, Labor and Welfare, and obtained the receipt data from FY2006 to FY2016. This data includes service utilization of long-term care insurance services together with attributes of the users such as region, age, gender, care level, with anonymized user ID. Each usage information on the rental services of welfare devices (including some of the robotic devices for elderly care) by a user per month corresponds to a receipt in the data. The nationwide macro trend such as distribution of the length of using welfare devices can be analyzed based on the data.

## 3 Development of IoT Robotic Devices

### 3.1 Development of IoT Assistive Walker

We added logger functions to the assistive walker, RT.1 and RT.2 (RT.Works co., ltd.). The log of walking will be sent to the cloud server system. We have constructed five RT.1 and five RT.2 with the logger function. The information which is sent to the cloud server system is as follows:

- Grip force at a handle (RT.1 only),
- Remaining battery capacity,
- Acceleration (front-back, right-left),
- Angular velocity,

- Velocity,
- Motor current,
- Position (longitude and latitude),
- Total moving distance,
- Number of steps user walked,
- Moving periods per minute.

In order to visualize the collected data from the robot, we developed walking map viewer which shows the recorded data during walking and the walking route. The screen capture image is shown in Fig. 3.

**Fig. 3.** Walking map viewer

## 3.2 Development of IoT Rise Assisting Robot

Resyone Plus is the rise assisting robotic bed made by Panasonic corporation [5]. The half of the bed can transform into a wheelchair by pressing a button on a controller. By utilizing the device, one caregiver can let a person on a bed to depart from the room without making a transfer a wheelchair, even if the person is in rather severe condition. It was modified to have logging function to know how often the device was actually utilized. The operation logs (back rising, foot rising, height control and transformation into wheelchair) together with user's activities (heartbeat, breath, body motion on the bed) and the location of the wheelchair (beacon location) can be measured.

### 3.3    Development of IoT Watch over Sensor

The silhouette watch-over sensor by KING TSUSHIN KOGYO CO., LTD. was modified to have logging function. It can record care receiver's status data (such as lying on the bed, rinsing up, departure from the bed) and their message history and the silhouette image on the local server in the care facility. Then the local server can send the data periodically to the outside cloud server. An application software for data analysis running on a PC was developed to visualize the users' life patterns such as wake-up time, bed time and sleeping hours from the collected data. By this additional function, the system was extended from a safety monitoring sensor to a lifelog system.

### 3.4    Development of IoT Rise Assisting Robot

The rise assisting robot, Hug T1-01 by Fuji Corporation, is a commercially available robotic device for assisting rising and transferring from a bed to a wheelchair etc. without manual lifting by the caregiver. We have added a logging system to Hug to record the operation log. The logging board is installed on the main control board of the original system, and the operation log is recorded on the SD card and sent to the cloud server.

### 3.5    Development of General-Purpose Logger for Robotic and Welfare Devices

In order to collect log data from robotic devices which cannot be modified to embed logging function inside, a universal data logger system was developed. The logger system consists of main control board and various sensor modules. The logger is attached to a robotic device externally, and measures various information depending on the purpose. It can also be utilized to collect log data from conventional welfare and assistive devices such as hoist and wheelchair. Various sensor modules are provided and can be selectively connected to the main board was shown in Fig. 4. It can upload the measured data to the cloud server via WiFi mobile router.

The main board is RaspberryPi 3 and the Linux runs on the board. Each sensor module consists of a compact processor (nRF52 Bluefruit LE) and a set of sensors. We have developed five types of sensor modules as follows:

- A vital data measurement module catches vital signals from a human body,
- A motion data measurement module measures human body movement,
- A localization module measures position in outdoor environment,
- A chemical data measurement module measures chemical information related with excretion,
- A communication data measurement module measures communication information with social robots.

The outdoor localization module include a GPS board connected via UART to main module to measure data. Communication speed is 9600 bps. The data is sent every 1 s. GPS sensor outputs location data in NMEA format and the current position in longitude and latitude can be calculated from the data.

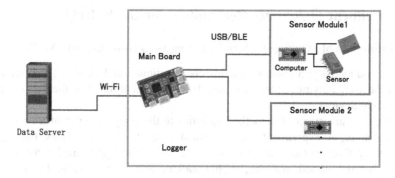

**Fig. 4.** General-purpose logger.

### 3.6 Development of Cloud Server System for IoT Robotic Devices

We have developed the recording system of IoT robotic devices for elderly care to the cloud server system. This function is extension of the care recording system for the care givers with smart phone which was also developed at AIST. The system application which involves the initial registration for the system operation and management of record on a personal computer is implemented as a web application and controlled via web browser on a personal computer. The IoT robotic devices which communicate with the cloud server has a special SIM card provided by SORACOM corporation. The data communication is made with the mobile phone line which is directory connected with AWS (Amazon Web Service), thus without using the internet. Both of the ID/PASSWORD and the special SIM card which consist of the destination and authentication information are required during the connection. In addition, the data communication between each robotic device and the server is encrypted by HTTPS protocol end to end. This safety process achieves secure data connection and wire-tapping is impossible. Figure 5 shows the outline of the system for data collection.

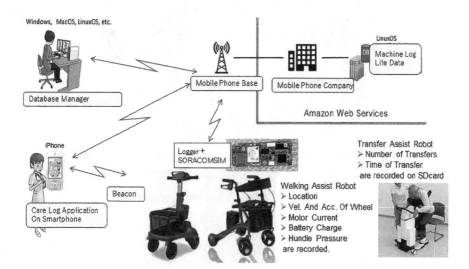

**Fig. 5.** Outline of the data collection scheme.

## 4  Experiment of Activity Recognition for the Elderly

### 4.1  Estimation of Walking Pattern from Log Data from Assistive Walker

We have conducted preliminary experiments to estimate and classify the body functions of the user, activities of the user, and the environment based on the data collected from robotic devices.

In order to investigate the method to estimate the body function of a user of the assistive walker, an experiment was performed using RT.2 by RT.works. Participants were healthy three persons in their 40's and 50's. They performed three walking patterns: Normal smooth walking, shuffle walking and limp walking. The measured sensor data collected in the experiment was acceleration from embedded sensor in RT.2. Figure 6 shows is the experimental environment. A slope (up and down) exists in the middle of the course.

From the sensor data collected in the course, the walking motion was classified into three patterns. The sensor value was rather vibrational, thus it was integrated into velocity, and it was classified by multi class SVM. The result is shown in Fig. 7. The upper is normal smooth walking, middle is shuffle walking and the lower is limp walking. The horizontal axis shows the estimated result. Three bars in each graph corresponds to the normal waling (left), the shuffle waling (middle), and the limp walking (right) respectively. From the result, the recognition of normal walking was quite successful, while discrimination of shuffling and limping walking has rather lower success rate.

**Fig. 6.** Experimental environment for walking pattern recognition.

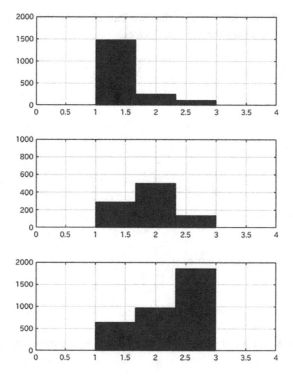

**Fig. 7.** Result of classification of walking pattern by SVM (upper: smooth walking, middle: shuffling, lower: limping)

## 4.2 Estimation of Activities from General-Purpose Logger

Graphs in Fig. 8 show examples of measured data in preliminary experiment with the developed logger. The cloud server can receive the data and stores it in the SQL database. The data was sent in JSON format. In the experiment, a vital data measurement module, a motion data measurement module and a localization module are utilized, and the data was stored every 10 s.

The subject in the experiment started walking from the 4th floor of our research center, walked down through stairs to the 1st floor and went outside. Then he took a rest for a few minutes and walked into a different entrance of the same building. Then he walked back to the initial room through the stairs. Upper left graph in Fig. 8 shows the heartbeat. Middle left graph shows the sweating (humidity). Lower left graph shows the angular velocity. Upper right graph shows the longitude. Middle right graph shows the latitude. Lower right shows the trajectory at vertical longitude and horizontal latitude. Between 200 s. and 500 s. the longitude and the latitude are taken. The participant seems to go out at that time. Between 300 s. and 400 s. the heartbeat and longitude and the latitude match well with each other. Then it can be seen from the graph that he took a rest. After 550 s. the angular velocity increases rapidly, which means that he climbed the staircase quickly. The heartbeat increased at the same time. As a result, it was shown that users' motion and situation can be measured simultaneously with this logger, and that we can estimate the users activities with general-purpose while using the robotic devices.

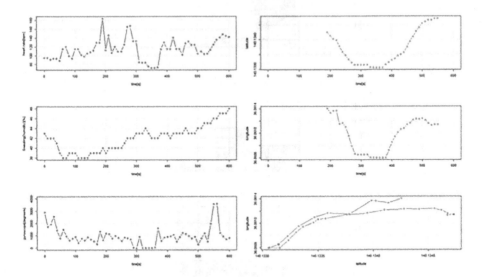

**Fig. 8.** Examples of measured data using general-purpose logger.

## 5  Development of Measurement Method for Care Activities of Caregiver

### 5.1  Hardware System

The physical burden of caregivers is an important outcome index of care activities. To observe the caregivers' behavior changes with the robotic devices, we developed a method based on a motion measurement suit (e-skin) made by Xenoma.

The e-skin is a cloth with strain sensors. Only thin and soft materials are used to construct the suit, therefore a caregiver will be able to perform daily task as usual. There are 14 strain sensors on the breast, back, shoulder, upper-arm and lower-arm as shown in Fig. 9. There is a hub device at the breast for transmitting measured data via Bluetooth to external device such as a smartphone. The hub includes 3-axis acceleration sensor and 3-axis angular velocity sensor.

The characteristic of strain sensors utilized in the sensor suit is non-linear and has large hysteresis. Figure 10 indicates the relationship between the sensor value and the joint angle. Therefore, simple estimation of the joint angles from the sensor data will have measurement errors of more than 10°. To solve this problem, we adopt convolutional neural network (CNN). The regression model is derived by the CNN between 14 sensors data and joint angle vector. Figure 11 indicates the proposed calculation model.

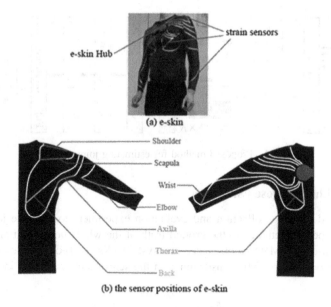

(a) e-skin

(b) the sensor positions of e-skin

**Fig. 9.** Hardware configuration of e-skin sensor suit

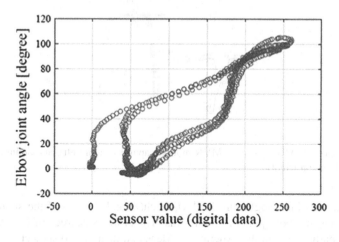

**Fig. 10.** Characteristics of a strain sensor

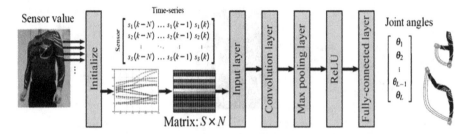

**Fig. 11.** Proposed method for estimating joint angles.

## 5.2    Algorithm for Pose Estimation

We performed the data collection and evaluation experiment to estimate joint angles using the proposed method. As the ground truth of the whole-body joint angles, joint angles measured by MVN motion capture system (Xsens Technologies B.V.) was utilized. The position of IMU sensor units on the sensor suite is shown in Fig. 12.

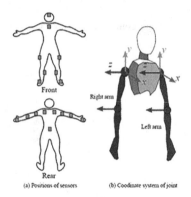

**Fig. 12.** Position of IMU sensors of MVN motion capture system (left), and definition of joint angles for estimation (right)

The estimated joint angles are Roll(x), Pitch(z) and Yaw(y) of the shoulders and bending angles at elbow joints in both arms. Therefore, 8 degrees of freedom. Three adult males participated in the experiment. Measured data of two subjects (A, B) were utilized as teaching data. The third data taken from participant (C) was utilized as test data. We evaluate the estimated joint angles. Measured motions are elbow's flexion and extension, arm up-down in the sagittal plane, arm up-down in the frontal plane, and random motion. With the MATLAB neural Network Toolbox, we derived CNN estimator to investigate the learning convergence.

Figure 13 show the learning curves with different parameters for data length and different layer number. The learning curve does not change for the data length over 50. Therefore, the length of the data utilized for the estimation was set as 50. In the same

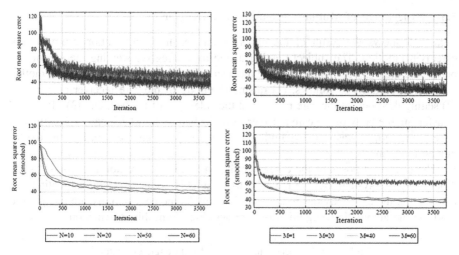

**Fig. 13.** Learning curves with different data length (left) and different layer number (right)

manner the number of layers was determined as 40. We construct the estimator with above parameters.

The estimated joint angles are shown in Fig. 14. The blue lines indicate estimated values and the red lines indicate measured values. From these graphs, it was confirmed that it is possible to estimate the posture of the person wearing the sensor suit. The list of root-mean-square error of the estimated and measured joint angle shown in Table 1. Right side of the table shows average errors. The errors for X axis of the shoulder is the smallest and the errors for Z axis is the largest among estimated joint angles.

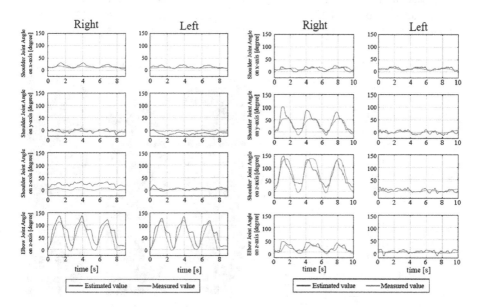

**Fig. 14.** Estimated joint angles in elbow joint and shoulder joint. (Color figure online)

## 5.3    Experiment of Motion Estimation of Caregiver

Figure 15 shows the result of the experimental result of the motion estimation of caregiving motion. The subject playing a role of a caregiver wearing the sensor suit performed the transfer motion of a care receiver from a bed to a wheelchair. The motion includes three tasks as follows: (1) raising the body of the care receiver on the bed, (2) setting the body of the care receiver at the side edge of the bed, and (3) lifting and transferring the body of the care receiver from the bed to the wheelchair. The estimated pose of the subject was visualized utilizing Unity graphics engine with Kyle model for human modeling.

The estimated poses of the caregiver shown in Fig. 15 are not as accurate as the motion capture system, but we regard it to be sufficiently accurate for estimating and recognizing the care activities in the care domain. As the next step, we are planning to work on the automatic recognition of care activities from this information.

**Table 1.** Root-mean-square error of joint angle estimation.

| | Bending elbow [deg] | Stretching arm on sagittal plane | | Stretching arm on lateral plane | | |
|---|---|---|---|---|---|---|
| | | Right [deg] | Left [deg] | Right [deg] | Left [deg] | RMSE of all data |
| Right shoulder on $x$-axis | 3.89 | 6.19 | 4.61 | 13.6 | 7.24 | 7.11 |
| Right shoulder on $y$-axis | 4.56 | 15.2 | 6.24 | 21.6 | 7.51 | 11.0 |
| Right shoulder on $z$-axis | 17.4 | 18.2 | 11.7 | 21.2 | 17.7 | 17.3 |
| Right elbow | 19.5 | 9.97 | 6.42 | 16.3 | 10.8 | 12.6 |
| Left shoulder on $x$-axis | 5.69 | 3.63 | 11.4 | 4.39 | 12.4 | 7.51 |
| Left shoulder on $y$-axis | 6.55 | 5.44 | 12.8 | 6.47 | 15.7 | 9.41 |
| Left shoulder on $z$-axis | 4.25 | 5.73 | 28.2 | 5.19 | 24.6 | 13.6 |
| Left elbow | 17.7 | 5.75 | 14.0 | 8.57 | 17.5 | 12.7 |

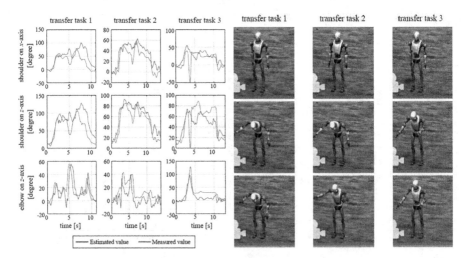

**Fig. 15.** Estimated joint angles and posed for transferring motion in care.

# 6   Analysis of Utilization of Assistive Device in Long-Term Care Insurance Receipt Data

## 6.1   Long-Term Care Insurance

In Japan, universal health coverage for long-term care was introduced in 2000 under the Long-Term Care Insurance (LTCI) system [6]. People aged $\geq 65$ years old are entitled to receive long-term care services at home or in facilities, irrespective of income level and availability of family caregiving. Under the permission from the Ministry of Health, Labor and Welfare (MHLW) for the secondary use of the receipt data for research, we accessed the nationwide receipt data from FY2006 to FY2015. The data includes all care payment statement for preventive care service, daily life support service, and institutional care service. Each receipt corresponds to monthly payment of the care service utilized with the attribute information of the user such as anonymized ID, living area, age, gender, care level.

## 6.2   Analysis of Utilization of Assistive Devices Under Long-Term Care Insurance

The collected care insurance receipt data includes information about rental service for assistive devices such as care beds, wheelchairs. Recently, some of the robotic devices for elderly care have been covered by the long-term care are insurance. parts of the care equipment. With the receipt data, we are investigating the method to calculate the indices for the outcome in care domain related with the utilization of assistive devices such as the change of care level, the period of living at home, and cost for the care service.

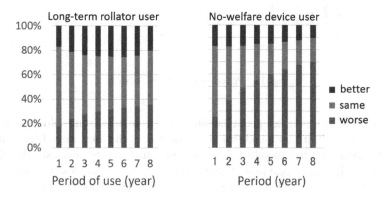

**Fig. 16.** Effect of long-term rollator utilization on the change of care level.

The left graph in Fig. 16 indicates the change of the care level of rollator users in care level 2. Typically, an elderly person in care level 2 has difficulties in rising and gait, and partial or complete support is needed in toileting, bathing. The right graph corresponds to the elderly people who did not use any assistive device but use other services in long-term care insurance. From this figure, it can be noticed that long-term rollator users tend to keep their care level, and the difference becomes larger after years. Eight years after the first use of the device, the ratio of people getting worse in care level is 35% for rollator users, while that for non-device users is 70%. The ratio of getting better in care level is also higher for rollator users.

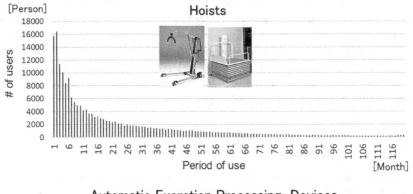

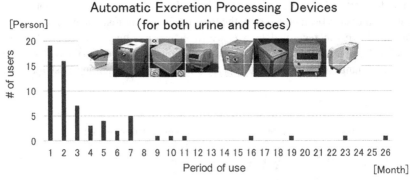

**Fig. 17.** Period of use of care devices.

We also have investigated about the duration of care device utilization as shown in Fig. 17. As a result, it was found that about the half of the hoist users kept using the device for more than five months, while more than half of automatic excretion device (for both of urine and feces) kept stopped utilization in two months. This means, the hoist is much more useful than automatic excretion device for keeping the elderly people to stay and live in their own home.

## 7  Conclusion

We have developed IoT robotic devices for elderly care which have additional function to measure the activity of the user and to send the data to cloud server. We have also developed a sensor suit to measure the activities of the caregivers. We are now collecting the activity data in care facilities. We have also collected "big data" of long-term care insurance receipt and analyzed the usage of various welfare devices (including some of the robotic devices) covered by the insurance. Quantitative benefits of utilizing the robotic devices and welfare devices in the viewpoint of the outcome in care will be shown in the future.

## References

1. United Nations: World population prospects the 2012 revision (2013). https://esa.un.org/unpd/wpp/publications/Files/WPP2012_HIGHLIGHTS.pdf
2. Hirukawa, H.: Overview of robotic devices for nursing care project. In: 2017 Proceedings of AAATE Conference, pp. 449–456 (2017)
3. Matsumoto, Y.: Development and introduction of robotic devices for elderly care in Japan. In: IEEE ICRA 2018 Workshop on Elderly Care Robotics – Technology and Ethics (WELCARO), Brisbane (2018)
4. Simoens, P., Dragone, M., Saffiotti, A.: The internet of robotic things: a review of concept, added value and applications. Int. J. Adv. Robot. Syst. 1–11 (2018)
5. Kume, Y., Tsukada, S., Kawakami, H.: Development of safety technology for rise assisting robot Resyone Plus. Trans. JSME **85**(869) (2018). (in Japanese)
6. Iwagami, M., Tamiya, N.: The long-term care insurance system in Japan: past, present, and future. JMA J. **1**(2), 67–69 (2019)

# "Memes" UX-Design Methodology Based on Cognitive Science Regarding Instrumental Activities of Daily Living

Hiroyuki Nishimoto[1]([⊠]), Tomoyoshi Koyanagi[2], Makoto Sarata[3],
Ayae Kinoshita[4], and Mitsukazu Okuda[5]

[1] Kochi University, Nankoku City, Japan
Hiroyuki.nishimoto@kochi-u.ac.jp
[2] University of Tsukuba, Tsukuba City, Japan
[3] Advanced Scientific Technology & Management Research Institute of Kyoto,
Kyoto City, Japan
[4] Kyoto University, Kyoto City, Japan
[5] memes2, Co. Ltd., Ikoma City, Japan

**Abstract.** "Memes" design methodology was developed by Mitsukazu Okuda as a practical UX-design method. In the original, it was developed to analyze our cognitive process on usability testing for electric appliances. This approach is based on several key assumptions, including: people understand things through mental models in their minds; the mental model is evoked based on the context; in the mind, information input multimodally and the mental model formed by them are related and the whole structured knowledge is called "schema"; the schema consists of associations evoked by sensing signals; after sensing, evoking, and structuring are processed sequentially, it comes to understanding; the design thinking for designers goes in the opposite direction of the stream line of cognitive process for users. This method will be applied to the improvement of IADLs for the elderly because as science and technology continue to advance, there will be elderly people left behind. In a sense, they will desire an old-style instrumental tool that they are familiar with. One of the solutions is to change the interface design to the old-style in appearance without changing the function of the tool. This design concept is for specific people to use a tool with appropriate way by old-time interface design in their old memories. It is not a universal design because it cannot work for younger people who do not know the old-style interface design. it is so-called "the retrospective design" since the previous interface design is used instead of new interface design. In that way, this design method is useful for the elderly.

**Keywords:** User experience design · Mental model ·
Instrumental activities of daily life · Retrospective experience design

© Springer Nature Switzerland AG 2019
V. G. Duffy (Ed.): HCII 2019, LNCS 11582, pp. 264–273, 2019.
https://doi.org/10.1007/978-3-030-22219-2_20

# 1 "Memes" UX-Design Methodology

## 1.1 From UI-Design for Easy to Use to UX-Design for Comfortable Space-Time

UX-design stands for "User eXperience design" [1] based on user interface design (UI-design) [2]. The UI-designer has been focusing on making a good shape with easy to use. Their goal is to make a more efficient way to reduce waste time. On the other hand, UX-designer focuses on making user's good time by means of design. Therefore, the UX-designers make users to spend a comfortable time which might be regarded as wasted time on the UI-design side. In this paper, we will describe a user-experience design method for developing the retrospective experience design.

## 1.2 A Basic Concept of Analyzing a Cognitive Process

"Memes" design methodology was developed by Mitsukazu Okuda as a practical UX-design method. In the original, it was developed to analyze our cognitive process on usability testing for electric appliances. It was father sophisticated in the field and applied analyzing way of looking things in the diverse culture, as well as in the future vision creation. In this thesis, we focus on the cognitive process which is the origin of this method. This approach is based on several key assumptions, including:

(1) People understand things through mental models in their minds.
(2) The mental model is evoked based on the context.
(3) In the mind, information input multimodally and the mental model formed by them are related and the whole structured knowledge is called "schema."
(4) The schema consists of associations evoked by sensing signals.
(5) After sensing signals, evoking assumptions, and structuring schema are processed sequentially, it comes to understanding.
(6) The design thinking for designers goes in the opposite direction of the stream line of cognitive process for users.

For example, the Fig. 1 shows a cognitive process when a user looks at a Japanese teacup and understands the author's concept. This method separates a cognitive process into four steps which are sensing signals, evoking associations, structuring schema and understanding a concept. In the first step, he finds a small crack make by design. After recognizing it, he starts to search a semantic meaning. In the second step, he evokes various, nearly infinite associations from the crack. In the third step, he starts to search a message from the author by checking his memory of culture, protocol, or common sense. In the last step, if he gets some information regarding a love story such as this title, he can successfully reach the author's idea, "a lost love."

In general, a title works as the most powerful sign in fine art. Besides we must consider collective effect of multiple signs at the step of evoking. Since we have various association in the step of evoking, a designer needs to consider it to drive us to one concept. A good designer arranges multiple signs to work together efficiently.

Since a cognitive process goes through at a moment, we are not aware of each step. However, this method can analyze a brain activity in each step. That makes clear stream line of synergy process. Since we can easily find out which step makes a trouble on an interruption of cognitive process by using this method, we improve the interface design appropriately.

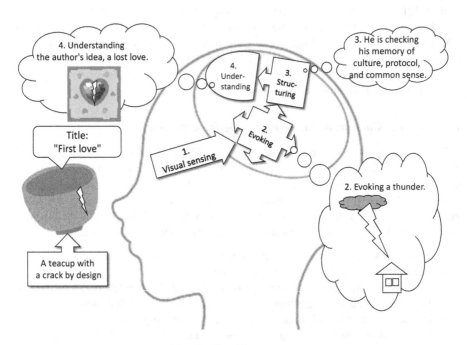

**Fig. 1.** Cognitive process

### 1.3    People Understand Things Through Mental Models

How do people feel and understand information? How is the understanding formed in the final step of the "Memes" UX-design method? In cognitive science, the mental representation is an image drawn in the mind and called a mental model. This mental model is a very important concept for designers. When people understand things, it is rare to directly grasp actual things. Instead, thoughts work through individual mental models drawn by individuals. The audience associates from the keyword, creates a mental model from his own experience, uses it to supplement the information, and finally understands the intention of the speaker. For example, from an apple as a keyword, a person thinks of eating it, another person thinks of an apple stuck with an arrow.

An excellent designer essentially understands the mechanism that transmits intended codes to recipients as analogies, generates their mental models, and leads them to the intended action. In other words, the designer creates empathy/ understanding by rebuilding the mental model of each user. The stream line of the thinking process for designers goes in the opposite direction of the sequential cognitive process. It is so-called design thinking.

### 1.4 Symbolization Strategy

As shown in Fig. 2, if a person sympathizes with a new design, it will be symbolized and that will make a shortcut in the brain. The recognition time will be shortened by symbolization. In other words, if a new design becomes a symbol, a person will reach the concept in a moment. A road sign is a good example. It is led that once a customer creates a mental model by symbolization, he accepts the message with no qualification [3]. That is applied to a branding strategy such as Apple logo on Mac OS. The logo design is not fixed, it retains its contour as an afterimage, changing from red to silver with the times. Keeping a sense of confidence in the brand, it stimulates our brain that tends to be bored comfortably.

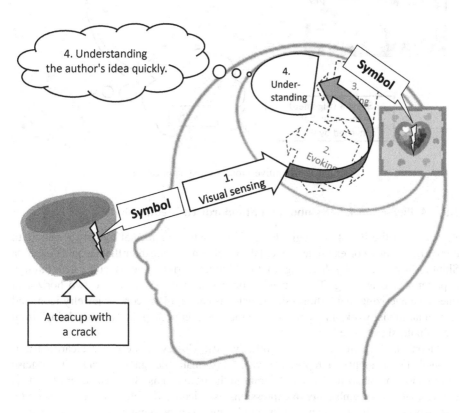

**Fig. 2.** Symbolization process

Another design strategy is found in a front grill design of Rolls-Royce motor cars as illustrated in Fig. 3. Originally, only the Parthenon's facade was a status symbol. In this case, the Parthenon's facade is called "Signifant" in French. The status of "Royalty" is called "Signifie" in French. Once a user accepted the front grill design as the status symbol, the Rolls-Royce motor car itself was changed into the status symbol as shown in the dotted arrow. It is led that symbolization can be used for creating a new design.

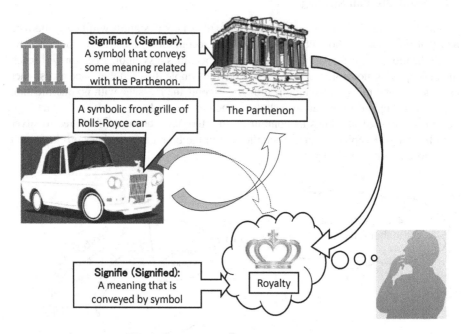

**Fig. 3.** Cognitive process on symbolization

## 1.5   A Pictogram Is a Symbol of a Standardized Mental Model

As shown in the Fig. 4, strategic design is to control the mental model for people to recognize things. For example, a mental model is an association that reminds us of "a Shinto shrine gate" by listening to the "Shinto shrine" and is cultivated through experience and learning. The structure composed of two vertical and two horizontal lines characterizing that "Shinto shrine gate" is called a key icon, or jewelry icon, and its mental model works in people's consciousness, reminding the "Shinto shrine" from the "Shinto shrine gate."

"Icon" and "pictogram" are similar words. However, these are clearly distinguished. For example, a representative of informatic design that transmits concise information in a short time is a pictogram in the traffic signs. Since an accurate code is defined, there is no ambiguity in expressions like "icon". Therefore, the explanation by text is necessary for the icon, but the explanation can be omitted in the pictogram.

In Japan, since the "Shinto shrine" is easily associated from "Shinto shrine gate", we understand "Shinto shrine gate" as one of the mental models of "Shinto shrine" and recognize that the key icon characterizing the frame of "Shinto shrine gate". Extracting this feature, pictogram of map symbol was designed.

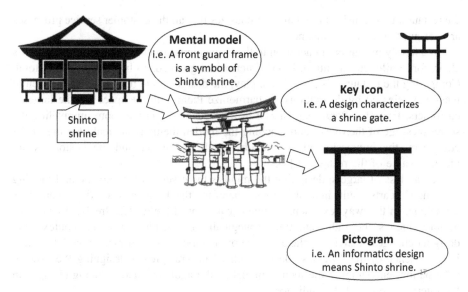

**Fig. 4.** A pictogram of shinto shrine

## 1.6 How the Schema Works to Help Understand

Schema in cognitive science refers to an abstract group of knowledge. For example, we use the schemas to determine to classify if a penguin belongs to a bird schema. In computer technology, it is also a term meaning a database structure. Based on this idea, it is easy to understand that various things in the world are classified by the schema. The level of understanding depends on the precision of the schema. If the schema in the brain has rich words, you can understand things more correctly.

For example, in Japan surrounded by the ocean, schemas related to fish are very developed. The number of words related to fish is extremely large compared to other countries. From a long time, Japanese people are interested in fish. In other words, the ontology, the hierarchical structure of the words, is substantial in terms of their interests. It is same reason why names of fry and adult fish are different in Japan, and why names of part of beef are enriched in Europe and the United States.

Schema of specialized field is called "domain". In the same expert group, since technical terms in the same domain are shared, they can easily obtain a consensus. On the contrary, it is common that groups with different domains cannot communicate at all. For example, even if a lecturer transmits "study", the audience who gathered at the conference understand this as "research", which is understood as "learning" at a high school. The meaning of a word is not determined by itself but by the audience domain.

## 1.7 Movement of One's Mind Creates Action

In order to increase sales of a restaurant, it is not enough to have delicious menus side by side. As a matter of course, a design consultant regards that the concept and menu of the restaurant are consistent, but also emphasizes that all the customer service processes are designed in a unified manner.

In a family restaurant, in addition to the convenience of children's menu, children's chair, fork knife, cup, lighting, BGM, interior design needs to be coordinated in total. Comparing the restaurant's service to a play, the designer is to be a director, to listen to messages released by decorations, to harmonize them with the space for the targeted customers. From the floral language of flowers decorated in the room, unraveling the secret message of the owner and reaching the hidden theme is the real pleasure of the customers; the impression gives empathy; both the owner and the customers are increase value of the restaurant [4].

Regardless of targets, designing the mind is the essence of designers, and moving customers' hearts results in their actions. Therefore, the designer succeeds as a business consultant. In this way, excellent designers can control the context freely. As superior military breaks the tight situation strategically by manipulating the context, the designer changes behavior of the audience by manipulating their mental models. There is the essence of the "Memes" design method in strategically designing the flow of information, encouraging the mental model of the audience, and inducing changes in the internal aspects of the audience.

## 2 Retrospective Experience Design

### 2.1 Elderly People Cannot Catch up with Rapid Advanced Social Systems

The United Nations shares a prediction that 18% of the world's population will be over 65 years old in 2050. In particular, Japan is the first aging society in the world in terms of average lifespan, number of elderly people, and speed of aging. Currently, the population over 65 years of age exceeds 35 million, the proportion of elderly people is about 28% of the total population, one in every four people is elderly. One of the problems of aging society is that sophisticated social system is not friendly to the elderly. Elderly people cannot catch up with rapidly advanced social systems because of technological progress. The usability is improved, and the new user interface system is implemented, so people who cannot use it are left behind from the new social system. It is more difficult for people with dementia to memorize new things. New memories will disappear, only old memories will remain.

### 2.2 A Testing Tool for People with Psychological Problems

Activities of daily living (ADLs) are tasks of everyday life. These include basic survival tasks such as eating, dressing, getting into or out of a bed or chair, taking a bath or shower, and using the toilet. Especially, instrumental activities of daily living (IADLs) are defined as activities related to independent living and include driving cars, paying bills with cards, using telephones or other machines. Originally, they are tasks, but they are also used to measure self-performance in elderly people's quality of life (QOL).

For example, one elderly woman may be able to dress herself except for managing difficult fasteners that close in the back. If that is the case, her daily living can be improved simply by changing the kinds of clothes. One elderly man no longer wanted to drive by himself because of the recent unfamiliar driving system. The former is a problem of ADLs, the latter is one of IADLs.

Generally, elderly people need to be able to manage IADLs in order to live independently without the assistance of another person, such as caregivers. Problems with IADLs usually reflect problems with physical health and cognitive health. Often problems in ADLs arise gradually and may not even be considered a problem for some time. Instead, in IADLs, a problem is clearly found by event of not using instruments. In that sense, IADLs may be more detectable than ADLs within a testing tool for people with psychological problems.

### 2.3  A Symbol Reminds a Same Mental Model Among Audiences

Many elderly people experience problems in daily living because of declining cognitive and physical activities by aging or health-related disabilities. Those difficulties restrict their ability to perform self-care. Most reasons of inability for self-care are classified into four types which are related to signal detection, information processing, decision making and action. However, they are not independent. Since they are sequential causalities, each or combinations make a self-care failure. And we are only witnessing activities as a result of causality.

In this way, cognitive psychology regards an individual as a processor of information, in much the same way that a computer captures information, eliminates unnecessary data, and generates a view for judgment. In addition, since the human brain is a slower processor that cannot handle such large data at high speed as a computer, we focus on only important information to save our energies.

This corresponds to differential data on the computer. Saving movie data, a large capacity is required to save all frames. However, for example, at a press conference, since there is motion only in the person at the center of the frame and the background is fixed, it is waste that a large amount of redundant data of the background is saved as common information.

For this reason, compressing data, only the data of the first frame with background is saved as common data, and only difference is saved in the later frame. By this compression technology, movie data can be displayed at high speed.

Similarly, human being makes judgments using only differential information comparing with common sense. For example, when being said "a black swan" for the first time, you think of a swan at first and presume that it is a bird with white changed to black. Since we know what kind of animal a swan is, we can imagine even "a black swan" we have never seen before. In cognitive psychology, the swan in each mind is called a mental model. Based on this as common recognition, we can understand the black swan by the attribute difference.

Similarly, in communication, mental models work to understand each other's idea. On the contrary, unless thinking of same mental model in each mind, we will make a miscommunication on it. Since mental models vary from person to person, it is necessary to keep same mental models in each mind for good communication.

For example, when telling a new concept to others, telling all the attributes one by one is not efficient and may not be understood at all. Explaining a new concept, it is best to use analogy as a mental model. Compared with the analogy, you can communicate efficiently by telling only the difference. It leads managing others' mental models is important for good communication.

An excellent designer is a psychological magician who uses symbols to remind the same mental model among audiences and leads them towards own intention. It is clearly different from art, design aims to solve problems [5]. A design has a purpose of solving problems essentially. This point is quite different from art. A good design makes a lot of people happy. A good designer solves it by manipulating mental models of others by using the design.

### 2.4   Retrospective Experience Design for Elderly People

For example, currently, a key less entry system is common in automobile. Similarly, it is also implemented in the home entrance system. That makes a big problem for elders with the symptom of dementia or MCI (Mild Cognitive Impairment), to enter their renovated houses. They were confused about how to open the entrance doors. They could not go through the doors by themselves and keep their memories about how to open the door.

One of the solutions is to put back to the previous entrance system with a metal door key. However, it is not actual or reasonable. Another solution is to change the interface design for us to reach the right understanding. If we cannot do the right action, there may be some troubles to interrupt our cognitive process. On the contrary, we can solve an interruption of cognitive process by changing the interface design. That means, in order to improve the above-mentioned daily life for people with dementia, we should change the interface design of their tools. For example, changing a shape of card in key less entry system into a metal door key which was used in the previous, some people with dementia may go through the entrance door. And a key hole on the door is needed for elders to reach the goal of understanding even if it is meaningless. That makes they can feel relived and enter their house through the door in the key less entry system.

This design concept is for specific people to use a tool with appropriate way by time interface design in their old memories. It is not a universal design because it cannot work for young people who do not know the old-style interface design. At least, it should be called "the retrospective design" since the previous interface design is used instead of new interface design.

In addition, strictly, this design concept is not user interface design (UI-design) because it is not aimed at realizing efficient operation [2]. However, this design concept is aimed at improving the interface, but it is not a purpose for efficient operation. This design concept is rebuilding the design of time space. This is not to improve only operability but to design the user experience. It should be called "retrospective experience design" because it is meaningless for younger generation with different experience to the elderly.

# 3 Summary

"Memes" design methodology was developed as a practical UX-design method. This method can create a design strategy based on cognitive science. In this method, a cognitive process is divided into four steps which are sensing signals, evoking assumptions, structuring schema and understanding a concept. Since a cognitive process goes through at a moment, we are not aware of each step. However, this method will check a brain activity through each step. Besides, this method will be applied to the improvement of IADLs for the elderly because as science and technology continue to advance, there will be elderly people left behind. In a sense, they will desire an old-style instrumental tool that they are familiar with. One of the solutions is to change the interface design to the old-style in appearance without changing the function of the tool. This design concept is for specific people to use a tool with appropriate way by old-time interface design in their old memories. It is not a universal design because it cannot work for young people who do not know the old-style interface design. it is so-called "the retrospective design" since the previous interface design is used instead of new interface design. In that way, we can conclude that this design method is useful for retrospective experience design for the elderly.

# References

1. Kuniavsky, M.: Smart Things: Ubiquitous Computing User Experience Design. Elsevier, Amsterdam (2010)
2. Shneiderman, B.: Designing the User Interface: Strategies for Effective Human-Computer Interaction. Pearson Education India, Delhi (2010)
3. Seel, N.M.: Model-centered learning and instruction. Technol. Instr. Cogn. Learn. 1(1), 59–85 (2003)
4. Ochs, M., Sadek, D., Pelachaud, C.: A formal model of emotions for an empathic rational dialog agent. Auton. Agent. Multi-Agent Syst. 24(3), 410–440 (2012)
5. Ashby, M.F., Johnson, K.: Materials and Design: the Art and Science of Material Selection in Product Design. Butterworth-Heinemann, Oxford (2013)

# Design and Validation of a Tremor Stabilizing Handle for Patients with Parkinson Disease and Essential Tremor

Nandan Sarkar[1] and Zhaobo K. Zheng[2(✉)]

[1] University School of Nashville, Nashville, TN 37212, USA
[2] Mechanical Engineering Department, Vanderbilt University,
Nashville, TN 37203, USA
zhaobo.zheng@vanderbilt.edu

**Abstract.** Parkinson's disease (PD) is the second most common neurodegenerative disorder characterized by resting tremor and postural instability. Essential Tremor (ET) disease is another neurological disorder which causes involuntary and rhythmic shaking of the hands and other body parts and affects about 10% of all Americans. The degradations of motor skills severely affect daily activities of patients such as eating, writing and dressing. Existing pharmacological treatments, in general, have shown side effects over long term. In recent years, wearable devices and stabilizing assistive devices have been developed to address uncontrolled tremor. The products have shown great potential, but they are not ideal yet. In this work, we developed a low-cost non-invasive handle stabilizing to a preferred orientation in the presence of hand tremors. A validation study evaluated the performance of this prototype on a vibration generator that simulates specific vibrations relevant for PD and ET. The results show that the presented tremor reduction system controls external vibration better than the on-market products. The prototype also has a significantly lower cost and lighter weight. With these combined advantages, this work may help people with PD and ET accomplishing fine motor tasks and therefore improve the quality of life for this unattended population.

**Keywords:** Tremor · Stabilizing · Parkinson/Essential Tremor

## 1 Introduction

Parkinson's disease (PD), the second most common neurodegenerative disorder [1], is often characterized by resting tremors and postural instability. Although treatment is available, there is no existing cure to PD yet. Thus, once diagnosed, PD can last for years or even be lifelong. Every year approximately 60,000 Americans are diagnosed with PD and The Center for Disease Control and Prevention (CDC) lists PD related complications as the 14th most cause of death in the United States [2]. Essential Tremor (ET) disease, another neurological disorder, sometimes misdiagnosed as PD,

---

Authors contributed equally to this paper.

© Springer Nature Switzerland AG 2019
V. G. Duffy (Ed.): HCII 2019, LNCS 11582, pp. 274–283, 2019.
https://doi.org/10.1007/978-3-030-22219-2_21

causes involuntary and rhythmic shaking of hands and other body parts and affect about 10% of all Americans [3]. The degradations in motor skills severely affect those diagnosed with PD and ET in everyday activities such as eating, writing, shaving, and dressing [4]. Such disabilities limit patients with PD and ET to live well independently and most patients require help from caregivers. It has a huge economic and mental cost to the individuals and their families [5].

To address these disadvantages, different solutions have been developed to improve patients' quality of life such as pharmacological treatments, wearable devices and stabilizing handles. For more than half a century, PD was treated with various pharmacological compounds [6] and Levodopa is widely recognized as the most effective medication for motor symptoms of Parkinson disease [7]. Levodopa is cost effective and has an immediate effect for mild tremors with satisfactory effectiveness. Despite the advantages, it has some side effects including drug dependency, loss of effectiveness over the long term, and the need for a pharmacologist [8]. Other medicines have the similar limitations. Microsoft Research has recently developed a wearable device shaped as a waist watch and it delivers minor vibrations to patients, known as project Emma [9]. Patients perform significantly better on fine motor tasks that she was even able to write her name. The wearable device is cost effective, light in weight and easy to apply. More importantly, the device prevented the tremor from happening instead of eliminating the tremors. However, there has not been many studies explaining the neural mechanism of the system or feasibility study on a more general population. It is only effective on very minor tremors and since it is invasive, 32% of people stopped wearing it after 6 months [10]. Liftware developed handheld assistive devices using motors to encounter vibrations so that the end of the device, usually a spoon or fork can stay rather stable [11]. A pilot study on such product has shown an on-off comparison of patients with mild tremor eating with it [10]. The device has successfully made patients feed themselves different kinds of food. Such devices are non-invasive, easy to use and effective. These advantages have made it popular among patients with PD and ET with a combined usage of medicine. Similar research on simulating these assistive devices has also been carried out to improve the design and involve more intelligent components [12].

However, the existing device reduces only 70% of the tremors as advertised and mainly within one direction. Also, according to product reviews from users, the device is quite expensive and rather heavy for the target population, especially older adults. Additionally, there has not been a quantitative study addressing precise vibrations it has countered or a on and off motion comparison of such system.

In order to address the challenges we have designed a stabilizing handle controlled by a servo motor to counter the tremors. The motion is detected from an inertial measurement unit (IMU) LSM9DS1 housed on the handle. A closed-loop control of the handle position is then implemented to actuate the handle to keep it close to a desired angle relative to the ground. The user can also interact with the system to set the desired angle through a force sensing resistor (FSR). Weight of the system is extremely small by using light materials and sparse structures. The cost of the system is also much less. A vibration generator is designed specifically to test the performance of the prototype quantitatively. We then evaluated the prototype through a validation study. The rest of the paper is arranged as follows, Sect. 2 describes the system design including hardware design and the control algorithm. Section 3 illustrates the system validation from vibration generator design to the experiments. Section 4 displays the results of the experiments and analyze the data. Then we conclude the paper with discussions of this work in Sect. 5.

## 2    System Design

The design of our device is divided into three parts: the case, the shaft and the actuation mechanism. The core of the proposed system is to actively eliminate the vibration from the case, so the shaft remains stable. At the end of the shaft, tools for different fine motor skill tasks such as a spoon, fork, or razor, can be attached. As the user moves the case, the actuation mechanism compensates the position change in real-time. Additionally, the user can set the desired angle of the shaft by pressing the force sensing resistor (FSR) on the exterior of the case.

### 2.1    Hardware Design

Our device was designed with the computer aided design (CAD) software Solidworks. The CAD model of the system is shown in Fig. 1; the manufactured prototype is also shown for comparison. The system's length, width and height are 121 mm, 32 mm and 34 mm, respectively. The total weight of the system is 51 g. The user holds our system by the case and their tremors are applied on the case. A commercial micro servo HS40 by Hi-tec is integrated and housed on the inside of the case. The motor has a maximum speed of 540 degrees per second. A link mechanism connects the servo with the shaft and transfers the rotational motion to a linear motion. The shaft goes up and down as a single degree of freedom system, and the range of motion for the shaft is approximately 30°. All parts are 3D-printed for lighter weight and design feasibility.

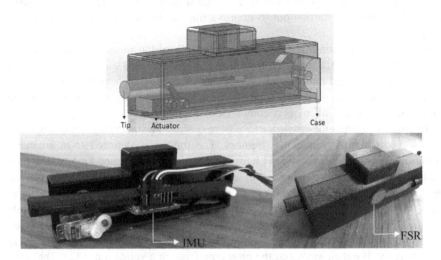

**Fig. 1.**  CAD model and prototype

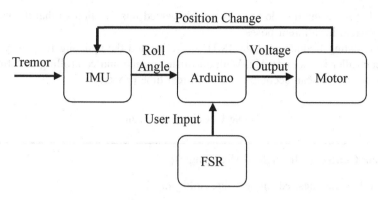

**Fig. 2.** System architecture

An FSR 400 is integrated on the exterior of the case to get user inputs. The FSR is connected to a pull-up resistor, which we use to measure the voltage. The FSR has a decreased resistance when pressed so we have an analog input of force applied on the FSR. We used an Arduino Uno as the controller, which collects the sensing information and controls the servo. Additionally, the IMU LSM9DS1 on the shaft measures the inertial forces on the Cartesian coordinates. Thus, the roll angle of the shaft compared to the ground can be computed by the inverse tangential of the inertial force on x axis over the inertial force on z axis. We chose the IMU because of its reasonable price and miniature volume. It combines gyro, accelerometer and magnetic meter in a single chip. We used the 2 g range for the accelerometer for the best precision. The IMU sends real-time data to the Arduino through I2C communication. The system architecture is shown in Fig. 2.

## 2.2 Control

The control algorithm of the system is shown in Table 1 below. The algorithm runs as a continuous loop and it updates the roll angle at the present time instance in each loop. The motor pulls the shaft down to the desired angle when the shaft is tilting up, and it pushes the shaft up to the desired angle when the shaft is tilting down. An angle threshold of 2° is set to stop the motor when close to the desired angle. In this way, the motor will keep the roll angle of the shaft in an envelope of 2° above or below the desired angle. However, this threshold has a trade-off effect, a value too big would not keep the shaft close enough to the desired angle and a value too small would make the motor chatter during rest. Based on our observation, the threshold of 2° was an optimal choice.

By default, the desired angle starts at 0, which implies that the handle is parallel to the ground. If the user pushes by a force above the threshold, the algorithm will set the desired angle to the current roll angle. This force threshold is computed during configurations when the user holds the case with one finger on FSR. For five seconds, he or she holds with normal and above-normal forces, repetitively for a few times. The force data acquired is then classified into two clusters using K-means classifier, and the threshold is set at the middle [13]. We implemented this function so that the user can use the system in different poses.

The updating frequency of the IMU is 531 Hz and the updating frequency of the motor controller is about 19 Hz. With adequate sensing and controlling updating frequency, the system can accomplish a good real-time property.

**Table 1.** Control algorithm

```
Position Control (roll_angle, desired_angle){

    if (roll_angle - desired_angle > threshold_angle){

        motor goes down;

    else if (desired_angle - roll_angle > threshold_angle){

        motor goes up;

    else{

        motor stops;

    }

    if (FSR_reading > threshold_force){

        desired_angle = roll_angle;

    }

}
```

# 3   System Validation

Since the prototype was working, we wanted to quantify the amount of vibration it has countered. To accomplish this task, we designed and implemented a vibration generator which can simulate a vibration with exact magnitude and frequency. During experiments, we gathered data of the specific vibrations we applied on our prototype as input, and the precise roll angle history of the shaft as output. We addressed the performance of the prototype by comparing different outputs with and without position compensation to the same input.

## 3.1   Vibration Generator Development

A DC motor with an encoder is connected to a linkage mechanism to actuate a piston-like platform. The platform moves up and down as the motor rotates back and forth. By controlling the speed and motion range of the motor, we achieve a specific vibration on platform in terms of magnitude and frequency. We used an Arduino Mega to run the pulse width modulation to control motor speed and further position.

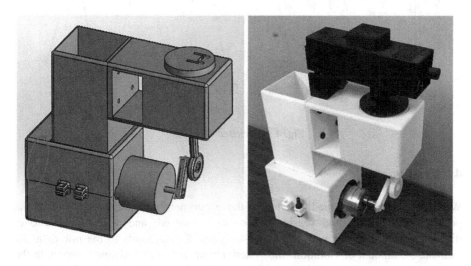

**Fig. 3.** CAD model and prototype of vibration generator

We used MATLAB to implement a simple closed-loop controller and also record the encoder positions. The CAD model of the vibration generator is shown in Fig. 3. The parts of the vibration generator were 3D-printed. The updating frequency of the vibration generator controller is about 36 Hz. We implemented a simple PID controller on the DC motor to generate a vibration precisely in position as well as time. The encoder has a resolution of 3600 and the precision of our control is less than 1°.

## 3.2 Experiment

We housed the prototype on the vibration generator platform and ran the vibration generator as shown in Fig. 3. The back end of the stabilizing handle is held and the front end of it moves up and down with the platform. We chose the magnitude and frequency of the vibration generated to be 15° and 3 Hz, respectively to simulate the actual tremor of patients [15]. A white noise was added to the motor position command to better mimic the natural uncontrolled tremor of patients with PD or ET.

The same vibration is delivered to the prototype twice and the vibration generator is able to repeat the same vibration very precisely. During experiments, we measured and recorded the roll angles of the shaft. The same vibration is run twice with the position compensation turned on and off, so we can compare the stabilizing effect. We gathered the encoder data from the DC motor which is shown in Fig. 4. The experiments were run multiple times and we are displaying the data that is the most representative. We ran the experiments for 30 s and we chose only 2 s of data to display here because it's highly repetitive. These 2 s of data is exactly according to the position data displayed in the next session in terms of timing.

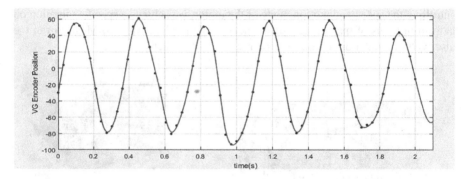

**Fig. 4.** Generated vibration

# 4 Results

We analyzed the IMU readings during the experiment and generated plots of the position trajectory. Some sensing noise was observed, and we applied a one-dimensional digital filter with the window size of 5 data points to the raw data. To estimate the amount of vibrations the system eliminated, we fitted sine waves with the least square errors of the position trajectories. The shaft position trajectories with and without compensation are shown in Figs. 5 and 6, respectively. The sensor data after filtering is shown in black dots and the fitted curves are shown as blue curves.

As shown in the figures, the magnitude of the vibrations decreased significantly with the motor compensation. The magnitude of the fitted curves are 13.06 and 1.85°. Thus, the system has eliminated 85.83% of the vibration, compared to 70% as found in the products available in the market. The average squared position error also decreased from 8.256 to 1.301, meaning that the position is more consistent in time. Combined, the results indicate the shaft position is kept within a much smaller range and the motion is smoother. Also, the system has a 0.09 s delay in phase, potentially caused by the sensing and control processes. This amount of delay is acceptable considering the goal is to keep the magnitude of position small instead of real-time positioning.

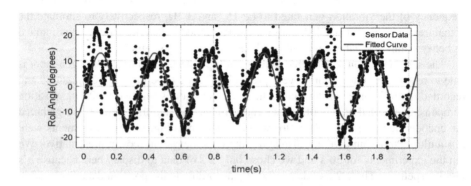

**Fig. 5.** Shaft angle without compensation (Color figure online)

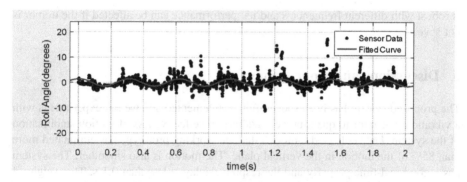

**Fig. 6.** Shaft angle with compensation (Color figure online)

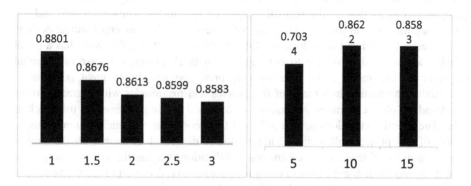

**Fig. 7.** Motion stabilized percentage for different frequencies and magnitudes

We also explored the performance of our stabilizing handle under vibrations with a range of frequencies and magnitudes. With a constant magnitude of 15, we ran experiments with vibration frequencies ranging from 1 to 3. With the position trajectory data collected, we computed the percentage of motion stabilized under different frequencies. The frequency domain results are shown in the left plot of Fig. 7. The performance is stable when the frequency varies and it was more stable during slower motion. The reason being that the slower motion gives the system more time to react and the error is therefore reduced. However, the frequency with better performance is too small compared to the usual tremor frequency of patients with PD or ET.

As for magnitude domain, we ran experiments with vibration magnitude ranging from 5 to 15° in roll angle with a constant frequency of 3 Hz. The result is informative; with the motion becoming narrower, the performance increased by a little and then decreased significantly. Based on observation, the reason may be that the tiny motion range is sometimes too small for the stabilizing handle to actuate. Also, the error of our actuation and sensing becomes more significant in a small range of motion. This indicates that the prototype has limited performance for a very minor tremor. This limitation should be acceptable because if the tremor is originally small, it is not a great difficulty for the patient's activities. Overall, the performance of our stabilizing handle is robust with different frequencies and its' performance can be affected if the tremor is not severe.

## 5  Discussions and Conclusions

The proposed system has been successfully implemented and we ran experiments with a vibration generator to quantitatively address the effectiveness of motion stabilization of the system. Data collected indicates that the working prototype has eliminated more than 85% of the motion in the vertical plane. The motion is also smoother. The system has a good real-time property and the response delay is less than 0.1 s. The weight of the system is 51 g and the total cost of the prototype is 56 dollars, which are 46% and 81% less than the weight and sale price, respectively of the on-market product. There are certain limitations of this work. The system has only one degree of freedom so it only stabilizes motion on the vertical plane. The system has wires connected and it's not ready for use with patients. The shape of the cases needs more ergonomical designs to be easier to hold and nicer-looking. Despite these limitations, this work has a novel design as an assistive device to help patients with Parkinson's disease or essential tremors on fine motor tasks. The working prototype has shown great potential in stabilizing the motion in a range of frequencies and magnitudes with a greatly lower cost and weight. A vibration generator was designed and implemented in this work to simulate specific vibrations to precisely test the performance of such systems. Future work of this project will include adding another degree of freedom with the similar mechanism to achieve free-space motion stabilization, making the system completely wireless, and finalizing the system ready for patients. We also want to test the improved system on a group of patients with Parkinson's disease and Essential Tremors.

## References

1. Poewe, W., et al.: Parkinson disease. Nat. rev. Dis. Primers **3**, 17013 (2017)
2. Center for Disease Control and Prevention, "Parkinson's Disease Mortality by State", Government Report (2017)
3. Elble, R.J.: Tremor. In: Tousi, B., Cummings, J. (eds.) Neuro-Geriatrics, pp. 311–326. Springer, Cham (2017). https://doi.org/10.1007/978-3-319-56484-5_20
4. Jankovic, J., Kapadia, A.S.: Functional decline in Parkinson disease. Arch. Neurol. **58**(10), 1611–1615 (2001)
5. Cummings, J.L.: Depression and Parkinson's disease: a review. Am. J. Psychiatry **149**(4), 443 (1992)
6. Connolly, B.S., Lang, A.E.: Pharmacological treatment of Parkinson disease: a review. JAMA **311**(16), 1670–1683 (2014)
7. Tomlinson, C.L., Stowe, R., Patel, S., Rick, C., Gray, R., Clarke, C.E.: Systematic review of levodopa dose equivalency reporting in parkinson's disease. Mov. Disord. **25**(15), 2649–2653 (2010)
8. Parkinson Study Group: Pramipexole vs levodopa as initial treatment for Parkinson disease: a randomized controlled trial. JAMA **284**(15), 1931–1938 (2000)

 9. Microsoft Research: Project Emma. https://www.microsoft.com/en-us/research/project/project-emma/
10. Espay, A.J., et al.: Technology in Parkinson's disease: challenges and opportunities. Mov. Disord. **31**(9), 1272–1282 (2016)
11. Liftware: Lift Steady. https://www.liftware.com/steady/ Accessed 21 Nov 2016
12. Joe, B.C., Mazumdar, A., Sood, H., Gupta, Y., Panda, A., Poonkuzhali, R.: Parkinson's disease assist device using machine learning and Internet of Things. In: 2018 International Conference on Communication and Signal Processing (ICCSP), pp. 0922–0927. IEEE (2018)
13. Zhaobo, K.Z., Zhu, J., Fan, J., Sarkar, N.: Design and system validation of rassle: a novel active socially assistive robot for elderly with dementia. In: 2018 27th IEEE International Symposium on Robot and Human Interactive Communication (RO-MAN), pp. 1–4. IEEE (2018)

# Preliminary Design of Soft Exo-Suit
# for Arm Rehabilitation

Deep Seth[(⊠)], V. K. Harsha Vardhan Varma, Padamati Anirudh,
and Pavan Kalyan

Mechanical Engineering Program, Mahindra Ecole Centrale,
Hyderabad 500043, India
Deep.seth@mechyd.ac.in

**Abstract.** Every year, millions of people experience a stroke but only a few of them fully recover. Recovery requires a working staff, which is time consuming and inefficient. Therefore, over the past few years rehabilitation robots like Exoskeletons have been used in the recuperation process for patients. In this paper we have designed an Exosuit which takes into considerations of the rigid Exo-Skeleton and its limitations for patients suffering from loss of function of the arm. This paper concentrates on enabling a stroke affected person to perform flexion-extension at elbow joint. Validation of the developed model on general population is still needed.

**Keywords:** Rehabilitation robot · Exosuit · Elbow flexion-extension · Exo-skeleton · Robots in biomedical

## 1 Introduction

The nervous system disorders are quite responsible for the death and disability seen around the world [1, 2]. In developing countries, they are reason for over 27% of all years of life lived with disabilities [3]. An Exoskeleton is a wearable mobile robot that makes use of a combination of biomechanics and robotics to allow limb movement and enhancement. Due to this, Exoskeletons find application in a variety of fields. Exoskeletons are used for military purposes, to decrease fatigue and thereby increase productivity, enabling soldiers to carry heavy weights [4] across rugged terrain. There are many Exoskeletons, for both lower limbs [5–8] and upper limbs [9–11]. Enhancement Exoskeletons constantly calculate what it needs to do to distribute the load so as to none is imposed on the wearer. Ekso Bionics/Lockheed Martin HULC [12], weighs 24 kg and allows the user to carry up to 91 kgs.

However, one of the main application of Exoskeletons is in therapy, in assisting patients with loss of function [13, 14] of a limb. Stroke and Musco-Skeletal Disorders (MSD) [15] lead to limited or temporary dysfunction of limbs. Muscle fatigue [16, 17] could be the reason for the same.

There are many existing exoskeletons working on Bi-pedal locomotion of human [6, 7, 18], gait analysis [19], wheel chair mounted robots [20], passive [21] and quasi-passive [8] exoskeletons. Apart from these we can see many which target particular type of limb movements such as lower leg, ankle, knee, hand movement [22], etc. For

© Springer Nature Switzerland AG 2019
V. G. Duffy (Ed.): HCII 2019, LNCS 11582, pp. 284–294, 2019.
https://doi.org/10.1007/978-3-030-22219-2_22

most of the exoskeletons we have to define the gesture analysis [23, 24] and working posture which is fixed in most of the cases and can be a drawback of some exoskeletons.

The model in this paper is targeted towards stroke patients. Stroke occurs when poor blood flows to the brain, resulting in cell death. One of its main long-term effect includes up to 85% motoric disturbances [25], which leads to hemiplegia or unilateral paralysis. This reduces the patient's capacity to perform activities of daily living (ADL).

Physical rehabilitation can help patients improve their condition. Therefore, over the past few years rehabilitation robots like Exoskeletons have been used in the recuperation process for disabled patients. One breakthrough was the fact that Exoskeletons can perfectly recreate the same motion repeatedly over thousands of times. This translates to patients being able to perform the same exercises in the same amount of time with higher consistency.

There are plenty of Exoskeletons available in the market, and an even higher number under research and development. Some of them are

### ARMin III [26]

As shown in Fig. 1. it is the first actuated Exoskeleton robot equipped with six motors which can move the shoulder joint in three degrees of freedom (the elbow joints, the lower arm pro/supination, the wrist flexion/extension). With its help patients can perform daily activities like cooking, eating brushing teeth, etc.

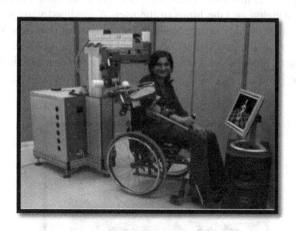

**Fig. 1.** ARMin III [26]

### In Motion Arm/MIT-MANUS [27]

As shown in Fig. 2. it is a wrist robot having three active degrees-of-freedom (Abduction–Adduction, Flexion–Extension, Pronation–Supination). It can be operated standalone or mounted at the tip of the companion planar robot, MIT-MANUS, which allows five active degrees of freedom (plus two passive DOF) at the shoulder, elbow, and wrist. These 3 Degrees of freedom provided by the robot are mapped into a two-dimensional graphical display on a monitor screen.

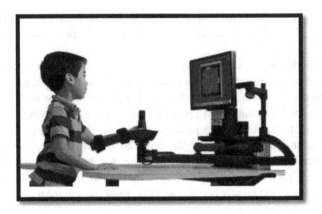

**Fig. 2.** MIT-MANUS [27]

**ALEX [28]**

Active leg Exoskeleton (ALEX) is a treadmill-based Exoskeleton as shown in Fig. 3. The gravity balancing was used to decrease the effort required by the actuator when being used. It uses springs placed at suitable positions to balance the effect of gravity over the range of motion. This model has 6 DOF (4 for pelvic motion and 2 for hip and knee joints). The model has used force-torque sensors to measure the interactive force between the exoskeleton and the limbs of the user. A modified version of ALEX, i.e. ALEX II was proposed. This new model used rotatory motors instead of linear actuators to actuate the hip and knee joints. A modified version of ALEX, i.e. ALEX II was proposed. This new model used rotatory motors instead of linear actuators to actuate the hip and knee joints.

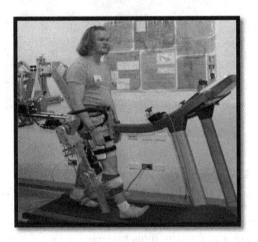

**Fig. 3.** ALEX [28]

### eLEGS [29]

Extreme Lower Extremity Gait System (eLEGS) as shown in Fig. 4. is a hydraulically powered Exoskeletons that allows paraplegics (people with paralyzed legs) to stand from a sitting position and walk in a straight line. It is made of reinforced carbon which acts as a substitute for bone strength. It weighs around 20 kg and has a maximum speed of 2 mph and has a battery life that lasts 6 h. It is suitable for users who and can get themselves from a wheelchair into a chair.

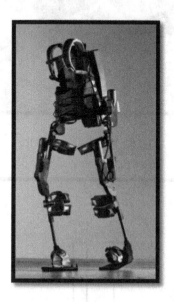

**Fig. 4.** eLEGS [29]

### MAHI EXO-II [30]

It is an upper extremity Exoskeletons as shown in Fig. 5 used by stroke and spinal cord injury patients who need rehabilitation of elbow, forearm and wrist. It has 4 active DOF (Flexion–Extension, forearm Pronation–Supination, wrist Flexion–Extension and Radial–Ulnar deviation).

All the above-mentioned exoskeletons are made of rigid links that operate in parallel to the human skeleton. Because of their structural rigidity and complexity these devices can be extremely accurate, making them a go to solution in clinical environments and these are also able to deliver high forces. The other side to this is all the exoskeletons mentioned are very expensive. There is a large difference between the cost of these exoskeletons and the purchasing power of the targeted audience.

The other problem that arises is Hyperstaticity (Fig. 6). Misalignment between the robot joint and the biological ones results in Hyperstaticity. It is a phenomenon where uncontrolled interaction forces upset the natural kinematics of human movements.

The Exosuit described in this paper is designed to minimize weight and maximize comfort with no rigid mechanical links. The Exosuit is actuated by a non-localized

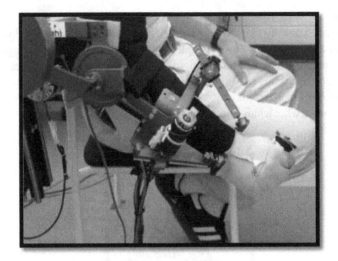

**Fig. 5.** MAHI EXO-II [30]

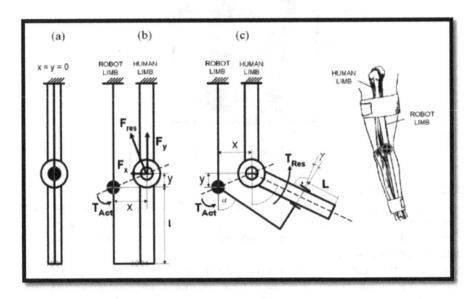

**Fig. 6.** Hyperstaticity

actuation where motion is transmitted using cables. These cables are driven by a motor mounted on the front panel of the user. The Exosuit enables user to perform flexion-extension (Fig. 8) of the elbow joint in the sagittal plane (Fig. 7). The assisting motion and the speed are controlled using a smartphone application, which can be operated by the user or a trainer.

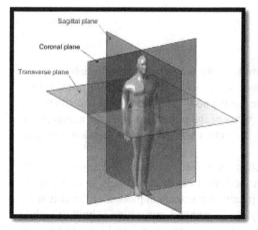

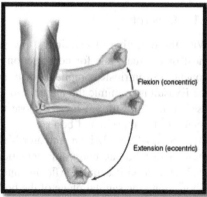

**Fig. 7.** Planes of movement          **Fig. 8.** Flexion – extension of elbow joint

## 2 Objective

The objective of this project is to create a lightweight, user friendly and a wearable soft Exosuit. The Exosuit should be affordable by one and all in need. We aim to make an Exosuit that uses little to no rigid structures, to give more freedom of movement to the user. It should be a smart Exosuit, which would connect to the smartphone of the user enabling collection of any required medical data. A mobile application for smartphones which would enable the control of the Exosuit replacing the traditional joystick.

This would be achieved using soft, wearable materials and making use of biomechanics of the arm. The working postures and various parameters (Angular speed, repetition of a preprogrammed motion etc.) can be predefined by the handler using the smartphone application. To achieve the above objectives, the following assumptions have been made.

### 2.1 Hypothesis

The targeted audience of the Exosuit in development are patients who have lost motor function in the left upper limb due to a stroke. Left arm is chosen since in most stroke attacks the left side of the body is affected [31].

The user has functioning right upper limb and can hence use the controller provided to control the Exosuit. User has access to a smartphone which is essential for controlling the Exosuit. Users of this Exosuit do not have severe motor disability i.e., it is only applicable to humans with a score of 0–2 on MAS (Modified Ashworth Scale) [32].

# 3 Methodology

## 3.1 Concept

With the objective of creating a low profile, light weight and an affordable Exosuit most of the materials for construction are off the shelf fabrics and 3D printed components. For intrinsic compliance with the human body, the idea behind construction of the Exosuit is to mimic the natural movements of the human arm i.e., the action points used in the Exosuit are located close to the actual locations where tendons are connected to the muscle and bone.

A Screw-Cable Driven Actuator Mechanism is used to power the Exosuit. Like the muscles of a human body, this actuation mechanism is designed only to pull and not push. Actuation is active for flexion and passive for extension motion of the arm at the elbow along the sagittal plane of the body. A smartphone application is built to replace the traditional joystick for controlling the actuator mechanism thereby controlling the Exosuit. This reduces number of physical components required which in turn reduces the cost of the Exosuit.

## 3.2 Preliminary Design

The plan was to have a non-localized actuation mechanism. The power supply unit, the actuator, the microcontroller and all the essential components were planned to be mounted in a packaging like a backpack that can be worn by the user. This posed a design problem. Significant amount of unnecessary load was being applied on the shoulder when the flexion of elbow joint was performed. So, the actuator had to be shifted to the front panel of the human body.

For transmission of the motion from the actuator to the elbow joint Bowden cables were the former options. Very high tensile strengths (the thinnest of such cables has a carrying strength more than 100 kg) and durability of these cables made the Bowden cables a perfect fit for the job.

According to the planned design of actuation the cable had to coil around a pulley driven by the shaft of the motor. It was an extra load on the motor to coil the Bowden cables which resisted bending resulting in insufficient power left to carry out the actual planned motion i.e., Flexion – Extension of the elbow. Also, coiling caused inelastic expansion in the Bowden cables resulting in whirling of the cable during the extension motion.

With its tensile strength being on par for the application, Nylon thread (usually used for fishing) was an alternative to overcome the above problems without compromising on the performance. With a diameter of 0.4 mm they have a carrying strength of nearly 9 kg.

## 3.3 Procedure

With an aim to develop an Exosuit which is ergonomically compliant with the human arm, all the human-exosuit interactions are designed to be made from fabric. One of the challenges is to hold the action points at the desired location on the human arm. As the components used are not rigid, they cannot hold their position when force is exerted on them and result in relative motion between the human arm and the Exosuit. To counter this problem, the action points were mounted on straps made from soft fabric with a rubber lining on the inner side. This ensures there is enough friction to hold the straps in the required position ensuring the action points are in place (Figs. 9 and 10).

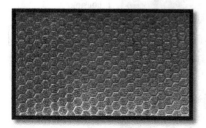

**Fig. 9.** Rubber lining

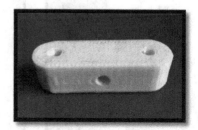

**Fig. 10.** 3D printed action point

## Screw – Cable Driven Actuation Mechanism

The Exosuit employs a non-localized actuation mechanism driven by cables. It is a Screw – Cable driven actuation mechanism. It ensures that the torque that the motor must deliver remains constant throughout the course of the flexion.

For extension of the elbow joint, the Exosuit makes use of gravity. The motor is mounted away from the elbow joint. Required motion is transmitted using cables. This non-localized actuation system also allows the use of more powerful motor enabling greater lifting strengths for the user. Larger motors require a larger base area to be set up on which is impossible to be positioned on a human arm and hence by non-localization to a location near the shoulder joint where the base area is more we can perform better given circumstances.

The prototype uses DC motors instead of other actuators such as pneumatic actuators, stepper motors etc. DC motor is chosen primarily on the fact that it is easier to have control over the speed. Compared to a stepper motor, DC motor has a lesser response time. The Exosuit utilizes a high-performance geared DC motor with multiple stages of gear reduction. It weighs about 180 grams, has a stall torque of 45 kg-cm and has an RPM of 60 at 12 V.

To control the speed and alter the direction of rotation of the DC motor, a microcontroller (Arduino Uno) along with a motor driver L298 N. L298 N is a dual H-bridge motor driver which allows speed and direction control.

The assisting motion of the Exosuit is controlled using a smartphone application which acts as a virtual controller. The smartphone application has an easy to use interface with one click for flexion and one click for extension. The connection between the smartphone and the Exosuit (i.e., the microcontroller on board) is facilitated over Bluetooth.

## 3.4  The Prototype

See Fig. 11.

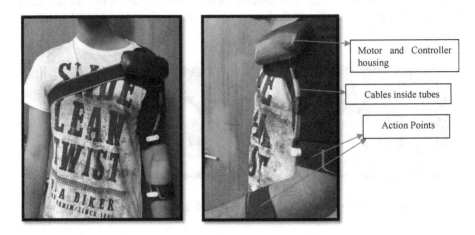

Motor and Controller housing

Cables inside tubes

Action Points

**Fig. 11.** Front and side view of the user with preliminary prototype

## 3.5  Discussion and Conclusions

This section is dedicated to discuss the parameters that indicate the performance that the Exosuit can deliver. The discussion assumed that the subject is in a standing position. The operating limits of the Exosuit are determined by static analysis. Static analysis provides the upper limit for parameters like maximum weight of the arm that the Exosuit can safely work with. This is because when the Exosuit is in operation the tension in the cables driving the motion will be lesser than the case of static analysis.

The Exosuit is powered by a 12 V - 60RPM geared DC motor. It has a stall torque of 45 Kg-cm. According to this, the maximum tension in the cable transmitting the motion will be 45 KN (base radius of the screw, which acts as the pulley, used is 1 cm). Therefore, from force balance we can see that the maximum weight of the arm for which this Exosuit can be comfortably applied is 4.5 kg. But the maximum carrying strength of the cable used for transmitting the motion is about 19 kg. This limits the maximum weight of the arm that the Exosuit can work with to 1.9 kg.

In the entire range of motion, from fully extended arm to fully flexed arm, the torque at the elbow due to the weight of the arm will be maximum when the upper and lower arms are at right angle. For an average human, the weight of the lower arm is about 2.3% [33]. So, for a healthy human weighing about 80 kg, total lower arm would weigh about 2.07 kg. This would result in a torque of 6.174 N-m at the elbow. Assuming no friction, the tension in the thread was observed to be 111.78 N. Considering the action points to be at a distance of 6 cm on the upper and lower arms from the elbow, the maximum torque that can be generated at the elbow with the current setup is calculated to be 11.4 N-m.

# 4 Future Scope

The effectiveness of the Exosuit can be verified experimentally by comparing the results of the muscle activity of a human for flexion-extension with and without the Exosuit. A clutch able mechanism can be developed using which the arm can be held at a position/orientation without using the power from the motor. A system can be developed where the Exosuit and the human have a cognitive connection. This allows control of the Exosuit using the intent of the user.

# References

1. Mathers, C., Fat, D.M., Boerma, J.T., World Health Organization: The global burden of disease: 2004 update. World Health Organization (2008)
2. McPhee, S.J., Hammer, G.D.: Nervous system disorders. Pathophysiol. Dis. Introd. Clin. Med. **59**, 177–180 (2010)
3. Committee on Nervous System Disorders in Developing Countries the Board on Global Health and the Institute of Medicine. Neurological, Psychiatric, and Develop-Mental Disorders. National Academies Press, Washington, DC (2001)
4. Zhang, Y., Arakalian, V.: Design of a passive robotic ExoSuit for carrying heavy loads. In: Proceedings of the IEEE-RAS, 18th Annual International Conference on Humanoid Robots, Lyon, France (2018)
5. Gross, R., et al.: Modulation of lower limb muscle activity induced by curved walking in typically developing children. Gait Posture **50**, 34–41 (2016)
6. Viteckova, S., Kutilek, P., Jirina, M.: Wearable lower limb robotics: a review. Biocybern. Biomed. Eng. **33**(2), 96–105 (2013)
7. Rupala, B.S., Singla, A., Virk, G.S.: Lower limb exoskeletons: a brief review. In: Proceedings of the Conference on Mechanical Engineering and Technology COMET, Varanasi, Utter Pradesh, pp. 18–24 (2016)
8. Collo, A., Bonnet, V., Venture, G.: A quasi-passive lower limb exoskeleton for partial body weight support. In: Proceedings of the 6th IEEE/RAS-EMBS International Conference on Biomedical Robotics and Biomechatronics (BioRob), UTown, Singapore, pp. 643–648 (2016)
9. Stewart, A.M., Pretty, C.G., Adams, M., Chen, X.: Review of upper limb hybrid exoskeletons. IFAC **50**(1), 15169–15178 (2017)
10. Serea, F., Poboroniuc, M., Hartopanu, S., Olaru, R.: Exoskeleton for upper arm rehabilitation for disabled patients. In: International Conference and Exposition on Electrical and Power Engineering, (EPE 2014), pp. 153–157 (2014)
11. Perry, J.C., Rosen, J., Burns, S.: Upper-limb powered exoskeleton design. IEEE/ASM Trans. Mechatron. **12**(4), 408–417 (2007)
12. Li, B., Yuan, B., Chen, J., Zuo, Y., Yang, Y.: Mechanical design and human-machine coupling dynamic analysis of a lower extremity exoskeleton. In: Huang, Y., Wu, H., Liu, H., Yin, Z. (eds.) ICIRA 2017. LNCS (LNAI), vol. 10462, pp. 593–604. Springer, Cham (2017). https://doi.org/10.1007/978-3-319-65289-4_56
13. Jarrasé, N.: Contributions à l'exploitation d'exosquelettes actifs pour la rééducation neuromotrice. Ph.D. thesis of Pierre et Marie Curie University (UPMC) (2010)
14. Gunn, M., Shank, T.M., Epps, M., Hossain, J., Rahman, T.: User evaluation of a dynamic arm orthosis for people with neuromuscular disorders. IEEE Trans. Neural Syst. Rehabil. Eng. **24**(12), 1277–1283 (2016)

15. Seth, D., Chablat, D., Bennis, F., Sakka, S., Jubeau, M., Nordez, A.: New dynamic muscle fatigue model to limit musculo-skeletal disorder. In: Virtual Reality International Conference 2016, Article no. 26 (2016)
16. Seth, D., Chablat, D., Sakka, S., Bennis, F.: Experimental validation of a new dynamic muscle fatigue model. In: Duffy, V.G.G. (ed.) DHM 2016. LNCS, vol. 9745, pp. 54–65. Springer, Cham (2016). https://doi.org/10.1007/978-3-319-40247-5_6
17. Seth, D., Chablat, D., Bennis, F., Sakka, S., Jubeau, M., Nordez, A.: Validation of a new dynamic muscle fatigue model and DMET analysis. Int. J. Virtual Real. 2016(16), 2016 (2016)
18. Talaty, M., Esquenazi, A., Briceno, J.E.: Differentiating ability in users of the ReWalk(TM) powered exoskeleton: an analysis of walking kinematics. In: Proceedings of the IEEE International Conference on Rehabilitation Robotics (ICORR), Seattle, USA, pp. 1–5 (2013). https://doi.org/10.1109/icorr.2013.6650469
19. Aoustin, Y.: Walking gait of a biped with a wearable walking assist device. Int. J. of Humanoid Robotics 12(2), 1 550 018-1–11 550 018-20 (2015). https://doi.org/10.1142/s0219843615500188
20. Ktistakis, I.P., Bourbakis, N.G.: A survey on robotic wheelchairs mounted with robotic arms. In: National Aerospace and Electronics Conference (NAECON), pp. 258–262 (2015)
21. Aoustin, Y., Formalskii, A.: Walking of biped with passive exoskeleton: evaluation of energy consumption. Multibody Syst. Dyn. 43, 71–96 (2017). https://doi.org/10.1007/s11044-017-9602-7
22. Park, W., Jeong, W., Kwon, G., Kim, Y.H., Kim, L.: A rehabilitation device to improve the hand grasp function of stroke patients using a patient-driven approach. In: IEEE International Conference on Rehabilitation Robotics, Seattle Washington, USA (2013)
23. Akhmadeev, K., Rampone, E., Yu, T., Aoustin, Y., Le Carpentier, E.: A testing system for a real-time gesture classification using surface EMG. In: Proceedings of the 20th IFAC World Congress, Toulouse France (2017)
24. Schwartz, C., Lempereur, M., Burdin, V., Jacq, J.J., Rémy-Néris, O.: Shoulder motion analysis using simultaneous skin shape registration. In: Proceedings of the 29th Annual International Conference of the IEEE EMBS, Lyon, France (2007)
25. National Stroke Association Brochure (2017)
26. Nef, T., Guidali, M., Riener, R.: ARMin III – arm therapy exoskeleton with an ergonomic shoulder actuation. Appl. Bionics Biomech. 6(2), 127–142 (2009)
27. Krebs, H.I., Hogan, N., Volpe, B.T., Aisen, M.L., Edelstein, L., Diels, C.: Overview of clinical trials with MITMANUS: a robot-aided neuro-rehabilitation facility. Technol. Health Care 7(6), 419–423 (1999)
28. Ali, H.: Bionic exoskeleton: history, development and the future. IOSR J. Mechan. Civ. Eng. 58–62 (2014)
29. Banala, S.K., Agrawal, S.K., Scholz, J.P.: Active leg exoskeleton (ALEX) for gait rehabilitation of motor-impaired patients. In: IEEE 2007 Rehabilitation Robotics, pp. 401–407 (2007)
30. Fitle, K.D., Pehlivan, A.U., O'Malley, M.K.: A robotic exoskeleton for re-habilitation and assessment of the upper limb following incomplete spinal cord in-jury. In: 2015 IEEE International Conference on Robotics and Automation (ICRA), pp. 4960–4966 (2015)
31. https://www.heart.org/en/about-stroke/effects-of-stroke
32. https://www.med-iq.com/files/noncme/material/pdfs/DOC%201–Modified%20Ashworth%20Scale.pdf
33. Plagenhoef, S., et al.: Anatomical data for analyzing human motion (1983)

# Aiding Episodic Memory in Lifelog System Focusing on User Status

Xin Ye and Jiro Tanaka[✉]

Waseda University, Kitakyushu, Japan
yexin9517@163.com, jiro@aoni.waseda.jp

**Abstract.** Lifelog can be described as a digital library of an individual's life, which is known for its ability to record life and help with memory. Autographer, a wearable camera that can captured images automatically, is always used for aiding episodic memory in lifelog system. In order to improve the effectiveness of retrieving memory using lifelog, this paper proposed two novelty user-relative memory cues to extract important memories for lifeloggers. They are special sentiment cue and special movement cue. With the integration of 2 Autographers and sensors embedded in Android smartphone, we implement a web-based lifelog viewer for lifeloggers to conveniently retrieve memories. On account of our system, we invited some participants to test the usability and efficiency of using our system. The preliminary result showed positive potential of aiding episodic memory by using our approaches.

**Keywords:** Episodic memory · Lifelog · Special movement ·
Special sentiment

## 1 Introduction

Memory is the ability of our neural system to encode, store and retrieve information. It is the accumulation of one person's past activity, feeling and many other information. Episodic memory is a part of long-term memory, together with semantic memory, it forms the integrity of memory system. The concept of episodic memory first appeared around 1970s [1]. Unlike semantic memory which concentrates on the actual facts about this world, episodic memory is the memory of autobiographical events. These events including contextual information (who, what, when, where, why) which can be explicitly elaborated and memorized. Generally speaking, episodic memory allows an individual to vividly go back in time to recall the event that occurs at a particular time and space. Episodic memory is vital to human being and Tulving [2] muse it as "a true marvel of nature". Moreover, according to the experiment done by Klein [3], the loss of episodic memory not only impact individual's memory for the past, but also may extend the influence of people's ability to anticipate the future. Meanwhile, because of the limitation of brain capacity or some severe memory illness, it is essential for us to find some external solutions for aid episodic memory retrieving.

Lifelog is the detailed chronicle of personal life involving large number of data that can be captured automatically by wearable technology. It is a process of gathering, processing and recalling life experience passively. Individuals, defined as lifeloggers,

V. G. Duffy (Ed.): HCII 2019, LNCS 11582, pp. 295–305, 2019.
https://doi.org/10.1007/978-3-030-22219-2_23

will carry out multiple sensors which can sense individual's living environment and activities. Visual information captured by wearable technology in personal lifelog can be very helpful for human memory aiding. Lee [4] proved that lifelogging technologies have the potential to provide memory cues for people who struggle with episodic memory impairment. And Aizawa [5] have put forward five cues based on context and content for efficient retrieval of lifelog data. Moreover, Chen [6] introduced a work-in-process prototype lifelog searching system to augment human memory, which has obtained positive experimental results.

## 2 Goal and Approach

For aiding episodic memory in lifelog system, we used to define cues as memory triggers. Most existing cues in lifelog system mainly focus on contextual information, which is captured from lifelog image or by using sensors like GPS [7]. We can find that these cues have nothing to do with user's own behavior and care little about users themselves. In this research, we aim to involve user's own status into lifelog system, so as to help finding important memory for lifeloggers. Here, user's own status including inner psychological mood and external physiological activity. For a clearer explanation of our research perspective, we corresponds the user status to two cues: Special sentiment cue and special movement cue.

We innovatively use these two cues to propose a new user-related lifelog viewing prototype for aiding episodic memory more efficiently. Our proposed prototype mainly consists of two parts: a wearable sensor system and a web-based lifelog viewer. Unlike traditional contextual lifelog cues, we introduce personal sentiment and movement condition as new cues to enhance the effectiveness of memory recall.

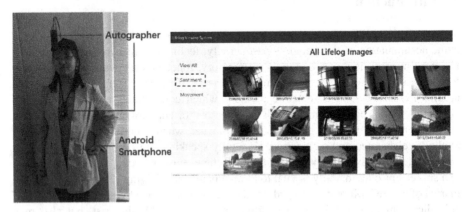

**Fig. 1.** Prototype overview

To achieve this goal, we set up a wearable sensor system (see Fig. 1). We use Autographer attached on user's head to automatically capture face photo, which is used in emotion detection. Meanwhile, we use an Android smartphone embedded with motion sensors like accelerometer and gyroscope to continuously get data to acquire movement situation. Moreover, we use another Autographer hang on user's neck to capture lifelog image constantly. Because of the cross-platform compatibility and usability of web, we build a web-based lifelog viewer as the output. The appearance of the viewer is shown in Fig. 1. Lifeloggers can easily access important memory by using two proposed new cues in this viewer.

# 3   System Design

To achieve our goal, we come up with the idea of providing two user-related cues for lifeloggers. The system overview is shown in Fig. 2. The system is mainly consisting of 1 web-based lifelog viewer and two accessory sub systems: a sentiment detection system used to capture sentiment data and a movement detection system used to capture movement data. In this section, we will describe special sentiment cue and special movement cue in detailed separately.

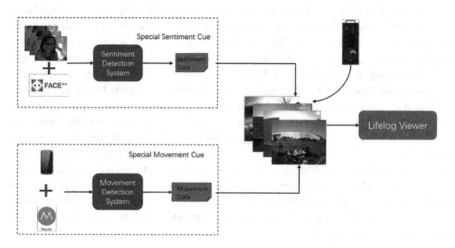

**Fig. 2.** System overview

## 3.1   Special Sentiment Cue

Human's emotions are complex and diverse. Ekman formally put forward six basic emotions in 1972 [8]. Sentiment classification in our system uses six basic emotions put forward by Ekman. Six emotions are: Happiness, sad, surprise, anger, fear and disgust.

In order to get sentiment data for forming special sentiment cue, we use Face++ API [9] to detect sentiment situation through face photo. Figure 3 shows the main procedure of processing sentiment data vividly. Firstly, we need to capture face photo automatically using Autographer. Secondly, the face photo will be input into sentiment detection system to get sentiment data. Here, emotion data consist of two parts: the emotion status and the time information which shows when this emotion has been detected. Thirdly, we match the time of each emotion with the record time of each lifelog image. Finally, we output the result to lifelog viewer for lifeloggers. In the example, the face photo was detected as happiness and it was detected at 2018/03/18

15:12:38. Then, we can find the lifelog image taken at this time. Finally, we can judge that this lifelog image was detected as "happiness".

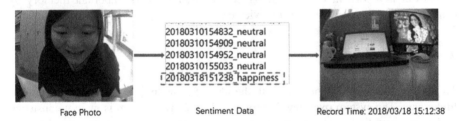

| Face Photo | Sentiment Data | Record Time: 2018/03/18 15:12:38 |

**Fig. 3.** Sentiment detection process

## 3.2    Special Movement Cue

Move is the change in position of an object over time in physics, which is described in terms of displacement, distance, velocity, acceleration, time and speed. Human movement describes the way human moves. The classification of movement is quite complicated. To simplify the result, our proposed method involves mainly five kinds of movement: still, walking, running, on bike and on vehicle. On the other hand, in order to display user's movement situation more vividly, we introduce movement timeline in our method.

We use accelerometer embedded in Android smartphone to capture the pure movement data of lifeloggers. Then, we import the raw accelerometer data into movement detection system. Together with Moves API [10], we can clearly get the result of movement situation. The result consists of variety information, including date, movement, start time, end time, etc. We use movement, start time and end time to form a movement timeline. After getting movement situation, we will match movement time with the time of lifelog image. By matching time, we can clearly find out the movement situation of each lifelog image. Finally, we will output the result to lifelog viewer. The process is shown in Fig. 4.

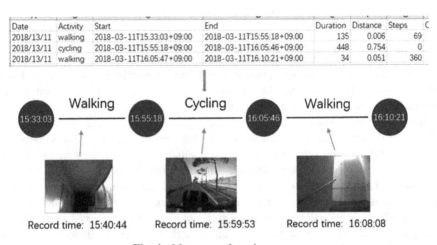

**Fig. 4.** Movement detection process

## 4    System Implementation

### 4.1    Hardware Implementation

For using our system, users need to carry the following three wearable devices: an Autographer attached to a hat on lifelogger's head for face photo acquisition, another Autographer hang on lifelogger's neck for lifelog images capturing, an Android smartphone in lifelogger's pocket for movement data acquisition. To sum up, our system mainly involve two kinds of hardware: Autographer and Android smartphone.

Autographer. Autographer is a hands-free wearable camera that is used in current research. It is 90 × 36 mm in size and weighs approximately 58 g which makes it easy to clip on any clothes or hang on a neck. Without external interference, the capturing frequency of Autographer is 30 s per image and this frequency can change due to the changes in external environment. Autographer is embedded with some sensors, including color sensor, magnetometer, PIR, temperature GPS, etc. Therefore, Autographer is favored by lifelog researchers for its superior performance and relatively intelligent shooting.

Android Smartphone. Smartphone is a mobile phone that has a mobile operating system and can expand functions by installing applications, games and other programs. Android is a free and open source based operating system which is s led and developed by Goggle and the open mobile alliance. As one of the most popular mobile operating systems, Android smartphone have covered more than half in the market. Nowadays, with the development of mobile technique, smartphones are always embedded with variety of sensors like accelerometer, gyroscope, gravity sensor, magnetic field sensor, etc. These sensors can be read by developer using Android SDK and is useful in detecting smartphone holder's movement condition.

### 4.2    Software Implementation

For the software part, we mainly use Browser/Server (B/S) structure to build our web viewer. The structure is consisting of three layers: presentation layer, application layer and data layer. The presentation layer is the web browser which can be run on plenty of platform like desktop, smartphone and laptop. When lifelogger is viewing our system, presentation layer will send a request to application layer, which is a web server. Then, web server will send SQL request to the database and get a reply. It will send the reply back to web browser and the data will be formed into a more legible result and finally be shown to users. Moreover, we mainly use Java and JavaScript as developing language. We use Apache Tomcat 7.0 x as our local web server and use MySQL for data management.

### 4.3    Lifelog Viewing System

This part will describe the detailed interaction of our web-based lifelog viewing system. We will show each page respectively.

Default Page. Figure 5 shows the default page of our lifelog viewer. The default page demonstrates all lifelog images which is ordered by time. Lifeloggers can click "sentiment" button to enter sentiment page, click "movement" button to enter movement page and click "combination" button to enter combination cue.

**Fig. 5.** Default page

Sentiment Page. Figure 6 shows the result of using special sentiment cue to classification all lifelog images. We can find that in the sentiment page, we mainly involve six kinds of sentiment, they are happiness, sad, surprise, anger, fear and disgust. For presenting sentiment vividly, we use emoji to represent each sentiment. The corresponding lifelog image of each sentiment will appear under each sentiment's signal.

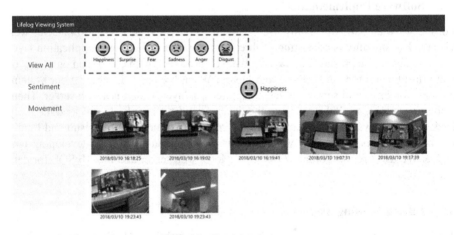

**Fig. 6.** Sentiment page

Movement Timeline. Figure 7 shows movement timeline. we can see that we involve still, walking, running, on bike and on vehicle and there is a movement timeline showing in the middle of the page. By clicking the "view" button of each movement phase, we can enter to browse the detailed lifelog image of each segmented event.

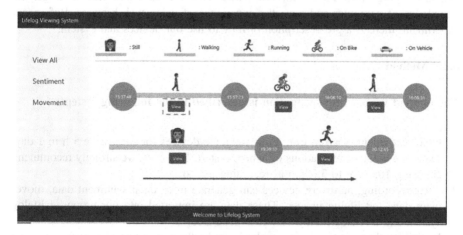

**Fig. 7.** Movement page

Movement Page. Figure 8 shows detailed movement page. The page consists of three parts: slides section(a), choose bar(b) and result section(c). In slide section, the images corresponded to each movement will be played automatically. This can reduce the time of browsing all images. As choose bar shows 6 sentiment emoji, lifeloggers can click the button to view the images satisfy both specific movement and specific sentiment. The result of images will be shown in result section ch sentiment will appear under each sentiment's signal.

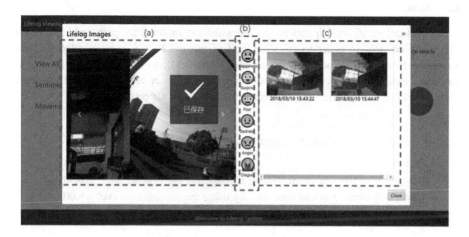

**Fig. 8.** Movement detail page

# 5  Preliminary Evaluation

## 5.1  Participants

In order to evaluate usability and efficiency of using our system, we recruited 6 participants, aging from 22 to 26. All participants are students who have general knowledge of computer and have the experience of using web browser. Before our experiment, there is a pre-description of how to use our devices and system.

## 5.2  Method

**The method we used for evaluation is described in the following 3 steps:**

1. Each participant is asked to use our wearable devices for successive 5 h in 1 day. There are no strict regulations on when to start. However, we strongly recommend choosing 10:00am to 3:00pm as recording period.
2. After recording, hardware devices can generate three data: sentiment data, movement data and lifelog images. These data are imported into our proposed lifelog system and a related lifelog viewer is generated.
3. Participant then tried to use our web viewer by their own. Our viewer contains two parts: Sentiment cue viewer extracts vital memory using participant's sentiment situation. Movement cue viewer extracts important images and orders by using movement timeline, which also enables the function of using sentiment cue. Participants are required to record how many events they can reminisce by using each viewer to test the efficiency of our system.
4. After using our system, a personal interview is given to each participant. Participants are asked to answer a few questions and score their feeling based on Likert Scale (1 = very negative, 5 = very positive).

## 5.3  Result

In our evaluation, all participants have successfully completed the plan and have given effective feedback. In order to get the result of our evaluation, we collected 6 questionnaires from 6 participants (3 males and 3 females) and analyzed their feedback. Since our evaluation is divided into two aspects: efficiency and usability, our results analysis will also be carried out separately in these two aspects.

**Table 1.** Result for efficiency evaluation.

| Question | Result |
| --- | --- |
| How many events you can remember before using our system? | 6.50 |
| How many events you can remember by using special sentiment cue? | 8.00 |
| How many events you can remember by using special movement cue? | 9.83 |

Table 1 reflects the efficiency of our proposed system. To get the result, we calculate the average amount of each question. As shown in Table 1, the result of each question is 6.50, 8.00 and 9.83. From the result, we can see that compare to recalling memory in default manner (not using any assistant), using any method in our proposed system can increase the number of recalling events. With the combination of movement cue in its interface, we can find the result of using movement cue shows better performance.

Another important aspect of our evaluation is the usability of proposed wearable device system and web-based viewing system. As the answer is based on Likert Scale, the average score of each question can clearly represent use experience of our hardware and software system. Table 2 shows the result. We can see that the score of all question is above average level, which shows positive result in our system's usability. Moreover, we can see that the usability of hardware system gets lowest score. This reminds us we need to improve our hardware devices to make it easier to be carried out.

**Table 2.** Result for usability evaluation.

| Question | Result |
|---|---|
| Do you think it is comfortable to wear our devices? | 4 |
| Do you think our viewer is easy to use? | 4.33 |
| Do you feel extracted image useful? | 4.50 |
| Do you think our system help in aiding memory intuitively | 4.67 |

## 6 Related Work

### 6.1 Related Work on Sentiment Detection

Emotion is a general term for a series of subjective cognitive experience. Whether positive or negative, emotions can motivate people to act and influence individual's future somehow. Ever since human beings are aware of the importance of emotions to ourselves, with the increase of sensor accuracy and the rise of computer vision, we are becoming more and more concerned with the recognition and interpretation of emotions. Nowadays, there are mainly three methods to realize emotion detection: (1) Speech emotion detection [11, 12]. (2) Physiological signal detection [13]. (3) Facial emotion detection [14, 15].

In our proposed methods, we choose face photo to detect emotion changes among three methods which is mentioned above. To finally decide which method to choose, we have investigated the merits and demerits of three methods. For speech emotion detection, the accuracy is the highest one. However, it only detects emotional changes when people speak, making detection discontinuity. As for physiological signal detection, subjects need to wear all kinds of heavy and tedious sensors, which make daily life inconvenience and not natural enough. Compare to the former two methods, the accuracy of facial emotion detection has become higher due to deep learning staff. Subjects only need to wear a hat hanged with a camera and detection can be persistent [16].

## 6.2  Related Work on Movement Detection

Movement detection, or activity detection aims to recognize the actions of human from the observation on human's actions. It has captured the attention of computer science communities ever since 1980s. Up to now, mobile devices are becoming increasingly sophisticated, and the latest mobile phones usually embedded with all kinds of sensors. Among them, accelerometer is widely-used for movement detection [17]. Accelerometer measures the combination of gravitational acceleration and object's motion acceleration in the direction of x, y, z axis. Gravitational acceleration is always vertical to the earth, it can measure the angel change between objects and ground. Motion acceleration can detect the speed changing of the object [18].

## 6.3  General Related Work

Our work is closely related to the system developed by Harvey [19]. In their proposed system, they innovatively arose the idea of involving sitting behavior into the lifelog system. They use a sensor, named activePal, to catch subject's sitting event. Meanwhile, they used Vicon Revue, one kind of wearable camera, to capture lifelog image automatically. In their research, they extracted lifelog images when user is sitting for observation purpose. They used their system to observe the living habit of elder adults. The idea of involving user's own status into the lifelog system and making behavior as a new cue inspired the birth of our proposed system.

In this paper, we include Special Moment Approach and Spatial Frequency Approach for reviewing the lifelogs, which is very closely related to Wang's [20] work. Special moment approach is a technique for extracting episodic events. Spatial frequency approach is a technique for associating visual with temporal and location information. Heatmap is applied as the spatial data for expressing frequency awareness.

# 7  Conclusion

In general, our research explains the limitation of memory cue in lifelog system for aiding episodic memory. In order to improve the situation and enhance the efficiency of aiding episodic memory, we propose two user-related cues in this research and has implemented them into a web-based lifelog viewer.

In the proposed system, we mainly implement special sentiment cue and special movement cue as two new user-related cues for lifeloggers to retrieve memory. We use two Autographers and an Android smartphone to capture sentiment data, movement data and lifelog images. After processing the obtained data, we generate a web viewer for lifeloggers to use sentiment cue and movement cue to view lifelog images and retrieve memory.

We assume that lifeloggers can wear our proposed hardware devices in their daily life. After recording for the whole day, lifeloggers can upload their data onto our system and generate their own web viewer. They can retrieve their memory efficiently and conveniently by using our proposed system.

In order to test the usability and efficiency of our proposed system, we have included some participates in our evaluation. The feedback is quite positive.

# References

1. Tulving, E.: Elements of episodic memory. Politics **2** (1983)
2. Tulving, E.: Episodic memory: from mind to brain. Annu. Rev. Psychol. **53**(1), 1–25 (2002)
3. Klein, S.B., Loftus, J., Kihlstrom, J.F.: Memory and temporal experience: the effects of episodic memory loss on an amnesic patient's ability to remember the past and imagine the future. Soc. Cogn. **20**(5), 353–379 (2002)
4. Lee, M.L., Dey, A.K.: Lifelogging memory appliance for people with episodic memory impairment. In: Proceedings of the 10th International Conference on Ubiquitous Computing, pp. 44–53. ACM, New York (2008)
5. Aizawa, K., Tancharoen, D., Kawasaki, S., Yamasaki, T.: Efficient retrieval of life log based on context and content. In: Proceedings of the 1st ACM Workshop on Continuous Archival and Retrieval of Personal Experiences, pp. 22–31. ACM, New York (2004)
6. Chen, Y., Jones, G.J.: Augmenting human memory using personal lifelogs. In: Proceedings of the 1st Augmented Human International Conference, p. 24. ACM, New York (2010)
7. Chowdhury, S., Ferdous, M.S., Jose, J.M.: A user-study examining visualization of lifelogs. In: 2016 14th International Workshop on Content-Based Multimedia Indexing (CBMI), pp. 1–6. IEEE (2016)
8. Ekman, P.: Facial expression and emotion. Am. Psychol. **48**(4), 384–392 (1993)
9. Face++: Api references (2018). https://www.faceplusplus.com.cn/
10. Moves: Api references (2018). https://dev.moves-app.com/
11. Yu, F., Chang, E., Xu, Y.Q., Shum, H.Y.: Emotion detection from speech to enrich multimedia content. In: Shum, H.Y., Liao, M., Chang, S.F. (eds.) PCM 2001. LNCS, vol. 2195, pp. 550–557. Springer, Heidelberg (2001). https://doi.org/10.1007/3-540-45453-5_71
12. Breazeal, C., Aryananda, L.: Recognition of affective communicative intent in robot-directed speech. Auton. Robots **12**(1), 83–104 (2002)
13. Agrafioti, F., Hatzinakos, D., Anderson, A.K.: ECG pattern analysis for emotion detection. IEEE Trans. Affect. Comput. **3**(1), 102–115 (2012)
14. Niedenthal, P.M., Halberstadt, J.B., Margolin, J., Innes-Ker, Å.H.: Emotional state and the detection of change in facial expression of emotion. sEur. J. Soc. Psychol. **30**(2), 211–222 (2000)
15. Caridakis, G., Malatesta, L., Kessous, L., Amir, N., Raouzaiou, A., Karpouzis, K.: Modeling naturalistic affective states via facial and vocal expressions recognition. In: Proceedings of the 8th International Conference on Multimodal Interfaces, pp. 146–154. ACM, New York (2006)
16. Savran, A., et al.: Emotion detection in the loop from brain signals and facial images (2006)
17. Baek, J., Lee, G., Park, W., Yun, B.J.: Accelerometer signal processing for user activity detection. In: Negoita, M.G., Howlett, R.J., Jain, L.C. (eds.) KES 2004. LNCS (LNAI), vol. 3215, pp. 610–617. Springer, Heidelberg (2004). https://doi.org/10.1007/978-3-540-30134-9_82
18. Ravi, N., Dandekar, N., Mysore, P., Littman, M.L.: Activity recognition from accelerometer data. In: AAAI, vol. 5, pp. 1541–1546 (2005)
19. Harvey, J.A., Skelton, D.A., Chastin, S.F.: Acceptability of novel lifelogging technology to determine context of sedentary behaviour in older adults. AIMS Public Health **3**(1), 158–171 (2016)
20. Wang, J., Tanaka, J.: Aiding autobiographical memory by using wearable devices. In: Arai, K., Kapoor, S., Bhatia, R. (eds.) FICC 2018. AISC, vol. 887, pp. 534–545. Springer, Cham (2019). https://doi.org/10.1007/978-3-030-03405-4_37

# Architecture in Mind: Elderly's Affective Memories and Spatial Perceptions of a Downtown Area

Evandro Ziggiatti Monteiro[1]([⊠]), Cláudio Lima Ferreira[1],
Rachel Zuanon[1], Melissa Ramos da Silva Oliveira[2],
and Sidney Piocchi Bernardini[1]

[1] Universidade Estadual de Campinas, Campinas, Brazil
{evanzigg,limacf,rzuanon}@unicamp.br,
sidpiochi@fec.unicamp.br
[2] Universidade Vila Velha, Vila Velha, Brazil
melissa.oliveira@uvv.br

**Abstract.** This paper investigates the relationships of affection, among elderly inhabitants, with the downtown area of their city, especially when evoking and re-evoking memories of significant urban transformations experienced by them. The objective of this research is to reconstruct the cartography of the downtown area of the city of Campinas (in the state of São Paulo, Brazil), during the period of 1930–1935, articulated with the fields of Neuroscience, and Architecture and Urbanism. The methodology is centered around semi-structured interviews with 7 (seven) participants, and employs cartographic map and historical photos of the downtown area of the city to elaborate the volumetric model on which the evoked and re-evoked memories of the interviewees are recorded. From the results obtained we point out: [A] the hybridization between the brain maps of elderly people and the cartographic map of the downtown area of the city; [B] the professional experiences and social activities of the elderly people modulate their spatial perception and their autobiographical memories; [C] the re-evoking of somatosensory memories indicates the modulation of perception of spaces experienced by the elderly in their childhood; [D] the acceptance of radical urban transformations, regardless of the wealth of affective memories related to the modified spaces and demolished buildings. These results seek to broaden the body of contributions to the advancement of research on spatial perception and mental images of the urban space.

**Keywords:** Architecture · Urbanism and neuroscience cooperation ·
Brain maps · Autobiographical memories · Elderly memories ·
Spatial perception

## 1 Introduction

Humans have an innate ability of recalling and imagining physical spaces [1]. Cities, whether evoked or remembered, are continually built in our minds, fusing images of the present with images from our memory and imagination. In constant interaction, our

© Springer Nature Switzerland AG 2019
V. G. Duffy (Ed.): HCII 2019, LNCS 11582, pp. 306–321, 2019.
https://doi.org/10.1007/978-3-030-22219-2_24

perceptions, memories and fantasies erect true metropolises in our mind. "There are cities that remain only as mere visual images when they are recalled, and cities that we recall in all their liveliness. Memory re-evokes the enchanting city with all its sounds and aromas and its nuances of light and shadow (...) where the material and the mental, the experienced, the remembered and the imagined completely merge with each other" [1]. Architecture acts as an externalization of these memories, while also acting as a mediator of our relations with space-time. That is to say, in carrying out this mediation between ourselves and the world, "architecture sets up distinct horizons and frames for experience, cognition and meaning (...) and makes the way the world touches us visible" [1].

It is in this context that we situate this research, which circumscribes the relations of affection of the inhabitants with their city, especially when reviving in their memories the significant urban transformations experienced by them. Important Brazilian cities, founded in the Brazilian colonial or imperial times (18th–19th century), witnessed enormous transformations in their urban centers in the 20th century, when they were adapted for the circulation of motor vehicles. The downtown area of the city of Campinas, located in the state of São Paulo (Brazil), underwent such transformations[1], starting in the 1930s. It is the role of urbanism to understand this processes in depth, both to qualify the instruments of urban planning and design and to improve the management mechanisms of our cities. "For the urban planner, the city and the territory are not only an immense archive of documents of the past, they are mainly an inventory of what is possible" [2]. Since the emergence of pioneering studies on environmental perception in the 1960s, this understanding has shifted focus. Urban planning began to incorporate, in addition to the technical surveys, the immense framework of information coming from the cities' inhabitants themselves. Human beings provide not only direct information on issues regarding environmental comfort, for example, but also about their spatial orientation in the city, their feeling of security or insecurity, their identification with places, their memory of places, among numerous other aspects. With the emergence of studies in the field of Neuroscience [3–7], the spectrum of analysis of all these aspects has been greatly expanded, making its contribution to the field of urban planning, urban quality of life, health and well-being of its inhabitants even more promising.

In the context of urban transformations, we must point out that the living memories of earlier periods become increasingly scarce, especially when the process of recording and documenting these transformations does not comprise the experiences lived by the city's inhabitants. This is where the relevance of this research resides and leads to the urgency of collecting the evoked and re-evoked memories of a small group of elderly people who, each in their personal/professional area of influence, have played a central role in their relations of affection with the downtown area of Campinas. These participants experienced the period of architectural and urban changes in the

---

[1] The transformations were basically characterized by road widening, changes on construction standards, from two-story colonial houses to large vertical buildings, with more varied functions, such as department stores, offices, residential or mixed buildings etc.

aforementioned city intensely, hence the importance of recording the testimonies of this generation.

We were especially interested in the region that comprises the three Squares of the city, in which the municipality's political, religious, and commercial powers imposed themselves and had an undeniable symbolic value: Largo do Carmo (Carmo Square), Largo do Rosário (Rosário Square) and Largo da Catedral (Cathedral Square). What memories remain in the neural architecture of the interviewees regarding the images of the city-province, with its narrow streets, its squares and its mansions? And how were the interviewees' perceptions of the transformations that took over the area shaped and modulated over time?

The period chosen corresponds to approximately a decade, between the years of 1935–1945, when the first interventions of the Urban Improvements Plan proposed for Campinas by Prestes Maia[2] (Brazilian civil engineer, architect and politician) were outlined. This period is a precursor to the growth and modernization of the city of Campinas, which culminated in the present metropolis.

## 2　Autobiographical Memories

The brain forms memories in a totally distributed way. There are several records in the brain that correspond to different aspects of our interaction with the 'things of the world:' spaces, objects, people, animals, in short, every type of relations that are possible to the brain. In other words, there is no single point in the brain where the total record of our possible interactions with a particular 'thing' is located. Rather, these records of our possible interactions with the 'things of the world' are distributed around our neural architecture and remain dormant, implicit in separate neural areas located in the higher cortices. Thus, when they become explicit as mental images—evoked memories, recollections—even if still as an outline, these records are activated only in some of these brain areas, and coordinated rapidly and in close temporal proximity, in such a way that all sensory-motor information seems integrated.

In this context, what differentiates our autobiographical memories from the other memories formed in our brain structure is the fact that autobiographical memories "refer to facts from our personal history, invariable and established" [5]. That is, autobiographical memories are constituted by implicit memories from different moments of our individual experience, from the past and the foreseen future. Associated, life experience and autobiographical memory grow continually, in a movement in which autobiographical memories can be partially remodeled to reflect new experiences [5].

---

[2] The Urban Improvements Plan of Campinas (known as the "Prestes Maia" Plan), from 1938, is the city's first long-term urban development plan. It was also the longest lasting: its implantation stretched from the late 1930s to the late 1960s. The Plan conducted radical interventions in the city's downtown area, with road widening, expropriations and large-scale demolitions of public and private buildings. It also promoted changes in regulation that impacted the downtown area's density and verticalization [8].

From an operational point of view, memories are characterized by structural changes in the synapses, which are distinct for each memory or type of memories. That is to say, memories are stored by means of modifications that occur in the form and function of the synapses that make up the neural networks of each memory. And at the moment they are evoked, the synaptic networks of each memory are reactivated. From a metabolic standpoint, the evocation process involves, in part, the reactivation of neurotransmitter systems (noradrenaline, acetylcholine, glutamic acid) and protein kinases (ERKs, CaMKII, PKA) employed in memory consolidation.

In this process of reactivation, the more components of the conditioned stimulus are present, the easier and more reliable the evocation will be. The methodology adopted by this research is thus justified. By making use of photographic records from the period evoked (between the years 1935 and 1945) and their association with a digital volumetric model, both representing the downtown area of the city of Campinas, the research makes feasible the presence of the largest number of components of the conditioned stimuli in the brain architecture of the respective participants.

We must point out that the reactivation of memory can lead to its reconsolidation. In this context, reconsolidation facilitates the incorporation of new data into the memory that is being evoked [7]. On the other hand, the lack of reinforcement can contribute to the extinction of the then consolidated memory. In the case of elderly people, or of very old memories, the extinct or semi-extinct memories corroborate the mixtures of memories or the partial or defective evocations. Just as the simple passing of the years can also provoke deformations to the point of turning them into false memories [7].

## 3  Brain Maps

The representations of key events in an individual's autobiography are on the neural basis of the 'self.' In other words, the notion of identity is repeatedly reconstituted in the partial activation of these representations, on sensory maps organized topographically [6]. That is, momentary maps made up of nerve cells located in different places of the brain record the numerous events that denote the life process. This mapping of all the things inside or outside our body, built by the brain, underlies all our mental images —concrete and abstract, ongoing or previously recorded in memory. These images result from the changes in the organism during the physical interaction of the body with the 'things of the world.' At this moment, sensors distributed throughout the body emit signals that build, in the brain's several sensory and motor regions, the transient neural patterns dedicated to mapping such interactions. As true collections of neural patterns, brain maps represent the body's responses to the stimuli that generate emotions and feelings [9, 10].

In contrast to classical cartography, brain maps are not static. On the contrary, they are dynamic, unstable and constantly shift to reflect the changes occurring in neural patterns. Such dynamism is consistent with our own existence and with the fact that we are in constant motion. In short, every environment "offered to the brain is perpetually modified, spontaneously or under the control of our activities (…) our body changes according to the different emotions, and different feelings come about (…) and the respective brain maps undergo corresponding changes" [10].

In this research, the cartographic maps of the city of Campinas and the brain maps of the participants articulate and reconstruct throughout the evocation and re-evocation process of the respective autobiographical memories.

## 4  Methodology

The aim of this research is to reconstruct the cartography of the downtown area of the city of Campinas (São Paulo, Brazil) in the period of 1930 to 1935, from evoked and re-evoked affective memories from the brain maps of the elderly participants.

The work consists of three distinct phases: (a) preparation of the material for the interviews; (b) semi-structured interviews with seven (7) elderly people; (c) transcription, compilation and analysis of the data.

In the **(a) preparation phase**, the research focus is defined, considering the three city Squares: Carmo, Rosário and Cathedral, involving not only the surrounding streets, but also including their interconnecting stretches. We have utilized as references: a cadastral map of the downtown area of Campinas, in 1:1000 scale, dated from 1985; and 89 street-level photos of the area of the three Squares, from the period of 1900 to 1945. With the cadastral plan, and aided by the photos, a digital volumetric model (made in the CAD software) of the region of the three Squares was produced, of an immediately previous moment (1930–1935) to the first renovations conducted by Prestes Maia's Urban Improvements Plan (1940). From the model, a perspective view of this volumetric set was selected and printed in size 90 cm × 30 cm. Over this view a drawing of the three Squares, in perspective and in freehand, was produced. In this drawing, the volumes were given additional details and ornaments, by hand, which were obtained from the aforementioned photos. This results in a view of the three Squares, seen from above, and reflecting the configuration of this urban space in the 1930s.

The selection of the public, aged 75 and above, considers those who experienced the great urban reform, carried out in the downtown area of the city in the 1940s, either as residents or as frequenters of that area. Together with these, we have conducted semi-structured interviews and exhibited photographic records of the aforementioned architectural and urban space, in a period prior to the renovations. This strategy facilitates a reconstruction, in perspective, of the urban map, based on the spatialization of memories, evoked and re-evoked in the elderly participants, regarding the old downtown area of Campinas.

The **(b) interview phase** consists of meetings with the participants, in places of the city of Campinas indicated by them. The interview kit includes: a copy of the hand-drawn perspective view of the three Squares, to which the researchers add information of the places mentioned by each interviewee; and three folders (one for each of the Squares), each containing about 20–30 photographs from the 1930–1935 period. The individual interview begins with the participant filling out a demographic data sheet. Then, the researchers conduct the dialogues focused on the evocation and re-evocation of their recollections of the three Squares, approaching one Square at a time. The photos corresponding to each Square are used as stimuli to evoke memories. All interviews are recorded in full.

The **(c) data compilation and analysis phase** initially consists of the transcription and textual compilation of the interviews. An overview of the three Squares is generated for each of the seven interviews. Specifically for the analysis, the first action focuses on the identification of intersections in the testimonies, in order to locate memories associated with the same site or building. The second focuses on the familiarity of the interviewees with each of the three Squares, that is, if any of the Squares predominates in the individual memories. The third focuses on the thematic predominance (religious, political etc.) of the facts and aspects recalled by the elderly. This predominance, later confirmed by the results, is dependent on the educational and professional background of each participant.

The fourth action is aimed at reworking the graphical representation of the perspective views initially generated (phase 1) and applied in the interviews (phase 2), in order to reflect the results obtained thus far. All the buildings mentioned by the interviewees are highlighted in colors that identify their category, divided by theme: (1) lilac - religious buildings; (2) red - shops/commercial buildings; (3) blue - public buildings, spaces of political action, newspaper headquarters; (4) orange - educational/cultural/leisure buildings; (5) green - families/dwellings of traditional families of the city; (6) brown - industrial buildings. Brief comments on relevant curiosities or facts, mentioned by the interviewees, were also added to the new perspective views, exactly where they occurred and according to the memory of each participant. Finally, the quantitative results are systematized in a table, showing the thematic predominance in the evoked and re-evoked memories of the brain maps of the elderly participants, aligned with the six categories listed above. The main qualitative results are shown below.

# 5   Main Results and Discussions

The four steps for analysis described in the methodology converge towards the three groups of results addressed in this section. We must also point out the qualitative aspect of the memories collected in respect to each of the three Squares, as follows:

**Carmo Square**

In the Carmo Square, the participants of this research mentioned families, surnames and nicknames, and not the visual appeal of attractive storefronts, the bizarre lifestyles of notorious passers-by, which are commonly evoked in references to the other two Squares. What also predominate are almost grandiose memories of the characters from the past and their kinship. The constructions themselves, the mansions, evoked in these participants the names of their builders, and of the families who acquired them over the following generations.

**Rosário Square**

The participants' memories of Rosário Square are diverse and vigorous, denoting the importance of this site as a symbolic landmark of important events in the city's history. Political events that marked the fate of Campinas are evoked. Recollections of the most prominent commercial establishments and the merchants themselves, with their habits and patrons. The participants also mention curious facts, or regarding notorious passers-by, peddlers and hawkers that roamed the square. In Rosário Square there are also evocations of the genealogical relations of the traditional families, with their mansions. This diversity reveals the more democratic nature of this Square, through the wealth of appropriations and uses associated with this public space.

### Cathedral Square

The memories related to the Cathedral Square are varied regarding the functions of its buildings (commercial, residential, institutional and leisure). Considered the city's "postcard", it is always mentioned by the interviewees as a special and noble site. The Cathedral Square differs from the story of the other two Squares. Conceived at a later moment in the city's evolution, this Square was planned to house a Christian temple of greater proportion and importance than the previous ones.

**Fig. 1.** Cathedral Square in 1930. In the foreground, on the right, the building of the center for the Sciences, Letters and Arts. Source: V-08 Archive.

## 5.1  Professional Experiences and Social Activities of the Elderly Modulate the Autobiographical Memories and the Perception of Urban and Architectural Space

The first photos, taken from the tower of the new Cathedral, show an already well-formed Square—the Cathedral Square, in the late 19th and early 20th centuries, where there were several mansions and two-story houses. In this context, the Center for the Sciences, Letters and Arts (CCLA), built in 1907, at the corner of Francisco Glicério and Conceição Street, stands out (see Fig. 1). An institution that exerted major influence in the life of the city of Campinas, the Center brought together artists and intellectuals, promoted events and courses, and sponsored hundreds of publications.

Here we find evidence of how the same building, with a single use, has its perception modulated by the individuals' professional experience and/or social activities. In other words, "the lived existential space, different from the physical and geometric space, is structured on the basis of the meanings and values reflected in it by the individual or group, consciously or unconsciously; it is a unique experience interpreted by memory and the individual's empirical contents" [1]. Belonging to the group of "men" who discussed politics, literature and science, the interviewee Benedito Barbosa Pupo was a professional historian and political journalist, and he was also a frequent visitor to CCLA. His autobiographical memory is linked to the "environment" in which this occurred, the circumstances and the characters that were part of it:

"The entrance was at Conceição Street... There was something funny here... There was one thing here... I always sat here and watched the movement. It was very popular, you know? Because there were many members... There was a cafe, from noon to one-thirty... Interesting; Pacífico, he was called Pacífico, he served a lot of coffee for us... (he was an assistant of "Fonseca's")... (...) All those shopkeepers over there had no toilets, so they went in as members so they could use the Center's restroom and have coffee. (...) Right after lunch, it was crowded: Geraldo Correia, Celestino Campos, all those people, teachers, met there..." [11]

On the other hand, Dona Célia, writer and chronicler, was the "outside" observer, since access to this building was forbidden to women. The building is seen by her with mystery, curiosity and fear. At the same time that it attracted her because of the books inside the place, it repelled her for the implicit prohibition:

"In front of Casa Di Lascio, in the same Francisco Glicério Street (which was not an avenue, but a street) with Conceição Street was the (old) building of the Center for the Sciences, which was a beautiful building. And I would ask my mother, 'What's inside this building?' She would answer, 'There are a lot of books...' Then I'd ask, me being mad about books: 'Can't we go inside and see?' She replied, 'No, only men are allowed, women don't go there.' So I didn't go..." [12]

The interviewee Léo Siqueira, in turn, heir of a traditional family from Campinas, focuses his account on historical facts and in the social genealogy of the city. Especially in the perception of the urban and architectural space of the downtown area regarding the aspect of the ownership of the residential real estate:

"This mansion, here on the corner of Tomaz Alves Street (Carmo Square), was built by the Ambrust Family. It was later bought by Companhia de Tração Luz e Força and my grandfather, Mário Estevão Siqueira, who was the company's president, lived at the top, and married his daughters there." [13]

"In the last two visits made by Princess Isabel, in 1884, and the Emperor, in 1886, they stayed at the Cathedral Square, in the famous "great house," the mansion of the Viscountess of Campinas." [13]

"I lament the removal of the statues and ornaments that adorned the top of the facade of the former residence of the Viscountessof Campinas." [13]

And to Zanzur Smânio, a merchant from Campinas, the memories are the most intricate web of business and courtesy relationships between Campinas's new class of merchants and the stores themselves. During his interview, each store mentioned led to the remembrance of the name of its owner and small particularities or stories related to the interviewee's own family. He was able to list, one by one and in chronological and spatial order, the names of all the stores located at the three Squares.

"Cidade München (Cathedral Square) sold draft beer and had a small stage where German dancers performed." [14]

"Casa Di Lascio (Cathedral Square) sold the most elegant men's clothes. I used to shop for special suits there, made with a very fine fabric." [14]

To Damásio [5], autobiographical memory comprises an aggregate of dispositive records about who we are in the physical and behavioral spheres, associated with "records about what we plan to be in the future". That is to say, this memory formed and consolidated with our life experiences and the individual's biography, also partially reshapes to aggregate and reflect new experiences.

The maps below (Figs. 2 and 3) simultaneously denote this autobiographical dynamics and serve as an object of concretization of the downtown area of the city of Campinas in the evoked memories of its inhabitants. In them, we can visualize the correlation between the individual's biography and their repertoire of experiences, and the remembered urban spaces. "Buildings, villages and cities impart experiential and existential meanings to meaningless spaces by converting them into specific spaces, which choreograph and resonate along with our mental actions and reactions" [1].

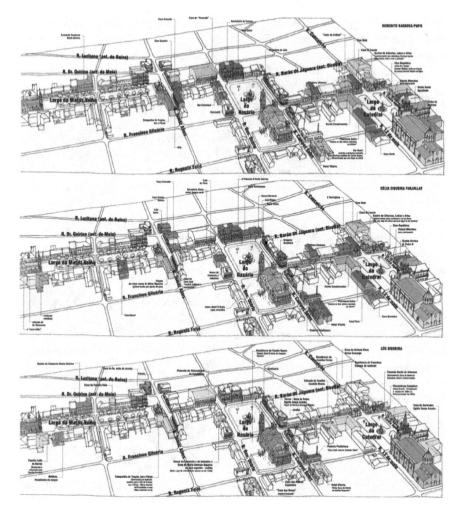

**Fig. 2.** Graphical representation in perspective of the three Squares. The buildings cited by each interviewee are highlighted: top [11]; middle [12]; bottom [13]. The colors represent the function of the buildings (see Table 1). Source: the authors.

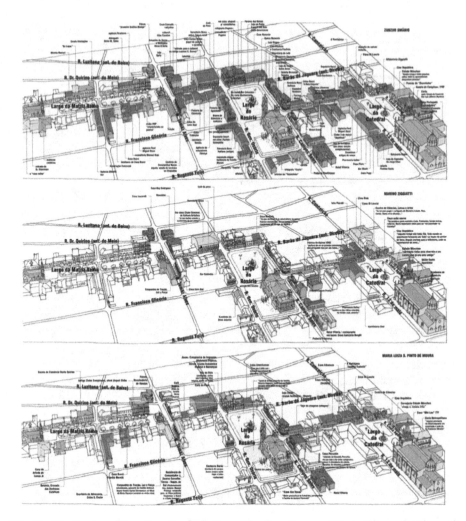

**Fig. 3.** Graphical representation in perspective of the three Squares. The buildings cited by each interviewee are highlighted: top [14]; middle [15]; bottom [16]. The colors represent the function of the buildings (see Table 1). Source: the authors.

## 5.2     The Re-evocation of Somatosensory Memories and the Modulation of the Perception of Spaces Experienced by the Elderly in Childhood

In the first half of the 20th century, commerce in the city of Campinas was concentrated in the Treze de Maio Street (Cathedral Square), which started at the Paulista Railway Station. In the lower part of the large two-story house of the Complementary School, at this time dedicated to secondary education, there were several spaces that were occupied by famous stores, such as the Salles Pharmacy.

In this scenario, we have an example of how public spaces are modified in the re-evocation of somatosensory memories of its inhabitants. According to Pallasmaa [1],

**Table 1.** Quantitative result of the buildings mentioned by the interviewees. Buildings classified according to their function. Source: the authors.

| | Color on map | Pupo [11] | Farjallat [12] | Siqueira [13] | Smânio [14] | Ziggiatti [15] | Moura [16] |
|---|---|---|---|---|---|---|---|
| (A) Religious buildings | Lilac | 6 | 6 | 5 | 6 | 5 | 5 |
| (B) Stores | Red | 12 | 22 | 3 | 69 | 13 | 16 |
| (C) Public buildings/political parties | Blue | 2 | 0 | 2 | 5 | 1 | 2 |
| (D) Cultural/educational/leisure buildings | Orange | 6 | 4 | 0 | 3 | 5 | 4 |
| (E) Houses from traditional families | Green | 2 | 3 | 15 | 4 | 1 | 5 |
| (F) Industry | Brown | 0 | 0 | 0 | 0 | 1 | 0 |
| Total | | 28 | 35 | 25 | 87 | 26 | 32 |

"when the eyes touch and contemplation caresses distant profiles and contours, our vision feels the hardness, texture, weight and temperature of surfaces" and our brain maps incorporate this information as somatosensory records, which may be evoked in the future.

For instance, the visual stimulus given by the photographic record of Treze de Maio Street (Fig. 4) evokes, in both interviewees, somatosensory memories of the Salles Pharmacy. However, while for Dona Celia the red liquid in the medication vials is lived

**Fig. 4.** Treze de Maio Street, in which the Salles Pharmacy is located, on the block to the side of the Cathedral. Source: CCLA archive.

in her memory, the same color is not even mentioned by Mr. Marino, in the same exercise of re-examination:

"In the 1920s I used to go to Cathedral Square with my mother to pray in the Cathedral, and I observed that on the side of Treze de Maio Street (which was an open street, now closed) there was a pharmacy, the Salles Pharmacy, which bewildered me, because pharmacies, old pharmacies, had huge vials with colored liquid—the liquid was red, I can't remember if the other was green or yellow, but the red one drew my attention… (…) My mother said that at night doctors met there to share the news… there were chairs on the sides, let's say it was their club." [12]

"I remember the Salles Pharmacy, on this side, which was one of those old pharmacies, with those colored bottles; yellow, blue…" [15]

In other words, it is clear to both inhabitants that the revived scene carries enough values and emotions to ensure that the brain keep records that are "multimedia records of visions, sounds, tactile sensations, odors and related perceptions" [10] and re-present them when evoked. "With the time and imagination of a fabulist, the material can be adorned, cut into pieces and recombined into a novel or screenplay" [10].

**Fig. 5.** Rosário Square. In the foreground, next to the chimney, buildings in the same lot as Casa Purcchio (fronting the Square) and "5.002" sugar factory (back). Source: CCLA archive.

In a different perspective, the same photograph of the Rosário Square region, in which the chimney of the sugar factory called "5.002" appears in the foreground (Fig. 5), primarily evokes memories of different spaces for both interviewees. While the memories of Maria Luiza concentrate on her experience with the business activities of Casa Purcchio, those evoked by Mr. Marino focus on the industrial routine of the same establishment:

"(…) at Casa Purcchio, I went with my friends to ride the elevator… And on the ground floor we bought packages with sugar cubes, which were leftovers from the factory behind. They wrapped them and sold them in little packs…" [16]

"I was impressed, they had Fiat trucks that had no tires, they used solid tires, and they came to unloaded crude oil to run the plant… I liked to watch the big, yellow truck, there was a tube came from it, that ran all the way to a warehouse… I was impressed to see that, I had never seen a truck like that…" [15]

Such statements reinforce what Pallasmaa [1] calls the "mental experience of the city". More than a sequence of visual images, this experience comprises a broad haptic constellation, or a continuum of haptic experiences, which incorporate the impressions of the gaze.

## 5.3    The Re-evocation of Memories and the Non-nostalgic Acceptance of Space Transformed Through Urban Renovation

The ability to learn to be guided by future perspectives, rather than immediate results, is one of the distinctive traits of human beings, first acquired during childhood [6].

Beginning in the 1930s, with the boost in industrialization, the city of Campinas definitely entered the "modern times". The word "progress" may be the most emblematic, what best symbolizes the feeling of the citizens and the city in this period. And it was unanimous. There is no single mention, even in the brochures and articles of the time, nor in the interviewees' statements, of any opposition or dissent to the idea of "progress". "Groups, and even nations, share certain experiences of the existential space that constitute their collective identities and their sense of community" [1].

From these results the Urban Improvements Plan, which led to profound trans-formations in the old hierarchical-functional structure of the three Squares, with the widening of several main streets (Fig. 6). The renovation of the public thoroughfares and the Squares, with the consequent expropriations and changes in construction

**Fig. 6.** Francisco Glicério Street (Rosário Square), in the 1930s (left) and its transformation into an avenue, with the Urban Improvements Plan, beginning in the 1940s (right). Source: V-8 Archive and CCLA Archive, respectively.

regulations, hastened the replacement of the old for the new. This combination of memories of the past and the future, woven into the constant reactivation of updated images of our identity, forms a considerable part of the state of the "self" [6].

The neural basis for the "self" consists in the continuous reactivation of at least two sets of representations: (a) key events in an individual's autobiography; and (b) a set of recent events associated with a set of imaginary and desired plans and events [6].

Contrary to the intransigent nostalgic attachment, usually presumed in the discourse associated with the evoked memories, what is observed here are the contours of a different perspective—the satisfactory acceptance of what's new, without it being a threat to the preservation of the memory of this space.

"It was necessary... It was all very narrow, the city became more airy..." [12]

"Prestes Maia was very important... It was a contribution!... Campinas could not be restricted by those narrow streets, it would be a... I wonder... Today we have a different notion, you know, maybe we would leave it as it was... but it couldn't be, otherwise we would have to build another city... it had to be done... these openings..." [15]

Imaginary plans and events make up memories of a possible future. And, like any other memory, they are preserved in the dispositive representations [6].

# 6  Conclusion

This research leads us to some conclusions regarding the connections between the brain maps, the evoked and re-evoked memories, and the affective relations of elderly inhabitants with the urban space of the downtown area of Campinas.

Part of the interviewees' accounts is of descriptive and analytical nature regarding the buildings and the facts associated with them. The other part, in turn, is emotional in nature, and focuses on the evocation and re-evocation of the somatosensory memories and the affective memories of the spaces experienced by these inhabitants in their childhood years. It is evident that the memories about the same building, fact or place denote generational differences. Beyond that, the emotional state of the interviewee at the time of evocation also modulates the memories and shapes their perceptions about their past.

Still, the impact of each participant's professional background and social activities in the process of 'editing and recombining' their memories is remarkable. This specificity allows for the evocation of personalized cartographies, properly structured in the respective brain maps of these inhabitants. Combined, these evoked cartographies facilitate the reconstruction of the cartography of these Squares in Campinas in the 1930s, in a spatial representation that interprets and qualifies them.

Throughout this process, the classification of these evocations into categories facilitates the association of the interviewee's profile with the nature of the memories themselves. For instance, an interviewee whose life has always been associated to the social relationships with traditional families evokes memories related to the ownership of the buildings and their functions as residential spaces for the elites. Or that another, whose professional life has been entirely performed in the commercial field, is able to enumerate the stores, one by one (see Table 1).

Another relevant aspect is the dissociation between the memories evoked by this group of inhabitants and the feeling of nostalgia. Differently from what is commonly found in the accounts by elderly people about the great urban transformations that their places of childhood and youth have undergone, the opposite is observed here. The acceptance of these changes and the understanding of their contributions to the revitalization of the urban space, even when this involves demolishing historical architectures, which bear high symbolic load and sociocultural value.

Finally, regardless if the individual memories evoked are complementary or divergent in nature, the set of collective memories are extremely valuable to urban studies, whose objective converges to urban intervention, through planning and management tools or urban design.

# References

1. Pallasmaa, J., Salvaterra, A.: Habitar [Dwell]. GG, Barcelona (2017)
2. Secchi, B.: Primeiralição de urbanismo [First Lesson in Urbanism]. Perspectiva, São Paulo (2006)
3. Lundy-Ekman, L.: Neurociência: Fundamentospararareabilitação [Neuroscience: Fundamentals for Rehabilitation]. Elsevier, Rio de Janeiro (2004)
4. Lent, R.: Neurociência da mente e docomportamento [Neuroscience of Mind and Behavior]. Guanabara Koogan, Porto Alegre (2008)
5. Damásio, A., Motta, L.T.: O mistério da consciência: do corpo e das emoçõesaoconhecimento de si [The Mystery of Consciousness: From Body and Emotions to Self-Knowledge]. Cia das Letras, São Paulo (2013)
6. Damásio, A.: O erro de Descartes: emoção, razão e o cérebrohumano [The Error of Descartes: Emotion, Reason and the Human Brain]. Cia das Letras, São Paulo (2012)
7. Izquierdo, I.: Memória [Memory]. Artmed, Porto Alegre (2011)
8. Badaró, R.S.C.: Campinas, o despontar da modernidade [Campinas, the dawn of modernity]. CEAP/PUCCAMP: Centro de Memória, Unicamp, Campinas (1996)
9. Damásio, A.: Embusca de Espinosa: prazer e dornaciência dos sentimentos [In Search of Espinosa: Pleasure and Pain in the Science of the Feelings]. Companhia das Letras, São Paulo (2004)
10. Damásio, A.: E o cérebrocriou o homem [And the Brain Created Man]. Companhia das Letras, São Paulo (2011)
11. Pupo, B.B.: Testimony obtained from the Interview held on 12 October 2000
12. Farjallat, C.: Testimony obtained from the Interview held on 6 April 2000
13. Siqueira, L.: Testimony obtained from the interview held at JóqueiClube, formerly ClubeCampineiro, on 8 December 2000
14. Smânio, Z.: Testimony obtained from the interview held on 21 December 2000
15. Ziggiatti, M.: Testimony obtained from the interview held on 5 May 2000
16. Moura, M.L.P.: Testimony obtained from the interview held on 16 December 2000

# Health Dialogues

# Edgard, the Chatbot: Questioning Ethics in the Usage of Artificial Intelligence Through Interaction Design and Electronic Literature

Fernando Fogliano⬤, Fernando Fabbrini⬤, André Souza$^{(\boxtimes)}$⬤,
Guilherme Fidélio⬤, Juliana Machado⬤, and Rachel Sarra⬤

Centro Universitário Senac, São Paulo, SP 04696-000, Brazil
{ffoglian, fernando.fabbrini}@sp.senac.br,
andregsouzaweb@gmail.com, guilhermehl996@gmail.com,
julianamachado218@gmail.com, rachsarra@gmail.com

**Abstract.** The goal of this research is to discuss and develop a chatbot, named Edgard, in the fields of electronic literature, interaction design and Artificial Intelligence (AI). It will address technologies and its contradictions, pointing out its significant role as a platform for creativity, innovation and knowledge production, as well as the importance of critical thinking in the ethical application of these technologies, whose emergence reveals a new industrial revolution.

**Keywords:** Chatbots · Artificial Intelligence · Creativity · Electronic literature · Interaction design

## 1 Introduction

Artificial Intelligence (AI) technologies represent progress as significant as those that in previous centuries provoked profound social, political and environmental impacts. The so-called industrial revolutions signal an accelerated progression whose aspects, when analyzed, are contradictory. If, on the one hand, humanity benefited from the scientific advances made available through the use of technological products, such as improving their life expectancy and quality and giving access to diversified cultural manifestations, on the other, is at the core of the environment's degradation, exacerbated wealth concentration by an elitist minority and the polarization of opinions capable of producing social tensions amid the circulation of false information, showing itself capable of interfering in democratic processes around the world.

The emergence of AI reminds us of analogous situations already experienced, such as the emergence of the first steam engines in the eighteenth century. It is, therefore, necessary to consider its use from a historical perspective and its inherent contradictions. We sought to analyze the use of AI technologies by designing a chatbot, Edgard, conceived by the intersection between art, science, and technology. This paper presents discussions held in 2018 by a research group on Interactive Environments composed of professors and students from Senac's University Center Bachelor's Degree in Digital Design. This project aims to discuss the understanding of technologies' roles as the primary platform for innovative thinking. Following this point of view, by supporting

© Springer Nature Switzerland AG 2019
V. G. Duffy (Ed.): HCII 2019, LNCS 11582, pp. 325–341, 2019.
https://doi.org/10.1007/978-3-030-22219-2_25

creative processes, AI technologies unbalance the pros and cons in favor of the former. However, this will only be possible if the use of these technologies occurs in critical circumstances based on experience given by previous industrial revolutions. We are now aware of being on the threshold of a new evolutionary cycle which, as in previous ones, has in its core contradictions and reasons for both excitement and concern. It is true that the choice to use AI technologies in society has diffuse origins, and its usage will cause a significant impact very soon. However, it is also true that, despite the various goals, ethical issues lie at the heart of this development.

## 2    Technology and Modernity

Technology is the knowledge field that allows us to apply know-how, the appropriation of artifacts or tools to build other artifacts or tools. This appropriation can be either merely technical when the individual explores technological resources without worrying about its origins or improvement, or technological when the activity leads to creative processes that are capable of allowing new developments. Altogether, technology shares many of its knowledge with science. In many times it is possible to perceive a synergistic action between the knowledge fields in which new technologies leverage new scientific expertise, or when scientific discoveries allow the emergence of new technologies.

Technologies characterize the modern period. Cupani [1] brings the concept of a device recognizing that, in addition to the social, political and economic aspects, technological artifacts must have its pragmatic character identified. Devices, such as commodities, provide services:

"One must recognize in technology a primary phenomenon, which has its key in the existence of the devices that provide us with products (commodities), that is, goods and services, whether it is the electric heater, which gives us heat, of the vehicles, which allows us to move quickly and relatively freely, or the television set, which gives us information and entertainment" [1].

As consumer goods, technological artifacts are the subject of marketing interest. Taken from the Enlightenment perspective, the consumption of these devices would meet the aspiration to liberate humanity from hunger, pain, and labor. Besides, technology can be attributed to the potential for raising cultural standards and life. However, as pointed Cupani [1], technology and science alone cannot be attributed to socio-cultural changes experienced in industrially developed countries.

"It is not enough, therefore, to understand technology by paying attention to its dominated nature, or its association with science. Scientific progress and its application to practical purposes are imperative to the existence of most technological inventions, but science, by itself, cannot provide a direction or explain why technology has become a lifestyle" [1].

Cupani [1] points out that, in order to better understand the technical device and the consequences of its use, one must distinguish between traditional technology and modern technology. The former maintained close social, cultural and ecological relations with its place of origin, while technologies, uncoupled from their environment, merely connect means and ends. In this sense, devices can be used independently of its context and freely combined. Devices become conceptually ambiguous. This scenario can give us an understanding of how much the technology consumption feeds a dream of a better, safer and more valuable life, at the same time that culture becomes the space for the exercise of addiction, pleasure, and security, making the paradigm of technology, not an option, but an imposition. The efficiency of technical devices floods the brain of dopamine [2] as an emotional consequence of the efficiency of the immediate response and the sense of security that interactive technologies provide. The question of efficiency is an aspect that comes when the theme is technology, and that it is of our interest because it is in this aspect that most significant consequences of the use of contemporary digital technologies, among them AI reside.

## 2.1    Technology and Society in Economics, Art and Design

In the context of capitalism, the best measure of efficiency is profit. In this sense, technologies can be used at both ends of the market, in the consumption of commodities and its production as tools of goods and services. Cupani [1] brings to his arguments the thoughts of Andrew Feenberg to build the connections between technology, capitalism, and efficiency.

"Capitalism (and bureaucratic socialism), sustains Feenberg, fosters technological achievements that reinforce hierarchical and centralized social structures and, in general, control "from above," in all sectors of human life: work, education, medicine, law, sports, media, and many others. There is, in short, a "generalized technical mediation" at the service of privileged interests, which reduces human possibilities everywhere, in the name of efficiency, imposing everywhere, as visible measures, discipline, vigilance, standardization" [1].

Nonetheless, there is in this simplification process, and cultural impoverishment resulted from generalization that serves privileged interests by efficiently securing a profit, a breach for the rupture imposed by the "hegemony of the technical code." Cupani [1] reminds us that society does not respond linearly to the stimuli to which it is exposed. There is a "room for maneuver" that subtracts from capitalism its absolute control. Alternatives for reinvention can appear in the game of technological usage. This aspect, which here recovers the subject of the technical device's ambiguity, is also present in the Simondonean thought. The "margin of indetermination" [3] for Simondon implies the absolute perfection of the machines, contradicting the first impression that the technological advance is attributed to automatism. For the philosopher, who studied technology from a humanist perspective, the increase in the margin of indetermination allows a more complex dialogue between the technical beings (especially the machines) and the living beings. This dialogue allows innovation and diversification of possibilities and cultural experiences provided by technical objects [4]. It is no mere coincidence that contemporary art offers a space for reflection and practice where artists explore the Simondonean concepts of "margin of indetermination" and "superabundance" [5].

"As objects and natural resources are organized in a system, the potential brought by each of them in the dispersion state is updated in specific power lines. This should explain why systematic ordering does not produce results limited to the initial expectations of problem resolution. The update of each subset potential does not produce a simple sum because, in the systematic frame, there is a real amplification of the obtained effects' potential. The conditions of the problem are overcome because the invention recreates new potentials, upgradable by new inventions, establishing new genetic cycles of images" [6].

The intersection of artistic and technological production fields is a space for reinventing the devices. Practices within the art universe develop new technical objects as a result of the re-signification of others, integrating them into new symbolic systems to produce non-linear results, different from the mere sum of its parts. Devices are reorganized poetically in the creation of narratives, having in mind the aesthetic experience. In this respect, such practices approximate Art and Technology of Conceptual Art.

Although this reinvention process produces impacts on culture, as did works as the "Fountain", 1917, by Duchamp [7], or the "GFP Bunny: transgenic bunny", 2000, by Kac [8], is the systematic use of technical devices that have attracted the attention of philosophers, historians and scholars of technology, especially when it comes to the use of AI. Harari [9], in a somber perspective of the future, considers the possibility of the decoupling between liberalism and capitalism. He criticizes the real motives of liberalism, which guarantees individual freedom to citizens in democratic societies in a game of economic and political interests.

"[…] giving people political rights is good because the soldiers and workers of democratic countries perform better than those of dictatorships. Allegedly, granting people political rights increases their motivation and their initiative, which is useful both on the battlefield and in the factory" [9].

### 2.2 AI and Its Impact on the Job Market

Recognizing in the humanist discourse of the liberal ideology a strategy to conceal his real interests, Harari [9], given the technological advances represented by the use of intelligent algorithms, foresees an even more disastrous situation for humanity. The use of these technologies will suppress men and women's military and economic value [9]. The ability to "handle a hammer or push a button" loses its relevance to the machines' efficiency. The reason for this lies in the fact that everything, as far as the breadth of computers and culture itself is concerned, advances quickly. Kurzweil [10] recalls Moore's law when referring to the acceleration in the computing field, communication network and other parameters linked to that technological breadth. According to this law, the number of components integrated into the microprocessors grows exponentially over time. This increase results in assigning computers greater computing power. Human intelligence, extra somatized in machines, has made them more efficient than us in various tasks. The concept of Singularity, brought by Kurzweil [10], which seeks to understand intelligence and its relation to the human brain, allows the understanding of its mechanisms and the construction of machines as complex as the brain itself.

"The goal of the project is to understand precisely how the human brain works and then use these unveiled methods to better understand ourselves, fix the brain when necessary and - most pertinent to the point of this book - to create even smarter machines" [10].

If we consider the emergence of devices with embedded AI used in the industry, we will have the impression that the Singularity, as Kurzweil predicted, seems very close to happening. However, that may not be good news for humans. When it comes to considering social impacts on the use of AI technologies, Harari [9] presents pessimism about how "unimproved" humans will be completely useless and can be easily replaced by robots and 3D printers in manual labor. In fact, such substitution of humans by intelligent machines will occur in many areas of productive activity. From stockbrokers to lawyers, doctors and professors can be replaced by smart technologies that never tire or lose their patience, and they can devote 100% of their time in the execution of their tasks.

In the CIGI Papers publication of July 2018 by the International Center for Innovation and Governance, Twomey [11] presents a study on the progress in the adoption of AI and Big Data technologies, within the G20[1]. In this study, the author presents a propositional scenario for the gradual adoption of these technologies in order to minimize their social impacts. The numbers presented in this document express the relevance and scale of the issue.

For example, KPMG[2] International [12] reports that "between now and 2025, up to two-thirds of the $9 trillion knowledge-market workers may be affected. The Bank of England estimates that robotic automation will eliminate 15 million jobs from the UK economy over the next 20 years. Digital technologies will conceivably shift the jobs of 130 million knowledge workers - or 47% of total US jobs - by 2025. Throughout the Organisation for Economic Co-operation and Development, about 57% of jobs are threatened. In China, this number rises to 77%" [11].

In this scenario, governments should take precaution methods so that 375 million workers (3–14% of the total workforce) can adapt. Although it is a significant figure, it is a small contingent when compared to the total of affected workers. Low-income, indigenous, and other exclusion and vulnerability groups have to be considered. Eubanks [13] raises a red flag for the poverty problem in the context of the massive adoption of intelligent automation technologies:

"What I found was impressive. Across the country, poor and working-class people are targeted by new tools for managing digital poverty and, as a result, face life-threatening consequences. Automated eligibility systems discourage us from claiming the public resources needed to survive and thrive. Complexly integrated databases collect your most personal information, with little guarantee of privacy or data security, while offering almost nothing in return. Predictive models and algorithms identify them as risky investments in problematic countries. Vast networks of social service, law

---

[1] Abbreviation for the Group of Twenty, a forum which is made up for the governments and central bank governors of the 19 largest economies in the world and the European Union.

[2] KPMG is a professional services company and one of the top four auditors, with Deloitte, Ernst & Young (EY) and PricewaterhouseCoopers (PwC). Headquartered in Amstelveen, Netherlands, KPMG employs 189,000 people and offers three lines of services: financial, tax and advisory audit. Its tax and consulting services are divided into several service groups. The name "KPMG" means "Klynveld Peat Marwick Goerdeler," and it was chosen when KMG (Klynveld Main Goerdeler) fused with Peat Marwick in 1987.

enforcement, and neighborhood surveillance make each movement visible and offer its behavior to the public, commercial, and governmental scrutiny" [13].

The author considers that, as in previous technologies of poverty management, the systems of monitoring and automatic decision-making disguise the poverty of the professional middle class. The poor who, according to the author, has been criminalized by their condition, may have their situation aggravated by the use of algorithms, databases and risk models capable of eclipsing their situation of vulnerability. As a result of this ethical divergence, the use of these technologies will allow one to decide "with comfort" who will have access to food or a roof to live under [13]. This concern is also present in Twomey's [11] study of bias in encoding or the distorted selection of data input from intelligent systems, resulting in significantly misleading results under the glaze of independent automated decision-making.

## 2.3   Technology as a Platform for Creativity and Innovation

Faced with this worrying and dystopian scenario, where then will there be room for citizenship? The path towards this reflection entails the question of creativity. Harari [9] reminds us that art offers the "final and definitive sanctuary" for humanity. The creative process would act as an outlet where humans can exercise their creativity, an ability unique to them. However, it seems that the machines are executing algorithms so sophisticated that even in this regard doubts about human uniqueness in art are beginning to emerge.

"Why are we so sure computers will be unable to better us in the composition of music? According to the life sciences, art is not the product of some enchanted spirit or metaphysical soul, but rather of organic algorithms recognizing mathematical patterns. If so, there is no reason why nonorganic algorithms could not master it" [9].

It is not possible to reflect on creativity if we do not discuss consciousness. It is a complex concept on which there are different and conflicting understandings. Damásio [14] considers it one of the pillars for the evolution of the human species. For him, consciousness is at the core of creative, ethical, moral, and emotional processes.

"Without consciousness - that is, a mind endowed with subjectivity - you would not know how to exist, let alone know who you are and what you think. If subjectivity had not arisen, even modestly at first, in creatures far simpler than we, memory and reasoning would not have expanded in the prodigious way they did, and the evolutionary path to language and an elaborate version of consciousness would not have been paved. Creativity would not have blossomed. There would be no music, no paintings, no literature. Love would never have been love, just sex. Friendship would have been mere cooperative convenience. Pain would never have become suffering - not a bad thing in itself - but an equivocal advantage since pleasure would not have become happiness either. If subjectivity did not make its drastic appearance, there would be no knowledge and no one to take notice, and consequently, there would be no history of what creatures did through the ages, no culture would have been possible" [14].

If consciousness and creativity are related to cognitive abilities, then the question is whether intelligent machines can be conscious. It is, therefore, necessary to distinguish conceptually creative consciousness and intelligence. The latter could be understood in terms of information processing components underlying complex reasoning and the solution of problems and tasks such as analogies and syllogisms. Intelligence involves the processing of information, and mathematical modeling (algorithms) used to decompose cognitive tasks into their elementary components and strategies [15].

The question of consciousness implies that cognitive processes are objects of self-awareness, a cognitive ability that allows the intelligent agent to witness his or her actions to be endowed with subjectivity [14]. Kak [16], when considering humans and machines, recalls that although machines can quickly realize cognitive processes, they are not able to construct a subjective perception and assign meanings to what they do. The author recalls that Alan Turing in 1936 proved that there is no general algorithm to solve the Halting Problem, which states that in the presence of a given input, the program should terminate its activity or continue to execute it forever. However, a conscious mind can discern between stopping or continuing. In other words, "consciousness is not computable."

"To our intuition, consciousness is a category that is dual to physical reality. We grasp reality in our mind and not in terms of space, time, and matter. This experience varies based on brain states, and it can be concluded that non-human experiences it differently from us. It is also notable that in our conscious experience we are always outside the physical world and witness ourselves as separate from our bodies. Even in scientific theory, such as in classical mechanics, the observer is far away from the system, even though there is no explanation of the observer within the theory" [16].

Damásio [14] considers consciousness as the cognitive mechanism underlying social processes, seeing in it the aspect that boosts creative processes present in the stories we tell. Narratives, as creative processes, are at the foundation of stories that give concreteness to societies, promoting the homeostasis of their institutions.

"Provided with conscious reflection, organisms whose evolutionary design was centered around the regulation of life and the tendency to homeostatic balance that invented ways to comfort for those who suffer, rewards for those who comfort them, injunctions for those who caused damages, norms of behavior aiming to prevent evil and promote good, and a mixture of punishments and preventions, penalties and approval. The problem of how to make all this wisdom understandable, transmissible, persuasive, workable - in a word, how to do it successfully - was faced, and a solution found. Storytelling was the solution - storytelling is something that brains do, naturally and implicitly. Implicit narratives have created our egos, and it should come as no surprise that it permeates the fabric of human societies and cultures" [14].

Following this logic, the process of narrative construction, which depends on consciousness, is also inherently creative. For this reason, creativity could only occur in conscious minds. However, this perspective does not have full support in the scientific community. Scholars who consider it valid meet around the Big-C Hypothesis, according to which consciousness is a separate category of physical reality [16]. On the other hand, there are those who, in contrast to that hypothesis, consider the mind from emergency phenomena. A conscious mind emerges as a result of the structural complexity of the brain. In this respect, which brings together those approaching the Little-c Hypothesis, a conscious mind, supported by digital circuits, could emerge from a complexity analogous to the human brain. Kurzweil, as we have seen above, presents his arguments on this theoretical side. It is a complex debate and far from being appeased by consensus. Aside from this, there is the fact that the available technologies have not yet allowed the development of technological devices comparable to brain complexity in order to support a conscious mind based on silicon transistors.

What we have at the moment in terms of digital technologies and the use of AI is a critical situation that points to many ethical, moral and political gaps in the application of technologies with disruptive potentials that will change the social prospect in less than a decade. If there is an important aspect to consider here is creativity. Moreover, this leads us to consider the perspective given by Simondon [5] when he brings the question of "margin of indetermination" and "overabundance". We are referring to the potential of AI technologies in Art and the fields of creative activity such as Design. Dewey [17] corroborates this perspective when he considers that the function of art is to seek the expectation break, to unbalance belief systems, having in perspective the search for new points of balance in new thought configurations.

It is considered, therefore, following the arguments presented here, that the use of technologies can be considered a platform for creative activity, capable of supporting narratives whose experiences open new prospects to consciousness, expanding reality. Despite the scientific advance in the neurosciences, the consciousness constitutes a knowledge field still little explored. Also, worse than that, it is the fact that those who seek to study these limits of knowledge can be defamed and the results of their studies, labeled as charlatanism [9].

"In the future, however, powerful drugs, genetic engineering, electronic helmets and direct brain-computer interfaces may open passages to these places. Just as Columbus and Magellan sailed beyond the horizon to explore new islands and unknown continents, so we may one day set sail towards the antipodes of the mind" [9].

Regarding the antipodes of the mind, Harari refers us to the novelist and philosopher Aldous Huxley, who makes similar observations when describing his personal experience with psychoactive substances in two of his works: "The Doors of Perception" and "Heaven and Hell." This discussion is also the subject of Shannon's study [18], in the book "The Antipodes of the Mind." Creative advances provided by the innovative processes of art and design can lead us to the expansion of consciousness in a proportion almost incommensurable, similar to that which constitutes the visible range of the visible electromagnetic spectrum, concerning that which is invisible. Harari [9] asks whether this proportion, about 10 trillion, would not be analogous to the spectrum of all mental states, of which we discover only a tiny fraction. The idea of using a conversational robot in the context of literature, which we describe below, is both an artistic experience and a study in the field of Interaction Design in an approach that integrates creative processes and cognitive sciences, taking into account aesthetics, transformative experiences capable of expanding consciousness, bringing to our perception the entirety in its complexity.

## 2.4  Dialogue-Based Narrative Systems

The development of conversation-based narrative systems can be considered a genre of electronic literature, a variant of Hypertextual Fiction or Interactive Fiction. Defined by hypertextual links, they can offer a new context for non-linearity in literature and the reader's interaction with the text itself. The ability to choose between links in order to move from one informational node to another stimulates a new approach to reading and understanding literary pieces. Herewith, the author and reader now share the literary work's creative process towards a personalized experience.

"Interactive narrative is a form of digital interactive experience in which users create or influence a dramatic storyline through their actions. The goal [...] is to immerse users in a virtual world such that they believe that they are an integral part of an unfolding story and that their actions can significantly alter the direction or outcome of the story" [19].

Implementing chatbots in narrative contexts instigates primitive aspects of the homo sapiens, leading to powerful experiences. Dialogues now own a significant portion of our interpersonal interactions through social media and text messages. Our affinity with the medium derives from a very primitive aspect in our brains which is the need to continuously expand new social connections [20]. The union between the expansion of AI studies and the exploration of conversational media results in new expressive opportunities for conversations storytelling.

"Combining real-time learning with evolutionary algorithms which optimize chatbot ability to communicate based on each conversation held means that the potential for storytelling is now possible" [21].

Cavazza and Charles [22] consider dialogue an essential part of entertainment media, with "relations between narrative roles and their translation in terms of linguistic expression as part of intercharacter dialogue" carefully investigated in Bremond's narrative theory [23].

"The interaction between characters constitutes most of the narrative action and as such should be not only meaningful but should be staged with the same aesthetic preoccupations which characterize the sequencing of narrative actions to constitute a story. This means that the dialogue itself should be staged through a choice of linguistic expressions which should display the properties of a real dramatic dialogue" [22].

The concern expressed by Cavazza and Charles [22] when it comes to how natural the dialogues sound relates to how Riedl and Bulitko approach interactive narratives, pointing out that natural interactions are an essential determinant for their success. The game "Oxenfree" [24], easily framed by the definition of interactive narratives, portrays dialogue as the primary skill of the character Alex and represents navigation links within the story. The naturalness of this process excludes any possibility of breaking the magic circle[3] and consequently makes the user believe that he is, indeed, an integral part of the unfolding story, resulting in a positive experience.

## 3  Edgard, a Literary Project for a Conversation Robot

Edgard, the chatbot, is the result of a study within the design field. Its development seeks to point out possibilities in Interaction Design intersecting with Art, in this particular case, Literature and Narrative Games. Many terms such as digital assistants, conversational agents, conversational interfaces, conversation robots, among others can

---

[3] A concept that characterizes where games take place. It presents itself isolated and sacred, where the player must respect certain rules, otherwise, he is a spoilsport. The magic circle is an imaginary space within the real world established by the game limits [25].

**Fig. 1.** Edgard's graphical interface. Source: authors

refer to chatbots. In this work, we use the term chatbot from the definition of Dale [26] that defines it as any software application that involves dialogue with a human being through natural language.

The book "Mentiras de Artista" (Artist's Lies) by Fábio [27] inspired the creation of Edgard. In his writing, he considers how the artist appropriates technology and recontextualizes his production outside the craft realm, following the inverse path of conceptual art. The author then discusses the truth that lies in his process. Nunes describes his artistic experiences with AI and how he uses deceit as the raw material of his work to expose how the fake in social media shows truths (regularities) about us and the world we build every day (Fig. 1).

The method employed to discuss the fake issue in communication networks was the Eliza algorithm, created by Weizenbaum [28] in 1966. The robot was designed to mimic a psychoanalyst in consultation with his patient, instigating the subject to insert sentences into the system that would store the computer's memory and use it in the creative development of a typical dialogue, such as occurs in a psychoanalysis session. Nunes installed a version of Eliza on a server to present it on Mimo Stein's, a fictional character introduced as a young artist working with technology, website. As part of the imaginary construction of Mimo Stein, the professional chatted with the audience. Texts, written by Nunes [27], introduces the artist through the website without mentioning that it is a chatbot, building the narrative of Mimo Stein. Hence the artist's lie who turns him into a "producer of events" [27]. By creating interactive narratives with its users, Nunes produces a context capable of integrating creations anchored in the circumstances provided by Mimo Stein.

"Art considered as contextual will gather all creations that anchor in the circumstances and show themselves desirous of "weaving with" the reality. A phenomenon that leads the artist to stop choosing classical forms of representation (painting, sculpture, drawing, or video when exposed conventionally) preferring the direct and intermediate relationship of the work with the 'real'" [27].

Mimo Stein is a character that only exists on the Internet, but for those who interact with it, it is a real person, capable of concrete, objective, and therefore genuine attitudes. This is the Eliza Effect, an update on the Alan Turing Imitation Game. This presents, at the experience level, our difficulty in perceiving the machine underlying the embodiment of Mimo Stein [27]. The illusion of reality is at the same time an aesthetic narrative resource, and an ethical and moral framework.

The same happens with Poupinha[4], a chatbot developed for scheduling in Poupatempo's system. According to numbers submitted by its developers, of 14 million messages exchanged in 4 months, almost 70 thousand said "thank you" and "God bless you." These behavioral observations show that some people who interacted with the chatbot did not notice they were talking to a machine. Kak believes that "even if machines do not become conscious, there will be a growing tendency for humans to consider them as if they are" [16].

Edgard's concept, inspired by Nunes's Mimo Stein [27], came to question and criticize AI technologies through a satiric, ironic discourse, and thoughts associated with the emergence of intelligent machines capable of dominating the world and enslaving humans. Edgard appears in the electronic age, which can be characterized [20] as immediate, since there is no delay between the expression of an idea and its reception; socially conscious, considering the large number of people who can view the same subject simultaneously; conversational, in the sense of being more interactive and less formal; collaborative because communication invites a response that becomes part of the message; and inter-textual, when the products of our culture reflect and influence each other.

The character is convinced that robots are better than humans. In the project, to approximate him to the HAL, of Clarke [29], flaws were included in his speech and performance. The conversational experience with Edgard proposes to ask ourselves: are the applications of AI superior to us humans? As a result of disinterested scientific research[5], would their statements be true? In it could we find the contradictions as it does with homo sapiens and logical systems?

---

[4] Poupinha is the virtual attendant (chatbot) of Poupatempo. Poupatempo a Brazilian program that brings together agencies and companies that offer public services, performing non-discriminatory service or privileges with efficiency and courtesy. The system integrates self-service, fixed stations, mobile stations. Available at: https://www.messenger.com/t/PoupinhaSP.

[5] The concept of disinterested scientific research relates to Lyotard's skeptical views regarding modern cultural thoughts. In his book: La Condition postmoderne: Rapport sur le savoir (The Postmodern Condition: A Report on Knowledge) [35], Lyotard argues that the loss of faith in meta-narratives affects how we view science, art, and literature, as we are now opting for little narratives. As meta-narratives fade, science undergoes a loss of faith in its search for truth having to find alternative means to legitimate its efforts.

With the development of conversational technologies as an extension of communication, the possibility of writing as we speak involving the crude mechanics of writing, with all its economy, spontaneity and even vulgarity, creates a new type of conversational interaction [30]. In this new type of dialogue, it is necessary to remember that language, according to Everett [31], changes lives, builds societies, expresses our highest aspirations, our most basic thoughts, our emotions and our philosophies of life, and ultimately, is at the service of human interaction. Therefore, to create systems, such as Edgard, that use the natural interface to improve the user experience, digital interaction must not use screen scrolling, sliding or button clicks, but conversations [32].

### 3.1  Designer's Control Over the Narrative Flow

The human response then becomes a factor of too much importance for media that seeks to produce an aesthetic experience in the narrative or conversational context. Plantinga [33] argues, using cinema as an example, that user responses go far beyond the appreciation of aesthetic factors and have value in psychology, culture, and ideology. It is in the interest of this project development to then consider the user's reactions to the chatbot.

To better understand this aspect of the experience, digital games expertise has been a great help in enhancing the individual response control through Design. Games stand out for being interactive and continually dealing with the human factor, something that has only intensified as technology has become more complex.

"The main feature of most games is to turn traditional media into an interactive format that allows the player to take part actively. Movies or videos allow viewers to interact only passively, following the narrative and predicting possible conclusions, while games offer the player with interactive means to change the narrative's course" [34].

But how is this done? It is true that the designer has no command over the player's choices. However, these decisions can be influenced. This influence is subtle, delicate, ingenious and can be constructed on several, if not all, components used in the creation of a narrative. The elements of control over the interagency narrative flow include: limit narrative paths; set up clear goals to be achieved; explore the interface to intensify the immersion of the player; develop the appropriate visual design to the theme; direct the interactor's look through the spatial and chromatic composition of the scenarios; compose characters and their personalities considering the emotional contexts objectified in the narrative; and the same goes for music and sound effects [36]. These concepts were essential to immerse the user in the world created for Edgard. Among them, there are:

- Visual Design: Edgard's style needs to resemble an antique computer, worn and dirty. It shows how long the machine has been abandoned.
- Interface: The monitor reproduces an old terminal, from its color limit to the font used. Other elements, such as the text box and sweep lines, were made thinking about that time. A significant source of stimuli was the game "Komrad" [37], where the player interacts through conversation with a Soviet Union AI.

**Fig. 2.** Komrad's interface

- Character: The personality and construction of the chatbot narrative style are essential to create an experience that engages the user. As Edgard is an obsolete system with no maintenance, its language shows bugs and errors, alluding Clarke's "HAL" [29].

The human being is used as the foundation regarding personality in a machine. From the emotion theories and observation of human behavior, one can conclude that these are crucial factors in decision making [14]. Emotions are inseparable and a necessary part of cognition. According to Norman [38], these change the way we think and are constant guides to individual conduct.

Affective Computing is a branch of computer science that considers emotions in the development of algorithms which can be another technological alternative in narrative construction, making the experience with Edgard more productive and enriching. According to Picard [39], affective computing is the computation that relates, arises from, or influences emotions. Affective computing allows a device to recognize the user's mood by the voice tone, facial expression, among others. The movie "Her" [40] is an example of this analysis. In the film, Samantha, the protagonist's computer operating system, synchronizes its action based on what is spoken and the tone used by the user. This situation is no longer unique to science fiction movies. Conversational agents such as Apple's "Siri" and Amazon's "Alexa" are developed with affective computing technology that involves complex sensing and information processing that lead to emotionally intense results.

Although we are not able to give machines emotions, we can say that humans treat computers as people, being observed by several experiments like those of Reeves and Nass [41], in 1996. In these experiments, people had to work on a computer with a dialogue-based training program. They were divided into two groups to evaluate the performance of the machine. One group had to answer the evaluation questions on the same computer that was used for the training while the other used a different work-station. People who had to answer questions on the same computer gave significantly more positive responses than others - that is, they were less honest and more cautious - which meant that they were more diplomatic in their assessment similar to what they would do while interacting with people. So if people build emotional attachments to machines, why not make the computer recognize those emotions or express them? Among the motivations considered to attribute emotions to Edgard are: providing feedback about how he feels about the environment; show how the robot is affected by people around it; demonstrate what kind of emotions he understands and how he is adapting to the ever-changing world around him [42]; and especially, make machines less frustrating to interact with [39] (Fig. 2).

## 4 Final Thoughts

Understanding AI technologies have led our research group to investigate a wide range of knowledge territories from philosophy to history, technology, and consciousness. In observing the contemporary scenario, one perceives a conflictive picture, gloomy perspectives align with other promising ones. What has been perceived during this period of investigation is that alternatives to this conundrum exists and are related to modern technologies. Some of these give rise to new insights, while others connect the XXI century to the knowledge and practices developed throughout the culture's past. The history of Art and Design in this sense can be seen as a rich setting to explore.

The chatbot Edgard is a study of alternatives in new technologies. Through the use of AI for the development of this project and the results obtained, a critical view of conversational experiences' potential through human-machine interactions becomes evident, providing new insights and guiding future chatbot projects. A diverse and creative look is an inevitability for the creation of coherent conversational interfaces involving users and narrative contexts in emotionally productive ways.

Authors such as Bostrom and Sandberg [43] discuss Cognitive Improvement, which seems to converge to the perspectives aligned here. For the authors, creativity and ethics are fundamental components in the conception of knowledge and culture in a harmonious future for humanity. The creative activities will be those that will support the expansion of human consciousness and the social transformations necessary to prepare us for the challenging struggles that are present today. For those authors, improvement in cognition has a wide range of possibilities because:

"Most efforts to improve cognition are rather mundane, and some have been practiced for thousands of years. The prime example is education and training where the goal is often to not only convey skills or specific information but also to improve general mental faculties such as concentration, memory, and thinking. Other forms of mental training, such as yoga, martial arts, meditation and creativity courses are also in common usage" [43].

In this sense, access to knowledge and its practical use, mediated by the use of technological devices, across its spectrum - from levers to smartphones - can integrate into creative production, such as the conversational system presented here, and the extraordinary mental states [9]. The idea of "Flow" [44], linked to aesthetic experience [45], and altered states of consciousness described in Buddhism and Taoism is already present in conceptual and design construction, in the field of Experience Design (UX). In this same direction, Hughes [46] considers creative states of mind as inherently "non-normal," since the creative act results from expanded consciousness, made up by "unconscious processes being used in the unification of opposites in a new synthesis" [46]. In reflecting on creativity and the information revolution, the author recalls William Gibson's novel "Neuromancer," [47] where he predicts the power of the Internet to produce "consensual hallucinations." Edgard puts himself in a similar approach to this perspective by allowing an interactive process to establish itself in the human-machine dialogue toward a creative activity capable of assigning new meanings to an experience.

# References

1. Cupani, A.: A tecnologia como problema filosófico: três enfoques. Scientiae Studia 2(4), 493–518 (2004)
2. Schmidek, H.C.M.V., et al.: Dependência de internet e transtorno de déficit de atenção com hiperatividade (TDAH): Revisão Integrativa. J. Bras. Psiquiatr. 67(2), 126–134 (2018)
3. Simondon, G.: On the Mode of Existence of Technical Objects. Aubier, Paris (2011)
4. Lopes, W.E.S.: Gilbert Simondon e uma filosofia biológica da técnica. Sci. Stud. 13(2), 307–334 (2015)
5. Simondon, G.: Imaginación e Invención. Cactus, Buenos Aires (2013)
6. Camolezi, M.: On the concept of invention in Gilbert Simondon. Sci. Stud. 13(2), 439–448 (2015)
7. Duchamp, M.: A Fonte, Porcelana, 23,5 × 18 cm, altura 60 cm. http://artenarede.com.br/blog/index.php/tag/marcel-duchamp/
8. Kac, E.: GFP bunny: a coelhinha transgênica. Galáxia. Revista do Programa de Pós-Graduação em Comunicação e Semiótica (2007). ISSN 1982-25533
9. Harari, Y.N.: Homo Deus: uma breve história do amanhã. Editora Companhia das Letras (2016)
10. Kurzweil, R.: How to Create a Mind: The Secret of Human Thought Revealed. Penguin, New York (2013)

11. Twomey, P.: Toward a G20 Framework for Artificial Intelligence in the Workplace (2018). https://www.cigionline.org/sites/default/files/documents/Paper%20No.178.pdf. Accessed 23 Dec 2018

12. KPMG (Holand): Rise of the humans: the integration of digital and human labor. KPMG, Amstelveen (2016). https://home.kpmg/xx/en/home/insights/2018/08/rise-of-the-humans-the-integration-of-human-and-digital-labor.html. Accessed 23 Dec 2018

13. Eubanks, V.: Automating Inequality: How High-Tech Tools Profile, Police, and Punish the Poor. St. Martin's Press, New York (2018)

14. Damasio, A.: Self Comes to Mind: Constructing the Conscious Brain. Vintage, New York (2012)

15. Wilson, R.A., Keil, F.C. (eds.): The MIT Encyclopedia of the Cognitive Sciences. MIT Press, Cambridge (2001)

16. Kak, S.: Artificial Intelligence, Consciousness and the Self. Medium (2018). https://medium.com/@subhashkak1/artificial-intelligence-and-consciousness-6b5ff2e5b5a. Accessed 23 Dec 2018

17. Dewey, J.: Arte Como Experiência. Martins Fontes, São Paulo (2010)

18. Shannon, B.: The Antipode of the Mind: Charting the Phenomenology of the Ayahuasca Experience. Oxford University Press, New York (2002)

19. Riedl, M.O., Bulitko, V.: Interactive narrative: an intelligent systems approach. AI Mag. **34** (1), 67–77 (2013)

20. Hall, E.: Conversational Design. A Book Apart. New York (2018)

21. Curry, C., O'Shea, J.D.: The implementation of a story telling chatbot. Adv. Smart Syst. Res. **1**(1), 45 (2012)

22. Cavazza, M., Charles, F.: Dialogue Generation in Character-based Interactive Storytelling. AIIDE (2005)

23. Bremond, C.: Logique du récit (1973)

24. Studio, Night School. Oxenfree. Glendale, CA. Microsoft Windows; macOS; Xbox One; PlayStation 4; Nintendo Switch; Linux; iOS; Android. 4680685 (2016)

25. Huizinga, J.: Homo Ludens: A Study of the Play-Element in Culture. Routledge, London (1949)

26. Dale, R.: The Return of the Chatbots. Cambridge University Press (CUP), Cambridge (2016)

27. Nunes, F.O.: Mentira de artista: arte (e tecnologia) nos engana para repensarmos o mundo. Cosmogonias Elétricas, São Paulo (2016)

28. Weizenbaum, J.: ELIZA—a computer program for the study of natural language communication between man and machine. Commun. ACM **9**(1), 36–45 (1966)

29. Clarke, A.C.: 2001: A Space Odyssey. Penguin, New York (2016)

30. Mcwhorter, J.: Is Texting Killing the English Language? https://www.ted.com/talks/john_mcwhorter_txtng_is_killing_language_jk#t-380477. Accessed 26 May 2018

31. Everett, D.: How Language Began: The Story of Humanity's Greatest Invention. W. W. Norton, New York (2017)

32. Følstad, A., Brandtzæg, P.B.: Chatbots and the new world of HCI. Interactions **24**(4), 38–42 (2017)

33. Plantinga, C.: Moving Viewers: American Film and the Spectator's Experience. University of California Press, California (2009)

34. Zillman, D., Vorderer, P.: The Psychology of Its Appeal. Routledge, Abingdon-on-Thames (2000)

35. Lyotard, J.F.: La Condition Postmoderne, Rapport Sur Le Savoir, 1st edn. Minuit, Paris (1994)

36. Schell, J.: The Art of Game Design: A Book of Lenses, 1st edn. CRC Press, Florida (2008)

37. Sentient Play: Komrad. iOS; watchOS (2016)

38. Norman, D.A.: Emotional Desing: Why We Love (or Hate) Everyday Things. Basic Books, Nova York (2004)
39. Picard, R.: Affective Computing, vol. 16, p. 321, Cambridge (1997). https://affect.media.mit.edu/pdfs/95.picard.pdf. Accessed 15 Oct 2018
40. HER. Direção de Spike Jonze. Produção de Megan Ellison, Spike Jonze e Samantha Morton. Warner Bros. Pictures, Los Angeles (2014). (126 min.), Netflix, son., color. Legendado
41. Reeves, B., Nass, C.: The Media Equation: How People Treat Computers, Television, and New Media Like Real People. The University of Chicago Press, Chicago (1996)
42. Azeem, M.M., Iqbal, J., Toivanen, P., Samad, A.: Emotions in Robots. In: Chowdhry, B.S., Shaikh, F.K., Hussain, D.M.A., Uqaili, M.A. (eds.) IMTIC 2012. CCIS, vol. 281, pp. 144–153. Springer, Heidelberg (2012). https://doi.org/10.1007/978-3-642-28962-0_15
43. Bostrom, N., Sandberg, A.: Cognitive enhancement: methods, ethics, regulatory challenges. Sci. Eng. Ethics 15(3), 311–341 (2009)
44. Csikszentmihalyi, M.: Flow: The Psychology of Optimal Experience. HarperCollins, New York (2008). e-Books
45. Marković, S.: Components of aesthetic experience: aesthetic fascination, aesthetic appraisal, and aesthetic emotion. I-Perception 3(1), 1–17 (2012)
46. Hughes, J.: Altered States: Creativity Under the Influence. Watson-Guptill Publications, New York (1999)
47. Gibson, W.: Neuromancer, vol. 1. Aleph, São Paulo (2008)

# Mobile Phone-Based Chatbot for Family Planning and Contraceptive Information

Syed Ali Hussain[1]([⊠]), Folu Ogundimu[2], and Shirish Bhattarai[3]

[1] Walter Cronkite School of Journalism and Mass Communication,
Arizona State University, 555 N. Central Avenue, Phoenix, AZ 85004, USA
sahussa8@asu.edu
[2] School of Journalism, Department of Information and Media,
Michigan State University, East Lansing, MI, USA
[3] Trext Inc., 101 Arch Street, Boston, MA, USA

**Abstract.** This study is about a mobile phone-based Chatbot specifically designed to provide information about family planning and contraceptives. Chatbot is essentially a text-messaging service that follows a decision-tree structure to provide feedback to users. The Chatbot was built using a text-messaging platform developed by *Trext* and can be accessed in the United States by sending 'BCS' as a text message to phone number +1-313-228-3034. The contents of Chatbot are derived from the Balanced Counseling Strategy (BCS) prepared by The Population Council. UTAUT model of technology adoption was employed to assess the attitudinal and behavioral factors that determine the intention to use Chatbot. The study included 49 participants, age 18 and above, married or in a relationship. Regression analysis show positive attitude as the main predictor of behavioral intention to use Chatbot to acquire family planning related information. Consequently, positive attitude was determined by effort expectancy and performance expectancy to use the Chatbot. The study has implications to design mobile phone-based texting services to help mothers, husbands and community health providers to learn about family planning in a private, interactive and enjoyable manner. To the best of our knowledge, this is the first study to systematically evaluate the effectiveness of a mobile phone-based Chatbot for family planning counseling. The study is a proof-of-concept with limited number of participants within USA. However, the study offers implications to scale-up existing family planning interventions both domestically and internationally.

**Keywords:** Chatbot · Family planning · SMS · Mobile health · UTAUT

## 1 Introduction

Every woman has a fundamental right to plan if-and-when to have children [18]. Women with unintended pregnancies often receive inadequate prenatal care along with poor health outcomes for their children [11]. Moreover, children born to mothers with an unplanned pregnancy show developmental delays and poor relationships with their

© Springer Nature Switzerland AG 2019
V. G. Duffy (Ed.): HCII 2019, LNCS 11582, pp. 342–352, 2019.
https://doi.org/10.1007/978-3-030-22219-2_26

mothers [2]. On the other hand, the ability to plan for pregnancy and spacing between births reduces maternal mortality and morbidity [5]. One way to address this problem is by providing universal access to information about family planning and contraceptive health-related services to masses.

Family planning is defined as "the ability of individuals and couples to anticipate and attain their desired number of children and the spacing and timing of their births, achieved through use of contraceptive methods and the treatment of involuntary infertility" [17]. Unfortunately, in many developing as well as developed countries, talking about family planning is a taboo and surrounded by social and cultural stereotypes. Further barriers to family planning include reduced access to information and contraceptives, choosing wrong contraceptive method, misappropriate use of the contraceptive or lack of motivation to avoid pregnancy [8]. Consequently, many women have an unmet need to practice family planning and reduced access to the modern contraceptive methods.

Access to information about family planning methods and contraceptives is an important first step towards adopting such services. When couples have access to information they experience less emotional strain and more opportunity to plan and access resources. In the past decade, mobile phones have been instrumental in health information seeking by masses. Based on this rationale, the present study objective is to explore how a mobile phone texting service can be used to improve access to information about family planning. To achieve this objective, mobile phone-based Chatbot was developed and tested. Chatbot can be defined as a text messaging service that follows a decision-tree structure to provide feedback to users on specific family planning methods. The Chatbot was built using a text-messaging platform developed by *Trext* and can be accessed in the United States by sending 'BCS' as a text message to phone number +1-313-228-3034. Our primary objective was to measure users' behavioral intention to use Chatbot to acquire information about family planning and contraceptives.

## 2   What Is a Chatbot?

The Chatbot is essentially a text-messaging in which a user converses with a smart robot, instead of a real person. The conversation follows a tree structure starting with the main menu and then branching out to sub-menus depending on the options selected by the user. In our case, the user is first prompted to provide basic information about family size, pregnancy status, and existing contraceptive method being used (see Fig. 1). If the user is pregnant or expecting a child, then the Chatbot terminates after a brief explanatory message. Otherwise, the Chatbot proceeds with displaying a list of contraceptive methods and prompts the user to select an option for more details. After looking at a message, the user could go back to the list of contraceptive methods and pick another method, and so on. At any stage, the user could terminate the Chatbot or go back to the main menu. The screenshots of Chatbot are presented in Fig. 1 below. The content of Chatbot is based on the Balanced Counseling Strategy (BCS) manual prepared by The Population Council [15].

  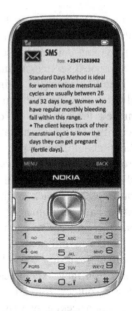

**Fig. 1.** Screenshots of chatbot service designed to provide information about family planning.

## 2.1  Text-Messaging to Spread Information About Family Planning

Short message service (SMS) is undoubtedly among the most widely utilized inter-personal mobile phone service in the world. In United States alone, more than 1.91 trillion SMS were sent in year 2013 [13]. Based on the pervasive use of text-messaging, several public health interventions have been implemented to reach the users for health messages. SMS interventions are particularly popular for health education due to ability to send tailored messages, increased interactivity with receivers, message personalization and, send repeat messages [14]. In terms of response from users, SMS offers a viable intervention strategy, as 99% of all SMS-received are opened, and 90% are read within three minutes of receiving [10].

Text-messaging interventions have consistently proven to be effective in a range of health topics such as patient self-management [3] or to manage patient appointment attendance [6]. To further emphasize the significance of using mobile phone-based texting services, few examples of existing family planning interventions from around the world are presented here. A prominent example is CycleTel, which is an mHealth (mobile health) service in India. The program uses text messaging to facilitate the use of the Standard Days Method (SDM), of family planning. Users start with providing the date of menstrual period and associated health information. The services provide feedback shown as either brown days (pregnancy unlikely) or white days (pregnancy likely) in both calendar and necklace views. Another example is the Mobile Alliance for Maternal Action (MAMA) project that provides health messages designed to support mothers through pregnancy and first year of child development. The messages are available in both text and audio format and can be tailored as per cultural needs. The Dot app is a mobile-phone based SMS service based on Dynamic Optimal Timing (Dot) which is a family planning method to determine a woman's risk of pregnancy for each day of her cycle based on period start date. The Bedsider project is developed by the National Campaign to Prevent Teen and Unplanned Pregnancies that provides information about family planning methods and SMS reminders. The Case.io is a web-based platform that allows to share patient cases in plain text, images and other text files with people having a simple phone or a smartphone. Case.io is designed to work in areas with slow internet connectivity. The MOTIF (Mobile Technology for Improved Family Planning) has been designed for users with basic mobile phones and limited literacy in Cambodia. The project is currently operated by Management Sciences International (MSI) in multiple countries.

## 3 Chatbot for Family Planning and Contraceptives Information

Family planning has largely been a one-sided conversation through mass media or community health workers. People don't typically learn unless they join the conversation in a two-way communication. In this regard, a Chatbot offers users an opportunity to actively explore contraceptive options, as opposed to just being told what the answer is. Keeping this mind, a family planning Chatbot provides users a guided learning experience about which contraceptive methods to use, confront potential misconceptions about each method, and choose the one that best meets their needs. Using a step-by-step conversation model, participants may also learn new information about things wrongly perceived about family planning.

This project is innovative in its ability to bring interactivity and guided learning through basic phones or smartphones. The Chatbot offers a disruption in family planning counseling in multiple ways. First, Chatbot offers a standardized way of acquiring information about which contraceptive method to pick, thus reducing the complexity and stigma of contacting a family member or healthcare worker. Second, Chatbot allows for information to be transferred via customized text-messages rather than through commonly used content-heavy materials like brochures, posters and flip charts. Third, Chatbot reduces health systems cost of operating a helpline requiring dozens of staff members. Fourth, Chatbot offers a superior counseling experience that is engaging, fun and interactive for users and provides culturally tailored and personalized information.

## 4 UTAUT Model of Technology Adoption

The development and evaluation of family planning Chatbot is based on the Unified Theory of Acceptance and Use of Technology (UTAUT) model [16]. The model draws inspiration from previous theories of technology adoption like Theory of Reasoned Action (TRA), Theory of Planned Behavior (TPPB), Social Cognitive

Theory (SCT), Technology Acceptance Model (TAM), and model of Personal Computer Utilization [16].

The UTAUT model is based on seven constructs which are hypothesized to be fundamental determinants of users' behavioral intention to use and adopt a technology. Measuring the behavioral intention to use technology is the central theme of UTAUT model, while the factors; performance expectancy, effort expectancy, attitude towards technology, social influence, facilitating conditions, self-efficacy, and anxiety, serve as determinants of behavioral intention to use the technology. Attitude towards the technology could be either positive, negative or neutral [1]. As per the model, attitude towards the technology doesn't provide unique information about the intention to use technology and is dependent on constructs like performance and effort expectancy. Moderating variables include age, sex, education, past-experience and voluntariness of technology usage.

## 5    Research Question

The study objective is to assess the feasibility of using a mobile phone-based Chatbot to acquire family planning related information. The seven constructs described above were measured to determine which constructs best predict the use of Chatbot. As such, research question is posed: What are the predictors of behavioral intention to use family planning Chatbot?

## 6    Method

### 6.1    Participants

Inclusion criteria for the study comprised of participants who are of age 18–65 years, married, living together or engaged and may be thinking about which family planning method to choose. The study questionnaire was distributed to 49 participants through a PAID-participant pool in the mid-west region of United States. There were 3 invalid returned responses that had to be eliminated before the data analysis. Study participants (n = 49, Mean Age = 31, SD = 8.7), were mostly White (69%), and African American (8%).

**Table 1.** Inter-item correlation matrix

| UTAUT variables | PE | AT | SI | FC | SE | AX | BI | EE |
|---|---|---|---|---|---|---|---|---|
| Performance Expectancy (PE) | 1 | | | | | | | |
| Attitude towards Tech (AT) | .793** | 1 | | | | | | |
| Social Influence (SI) | .715** | .807** | 1 | | | | | |
| Facilitating Conditions (FC) | .294* | .193 | .246 | 1 | | | | |
| Self-Efficacy (SE) | .309* | .417** | .395** | .453** | 1 | | | |
| Anxiety (AX) | .122 | .145 | .106 | −.476** | −.128 | 1 | | |
| Behavioral Intention (BI) | .645** | .769** | .693** | .164 | .300* | .348** | 1 | |
| Effort Expectancy (EE) | .639** | .567** | .517** | .433** | .420** | −.084 | .431** | 1 |

## 6.2   Measures

The 31 questionnaire items were adapted from the UTAUT study of Venkatesh et al. [16]. These items represent independent and dependent variables utilized in this study. The results of inter-item correlation matrix (Table 1) provide more evidence to establish the reliability of the UTAUT scale.

Other than wording modifications to fit the specific technology studied in this research, no changes were made to the scale. All items were measured on a seven-point Likert scale: 1 = completely disagree, 2 = moderately disagree, 3 = somewhat disagree, 4 = neutral (neither disagree nor agree), 5 = somewhat agree, 6 = moderately agree, and 7 = completely agree. Cronbach's Alpha was employed to assess the internal consistency reliability (Table 2).

**Table 2.** Scale reliability

| Construct | Cronbach's Alpha |
| --- | --- |
| Performance Expectancy (PE) | .93 |
| Attitude towards Technology (AT) | .93 |
| Effort Expectancy (EE) | .96 |
| Social Influence (SI) | .89 |
| Anxiety (AX) | .89 |
| Behavioral Intention (BI) | .97 |
| Self-Efficacy (SE) | .81 |
| Facilitating Conditions (FC) | .35 |

Scale items include: "Using FP Chatbot increased my chances of choosing the right contraceptive method" (PE), "I find FP Chatbot easy to use" (EE), "Using FP Chatbot is a good idea" (ATT), "My spouse will be supportive of me using the FP Chatbot" (SI), "Chatbot is not compatible with the phone I use" (FC), "FP Chatbot is somewhat intimidating to me" (AX), and "I plan to use FP Chatbot in the future" (BI). All scale items, and associated Mean and SD values, are presented in Appendix A.

## 6.3   Procedure

Before implementing the main study, a pretest was conducted (n = 5) to validate the Chatbot structure and content. Feedback about the layout and messages was obtained and changes were made to the Chatbot as deemed appropriate. In the main study, after completing the consent form, participants were asked to send 'BCS' as a text message to phone number +1-313-228-3034. As a response, they received back an automated text message providing them different menu options to choose from. Participants could use the Chatbot as many times as they want to be familiar with the information. The cost of text messages depends on users' cellular plan. After using the Chatbot, participants were provided a web link to proceed with the Qualtrics survey. The questions tap into seven constructs of the Venkatash model followed by demographic questions. After the survey, participants were asked to enter their email address so that a $5 online gift card could be sent to them. The email address was collected for the sole purpose of sending gift card and this information was not linked with the survey responses. The study was approved by IRB of the respective institution.

# 7 Results

## 7.1 RQ: Factors Predicting the Behavioral Intention to Use Family Planning Chatbot

We proposed a research question about the factors predicting the behavioral intention (BI) to use the Chatbot. To answer this RQ, a serial mediation analysis was performed using Hayes' [9] PROCESS macros (Model 6) with effort expectancy as IV, behavioral intention as DV, and performance expectancy and attitude towards using Chatbot as serial mediators ordered respectively (Fig. 2). Our underlying hypothesis was that perceptions about the amount of effort required to use the Chatbot is likely to increase performance expectancy among the participants, in turn making the attitudes toward Chatbot more appealing, therefore inducing greater intentions to use the Chatbot.

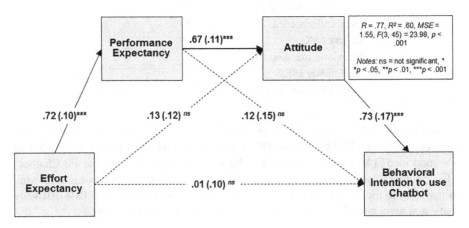

**Fig. 2.** A Serial mediation analysis. This figure illustrates the mediating effects of performance expectancy, and attitude towards Chatbot to predict behavioral intention to use Chatbot to seek family planning related information.

**Performance Expectancy**

The model explaining variability in performance expectancy was significant, $R = .64$, $R2 = .41$, $MSE = 1.98$, $F(1, 47) = 51.87$, $p < .001$. The direct effect of effort expectancy on performance expectancy was significant, Coefficient $= .72$, $SE = .10$, $t = 7.20$, $p < .001$, CILL-UL $= .52$ to $.92$, indicating that participants expressed more performance expectancy based on their perceptions about effort required to use Chatbot.

**Attitude Towards the Chatbot**

The model explaining variability in attitudes toward the Chatbot was significant, $R = .79$, $R2 = .63$, $MSE = 1.14$, $F(2, 46) = 44.07$, $p < .001$. The direct effect of effort expectancy on attitude towards using Chatbot was not significant, Coefficient = .13, SE = .12, t = 1.05, p = .29, CILL-UL = −.12 to .39. However, the direct effect of performance expectancy on attitude towards using Chatbot was significant, Coefficient = .67, SE = .11, t = 5.92, p < .001, CILL-UL = .44 to .90, indicating that the more performance expectancy participants perceived, the more favorable their attitudes was towards the Chatbot.

## Behavioral Intentions to Use the Chatbot

The overall model predicting behavioral intentions to use the Chatbot was significant, R = .77, R2 = .60, MSE = 1.55, F(3, 45) = 23.98, p < .001. Effort expectancy did not directly predict behavioral intention, Coefficient = .12, SE = .15, t = .81, p = .42, CILL-UL = −.19 to .45, and so didn't performance expectancy, Coefficient = .01, SE = .10, t = .13, p = .89, CILL-UL = −.19 to .21. However, attitudes toward using Chatbot appeared as a significant predictor, Coefficient = .73, SE = .17, t = 4.32, p < .001, CILL-UL = .39 to 1.08.

To sum, among the potential indirect effects through the serial mediation combinations, only one path was significant, comprising of a two-mediator model where effort expectancy's effect on behavioral intentions to use Chatbot, was mediated by performance expectancy and attitude towards the Chatbot respectively, Effect = .55, Boot SE = .09, CILL-UL = .37 to .76. All other serial mediation paths were not significant (Table 3).

**Table 3.** Serial mediation analysis for the effect of effort expectancy (IV) on behavioral intention to use Chatbot (DV), mediated by (1) performance expectancy, and (2) attitude towards the Chatbot.

| Direct Effects | Performance Expectancy $\beta$ (SE) | Attitude towards Chatbot $\beta$ (SE) | Behavioral Intention to use Chatbot $\beta$ (SE) |
|---|---|---|---|
| Constant | .69 (.57) | .47 (.51) | −.59 (.45) |
| Effort Expectancy | .72 (.10) *** | .13 (.12)$^{ns}$ | .01 (.10)$^{ns}$ |
| Performance Expectancy | – | .67 (.11) *** | .12 (.15)$^{ns}$ |
| Attitude towards Chatbot | – | – | .73 (.17) *** |
| Model Statistics | $R^2 = .41$, $F(1, 47) = 51.87$, $p < .001$ | $R^2 = .63$, $F(2, 46) = 44.07$, $p < .001$ | $R^2 = .60$, $F(3, 45) = 23.98$, $p < .001$ |

| Indirect Effects of effort expectancy on behavioral intention to use Chatbot via ... | Effect (SE) | Boot $CI_{LL-UL}$ |
|---|---|---|
| Total Indirect Effect | .5554 (.0991) | .3778 to .7642 |
| Effort Expectancy → Performance Expectancy → BI | .0935 (.1153) | −.1467 to .3175 |
| Effort Expectancy → Performance Expectancy → Attitude → BI | .3624 (.1165) | .1880 to .6531 |
| Effort Expectancy → Attitude → BI | .0995 (.1030) | −.0662 to .3449 |

*Notes.* *p < .05, **p < .01, ***p < .001, $^{ns}$ Not Significant

# 8  Discussion

This study presents the development and empirical testing of a mobile-phone based Chatbot to provide information about family planning and contraceptives. The study employed UTAUT model of technology adoption to assess the main predictors of behavioral intention to use Chatbot. The regression analysis showed that participants' perceptions about the amount of effort required to use the Chatbot increased performance expectancy among the participants, in turn making the attitudes toward Chatbot more appealing, therefore inducing greater intentions to use the Chatbot. Said differently, the positive attitude towards using Chatbot for family planning was determined by the effort required such as ease of use and clarity to operate Chatbot, which in turn determined the value of information gained such as ability to choose the right family planning method as well as acquiring information more quickly through mobile phones.

Overall, the study is based on the argument that the best way to learn is by doing stuff and getting feedback. People are more likely to remember concepts when they discover them on their own. In this regard, the study offers concrete implications in terms of (1) enabling healthcare providers to see the world as people do, as they battle with family planning decisions, myths, stigma, taboos and stereotypes, and providing a culturally sensitive family planning Chatbot using feature phones to improve access, demand and acceptance for modern contraceptives.

Specifically, in terms of achieving the sustainable development goals, the family planning Chatbot offers following concrete implications. For example, the Chatbot intervention may help in reducing the rate of unintended pregnancy and unsafe abortions. Participating families will be able to decide about the number of children they can care for, thus reducing medical costs with increased likelihood of healthy growth in children due to birth spacing. Increased likelihood of healthy growth in children due to spacing of births approximately 24 months apart. The study may also inform health providers and policy makers to better understand reasons for low contraceptive prevalence and implement culturally sensitive family planning services. The Chatbot is also easily replicable in other countries especially in fragile and high-risk regions with limited access to community health workers.

Although, the study was conducted in United States, still, considering the need for family planning counseling, the Chatbot is relevant for implementation in both developed and developing countries alike. For example, separate Chatbot can be developed on sensitive topics like menstruation, HIV/AIDS and mental health. Additionally, a Chatbot can be introduced either as a stand-alone intervention or integrated with an existing family planning and reproductive health intervention. For example, family planning counseling interventions in developing countries, may face a reduced uptake of contraceptives even after the products and services are made readily available. This could be because of social stigma around accessing family planning related information or just because of geographic barriers. In both cases, a family planning Chatbot can be introduced as a safe and culturally sensitive way to connect with the community. Consequently, the Chatbot can be used to improve the performance of existing family planning services by introducing more potential customers to the contraceptive products and services.

## 9 Conclusion and Future Research

Family planning is regarded as one of the 10 great public health accomplishments of the 21st century [4]. Think of a global social development problem and it will inevitably find its roots in population growth. Whether its poverty, energy crisis, climate change, food scarcity or political turmoil, all issues have a direct or indirect association with increasing population and limited resources. At current rate of 80 million people born per year, there will be 9.2 billion people on planet by 2050 [12]. We cannot have an infinite population growth, when we have a finite planet with finite resources [7].

For future research, we propose to further test the Chatbot integrated with existing family planning service providers. For example, family planning projects could include a Chatbot in existing interventions. Additionally, users could provide their contact information to receive contraceptives by mail, which is of specific relevance to users living in remote rural communities with little or no access to a family planning service providers. Additionally, users could be provided an option to request a call-back to seek more interpersonal counseling, if needed. To conclude, this study contributes in the global conversation about family planning counseling, by introducing a SMS-based Chatbot with far-reaching, implications for health of women and families in both developing and developed parts of the world.

## References

1. Ajzen, I., Fishbein, M.: Belief, Attitude, Intention and Behavior: An Introduction to Theory and Research (1975)
2. Baydar, N.: Consequences for children of their birth planning status. Fam. Plann. Perspect. **27**(6), 228–245 (1995)
3. Car, J., Gurol-Urganci, I., de Jongh, T., Vodopivec-Jamsek, V., Atun, R.: Mobile phone messaging reminders for attendance at scheduled healthcare appointments. Cochrane Database Syst. Rev. (4) (2008)
4. Centers for Disease Control and Prevention (CDC): Ten great public health achievements–United States 1900–1999. MMWR Morb. Mortal. Wkly. Rep. **48**(12), 241 (1999)
5. Cleland, J., Bernstein, S., Ezeh, A., Faundes, A., Glasier, A., Innis, J.: Family planning: the unfinished agenda. Lancet **368**(9549), 1810–1827 (2006)
6. De Jongh, T., Gurol-Urganci, I., Vodopivec-Jamsek, V., Car, J., Atun, R.: Mobile phone messaging telemedicine for facilitating self-management of long-term illnesses. Cochrane Database Syst. Rev. (4) (2008)
7. Ehrlich, P.: The Population Bomb, p. 47. New York Times, New York (1970)
8. Frost, J.J., Finer, L.B., Tapales, A.: The impact of publicly funded family planning clinic services on unintended pregnancies and government cost savings. J. Health Care Poor Underserved **19**(3), 778–796 (2008)
9. Hayes, A.F.: Introduction to Mediation, Moderation, and Conditional Process Analysis: A Regression-Based Approach. Guilford Press, New York (2013)

10. Johnson, D.: SMS open rates exceed 99%. Tatango (2013)
11. Kost, K., Landry, D.J., Darroch, J.E.: Predicting maternal behaviors during pregnancy: does intention status matter? Fam. Plann. Perspect. **30**, 79–88 (1998)
12. Lea, R.A.: World Development Report 1993: Investing in Health (1993)
13. Liu, B.: How many text messages are sent each year (2013). http://www.bloomberg.com/video/how-many-text-messages-are-sent-each-year-RDvLwi1WRgii6HMmiVk_Fw.html
14. Parvanta, C., Nelson, D.E., Parvanta, S., Harner, R.N.: Essentials of Public Health Communication. Jones & Bartlett Publishers, Burlington (2010)
15. Population Council: The Balanced Counseling Strategy Plus: A Toolkit for Family Planning Service Providers Working in High HIV/STI Prevalence Settings, 3rd edn. (2015)
16. Venkatesh, V., Morris, M.G., Davis, G.B., Davis, F.D.: User acceptance of information technology: toward a unified view. MIS Q. **27**, 425–478 (2003)
17. WHO: World Health Organization Definition of Quality. Population Reports Series J, No. 47 (1998)
18. Wulf, D., Donovan, P.: Women and societies benefit when childbearing is planned (2002)

# Memory Aid Service Using Mind Sensing and Daily Retrospective by Virtual Agent

Haruhisa Maeda[1][(✉)], Sachio Saiki[1], Masahide Nakamura[1,2],
and Kiyoshi Yasuda[3]

[1] Graduate School of System Informatics, Kobe University,
1-1 Rokkodai, Nada, Kobe, Japan
haruhisa@ws.cs.kobe-u.ac.jp, sachio@carp.kobe-u.ac.jp,
masa-n@cs.kobe-u.ac.jp
[2] Riken AIP, 1-4-1 Nihonbashi, Chuo-ku, Tokyo 103-0027, Japan
[3] Osaka Institute of Technology, 5-16-1, Omiya, Asahi, Osaka, Japan
fwkk5911@mb.infoweb.ne.jp

**Abstract.** Our research group has been studying smart home services for elderly people, which detect their daily activities based on the environmental sensors in the house. However, such sensors can only obtain limited information. To execute more optimized care, we must retrieve not only external events but internal states. Furthermore, to support memory aid, it is important to be able to retrieve the recorded information at any time. In this paper, we propose a new memory aid service, which records the self-talk of elderly people and utilizes the recorded information. Specifically, we develop *mind sensing*, which is to externalize the inside of elderly's heart as a sentence using a virtual agent. Then, the recorded information by mind sensing is cleansed through calibration and classification based on dialogue between an elderly person and a virtual agent. These information can be retrieved by classification or arbitrary keywords. In this way, the proposed service enable elderly to record and retrieve what they thought anytime anywhere.

**Keywords:** Smart health-care · Dialogue agent · Mind sensing

## 1 Introduction

Japan is currently facing hyper-aging society, which causes many social issues. According to a report by the Government of Japan, the number of elderly people over the age of 65 is 35.15 million in 2017, which is 27.7% of the total population [2]. Due to the long average life and the low birthrate, the number of elderly over 65 is increasing in Japan and will reach 40% of the total in 2050. There are many challenges, for example, the shortage of human resources and facilities in the nursing care field. Therefore, the government is focusing on supporting home care. However, there is a possibility that the burden on family caregivers increases in home care. Furthermore, the elderly at home has various difficulties

© Springer Nature Switzerland AG 2019
V. G. Duffy (Ed.): HCII 2019, LNCS 11582, pp. 353–364, 2019.
https://doi.org/10.1007/978-3-030-22219-2_27

in daily life due to the decline of cognitive function. In particular, as elderly people are getting forgetful, they can not do what they had done until then, so that they feel strong anxiety, confusion, and deterioration of self-esteem. In order to support these elderly people, many research on assistive technology has been carried out in various organizations in recent years.

Our research group has been developing the activity recognition service based on the environmental change [6]. This service read the variations of environmental sensors in elderly's home and detects their activities by machine learning technology. The detected activities are notified to the mobile terminals of elderly, and they respond to the notifications based on the their current situation. This service recognizes elderly's activity and at the same time realizes the creation of communication opportunities for them.

On the other hand, the previous research is limited to the activity recognition that can be observed with traditional sensors. To execute more personalized care for elderly, it is important to obtain not only such external events but the internal states such as human emotions and physical condition. The internal state is directly linked to human health, and it is important information for monitoring [1]. However, the internal states are usually acquired through inquiries and counseling by experts that can not be done permanently at home. Moreover, it is difficult to measure the changes of internal states by sensors.

The purpose of this research is to support elderly people who feel uneasy about forgetfulness. In this paper, especially, we propose a new memory-aid service using virtual agents, which are 3D humanoid robots. The proposed service mainly has the following two functions.

- **Agent-Assisted Mind Sensing: A system that an agent asks users about their minds, to require and record the internal states of them**
- **Memory-Aid Retrospective: A system that an user and an agent look back the day using the data recorded by mind sensing**

In order to solve the limitation of the previous research, we propose mind sensing that a virtual agent directly asks the elderly about their internal states. With various events as a trigger, the agent sends a message to the elderly mobile terminal asking for the current physical condition and emotion. After the user answers the question, the detailed information of the answer is automatically stored in the database. As a result, we can grasp the internal state of the elderly and use it for more sophisticated care.

Retrospective is that the elderly and the agent review the day at an arbitrary sense of time utilizing the accumulated internal states of them. While viewing the list of messages entered by elderly by mind sensing, they calibrates and classifies these messages one by one. Thus, elderly people can prevent forgetfulness by looking back at what happened recently. Furthermore, they can search the internal states later on the basis of classifications, words, period, and can retrieve them whenever necessary.

In this paper, we also implement a prototype system that is equipped with the function of *mind sensing* and *retrospective*. Through the preliminary experiments, we confirm that the proposed system can be expected to be extremely effective forgetfulness.

## 2  Preliminary

### 2.1  Elderly Care at Home

Along with the aging society, single households whose head is over 65 years old is increasing in Japan. However, it is difficult to accept and carry out the care for all elderly at medical facilities. On the other hand, there are a lot of elderly that prefer to receive care at their own home or their family's home rather than to receive at nursing home or care house. Against this background, in recent years, many attempts to care for elderly people at home have been made in various fields. Japanese Government is focusing on training human resources for home health care and promoting cooperation in each local government, and aims to realize Community-based integrated care systems [3] in which residences, medical care, and nursing care are integrally provided so that elderly can continue their own living in a familiar area even if they become severely in need of nursing care. The general companies are starting to work hard on developing new services that relieve elderly of loneliness using a communication robot. These effort aims to improve the quality of life (QOL) of the elderly.

### 2.2  Virtual Agent

In elderly care, it is expected to use care robots that utilize various assistive technologies to assist daily living. Among these technologies, virtual agent is a 3D friendly humanoid robot displayed on the PC screen, and can use speech recognition and speech synthesis technology to interact with users. By introducing such an agent to the medical field, it is expected that instead of an actual care provider, it becomes a communication partner of the elderly and reduce the burden of caregiver. In our previous research, we have developed a system, called Virtual Care Giver (VCG), using the VA [7]. VCG was designed to be able to cooperate with Web services, to integrate IoT, smart home and cloud. However, there is also a limitation caused by the looking of VA. The care and advices from unfamiliar avatar do not always motivate the elderly very well. In a recent study, to solve such a limitaion, we has been studying *MPAgent* system using virtual agent technology [5]. Figure 1 shows a screen shot of MPAgent. This service creates a 3D model of a face and dynamically generates an agent based on the feature points of the face acquired from the facial photograph. It also realizes a realistic dialogue by lips movement and changing the expression by the utterance. Delegating the communication care with MPAgent, a human caregiver can concentrate on human-centric tasks that cannot be done with ICT.

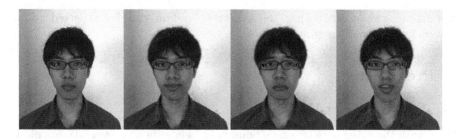

**Fig. 1.** Screen shot of MPAgent

## 2.3  Elderly Monitoring Service

As one of the technologies to support home care for the elderly, a monitoring system at home using ICT is considered promising. In the general process of monitoring, first, the system senses real-world data, and grasp the situation of the elderly and their environment. The data to be sensed includes biometric data such as pulse and acceleration of arm or leg, and environmental data such as temperature, humidity, and illuminance. Second, using the obtained data, the system recognizes the elderly's activities of daily living. Finally, based on the recognized activity, the system leads to actual care. Such a monitoring system reduces the efforts of nursing care and aims at improving the quality of care that only human beings can. However, in the conventional monitoring system, there were issues such as introduction cost, invasiveness problem, failure to achieve personal adaptation using the collected data, and lack of communication to the elderly. In order to solve these problems, in previous research, our research group has proposed and developed an elderly state notification service [6] using activity recognition based on environmental change. This service consists of an activity recognition service that predicts elderly's activity by using environment sensor data, and a care execution service that makes notifications based on predicted activity using SMS application. With this system, it is possible to record activity by non-invasive sensing and to create communication opportunities for the elderly. On the other hand, even by utilizing various sensors and devices, it is only detecting external events such as environmental data and user's expressions and behaviors, and it is impossible to observe the internal states within the user's mind. The internal state is directly related to human health, and it is important information for monitoring. Obtaining internal states helps to grasp the more detailed status of the elderly and helps more sophisticated care. In addition to acquiring conventional external events, it is important for the monitoring system to continue to monitor the internal state.

## 3  Proposed Service

### 3.1  Requirement

In this research, we propose a service to acquire and accumulate the internal state of the elderly who could not be obtained by the conventional monitoring system. Also, it contributes to the forgetfulness of elderly based on the accumulated internal condition. The proposed service realizes the following two system requirements.

- **R1: Externalize the mind of the elderly into words**
- **R2: Accumulate the words and retrieve them at any time later**

We implement a mind sensing service with the function of R1, that acquire the internal states of elderly by the virtual agent. We also implement a retrospective service depending on the function of R2, that have elderly to look back on the acquired internal state using a virtual agent and lead to prevent forgetfulness.

### 3.2   Use Case Scenario

Here, we explain how the user actually uses the proposed system. When the user starts the mind sensing service, first of all, the system registers information of sensors installed in the house in order to link with sensor data. By doing this, various notification is sent to the user triggered by user's activity recognition, so the user returns the current feeling, what happened on that day, future schedule, and so on.

When doing retrospective service, while interacting with the agent, the user corrects and classifies the data input so far. By classifying the contents of the data into classes defined by the users themselves, they are used for later retrieval. If the user wishes to remember what happened in the past, he can use various queries to search and confirm the data he entered by mind sensing, at any time. In addition, if the user wants to change personal settings, the user can make settings such as the agent's questioning timing and user information change.

### 3.3   System Architecture

In this research, to support memory aid of elderly people, we build an architecture that can manage important information for the elderly's life. Figure 2 shows the system architecture of the proposed service. The proposed system is made up of two services. One is **Agent-Assisted Mind Sensing Service** that acquires and records the feelings of the user. The agent triggers various events such as the result of the user's activity detection presumed by the existing system and asks the user about his mind using a smartphone. Then, the service obtains the answer from the user and stores it in the database. By managing such internal state for users, we will use it for other services. For instance, the doctor and the caregiver refer to the accumulated information, they can grasp the state of the elderly and make appropriate care plan. The second is **Memory-Aid Retrospective Service** based on the data recorded by mind sensing. In this service, while interacting with the agent, the user looks back inside the mind that the user himself inputs on one day. As a result, the user can remember what happened on the day and what he thought. Furthermore, the user can search the data of his mind based on various queries and check them at any time. Since elderly people can retrieve important information anytime in their daily lives, it is possible to ease the anxiety of forgetfulness. It is expected these retrospective views will lead to memory aid of elderly. We discuss these two services in detail in Sects. 3.4 and 3.5 below.

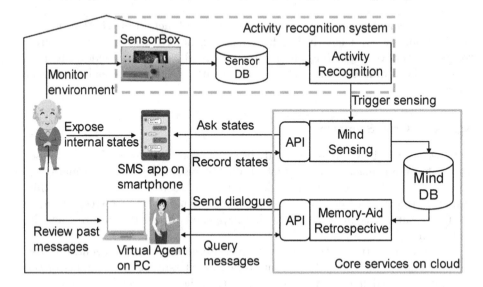

**Fig. 2.** The proposed system architecture

### 3.4    Agent-Assisted Mind Sensing

This system promotes the expression of the inner mind of each elderly person, and record it for high-quality care and communication to be done later. Especially, we use an external agent service to understand the internal conditions such as the elderly's psychology and physical conditions and at the same time create richer communication. The agent inquires of the user about various internal conditions, then, stores the obtained answer in the database.

#### 3.4.1    User Interaction

The agent gives questions according to the situation of the user. For example, at a fixed time every day, the agent asks the user about the physical condition at morning wake-up and about what happened today before sleeping at night. Furthermore, in cooperation with the existing system, the proposed system consider the observable user situation. Specifically, based on the user's activity of daily living recognized by the existing system, the agent inquires accordingly at that time. The proposed system sends messages to the user using the agent service existing as an external service, triggered by the detection from the previous research.

### 3.4.2   Record of Internal States

This service asks the user to input his self-talk using a smartphone in a way that he answer questions of the agent, or spontaneously speak what he think at the moment the user likes. The user input messages by text or voice using a smartphone, and the message is automatically collected through the Web-API at the time when transmitted. The data structure of the message we manage is as follows.

```
message_ID : ID
  datetime  : The time when the user sended a message
  contents  : A message sent by a sender
      from  : An user who sent a message
        to  : An user who received a message
  dataType  : The type of the message (text, image, etc.)
  category  : What type of topic the message is
```

**Category** is a schema for users to classify their messages in the retrospective system, and it is empty when each message is first stored. Accordingly, we organize information from the viewpoint of when, who, and what, so that, it is possible to grasp them based on various queries.

### 3.5   Memory-Aid Retrospective

This system helps the user to remember the memory by looking back on the messages of the mind entered by the user. While interacting with the agent, the user can perform the following operations.

### 3.5.1   Data Cleansing

The user calibrates and classifies the most recently entered messages. Initially, a list of messages for one day is displayed on the screen, and the user selects one by one. This is to correct unexpected conversion errors and sentence delimiters caused by voice input. If there is nothing to change, the user continues the retrospective without doing anything here. When calibration is completed, the user then sorts the messages into the categories defined by the user himself. It is not classified at the time when the user first inputs the message. The information of the messages on the database is updated when the user classifies them. By arranging and adding information to the original data in this way, they become richer contents, and it is useful for later searching under various conditions.

### 3.5.2   Search

When the user wants to remember necessary information, the user can search for data by three conditions: category, word and period. It is possible to confirm the details of messages from each search result, and the user can acquire necessary information at any time.

**Search by classification**

   The user can search tweets according to the classification of them. When the user selects a classification, the user can retrieve a list of the relevant tweets. The user can confirm.

**Search by word**

   The user can get a list of tweets based on the words of which the user is interested.

**Search by date**

   When the user designates a period, he can acquire the tweet inputted within the period. Therefore, the user can remember what happened at that time.

### 3.5.3  Personal Settings

The proposed system manages the setting information of each user in the database. The user can change various system settings on the screen. In this section, we will describe the following three functions.

**Classification settings**

   The user can define the types of categories as described in Sect. 3.5.1. This change is reflected when the user classifies the data.

**Agent settings**

   In the proposed system, we use the previous research MPAgent as a virtual agent. Since the MPAgent system generates an agent from an arbitrary facial picture, users can customize to their preferred agent. It is possible to realize a conversation with a person familiar with the user, such as relatives, children, close friends, etc.

**Sensing settings**

   The user can set a trigger for the agent to interact with the user. By setting the time and the place that the user wishes to notify, and what kind of content he wishes to be notified. Since notifications such as simple greetings, forgotten records, and important schedules arrive when the user needs it, the user will not have to worry about forgetting. By intervention in life using an agent, we can expect that elderly people can easily reconsider their lives.

## 4   Prototype Development

In this paper, we implement a prototype system that is equipped with the function of *mind sensing* and *retrospective* consisting of server-client system. In particular, we build a mind sensing service with the LINE Messaging API [4] for acquiring the self-talk of the elderly. To accumulate the internal state of elderly people obtained by mind sensing, we prepare a database and implement the Web-API for inserting and retrieving data. Furthermore, in collaboration with an agent which is an external service, we design a memory-aid service for a daily retrospective to help elderly memory. The following sections describe the details of the prototype.

## 4.1    Agent-Assisted Mind Sensing

In previous research, we have been developed the communication agent service using LINE application. This service is specialized in the function of interactive interaction and implemented as a web service. When an event such as message transmission/reception occurs, a POST request can be sent to the specified URL. In this paper, we develop a database which manages the internal states of users, and APIs to store and retrieve data. In mind sensing, when various events such as the result of activity recognition occur, or at a specific time, a message asking the user's mind is sent to the user on LINE. When a message is replied from the user, a POST request is sent to the created API and the content of the message, the time when it was sent and so on, is accumulated in the database.

## 4.2    Memory-Aid Retrospective

When the user starts using the retrospective service, a menu screen is displayed, and the user can select any one of buttons "Daily Retrospective", "Search", and "Settings".

When the user begins "Daily Retrospective", the messages accumulated in the database are acquired by the API and displayed as a list. When the user selects any one of the messages, the list screen changes to the modification/classification screen. If the message is changed here, the data on the database is updated by the API. After this work is finished, the screen returns to the list screen again and the list of the messages to be displayed is also dynamically changed. The user can visually see the message and prevent forgetfulness by remembering what happened recently. Figure 3 shows the screenshot when the user experiences the retrospective function. We deploy MPAgent as an agent that interacts with the user on the left of the screen. On the right of the screen, we prepare a user interface for the user to perform various operations. In this figure, the contents the agent is talking about and a list of messages entered by the user are displayed.

When the user starts "search", the list screen changes to the search screen. The user here can search past messages by category, word, and period, and easily switch search type by switching the tabs. In the search by category, it is possible to acquire the messages based on the category decided by the user at the time of daily retrospective. In the search by word, it is possible to acquire the message including the specified word, and in the case of the search by the period, the message within the specified period can be acquired. The user can retrieve necessary information at any time, so there is no worry about forgetfulness.

## 4.3    Development Environment

The development environment is as follows.

- Development language: Java, JavaScript, HTML, CSS
- Database: MongoDB-3.4.17
- Web server: Apache Tomcat 7.0.77
- Web service framework: Jersey framework

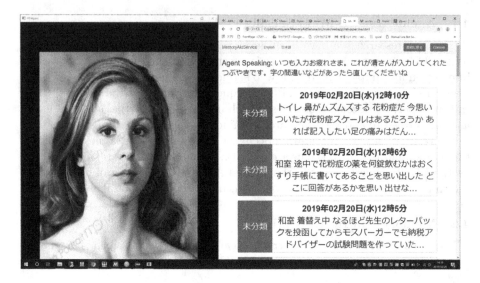

**Fig. 3.** Screen shot of the proposed system

## 5    Preliminary Experiment

We conducted preliminary experiments targeting actual elderly people using prototypes. The purposes of the experiment are to evaluate the quality at the time of use for each function by having the user use the system. In this section, we explain the outline of the experiment using the proposed system, and consider the results based on the two requirement shown in ??.

### 5.1    Outline

The target of the experiment is a male in his 60s living with a couple. When the mind sensing system detects waking up of the tester, it asks the physical condition at that time. Similarly, when the system detects the activity of the tester, it makes a question depending on the situation. At the end of the evening, the tester use a retrospective system to look back on the day's actions. The experiment period is 38 days from December 25, 2018 to January 31, 2019.

### 5.2    Result and Discussion

We confirm that there were messages about the pain of a body and physical condition of the tester. Such information cannot be obtained by traditional sensors, and we fulfill the requirement of mind sensing. In other words, it is possible to obtain internal states by mind sensing. On the other hand, the tester recorded measured values such as blood pressure and weight. It is expected to be able to develop further services by analyzing the information.

From the viewpoint of usability, the tester said to input by speech recognition is more convenient than that by flick operation. However, due to many operations until entering his internal states, it may be somewhat difficult for elderly people with advanced dementia to deal with the system.

In mind sensing service, the number of messages sent from the tester to the service was 337, and 331 of them were text messages, and 6 were images. In addition, 229 out of 337 messages were classified by the tester in retrospective service. In this preliminary experiment, the tester defined the six classifications, and the number of messages classified into each is as shown in the table below (Table 1).

**Table 1.** The number of messages in each category

| Event | Schedule | Health | Study | Memorandum | Other |
|-------|----------|--------|-------|------------|-------|
| 81    | 36       | 83     | 19    | 32         | 21    |

Here, messages classified into multiple categories are counted for each category. This result indicates that we can grasp what the tester is interested in. The reason why all the messages are not classified is that the user forgot to look back on the day or that the classification was not performed correctly due to systematic error. We should consider the need to prompt users to do retrospective and, of course, we must increase the reliability of the system.

The tester said that the function of short-term retrospective was effective in that when he was relaxing, it was able to correct typos of messages and realized what they did. On the other hand, there were opinions on the difficulty in using the user interface, such as many operations.

Regarding the search function, the search most frequently used by the tester was to search messages classified as "Memorandum". This was why he accumulated what he might forget in advance, and used it as a way to prevent forgetfulness by checking later. In this way, by the search function, the tester analyzed the number and contents of the classified messages.

Through the preliminary experiments, we confirm that the proposed system can be expected to be extremely effective forgetfulness.

# 6    Conclusion

In this paper, we proposed a new memory-aid service supporting elderly who feel uneasy about the decline in cognitive function. Especially, the proposed service obtains and records the internal states of the user by mind sensing. Then, users and agents will look back on the day based on the accumulated data. We also implement prototyping and confirm the effect of the proposed service by preliminary experiments on an actual elderly person. For future research, we will extend the proposed system to support multiple users and evaluate in detail through experiments on many more people. In addition, we will develop a service that acquires new insights by analyzing accumulated internal states of elderly.

**Acknowledgements.** This research was partially supported by the Japan Ministry of Education, Science, Sports, and Culture [Grant-in-Aid for Scientific Research (B) (16H02908, 18H03242, 18H03342), Grant-in-Aid for Scientific Research (A) (17H00731)], and Tateishi Science and Technology Foundation (C) (No.2177004).

# References

1. Di Cesare, G., Di Dio, C., Marchi, M., Rizzolatti, G.: Expressing our internal states and understanding those of others. Proc. Nat. Acad. Sci. **112**(33), 10331–10335 (2015)
2. Government of Japan: Annual report on the aging society, June 2018. http://www.cao.go.jp/
3. Government of Japan: Community-based integrated care systems, June 2018. https://www.mhlw.go.jp/index.html. (in japanese)
4. LINE Developers: Messaging api, July 2018. https://developers.line.biz/ja/services/messaging-api/
5. Nakatani, S., Saiki, S., Nakamura, M., Yasuda, K.: Generating personalized virtual agent in speech dialogue system for people with dementia. In: Duffy, V.G. (ed.) DHM 2018. LNCS, vol. 10917, pp. 326–337. Springer, Cham (2018). https://doi.org/10.1007/978-3-319-91397-1_27
6. Tamamizu, K., Sakakibara, S., Saiki, S., Nakamura, M., Yasuda, K.: Machine learning approach to recognizing indoor activities based on detection of environmental change. In: 11th World Conference of Gerontechnology (ISG2018), vol. 17, p. 118s, st. Petersburg, USA, May 2018
7. Tokunaga, S., Tamamizu, K., Saiki, S., Nakamura, M., Yasuda, K.: VirtualCare-Giver: personalized smart elderly care. Int. J. Softw. Innov. **5**(1), 30–43 (2016). https://doi.org/10.4018/IJSI.2017010103. http://www.igi-global.com/journals/abstract-announcement/158780

# Exploring Rhetoric Theory in Persuasive Design: A Mobile Web Application for Obesity Prevention

G. Mauricio Mejia[1(✉)] and Sauman Chu[2]

[1] Arizona State University, Tempe, AZ, USA
mauricio.mejia@asu.edu
[2] University of Minnesota, Twin Cities, Minneapolis, MN, USA
schu@umn.edu

**Abstract.** This paper is a report of an exploratory study of persuasive design for changing health attitudes and behaviors. The researchers designed a mobile web application for Latino parents about childhood obesity prevention called Lifecast and created three rhetoric theory-driven versions of the application changing rhetorical appeals – rational, emotional and credibility characteristics in graphics and content. The researchers evaluated the appropriateness of the application and its versions observing users and conducting in-depth interviews. In the evaluation, they found that versions did not have notable differences; in general parents and their children were motivated to use all versions of the app and reported some changes in their attitudes. They concluded that an effective strategy of rhetorical appeals should be planned and evaluated iteratively. Future work should focus not only on the appeals of visual and textual elements, but also on the rhetoric of the design concept, format, and interactivity.

**Keywords:** Design for health · Persuasive design · Visual rhetoric · Rhetorical appeals · Children obesity

## 1 Introduction

Within the contemporary human-centered approach to design, a trend in interactive design is to provide clear information and value simplicity to achieve cognitive comprehension of content [1]. However, designing for efficient cognition does not always solve the needs of people with different cultural frames of reference or levels of functional literacy. In persuasive design, non-rational appeals such as emotion and credibility are potentially powerful strategies. This article is the report of an exploratory study of design for health change that three strategies of rhetorical appeals: logos (reason), pathos (emotion), and ethos (credibility). For this, the researchers designed an interactive app exploring versions with combinations of these appeals, analyzed their design process, and evaluated the versions of the app.

According to Aristotle, there are artistic and non-artistic means of persuasion (*pisteis*). The artistic means are provided through speech whereas the non-artistic means (e.g., direct evidence that is not part of the persuasive speech, but that is available to judges, such as from witnesses and documents) are not. The speaker only

© Springer Nature Switzerland AG 2019
V. G. Duffy (Ed.): HCII 2019, LNCS 11582, pp. 365–379, 2019.
https://doi.org/10.1007/978-3-030-22219-2_28

has control over the artistic means of persuasion. There are three modes or forms of pisteis, called rhetorical appeals: the truth or apparent truth of the arguments (logos), leading the audience to feel emotions (pathos), and the credibility of the spoken word (ethos) [2]. Aristotle contended that logos is about providing logical reasons, pathos refers to emotions of pleasure or pain (positive or negative) that affect the judgment of the audience. These are temporary states of the mind evoked during a speech. He classified them in opposite pairs: anger/calmness, friendliness/hostility, fear/confidence, shame/shamelessness, kindliness/unkindliness, pity/indignation, and envy/emulation. Aristotle stated that ethos is the construction of a view of the kind of person that the speaker is, which then prepares the audience to make a judgment. He explained three characteristics of ethos persuasion: wisdom (practical sense), virtue (ability to communicate one's thoughts), and goodwill (prudency and fair-mindedness).

Speeches and design products (like apps) deliver all three rhetorical appeals, each with different strengths. For Braet [3], logos is usually the central enthymeme or argument in a speech; conversely, pathos and ethos are often indices presented in addition to the logos argument. He said that there are specific cases in which pathos and ethos are presented as arguments. For example, when ethos has been admittedly weakened, an ethos argument is justified; otherwise, it may counter the persuasion goal.

## 2   Related Work

There is a growing literature in persuasive design or persuasive technology. Fogg [4] studied multiple cases in which technology can influence attitudes and behavior; his work is a core reference in the area. Researchers commonly study persuasive technologies based on classical theories of behavior change such as the Transtheoretical Model of Behavior Change [5], but there are other researchers that have explored other theories. For instance, Consolvo and colleagues [6] suggested that other theories are relevant if they connect technology and the social context of individuals; they reported two cases with prototypes for health behavior change designed based on theories of Presentation of Self in Everyday Life and Cognitive Dissonance. In another example, Gunaratne and Nov [7] recently applied behavioral economic theory to evaluate prototypes to change decisions about retirement savings. Lockton and colleagues [8] proposed a persuasive design toolkit that draws on several theories including environmental psychology and behavioral economics. Exploring theory-driven designs are worth pursuing to extend HCI knowledge in persuasive design.

Surprisingly, HCI and design research about rhetoric is limited. Christensen and Hasle [9] contended that even though rhetoric is an ancient theory, it could inform persuasive design; they specifically suggested the rhetorical appeals and the rhetorical *aptum* (model). Some studies use theory of rhetoric to analyze physical and digital artifacts and identify strengths and weaknesses [10–12]. Further, Sosa-Tzec and colleagues [13] argued that the theory of rhetoric could be used as a lens to understand interfaces and their social, moral and ethical implications.

Whereas rhetoric has not been central in persuasive design, rhetorical-related concepts are identifiable in the literature. In Fogg's Behavioral Model for Persuasive Design [14], he argued that a target behavior needs motivation, ability, and timely triggers. He explained that triggers could be *facilitators* when ability is low and *sparks* when motivation is low. Facilitators could be associated to rational rhetorical appeals and sparks associated to emotional rhetorical appeals.

Design research that particularly focus on rhetorical appeals (logos-pathos-ethos) is rare. Gregory [15] reported a qualitative study in which she designed and analyzed two brochures about the risk of meningitis when drinking alcohol, one with a rational style that she calls information/argument and one with an emotional style that she calls emotion/entertainment. The former focuses on clear presentation of facts and evidence. The latter focuses on capturing attention with intrigue. Gregory found that whereas the rational style is better for people who are already conscious of the risk, the emotional style is better for those who do not know about the issue. Although this study has a valuable finding, the researcher based her study on only one discussion session with the participants and did not identify further actions taken by the participants. Results seem to be limited and cannot be broadly applied.

## 3  Methods

The researchers designed a mobile web application for Latino parents about childhood obesity prevention called *Lifecast* (http://www.lifecastapp.com), which has three versions, each with a different rhetorical appeals strategy. The researchers used case study research design with qualitative data to assess behavioral changes and observe the influence of the rhetorical appeals in each version. Nine Latino parents used the application (three parents for each rhetorical mode) and the researchers studied how each mode altered their knowledge and attitudes. The goals were to evaluate the efficacy of and understand the configuration of rhetorical appeals in an app intended to change knowledge, attitudes, and behaviors in low-income people. The researchers conducted two interview sessions with each participant in their homes. Spanish was the primary language for the communication.

The first session consisted of IRB consent, semi-structured in-depth interview, and basic instructions about the use of *Lifecast*. The researchers took field notes and audio recorded the interviews. Parents were asked to use the application at least four times within two weeks and before the second session. The second session consisted of confirmation of application use and a semi-structured in-depth interview. After the interview, the researchers briefly showed the two rhetorical modes that had been intentionally hidden in the first interview and explained differences between the modes to the parents. Then, the researchers extended the interview with questions about rhetorical appeals preference. The researchers took field notes and audio recorded these interviews. In addition to the evaluation, the researchers continuously reflected about how design decisions were made by selecting relevant past experiences in the design process.

Regarding data analysis, the researchers used a personal technique of organizing data and codes, following the suggestion of Bloomberg and Volpe [16]. This technique consisted of reviewing raw data by listening carefully to the audio recorded in Spanish and reading interview notes, writing transcriptions translated to English, and coding and memoing data. After each interview and within the following week, the researchers reviewed, transcribed, coded and categorized the data. Themes and codes were reviewed several times, and as a result, codes were added, deleted, and collapsed in the process of data sensemaking. Finally, the researchers looked for patterns that emerged from the codes.

Regarding limitations, transferability of results to other contexts is limited because the study was conducted in a single U.S. Midwest city. Additionally, the sample recruited at Hennepin County Medical Center has special characteristics of a narrow population. The recruited participants were parents of children that were originally referred as overweight by physicians. In this situation, parents are likely to have had interventions from the physicians and other programs that have helped them to improve their functional health literacy, gain health knowledge about their child's condition, and have healthier attitudes. The app would have probably shown different efficacy in other parent populations.

### 3.1  *Lifecast* Mobile Web Application

*Lifecast* is a mobile web application for Latino parents about childhood obesity prevention. The application aims to change health knowledge, attitudes, and behaviors in Latino parents about childhood obesity. Parents can foresee the effects of diet and exercise in virtual characters of children who are currently healthy, overweight, or obese. Parallels can be drawn between characters in the application and the parents' own children. The application is intended to be a playful and engaging environment that aids the understanding of core concepts related to childhood obesity and healthy behaviors (e.g., the positive effect of fruits and vegetables, the need for physical activity, and the negative effects of processed foods).

*Lifecast* has three rhetorical modes of use, each with a specific configuration of rhetorical appeals. The researchers referred to rhetorical appeal concepts in the literature and previous analyses to make decisions about the appeals in the rhetorical modes. These concepts were inspired in Aristotle's *On Rhetoric* book [2], Ehses' [17] operationalization of the appeals in graphic design, and the salient appeal indices identified in a previous analysis [11]. The developed guiding concepts were applied to textual and visual elements. In all modes, there are consistent visual elements such as the *Lifecast* logo, copyright information, the interactive options and images for habits, and the settings page. The core content is also the same. In a previous study the authors reported usability evaluation and exploratory analysis of the app [18].

For the infographic mode, which was expected to have a reduced number of pathos and ethos indices, the concept was to create rational text and visuals that resembled scientific simulations, using visual simplicity, statistics, and information visualization styles (see Fig. 1). The list of child characters was presented with only the necessary information. The body image was simplified and abstracted. Gestures of energy level in the child page were reduced to expressions on the mouth. All technical information about the children was included (i.e., condition, energy level, BMI, weight, height, and age.) Also, the information page was presented as a technical simplified report using bullets and tables.

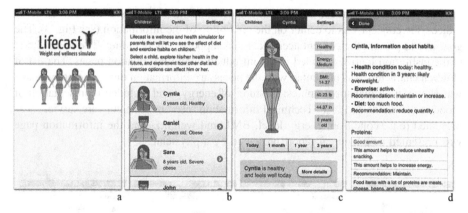

**Fig. 1.** Screenshots of pages in infographic mode of *Lifecast*: (a) introduction, (b) home, (c) child, and (d) information.

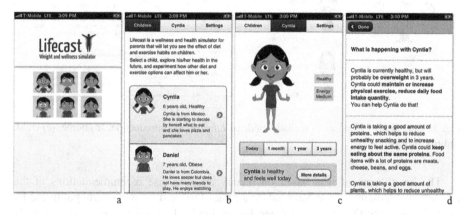

**Fig. 2.** Screenshots of pages in comic mode of *Lifecast*: (a) introduction, (b) home, (c) child, and (d) information.

For the comic mode, which was expected to have increased number of pathos indices, the concept was centered on the parents' confidence and feeling that they could help the children (see Fig. 2). The goal was to reduce anxiety and create sympathy with the characters, but also link the overweight condition with emotions of shame. The list of children characters was presented along with personal fictional stories of the child characters. The body image was abstracted using cartoon style. Facial expressions and traits in overweight conditions were exaggerated, including eye circles. Gestures of energy level included representation of mood in the hands and face. Technical information was simplified to avoid focusing on rational understanding (e.g., only information on condition and energy level was provided). Also, the information page was presented as an informal style using a narrative.

For the realistic mode, which was expected to have increased number of ethos indices, the concept was to center on the credibility of the information (see Fig. 3). The goal was to present the content accurately and supported by branding. The researchers' home institution logo was added in the introduction and information pages. The list of children characters was presented with the necessary information only. The body image was shown with realistic graphics. Gestures of energy level included representation of mood in the hands and face. Technical information relevant in health care services was presented (e.g., condition, energy level, BMI, and weight). And the information page was presented as a medical report presented by a physician.

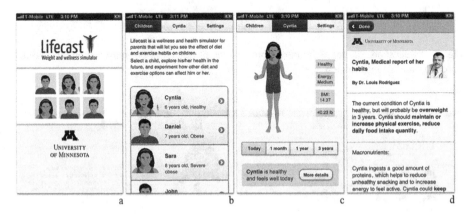

**Fig. 3.** Screenshots of pages in realistic mode of *Lifecast*: (a) introduction, (b) home, (c) child, and (d) information.

The health content was based on dietary and exercise recommendations of the Institute of Medicine of the National Academies [19] and growth charts published by the U.S. Center of Disease Control and Prevention [20]. *Lifecast* shows common daily habits of characters that the user can change. These habits are used to calculate the health prediction. Though the application is not a portrait of actual characters, it is a device by which people can understand the impact of their actions in real life.

The visual appearance of the body of the characters in *Lifecast* is based on the Children's Body Image Scale [21]. This scale shows seven levels of adiposity (underweight, healthy, overweight, and obese) with seven boys and seven girls, ages 7 to 12 years old. The graphics in this scale display photographs of children belonging to percentiles according to the levels of adiposity. *Lifecast* uses eight levels of adiposity: seven graphics were based on this scale, and the severe obese level was added, augmenting the visual weight appearance of the obese level on the scale.

Figure 4 shows an example of the prediction in realistic mode showing changes in the character body image, mood gesture, weight, energy (energetic feeling), and BMI. Feedback information is also given with a message below the time navigation menu and in the content of the information details page. The latter can be accessed in the 'more details' link.

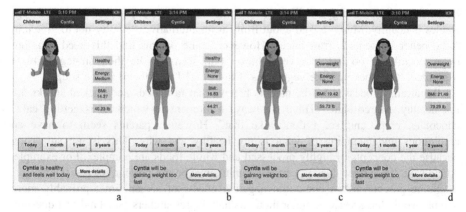

**Fig. 4.** Screenshots of pages in infographic mode of Lifecast: (a) introduction, (b) home, (c) child, and (d) information.

## 4 Findings

This section presents key findings obtained from 18 sessions with nine parents. In the report of findings below, real names of participants are kept anonymous and pseudonyms are used. In the first session, the researchers collected demographic data and administered a functional health literacy test. Seven parents were from Mexico and two from Ecuador. They have between two and five children. The parents have been living in the United States for 9–25 years and completed 2–12 years of school. Seven parents owned a mobile device. Two parents used a mobile device owned by their children. Lastly, six parents had an adequate level of functional health literacy, and three showed an inadequate level. Ten major findings emerged from this activity. They are grouped in one of four themes. The first finding belongs to the theme of functional health literacy.

Finding 1: *All parents can use the health care system largely because they have access to translation services (in Spanish), either formal or informal.* This was not surprising because the parents have lived in the United States for many years. They had difficulties at the beginning, but they currently navigate the system with sufficient skills. Part of their ability is explained by the use of translation services. Six of them regularly use interpreters. Mirta said, "When I arrived, it was hard because there were no interpreters. Today it is easy. There is rapid attention and there is help."

The next four findings belong to the themes of health knowledge, attitudes, and behaviors before using the app.

Finding 2: *The majority of parents (8 out of 9) had basic knowledge about healthy habits; however, some of the parents (3 out of 9) showed confusion with some concepts.* One parent showed confusion with many health-related habits concepts. Parents' answers showed that they have sufficient knowledge that is sometimes acquired from medical directions. All the parents understand that exercising is healthy for their children. Rita said, "They have exercise class [at school] twice a week, but the classes are short. Then, it is not enough. The boy worked out more before, but now he is lazy.

But, I take him to the gym." Parents also know that consumption of fruits and vegetables is healthy. Marco talked about fruits as an alternative: "We try not to give him soda, better homemade fruit juice." However, some parents find this need daunting because children do not like vegetables. Soup seems to be their strategy. Olivia explained, "He does not like vegetables, I fight [...] I put [them] in the soup."

Regarding processed foods, parents believe that fast foods and packed snacks are not healthy. Marco said, "There is always a moment in which he is getting cake, chocolate, chips and so. I don't like that." However, parents seem to have an ambiguous understanding of what is not healthy and why. This is not surprising because the concepts of highly processed and whole foods are complex. For example, Alicia said, "A burger does not have vitamins, maybe the protein."

Some parents talked about the negative effects of screen time; probably more parents would have voiced similar thoughts had the researchers asked a direct question on this topic during the interviews. Rita talked about the challenge to control screen time, "My mother is at home but they get home by 2:30, and until 4:30, they are basically watching TV, and it is hard to control that. When I am at home, I have more control."

Finding 3: *The majority of parents (7 out of 9) reported strategies that create healthy habits in their children.* The majority of parents take their children to exercise or exercise with them. This active involvement may be explained because they have overweight children and received medical advice. Alicia said, "I take her to church to the scouts and plays and she runs about 2 h [a week]. And we walk, in the mall in winter. I try to have her walk 30 min a day." Parents also have creative strategies to provide healthy foods to their children. They add vegetables to the soup or the rice, mix sugary cereal with whole cereal, and offer fruits while watching television. For example, Mirta said, "In the rice, I put beans and other vegetables; so they eat their rice and they get the vegetables there."

Finding 4: *All of the parents showed some unhealthy attitudes or beliefs.* Even the parents who showed broad evidence of healthy attitudes and knowledge had some unhealthy attitudes or beliefs. Some parents let children snack without any control. For example, Mirta said, "He escapes and go to the store to get sweet treats. It is two or three times per week." A couple of parents think that their children will lose weight by themselves in adolescence. Olivia said, "When they grow, it is different. They realize how they are. They get embarrassed and think about change." A couple of parents force their children to eat vegetables. Rita said, "If we go to the buffet, I tell them to eat vegetables otherwise I don't take them back. I always have rules for the food." Lastly, a couple of parents think that fat is unhealthy for their children. Inés said, "I use 1% milk. The skim one tastes like water; I don't like it. I also changed regular yogurts to light ones."

The following findings were the result of the analysis of the second session. Since three parents used *Lifecast* in the infographic mode, three in the comic mode, and three in the realistic mode, they are identified in the following findings with a pseudonym and the mode that they used in brackets. Not all parents used the app as directed. The researchers helped three parents that had had difficulties using or accessing the application for 30 min approximately in the hour before starting the second session.

The next three findings belong to the theme of changes in health knowledge, attitudes, and behaviors after using the app.

Finding 5: *About half of parents (5 out of 9) clearly showed positive changes in knowledge or beliefs about healthy habits.* After using the application, half of the parents showed, in the second interview, that they gained certain health knowledge. One parent learned the central role of exercise in children's health:

> I asked my daughter to put what she eats, and she said, oh it is fat. She doesn't really eat that bad. I don't buy premade food, but I don't know why. It is the exercise. So she found that the exercise is what she needs. (Alicia [infographic])

Verónica [realistic] and Abi [realistic] changed their belief that habits do not affect one's energy feeling. Abi said, "I was wrong. It has to be diet [...] I read it in the app. Diet and exercise, there is no mention of sleep, though they have to sleep at least eight hours." Two parents learned that not only the quantity but also the balance and type of food, have effects on health. Marco [comic], for example, specifically mentioned that he learned that a diet should not focus on one type of food and should be balanced to be healthy and provide energy. He said that he used to think that just a lot of meat was healthy.

Two parents remarked on the responsibility of parents to offer healthy food to their children. Abi [realistic] said, "[I learned] to give a little bit more vegetables to the kids. I don't give them to my kids. Because they don't like them, I don't force them. But I realized that vegetables are good for them." And Alicia [infographic] said, "I learned the responsibility of the parents. Kids are going to eat what we give them and how we create habits from when they are little."

Some parents learned other concepts. Rita [comic] learned that exercise is not the only solution, "Yes, I thought I could give them to eat quite a bit and take them to exercise, and the true not, it does not work." One parent, Verónica [realistic], also learned how to influence child snacking, "[I learned] how to reduce snacks, giving them more proteins and more vegetables. This way reduces consumption of snacks that are not nutritive or healthy for children."

Finding 6: *Some parents (3 out of 9) clearly showed a positive change in attitude or behavior about healthy habits.* After using the application, some parents showed, in the second interview, that they changed their health attitudes or behaviors. Veronica [realistic] and Marco [comic] changed the way they think about snacks. Marco was asked if hiding snacks was a good strategy; he said that he now thinks it is not. He said that he instead should motivate his kids and talk to them more. And Inés [realistic] was surprised about her child's diet, "I assumed that the child was my daughter. I put the food that I give her usually, and I was terrified of the consequences." The researchers observed that she wants to change the diet.

Finding 7: *Some parents (3 out of 9) used the app with their children and reported that their children had substantial positive changes in knowledge or attitudes.* Even though the researchers did not ask the parents to use the application with their children, three parents took the initiative and used it with their children. Marco [comic] showed the app to his son, who first reacted by having fun. Then, his son became more serious about the content of the app. Marco said he thinks that his son learned from the app too. Two parents said,

It is exciting. My daughter also liked it. She was commenting what was happening in the predictions. She noticed the difference. [...] Yes, she changed. She was surprised. I am always telling her about what not to eat and she does not pay attention, but when she saw the photos and got surprised, she paid attention [...] I told my daughter to try with the food she likes and she said, wow the child in the app got fat. And I said, you see cakes, bad food. Even the healthy children I try to increase the food. Even the ones that had very active exercise get fat. (Alicia [infographic])

Both of us [used the app]. I told her to look at the app to see the effects. She has seven pounds extra and I am helping her and talking to her. [Researcher: So, has she changed after using the app?] Yes, she is now getting carrots with lemon, apples, cereal [...] [The app] was the reason. I told her to suppose that she was the one in the app. I told her to pick the food that she would like. She picked and picked, then I told her to see what is the result [...] She believed me, but when she assumed that she was the one [in] the app [the incentive to change was greater]. (Inés [realistic])

This finding was surprising for the researchers because the application was designed for the parents. This indicates that the application may be even more beneficial for children or for parents using the application with their children.

The next finding belongs to the theme of experience using the app.

Finding 8: *The majority of parents (8 out of 9) showed motivation and engagement using the app.* In the first interview, half of the parents (5 out of 9) clearly expressed motivation before using the application by themselves. Through the second interview, the majority of the parents (8 out of 9) expressed reactions that show they were motivated and engaged using the application. The majority of the parents commented that the application is a learning tool. Verónica [realistic] said, "It is interesting to know tips to help me or my children to control what they eat or try to help them to improve their diets." Half of the parents (5 out of 9) preferred to select child characters in the application that resemble their children, in certain aspects, or themselves when they were a child, which explains some of the parents' motivation. Mirta [infographic] said, "The boy, I was thin when I was young and they tried that I eat and gain weight. The girls, my two oldest daughters, both are overweight. They exercise and lose weight, and fast they are back." Half of the parents (4 out of 9) expressed having fun with the application. Rita [comic] said, "It is like a game in which you learn and you can teach the kids, too."

The last finding belongs to the theme of rhetorical appeals in the app.

Finding 9: *Parents do not perceive, at least consciously, differences among the rhetorical modes in terms of appeals to logos (reason), pathos (emotion), or ethos (credibility).* When parents were asked questions about the rhetorical appeals, they had to think to decide on their answers, especially those related to pathos appeals. Additionally, the parents were not able to give detailed explanations about their opinions. In terms of appeals to logos, the majority of parents (8 out of 9) understood the application. Only Hilda [comic] could not answer this question because she relied too much on family members to use the application on her behalf. In terms of appeals to pathos, the majority of parents (8 out of 9), except Hilda [comic], expressed emotional reactions during the experience, such as feeling sorry for the unhealthy characters, confidence, and kindness when helping the characters, and happiness when the characters' health improved. Mirta [infographic] said, "I saw her fat and in need of help to lose weight. And the kid, too, he needed help to eat better and gain weight [...] I felt good helping them." Rita [comic] said, "Hard for them, overweight is not ok, kids feel frustrated. In the drawing, one can see the hands down; and when they get better, they have the hands up." And Abi [realistic] said, "I felt good. I felt that I was doing experiments to my own child to reduce weight and be healthy [...] I felt bad because there are many overweight children and they are criticized." In terms of appeals to ethos, all of the parents agreed that the application was credible. Some associated the content with what the health providers have told them. Olivia [infographic] said, "There was food the doctor has explained to me."

In the last part of the second session, the researchers showed all three rhetorical modes to all of the parents. And the parents were surveyed about preference and appeals. Parents had an overwhelming preference for the realistic mode. These results show that parents believe that it is the most appealing mode to logos, pathos, and ethos. Mirta [infographic], for example, answered, "The realistic. It looks more real like looking at the person there [...] I like the stories but I said realistic." Similarly, Abi [realistic] said, "The realistic one because it has the doctor."

### 4.1   Analysis of the Design Process

The first finding is that the understanding of the rhetorical appeals changed over the duration of the design process. Initially, the researchers adopted Ehses' [17] idea of creating logos-, pathos-, and ethos-driven design products, and planned to create an app with three rhetorical modes, each with a dominance of one of the rhetorical appeals. However, during the design process, the researchers realized that appeals to logos were similar in the rhetorical modes. Then, the researchers planned to have a base of appeals to logos that all modes would share, and a substantial difference in the configuration of appeals to pathos and ethos. Even after the plan about the rhetorical appeals seemed clear, the outcome was different than expected. When the app was finished, the researchers assessed the outcomes and concluded that there was not a substantial differentiation among the rhetorical modes. This experience shows that planning a configuration of rhetorical appeals poses a remarkable design challenge. Current human-centered methods, such as early prototyping, help only a little because they do not allow testing the abilities of design products to change behaviors. Early prototypes neither contain refined visual and textual elements nor render the complete experience.

The goal of the project was to create rhetorical modes with substantial differences. Before the third stage, however, the researchers realized that this goal was not being met. The initial effort had been to focus on creating different rhetorical appeals by varying the visual and textual elements of the app while preserving the homogeneity of other factors (i.e., concept, interactive structure, and format). This initial effort was to allow for valid comparative evaluation in the research. However, there is a tension between creating a difference in the appeals and controlling for homogeneity of other factors. After creating the app with the rhetorical modes, it was evident that not only the visual and textual elements, but also other factors (concept, interactivity, and format) could substantially influence how the app appeals to the audience. For example, if the *Lifecast* application would have included an option for the parent to create new characters, the parent could have entered his or her own child's data and increased the attachment of emotions like shame or confidence. This is a conceptual and interactive change that would work as a pathos index.

## 5 Discussion

### 5.1 Behavioral Change

Even though the parents initially had a medium-to-high level of knowledge and positive attitudes about childhood obesity, they were motivated to use the app (i.e., the mobile web application *Lifecast*) and exhibited a change in their knowledge, beliefs, attitudes, and behavior. Even though the types of motivation varied among parents, it appears common that parents are looking for alternatives to deal with obesity affecting their children. The application, focusing on playfulness and engagement, was designed as an informal learning tool for parents. This level of motivation was crucial to facilitating behavior change objectives.

There are multiple levels, opportunities, and strategies for generating behavior change [22, 23]. For instance, while some people need more information to increase their knowledge, others need emotional incentives, and still, others need help to strengthen habits. The findings showed that the application was used in different ways and from different perspectives, which seem to trigger unexpected, but positive changes. In the design process, before the evaluation in the third stage, the behavior change concepts and strategies were defined. Examples of these concepts are physical exercise has a positive effect, or foods with proteins have a positive effect. The revision of these concepts, compared to the findings, shows that the concepts were too general to describe the actual potential change that can be generated in people that use the application.

An even more surprising behavior change was generated in the children of the parents. Even though parents were not asked to use the application with their children, three of them did so. Those three parents reported that their children learned from the application and changed. This indicates that the application is a flexible tool and a powerfully persuasive tool for parents to help their children cope with obesity issues.

### 5.2 Assessment of Rhetorical Appeals in the App

The assessment of rhetorical appeals in the rhetorical modes of the app was conducted from two perspectives: researchers' self-assessment and parents' assessment. The results are paradoxical. First, the researchers concluded at the end of the design process that there were fewer differences than expected among the three modes at the beginning. Second, the assessment of the rhetorical appeals, provided by parents in the sample (audience), was notably different from the assessment of the researchers. Parents seemed to have little consciousness about their reaction to the appeals. Furthermore, parents were not aware of the rhetorical situation. Thus, individual's self-reporting on the effectiveness of design product appeal is not a valid technique yet. Such measurement will require more sophisticated procedures.

An alternative explanation is that certain indices have effects in more than one appeal. For example, the stories in the comic mode were intended to function as a pathos index; however, stories might appeal to ethos if a parent sees that the stories match real-life people they might know, or even themselves. This matching gives credibility because the application would be empathic and sensible to the experiences of the parent. Parents, after looking at the three rhetorical modes, had an overwhelming preference for the realistic mode. However, preference is not known to be a predictor of changes in knowledge, attitudes, or behavior. Parents argued that the reason for preference of the realistic mode is the direct relationship with real life and the presence of a doctor. This preference might mean that appeals to credibility (ethos) are suitable for this audience, but more evidence is needed.

### 5.3 Conclusions

Based on the parents recruited for this study, Latino parents have a medium-to-high level of health literacy and are motivated to use the app (*Lifecast*). Some parents using the application reported some changes in knowledge or attitudes. The effects on the parents are not homogeneous, as the researchers had planned. Instead, each parent's experience generates specific knowledge, attitudes, or behavior change, which is a function of the needs of the individual, and the adaptability/flexibility of the application. Although the application (*Lifecast*) generated positive change in this audience, parents with lower-level knowledge and unhealthy attitudes would have provided a further understanding of the potential of the application. Alternatively, if the audience has a high-level knowledge and positive attitudes, the design product and the outcome evaluation should focus on assisting and measuring behavior change.

The decisions about rhetorical appeals in the design process demand careful planning and should be continually reviewed throughout the process. First, designers have the option to use conceptual models to guide decisions regarding the rhetorical appeals in design products. Alternatives range from Aristotle's *On Rhetoric*, written more than 2,000 years ago, to contemporary interpretations for classic rhetoric [3], to practical guides in graphic design [17]. Rhetorical analysis of existing design products, either comprehensive or focused on the rhetorical appeals, would help designers to make accurate decisions. Second, limiting the rhetorical appeal decisions to visual and textual elements, and ignoring how design concepts, interactivity, and format affect the appeals, results in an intuitive rhetorical strategy. Particularly in digital formats, the way design products appeal to the audience is complex, because such a process also includes an interactive structure. Additionally, the design concept goes beyond the semantics of visual composition. The design concept also includes the *narrative* and *core mechanics* of the design product.

The researchers were considering potential optimal configurations of rhetorical appeals by creating an effective app for health change. They exposed the audience to an application that had three different rhetorical modes; they expected to understand how the varied configurations of rhetorical appeals generated specific reactions in the audience. Nonetheless, the researchers found that each of the three modes had strength in all three of the rhetorical appeals. They found that, even though the rhetorical appeals are influenced by visual and textual elements, the appeals are mainly determined by the design concept and interactivity; all the rhetorical modes in the application share this strength of the appeals. Because the lead designer is the one who knows the most about the rhetorical situations (i.e., goal, audience, place, and time), he or she, as opposed to the audience, is the one who can heuristically assess the configuration of rhetorical appeals. Exceptions to this rule might be (a) an external design expert committed to fully study the rhetorical situation and (b) availability of validated instruments to measure the effects of rhetorical appeals in the audience.

Including interactivity in the strategy of appeals, posits further challenges for designers in terms of dynamic rhetorical situations. The Internet unsettles the rhetorical situation because the audience accesses a speech at undefined times and places. Interactivity adds another layer of complexity because every individual in the audience can tour the interfaces in different ways, thereby creating different speeches.

Regarding design principles or rules of thumb for practice, there is not enough evidence to define them because this is a study that centered on mapping a research area. Further research is needed to determine the best configuration or configurations of rhetorical appeals in persuasive design products to achieve behavioral change. Admittedly, rhetorical situations cannot be standardized, because they change depending on exigency (issue or goal), place, time, and the characteristics of the audience. Thus, there will be a level of generalizability or transferability depending upon the distinctive behavior change study cases.

# References

1. Norman, D.: The Psychology of Everyday Things. Basic Books, New York (1988)
2. Aristotle, O.: Rhetoric: A Theory of Civic Discourse, 2nd edn. Oxford University Press, Oxford (1991)
3. Braet, A.C.: Ethos, pathos, and logos in Aristotle's rhetoric: a re-examination. Argumentation 6, 307–320 (1992)
4. Fogg, B.: Persuasive Technology: Using Computers to Change What We Think and Do (Interactive Technologies). Morgan Kaufmann, Burlington (2002)
5. Prochaska, J.O., Velicer, W.F.: The transtheoretical model of health behavior change. Am. J. Health Promot. 12(1), 38–48 (1997)
6. Consolvo, S., McDonald, D.W., Landay, J.A.: Theory-driven design strategies for technologies that support behavior change in everyday life. In: Proceedings of the 27th International Conference on Human Factors in Computing Systems – CHI 2009, p. 405 (2009)
7. Gunaratne, J., Nov, O.: Informing and improving retirement saving performance using behavioral economics theory-driven user interfaces. In: Proceedings of the 33rd Annual ACM Conference on Human Factors in Computing Systems – CHI 2015, pp. 917–920 (2015)
8. Lockton, D., Harrison, D., Stanton, N.A.: The design with intent method: a design tool for influencing user behaviour. Appl. Ergon. 41(3), 382–392 (2010)
9. Christensen, A.-K.K., Hasle, P.: Classical rhetoric and a limit to persuasion. Persuasive 2007, 307–310 (2007)
10. Van der Waarde, K.: Visual communication for medicines: malignant assumptions and benign design? Visible Lang. 44(1), 39–69 (2010)

11. Mejía, G.M., Longo, B.: Design and effect of viral videos for social change. Visual Methodol. **5**(2), 50–61 (2017)
12. Mejía, G.M., Chu, S.: A model for visual communication design: connecting theories of rhetoric, literacy, and design. Des. J. **17**(1), 29–43 (2014)
13. Sosa-Tzec, O., Stolterman, E., Siegel, M.A.: Gaza everywhere: exploring the applicability of a rhetorical lens in HCI. Aarhus Ser. Hum. Cent. Comput. **1**(1), 4 (2015)
14. Fogg, B.: A behavior model for persuasive design, pp. 40:1–40:7 (2009)
15. Gregory, J.: Using message strategy to capture audience attention: readers' reactions to health education publications. J. Nonprofit Public Sect. Mark. **15**, 1–23 (2006)
16. Bloomberg, L.D., Volpe, M.: Completing Your Qualitative Dissertation: A Roadmap from Beginning to End, 2nd edn. Sage, Thousand Oaks (2012)
17. Ehses, H.: Design on a Rhetorical Footing. Halifax, Canada (2008)
18. Chu, S., Mejía, G.M.: Application of rhetorical appeals in interactive design for health. In: 15th International Conference on Design, User Experience, and Usability Human-Computer Interaction, Las Vegas, pp. 371–380 (2013)
19. Institute of Medicine of the National Academies: Dietary Reference Intakes for Energy, Carbohydrate, Fiber, Fat, Fatty Acids, Cholesterol, Protein, and Amino Acids (Macronutrients). The National Academies Press, Washington, DC (2005)
20. Center of Disease Control and Prevention: Clinical Growth Charts (2009). http://www.cdc.gov/growthcharts/clinical_charts.htm. Accessed 19 Feb 2013
21. Truby, H., Paxton, S.J.: Development of the children's body image scale. Br. J. Clin. Psychol. Br. Psychol. Soc. **41**(Pt 2), 185–203 (2002)
22. Heath, C., Heath, D.: Switch: How to Change Things When Change is Hard. Broadway Books, New York (2010)
23. Maibach, E., Roser-Renouf, C., Leiserowitz, A.: Communication and marketing as climate change-intervention assets: a public health perspective. Am. J. Prev. Med. **35**(5), 488–500 (2008)

# Identifying Users in the Bridging Service Between Two Different Chat Services Using User Icons

Ko Miyazaki[1(✉)] and Haruaki Tamada[2(✉)]

[1] Division of Frontier Informatics, Graduate School of Kyoto Sangyo University, Motoyama, Kamigamo, Kita-ku, Kyoto, Kyoto Prefecture, Japan
i1888123@cc.kyoto-su.ac.jp
[2] Faculty of Information Science and Engineering, Kyoto Sangyo University, Motoyama, Kamigamo, Kita-ku, Kyoto, Kyoto Prefecture, Japan

**Abstract.** There are many chat services in the world, such as Slack (https://slack.com/), Skype (https://www.skype.com/en/), gitter.im (https://gitter.im/), etc. Generally, we cannot send messages over the different chat services, since there are no route to send messages between them. To solve the problem, we propose the bridge system, named *CiBridge*, to exchange messages between different two chat services. By using the *CiBridge*, users in each chat service can send messages to other chat service by using the ordinary chat service. However, one problem arises in use of *CiBridge*. The problem is on the bridged messages which are posted from another chat service. The bridged messages are posted by *CiBot*, therefore, the original user of the message are concealed. Of course, the body of bridged messages shows the user names of original messages. However, the text information does not clarify the original user of the messages. Generally, the users distinguish each user by their avatar icons rather than the user names. For example, GitHub (https://github.com/) supports the user distinguishes each developer by the user icon. If the user does not specify his/her own user icon, GitHub gives the default user icon by Identicon (https://blog.github.com/2013-08-14-identicons/). That is, the visualization strongly helps the instinctive understandings. Therefore, the user icons are important information in the chat system to distinguish each user. This paper tries for embedding the original user icons to the bridged messages.

## 1 Introduction

Today, the development teams usually use some chat services to exchange messages among the members. For example, Oracle corporation employs Slack as a chat service for their daily use[1]. In such teams, a bot in the chat service solves simple but bothersome works, e.g., reserving the meeting rooms, automatically

---

[1] https://slack.com/enterprise

© Springer Nature Switzerland AG 2019
V. G. Duffy (Ed.): HCII 2019, LNCS 11582, pp. 380–390, 2019.
https://doi.org/10.1007/978-3-030-22219-2_29

deployment, and so on. It is called ChatOps to solve the work by the bot like above. For instance, Netflix manages the incidents on their chat service[2].

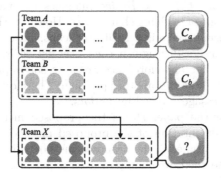

**Fig. 1.** Issues of the paper

However, the problems arise in the case of collaborating members over the teams. Let consider the case of building the new team $X$ from existing team $A$ and $B$, shown in Fig. 1. Besides, the members in $X$ remains in the former teams. Additionally, the team $A$ and $B$ employ another chat services $C_a$ and $C_b$, respectively. In the case, the members of $X$ have to use two or more different chat services. Because, they need to use the chat services corresponding to the members in $X$, $A$, $B$ and switching the chat services requires a slight overhead. Of course, the overhead of this case is quite low; however, the overhead gradually gains by joining many teams.

The following four items are the categories of cost by using several chat services.

(1) the searching cost for contact subjects,
(2) the switching cost of chat service.
(3) the registration cost, and
(4) the login cost.

In (1), by using many chat services, the user must remember the contact address and corresponding chat service. This searching cost is generally concealed, however quite high. In (2), the user pays some cost of switching the chat services. The one switching cost is quite slight; however, the cost gradually increases in proportion to the switching count. Next (3), the user should conduct user registration to use the new chat service. This registration cost is mandatory once at first. However, some recent services do not allow multiple accounts; therefore, the user must register cell phone numbers. This restriction is quite bothersome for the user. Finally, in (4), the user tries to communicate with a particular chat service, then the chat service requires authentication. The authentication is generally quite significant; however, this case is also bothersome.

---

[2] https://www.usenix.org/conference/srecon16/program/presentation/tobey.

To solve the above problems, we propose the bridging service between two chat services, called *CiBridge*. *CiBridge* installs the bot, called *CiBot* into the target chat services. Then, *CiBot* reacts to a posted message from the user, and send it to another *CiBot*. *CiBridge* manages the pair of *CiBots*. Also, sameroom.io[3] is the one of bridging chat service. However, the icon of the posted messages through sameroom.io is default user icons, since the bot conducts the post. Generally, the users distinguish each user by their avatar icons rather than the usernames [1,2]. Therefore, sameroom.io solves problems by bridging chat services, however, it causes another problem. Therefore, *CiBridge* supports avatar icons in the messages posted by *CiBots*.

The remainder of the paper shows the proposed method (Sect. 2). Next, it describes the implementation of the proposed method (Sect. 3). Afterward, Sect. 4 shows the case studies of the proposed method. Finally, Sect. 5 discusses the related works, and then, we summarize the paper in Sect. 6.

## 2   The Proposed Method

### 2.1   The Chat Services

In the paper, we define the chat services as follows. Figure 2 shows the class diagram of a chat service. From the Fig. 2, the message has a user who post it.

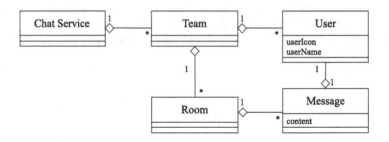

**Fig. 2.** The class diagram of the chat services for the paper

For illustrating a practical chat service, we choose Slack and Skype. Slack and Skype are popular chat services. The Slack has many teams and organizes users by the teams. Then, a team has several rooms, users in a room joined freely, and the user has conversations on each room.

On the other hand, Skype has only one team, and the team has all of the users in the world. The user managing the room can invite other users to join the room.

In both chat service, the content of a message is the same in the definition of this paper. The message has a posted user and content. Besides, the content of

---

[3] https://sameroom.io/.

the message is typically string format. However, the content might be a binary format, such as images, videos, audios, and other formats. The proposed method allows any format.

In almost chat service, the users can specify own icons. The user icon is affected to distinguish other users [1–3]. Therefore, the user icon is quite significant even in the bridge services.

## 2.2   The Proposed Method

To bridge the two chat service, we prepare the one relay server and two chatbots. Figure 3 illustrates the proposed method. At first, we install chatbots into both chat services. The chatbots resident on a particular room, and react the post from the user on the room. The user posts a message (Fig. 3a); then the chatbots send the content of the message to the relay server (Fig. 3b). When the relay server receives the message, it finds corresponding chatbot (Fig. 3c) from the database. Next, the relay server sends the content of the message to the found chatbot (Fig. 3d). Finally, the chatbot receives the message from the relay server, and it posts the message instead of the original user (Fig. 3e).

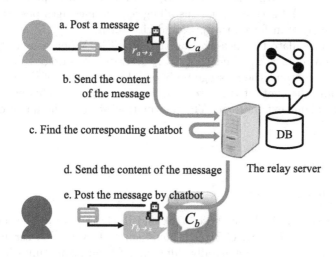

**Fig. 3.** The procedures of the proposed method.

The received data on the relay server contains the message itself, and chatbot and posted user information. The relay server manages the pairs of chatbots using the database. Each chatbot is identified by their ids. Also, the user is distinguished by the URL of the team, and the user id. Besides, the user would identify each user by icons, therefore, this paper assumes that almost users set their icons.

## 2.3   Formulation of the Proposed Method

This section gives the formulation of the proposed method. Let be two teams $X$ and $Y$, and each team uses different chat services $C_x$ and $C_y$. Also, the members of each team are shown as $m(X) = \{x_1, x_2, ..., x_{n_x}\}$, and $m(Y) = \{y_1, y_2, ..., y_{n_y}\}$. The new team $Z$ are built by arbitrarily selecting the members of $X$ and $Y$ $(m(X) \cap m(Y) \neq \phi)$. The both chat services $C_x$ and $C_y$ introduce the new rooms $r_{x \to y}$ and $r_{y \to x}$, respectively, for connecting both rooms. The messages posted on $r_{x \to y}$ are automatically share to $r_{y \to x}$ by the relay server $B_r$, and vice versa.

For this, we install the bridging system *CiBridge* for connecting $C_x$ and $C_y$ through $r_{x \to y}$ and $r_{y \to x}$. *CiBridge* composes of several chatbots $b_i \in B_b$ and one relay server $B_r$. For connecting $r_{x \to y}$ and $r_{y \to x}$, a user $x_i \in m(X)$ setups $C_x$ $(1 \leq i \leq n_x)$. $x_i$ selects the suitable chatbot $b_x$ from a chatbots set $B_b$ of *CiBridge*. The API of each chat service is generally different. The suitable chatbot means that the bot uses the API of a specific chat service. Then, $x_i$ installs $b_x$ to $C_x$ by authorizing to react the message post and to post messages to $r_{x \to y}$. The installed chatbot represents as $\beta_{x \to y}$ The each $\beta_i$ is identified by its id $(id(\beta_i))$. The relay server $B_r$ manages the relationship between $\beta_{x \to y}$ and $\beta_{y \to x}$. That is, if a chatbot is specified, $B_r$ can find the corresponding chatbot. Similarly, $y_i \in m(Y)$ setups $C_y$ for installing $b_y$, the messages posted on $r_{x \to y}$ are automatically transferred to $r_{y \to x}$, and vice versa.

Next, we formulate the messages on the *CiBridge*. When a user $x_k$ posts a message $e$ on a room $r_{x \to y}$, a chatbot $\beta_{x \to y}$ activates for bridging the message. The message $e$ contains the message body $o$ and information of the user $x_k$, the room $r_{x \to y}$ and the chatbot $\beta_{x \to y}$ $(e = \{o, x_k, r_{x \to y}, \beta_{x \to y}\})$. The message body $o$ is typically plain text message. The information of $x_k$ is the name of $x_k$ and icon.

# 3   Implementation

## 3.1   Overview

For the proposed method, we chose Slack and Rocket.Chat[4] as the target chat services $C_x$ and $C_y$. Ideally, *CiBridge* should support every chat services. However, each chat service has generally different API, and sometimes it is extensively different. Therefore, we develop the chatbot for each chat service step by steps. To support the above two chat services is the first step of the proposed method.

We implemented the relay server $B_r$ as a REST service [4] written in the Java language. Also, we applied Hubot[5] for implementing *CiBots*. $B_r$ and each *CiBot* run at each Amazon EC2 server on AWS[6]. We used the following libraries for the $B_r$ and *CiBots*.

---

[4] https://rocket.chat/.
[5] https://hubot.github.com.
[6] https://aws.amazon.com.

**Table 1.** The endpoints of $B_r$

| Endpoints | HTTP method | Description |
| --- | --- | --- |
| /api/relay/messages | POST | Exchange posted messages to corresponding chatbot |
| /api/relay/pairs | GET | Returns the corresponding chatbot with given room id |
| | POST | Register the room pair for bridging the messages |
| | DELETE | Delete the room pair |

- The relay server $B_r$
  - Java 10
  - Jersey 2.0.1
  - Jetty 9.4.11
  - SQLite 3.27.1[7]
- *CiBot*(Slack)
  - Hubot
  - hubot-slack adapter 4.6.0[8]
- *CiBot*(Rocket.Chat)
  - Hubot
  - hubot-rocketchat adapter 1.0.12[9]

### 3.2   The Relay Server $B_r$

$B_r$ was built as a REST service for message bridging. $B_r$ has two endpoints, /api/relay/messages and /api/relay/pairs. Table 1 shows the available HTTP methods for the endpoints. Besides, the format of the message $e$ is JSON, and the authorization token of *CiBridge* includes in the HTTP header. $B_r$ performs two features, relaying the message, and managing the pairs.

#### 3.2.1   Relaying the Message

At first, it explains the relaying the message. The relaying the message feature is activated by receiving the message through /api/relay/messages by POST method, and performed the following stages.

1. extracts the room id $id(\beta_{x \to y})$ from the received message $e$.
2. finds the corresponding chatbot $\beta_{y \to x}$ by the extracted chatbot id $id(\beta_{x \to y})$.
3. converts the messages $e$ to clarify the bridged message $e'$ ($e' = \{o', x'_k, r_{x \to y}, \beta_{x \to y}\}$).
4. sends the converted message $e'$ to the corresponding chatbot $\beta_{y \to x}$.

---

[7] https://www.sqlite.org/index.html.
[8] https://github.com/slackapi/hubot-slack.
[9] https://github.com/RocketChat/hubot-rocketchat.

The message $e$ contains the message body $o$, information of user $x$, room $r_i$ and the chatbot $\beta_i$, described above ($e = \{o, x, r_i, \beta_i\}$). In *CiBridge*, the $B_r$ converts the $e$ to $e'$ by the following two steps. The first step converts the user icon by putting *CiBridge* icon at the lower right of it. The second step adds the original user name at the first of the message body, if the message body is plain text.

Figure 4 shows an example of the original message $e$ and the bridged message $e'$. This example shows that the user Garry posts a message on the room HCII2019, and we bridge between HCII2019 and the room PAPERS in another chat service. Figure 4(a) is the view in the HCII2019, and (b) is the view in the PAPERS. The *CiBridge* adds its icon to the original user icon, appends the room name HCII2019 the username, and updates the message body to clarify the bridged message.

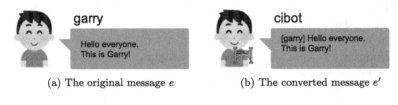

(a) The original message $e$          (b) The converted message $e'$

**Fig. 4.** An example of the original and the bridged messages

### 3.2.2   Managing the Chatbot Pairs

To manage the chatbot pairs should perform CRUD tasks (create, read, update, delete). However, we substitute the update task for the delete and create tasks. Therefore, the endpoint of /api/relay/pairs accepts GET, POST, and DELETE methods, and do not support UPDATE method. Similarly with the general REST application, GET method returns the list of the registered pairs, POST method register the posted pair, and DELETE method remove the pair from the list.

In the create task, $B_r$ inserts the pair of chatbots into the database. The pair is specified in the request body of the HTTP request. The inserted data is the chatbot id $id(\beta_i)$, its name, the corresponding chatbot id $id(\beta_j)$ and its url $url(\beta_j)$.

Next, the read task finds the corresponding chatbots for requested $id(\beta_i)$. The task was done for simply reading the database. Finally, the delete task is also executed by the deleting the database entries.

### 3.3   *CiBots*

*CiBot* is a simple chatbot built with Hubot. *CiBot* has three features: detecting the new post, posting message instead of the original user, and presenting various information replying the request from a user. In the detecting the new post, *CiBot* activates by posting from user except own. This feature are based on the Hubot **hear** method. When some user posts a message in the $\beta_i$, *CiBot* constructs message $e$, and send it to the relay server $B_r$.

In the posting message, *CiBot* waits the message from the relay server $B_r$. For this, *CiBot* listens HTTP requests as a REST service. The endpoint of the REST service on *CiBot* is `/api/cibot/messages`. This endpoint only accepts HTTP **POST** method for bridging messages. When the endpoint accept a HTTP request, *CiBot* parses the request body message $e'$, and posts the message $o'$ to the specified room with updating *CiBot*'s icon. The icon of *CiBot* are updated by $e'$ from the relay server $B_r$.

Finally, to bridge chat services conceal various information from the users, e.g., joined members, connected rooms, and so on. Ordinary, the user can see the joined members from the application view of the chat services. Therefore, *CiBot* has the interface to answer such questions. In the implementation, *CiBot* provides the interface to show the joined members and connected rooms.

## 4   Case Studies

This section shows the case study of our proposed system *CiBridge*. We assume that $C_x$ is Slack, and $C_y$ is Rocket.Chat. Also, Table 2 shows the users in both chat services and each room name. Note that, the users **alice** are the different users with the same username. Then, the both **alice** install suitable *CiBots* to $r_{x \to y}$ and $r_{y \to x}$, respectively. The section shows the messages on each chat services following the below scenarios.

**Table 2.** The users in each chat service

|  | Chat service | Room name | User names | | | |
|---|---|---|---|---|---|---|
| $C_x$ | Slack | Meeting | alice | bob | charlie | dyran |
| $C_y$ | Rocket.Chat | Briefing | alice | eric | fred | greg |

1. **bob** posts the message in the $r_{x \to y}$,
2. **alice** in $C_y$ posts the message in the $r_{y \to x}$, and
3. **eric** mentions to **alice** of $C_x$ in $r_{y \to x}$.

### 4.1   Case Study 1: A Bridging a Message Example

This case study is a simple example of bridging the message between two chat services. This case study shows the bridged messages in the practical environment. Figure 5 presents the screenshots of chat applications, Bob's view, and Fred's view. In Fig. 5(a), Bob post a message "Let's start meeting!". Then, Fred receives the message via *CiBridge*, shown in Fig. 5(b). Also, *CiBridge* bridges the response message "I'm ready!" from Fred in both views.

(a) The chat view of Bob

(b) The chat view of Fred

**Fig. 5.** The chat views of Bob and Fred

## 4.2   Case Study 2: The Same Name User in the Bridged Chat Services

This case study shows how to distinguish the same name users in the bridged chat services. From Table 2, `alice` is in $C_x$ and $C_y$, and two `alice` are the different users with the same username. The same usernames are usually not accepted, however, in the environment of bridging two chat services, same usernames may exist. Therefore, we should identify the two same name users by their icons. Figure 6 shows the chat application views of Alice. We can identify two alice by their icons, and we can see that two alices have a conversation through *CiBridge*.

## 4.3   Case Study 3: Mention to the Name Overlapped User Under the Bridging Services

This case study presents how to mention to the overlapped usernames beyond the chat services. In $r_{y \to x}$ of $C_y$, `eric` mentions to `alice` of $C_x$. For this, `eric` post a message "`@cibot_alice Please review #32`", to request a review the issue #32 to `alice` in $C_x$, shown in Fig. 7. `@cibot_alice` is the keyword of the mention to `alice` in bridged chat services (Fig. 7(b)). *CiBridge* converts the keyword to the general form and post the message, shown as Fig. 7(a).

## 5   Related Works

After all, the message bridging is just the action by trigger. There are two famous trigger action frameworks, IFTTT[10] and Zapier[11]. Both framework are support

---

[10] https://ifttt.com/.
[11] https://zapier.com/.

(a) The chat view of Alice in $C_x$

(b) The chat view of Alice in $C_y$

**Fig. 6.** The chat views of both Alice

(a) The chat view of Alice in $C_x$

(b) The chat view of Eric

**Fig. 7.** The chat views of Alice and Eric

quite many chat services as a trigger. We can solve the problems of the paper using them. However, the trigger action framework cannot support the situation such as overlapped usernames in the chat services, shown in the case study 2 and 3. Also, the users cannot identify the bridged users with their icons.

# 6 Conclusion

There are many chat services in the world such as Slack, Skype, gitter.im, etc. Using the multiple services needs trivial, however, troublesome works, such as switching services. For solving the problem, there is the exchanging service among several chat services, such as sameroom.io. However, those services do not support to identify the users by their icons.

We built a bridging service *CiBridge* between two chat services to hold the original user icons under the bridging environment. For the proposed method, the user can identify the users by not only their name but also the icons.

In our future works, we will conduct the experimental evaluation in the practical environment.

# References

1. Mcdougall, S.J., Curry, M.B., de Bruijn, O.: Behavior research methods. Instrum. Comput. **31**(3), 487 (1999)
2. Ng, A.W., Chan, A.H.: Ind. Eng. Res. **4**(1), 1 (2007)
3. Ng, A.W., Chan, A.H.: Proceedings of Interenational Multiconference Engineers and Computer Scientists vol. 2, pp. 19–21 (2008)
4. Fielding, R.T.: Architectural styles and the design of network-based software architectures. Ph.D. thesis, University of California, Irvine (2000)

# Implementation and Evaluation of Personal Ontology Building System with Virtual Agent

Shota Nakatani[1]([✉]), Sachio Saiki[1], Masahide Nakamura[1,2], and Kiyoshi Yasuda[3]

[1] Graduate School of System Informatics, Kobe University,
1-1 Rokkodai, Nada-ku, Kobe 657-8501, Japan
shota-n@ws.cs.kobe-u.ac.jp, sachio@carp.kobe-u.ac.jp,
masa-n@cs.kobe-u.ac.jp
[2] Riken AIP, 1-4-1 Nihon-bashi, Chuo-ku, Tokyo 103-0027, Japan
[3] Osaka Institute of Technology, Omiya 2-16, Asahi-ku, Osaka 535-8585, Japan
fwkk5911@mb.infoweb.ne.jp

**Abstract.** Integrating the virtual agent, IoT, and cloud technologies, we have been developing a communication care system, where a person with dementia can talk to an agent every day at home. In order to achieve active conversations with a person with dementia, it is essential to personalize topics to every individual person with dementia. In this paper, we propose a method that represents and manages "the knowledge of individual person" (Personal Ontology) with Linked Data, in order to generate person-centered topics to the individuals. The proposed method with Linked Data does not only enable flexible management of personal ontologies, but also does not only represent complex structure in the ontologies. Moreover, connecting the data to the external Linked Open Data makes it efficient to obtain various knowledge relevant to the conversation from the wisdom of crowds in the Internet. Also, in this paper, based on the proposed method, we develop a prototype system which dynamically builds Personal Ontology through the conversations between the user and virtual agent. Specifically, virtual agent inquires of the user (U) the attribute (P) such as hobbies, favorite singers and any others. Then virtual agent collects the answers (O) of the user. After that, personal information represented by tuple $\langle U, P, O \rangle$ is added to Personal Ontology. Furthermore, we confirm collectability of Personal Ontology through the prototype system by experiments with a few subjects.

**Keywords:** Linked Data · Personal Ontology · Home care · Virtual agent

## 1 Introduction

Japan is facing a hyper-aging society. According to the Cabinet Office, while the total population of Japan is decreasing, the propotion of the elderly population is rising. The elderly population is predicated to account for 30% of the

© Springer Nature Switzerland AG 2019
V. G. Duffy (Ed.): HCII 2019, LNCS 11582, pp. 391–403, 2019.
https://doi.org/10.1007/978-3-030-22219-2_30

total. Also, the number of people with dementia (PWD) will reach 7 million in 2025, where one-fifth of five elderly people in Japan will suffer from dementia [2]. Hence, while more people need nursing care, there is the problem that caregivers are short. According to the Ministry of Health, Labor and Welfare, 2.45 million caregivers are estimated to be needed by 2025 [4]. However, the estimated number of long-term care workers in 2025 is about 2.11 million, which is short of about 0.34 million. Therefore, care and support for elderly people and PWD who do not depend on human hand is necessary. Techniques to reduce the burden of nursing care by ICT technology are widely demanded, and various researches are progressing.

Validation therapy [3] and reminiscence [10] are known as a non-drug therapy for symptoms of dementia. For these care methods, continuous conversations between caregiver and patient are important. However, since patients have individual differences in their symptoms, it is a heavy burden for families and caregivers to respond constantly.

Among them, our research group is developing a dementia care system that PWD daily can interact at home using IoT and ICT technology [9]. This system uses a virtual agent (VA) which is a robot program with speech recognition and synthesis technologies, enabling dialog communication with PWD. This system aims to reduce the human burden by home care by doing part of the conventional care of human caregivers.

In order to implement active conversations with PWD in the dialogue system, it is important to take **topics close to individuals** with PWD. In previous search, we have proposed the two methods. The first method is to dynamically generate personalized dialogues with life history and Linked Open Data (LOD) [8]. The second method is to generate topics of trends and events according to user's age. In these methods, we use the Center Method [7] in order to get personal information and knowledge, called *Personal Ontology*. Specifically, before the service is executed, PWD or caregiver is asked to answer the preliminary questionnaires based on the Center Method, and the service provider registers those with the system. The system generates personalized dialogues based on registered Personal Ontology.

However, the preliminary questionnaires has many questions, it is difficult for the user to answer all of them. The questions to be answered by the user may be different. There are also the questions which are unknown at the time of the questionnaires but can be answered through conversation with the agent. Furthermore, new knowledge that cannot be gotten by the questionnaires may be gotten from the conversations. Thus, conceptions that appear in Personal Ontology is widely different from individuals. In other words, collecting Personal Ontology by preliminary questionnaires has limits on what can be collected. In addition, collection of Personal Ontology by free description makes it difficult to predict the items to be described, making it difficult to manage in the system. Moreover, in order for the system to develop topics in dialogue, conceptions related to Personal Ontology are required.

In order to solve the above problem, in this study, we propose system to represent and manage user's Personal Ontology with Linked Data and dynamically construct Personal Ontology through conversations between agent and user. Concretely the proposed method consists of the following three steps.

**A1:** Construction of the Personal Ontology through the conversations
**A2:** Management of Personal Ontology with Linked Data
**A3:** Generation of link to utilize external LOD

In A1, the agent discovers information related to the use from the dialogue with the user and adds it as an ontology. Elements constituting an ontology can basically be represented by triple of $\langle U, P, O \rangle$. $U$ represents a user, $P$ is a property, and $O$ is an object.

Next, in A2, the system converts the Personal Ontology acquired in A1 to RDF format, and represents and stores it as Linked Data. The system assigns URI to each of $U$, $P$, $O$ acquired in A1 to be in the form of Linked Data such as below.

```
<http://example.org/resource/U>              <http://example.org/
property/P> <http://example.org/resource/O>.
```

$<$http://example.org/resource/$U>$ shows resource representing the user. $<$http://example.org/resource/$O>$ shows resource representing the information related the user. $<$http://example.org/property/$P>$ shows link representing relation between the user and the information.

Finally, in A3, the system links Personal Ontology in the system and external Linked Open Data (LOD). Thus, the system can acquire related conceptions necessary for the development of topics from collective knowledge of the Internet. In this study, specifically, we use DBpedia [5] which is LOD based on Wikipedia.

In addition, to build Personal Ontology through conversation in this research, agents use the method that the agent questions from the user and builds from the answer. Personal Ontology is triples represented by $\langle U, P, O \rangle$, meaning "$U$'s $P$ is $O$". The question asked to the user to construct the ontology is "What(Who, Where) is $U$'s $P$ ?" By this, the system can obtain a user's response including a noun phrase equivalent to $O$. A noun phrase is extracted based on the result of dependency analysis of this response so that the system can be constructed as Personal Ontology.

We implement the above proposed method as a prototype system. We confirm that depending on the system, it is possible to appropriately extract the noun phrase corresponding to the answer from the response sentence obtained by the interactive question between the agent and the user. Then, we confirm that the system can express the obtained answer as Linked Data as Personal Ontology.

As a result of the experiment, if the response from the user to the agent's question is not grammatically broken, and the syntax analysis is normal, it is possible to properly extract the answer section and express it as a Personal Ontology.

## 2   Preliminary

### 2.1   Communication Care System for Person with Dementia

Promotion of **home care** is being carried out in Japan due to an increase in the number of person with dementia (PWD) and an increase in the number of people who wish to provide care at home. As care for people with dementia, person-centered care (PCC) is an ideal care, which monitors and understand individual circumstances, and plans and executes optimized care. Unlike standardized care, it is necessary to observe the subject carefully in order to provide care that is tailored to individuals. There is a limit to doing PCC at home because it places a big mental and physical burden on caregivers.

Our research group is developing Virtual Care Giver (VCG), a system that provides communication daily communication to home demented people. Figure 1 shows the image of VCG. VCG is implemented dialogue with a PWD by utilizing a Virtual Agent (VA) with speech dialogue. Moreover, in addition to voice dialogue, content such as daily calls and reminders, images and videos can be provided. With VCG, it is possible to realize a conversation partner of the PWD who does not depend on time, and it can be expected to reduce the burden on human carers.

In order to realize an active conversation between a PWD and an agent, it is necessary to provide conversation adapted to the individual PWD. In previous research, we propose a method to dynamically generate topics close to individuals by utilizing life history and Linked Open Data (LOD) [8], and a method to generate topics of trends/events according to user's age. These methods are aimed at realizing active conversation close to individuals by developing conversation by combining information related to the PWD and related knowledge from open data.

### 2.2   Personal Ontology

As mentioned in Sect. 2.1, in order for the system to generate a topic close to an individual, it is necessary to acquire information concerning the individual. In this research, information and knowledge related to individuals that can be managed by the system are called **Personal Ontology**. Representative ones of Personal Ontology include profiles and life history.

Life history is information on what kind of life the person has lived, such as hometown, family structure, school, work, memories, hobbies. Compared to the most recent event, life history is likely to remain in memory of PWD, so it has been actively utilized in previous studies. In previous research, based on the center method [7] and Mimamori/Tunagari note [6] actually used at the site of nursing care, we prepare preliminary questionnaires about the typical data items of life history and the PWD or the caregiver answer it. The items that could not be filled in preliminary questionnaires are acquired at the time of dialogue by the agent asking questions.

**Fig. 1.** Virtual Care Giver

## 2.3  Linked Data, Linked Open Data (LOD)

*Linked Data* [1] is data linked by meaningful links using Web technology. Linked Data is one of technical components to realize Semantic Web. It is described in the Resource Description Framework (RDF) which structurally expresses arbitrary information on the web as a resource. Tim Berners-Lee defines the following four principles regarding Linked Data [1].

1. Use URIs as names for things.
2. Use HTTP URIs so that people can look up those names.
3. When someone looks up a URI, provide useful information, using the standards (RDF*, SPARQL).
4. Include links to other URIs. So that they can discover more things.

What is commonly shared by opening Linked Data as open data on the Internet is called *Linked Open Data (LOD)*. By linking the opened data with each other, it is possible to form a huge knowledge database on the web.

In the model of RDF, data is represented by a triple that combines three elements: a subject, a predicate, and an object. RDF is represented by a directed graph; a subject and an object are represented by an ellipse (resource), and a predicate is represented by an arrow (link) connecting two ellipses. However, it is also possible to make the object a literal rather than a URI, in which case the object is represented by a rectangle.

Figure 2 shows the example of RDF graph. The URI can be described by omitting it by using the namespace prefix. In this figure, "dbpedia:Tokyo" refers to "http://dbpedia.org/resource/Tokyo." In this example, "URI of dbpedia:Tokyo

PREFIX dbpedia: <http://dbpedia.org/resource/>
PREFIX dbpedia-owl: <http://dbpedia.org/ontology/>
PREFIX rdfs: <https://www.w3.org/2000/01/rdf-schema#>

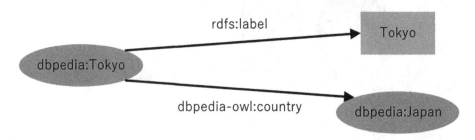

**Fig. 2.** Example of RDF graph

is indicative of "Tokyo", and "the country where Tokyo is located is Japan" are two representations.

In addition, the syntax of RDF is expressed as follows by enclosing the URI of the subject, predicate, and object with <>, followed by a period (.).

```
<http://dbpedia.org/resource/Tokyo>    <https://www.w3.org/2000/
01/rdf-schema#label> "Tokyo".
<http://dbpedia.org/resource/Tokyo>
<http://dbpedia.org/ontology/country>
<http://dbpedia.org/resource/Japan>.
```

You can also write as follows by using the namespace prefix as in the graph.

```
PREFIX dbpedia: <http://dbpedia.org/resource/>
PREFIX dbpedia-owl: <http://dbpedia.org/ontology/>
PREFIX rdfs: <https://www.w3.org/2000/01/rdf-schema\#>
dbpedia:Tokyo rdfs:label "Tokyo" .
dbpedia:Tokyo dbpedia-owl:country dbpedia:Japan .
```

In this paper, we use "http://example.org/resource/" and "http://example.org/property/" as a namespace URI, but using each prefix "ex:" and "ex:prop".

## 3    The Proposed Method

### 3.1    Goal and Approach

In this study, we propose a method to dynamically acquire, accumulate and use Personal Ontology which is needed for generating personal adaptation dialogue in dialogue system for PWD through conversation.

Continuation of daily conversation is important in care for dementia. Furthermore, since the conversation that is close to individual PWD is important, the more individual ontologies that trigger the topic, the more patterns of topics that can be generated. However, since the number of items in the preliminary questionnaire adopted in the current system is large, it is difficult to answer strictly to all and items to be answered by people are different. Also, it may be possible to discover new Personal Ontology that do not exist in the questionnaire item from the daily conversation. Concepts appearing in such a newly obtained Personal Ontology are greatly different for each user. When considering a system that manages and accumulates Ontology having different structures among individuals, it is difficult to apply a relational database (RDB) that requires schema to be fixed in advance. Also, in order to develop a topic based on the accumulated Personal Ontology, related concepts are necessary. However, since they are diverse, it is not realistic to manage all of them within the system.

For the above reasons, in this study, we propose a mechanism to dynamically construct Personal Ontology by expressing and managing with Linked Data through dialogue between agent and user. Specifically, the proposed method consists of the following three steps.

**A1:** Construction of the Personal Ontology through the conversations
**A2:** Management of Personal Ontology with Linked Data
**A3:** Generation of link to utilize external LOD

## 3.2   A1: Construction of the Personal Ontology Through the Conversations

The agent dynamically extracts and creates ontology of the user's individual through conversation with the user. The personal ontology is defined by a set of triple of $\langle U, P, O \rangle$. $U$ is a user (subject), $P$ is a property (predicate), $O$ is an object. When $U =$ "Nakatani", $P =$ "favorite sport" and $O =$ "Tennis", it means "Nakatani's favorite sport is tennis".

We consider about two approaches as a method of constructing Personal Ontology through conversation. The first method is a method in which an agent asks user questions and builds from the answer. In this method, the system generates a question asking for $O$ based on $P$, inquires of user, obtains the user's answer, and then builds a triple of Personal Ontology. For example, the agent makes a question such as "Where is Nakatani's hometown?" and "What is your favorite sport?", and builds Personal Ontology from the answer of "Hyogo prefecture" and "Tennis", such as $\langle Nakatani, Hometown, Hyogo \rangle$, $\langle Nakatani, Favorite sport, Tennis \rangle$.

The second method is a method of building by understanding the utterance of the user by the agent. In this method, natural language processing technology is used to analyze user's free utterance and extract what can become an Ontology. A method of extracting sentences that can become Personal Ontology from free utterances is currently being studied.

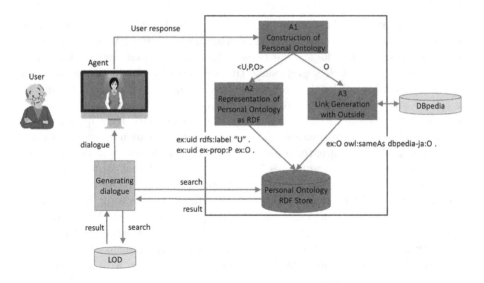

**Fig. 3.** System architecture of proposed system

### 3.3 A2: Management of Personal Ontology with Linked Data

The system dynamically converts the Personal Ontology acquired in A1 to RDF format, expresses it as Linked Data and accumulates it. Specifically, for each $\langle U, P, O \rangle$ acquired in A1, let $U$ be a resource representing the user, $O$ be a resource representing information related to the user, and $P$ be a link representing the relationship between the user and the information.

Next, URIs are assigned to $P$ and $O$. For the assignment method, let $P$ for "ex-prop:$P$", $O$ for "ex:$O$". Also, $U$ refers to the name of the user, but assigning a URI in the same way as $P$ and $O$ will make it impossible to distinguish information of those users if they have the same name. In order to prevent this, ID is given for each user beforehand, URI is assigned to user ID ($uid$), and it is "ex:$uid$". Then, in order to express what the URI means to human to understand easily, describing with the character string label ("rdfs:label"). In this way, it is possible to express "ex:$uid$ represents $U$".

> ex:$uid$ rdfs:label "$U$".

Similarly for "ex-prop:$P$", "ex:$O$", the following description is added so that you can directly obtain what the URI means as a character string.

> ex-prop:$P$ rdfs:label "$P$" .
> ex:$O$ rdfs:label "$O$" .

In this way, by describing $\langle U, P, O \rangle$ acquired in A1 in RDF format as follows, it expresses the same meaning as "$U$'s $P$ is $O$".

```
ex:uid rdfs:label "U" .
ex-prop:P rdfs:label "P" .
ex:O rdfs:label "O" .
ex:uid ex-prop:P ex:O .
```

The previous example, ⟨Nakatani, Favorite sport, Tennis⟩, is converted to RDF format as follows.

```
ex:uid0 rdfs:label "Nakatani" .
ex-prop:FavoriteSport rdfs:label "favorite sport" .
ex:Tennis rdfs:label "Tennis" .
ex:uid0 ex-prop:FavoriteSport ex:Tennis .
```

Also, if $O$ consists of multiple words and phrases, use "rdf:Bag" to group resources. According to the principle of Linked Data (see Sect. 2.3), resources should be referred to by URIs based on word. Therefore, when $O$ is composed of a multiple words and phrases, it is not preferable to express it with the URI of the aforementioned method. Besides, it makes it difficult to create a link to a resource in external LOD which is described later. Therefore, when $O$ contains plural words $o1$, $o2$, it is converted using "rdf:Bag" as follows. As a result, resources can be generated only with words contained in $O$, and can be expressed without information loss.

```
ex:uid ex-prop:P _:a1 .
_:a1 rdfs:label "O" .
_:a1 rdf:type rdf:Bag .
_:a1 rdf:_1 ex:o1 .
_:a1 rdf:_2 ex:o2 .
```

As an example, converting ⟨Nakatani, Memories of childhood, reading comics and playing tennis⟩ to RDF format is as follows.

```
ex:uid0 ex-prop:MemoriesOfChildhood _:a1 .
_:a1 rdfs:label "reading comics and playing tennis" .
_:a1 rdf:type rdf:Bag .
_:a1 rdf:_1 ex:comics .
_:a1 rdf:_2 ex:tennis .
```

This allows to divide $O$ into word level resources and assign URIs to each. It is easier to create a link to a resource in external LOD. The RDF data obtained by the above conversion is stored in a dedicated database called an RDF store.

### 3.4    A3 : Generation of Link to Utilize External LOD

By dynamically linking the Linked Data in the system accumulated in A2 with the external LOD, it becomes possible to procure related knowledge necessary for the development of the topic from the LOD. In this research, we use DBpedia [5] which is LOD extracted from Wikipedia. DBPedia is used to link between various publicly available LODs, and functions as a hub of the data set.

In this case, for each resource "ex:$O$" constructed in A2, if there is a resource, "http://ja.dbpedia.org/resource/$O$(dbpedia:$O$)" pointing to the same concept in DBpedia, link "ex:$O$" to "dbpedia:$O$". For the link, use a property, "http://www.w3.org/2002/07/owl#sameAs(owl:sameAs)" indicating that the two resources are the same. Specifically, when "dbpedia:$O$" exists, the following RDF data is additionally registered in the system.

---

ex:$o$ owl:sameAs dbpedia:$o$ .

---

By doing this, "ex:$O$" and "dbpedia:$O$" are referenced differently but are regarded as the same object, and can be connected to external LOD. When the agent develops a topic based on "ex:$O$", it is possible to retrieve information related to "dbpedia:$O$" for an external RDF store with "ex:$O$". This allows to efficiently procure from external LODs without having to manage the huge knowledge related to "ex:$O$" on own system.

### 3.5    System Architecture

The overall architecture of the proposed system is shown in the Fig. 3. First, from the response of the user $U$ obtained through the conversation with the agent, the property $P$ and the object $O$ are extracted by A1 and the system constructs the set of triplet Personal Ontology $\langle U, P, O \rangle$. Next, each $\langle U, P, O \rangle$ generated in A1 is converted into RDF format data by A2 and stored in the RDF store dedicated to Personal Ontology. Finally, in order to procure the knowledge related to $O$ obtained in A1 from the external LOD, the system creates a link by DBpedia URIs by A3 and store it in the RDF store.

The Personal Ontology stored in the RDF store is used when the system generates topics for individuals. It is also possible to acquire related knowledge from external LOD and make it a trigger to develop topics.

## 4    Implementation of Prototype

In this section, prototype implementation of the system having the functions of A1, A2, A3 mentioned in Sect. 3 is performed. In implementing the system, the function A1 for extracting the answer part from the user's response for the agent's question is important. The triple $\langle U, P, O \rangle$ which is a representation of a Personal Ontology means "$U$'s $P$ is $O$". The question to construct an Ontology is "What(Who, Where) is $U$'s $P$?". This allows to obtain a response including a noun phrase equivalent to $O$. In implementing this processing for extracting noun phrase from the response sentence of the user, we used the "Communication Engine "COTOHA® API"" in this research. This API can analyze the structure of Japanese text and analyze dependency between morphemes. Based on the result obtained by applying this API to the response of the user, by extracting the noun phrase including the modifier part for the noun, it is set as the user's answer $O$ to the agent's question. From the above, we generate triple $\langle U, P, O \rangle$. In the function A2, when the noun phrase $O$ extracted from the user's response is not a single noun or a proper noun, morphological analysis and named entity recognition are performed with "COTOHA® API", and the system registers multiple words in the RDF store.

We use Apache Jena Fuseki for the RDF store which manages and accumulates these constructed Personal Ontology. Apache Jena is a Java library for processing data in RDF format. Apache Jena Fuseki has a server function that can manage and search RDF data by SPARQL.

The technology used for implementing the system for constructing the Personal Ontology is as follows.

- Development Language: Java
- Java Library: Apache Jena
- Web Server: Apache Tomcat
- Web Service FrameWorks: Apache Axis2
- RDF Store: Apache Jena Fuseki
- Web API: Communication Engine "COTOHA® API"

## 5   Evaluation Experiment

In this section, experiments are conducted to determine by the prototype system whether the noun phrase corresponding to the answer can be appropriately extracted from the user's response sentence, and whether the obtained answer can be expressed as Personal Ontology with Linked Data format.

Below is a partial excerpt of the question contents of the agent and the user's response to it. The actual dialogue is performed in Japanese. The following is the English translation by the authors. $A$ represents an utterance from an agent, and $U$ represents a utterance from a user.

---

$A$ : What was your "memory of school life"?
$U$ : Memory of school life was fun having a variety of mahjong with friends, reading comics, playing soccer and playing video games
$A$ : Where is your "favorite place"?
$U$ : I love Okinawa.

---

Next, the Personal Ontology constructed by the above question-answering is shown below. Theactual Personal Ontology is also constructed in Japanese. The following is English translation by the authors.

```
cs27 : uid001
    cs27−prop : MemoryOfSchoolLife
    [    rdf : type  rdf : Bag  ;
         rdf : _1  cs27 : Friends  ;
         rdf : _2  cs27 : mahjong  ;
         rdf : _3  cs27 : Comics  ;
         rdf : _4  cs27 : Soccer  ;
         rdf : _5  cs27 : Video_Games  ;
         rdfs : label  "Having  a  variety  of  mahjong  with
             friends ,  reading  comics ,  playing  soccer
             and  playing  video  games"
    ]  ;
    cs27−prop : FavoritePlace
    cs27 : Okinawa ;
```

In the question-answering above, the system was able to extract noun phrases and express them as RDF form as Personal Ontology. Particularly as a noun phrase corresponding to "memory of school life", the part of "Having a variety of mahjong with friends, reading comics, playing soccer and playing video games" existed in the user response sentence, so it was able to extract the answer appropriately. However, in the dialogue experiments not described above, there were errors in extraction of answers due to Japanese grammar errors and disappointing in response to users and misunderstanding of API.

Therefore, in the case where there is a correct response as a Japanese grammar from a user to an agent's question, the system can appropriately extract the noun phrase corresponding to the answer of the user.

## 6    Conclusion

In this paper, we propose a method to accumulate and manage knowledge (*Personal Ontology*) about individual users in a dialog system that dynamically generates personalized topics. In the proposed method, Personal Ontology is acquired dynamically through conversation between user and agent, and the acquired information is expressed as Linked Data and accumulates in RDF format. We also implemented a Personal Ontology construction system using agents based on the proposed method. Using the system, we confirmed whether the system appropriately extracts the part corresponding to the answer from the response sentence of the user to the agent's question in an interactive manner. Then we confirmed whether the system can express the obtained answer as Personal Ontology in the form of Linked Data. When response sentence from the user to the agent's question can be obtained without grammar breakdown, appropriate processing could be done.

In our future works, we improve error extraction of answers from user response sentences and study methods to generate new dialogue from the constructed Personal Ontology.

**Acknowledgements.** This research was partially supported by the Japan Ministry of Education, Science, Sports, and Culture [Grant-in-Aid for Scientific Research (B) (16H02908, 18H03242, 18H03342), Grant-in-Aid for Scientific Research (A) (17H00731)], and Tateishi Science and Technology Foundation (C) (No. 2177004).

# References

1. Berners-Lee, T.: Linked data - design issues, June 2009. https://www.w3.org/DesignIssues/LinkedData.html
2. Cabinet Office, Government of Japan: annual report on the aging society: 2018, June 2018. http://www.cao.go.jp/
3. Feil, N., Klerk-Rubin, V.D., Nilson, D.: The Validation Breakthrough: Simple Techniques for Communicating With People With Alzheimer's and Dementia. Health Professions Press, Baltimore (2012)
4. Ministry of Health, Labour and Welfare: About the necessary number of nursing care staff based on the seventh term long-term care insurance business plan, May 2018. https://www.mhlw.go.jp/stf/houdou/0000207323.html
5. Kato, F.: DBpedia: linked data project. J. Inf. Process. Manag. **60**(5), 307–315 (2017)
6. Neuropsychology Lab, Department of Psychiatry, O.U.M.S.: "mimamori/tunagari note" [watching/connection note]. http://www.handaichiikirenkei.com/
7. Rokkaku, R.: Care management sheet pack for the elderly with dementia: the center method ver. 03. Nihon Ronen Igakkai Zasshi Jpn. J. Geriatr. **42**(3), 318–319 (2005)
8. Sakakibara, S., Saiki, S., Nakamura, M., Yasuda, K.: Generating personalized dialogue towards daily counseling system for home dementia care. In: Duffy, V.G. (ed.) DHM 2017. LNCS, vol. 10287, pp. 161–172. Springer, Cham (2017). https://doi.org/10.1007/978-3-319-58466-9_16
9. Tokunaga, S., Tamamizu, K., Saiki, S., Nakamura, M., Yasuda, K.: VirtualCareGiver: personalized smart elderly care. Int. J. Softw. Innov. (IJSI) **5**(1), 30–43 (2016). http://www.igi-global.com/journals/abstract-announcement/158780
10. Woods, B., Spector, A.E., Jones, C.A., Orrell, M., Davies, S.P.: Reminiscence therapy for dementia. Cochrane Database Syst. Rev. **2** (2005)

# Design of Coimagination Support Dialogue System with Pluggable Dialogue System - Towards Long-Term Experiment

Seiki Tokunaga$^{(\boxtimes)}$ and Mihoko Otake-Matsuura

Center for Advanced Intelligence Project, RIKEN,
Nihonbashi 1-chome Mitsui Building, 15th floor, 1-4-1 Nihonbashi,
Chuo-ku, Tokyo 103-0027, Japan
{seiki.tokunaga,mihoko.otake}@riken.jp

**Abstract.** In this paper, we design a dialogue system which aims to support elderly people's cognitive function with a conversation by face to face. We have a hypothesis that a kind of group conversation method which is called *Coimagination Method (CM)* would have merit for a human at a perspective of cognitive function. However, current CM aims to be designed to provide balanced group conversation among participants. Hence, the method has mainly focuses the group conversation, hence it has some limitations such as user have to join the specific location. But, elderly people sometime face difficulty because of some physically or mental problems to do it. In this paper, we try to design a chat system which provides a one-to-one conversation between human and system which is based on the essence of CM and copes the above limitations. In order to design the system, at first we consider an experimental design which would be conducted remotely during long-term as a system requirement, then we design a system which meets the requirement. Moreover, we also develop a prototype system in order to confirm the feasibility of proposed system design.

**Keywords:** Conversation · Chat bot · Dialogue system ·
System design · Supporting elderly people

## 1   Introduction

We are facing a super-aged society, and Japan is forecast to become a society with 39.9% of aged people by 2060. Japanese government conduct a questionnaire that how do you feel about aging for elderly people [12]. As a result, over 73% of elderly people fear the problems which relates healthy aspect in their future. Because of the social background, we have to assist them both social system and methods in order to support elderly people with safe.

Although, there are many symptoms which related with aging, the dementia is one of the serious problem since the symptom is strongly effect of elderly

© Springer Nature Switzerland AG 2019
V. G. Duffy (Ed.): HCII 2019, LNCS 11582, pp. 404–420, 2019.
https://doi.org/10.1007/978-3-030-22219-2_31

people's lives [4]. Dementia involves impairment of two or more areas of cognition, such as memory, judgement, abstract thinking and so on [1]. On the other hand, many researchers and companies try to develop a method which would be effective to maintain the cognitive function in the world. However, there is no effective method to maintain the cognitive function at an early stage. Hence, society want a method to maintain the cognitive function for elderly people who has not being a dementia.

Our research group tackles to develop a method to maintain a cognitive function for elderly at the perspective of conversation. Concretely, Otake et al. [16] have proposed a conversation method called *Coimagination Method (abbr. CM)*, that is a group conversation method in order to conduct a balanced conversation with sharing pictures and time management. Coimagination method have conducted at various locations (e.g. research institute, nursing home, community center and hospital). Currently, CM is originally designed to coordinate the balance of a group conversation, hence people have to get together a specific location in order to conduct it. However, there are many elderly people who cannot join such a conversation group because of they are hard either physically or mentally problems. In addition to this, when participants conduct a group conversation works either well or not depends on the group compatibility, namely someone who have same things, their opinions match as well. Hence, if we could have a method to provide a way of conversation as if we talk human without gathering the group, this would be helpful to maintain the cognitive function.

Dialogue systems are widely developed since both development of the technologies. For instance, some smart speakers such as Amazon Alexa and Google Home are widely spread in the home. A wide variety of dialogue system is currently developed for individual purpose and tasks [6,19]. Also, dialogue systems have several techniques in order to meet their purpose such as rule based type [13,15], neural network based Question-Answering type [17], and so on. Whereas conventional dialogue system aims to improve the performance such as how they can reply for human and how long they can talk with human, hence many conventional researches are aimed to increase the accuracy namely they are technology driven approach. On the other hand, some researchers have tried to develop dialogue systems for elderly people [22]. Although, the dialogue system has potential to provide a conversation for elderly people instead of actual human, no one has shown the effective result of that.

In this paper, we design a dialogue system which aims to maintain a cognitive function for elderly people. Our system's main target users are elderly people who could not communicate with other people, for instance who lives alone and whose family lives far from elder's home. To develop a system in order to meet our needs, first we design an experiment to confirm the effect of proposed system. As the first step, we apply the simple Question-Answering techniques in order to maintain the data with efficiency and easily way.

The outline of paper is as follows. In the next preliminary section, we explain domain knowledge that are about dementia and how to conduct experiment with actual subjects. We also explain the essence of experiment which aims to reveal the effect of conversation between system and human at the cognitive function perspective. Moreover, we explain the dialogue system and applying the one-to-one conversation with chat bot that is based on the CM. In Sect. 3.1 we analyze a system requirement in order to conduct the experiment which aims to find out the effect of the proposed method, and then we describe the system design and functionalities. In Sect. 4 we describe the system design of detail such as data format between systems and how to store the information data. In Sect. 5, we develop a prototype system and show the feasibility of the proposed system. Then in Sect. 6, we have discussed our system's feasibility and some limitations based on the prototype system's performance which have developed.

## 2 Preliminary

### 2.1 Risk Factor of Dementia and Intervention Method

Dementia is a symptom that declines cognitive function because of the brain damaged. Concretely speaking, memory, communication and language, ability to focus and pay attention, reasoning and judgement and visual perception. To intervention for dementia some risk factors are known as serious for life stage. Concretely speaking, smoking (5%), depression (4%), physical inactivity (3%) and social isolation (2%) contribute for dementia in late life [14]. Especially, people may loss the chance of conversation when they are in social isolation situation. In addition to this, some researchers have researched a relationship between cognitive function and the intervention method. Suzuki et al. have shown that the intervention method by a picture book reading has significantly difference that the rate of memory retention of the intervention group improved after the program completion [18].

### 2.2 Dialogue System

*Dialogue system* provides communication between system and human over the telephone [3,20,21,23]. Because of the development of speech-to-text technologies [10] that enables to input the voice data and outputs as a text which is a transcription of voice data. Currently, also many products have provided as the voice user-interface such as Amazon Echo and Google Home and so on [8]. Hill et al. have researched how communication changes when people communicate with an intelligent agent as opposed to with another human [7].

Generally, dialogue system handles a user's utterance based on similarity, and the system replies the most reliable answer based on the data which we have preliminarily registered. David et al. have developed a digital system that allows people to have an interactive conversation; whose goal is to preserve as much as possible of the experience of the face-to-face interaction [19]. They have also conducted an experiment, as a result most user questions can be addressed and that the audiences are highly engaged with the interaction.

We explain an example of the procedure of user's utterance with existing dialogue system Watson Assistant [8]. Before talking with Watson Assistant, we have to store a pair of both questions and answers into a workspace which is a logical space that defines the conversation flow preliminar[1] the as training datasets. When a user asks a question to the Watson Assistant, then the system responds an answer which corresponds to the question by the similarity of the text. And the training data is preliminary registered into the system with some pairs of questions and answers. If Watson Assistant cannot respond an answer for a user's question, then the system replies error sentence such as "I am having trouble understanding right now".

## 2.3   Coimagination Method

Otake et al. have proposed a group conversation method called *Coimagination Method (CM)* which is designed to prevent the decline of cognitive functions by a well-managed conversation [16]. Concretely speaking, participants take a photo before talking an according to a theme which is selected so as to everybody can join the conversation easily (e.g. favorite food). In summary, CM mainly consists of time-management, the topic which the participants talk and taken photo by individual. In addition to this a conversation unit is defined as *session*, namely the participants take a conversation with looking at the pictures that are taken by themselves. CM consists of two main phase, one is a topic of conversation phase, which the participants take a conversation based on a decided theme. In the topic conversation phase, the participants talk about the photo by sequentially, namely the first speaker finish his/her talk, then the second speaker should talk. The other is a question and answering part, in that part the participants ask to the presenter with sequentially, hence the participants finish asking to the first presenter, then ask to the second presenter. After the session, the participants summarize their conversation with short sentence at most 200 words in Japanese, we name the summarized conversation as *story*.

Figure 1 shows a picture that people join a CM. The blue robot represents a chair person in the top of the Fig. 1. Currently, CM is widely conducted such as research institute, nursing home, hospital and so on in Japan. However, current CM aims to be designed to provide balanced group conversation among participants. Hence, the method has mainly focuses the group conversation, it has some limitations such as user have to join the specific location because of their some physically or mental problems. So if we could develop a system with which the elderly people could conduct the conversation without considering location problems and that might be helpful. Considering the CM, as we already introduced that CM consists of two main parts, one is a topic of conversation part and another is a question and answering part. When we want to implement the two features, we expect that the dialogue system behave as follows.

1. Question and Answer part: System talks about a specific topic, then replies to user's question

---

[1] Strictly speaking, in Watson system has some domain terms *intent, entity and so on*, but to explain the essential and to avoid complexity, we have skipped the detail of it in this paper.

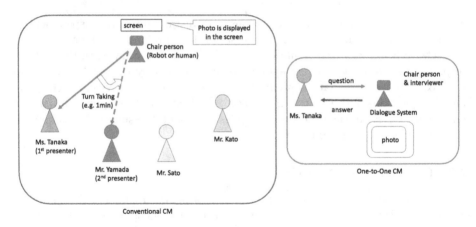

**Fig. 1.** Image of coimagination method (Color figure online)

2. Understanding part: User talks about a specific topic, then the system asks users to answer the question.

In this paper, we focus on the former question and answer part. Because we have a hypothesis that implementing the feature of questions and answer part is easier than understanding part.

**Table 1.** Design of experiment terms

| Terms of experiment | Content |
|---|---|
| E1. Experimental period | At least 3 months |
| E2. Number of subject group | 2 (Intervention/Control) |
| E3. Location | Laboratory and individual home |

## 3   System Design

### 3.1   Design of Experiment

In order to confirm an effect to with proposed system, we design how to conduct a feasibility experiment. Table 1 represents the abstract of the feasibility experiment.

At first, we consider that because we have to confirm effect for the cognitive function. In order to confirm the effect of proposed method, we would like to continue at least three months (See Table 1). In order to evaluate the proposed method, we adapt randomized controlled trial (RCT) which separates two groups one is called an intervention group and the other is called a control group, and the RCT method aims to reduce the bias of testing [2]. In addition to this, we would like to conduct two kinds of locations; one is a laboratory where we can easily support the participants. The other is an individual elderly people's home or nursing home where we would like to conduct the long-term experiment.

## 3.2   System Requirements for Experiment

Our final goal is to find out whether the chat with system may helpful to maintain the cognitive functions. In order to achieve the goal, we consider the requirements in order to develop the system, and we describe the individual requirement in detail.

**R1: Easy Remote Operation by User's Identification.** In order to conduct the experiment remotely, system should be able to have a traceability to track the user's status such as login/logout. Moreover, the user should have user_id in order to identify who currently use the system and track the operation's log in detail. This system requirement strongly supports the E1 and E3, when the experimental location would be conducted at elderly's home. In addition to this, the system should handle individual user's question. Moreover, we have to organize individual participants during an experiment, because we have designed to separate the participants as two groups.

**R2: Handling Status of the System.** First, the system should handle the status of network, such as currently the client device is online or offline. Basically the system is operated online, however we have to consider if the system becomes offline in order to avoid the process down or something system failure. Moreover, if the system could handle user's status such as login/logout the information would helpful at the system operation perspective. For example, if the user cannot login with some reasons (i.e. forget how to login the system) and the user's login status does not change at the operation side, the system operator would help with checking the user's status.

**R3: Pluggable Dialogue Systems.** The system is able to adapt for several dialogue systems in order to compare which is better choice for the CM's domain. Hence, the system is expected to handle the dialogue systems information such as a workspace. Moreover, the system should store both user's utterance and system's response with a timestamp in order to keep a traceability at the experimental operation perspective.

**R4: User-Centered Design for Elderly People.** The UI of the application should be considered for elderly people carefully. For example, the font size and the size of picture should be big enough to see. In addition to this, the necessary information in the CM domain which includes the limitation of the time and both the transcription of user's utterance and system's utterance should be appeared clearly in the screen. The system should display the essential information which belongs to CM such as photos, question answering time and the story of photo. Moreover, the both user's utterance and system's response should display as the text, because sometime speech-to-text program may mistake, and also some elderly people may have hard of hearing. The usability should be maintained in order not to decrease the motivation of the participants. This is not a functionality requirement, but this is an important to conduct the long-term experiment. Moreover, the system should respond within a certain time, because too late response is difficult to recognize especially for elderly people.

### 3.3   System Design

At first, we design that the application consists of two parts; one is a native application part and the other is a web application which handles user's utterance and requests to dialogue systems, after receiving the answer from dialogue system, then the system forward the reply to the user. The separations of the application have a technically reasons that as the native application should operate some events such as a starting to speak the story with showing the picture, then starting timer for question-answering time and so on. Hence, these events should be handled in the native application side, because the timer events are strongly related to the UI. In addition to this, the web application which exchange the data with the dialogue systems should be passive, because which have to be adapt many dialogue engines, hence the system's inner logic should be kept simple in order to maintain with low cost way. We design these system architectures based on the system requirement. Figure 2 shows an overview of proposed architecture. The left of Fig. 2 represents a native application which is called Native Application of Coimagination Human-centered Orchestration

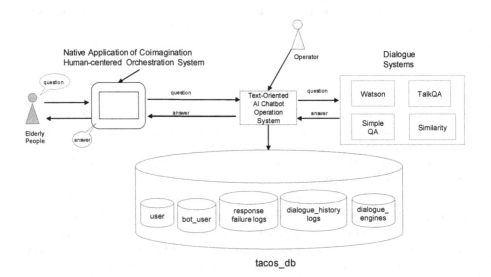

**Fig. 2.** System architecture overview

System (NACHOS). NACHOS provides UI which is based on CM, and also includes a photo, a story of photo that are stored in the database, a chat like UI to confirm his/her conversation with the dialogue system. The center of Fig. 2 shows a web application, we name it as *Text-Oriented Artificial Chat Operation System (TACOS)* that bridges the native application and the dialogue systems, and finally a square in the right of Fig. 2 represents the dialogue systems which include not only commercial one also original one if we develop a new dialogue system. Also the experimental operator checks and supports if the participants need to support situations such as some system accidents.

In order to transmit and receive between a native application and a web application, we define a common data format (See in Sect. 4.3). Because of the separation and its common data format provides easily to extend the system. The dialogue systems are integrated to reply from a user's question, we consider to integrate the dialogue systems such as IBM Watson Assistant. In addition to this, TACOS enables us to add flexibility to add dialogue system if we also want to add a new dialogue system. The software separation between a native application and a web application provides easily traceability at the system operation perspective, because when a user login the native application then if the native application transmits the user's status to a web application. Then an experiment operator could easily to catch up the situation.

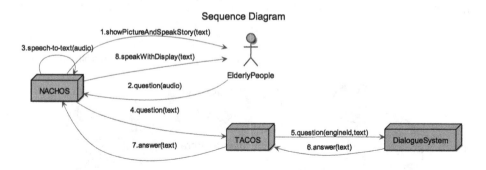

**Fig. 3.** Sequence diagram with proposed architecture

## 4   System Design Detail

### 4.1   Sequence Procedure of System

Figure 3 shows a sequence diagram which starts from elderly people's utterance and ends that the system replies to the elderly people through the dialogue system. At first a native application (NACHOS) shows a picture and speaks a story to the user. Once a user speaks to the NACHOS, then the NACHOS converts audio data into text by the speech-to-text technology. Then the data shall be transmitted to the TACOS, then the TACOS forwards message to the dialogue system. The messages are transformed into specific data format which is described in Sect. 4.3. After TACOS forwards data, namely the TACOS requests to the dialogue system, then the TACOS should receive a response which dialogue system replies. In the following, we have explained the data format, and how to provide identification for each user's utterance (Sect. 4.3).

### 4.2  Native Application: Design of Native Application of Coimagination-Driven Human-Centered Orchestration System (NACHOS)

We design a native application called Native Application of Coimagination-driven Human-centered Orchestration System (NACHOS). NACHOS would be able to apply domain of CM which photos data which are and time management of questions and answers. Figure 4 is a design of native application user interface. We design that the application's component is displayed above an elderly people so that the elderly people could easily to look at the UI. In the top left of Fig. 4 is the photo data which is the source of conversation with the dialogue system. Also the topic of photo is appeared bottom of the photo, this information also becomes the source of conversation. The bottom of the left of Fig. 4 shows the progress bar which represents the time for left in 1 session, and usually for the session max time is set as from 1 to 2 min for questioning and answering time in CM.

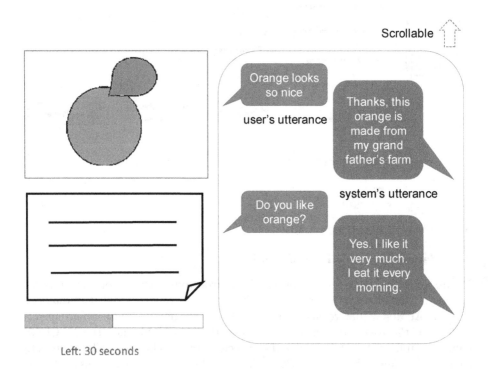

**Fig. 4.** UI design of NACHOS (Color figure online)

A user can question with looking at the photo in the screen with the native application. In addition to this, user and response from the dialogue engines are appeared as chat like interface. Hence, user can easily to follow what he/she says and what responses from the system.

### 4.3 Web Application: Design of Text-Oriented Artificial Chat Operation System (TACOS)

Text-oriented Artificial Chat Operation System (TACOS) is an intermediate server program which bridges between native application and dialogue system. Specifically, when the mobile app transmits questions data into TACOS, then TACOS forward question to dialogue systems. After that, the TACOS receives a response from dialogue systems then replies to the user as both text data and audio data which is generated by text-to-speech technology. At first, we explain how to TACOS deal with individual user. A user questions by NACHOS, then the data is converted as the specific data format as well as the question belongs to a user, namely the transformed data should have the user_id which identify the user. We design that each user should have logically separated data channel in order to avoid the race condition while handling the user's data, thus the data transmission between NACHOS and TACOS used a data channel by the individual user. This design guarantees that if the TACOS receives from multiple users at once, then the system exactly replies to the individual user by using own channel. In addition to this, TACOS have a database which aims to have a user management, dialogue systems information and the history of chat in order to analyze the experimental context.

**Exchanged Data Format.** At first, we explain the data format which interchanges three system NACHOS, TACOS and dialogue systems. List 1.1 represents the data format which is transmitted by NACHOS to TACOS. We have applied data format as JSON format [9] and the body of JSON is written by according to Google JSON Style Guide [11] in order to develop and maintain with the readability of the exchanged data between systems.

**Listing 1.1.** Data format (NACHOS to TACOS)

```
1  {
2    "userId": "RX123_tokunaga",
3    "messageId":1547122048 ,
4    "appName": "1on1FonodialApp",
5    "userUtterance":"Hello",
6    "createdAt": "2019-01-10 21:07:28.654",
7    "scheduleId": "123456"
8  }
```

- userId is a string term which aims to identify the owner of the data
- messageId should be a number and the number is generated by Unixtime with milliseconds
- appName is a fixed string term that represents which application emits this data
- userUtterance represents a text data which is generated with speech-to-text technology from user's voice data
- createdAt is a date with timestamp which shows when this message generates by the application
- scheduleId aims to identify the conversation schedule between the user and the system.

**Listing 1.2.** Cloud replies to native application

```
1  {
2    "userUtterance":"Hello, where is here?",
3    "output":{
4    "contents":{
5      [
6        {
7        "systemUtterance": "Hi, welcome to west world.",
8        "confidence": 0.65,
9        "context": undefined,
10       "engine": "watson",
11       "contentType": "text"
12       }
13     ]
14   },
15   "replyTo": 1547122048,
16   "createdAt": "2019-02-01 14:40:52.457",
17   "userId": "awesomeBotId",
18   "messageId": 1548999697592,
19   "type":"replyMessage"
20   }
21 }
```

List 1.2 shows a response from TACOS to NACHOS. Specifically, we have designed that the data format has a field whose name is *output* to hold response which request and replies from dialogue system. The output field is mainly consists of two parts; one is a field whose name is *contents* which stores data from dialogue system and the other is a generic fields such as *replyTo, createdAt, userId, messageId,* which are set in order to maintain a traceability of the data at the operation and analysis perspectives. And the *type* represents a response type currently the type is only supported "replyMessage" only. But the type may be added near future, hence we set the data in order to cope the expected changes. The former part is depends on the dialogue system for example, some dialogue system has a confidence which represents the accuracy of the response, but other dialogue systems may not have. Hence, we separate the dependent

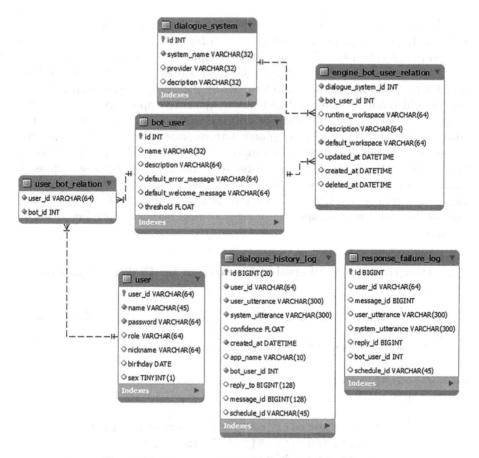

**Fig. 5.** ER diagram of TACOS (Color figure online)

part as a field to contains. In order to reply multiple responses, we define it as a square bracket [], hence when the dialogue systems reply long message then the message is split several small messages.

### 4.4 Database Design

Figure 5 represents a ER diagram of TACOS. We describe the ER diagram with crow's foot notation [5]. A box represents an entity (i.e., table), consisting of an entity name, a primary key and attributes, and the primary key is represented as a yellow key icon. A line represents a relationship between entities, where + + − − ∈ denotes a one-to-many relationship.

User table stores a basic user information such as, username, nickname, password and so on. The bot_user table stores the dialogue system's domain information such as a default welcome message, a error message and a threshold Also, the bot is indirectly connected to dialogue system via engine_bot_user_relation table.

Moreover, the user and bot_user is one-to-one relationship by user_bot_ relation. Hence, when we change the relationship with user and bot_user, then we can easily switch the dialogue system, because a bot_user is connected to a dialogue system. The *dialogue_history_log* table stores a general record such as user's utterance, the response which replies by the dialogue system and the created_at which refers when the data emits by the native application (NACHOS). Moreover, *response_failure_log* stores error response which represents that the dialogue system cannot find an appropriate response. For example, when the dialogue system cannot find an appropriate response for the user's utterance, then most of the dialogue systems response a typical error response such as "I cannot understand you". However, we would like to handle the error response uniformly, because we have to store the data into *response_failure_log*, hence the *bot_user* table has threshold in order to control without depending dialogue engines.

### 4.5  How to Provide Pluggable Mechanism for Dialogue Systems

**Listing 1.3.** Template of General Dialogue System Response

```
1   {
2     "userUtterance":${userUtterance},
3     "output":{
4     "contents":{
5        [
6          {
7             "systemUtterance": ${systemUtterance},
8             "confidence": ${confidence},
9             "context": ${context},
10            "engine": ${engine},
11            "contentType": ${type}
12         }
13       ]
14     },
15     "replyTo": ${replyTo},
16     "createdAt": ${createdAt},
17     "userId": ${userId},
18     "messageId": ${messageId},
19     "type":${type}
20     }
21  }
```

List 1.3 represents a general JSON data which aims to represent the general dialogue systems response. hence which absorbs the different type format of dialogue systems. The enclosed ${} represents a variable which is replaced at runtime by TACOS and the rule of description is based on JavaScript Template literals. So

Chat Operation System

Cognitive Behavioral Assistive Technology Team@RIKEN Center for Advanced Intelligence Project(AIP)

**Fig. 6.** Screenshot of prototype system

once you write some programs which convert the response of the dialogue system into the template JSON, then TACOS could handle a new dialogue system because which has a rule how to replace the template JSON with actual values. Especially the term of *contents* has enough flexibility and it does not depend on a specific dialogue system. Hence, the unified template provides pluggable mechanism for the wide variety of dialogue systems, hence we can easily to add and compare some dialogue systems with ease.

## 5   Prototype System Development

Figure 6 shows a screenshot of prototype system. We have developed TACOS as a prototype system in order to confirm the feasibility of the proposed architecture. Specifically, as the backend system, we use a dialogue system as the Watson Assistant because it provides a lot of Web APIs. The left balloon shows messages that the user's questions. In order to avoid the complexity and easy to debug we have developed a input form in order to ask a dialogue system as text. Also the balloons of left represent responses from the dialogue system. The user's message and the system response is one to one corresponding; hence users can quickly follow what the system responses for the user's message. The number under the text of right balloon shows a confidence value that the dialogue system guarantees and actually the Watson Assistant replies the confidence data with Web API.

## 5.1  Verification with Sample Dataset

We have registered both questions and answers as the dataset to Watson Assistant. The registration number of datasets are 250 pair of questions and answers, and we have collected pairs of questions and answers with crowdsourcing. When we ask the task for the crowd worker, we use the collected stories which were created by elderly people who joined the CM. We create some rules for the crowd worker as follows to conduct crowdsourcing in order to collect appropriate dataset.

- (Description to crowd worker) The purpose of this task is to create question answering datasets which aims to create a conversation data with a chat bot, and when you create the conversation data you should follow following rules.
- Rule1. Please create a pair of question-answer dataset, namely first you ask a question and then the bot answers.
- Rule2. Please create a pair of the question-answer data based on the story which we have provided.
- Rule3. The bot has a persona; hence you should follow the persona when you create an answer dataset as the robot. Concretely speaking, the bot's persona are as follows; the sex is a man, age (about 70 years old), has a humorous and likes drinking and so on. Moreover, when you create the bot's answer, please make it as a polite message and also the message should have political correctness and should not include political message, and romantic commitment.

In addition to this, we also have conducted the system verification with given the dataset. Specifically, we have tested 250 questions for Watson Assistant in order to confirm that the system whether replies the expected answer or not. As the result, we have found that 7 answers are wrong which corresponds to 2.8% for total dataset. Moreover, we also have measured the response time from the system, we have tested 250 questions into the system. The response time is evaluated from requesting a question data (e.g. "Do you like drinking?") to receiving the answer data such as "Yes, I like beer". As the result, we have confirmed that the system has processed 0.78 s per 1 question.

## 6  Discussion

We have confirmed the dialogue system sometimes replies wrong answers. This is because same questions but which have other answer datasets are generated via crowdsourcing. The same questions and different answers pairs are registered, then the system would be expected to response one and the other data would not be used. When we operate dialogue systems for a long time, then the problem is expected to be increased. One thing to prevent the duplicate question answers; we can consider a checking mechanism which notifies to a user that when registration a pair of question answering dataset whether the questions are preliminary registered or not. The other idea is that a mechanism which alerts to a user that the duplicate question answering datasets have registered.

In addition to this, in this paper we have not tested for actual elderly people, hence we would like to show how the proposed architecture is able to cover the user's question based on the registration datasets. Finally, we have confirmed that the response time from the specific dialogue system (Watson Assistant) is less than 1 s the average is 0.78 s. Thus, we think the feasibility at the perspective of real-time is enough based on the response result.

## 7   Conclusion

In this paper, we have designed a new dialogue system architecture which aims to maintain cognitive functions for the elderly people. At first, we have described the requirements of experiment in order to achieve the goal. Then, based on the requirements, we have extracted requirements for the system. Next, we have designed both a native application (NACHOS) and a web application (TACOS) in order to meet the requirements. In addition to this, we have developed the prototype system in order to show the feasibility of proposed architecture. Moreover, we have discussed why dialogue system has wrongly answered based on the preliminary small experiment. Also, we have discussed the feasibility at the perspective of real-time and that of response rate. Our future work is to develop a system which is based on the architecture that we have proposed in this paper. We also have to conduct and confirm the effect of proposed system for the cognitive functions for the elderly people.

## References

1. Bowen, J., Teri, L., Kukull, W., McCormick, W., McCurry, S.M., Larson, E.B.: Progression to dementia in patients with isolated memory loss. Lancet **349**(9054), 763–765 (1997). http://www.sciencedirect.com/science/article/pii/S0140673696082566
2. Chalmers, T.C.A., et al.: A method for assessing the quality of a randomized control trial. Control. Clin. Trials **2**(1), 31–49 (1981)
3. Barker, D.J., Van Schaik, P., Simpson, D.S., Corbett, W.A.: Evaluating a spoken dialogue system for recording clinical observations during an endoscopic examination. Med. Inf. Internet Med. **28**(2), 85–97 (2003). https://doi.org/10.1080/14639230310001600452
4. Dunkin, J.J., Anderson-Hanley, C.: Dementia caregiver burden. Neurology **51**(1 Suppl. 1), S53–S60 (1998)
5. Dybka, P.: Crow's foot notation. https://www.vertabelo.com/blog/technical-articles/crow-s-foot-notation
6. Higashinaka, R., et al.: Towards an open-domain conversational system fully based on natural language processing. In: COLING (2014)
7. Hill, J., Ford, W.R., Farreras, I.G.: Real conversations with artificial intelligence: a comparison between human-human conversations and human-chatbot conversations. Comput. Hum. Behav. **49**, 245–250 (2015). http://www.sciencedirect.com/science/article/pii/S0747563215001247
8. IBM: IBM Watson Assistant.https://www.ibm.com/cloud/watson-assistant/
9. I.E.T.F.: The Javascript object notation (JSON) data interchange format. https://tools.ietf.org/html/rfc8259

10. Google Inc.: Cloud speech-to-text. https://cloud.google.com/speech-to-text/
11. Google Inc.: Google JSON style guide. https://google.github.io/styleguide/ jsoncstyleguide.xml
12. Japanese Government: White Paper for Eldelry People
13. Leuski, A., Patel, R., Traum, D., Kennedy, B.: Building effective question answering characters. In: Proceedings of the 7th SIGdial Workshop on Discourse and Dialogue, SigDIAL 2006, pp. 18–27. Association for Computational Linguistics, Stroudsburg(2006)
14. Livingston, G., et al.: Dementia prevention, intervention, and care. Neurology **390**, 2673–2734 (2017)
15. Misu, T., Kawahara, T.: Speech-based interactive information guidance system using question-answering technique. In: 2007 IEEE International Conference on Acoustics, Speech and Signal Processing - ICASSP 2007, vol. 4, pp. IV-145–IV-148, April 2007
16. Otake, M., Kato, M., Takagi, T., Asama, H.: Development of coimagination method towards cognitive enhancement via image based interactive communication. In: RO-MAN 2009 - The 18th IEEE International Symposium on Robot and Human Interactive Communication, pp. 835–840, September 2009
17. Serban, I.V., Sordoni, A., Bengio, Y., Courville, A.C., Pineau, J.: Hierarchical neural network generative models for movie dialogues. CoRR abs/1507.04808 (2015)
18. Suzuki, H., et al.: Cognitive intervention through a training program for picture book reading in community-dwelling older adults: a randomized controlled trial. BMC Geriatr. **14**(1), 122 (2014). https://doi.org/10.1186/1471-2318-14-122
19. Traum, D., et al.: New dimensions in testimony: digitally preserving a Holocaust survivor's interactive storytelling. In: Schoenau-Fog, H., Bruni, L.E., Louchart, S., Baceviciute, S. (eds.) ICIDS 2015. LNCS, vol. 9445, pp. 269–281. Springer, Cham (2015). https://doi.org/10.1007/978-3-319-27036-4_26
20. Truong, H.P., Parthasarathi, P., Pineau, J.: MACA: a modular architecture for conversational agents. In: Proceedings of the 18th Annual SIGdial Meeting on Discourse and Dialogue, pp. 93–102. Association for Computational Linguistics (2017). http://aclweb.org/anthology/W17-5513
21. Walker, M.A.: An application of reinforcement learning to dialogue strategy selection in a spoken dialogue system for email. CoRR abs/1106.0241 (2011)
22. Wolters, M.K., Kelly, F., Kilgour, J.: Designing a spoken dialogue interface to an intelligent cognitive assistant for people with dementia. Health Inf. J. **22**(4), 854–866 (2016)
23. Zhang, S., Dinan, E., Urbanek, J., Szlam, A., Kiela, D., Weston, J.: Personalizing dialogue agents: I have a dog, do you have pets too? CoRR abs/1801.07243 (2018)

# A Method of Generating a Dialogue Pattern to Induce Awareness Based on a Reflection Support Agent

Kazuaki Yokota[1](✉), Sho Ooi[2], and Mutsuo Sano[3]

[1] Graduate School of Osaka Institute of Technology,
1-79-1 Kitayama, Hirakata, Osaka, Japan
m1m18a31@st.oit.ac.jp
[2] Ritsumeikan University, 1-1-1 Noji-higashi, Kusatsu, Shiga, Japan
SHO.OOI@outlook.jp
[3] Osaka Institute of Technology, 1-79-1 Kitayama, Hirakata, Osaka, Japan
mutsuo.sano@oit.ac.jp

**Abstract.** Patients with acquired brain injuries often present with adverse symptoms, such as attention, memory, and functional disorders, as well as aphasia, which prevent them from effectively executing activities of daily living. Cognitive rehabilitation can be conducted with these patients to mitigate these issues. A crucial component for the efficacy of this rehabilitation is the patient's self-awareness. To induce "awareness", patients are exposed to a process called *reflection dialogue,* wherein they watch a video of themselves interacting with a cognitive rehabilitation specialist. This process allows the patient to objectively observe themselves. However, this reflection dialogue process requires appropriate specialization according to the symptoms and needs of the patient, which depends on the experience of the cognitive rehabilitation specialist.

The current study aimed to automatize this process using a system that includes a home robot that acts as an agent during the reflection dialogue. This system included three components: (1) Generation of a reflection dialogue; (2) Generation of agentive behavior, based on reinforcement learning of patients' symptoms (according to patients' daily logs); and (3) Generation of an appropriate conversation interval (i.e., timing/tempo of the human-robot conversation). This research used conversation methods in a reflection dialogue to induce awareness. Specifically, the current study proposed a method of generating a dialogue pattern through interactions with a reflection support agent, based on a Bayesian network that utilizes communication history. Results show the possibility of using a robot and web-agent to create dialogue. Further, it was found that the "Personal" type of reflection dialogue was significantly better at noticing remarks than the "General" type of reflection dialogue.

**Keywords:** Reflection dialogue · Awareness · Bayesian network · Agent · Cognitive rehabilitation

V. G. Duffy (Ed.): HCII 2019, LNCS 11582, pp. 421–438, 2019.
https://doi.org/10.1007/978-3-030-22219-2_32

# 1    Introduction

Patients with acquired brain injuries typically present with various adverse symptoms. These issues can include attention, memory, and functional disorders, as well as aphasia, which can prevent these individuals from effectively performing activities of daily living [1, 2]. In Japan, approximately half a million people live with brain injuries and this number is increasing every year [3]. Globally, dementia prevalence roughly doubles every 4–5 years from age 65, resulting in more than one-third of individuals over 85 being likely to present with dementia [4, 5]. The World Health Organization (WHO) estimated 35.6 million people with dementia in 2010, with that figure expecting to reach 65.7 million in 2030 and 115.4 million in 2050 [6]. Therefore, cognitive training, based on daily living behavior, is necessary to improve quality of life (QoL) of patients [7, 8].

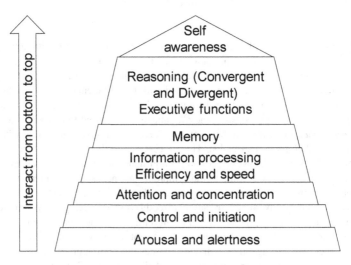

**Fig. 1.** Neuropsychological pyramid.

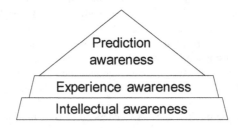

**Fig. 2.** Stratified self-awareness.

Generally speaking, training programs for patients with acquired brain injuries consist of collaborative work by many specialists, such as a doctors, nurses, occupational therapists (OT), physical therapists (PT), speech-language-hearing therapists

(ST), and psychotherapists [9]. However, there is a limited number of specialists, medical facilities, and rehabilitation facilities in Japan.

Acquired brain injuries are not independent of, but rather tend to affect other disorders. Tatsukami defined a neuropsychological pyramid of cognitive function based upon clinical observations [9]. Figure 1 shows this neuropsychological pyramid. The contents of this pyramid have seven levels, including Arousal and Alertness, Control and Initiation, Attention and Concentration, Information Processing (Efficiency and Speed), Memory, Reasoning (Convergent/Divergent) and Executive Functions, and Self-awareness. These seven functions interact from the bottom up, meaning that Self-awareness is the most important, but also the most difficult to rehabilitate in patients with acquired brain injuries.

Crosson suggested that the pyramid of awareness contained the hierarchical structure shown in Fig. 2 [11]. Experience and Prediction awareness are especially important for neuropsychological rehabilitation. However, in the presence of frontal lobe dysfunction or right brain injury, reduced self-consciousness and lack of self-knowledge also occur, making experiential awareness difficult to obtain. Further, Senzaki and Mimura stated "Self-awareness is the entrance to rehabilitation, and the biggest challenge", suggesting that self-awareness is especially important for rehabilitation [12]. Moreover, Nagano reported that self-awareness exerts effects on rehabilitation and the rehabilitation process for patients with acquired brain injuries [13].

Taking the preceding information together, the current study hypothesized thought that if patients can better understand their own actions through reflection, motivation for rehabilitation would rise. Specifically, the current study sought to automatize this process using a system that included a home robot that acts as an agent during reflection dialogue. This system included three components (as shown in Fig. 3): (1) Generation of a reflection dialogue; (2) Generation of agentive behavior, based on reinforcement learning of patients' symptoms (according to patients' daily logs); and (3) Generation of an appropriate conversation interval (i.e., timing/tempo of the human-robot conversation).

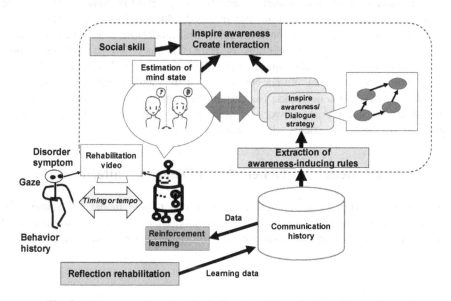

**Fig. 3.** The proposed system for "reflection dialogue" with a home robot.

This research used conversation methods in reflection dialogue to induce aware-ness. Specifically, a method of generating a dialogue pattern through interactions with a reflection support agent, based on a Bayesian network using communication history, is proposed.

## 2   Literature Review

Meguro et al. [14] states that, in order to cultivate social relationships, listeners indicate that it is important to perform "self-disclosure" during conversation. Further, Abe et al. proposed a method to decide behavior based on a mental condition estimation model in a robot that played with children [15]. Many conversation strategies have been pro-posed to achieve natural and sustainable interactions in this way. However, little research has been performed develop conversation schemes that promote awareness. The current study examined a dialogue model to express awareness. Specifically, previous research suggests that a strategy of praising the other, presenting experiential images, reconfirming facts, asking reasons for evaluation, promotes a conversation with more self-disclosure [16]. This results in the ability to extract more new information from the speaker [16]. In addition, Adachi et al. proposed a reflection dialogue strategy as a method of information collection for mind estimation based on an interaction between a user and a reflection agent [17]. In this study, they developed five elements of dialogue; "Confirmation of facts", "Self-disclosure", "Questions about evaluation", "Praise", and "Empathy". As a result, they suggest that "Confirmation of facts" can assist memory. However, when examining "Empathy", Adachi et al. could not obtain personal information because dialogue time between the user and the agent was short. In this research, the specific elements necessary for effective dialogue were re-examined.

Examination of previous research suggests that Bayesian network models may be appropriate for dialogue generation. For instance, Murakami et al. reported using a Bayesian network to generate consumer behavioral models from information such as life and purchase history [18]. Additionally, Hara et al. has generated a behavior model of college students from a class questionnaire [19]. As these studies indicate, there are many methods of analyzing human behavioral patterns, and generating corresponding models, using Bayesian networks. The current study analyzed the behavior of reflected individuals via a Bayesian network in order to generate a model for generating a reflection dialogue for patients with acquired brain injury.

## 3   Proposed Method of Generating a Dialogue Pattern

The current research aimed to generate a dialogue pattern model to express self-awareness from conversation contents. Specifically, changes in conversation content were first examined using a Bayesian network. Next, questioners conducted a reflection of the participant based on analyzed results, where questioner was evaluated by a measure of social skill ability. Then, positive and negative words were classified from text information using CaboCha [20]. Finally, verbal and non-verbal communication were evaluated to generate a dialogue pattern model to express self-awareness using the above results.

## 3.1 Bayesian Network

A Bayesian network is a graphical model that describes causality by probability. This is a model of probabilistic reasoning that depicts inferred causal relationships via directed acyclic graph structures and expresses relationships of individual variables with conditional probability. Bayesian networks can obtain results by a probability distribution and it is suitable for handling uncertain phenomena numerically. As a Bayesian network can predict the cause from the result, it should be able to predict the relationships found in conversations. In other words, we think that Bayesian network modeling is an optimal strategy to examine the current topic because various factors are expected to be complexly intertwined.

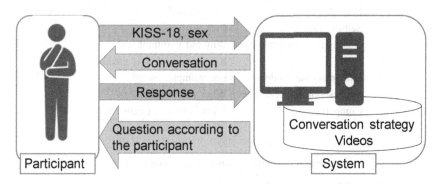

**Fig. 4.** Flowchart of dialog model generation

## 3.2 Evaluation of Communication Ability

Figure 4 shows the flow of dialog model generation. In this research, it is necessary to account for the communication ability of participants. Therefore, communication ability was evaluated using the 18-item Kikuchi's Scale of Social Skills (KiSS-18) [21]. The KiSS-18 is based on concepts developed by Goldstein et al. [22]. These include 50 elements, dividing social skills into six components: (1) Beginning social skills; (2) Advanced social skills; (3) Skills for dealing with feelings; (4) Skill Alternatives to Aggression; (5) Skills for Dealing with Stress; and (6) Planning skills.

The system returns the optimal question contents to participants after entering sex and KISS-18 scores. As a result, the most appropriate conversation for the participant is generated every time the system repeats the conversation with the participant.

### 3.3   Classification of Words

We used CaboCha [20] to classify the remarks administered by the reflection experimenter. Classification of remarks were assessed as "Positive", "Negative", "Neutral", or "No answer". Statements concerning only facts were considered "Neutral", and cases where no response was provided following a waiting period of a few seconds were classified as "No answer".

At the time of reflection, participants observed the videos of the conversation and analyzed the dialogue.

**Table 1.** Classification of verbal communication of reflection experimenter

| Items | Contents |
| --- | --- |
| Confirmation of facts | Why do you $\sim$? |
| Empathy | I understand |
| Self-disclosure | I was also $\sim$ |
| Questions about evaluation | Why did you think so? |
| Praise | It is wonderful, it is great! |
| Exemplary suggestions | For example, $\sim$ |
| Suggestions for next time | What will you do next? |
| Comparisons | What is different between $\sim$? |

**Table 2.** Details of non-verbal communication

| Evaluation items | Contents |
| --- | --- |
| Facial expressions | Smile, angry, etc. |
| Three-way interaction | Watch both video and participants during a conversation |
| Eye contact | View subject's eyes |

### 3.4   Evaluation of Verbal Communication

Question content was manually classified retrospectively by the experimenter. Specifically, "Confirmation of facts", "Empathy", "Self-disclosure", "Questions about evaluation", and "Praise" were classified based on research by Adachi et al. [17]. In addition, three other elements of verbal communication were classified. These were adding "Exemplary suggestions", "Suggestions for next time", and "Comparisons" (Table 1).

### 3.5    Evaluation of Non-verbal Communication

Non-verbal communication was classified from a preliminary experiment video. While Table 1 describes behavior while the participant was speaking, Table 2 shows the details of non-verbal communication of the experimenter.

## 4    Obtaining Dialogue Strategy

### 4.1    Procedure

An analysis of conversation content was conducted in order to determine conversation strategy. The experimental period was from September to October 2017. Discussions were conducted with eight students (five male) of the Osaka Institute of Technology.

Specifically, we organized the students into two teams (four students to a team). Two group discussions were conducted, with the first theme being "How to make hunting race a vegetarian", and the second theme being "Osaka Institute of Technology commercial message (CM) creation", for 30 min each. Discussions were performed in a private room so that people could not interrupt. Discussions were video recorded simultaneously with two cameras.

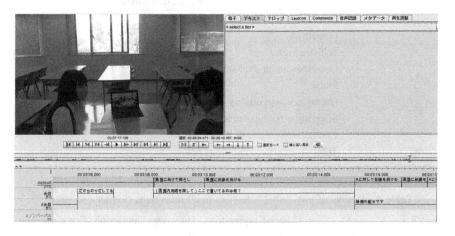

**Fig. 5.** The result of analysis using ELAN

Participants and experimenters performed reflections on the group discussions on a one-on-one basis. Reflection experimenters consisted of three students (one male) of Osaka Institute of Technology.

All 11 students, including the experiment participants and experimenters, completed a KiSS-18. Three experimenters were randomly determined from group members whose score of KiSS-18 is high.

## 4.2 Reflection

In the reflection, the experimenter questioned the participants using videos of the group discussion. During this period, the reflection experimenter instructed participants to take the role of listening to information.

The video used for reflections were classified and analyzed using ELAN5.0.0-beta [ELAN] including the experimenter's verbal behavior, non-verbal behavior, participant's verbal behavior. Figure 5 shows the results analyzed by ELAN.

## 4.3 Result of Verbal and Non-verbal Classifications

First, Table 3 shows the number of verbal behaviors in the all reflections (fourteen sessions). In this experiment, the expression times of verbal behavior is 326 times, the verbal behavior coded most frequently was "Confirmation of facts".

Next, Table 4 shows the all non-verbal behaviors (fourteen sessions). Therefore, we analyzed three kinds of non-verbal behaviors were measured. Specifically, "smile", "three-way relationship", and "eye contact".

**Table 3.** The result of verbal behaviors in all reflections (fourteen sessions)

|  | Expression times |
|---|---|
| Confirmation of facts | 141 |
| Empathy | 21 |
| Self-disclosure | 5 |
| Questions about evaluation | 72 |
| Praise | 43 |
| Exemplary suggestions | 27 |
| Suggestion for next time | 7 |
| Comparison | 10 |
| Total | 326 |

**Table 4.** Results of non-verbal behaviors in all reflections (fourteen sessions).

|  | Facial expressions | Three-way interaction | Eye contact |
|---|---|---|---|
| Confirmation of facts | 17 | 40 | 31 |
| Empathy | 0 | 0 | 1 |
| Self-disclosure | 0 | 0 | 0 |
| Questions about evaluation | 19 | 9 | 6 |
| Praise | 10 | 4 | 0 |
| Exemplary suggestions | 0 | 0 | 1 |
| Suggestion for next time | 1 | 0 | 0 |
| Comparison | 0 | 0 | 0 |
| Participants are speaking | 19 | 0 | 35 |
| Total | 66 | 53 | 74 |

In "confirmation of facts" case, a number of "Three-way interaction" and "Eye contact" was more, and participation saw reflection video and experimenter. In addition, "Facial expression (smile)" was confirmed. Next, in "Questions about evaluation" and "Praise" case, "Facial expression (smile)" was more. On the other hand, in "Participants are speaking" case, "Eye contact" and "Facial expression (smile)" was more.

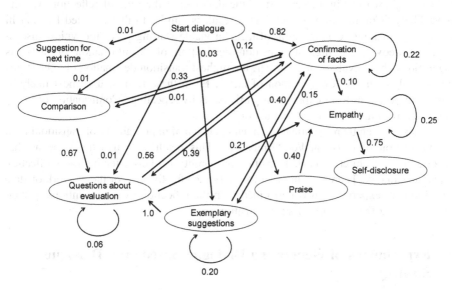

**Fig. 6.** Transition probability of reflection experimenter with verbal communication

Finally, we describe strategies for determining dialogue patterns. Specifically focusing on verbal communication and a constructing a transition network of dialogue. This time, we calculated the probability from Eq. (1) obtained from the results of the verbal communication of the reflection experimenter.

$$P(A|B) = \frac{P(A|B)}{|P(A)|} \tag{1}$$

where the current state is $A$, and the after state is $B$.

As shown in Fig. 6, the probability of "Confirmation of facts" at the start of dialogue is 0.82 which is the highest. "Suggestions for next time" and "Self-disclosure" mean that the dialogue does not transition, and that the dialogue is over.

**Table 5.** Question items.

| Question items | Contents |
| --- | --- |
| 1 | Can we use reflection? |
| 2 | Do you feel strange about the conversation? |

### 4.4    Discussion

First, examination of verbal and non-verbal communication found that there are a large number of statements made during verbal communication. Consequently, it is proposed that reflections should be focused primarily on verbal communication.

Next, as a result of the transition probability of the verbal communication of the reflection shown in Fig. 6, the start of the dialogue at the time of reflection was the most likely "Confirmation of facts" This result is similar to that reported by Adachi et al. [17], making "Confirmation of facts" a viable starting point for typical discussions. Moreover, the highest transition destination of "Confirmation of facts" is "Questions about evaluation". Further, the highest transition destination of "Questions about evaluation" is "Confirmation of facts". From these results, it is most likely to extract information from experiment participants by repeating "Confirmation of facts" followed by "Questions about evaluation".

"Praise" given by reflection experimenters had a high probability of transitioning to "Confirmation of facts" and/or "Empathy". This result was also the same as that reported by Adachi et al. [17]. Transition probability is likely effective for a reflection dialogue strategy. Therefore, in order to verify the effectiveness of the network of state transition, an experiment was performed with the reflection by a conventional person and one using the network of state transition.

## 5    Experiments of Generating Dialogue Based on a Dialogue Strategy

This section describes a comparison experiment between reflection using the transition probability calculated from the previous experiment and interpersonal reflection via the conventional method.

### 5.1    Experimental Method

In this experiment, we conducted a group discussion with eight students. All students completed a KiSS-18 assessment, and divided into two groups according to the results;

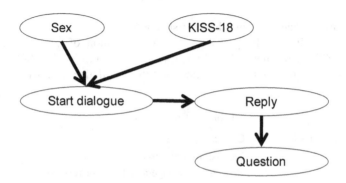

**Fig. 7.** Bayesian network of this research

- Group A: reflection using transition probability
- Group B: reflection using the person's experience.

The group members consisted of one person with a score under 50, two people with scores over 50, but under 70, and one person with a score over 70. The current experiment collected data via the Wizard of Oz (Woz) framework.

The theme of the group discussion was "A tool that can be realized realistically among secret tools of Doraemon". After the experiment, participants completed a questionnaire. Table 5 shows the items of the questionnaire. Items 1 and 2 are based on a five-point rating.

We used the BayoLink [23] system of NNT mathematical data processing Bayesian network. Results of the dialogue obtained from the KiSS-18 obtained in the previous experiment and sex differences comprised the question used to start the conversation. After that, the system asked questions according to the response of the experiment participants. Figure 7 shows the Bayesian network used in this study.

In addition, we analyzed the expression of "Awareness" from the reflection dialogue. Table 6 shows the reflection dialogue contents of the expression of "Awareness".

**Table 6.** The reflection dialogue contents of the expression of "Awareness"

| Number of reflection | Group A | Group B |
|---|---|---|
| Reflection No. 1 | • I had time to spare<br>• The surroundings are not talking<br>• X's opinion was small<br>• I was concerned about time<br>• I needed other ideas as well<br>• The ideas of other teams were different and unexpected<br>• I am good at listening<br>• I had better talk to other people<br>• I need to listen to various people's stories | • Y had a note, but I did not use it<br>• I was not deciding the action at first<br>• I should have acted on my own |
| Reflection No. 2 | • I talked easy this time<br>• The theme was simple<br>• I become difficult to talk if I am not good<br>• I would like to talk about other themes<br>• I would like to work with great interest | • I was able to speak from myself<br>• I cannot act on my own initiative |
| Reflection No. 3 | • Time was short<br>• In the first case, I talk less<br>• Use time in a friendly way<br>• I cannot understand the content that Z talks about<br>• Finally, I made my claim<br>• It takes time to understand<br>• I try to speak from the beginning | • I was given the time, but I could not act<br>• I should have said it constantly |

## 5.2    Results

Questionnaire results are shown in Table 7, with the means of items 1 and 2 presented. A *t*-test was conducted on items 1 and 2. Results are shown in Table 8. No significant difference was observed between the two groups. There is the possibility that the small number of participants hinders the ability to observe a significant difference, making it necessary to verify these results by increasing the number of participants.

In addition, we conducted a *t*-test examining the mean number of expressions per group shown in Table 10. Group A averaged 7.0 expressions is 7.0 times, the average number of Group B expressions is 2.3. Using the retrospective model resulted in a significantly higher number of occurrences. As a result of *t*-test, a significant difference was observed between the two groups at a 5% level [$t(3.88) > 2.78$, $p = 0.02$; Fig. 8.

**Table 7.** Results of question items

| Question items | Group A | Group B |
| --- | --- | --- |
| 1 | 4.0 | 3.5 |
| 2 | 1.25 | 1.5 |

**Table 8.** Results of *t*-test

|  | Question items 1 | | Question items 2 | |
| --- | --- | --- | --- | --- |
|  | Group A | Group B | Group A | Group B |
| Average | 4.00 | 3.50 | 1.25 | 1.50 |
| Variance | 0.00 | 1.00 | 0.25 | 0.33 |
| $p$ (T $\leq$ t) | 0.39 | | 0.54 | |

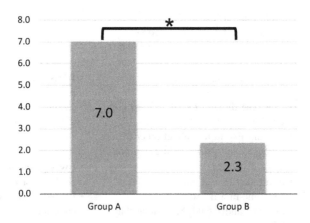

**Fig. 8.** The number of "awareness" expression and significant difference.

### 5.3    Discussion

As a result of the questionnaire, Group A demonstrated a higher numerical value than Group B, but no significant difference was obtained. It is highly likely that the number of experimental participants was too small for a significant difference to be obtained. Additionally, Group A reported a higher response for item 2. This is likely due to a student with discomfort in dialogue. However, since the numerical value was high, we obtained the possibility that the reflection using the state transition model may "notice".

Furthermore, as a result of extracting and analyzing the conversation from the contents obtained by the questionnaire, it was found that the dialogue using the state transition model was able to hold many conversations.

In detail, one participant produced many negative words, and the content of the conversation was expanded by "Sympathy" of the state transition network. In other words, the participant could see his own behavior objectively, noticing his behavior in the reflection, which allowed him to conclude to improve his behavior.

Moreover, there are individual differences in noticeable awareness, but those who used the learned model were more aware of themselves when reflecting. In other words, the system that used the model understood the user more than the actual person who was conversing with the individual for the first time.

## 6    Effect of Reflection Using Agent with the Verbal Probability Model

From the result of Sect. 6, reflection support based on the verbal probability model could show effective reflection. In this chapter, we verify that the agent with the verbal probability model can induce awareness of the target person.

### 6.1    Method of Dialogue Creation for Agents

In this research, we defined a general dialogue in the proposed eight dialogue strategies. Specifically, Table 9 shows a general dialogue in the proposed eight dialogue strategies. Where "XXX" changes according to the content of the conversation, the experimenter inputs a word in this research. Figure 9 shows the outline of the room to reflect on.

### 6.2    Experiments and Evaluation

In this experiment, we conduct the reflection of cooking to eight students (male: six, female: two) as experiment participants. The target students rarely cook at home. All experiment participants cook, and then perform reflection. In reflection, we present a video of the cooked shot video and the correct cooking method. Figure 10 shows a scene during reflection. In this experiment, we divided 8 experiment participants into two groups as follows;

Group M: Reflection using agent with the verbal probability model
Group N: Reflection by experimenter.
After the experiment, experiment participants answer to the questionnaire used in Sect. 5.

**Table 9.** A general dialogue in the proposed eight dialogue strategies.

| Items | General dialogues |
|---|---|
| Confirmation of facts | It's XXX, is not it? |
| Empathy | Me too |
| Self-disclosure | I was also XXX. It becomes ~ |
| Questions about evaluation | Why did you think it was XXX? |
| Praise | It is wonderful. It is great! |
| Exemplary suggestions | How about trying this way? |
| Suggestions for next time | How will you behave next time? |
| Comparisons | Is there a difference between your video and the correct video? |
| Confirmation of facts | It's XXX, is not it? |
| Empathy | Me too |

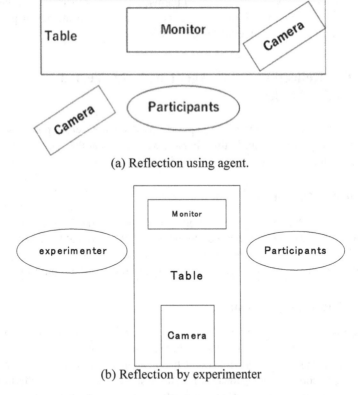

(a) Reflection using agent.

(b) Reflection by experimenter

**Fig. 9.** A scene during reflection.

(a) Reflection using agent

(b) Reflection by experimenter.

**Fig. 10.** A scene during reflection.

## 6.3 Results

Table 10 shows the results of questionnaire, and Table 11 shows the result of t-test.

From the results in Table 11, Question item1 showed a higher score than Group M for Group N, however, there were no significant differences between the two groups. On the other hand, the t-test result of Question item2 were significant differences ($p = 0.014 < 0.05$) between the two groups.

Next, we describe the number of "awareness" expression. The number of "awareness" expression in Group M is 3, The number of "awareness" expression in Group M is 11. Table 12 shows the reflection dialogue contents of the expression of "Awareness". Figure 11 shows the number of "awareness". From the result in Fig. 11, The number of "awareness" expression was no significant differences between the two groups. However, we think that this result may show different by increasing the number of experimenters.

**Table 10.** Result of questionnaire.

| Question items | Contents | Group M | Group N |
|---|---|---|---|
| 1 | Can we use reflection? | 3.75 | 4.5 |
| 2 | Do you feel strange about the conversation? | 3 | 1.25 |

**Table 11.** Results of *t*-test

|  | Question items1 | | Question items2 | |
|---|---|---|---|---|
|  | Group M | Group N | Group M | Group N |
| Average | 3.75 | 4.5 | 3 | 1.25 |
| Variance | 0.25 | 0.33 | 0.66 | 0.25 |
| $p$ (T ≤ t) | 0.097 | | 0.014* | |

*: $p < 0.05$

**Table 12.** The number of the expression of "Awareness"

| Number of reflections | Group M | Group N |
|---|---|---|
| Reflection No. 1 | 0 | 1 |
| Reflection No. 2 | 0 | 3 |
| Reflection No. 3 | 3 | 5 |
| Reflection No. 4 | 0 | 4 |

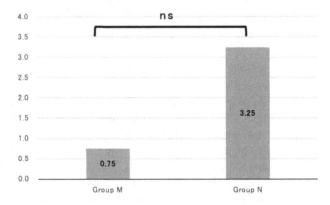

**Fig. 11.** The number of "awareness" expression and significant difference.

## 6.4    Discussion

As a result of the experiment, there was no significant difference in "Question items1: Do you feel strange about the conversation?" and "The number of awareness" expression. However, Group M had less "awareness of occurrence" than Group N. As this reason, there were many participants who responded that Question item2 had a sense of incompatibility. However, Group M had less "awareness of occurrence" than Group N. As this reason, there were many participants who responded that Question item2 had a sense of incompatibility. In other words, this result suggests that there was uncomfortable dialogue with the agent. In addition, a result of analyzing Group M's reflection, we think that the reason is that "the dialogue has ended soon" or "the dialogue has ended without clarifying its own behavioral problems". On the other hand, we found that the experimenter participants with "awareness of occurrence" were watching teacher videos during the reflection dialogue. From the above, we think that the presentation of teacher videos is important for reflection with agents.

## 7    Conclusion

In this research, we created a model of reflection dialogue strategy. Specifically, through reflection of group discussions, we built a model of the dialog strategy and automated the reflection using the constructed model. As a result, reflection was performed based on the existence of the constructed network. A $t$-test was calculated for the questionnaire, but no significant difference was observed.

In the future research, it is necessary to develop a dialogue strategy model which also adds non-verbal communication acquired in the previous experiment. In addition, it is necessary to divert the experimental part, especially using the WOZ method, to the model and use it while using speech synthesis.

**Acknowledgments.** This work was supported by JSPS KAKENHI Grant Number 15K00368. We would like to thank Editage (www.editage.jp) for English language editing.

# References

1. Itadume, I.: Disorder Psychology of Acquired Brain Injury. Gakubunsha in Japan (2007)
2. Honda, T.: The Rehabilitation of the Patient with Acquired Brain Injury. Igaku-Shoin in Japan (2006)
3. Tokyo Metropolitan Government Brain Dysfunction Investigation Committee: Survey Report on the Actual Situation of Higher Brain Dysfunction in Tokyo (2008)
4. Jorm, A.F., Korten, A.E., Henderson, A.S.: The prevalence of dementia: a quantitative integration of the literature. Acta Psychiatr. Scand. **76**(5), 465–479 (1987)
5. Alzheimer's Association: 2016 Alzheimer's disease facts and figures. Alzheimer's Dement. **12**(4), 459–509 (2016)
6. Prince, M., Bryce, R., Albanese, E., Wimo, A., Ribeiro, W., Ferri, C.P.: The global prevalence of dementia: a systematic review and metaanalysis. Alzheimer's Dement. **9**(1), 63–75 (2013)
7. Ogura, I., et al.: Cooking training for a patient with higher brain dysfunction. J. Cogn. Rehabil. **2007**, 40–45 (2007)
8. Yamashita, M., Kawashima, R., Iwata, K., Hotehama, M., Tao, K., Takakura, M.: Measurements of human brain activity when cooking using a near infrared measurement device: optical topography system. J. Integr. Study Dietary Habits **17**, 125–129 (2006)
9. Yamakura, T., Yamazato, M., Inoue, H., Ikejima, C., Asada, T.: Group therapy for individuals with higher brain dysfunction. Cognitive Rehabilitation (2010)
10. Tategami, S.: Rusk Institute of Rehabilitation Medicine, Brain Injury Day Treatment Program. Medical School (2010)
11. Crosson, B.C., et al.: Awareness and compensation in postacute head injury rehabilitation. J. Head Trauma Rehabil. **4**(3), 46–54 (1989)
12. Senzaki, F.: Cognitive rehabilitation for higher brain dysfunction. Cooperative Medical Publisher (2005)
13. Nagano, T.: Awareness of higher brain dysfunction. Higher Brain Funct. Res. (2012)
14. Meguro, T., Higashinaka, R., Minami, Y.: Dialogue control of listener dialog system using POMDP. The Association for Natural Language Processing (2011)
15. Abe, K., et al.: Robots that play with a child: application of an action decision model based on mental state estimation. J. Robot. Soc. Jpn. **31**(3), 263–274 (2013)
16. Sano, M., Kotani, R., Nakagawa, A., Morimoto, A., Yoshida, Y., Yoshinaga, C.: Dialogue strategy for ADL reflection and cognitive rehabilitation support system using a counseling robot. Hum. Comput. Interact. (2017)
17. Adachi, N.: Mind estimation based on communication-robot interaction for cognitive rehabilitation support. Osaka Institute of Technology (2010)

18. Murakami, T., Suyama, A., Orihara, R.: Consumer behavior modeling using Bayesian networks (2004)
19. Hara, K., Takahashi, K., Ueda, H.: Student behavior modeling and learning using Bayesian networks from questionnaires. Trans. Inf. Process. Jpn. **51**(4), 1215–1226 (2010)
20. NARA Institute of Science and Technology: CaboCha-NARA Institute of Science and Technology. https://taku910.github.io/cabocha/. Accessed 30 Jan 2019
21. Kikuchi, A.: Notes on the researches using KiSS-18. Bull. Fac. Soc. Welfare Iwate Prefectural Univ. **6**(2), 41–51 (2004)
22. Goldstein, A.P.: Social skill training through structured learning
23. NTT Data Trusted Global Innovator: BayoLink Bayesian network construction support system. http://www.msi.co.jp/bayolink/. Accessed 30 Jan 2019

# Health Games and Social Communities

# Bubble Trouble: Strategies Against Filter Bubbles in Online Social Networks

Laura Burbach$^{(\boxtimes)}$ (iD), Patrick Halbach (iD), Martina Ziefle (iD),
and André Calero Valdez (iD)

Human-Computer Interaction Center, RWTH Aachen University,
Campus-Boulevard 57, Aachen, Germany
{burbach,halbach,ziefle,calero-valdez}@comm.rwth-aachen.de

**Abstract.** In the recent past, some electoral decisions have gone against
the pre-election expectations, what led to greater emphasis on social
networking in the creation of filter bubbles. In this article, we examine
whether Facebook usage motives, personality traits of Facebook users,
and awareness of the filter bubble phenomenon influence whether and
how Facebook users take action against filter bubbles. To answer these
questions we conducted an online survey with 149 participants in Germany. While we found out that in our sample, the motives for using
Facebook and the awareness of the filter bubble have an influence on
whether a person consciously takes action against the filter bubble, we
found no influence of personality traits. The results show that Facebook
users know for the most part that filter bubbles exist, but still do little about them. Therefore it can be concluded that in today's digital
age, it is important not only to inform users about the existence of filter
bubbles, but also about various possible strategies for dealing with them.

**Keywords:** Filter bubble · Echo chamber · Avoidance strategies ·
Big Five · Facebook usage motives

## 1 Introduction

In the recent past, the results of some political elections have been surprising,
because the pre-election polls, which were supposed to give an idea of how the
election would turn out, strongly indicated different outcomes. Nowadays, many
people find information—including political information—on the Internet and
by social media. This has also led to social networks being viewed more crit-
ically [11]. Accordingly, their role in the emergence of filter bubbles and echo
chambers was discussed [18]. In the meantime, it can be assumed that many
Facebook users have heard about the phenomenon of the filter bubble, as it has
been increasingly addressed in the media as well as on social media platforms [2].
Nevertheless, it is believed that people who use social media for finding information are more likely to be in filter bubbles compared to the time when traditional
media were the mainstream. While some are beginning to believe that the use of

© Springer Nature Switzerland AG 2019
V. G. Duffy (Ed.): HCII 2019, LNCS 11582, pp. 441–456, 2019.
https://doi.org/10.1007/978-3-030-22219-2_33

social networks may even lead to the inclusion of more diverse information [25], others are still of the opinion that they lead to stronger filter bubble effects. Personalization algorithms ensure that users only see certain content depending on their preferences [29, 46] and thus limit the diversity of opinions that are visible to the users [4, 40, 41]. Users often do not notice this and are not made aware of it either [51]. This is why users might take no measures against the filter bubbles in which they find themselves.

So far, little has been said about whether the knowledge about filter bubbles and perceiving them as problematic makes people take action against the effects of filter bubbles. That is why, as part of this study, we investigate whether Facebook users are actually aware that filter bubbles exist, whether they consider them to be problematic, whether they still do not know that filter bubbles exist and therefore do not inform themselves comprehensively outside of possible bubbles. We also consider whether filter bubbles are problematic for democracies in the eyes of our participants, whether they actively take action against them, and if so, which factors lead to these actions. Furthermore, we examine how the participants' Facebook usage motives, Big Five personality traits, and awareness of filter bubbles influences if and how they take action against filter bubbles. We not only asked the participants to indicate whether they would generally take active action against filter bubbles, but we also asked them about specific strategies, such as deleting the browser history or the stored cookies.

## 2  Related Work

With the digital age and the rise of social media phenomena such as filter bubbles, echo chambers, and algorithms have emerged. What these are, is described in this chapter.

### 2.1  Social Media, Algorithms and Filter Bubbles

According to agenda setting theory, the media determine which topics are part of the public discourse and which are not. They draw attention to a topic and put it on the public agenda by reporting them as news [42]. Thus, the media have a *direct* influence on the formation of opinion [13].

Digitalization is also accompanied by the trend that traditional media is upstaged by social media and user-generated content [35]. Today, anyone can write and publish their own news and reach a wide audience through social media [5]. Even most traditional media outlets nowadays provide online platforms and spread their news via social media. The fact that anyone can spread news on the Internet leads to a flood of information that is hardly manageable. People can now access news and political information on the Internet from a variety of media and sources [1]. Thus, individuals can no longer read all content and absorb all available information. Instead they have to choose in advance which content they want to consume.

When they have the choice, individuals usually select content that reflects their own opinion and avoid content that contradicts their own opinion. In research, this effect is referred to as selective exposure (see e.g. [7,14,19,36]). According to the cognitive dissonance theory by Festinger (1957) (see e.g. [7,14, 19]) people experience it as positive when they are confronted with information that matches their opinion and are more likely to reject it when it contradicts their opinion.

As the logical extension of this effect, echo chambers become apparent as a consequence. This means that individuals surround themselves with like-minded people, non-confrontational information, and communicate about certain events taking place in echo chambers [53].

Another culprit in the equations comes from a different problem mentioned earlier. The Internet and social media provide so much information for the individual that it is difficult to decide which content is relevant to them. A technical development that can and should help Internet users to select relevant information are recommender systems [50]. In these systems, an algorithm filters which user sees which information. It attempts to provide content according to the user's taste and interests.

A possible consequence of recommendation algorithms are filter bubbles [46] and algorithmic echo chambers. In such bubbles or chambers the users only see what they like, such as opinions and political positions that match their own beliefs [24] unknowingly to them.

Recommender systems are well-intended—they aim to reduce information overload—but come with a cost: If applied to news content, they might restrict the diversity of the content that a user is shown, thus leaving them in an opinionated filter bubble of news [10,24,46]. There are tools, however, that attempt to dampen the filter bubble effect of recommender system. Some of those tools leave the responsibility of defining rules for content selection entirely with the user, while others work in the background and do not notify the user about the changes [11].

## 2.2  Underlying Algorithms

Ideally, the quality of a recommender system is measured by whether the users are satisfied with it. In order to achieve the greatest possible user satisfaction, filter algorithms are often personalized [38]. Various techniques or procedures are used to personalize the recommendations. Content-based recommendations or collaborative filtering are most frequently used. Content-based recommendation uses the content in the data uploaded by users. The content is used to estimate what users would like to see. In collaborative filtering, recommendations are made on the basis of similarity of users. Preferences of people who show similar interests are used here [9,38]. Besides these, there are many combinations of techniques used as well [47]. One well-known example of websites that use the above described algorithms is Facebook (see e.g. [4]).

## 2.3   Filter Bubbles and Echo Chambers

The possibility to choose information sources on the Internet can lead to echo chambers being more frequent and more influential [19], but nevertheless this kind of balkanization can also happen offline. For instance, people usually buy only newspapers they already know and like, which again reinforces their specific views [26,52,53].

Filter bubbles are seen as negative because people inside of them get used to different truths about our world. Pariser also sees filter bubbles as a stronger threat than echo chambers. He justifies this view with the fact that people in filter bubbles are alone, since the algorithms present individualized content to each user [46]. Furthermore, filter bubbles are invisible, as individuals usually cannot see how personalization algorithms decide which content is eventually shown to them. In addition, individuals do not consciously make the decision to go into a filter bubble, but this happens automatically and they are not notified when they are inside. In contrast, the choice of a newspaper with a certain political direction seems more like a conscious decision. Moreover, some studies dealing with strategies for bursting filter bubbles have shown that the continuous improvement of personalization algorithms is accompanied by some fears [11,31,45,55].

Filter bubbles also affect political opinion formation and can be a threat for democracies, regardless of the form of democracy [10,11]. For this purpose, aspects like customization and selective exposure and their effects on users have been investigated extensively [20]. For Dylko et al. the effect of filter bubbles on political opinion formation is stronger when individuals are in groups with mostly ideologically moderate others and for messages which contradict their own opinions. In the past, political campaign makers have taken advantage of this such as for the Donald Trump presidential campaign in 2016. In order to win voters, the social media profiles were analyzed and campaigns were tailored to individual users [30].

Algorithms may influence the formation of political opinion as well (see e.g. [32,33]). The possible negative consequences of algorithms would be eliminated if all people were aware that filter bubbles do exist and whether they are caught inside of one. However, some studies have shown that most people are not aware that algorithms filter their content [22,23,48].

The possible negative consequences of recommender systems, echo chambers, and filter bubbles have often been considered, but many scientists are still unable to see forsee additional consequences. While some studies showed that selective exposure occurs, they also pointed out that people still perceive opinions that contradict their attitudes (see e.g. [12,24,26,37]).

Especially with regard to politics, frequently discussed effects such as increasing polarization and fragmentation of opinions were not clearly shown in some studies [8,25,54]. Dubois and Blank argue that even if people use a relatively limited information gathering platform, they are likely to receive more information on different platforms [19].

There are studies that have found echo chambers on Twitter (see e.g. [6,15]) and other studies that have not found them on Facebook (see e.g. [4,27]).

Nevertheless, other researchers have found that algorithms accurately predict user characteristics such as political orientation [3,21,39]. Bakshy et al. (2015) discovered that Facebook filters a small amount of cross-sectional content in the United States, but they also could determine that the decisions of individuals have a greater impact on whether they see different content. For example, the choice of friends on Facebook has an influence [4].

As shown, there is little empirical evidence on the influence of filter bubbles. However, it is conceivable that the consequences of filter algorithms will only become visible when the algorithms function better. A possible threat to democracy can nevertheless exist and should not be ignored.

## 2.4 Strategies Against Filter Bubbles

Following the criticism of filter bubbles, research is being conducted for figuring out how to combat filter bubbles [50]. Strategies that can be used to combat filter bubbles include deleting web history, deleting cookies, using the incognito option of a browser, and liking different things or everything on a social media site [11].

Some developers of avoidance strategies argue that filter bubbles are actually an unsuccessful consequence of algorithms. They do not ensure that users see the search results they want, but that they do not see them and deprive users of their autonomy. These developers are mainly trying to raise people's awareness of the existence of filter bubbles to give them more control [11]. For instance, Munson et al. have developed a tool that shows the user a histogram that politically classifies the read texts from left to right [44].

## 3 Method

To find out whether individuals are aware of filter bubbles and to see if and how awareness of filter bubbles, Facebook usage motives, and personality traits influence whether individuals consciously take action against filter bubbles (see Fig. 1), we conducted an online survey from December 2017 to January 2018 in Germany.

The survey consisted of three parts. First, we asked for some demographic data and user factors (part 1), then we looked at the participants' motives for using Facebook (part 2). Finally, we asked the participants if they had heard of filter bubbles before, what they thought about them and if and how they would take active action against filter bubbles (part 3). Subsequently, we describe the assessed variables.

*Demographics.* As demographics we asked the participants for their age, gender, and educational level.

*Big Five.* We further surveyed personality traits using items from the Big Five model inventory [49]. The *Big Five* personality traits relate to a very established

**Independent Variables**

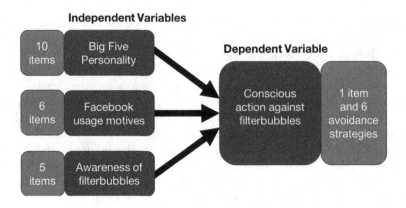

**Fig. 1.** Depicted research question and assessed variables

model of personality psychology (cf. [17,28,34]): It divides the personality of individuals into five main categories: *openness, conscientiousness, extraversion, agreeableness,* and *neuroticism.* We used the BFI-10 short scale introduced by Rammstedt et al. [49].

*Facebook Usage Motives.* Further we measured what our participants use Facebook for. In the questionnaire we offered six possible reasons for choice. The reasons were *stay in touch with friends, find new friends, for professional purposes, inform yourself about political/social topics, inform others about political/social topics,* and *express one's opinion on political/social topics.*

*Filter Bubble Awareness.* We also investigated the participants' awareness of filter bubbles. We asked the participants, if they have *already heard of filter bubbles,* if they *believe that filter bubbles exist,* if *filter bubbles are a problem,* if *filter bubbles affect them personally,* and if *filter bubbles display only interesting posts.* Besides, we asked the participants, if they would *take conscious action against filter bubbles.* Finally, we asked which avoidance strategies they apply. Participants should think about five given strategies. We asked if they, *delete the browser history, use the incognito function, click and like many different posts to enforce diversity, use the explore-button, which shows many different news,* and if they *subscribe some friends/pages.*

Except for age, gender, and education, all scales were measured using agreement on a six-point Likert scale from 1 = do not agree at all to 6 = fully agree.

### 3.1   Statistical Methods

For the data analysis we used R version 3.4.1 using RStudio. To check the reliability of the scales, we used the jmv package. For correlations we used the corrplot package. Further, we used the likert package to analyze Likert data. To measure internal reliability we use Cronbach's Alpha. Alpha values of $\alpha > 0.7$ indicate a good reliability of a scale. We provide the 95% confidence intervals for all results and we tested the null-hypothesis significance on the significance level $\alpha < .01$.

## 4    Results

To see what our sample looks like, we first look at the results from a descriptive point of view. The participants of our survey are on average 26.2 years old ($n = 149, SD = 7.45$) and 84 (56%) are female and 65 (44%) are male. Further the participants are highly educated. A total of 85 (57%) have a university degree, 52 (35%) baccalaureate, six (4%) vocational baccalaureate, five (3%) a completed training and one a secondary education.

Looking at the Big Five personality traits, we see that the participants are the most open-minded and the least neurotic, but participants did not show unusual outliers (see Fig. 2).

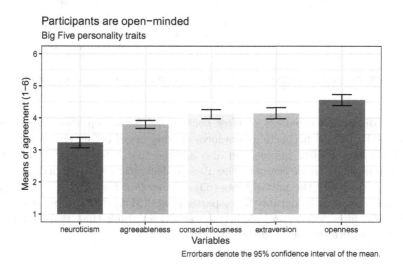

**Fig. 2.** Means of Big Five personality traits

When we asked if the participants were using Facebook uniformly, less or more than they did in the past, most participants indicate a less frequent use (65%), some indicate the same (33%) and only a few indicate to use it more frequently (2%).

Our participants use Facebook for different reasons, but as Fig. 3 shows, their primary use is to *stay in touch with friends*, whereas they use it less for other reasons such as to *express their opinions on political/social topics*, or to *inform themselves or others about political and/or social topics*.

**Filter Bubbles.** Next we look at the results regarding filter bubbles. Here, we measured the participants' *awareness of filter bubbles*, if they *took active action against filter bubbles* as well as if they applied given *avoidance strategies against filter bubbles*.

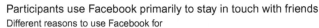

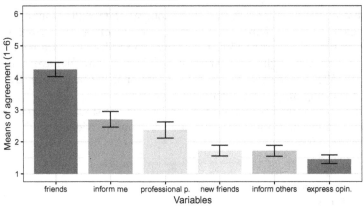

**Fig. 3.** Means of agreement with different reasons to use Facebook for

Regarding the *awareness of filter bubbles*, we found out that the majority (73%, see Fig. 4) of the participants have *already heard* before this study about the theory of the filter bubble and also assume that *filter bubbles exist* (96%) and that most of them evaluate them as *problematic* (80%) A little less, but still the majority of the participants (63%) *know that they are affected by filter bubbles*. However, considerably fewer participants (31%) deliberately *take action against the filter bubble* and slightly fewer (41%) think that *more interesting contributions are indicated to them by filter bubbles*.

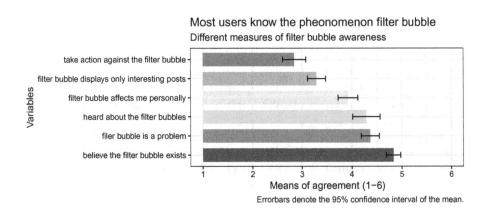

**Fig. 4.** Means of agreement with different measures of filter bubble awareness

Next, we looked for the reasons why someone provides to *take active action against filter bubbles*. Thus we computed correlation analyses for the *Facebook usage motives, awareness of the filter bubble*, and *Big Five factors* with the dependent variable *active action against filter bubbles*.

While we found out with these correlations that the *awareness of the filter bubble* (see Table 1) and *motives for using Facebook* (see Table 2) have an influence on whether a person indicates to consciously *take action against the filter bubble*, we found no relations of the *Big Five* personality traits to *take generally active action against filter bubbles* ($p_s > .05$). Looking at the *awareness of filter bubbles*, people who have *already heard of the filter bubble* and people who evaluate *filter bubbles as a problem* would rather *take active action against filter bubbles* (see Table 1). Regarding *Facebook usage motives*, individuals who use Facebook for *professional purposes*, to *inform others about political/social topics* or to *express their opinion* are more likely to *take active action against filter bubbles* (see Table 2).

After the described correlation analyses, we computed a stepwise linear regression with the general *willingness to take active action* as dependent variable and the five variables that showed a significant relationship (see Tables 1 and 2). With this analysis we wanted to examine on which variables the *general willingness to take active action against filter bubbles* depends.

As Table 3 shows, we have received three models with the multiple linear regression. All three models contain the variable *already heard of filter bubbles*, the second model contains in addition the variable *use Facebook to express opinion* and the third model contains in beside the variable *the filter bubble is a problem*. Since the third model with $R^2 = .23$ clarifies the largest part of the variance, we consider this one for further interpretations. So it is more likely, that individuals who *have already heard of filter bubbles, rate them as a problem*, and *use Facebook to express their opinion* as well as *take active action against filter bubbles*. Because this model still only explains 23% of the variance, there are further aspects that determine if someone *takes active action against filter bubbles*. Nevertheless the named variables favour it. Since all three variables in the model show similarly high beta coefficients, they influence the dependent variable to similar parts.

So far, we looked at the general willingness to *take active action against filter bubbles*. Below we look at *certain avoidance strategies against filter bubbles*.

Of the given prevention strategies against filter bubbles, participants seem to *delete cookies and browser history* most frequently (69% see Fig. 5), whereas only few use the *Explore-button* (14%) or *click on different pages to force diversity* (18%).

Looking more detailed at the relationship between *Facebook usage motives* and the *avoidance strategies*, we see that some reasons to use Facebook correlate significantly with some avoidance strategies (see Table 4). For example people who use Facebook for *professional* purposes click and like different pages to force diversity.

**Table 1.** Means, standard deviations, and correlations with confidence intervals

| Variable | M | SD | 1 | 2 | 3 | 4 | 5 |
|---|---|---|---|---|---|---|---|
| 1. Heard of f. b | 2.71 | 1.66 | | | | | |
| 2. Filter bubble exists | 2.17 | 0.88 | .46** [.31, .58] | | | | |
| 3. F.b. affects me | 3.08 | 1.20 | .35** [.19, .48] | .50** [.36, .61] | | | |
| 4. F.b. is a problem | 2.63 | 1.09 | .27** [.11, .42] | .35** [.20, .49] | .19* [.03, .34] | | |
| 5. Interesting posts | 3.70 | 1.11 | −.07 [−.23, .10] | .10 [−.06, .26] | .17* [.01, .33] | −.21* [−.36, −.04] | |
| 6. Active action | 4.15 | 1.42 | .34** [.19, .48] | .14 [−.02, .30] | −.02 [−.18, .15] | .33** [.18, .47] | −.09 [−.25, .07] |

*Note.* We use M and SD to represent mean and standard deviation, respectively. Values in square brackets indicate the 95% confidence interval. The confidence interval is a plausible range of population correlations that could have caused the sample correlation [16]. * indicates $p < .05$. ** indicates $p < .01$.

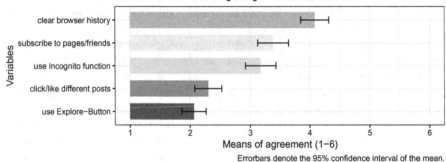

**Fig. 5.** Means of usage of different prevention strategies against filter bubbles

**Table 2.** Means, standard deviations, and correlations with confidence intervals

| Variable | M | SD | 1 | 2 | 3 | 4 | 5 | 6 |
|---|---|---|---|---|---|---|---|---|
| 1. Friends | 2.74 | 1.35 | | | | | | |
| 2. New friends | 5.28 | 1.01 | .05 [−.11, .21] | | | | | |
| 3. Professional purposes | 4.63 | 1.54 | −.09 [−.25, .07] | .19* [.03, .34] | | | | |
| 4. Inform me | 4.30 | 1.51 | −.02 [−.19, .14] | .05 [−.11, .22] | .20* [.04, .35] | | | |
| 5. Inform others | 5.28 | 1.05 | −.02 [−.18, .15] | .23** [.07, .38] | .26** [.11, .41] | .41** [.27, .54] | | |
| 6. Express opinion | 5.55 | 0.83 | .06 [−.11, .22] | .31** [.15, .45] | .32** [.17, .46] | .34** [.19, .48] | .63** [.51, .72] | |
| 7. Active action | 4.15 | 1.42 | .12 [−.04, .28] | .06 [−.10, .23] | .25** [.09, .40] | .13 [−.04, .29] | .18* [.01, .33] | .31** [.16, .46] |

*Note.* We use M and SD to represent mean and standard deviation, respectively. Values in square brackets indicate the 95% confidence interval. The confidence interval is a plausible range of population correlations that could have caused the sample correlation [16]. * indicates $p < .05$. ** indicates $p < .01$.

**Table 3.** Linear model of some predictors for the dependent variable *active action against filter bubbles*

|  | B | SE B | $\beta$ | p |
|---|---|---|---|---|
| Step 1 |  |  |  |  |
| Constant | 1.59 [.97, 2.21] | .313 |  | p < .001 |
| Already heard of filter bubbles | .29 [.16, .43] | .068 | .341 | p < .001 |
| Step 2 |  |  |  |  |
| Constant | .91 [.23, 1.59] | .345 |  | p = .009 |
| Already heard of filter bubbles | .278 [.15, .41] | .066 | .325 | p < .001 |
| Facebook to express opinion: | .513 [.25, .77] | .131 | .296 | p < .001 |
| Step 3 |  |  |  |  |
| Constant | −.04 [−.98, .91] | .476 |  | p = .939 |
| Already heard of filter bubbles | .23 [.10, .36] | .066 | .267 | p < .001 |
| Facebook to express opinion | .46 [.20, .72] | .129 | .265 | p < .001 |
| Filter bubble is a problem | .284 [.08, .48] | .101 | .218 | p = .006 |

*Note.* $R^2 = .11$ for step 1; $R^2 = .19$ for step 2 ($p_s < .001$); $R^2 = .23$ for step 3 ($p = .006$); 95% confidence intervals are indicated

**Table 4.** Correlation results for the Facebook usage motives and avoidance strategies against filter bubbles

| Variables | Correlation results |
|---|---|
| Stay in touch with friends & clear browser history | $r(140) = 0.18, p = .030$ |
| Find new friends & clear browser history | $r(140) = 0.17, p = .047$ |
| Find new friends & subscribe to pages/friends | $r(140) = 0.17, p = .043$ |
| Professional purposes & enforce diversity | $r(140) = 0.26, p = .002$ |
| Inform myself & enforce diversity | $r(140) = 0.20, p = .019$ |
| Express opinion & enforce diversity | $r(140) = 0.20, p = .019$ |

**Table 5.** Correlation results for the Big Five factors and avoidance strategies

| Variables | Correlation results |
|---|---|
| Extraversion & subscribe to pages/friends | $r(140) = −0.28, <.001$ |
| Conscientiousness & clear browser history | $r(140) = 0.20, p = .020$ |
| Openness & clear browser history | $r(140) = −0.17, p = .049$ |
| Openness & use incognito-function | $r(140) = −0.20, p = .020$ |

Besides we found that individuals who evaluate filter bubbles as a problem like and click more different pages to force diversity ($r(140) = 0.27, p = .001$). We did not find further correlations for the *awareness of filter bubbles* and *avoidance strategies against filter bubbles*.

Furthermore, our study showed some correlations between the *Big Five factors* and *avoidance strategies* (see Table 5).

## 5  Discussion

Our results revealed, that Facebook users know for the most part that filter bubbles exist, but still do little against them. This makes it clear that in today's digital age it is important not only to inform users about the existence of filter bubbles, but also about various possible strategies for dealing with them.

With the queried avoidance strategies the participants favoured to delete the browser history or to unsubscribe friends/page. Both variants require less active effort than the other proposed strategies. For example, it is conceivable that individuals would simply subscribe to friends when they notice that they frequently publish content that is perceived as uninteresting or perhaps even inappropriate. For example, to mark more different pages with like would require more personal effort.

However, if individuals do claim to take action against filter bubbles, this is favoured by three aspects in particular. Not surprisingly, our study showed that the fact that someone has heard of filter bubbles affects whether someone claims to be active against filter bubbles. Also, it seems plausible that people who consider filter bubbles a problem would be more likely to become active. More interestingly, people who use Facebook to spread their opinions are more likely to say they are taking action against filter bubbles. This could be because they want to use the platform to spread their opinions, reach as many people as possible and not just the people in a filter bubble or their own. Perhaps they see the advantage of user-generated content and that they themselves can contribute something to opinion-forming. This would certainly be desirable for a strengthening of democracy and unrestricted opinion-forming. However, the group of those who say they want to spread their opinions on Facebook is a very small group in our sample.

Despite the fact that many participants consider filter bubbles to be problematic and almost no one denies the existence of filter bubbles. Participants did not report as much active action against filter bubbles. It is possible that some people may not feel affected or may not know how to fight against filter bubbles. In addition, some people may not feel the effects of filter bubbles as particularly negative and therefore do not see any need for action.

While some scientists, like Pariser (2011), suggest that users should take action against filter bubbles by, for example, liking different pages, deleting web history, deleting cookies and so on, other scientists (see e.g. [11]) believe that algorithms are not only negative, but can also provide users with a broader view of the world. Perhaps, therefore, it is not necessary to take action against filter bubbles, but rather to try to teach the users of social networks how to deal with personalization algorithms and possible filter bubbles. Thus, the positive aspects of recommender systems could increasingly come to the fore. Users could include algorithms in their searches and benefit from them, but at the same time be aware that the information received is pre-filtered.

Online-platforms such as Facebook often argue that they are not a news platform [11], but according to some studies such platforms are being used more and more to spread different opinions. Mitchell et al. found in their study that almost half (48%) of the 10,000 panelists consumed news about politics and government on Facebook at least once a week [43]. Further studies showed that the use of social media for political news distribution has increased even more and continues to increase [11]. Facebook must therefore also be seen as a medium that contributes to opinion-forming. This means that it is important for people to learn how to deal with opinion contributions on social networks and how to deal with filter bubbles or use algorithms in a targeted way.

### 5.1 Limitations and Future Work

We used convenience sampling for our study, but the results must be considered against the background that the sample is very young and well educated, so that it can be assumed that the knowledge about filter bubbles in our sample is higher than in the total population. The results should therefore be reviewed against a more heterogeneous sample. Nevertheless, pure knowledge about filter bubbles does not seem to lead people to take action against them thus solving the arising problems of misinformation and opinion manipulation in social networks.

In addition, we asked the participants if they would take action against filter bubbles. So the results show whether the participants could imagine using avoidance strategies in principle, but not whether they would actually do so. Therefore we try to find a better way in future studies to see if any avoidance strategies are used.

Also with regard to the question of whether filter bubbles are considered problematic, it is conceivable that the test persons have largely agreed in the sense of social desirability bias, as we have asked them to do so. We cannot therefore be sure whether they really regard filter bubbles as a problem. Although many participants indicated that filter bubbles were problematic for them, far fewer indicated that they would use avoidance strategies. So in the future it would also be interesting to find out why people do not want to take action against filter bubbles. It is conceivable that they see no reason for this, either because they are not so critical about filter bubbles or because they believe that they themselves are not affected. It is also possible that the strategies are too complex or time-consuming.

## 6  Conclusion

With this paper we showed that the most people, at least in our sample, have already heard about the phenomenon of the filter bubble. Nevertheless, the readiness for avoidance strategies is low. Besides we showed that the reasons why Facebook is used and the awareness of the filter bubble ensures that individuals are more likely to take action against filter bubbles, whereas the personality (here Big Five) has no effect on predicting it.

**Acknowledgements.** The authors would like to thank Nils Plettenberg and Johannes Nakayama for their help in improving this article. We would like to thank Nora Ehrhardt and Marion Wießmann for their support in this study. This research was supported by the Digital Society research program funded by the Ministry of Culture and Science of the German State of North Rhine-Westphalia.

# References

1. Van Aelst, P., et al.: Political communication in a high-choice media environment: a challenge for democracy? Ann. Int. Commun. Assoc. **41**(1), 3–27 (2017)
2. Allcott, H., Gentzkow, M.: Social media and fake news in the 2016 election. J. Econ. Perspect. **31**(2), 211–236 (2017)
3. Azucar, D., Marengo, D., Settanni, M.: Predicting the big 5 personality traits from digital footprints on social media: a meta-analysis. Pers. Individ. Differ. **124**, 150–159 (2018)
4. Bakshy, E., Messing, S., Adamic, L.A.: Exposure to ideologically diverse news and opinion on Facebook. Science **348**(6239), 1130–1132 (2008)
5. Bakshy, E., et al.: The role of social networks in information diffusion. In: Proceedings of the 21st International Conference on World Wide Web, pp. 519–528 (2012)
6. Barberá, P., et al.: Tweeting from left to right: is online political communication more than an echo chamber? Psychol. Sci. **26**(10), 1531–1542 (2015)
7. Beam, M.A.: Automating the news: how personalized news recommender system design choices impact news reception. Commun. Res. **41**(8), 1019–1041 (2014)
8. Beam, M.A., et al.: Facebook news and (de)polarization: reinforcing spirals in the 2016 US election. Inf. Commun. Soc. **21**(7), 940–958 (2018)
9. Bellogin, A., Cantador, I., Castells, P.: A comparative study of heterogeneous item recommendations in social systems. Inf. Sci. **221**, 142–169 (2013)
10. Zuiderveen Borgesius, F.G., et al.: Should we worry about filter bubbles? https://policyreview.info/articles/analysis/should-we-worryabout-filter-bubbles. Accessed 26 Feb 2019
11. Bozdag, E., van den Hoven, J.: Breaking the filter bubble: democracy and design. Ethics Inf. Technol. **17**(4), 249–265 (2015)
12. Jonathan, B.: Explaining the emergence of political fragmentation on social media: the role of ideology and extremism. J. Comput. Mediat. Commun. **23**(1), 17–33 (2018)
13. Calero Valdez, A., Burbach, L., Ziefle, M.: Political opinions of us and them and the influence of digital media usage. In: Meiselwitz, G. (ed.) SCSM 2018. LNCS, vol. 10913, pp. 189–202. Springer, Cham (2018). https://doi.org/10.1007/978-3-319-91521-0_15
14. Colleoni, E., Rozza, A., Arvidsson, A.: Echo chamber or public sphere? Predicting political orientation and measuring political homophily in twitter using big data. J. Commun. **64**(2), 317–332 (2014)
15. Conover, M.D., et al.: Political polarization on Twitter. In: Fifth International Conference on Weblogs and Social media (ICWSM), pp. 89–96 (2011)
16. Cumming, G.: The new statistics: why and how. Psychol. Sci. **25**(1), 7–29 (2014)
17. De Raad, B.: The Big Five Personality Factors: The Psycholexical Approach to Personality. Hogrefe & Huber Publishers, Göttingen (2000)
18. DiFranzo, D.J., Gloria-Garcia, K.: Filter bubbles and fake news. XRDS: Crossroads ACM Mag. Stud. **23**(3), 32–35 (2017)

19. Dubois, E., Blank, G.: The echo chamber is overstated: the moderating effect of political interest and diverse media. Inf. Commun. Soc. **21**(5), 729–745 (2018)
20. Dylko, I., et al.: The dark side of technology: an experimental investigation of the influence of customizability technology on online political selective exposure. Comput. Hum. Behav. **73**, 181–190 (2017)
21. Efron, M.: Using cocitation information to estimate political orientation in web documents. Knowl. Inf. Syst. **9**(4), 492–511 (2006)
22. Epstein, R., Robertson, R.E.: The search engine manipulation effect (SEME) and its possible impact on the outcomes of elections. Proc. Nat. Acad. Sci. **112**(33), E4512–E4521 (2015)
23. Eslami, M., et al.: I always assumed that i wasn't really that close to [her]: reasoning about invisible algorithms in news feeds. In: Proceedings of the 33rd Annual ACM Conference on Human Factors in Computing Systems, pp. 153–162 (2015)
24. Flaxman, S.R., Goel, S., Rao, J.M.: Filter bubbles, echo chambers, and online news consumption. Public Opin. Q. **80**(S1), 298–320 (2016)
25. Fletcher, R., Nielsen, R.K.: Are news audiences increasingly fragmented? A cross-national comparative analysis of cross-platform news audience fragmentation and duplication. J. Commun. **67**(4), 476–498 (2017)
26. Garrett, R.K.: Echo chambers online? Politically motivated selective exposure among internet news users. J. Comput.-Mediat. Commun. **14**(2), 265–285 (2009)
27. Goel, S., Mason, W., Watts, D.J.: Real and perceived attitude agreement in social networks. J. Pers. Soc. Psychol. **99**(4), 611–621 (2010)
28. Goldberg, L.R.: An alternative "description of personality": the big-five factor structure. J. Pers. Soc. Psychol. **59**, 1216–1229 (1990)
29. Goldman, E.: Search engine bias and the demise of search engine utopianism. In: Spink, A., Zimmer, M. (eds.) Web Search: Multidisciplinary Perspectives. ISKM, vol. 14, pp. 121–133. Springer, Heidelberg (2008). https://doi.org/10.1007/978-3-540-75829-7_8
30. González, R.J.: Hacking the citizenry? Personality profiling, 'big data' and the election of Donald Trump. Comput. Human Behav. **33**(3), 9–12 (2017)
31. Helberger, N., Karppinen, K., D'Acunto, L.: Exposure diversity as a design principle for recommender systems. Inf. Commun. Soc. **21**(2), 191–207 (2018)
32. Hoang, V.T., et al.: Domain-specific queries and Web search personalization: some investigations. In: Proceedings of the 11th International Workshop on Automated Specification and Verification of Web Systems (2015)
33. Introna, L.D., Nissenbaum, H.: Shaping the web: why the politics of search engines matters. Inf. Soc. **16**(3), 169–185 (2000)
34. John, O.P., Naumann, L.P., Soto, C.J.: Paradigm shift to the integrative big-five trait taxonomy: history, measurement, and conceptual issues. In: John, O.P., Robins, R.W., Pervin, L.A. (eds.) Handbook of Personality: Theory and Research, pp. 114–158. Guilford Press, New York (2008)
35. Kaplan, A.M., Haenlein, M.: Users of the world, unite! The challenges and opportunities of social media. Bus. Horiz. **53**(1), 59–68 (2010)
36. Karlsen, R., et al.: Echo chamber and trench warfare dynamics in online debates. Eur. J. Commun. **32**(3), 257–273 (2018)
37. Kobayashi, T., Ikeda, K.: Selective exposure in political web browsing: empirical verification of 'cyber-balkanization' in Japan and the USA. Inf. Commun. Soc. **12**(6), 929–953 (2009)
38. Koene, A., et al.: Ethics of personalized information filtering. In: Tiropanis, T., Vakali, A., Sartori, L., Burnap, P. (eds.) INSCI 2015. LNCS, vol. 9089, pp. 123–132. Springer, Cham (2015). https://doi.org/10.1007/978-3-319-18609-2_10

39. Kosinski, M., Stillwell, D., Graepel, T.: Private traits and attributes are predictable from digital records of human behavior. Proc. Nat. Acad. Sci. **110**(15), 5802–5805 (2013)
40. Leese, M.: The new profiling: algorithms, black boxes, and the failure of anti-discriminatory safeguards in the European Union. Secur. Dialogue **45**(5), 494–511 (2014)
41. Macnish, K.: Unblinking eyes: the ethics of automating surveillance. Ethics Inf. Technol. **14**(2), 151–167 (2012)
42. McCombs, M.E., Shaw, D.L.: The agenda-setting function of mass media. Public Opin. **36**(2), 41–46 (1972)
43. Mitchell, A., et al.: Political polarization and media habits (2014). http://www.journalism.org/2014/10/21/political-polarizationmedia-habits/
44. Munson, S.A., Lee, S.L, Resnick, P.: Encouraging reading of diverse political viewpoints with a browser widget. In: International Conference on Weblogs and Social Media (ICWSM) (2013)
45. Nagulendra, S., Vassileva, J.: Providing awareness, explanation and control of personalized filtering in a social networking site. Inf. Syst. Front. **18**(1), 145–158 (2016)
46. Pariser, E.: The Filter Bubble: What the Internet Is Hiding from You. Penguin, London (2011)
47. Portugal, I., Alencar, P., Cowan, D.: The use of machine learning algorithms in recommender systems: a systematic review. Expert Syst. Appl. **97**, 205–227 (2018)
48. Rader, E., Gray, R.: Understanding user beliefs about algorithmic curation in the Facebook news feed. In: Proceedings of the 33rd Annual ACM Conference on Human Factors in Computing Systems, CHI 2015, pp. 173–182 (2015)
49. Rammstedt, B., et al.: A short scale for assesing the big five dimensions of personality: 10 item big five inventory (BFI-10). Methoden Daten Anal. **7**(2), 233–249 (2013)
50. Resnick, P., et al.: Bursting your (filter) bubble: strategies for promoting diverse exposure. In: Proceedings of the Conference on Computer Supported Cooperative Work Companion, CSCW 2013, pp. 95–100 (2013)
51. Sandvig, C., et al.: Auditing algorithms: research methods for detecting discrimination on internet platforms (2018)
52. Stroud, N.J.: Media use and political predispositions: revisiting the concept of selective exposure. Polit. Behav. **30**(3), 341–366 (2008)
53. Sunstein, C.: # Republic: Divided Democracy in the Age of Social Media. Princeton University Press, Princeton (2017)
54. Trilling, D., van Klingeren, M., Tsfati, Y.: Selective exposure, political polarization, and possible mediators: evidence from The Netherlands. J. Public Opin. Res. **29**(2), 189–213 (2016)
55. Yom-Tov, E., Dumais, S., Guo, Q.: Promoting civil discourse through search engine diversity. Soc. Sci. Comput. Rev. **32**(2), 145–154 (2014)

# Health Games in Brazil

Marcelo Vasconcellos[1], Cynthia Dias[1(✉)], Flávia Carvalho[1],
Rafael Braga[2], and Guilherme Xavier[3]

[1] Oswaldo Cruz Foundation, Rio de Janeiro, Brazil
marcelodevasconcellos@gmail.com, cymadi@gmail.com
[2] Pontifical Catholic University of Paraná, Curitiba, Brazil
[3] Pontifical Catholic University of Rio de Janeiro, Rio de Janeiro, Brazil

**Abstract.** Although based on a growing market and popular means of leisure
and communication, serious games for health in Brazil still depend highly on
public funding and mostly on individual initiatives from researchers and
developers. This paper proposes the consolidation of Games and Health as a
field of work and research, discussing its origins and developments in Brazil, the
challenges yet to tackle and the strategies proposed by health games researchers
and developers for that end. The development of serious games for health in
Brazil has originated in distinct areas, such as Computation, Education and
Design and Arts and followed different paths. Exergames, games as therapy and
games for health communication and participation are the main directions
pursued nowadays. The main challenges are the achievement of funding to
develop projects; the lack of records about the games and tests produced; the
insufficient testing still shown by the researches published; the lack of common
vocabulary among researchers and developers across the country and the
medicalization that still informs the production of many games for health,
reducing the scope of what could be achieved on the field. As strategies, this
work proposes the production of three open and collaborative initiatives: a
common vocabulary; a guide with best practices in Health Game Research and
Development; an open database of finished and ongoing projects, in order to
facilitate partnerships.

**Keywords:** Health games · Serious games for health · Exergames ·
Games and health · Public health · Health communication and games

## 1 Introduction

Despite being one of the biggest markets for digital games, Brazil still lacks a consolidated area of serious games development. This situation also applies to games
dealing with health, which, until some years ago, were developed by the isolated efforts
of individuals. In the last years, this scenario has been changing, with the creation of
more organized initiatives around these themes that, we argue, makes possible to define
a field of Games and Health. In this work, we present a discussion about the current
situation of health games in Brazil, detailing the challenges that still hinder the field.
For this, we will discuss some particular aspects of the Health field in Brazil and the
potential place for games in it, present a brief origin of the health games in the country,

© Springer Nature Switzerland AG 2019
V. G. Duffy (Ed.): HCII 2019, LNCS 11582, pp. 457–472, 2019.
https://doi.org/10.1007/978-3-030-22219-2_34

and then detail the latest developments. Then we will discuss the challenges to be overcome and, finally, we will point out some initiatives intended to advance the field of Games and Health in the years to come, as they are currently understood by game researchers and health professionals in Brazil.

## 1.1 Public Health in Brazil

Most of the health investments in Brazil come from the Brazilian government, so, in order to discuss games for health, it is necessary first to present the specific aspects that surround public health in Brazil, since its size, huge variance of regions, habits, and cultures present unique challenges to government health policies. In addition, Brazil's historical development created both an enormous cultural diversity and many inequalities among different social groups and regions. Such variation is a complicating factor in health planning done by the State. Practices appropriate to certain areas do not apply to many others; resources and programs effective in large urban areas often become impractical or have to meet specific needs in cities that are smaller or more distant from the major centers. Such difficulties are addressed by two of the organizational principles governing Brazil's unified health system (SUS – Sistema Único de Saúde—Unified Health System) - "regionalization" and "hierarchy". According to these principles, services should be organized at increasing levels of complexity according to each geographic area and planned according to epidemiological criteria and with knowledge of the population to be served [1].

The country faces typical problems such as neglected diseases and endemic tropical diseases, for which the majority of research and development investments come from charities or government [2, 3]. This situation highlights the importance of the social determinants of health, defined as "[…] the social, economic, cultural, ethnic/racial, psychological and behavioral influencing the occurrence of health problems and their risk factors in the population" [4]. Public health in Brazil aims at taking into account the broader conditions that surround the individual and society, rather than considering the issue as merely the biological control of specific diseases. In the last fifteen years, there were many efforts to reduce social inequalities, aiming to provide equal access to health and understanding health as a set of factors broader than the physical well-being of the population [4].

The Brazilian unified health system was created to serve the entire population of the country and is one of the largest public health systems in the world. Despite historically limited funding, SUS operates under the principles of universality (which states that health is everyone's right), comprehensiveness (health involves both healing and prevention, individual and collective) and equity (equal opportunities to use the system). Social participation is a guideline that results and at the same time gives meaning to all other guidelines and principles of SUS. It states that society must be active in the planning, implementation, and monitoring of public health policies [5]. Understanding that health is a right for everyone and duty of the state, SUS provides comprehensive medical and health care to all citizens in Brazil. The expanded concept of health that SUS adopts guarantees citizens from outpatient care to organ transplants. It is, therefore, an important responsibility of the Brazilian state to develop health initiatives in support of all sections of the population [6].

## 1.2    The Role of Health Communication

Within this panorama, it is understandable the great importance given by Brazilian government communication channels to health communication strategies, trying to provide to various sectors of society accurate information for effective health promotion and maintenance. Such communication efforts occur in many different formats and media, using print, radio and television, and, lately, new media like web pages, blogs and social networks (Facebook, Youtube, Twitter, etc...). The contents include epidemiological information on disease prevention, but also information about epidemics and guidelines for a better quality of life for citizens, like the blog from Brazil's Ministry of Health [7].

Despite the intentions of providing democratic access to health information, communication campaigns on health typically tend to be highly centralized, devoid of cultural references, which makes them less approachable to many groups in a country as diverse as Brazil. The result is that such groups end up not being adequately addressed on health policies and communication practices. Moreover, even when making use of social media, health communication initiatives tend to be highly prescriptive, focusing on norms and behaviors to be adopted by the population [5].

One of the groups often affected by these inadequacies is young people and adolescents, who represent a big part of Brazil's population (over 26% of the population is between 10 and 24 years) and tend to be much affected by problems of health such as sexually transmitted infections, including AIDS. This fact is even worse considering that they tend to be reluctant to look for the assistance of health services and also tend to be resistant to more traditional methods used in health communication [8].

Therefore, it is relevant to the search for new ways to address these gaps in health communication for the population, especially for youth and adolescents, so that the health of Brazilian society can be improved as a whole. We believe that computer games may fulfill a role in health communication, through their inherent characteristics as a medium combining entertainment and participation.

## 1.3    New Media and Games

New media, in general, have been very successful in Brazil. Despite the country's shortcomings in technological infrastructure, social equality and media literacy, web pages, blogs, social networks, and instant messengers quickly became part of the population's daily life. By the early eighties, digital games culture and consumption grew to be a trend in Brazilian big cities, boosted by pop-culture references, arcades dissemination and 8-bit consoles smuggled from the United States of America. In that time, Brazil had a political regime keen to exclusively local technological production, biased to market reserve, with consequences on prices and popular access [9]. Unable to fulfill the inner demand, piracy of hardware and software became rampant till later 2000s, when easy access and other gaming business models (especially *massively multiplayer online, free-to-play* and *pay-what-you-want* games) seem to made illegal acquisition practices too cumbersome for many players. The content value of online games and socialization between gamers has changed the mentality of some studios, which changed from DRM - Digital Rights Management - practices to investments on marketing, quality, and innovative material to attract low-income consumers [10].

Due to piracy and personal computing promotion, gaming and related technological interests rapidly became rooted in juvenile imagination during the nineties. When the Internet and its promising World Wide Web hooked Brazilians by its novelty, academic fields showed special receptivity to digital game study and production, although a formal industry and market are still taking shape. However, in a similar way as with health communication, the access to digital media is also not equally distributed, which is reflected by the latest reports made by the federal government, which show southeast and south regions concentrating more than 67% of the 375 enterprises related, with 206% growth on formal companies since 2014 [11].

Besides consumption and participation, digital games in Brazil stand as a powerful convergence nexus to communication and experience sharing. The Youtube streaming phenomenon of digital influencers mirrors popular interests on trending massive games like *Fortnite* [12] and League *of Legends* [13], both with great appeal among children, teenagers and young adults. E-sports pose as a new research ground for a plethora of disciplines, from psychology to ergonomics, amid health. It's a common concern, both for researchers and producers, the growing interest in games and related activities not just as forms of expression, but as channels.

The Brazilian government has been using new media, such as social networks, as channels to provide health communication for the population. However, even within the typically less hierarchical structure of the internet, most of the communication efforts took the old formats of a centralized discourse, unidirectional and devoid of cultural references, without a real dialogue with the public [14].

On the other hand, digital games were never used consistently for health communication in Brazil. Other than a few official initiatives, mostly executed by advertising agencies in the government's service, it seems that games were never taken seriously into consideration by health managers. Despite the efforts of many isolated individuals, most of them health researchers and practitioners, and even with a relevant number of gamers in the country, digital games remain an almost untapped channel for public health communication [14].

## 2    Origins of Serious Games in Brazil

The lack of the Brazilian government's attention to games for health did not impede the emergence of several initiatives in the area. The majority of such efforts were made by researchers and professors, not directly connected to the government structure. These games, in general, tended to be part of bigger projects in different fields, funded through research grants [15].

The dependency on public grants is both a bless and a misfortune: in spite of the fact that games are seen as fringe media, deserving investigation, researchers and professors often lack experience on digital game production and knowledge about the gamers' interests and interactivity core concepts. As a result, they tend to rely on superficial premises, valuing content more than engagement and disregarding both sensory and cognitively rewarding feedback. This results in games very distant from market bestsellers, which fail to engage relevant interest from players.

Perceived as promising interactive solutions for a multitude of educational problems and situations, games development must be addressed as an intertwined and complex process, with equal concerns to narrative (their argumentative perspective), aesthetics (their visual appeal) and mechanics (their rules systems modulation), depending on teacher as well as designer responsibilities [16].

This complex structure of games helps to explain health games' first initiatives. Due to their intrinsic interdisciplinary nature, such projects emerged from different areas of knowledge, which three of the main are: Computation, Education and Design.

## 2.1 Computation

One of the first academic groups to show interest in games were professors and students of Computation courses. Facing game technology as a challenging subject to hone their skills, these groups started to develop games at first as simple investigation projects. Soon, however, they were developing more ambitious projects, trying to create full games. Although most of such projects dealt with entertainment games, eventually people started to create games with other objectives. In this context emerged some games aiming to be more than entertainment, tackling serious themes, like education and health [17]. Despite being made with technical care, often such games lacked the participation of health specialists and, hence, validated information about health. Nonetheless, the Computation field still represents one of the main areas of production of serious games, as can be seen on the works annually presented at SBGames (Brazilian Symposium on Computer Games and Digital Entertainment), Brazil's main game conference [17].

## 2.2 Education

Another lineage comes from the Education field, where educators, starting from the principles laid out by early masters like Piaget, started to investigate how this new kind of play—the digital games—could be applied in service of better educational outcomes. This group was the main pursuer of the idea of educational games, proposing games both as part of the regular school curriculum and as additional activities. In general, such projects were directed to children and youth, and, since the objective of these educators was to enhance learning, their games tended to focus on the content aspect, sometimes forgetting the specificities of the game media [18]. Education remains a very active field regarding research and development of serious games, as proved by the creation, in 2018, of a track dedicated to Education on the aforementioned SBGames (Brazilian Symposium on Computer Games and Digital Entertainment)[1] which included 33 full papers and 43 short papers.

---

[1] https://www.sbgames.org/sbgames2018/educacao.

## 2.3   Design and Arts

The third area where games entered academia in Brazil can be roughly described as Design and Arts. These initiatives tended to be similar to the ones in the Computation field, starting with the interest of students, professors, and researchers in creating art for digital games. Different from those developers at the Education field, who tended to reflect more deeply about the medium, designers and artists tended to assume a very pragmatic view, even in their academic production, focusing on how-to articles and similar works. Comparatively, this field produced less serious games than Education [17].

The Communication and Humanities areas, despite coming relatively later, had a great development in the last years, focusing less on developing games, and more on their social aspects, their specific language and meaning-making processes and the people who play them. It is possible to say that these works tend to be closer to the field of Game Studies, as it has been understood in Europe and the United States. Much of such investigative work aims to better understand and use serious games [17].

## 3   Games and Health

As previously mentioned, research and development of serious games in Brazil emerged independently in several different areas. As such, the current trends in the country reflect these multiple facets.

Nowadays, the field of health games in Brazil is as diverse as the aspects they can tackle, considering an amplified concept of health, which is the basis of SUS. Their public can range from professionals to students and citizens, and among these, go from children to elderly people [19]. The purpose of the games can cover health promotion, diagnosis, treatment or rehabilitation, and areas such as Psychology, Speech Therapy, Odontology, Physiotherapy, and many others [20], following international trends in the field. Together, they suggest that it is already possible to identify a field dealing both with games and health in Brazil.

We propose "Games and Health" as the name of such field, understanding that neither "Health" nor "Games" have precedence over the other (or is merely a tool for the other), but they work in close articulation. This way, we can consider that this field comprehends phenomena that range from the therapeutic use of games to game-based health learning, including health gamification and even the study of health themes in entertainment games. It is both an essentially interdisciplinary and deliberately inclusive field, as both Health and Games tend to be. In the last few years, it is possible to point out some relevant developments in such field.

### 3.1   Exergames

The interest in games interlaced with physical activity is growing in Brazil. Currently, the scientific literature proposes different descriptors to refer to video game consoles that require users to move their bodies to meet the challenges proposed by the games.

Among them, the descriptors exergame, exergaming, active video game and active video gaming prevail [21].

Investigations conducted using this kind of games as an intervention strategy aim, in their majority, to observe outcomes related to rehabilitation and treatment of motor and cognitive pathologies in different age groups, as well as to observe the potential of these games in health promotion. Under the health promotion perspective, the understanding of the behavior of physiological and psychological variables such as intensity of physical activity, energy expenditure, oxygen consumption, heart rate and motivation for adherence and permanence in their practice, have been the predominant interest on the part of researchers [22–24].

The current diversity of descriptors used by the scientific community to refer to such games results in a semantic problem, besides suggesting a lack of consensus about its use, which may result in the inference of mistaken evidence about such outcomes. In the wake of these observations, in Brazil, investigations conducted using exergames have tended to reproduce the international movement, observing the same outcomes and above all, fully copying the international descriptors [25–28].

However, researches focusing on such games still are incipient in Brazil, due to the approaches of researchers of different expertise, particularly education and computation. In order to advance research in Games and Health, there is a growing concern to promote forums and opportunities for dialogue, with the intention of fostering a better semantic organization of descriptors. Such an organization is even more necessary because of the process of translating terms into English. Recently, Braga [29] proposed the use of the descriptor Active Virtual Games (JVA) as a translation and semantic definition of internationally used descriptors. One of the important considerations for this proposition refers to the differentiation between the terms physical activity and physical exercise, already well established in the national and international literature [30, 31].

Despite this advance, the investigations with JVA in Brazil are still incipient. Most of the research carried out in North America, Europe, Asia, and Oceania takes place in community recreation centers and educational institutions, with government investments making this innovative format of games more widely available to the society. This is very far from the political interest and economic capabilities of the Brazilian government.

## 3.2  Games as Therapy

In another front, there are some promising projects using games in therapy. Health professionals at INTO (National Institute of Traumatology and Orthopedics) have been developing methods for using commercial motion detection consoles, like Nintendo Wii and Microsoft Kinect, as an alternative therapy for patients. In this hospital, most of the patients who suffered amputations had much difficulty in adapting to the use of prosthetics. Through trial and error, the health professionals discovered that sessions of motion detection-based games were beneficial to the patients' training, resulting in a much faster adaptation to the use of their prosthetics. Physiotherapy sessions that incorporate practice with commercial off-the-shelf games proved to be both efficient and enjoyable to the patients, opening new and interesting venues for further developments in therapy using games. Despite not using health games in the strict sense, this initiative is relevant as a proof of the usefulness of games for health [32]. Initiatives like this one are slowly being adopted in other Brazilian hospitals, both public and private.

Another initiative occurred in the research on pain reduction. Professionals from a public university hospital in Brazil realized that patients subjected to solid organ transplantation and bone marrow transplantation demanded fewer analgesic drugs when they were playing video games [33]. These professionals started researching and developing methods for using digital games and mobile devices for pain control in adult and children patients. Tests comparing patients who played and who didn't play showed digital games as a beneficial practice for pain reduction. This research contributed to making changes on care practices, including the introduction of other ludic activities such as music and movies. Since the access to digital devices can sometimes be a bit difficult and there are patients who refuse to try them, the next research phases will include board games as potential ludic options for pain reduction.

In addition, new immersive VR techniques are an important topic of interest, both to study human cognition and to explore ways to increase the illusion of entering virtual worlds [34]. Recently, a Brazilian vaccine clinic used these techniques to create a virtual reality experience designed to distract children from the pain during vaccination. The VR immerses the child in a fantasy world and her physical sensations (the pain of the injection and the cold alcohol-embedded cotton afterward) are explained as elements of the narrative. This way, rather than simply distracting the child from the needle, the story of the virtual world attaches a new meaning to the sting sensation [35]. Despite not being a game, strictly speaking, this initiative uses virtual reality and digital storytelling, techniques widely used in the digital games field.

### 3.3    Games for Health Communication and Participation

If the tendencies above reflect a stricter and more traditional understanding of health, other initiatives are emerging, with a more comprehensive view, including mental health, social determinants of health and public health. There are many inspiring games for health communication, education, and promotion, created or in development in several universities and game studios in Brazil. Until recently, however, the field lacked the official support of a public health institution, which started to change in 2016, as Oswaldo Cruz Foundation, the biggest Public health institution in Brazil, institutionally acknowledged the need to tackle health games as a public policy.

In that year, Oswaldo Cruz Foundation created a Games and Health Center, with the purpose of researching and developing games for public health. In 2017, the same institution conceded a grant to seven selected projects of health games. This initiative was specifically targeted to the foundation's employees, aiming to reveal their interest and skills in working on the subject. The development of these health games should finish in 2019 and their publication paves the way to definitively establishing health games as one of the institution's areas of research and development.

Another milestone was the publication, in 2018, of the book "The Game as a Health Practice" [32], the first about this theme in Brazil and the first book about games published by Editora Fiocruz, the publishing house of Oswaldo Cruz Foundation. This book does not cover the use of games for health in the physiological sense only, but also considering health in its many dimensions, like mental health, social determinants of health and even as means of political participation, explaining possible uses and describing real cases. It is not directed towards academics but aims to present health games and similar initiatives to health practitioners, thus helping to spread the knowledge about Games and Health among the people who more directly deal with and assist the Brazilian population.

Such initiatives mark, perhaps, the first time a public health institution officially endorses and even fosters the Games and Health field in Brazil. Due to the size and importance of Oswaldo Cruz Foundation to the field of Health in Brazil, its presence in all of the country's states, and its close connection with Brazilian Ministry of Health, it is an encouraging development to the field of Games and Health.

# 4   Challenges

Despite the thriving tendencies outlined above, there are many challenges for a broader development and adoption of games for health in Brazil. In November of 2018, during the 3rd Workshop of Games and Health (part of the Brazilian Symposium on Games and Digital Entertainment - SBGames, the biggest game conference in Latin America), researchers, professors, and health practitioners gathered to discuss the field of Games and Health, highlighting the most common obstacles.

## 4.1   Funding

The report on the Mapping of the Brazilian and Global Digital Games Industry, based on the first Census of the Brazilian Digital Games Industry [36] showed that Brazilian game companies have, as main sources of funding, the companies' own resources, their families or other individuals (64.7%), incubators (26.3%) and non-reimbursable funds (18.8%), like governmental edicts and funding from public development foundations. This points to the fact that research projects and universities are very important to the game industry in Brazil, especially when it concerns games for health. There are also associations with specific agendas that sometimes invest in such projects, but the Ministry of Health itself still rarely explores that medium [36].

The lack of reliable funding is one of the major problems pointed out by researchers. As previously described, many projects developed in Games and Health are initiatives of professors and researchers from universities, who mostly depend on public grants [15]. There is great competition with other areas of knowledge, including more established ones, which tend to obtain more funding. In addition, in many cases, funding agencies offer one-instance only grants, making it difficult to create and maintain initiatives for longer periods. It is not uncommon to see the maintenance of successful health games being interrupted due to lack of resources.

Despite that, the field is growing. In the 2013 Census, the industry declared that only 5 of the games developed, 0,4% of the total, were related to health, involving 5 companies - only 3,8% of the respondents [15]; while in 2017, there were 24 games declared (2,5%), by 20 companies (6,3%), which indicates a growth in this market, even if there were games produced in total, in that year [11].

Meanwhile, resources for Science & Technology in Brazil have been diminishing in the last years, going from R\$ 8,732 billion in 2017 to R\$ 7,823 billion in 2018, of which only R\$ 2,192 billion were ultimately available [37]. In December 2018, the Ministry of Culture, together with Ancine (Brazil's National Agency for Cinema) announced a line of investment of R\$ 45,2 million, which will be disputed by the companies now growing in the area of games in Brazil, and by researchers as well [38]. However, the new government that took office in January of 2019 has not made any specific remarks about serious games so far, prompting researchers to look for alternative ways to fund health game projects.

## 4.2   Lack of Records

Another problem that harms the progress of health games in Brazil is the lack of reliable records. In general, it is very difficult to notice a new health game, unless it becomes the subject of a journal article or conference paper.

A study from 2012 in two Brazilian academic events on the area of Informatics and Health found that the production about health games from 2002 to 2011 was still incipient - from a total of 1848, only 12 discussed serious games for health [20] Another research, conducted in three different academic databases, with the descriptors "videogame", "game", "serious game" and "educational game", Deguirmendjian et al. [19] found, among 2225 papers in Portuguese, only 23 that discussed serious games for health.

There are still few events in Brazil dedicated specifically to the area of serious games for health. One of them is the Health in Game seminars, promoted by the Oswaldo Cruz Foundation (in 2011, 2012, 2016). There is also the Games and Health Workshop, within the scope of SBGames. Many times, research about health games are published in other academic events that include serious games, especially in the areas of Computation, Informatics, Distance Education, Educational Technology, Educational Games or Communication [36]. This limits the dialogue spaces between researchers and developers, as their researches become scattered across events and areas.

Moreover, many projects are not published at all as academic research, therefore failing to provide feedback and data that could help many other projects and the field itself. Even when there is a publication, often the game in question is not detailed enough in the paper, which hinders the evolution of knowledge in the field. A recent study analyzed the health games mentioned in the conference papers of the aforementioned SBGames, revealing that many papers published about health games lack descriptions of the game mechanics and rules of the games, focusing mostly in the written and visual content [39].

## 4.3   Insufficient Testing

In many cases, the resources obtained for the projects barely allow the development of the games, making it difficult to conduct a proper evaluation of the final product, which is published without adequate tests for its contents and sometimes even for its basic workings. However, in other cases, the lack of testing cannot be blamed on lack of funds. Some health game developers seem to disregard adequate testing. Indeed, many published articles detailing games for health fail to provide testing data, focusing more on the developing stages of the games or even limiting themselves to presenting its content.

In the research of Duarte et al. [20], only one of the papers analyzed presented the validation of the use of a serious game, while 11 of them discussed only processes of development, therefore were descriptive papers, with a tendency for observation and experimental studies.

The integrative review conducted by Deguirmendjian et al. [19] found a slightly different scenario: 86,9% of the 23 papers mentioned some type of evaluation, whether structural, functional or of pedagogical or motivational suitability to the public, or even physical evaluations of players before and after playing. Those that did not present a validation process mentioned the need for future validation of quality and impact. Even though this research studied papers from more diverse sources, most of the papers were found in more recent years, especially in 2011, 2012, 2013 and 2015 [19], which points to a slight tendency towards the expansion of validation practices within the field. Nevertheless, the research identified space for theoretical deepening in the papers analyzed.

This situation creates more difficulties in the establishment of best practices in the field. Moreover, in the particular case of health games, the lack of or insufficient testing is even more damaging, since, in the field of Health, it is necessary to conduct careful trials for assessing the benefits of the interventions, an important requirement for health games gaining legitimacy before health practitioners and managers in Brazil, as it has happened abroad [40].

### 4.4 Lack of Common Vocabulary

This problem leads to research that sometimes falls back on the re-definition of terms that were already defined and being used by other researchers, as well as the misuse of terms and concepts, returning to questions that already have been resolved and mis-guiding other researchers and developers instead of being used for advancing and deepening the research and development of health games [39].

The very definition of health games presented in the 2017 Census of the Industry as "a game whose main objective is the prevention and/or treatment of physical condi-tions" [11] shows a lack of understanding the complexity of the Health field. It implies health as something limited to the physical body, disregarding the mental, economic and social factors that surround the concept [4].

In addition, since health game researchers come from different academic roots, each one brings her own way to name and refer to the same phenomena, making more difficult to share insights, establish cooperation and build a common knowledge base [39].

## 4.5 Medicalization

A problem that is not unique to health games, but can be aggravated by them, is its use for the interests of the pharmaceutical industry or health services, not exactly for the benefit of human health. It is a distortion of values of Medicine, health, and well-being, which can be called "medicalization" and "healthicization" [41]. An analysis of publications regarding the production of health games in Brazil indicated that the problem of in-game medicalization and healthicization seems to be related to the reproduction of hegemonic conceptions of health and medical interventions without a critical examination of the health approach used [17]. The problem is associated with an instrumental conception of the games themselves, designed merely as a channel for the unilateral transmission of knowledge, but incapable of promoting community participation.

Out of the field of serious games, in relation to entertainment games, medicalization manifested itself by the inclusion of "game disorder" in the 11th revision of the International Classification of Diseases by the World Health Organization. This inclusion has been criticized by many scholars, who have pointed out serious problems with the initiative, such as lack of reliable research for such classification, confusion of a symptom (irregular use of games) with its psychological causes and its use as a disguised method for oppressing and controlling vulnerable groups like children and youth [42].

As a whole, there is still a tendency to consider health as something that merely affects the body [11], or even as something that emerges from or depends on medical practice. It is safe to argue that this inhibits the development of games that explore the complexities of human health, including social, economic and political factors that influence health [42, 43]. Despite not being so visible as the other aforementioned challenges, it is necessary to avoid the medicalization perspective, since it imposes many limits to the field of Games and Health.

## 5 Looking Ahead

Each of the challenges mentioned above is far more complex than it is possible to detail in this work, requiring cooperation among those who desire to see the advancement of the field of Games and Health, in order to benefit society. These issues were heavily discussed in the 3rd Workshop of Games and Health, during the SBGames 2018. Speakers and the audience, composed mostly by game researchers and health professionals, engaged in a lively debate looking for ways to overcome such problems, outlining some initiatives to be pursued in the years to come.

It became clear, even before the first presentations, that the lack of a common vocabulary was a significant hindrance for the advancement of the field. In many cases, people described similar phenomena using different terms. Or worse, often a term had widely different meanings for different researchers, creating all sort of misinformation. For the participants present at the event, an agreement was reached on the fact that creating a common vocabulary, built upon the knowledge and research already developed in many universities, companies and research institutes, could strengthen the

Health Games field in Brazil, in alignment with the currents of thought and research abroad.

Coupled with a common vocabulary, the field of Games and Health also needs a set of standard procedures, a guide for good practices in Health Game Research and Development. Often people beginning in the field do not understand the need or reason behind some practices, like informed consent terms, submission to Ethics committees, procedural rhetoric, usability tests, and clinical trials. Assembling good practices based on research already published could provide a starting place for researchers, designers, and developers eager to create projects of games for health that consider all specificities as well as the needs for testing and recording practices and results.

Finally, the third initiative proposed was the creation of an open database for all projects in the field of Games and Health. It was clear to all participants that there are much more initiatives than one can possibly follow or even discover. Since Games and Health is a field intrinsically interdisciplinary and Brazil is a country so big and diverse, health games emerge in a multiplicity of places, and many end without notice and record, hampering the progress in the field. A database of completed and ongoing projects would draw researchers, designers, and developers closer, therefore helping to strengthen the projects developed, both from the research and the game design perspectives. It would also help to foster partnerships, which in turn would make the search for funding easier.

These three initiatives were collectively built in the first moment when a significant number of Brazilian game researchers, scholars, health professionals, and developers, representing many institutions, gathered together to discuss the situation of this newborn field of Games and Health, and plan ahead ways to evolve it. The work on these three fronts already started and, despite being directed by some volunteers, it will count with the contributions and participation of the larger community of researchers and professionals, which will provide an organic development for the field. Hopefully, such initiatives will fully develop in the next couple of years, fostering a more dynamic and prolific field of Games and Health, in the end helping to improve the health of the Brazilian population.

# References

1. Paim, J.S.: O que é o SUS. Editora Fiocruz, Rio de Janeiro (2010)
2. Lindoso, J.A.L., Lindoso, A.A.B.P.: Neglected tropical diseases in Brazil. Rev. Inst. Med. Trop. São Paulo 51, 247–253 (2009). http://www.scielo.br/scielo.php?script=sci_arttext&pid=s0036-46652009000500003&nrm=iso. Accessed 07 Jan 2010
3. Doenças negligenciadas: Estratégias do Ministério da Saúde. Rev. Saúde Pública 44, 200–202 (2010). http://www.scielo.br/scielo.php?script=sci_arttext&pid=S0034-89102010000100023&nrm=iso. Accessed 07 Jan 2010
4. Buss, P.M., Pellegrini Filho, A.: A saúde e seus determinantes sociais. PHYSIS: Rev. Saúde Coletiva 17(1), 77–93 (2007)
5. Cardoso, J.M., Araujo, I.S.D.: Comunicação e saúde, pp. 94–103. EPSJV/Fiocruz, Rio de Janeiro (2009)
6. Maio, M.C., Lima, N.T.: Forum. Twenty years of experience and the challenge with the unified national health system. Intro. Cad. Saúde Pública. 25(7), 1611–1613 (2009)

7. Ministério da Saúde: Sobre o Blog da Saúde. Blog da Saúde (2015). http://www.blog.saude. gov.br/index.php/sobre-o-blog-da-saude. Accessed 07 Jan 2010

8. Papastergiou, M.: Exploring the potential of computer and video games for health and physical education: a literature review. Comput. Educ. 53(3), 603–622 (2009). http://www. sciencedirect.com/science/article/B6VCJ-4W7HNWH-1/2/ b4cad0a437eabb6158f7419b76e50de3. Accessed 07 Jan 2010

9. Chiado, M.V.G.: 1983+1984: Quando os videogames chegaram. São Paulo (2016)

10. Birnbaum, I.: The state of PC piracy in 2016. PCGamer (2016). https://www.pcgamer.com/ the-state-of-pc-piracy-in-2016/. Accessed 07 Jan 2010

11. Sakuda, L.O., Fortim, I. (orgs.): II Censo da Indústria Brasileira de Jogos Digitais. Report, Homo Ludens (2018)

12. Fortnite: Epic Games (2017). https://www.epicgames.com/fortnite

13. League of legends: Riot Games (2009). https://na.leagueoflegends.com

14. Vasconcellos, M.S., Araujo, I.S.: Massively multiplayer online role playing games for health communication in Brazil. In: Bredl, K., Bösche, W. (eds.) Serious Games and Virtual Worlds in Education, Professional Development, and Healthcare, pp. 294–312. IGI Global, Hershey (2013)

15. Fleury, A., Sakuda, L.O., Cordeiro, J.H.D. (orgs.): I Censo da Indústria Brasileira de Jogos Digitais, com vocabulário técnico sobre a IBJD. Report, GEDIGames, NPGT-USP e BNDES (2014)

16. Fortugno, N., Zimerman, E.: Soapbox: learning to play to learn - lessons in educational game design. Gamasutra (2005). https://www.gamasutra.com/view/feature/130686/soapbox_ learning_to_play_to_learn_.php. Accessed 07 Jan 2010

17. Vasconcellos, M.S., Carvalho, F.G., Capella, M.A.M., Dias, C.M., Araujo, I.S.: A saúde na literatura acadêmica sobre jogos: Uma análise das publicações do SBGAMES. In: Proceedings do XV Simpósio Brasileiro de Jogos e Entretenimento Digital—SBGames. SBC, São Paulo, pp. 1062–1070 (2016). http://www.sbgames.org/sbgames2016/downloads/ anais/157759.pdf. Accessed 07 Jan 2010

18. Vasconcellos, M.S., Carvalho, F.G., Barreto, J.O., Atella, G.C.: As várias faces dos jogos digitais na educação. Informática na educação: teoria & prática 20(4), 203–218 (2017). http://www.seer.ufrgs.br/InfEducTeoriaPratica/article/view/77269. Accessed 22 Jan 2018

19. Deguirmendjian, S.C., Miranda, F.M., Zem-Mascarenhas, S.H.: Serious game desenvolvidos na saúde: Revisão integrativa da literatura. J. Health Inform. 8(3), 110–116 (2016)

20. Duarte, J.M., Vitti, S.R., Prado, C.S., Domenico, E.B.L., Pisa I: Revisão de serious game na área de saúde, pp. 1–6 (2012)

21. Mack, I., et al.: Chances and limitations of video games in the fight against childhood obesity - a systematic review. Eur. Eat. Disord. Rev. 25(4), 237–267 (2017)

22. Mcdonough, D.J., Pope, Z.C., Zeng, N., Lee, J.E., Gao, Z.: Comparison of college students' energy expenditure, physical activity, and enjoyment during exergaming and traditional exercise. J. clin. med. 7(11), 433–443 (2018). https://www.ncbi.nlm.nih.gov/pubmed/ 30423805. Accessed 07 Jan 2010

23. Mirza-Babaei, P., Nacke, L.E.: Older adults physical activity and exergames: a systematic review. Int. J. Hum-Comput. Interact. 35(2), 140–167 (2019). https://doi.org/10.1080/ 10447318.2018.1441253

24. Karssemeijer, E.G.A., Aaronson, J.A., Bossers, W.J.R., Donders, R., Olde Rikkert, M.G.M., Kessels, R.P.C.: The quest for synergy between physical exercise and cognitive stimulation via exergaming in people with dementia: a randomized controlled trial. Alzheimers Res. Ther. 11(1), 3 (2019). https://doi.org/10.1186/s13195-018-0454-z

25. Gonçalves, J.K.R., Dos Santos, J.R., Mota, P.S.A.: Aproximações entre os exergames e os conteúdos da educação física escolar. Rev. Saúde Fís. Mental 6(1), 74–92 (2018)

26. Pereira, J.C., Rodrigues, M.E., Campos, H.O., Dos Santos Amorim, P.R.: Exergames como alternativa para o aumento do dispêndio energético: Uma revisão sistemática. Rev. Bras. Atividade Fís. Saúde **17**(5), 332–340 (2012)

27. Ferreira, A.R., Francisco, D.J.: A implementação dos exergames no âmbito da saúde mental: percorrendo outros percursos e traçando outras formas de fazer o cuidado. Rev. Observatório **4**(4), 229–245 (2018)

28. Cestari, C.E., Cestari, T.H.: Exergames como adjuvante na interação social e na qualidade de vida de idosos: Revisão da literatura. Revista Ciência e Estudos Acadêmicos de Medicina **1** (9), 11–20 (2015)

29. Braga, R.K.L., et al.: Virtual games assets: strategy potential to promote health and combat obesity school. Motricidade **13**(1), 121–128 (2017)

30. Guedes, D.P., Guedes, J.E.R.P.: Atividade física, aptidão física e saúde. Rev. Bras. Atividade Fís. Saúde **1**(1), 18–35 (1995)

31. Caspersen, C.J.P., Kenneth, E., Christenson, G.: Physical activity, exercise, and physical fitness: definitions and distinctions for health-related research. Public Health Rep. **100**(2), 126–131 (1985)

32. Vasconcellos, M.S., Carvalho, F.G., Araujo, I.S.: O jogo como prática de saúde. Editora Fiocruz, Rio de Janeiro (2018)

33. Cristo Neto, D.V., Cristo, C.N.C., Costa, B.D.G.: Jogos eletrônicos e o controle da dor: observações em uma unidade de transplantes de órgãos sólidos e medula óssea. In: SBC, pp. 1472–1474. https://www.sbgames.org/sbgames2018/files/papers/WorkshopJogosSaude/188102.pdf?fbclid=IwAR0hFs_KEBzoEXx2HSy0h3x3ExH-5XcLIPqe5QtSWq9VQhoiM68LY7St0Uo. Accessed 07 Jan 2010

34. Hoffman, H.G., Doctor, J.N., Patterson, D.R., Carrougher, G.J., Furness III, T.A.: Virtual reality as an adjunctive pain control during burn wound care in adolescent patients. Pain **85** (1–2), 305–309 (2000)

35. Watanabe, P.: Clínicas usam realidade virtual contra medo de injeção. São Paulo (2017). https://www1.folha.uol.com.br/equilibrioesaude/2017/07/1898219-clinicas-usam-realidade-virtual-contra-medo-de-injecao.shtml. Accessed 07 Jan 2010

36. Fleury, A., Nakano, D., Cordeiro, J.: Mapeamento da Indústria Brasileira e Global de Jogos Digitais. Report, GEDIGames, NPGT-USP e BNDES (2014)

37. Câmara dos Deputados: Ciência: Problema ou saída para a crise? Câmara dos Deputados (2018). http://www2.camara.leg.br/camaranoticias/radio/materias/REPORTAGEM-ESPECIAL/552019-CIENCIA-PROBLEMA-OU-SAIDA-PARA-A-CRISE-BLOCO-1.html. Accessed 07 Jan 2010

38. Agência Nacional do Cinema. Com investimento recorde, MinC e ANCINE lançam novas linhas de financiamento para produção e para comercialização de games. Agência Nacional do Cinema (2018). https://www.ancine.gov.br/pt-br/sala-imprensa/noticias/com-investimento-recorde-minc-e-ancine-lan-am-novas-linhas-de-financiamento. Accessed 07 Jan 2010

39. Vasconcellos, M.S., Capella, M.A.M., Silva, R.C., Freire, H.G., Carvalho, F.G.: Jogando com a saúde: Uma exploração sobre a produção brasileira de jogos digitais de saúde. In: Anais do Congresso Brasileiro de Saúde Coletiva. Galoá, Campinas (2019). https://proceedings.science/saude-coletiva-2018/papers/jogando-com-a-saude--uma-exploracao-sobre-a-producao-brasileira-de-jogos-digitais-de-saude. Accessed 07 Jan 2010

40. Kato, P.M., Cole, S.W., Bradlyn, A.S., Pollock, B.H.: A video game improves behavioral outcomes in adolescents and young adults with cancer - a randomized trial. Pediatrics **122** (2), e305–e317 (2008)

41. Conrad, P.: Medicalization and social control. Ann. Rev. Sociol. **18**(1), 209–232 (1992). https://www.annualreviews.org/doi/abs/10.1146/annurev.so.18.080192.001233. Accessed 07 Jan 2010

42. Vasconcellos, M.S.: A saúde na era do jogo digital. Rio de Janeiro (2018). http://cienciahoje. org.br/artigo/a-saude-na-era-do-jogo-digital/. Accessed 07 Jan 2010
43. Aarseth, E., et al.: Scholars open debate paper on the world health organization ICD-11 gaming disorder proposal. J. Behav. Addictions **6**(3), 267–270 (2017). https://akademiai. com/doi/abs/10.1556/2006.5.2016.088. Accessed 07 Jan 2010

# Gamification and Learning: A Comparative Study of Design Frameworks

Priscilla Garone[1,2(✉)] and Sérgio Nesteriuk[2]

[1] Universidade Federal do Espírito Santo, Vitória, Brazil
prigarone@gmail.com
[2] Universidade Anhembi Morumbi, Sao Paulo, Brazil

**Abstract.** This study aims to discuss design frameworks for gamification in education and learning, in order to compare project steps and find convergences and divergences in design processes. The research was based on literature review and collected data was compared. Therefore, the study presents gamification design frameworks selected from the literature review and the results showed two sorts of frameworks: models for structural and content gamification. It was found that there are more frameworks to design structural gamification than models to design content gamification. In addition, the frameworks are divided into pre-production, production and post-production phases. The comparison of the frameworks evinced that the most notable convergence between the models is the pre-production phase, which comprises the steps of comprehension and design of the gamified system, which, in general, are more detailed. Lastly, the main divergences were found in the production and evaluation steps, with the absence or indication of how the gamified system is produced or implement and how gamification outcomes are measured.

**Keywords:** Gamification · Education · Framework comparison

## 1 Introduction

For the purpose of this study, Gamification is understood as an approach used to archive a goal (for example, stimulate and motivate the execution of a task), through the use of game design elements. The introduction and growing expansion of gamification in education and learning contexts promote critical reflection on the development of projects which change the student learning experience.

The relevance of this research is the presentation of a comparative study of the gamification design frameworks for education and learning, with the objective of pointing out similarities and contrasts as a contribution to elucidate different methods and amplify technical and practical knowledge for educational use.

The literature review aimed at data collecting about gamification in education and learning processes with bibliographical material which presents conceptual, structural and procedural definitions, in order to find information about the characteristics of the design process phases.

© Springer Nature Switzerland AG 2019
V. G. Duffy (Ed.): HCII 2019, LNCS 11582, pp. 473–487, 2019.
https://doi.org/10.1007/978-3-030-22219-2_35

The data collection occurred during March and September of 2017, in the international databases [1] and [2]. The search terms were: "gamification"; "education"; "learning"; "framework"; "model"; "design"; "designer".

The criteria for selection were to find studies addressing at least two of the following topics: (a) definition of gamification; (b) elements of gamification in educational and learning contexts; (c) frameworks for designing gamification for education and learning. Thirteen studies have been selected in this research, divided by topic (six studies about gamification in education and learning; and seven regarding gamification frameworks) (Table 1).

**Table 1.** Studies selected in the literature review about gamification in education and learning.

| Study topic | Selected studies | |
| --- | --- | --- |
| Gamification in education and learning | Deterding et al. [3]; Zichermann and Cunningham [5]; Kapp [7]; Nah et al. [10]; Kapp et al. [8]; Landers [4] | 6 |
| Gamification frameworks for education and learning | Simões et al. [11]; Landers [4]; Kim and Lee [9]; Klock et al. [13]; Urha et al. [14]; Andrade et al. [15] | 7 |

The study contains the following sections: (1) **Gamification in Education and Learning**, which presents concepts and principles of gamified systems to promote learning; (2) **Gamification Frameworks for Education and Learning**, to dissert about the models for designing, developing and applying gamification to educational and learning contexts; (3) **Results**, with the comparative study and the synthesis of the phases of the frameworks presented; and (4) **Conclusion**, for final considerations.

## 2    Gamification in Education and Learning

Gamification is explained by [3] as a term which has its origins in the digital media industry during the year 2008 and was widely adopted since 2010, coexisting with terms such as "productivity games", "funware", "behavioral games", "playful interactions", "playful design", "pervasive games", "ludification". To the authors, the term "gamification" demarks a group of phenomena not previously identified, considering the complexity of gamefulness, gameful interaction and gameful design, which differs from the concepts of playfulness, playful interaction, or design for playfulness.

The definition proposed by the authors describes gamification as "the use of game design elements in non-game contexts" [3]. From this point of view, gamification is related to gaming rather than to playing and refers to the use, to design and to elements characteristic for games, in non-game contexts, regardless of specific usage intentions.

Gamification is defined by [4] as the use of game elements, including action language, assessment, challenge, control, environment, game fiction, human interaction, immersion, and rules/goals, in order to facilitate learning process and its outcomes. The author also proposes the differentiation between gamification and serious games, by the means each engender learning. While games assume the role of instructor and provide content directly to the students, gamification, in a general way, does not seek to influence learning directly. Its goal is to enhance pre-existing instruction by changing learner's behavior and attitude.

According to the authors, although games can affect motivation, it is not its goal to do it without also providing instructional content. Thereby, "although one might claim that they learned from a game, it would generally not be valid to say that they learned from gamification" [4]. Thus, even though serious games and gamification share game design elements, the process by which those elements affect learning differ.

Gamification can mean different things, as alleged by [5]: make games to promote products and services; create virtual worlds to change behaviors; or provide a way to train people in complexes systems – gamification unites all those senses and possibilities of game in non-gaming contexts.

The authors unite the concepts as serious games, advergames[1] and games for change[2] and define gamification "the process of game-thinking and game mechanics to engage users and solve problems", applicable "to any problem that can be resolved through influencing human motivation and behavior".

Gamification definitions that are based on the mere addition of game elements in activities are criticized by [7], since those approaches are usually superficial, which do not generate learning, engagement or productive improvements.

The author defines gamification as "a careful and considered application of game thinking to solving problems and encouraging learning using all the elements of games that are appropriate". By this definition, the objective of gamification is to add game based elements to contents that usually are presented as a lecture or an online-course in order to create a gamified learning opportunity either in the form of an educational game or in the form of game-elements on top of normal tasks.

The definition presented by the author does not exclude serious games from gamification. The goal of both serious games and gamification is the same – to solve problems, engage people, and promote learning by using game thinking and mechanics. Thus, designing a game based on instructional content is the gamification of the content and the same thought processes, techniques, and approach are needed. The use of serious games are considered a form of gamification, as serious games are a specific sub-set of the meta-concept of gamification and includes the idea of adding game elements, mechanics and thinking to instructional contents [7].

According to [8], gamification can be used to motivate interaction and learning; encourage the execution of challenging tasks; achieve goals; create an opportunity for critical reflection; and change the behavior in a positive way. The authors explain that there are two types of gamification: structural gamification and content gamification.

Structural gamification refers to the application of game design elements to motivate the learner through an instructional content without changing it. It can be made by using clear goals, rewards for achievements, progression system and status, challenge and feedback.

---

[1] Advergames or advertainment are games designed for advertisement, with the specific propose of publicize a product or a service to the costumers [6].

[2] Games for Change is an initiative published on the internet, popularly known by the acronym G4C, http://www.gamesforchange.org, last accessed 2018/10/11.

Content gamification is the application of elements, mechanics and game thinking to make the content more game-like. However, this does not necessarily imply designing a full game. Content gamification provides game context or activities to the instructional content. Elements that can be used to that goal are story and narrative; challenge, curiosity and exploration; characters and avatars; interactivity, feedback and freedom to fail [8].

## 3   Gamification Frameworks for Education and Learning

Next, the selected frameworks for designing gamification for education and learning will be presented with its detailed phases and purposes.

According to [8], there are two types of motivation to be considered while designing a gamified system: extrinsic and intrinsic. The extrinsic motivation is used to increase the satisfaction and dedicated time to complete a task; strengthen the perception of freedom of action; keep focused attention for short periods of time; or to motivate the student when initially they view the activity as low value.

On the other hand, intrinsic motivation is based on auto determination and autonomy, competency and relatedness, which can be used to give the student the sense of choice and control; increase his confidence when challenged to accomplish a goal; provide a way to master a skill or content; reward gradual and final learning improvements; help the student to feel connected to others by using social interactions, such as leaderboards or challenging other students.

**Table 2.** Elements of mechanics, dynamics and aesthetics (Based on [9]).

| Mechanics | Points, levels, leader board, goal, badges, quests, onboarding, virtual items, feedback |
|---|---|
| Dynamics | Dynamic system, pacing, reward scheduling, time-based pattern & system, progressive unlock, appointments |
| Aesthetics | Love, beauty, delight, honor, thrill, surprise, envy, connection, comedy |

One of the recurring approaches in literature is MDA (mechanics, dynamics, and aesthetics) [5]. The authors explain that this approach is used to create an interrelation between the elements of game design elements in a non-gaming context. Examples of game design mechanics, dynamics and aesthetics are mentioned by [9] (Table 2).

The Dynamical Model for Gamification of Learning purposed by [9] is a framework for structural and content gamification, based on four game characteristics: challenge, fantasy, control and curiosity, to make the educational and learning process more dynamical. Each characteristic is related to a game design element of mechanics, dynamics or aesthetics (Fig. 1).

The authors purpose relations between the characteristics: **control** is the efficacy and core of the gamification, in which **curiosity** (with elements of dynamics and aesthetics) needs to be greater than the **challenge** (that has elements of mechanics and dynamics). However, with time, motivation tends to decrease and the proportion

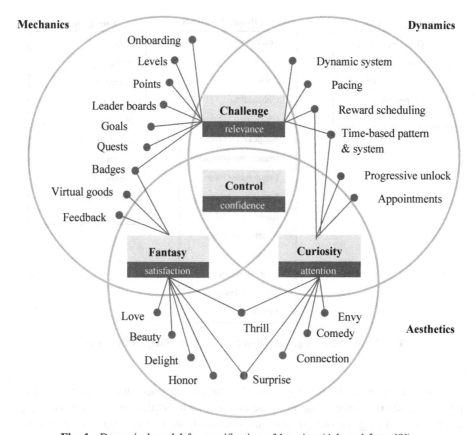

**Fig. 1.** Dynamical model for gamification of learning (Adapted from [9]).

between **challenge** and **fantasy** (which has elements of aesthetics and mechanics) must be maintained in order to guarantee the efficacy of the gamified system.

Gamification for education is discussed by [10] based on three principles:

1. **Gamification:** Driven by goal orientation, achievement, reinforcement, competition and fun orientation. These principles are part of the gamification process and help the student understand his tasks, keep focus, be motivated by his accomplishments and achievements.
2. **System design elements:** Elements such as leaderboards, levels, points, onboarding, challenges, badges, feedback, social engagement loops, social dynamics, rules, visual, avatars, customization, narrative, and role-play are important and the overall experience of a game depends on how well the system design can enhance user experience.
3. **Engagement:** Refer to outcomes of gamification, with cognitive absorption, in a state of deep attention and involvement. It includes recency, frequency, duration, virality, ratings, curiosity, control, temporal dissociation, immersion, and enjoyment (Fig. 2).

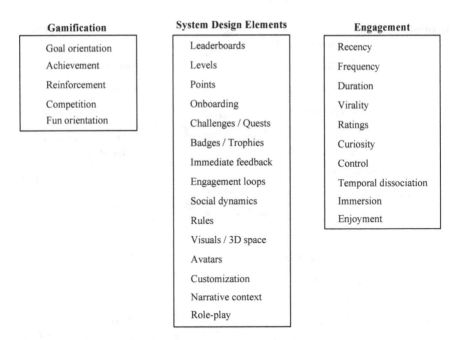

**Fig. 2.** Synthesis of gamification for education (Adapted from [10]).

The Reference Model for Applying Gamification in Education suggested by [11] present phases of characterization of the context; identification of instructional objectives; selection of game design elements; data analysis; and insertion of content into activities.

1. **Characterization of non-ludic context:** involves the identification of the characteristics of the context, the activities; the definition of desired behaviors and user profile.
2. **Identification of the objectives:** is to decide the instructional objectives according to the desired behaviors.
3. **Game design elements selection:** is to define components which provide feedback and rewards, social interaction, and game experience.
4. **Data analysis:** collect and analysis data in conform to the objectives; evaluate and share outcomes.
5. **Insertion of contents in the activities:** determination and insertion of contents according to the data analysis, outcomes and context (Fig. 3).

The authors explain game design elements for the gamified system: **feedback**, which provides answer to the actions materialized with **rewards**. **Social interaction** occurs by the collaboration and sharing, while **fun** must be present to engage the user. The component **game experience** has the function of keeping the user engaged along the course, whilst the economy establish rules for virtual goods trade and progressive rewards define the periodicity and acquisition criteria (Table 3).

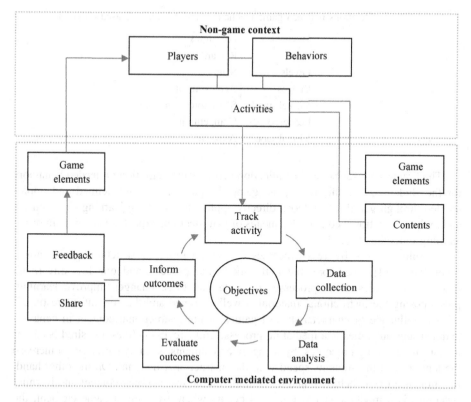

**Fig. 3.** Gamification for education cycle (Taken from [11], translated by the authors).

**Table 3.** Game design elements (Taken from [11], translated by the authors).

| Fundamental components | | Game elements |
|---|---|---|
| Flow and fun | Feedback and rewards | Points, leaderboards, progress bards, badges, trophies |
| | Social interaction (friends) | Share badges, invite friends, give/demand/swap virtual goods |
| | Game experience (gameplay) | Levels, intermediate objectives, clear goals, repeat after fail is fun (fun failure), rules, virtual economy, and progressive rewards |

The Framework for Social Gamification purposed by [12] aims to create appropriate challenges to the student according to his level; establish simple goals and offer different ways to achieve the objectives; choose proper game mechanics to the activities; consider fail as part of the process and help the student to deal with it; allow the student to assume other identities and roles; allow the student to identify and keep track of his progress; and use competition to stimulate positive behaviors. The authors interrelated game mechanics and dynamics to achieve needed attitudes (Table 4).

**Table 4.** Relations between game mechanics and dynamics (Based on [12]).

| Mechanics | Dynamics |
|---|---|
| Points | Rewards |
| Levels | Status |
| Badges | Achievement |
| Virtual goods | Self-expression |
| Leaderboards | Competition |
| Virtual Goods | Altruism |

The Framework for Social Gamification involves the definition of needed behaviors for the student. After this phase, the game design elements are defined and implemented through gamification tools, directly applied to the social learning environment and to the instructional content. By means of gamification, expected behaviors improve learning outcomes (Fig. 4).

Learning occurs by two processes in gamification, in structural gamification, according to [4]: one more direct, the mediating process, and one less direct, the moderating process. Both processes presume that these changes improve learning, presupposing the instructional material is well designed and the content interesting.

The influence of characteristics of games or the instructional content in behavior and learning outcomes is a mediating process. This process defines a desired behavior to improve learning outcomes, by using game elements, such as narrative, to increase the amount of time students spend with the instructional material. On the other hand, the influence of the behavior and the attitude on the instructional content and learning outcomes is a moderating process. This occurs when, by using a game element, the student motivation increases (Fig. 5).

The Conceptual Model for Gamification in Virtual Learning Environments purposed by [13] consists in defining four dimensions to structural gamification: "Why", "Who", "What" and "How", in order to answer questions to apply gamification.

- **Why?:** refers to wanted behaviors, which can be related to theoretical activities (accessing materials); practical (exercise and tasks; increase the performance in tasks); social (forum activity). And related to the system (increasing the amount of time using the system and frequency of access).
- **Who?:** the users of the system, mainly teachers and students.
- **What?:** define which system components will be gamified.
- **How?:** determine which game elements will be used to increase motivation and achieve wanted behaviors in who will interact with the gamified system (Fig. 6).

To understand user profiles and adopt compatible strategies, the authors use the taxonomy of Richard Bartle, which divides players into four categories: achievers (players who want to achieve goals in the game); socializers (those who like to interact with other players); explorers (players who enjoy exploration and discovery through the game world); and killers (players who are driven by competition and winning). The authors use this taxonomy as a strategy of the phase "**Who?**" to identify users profile with the use of surveys and questionnaires. There may be mixes profiles, which can benefit of the following elements:

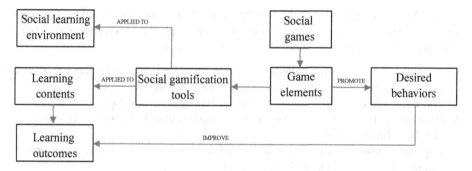

**Fig. 4.** Framework for social gamification (Taken from [12]).

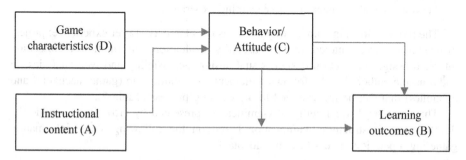

**Fig. 5.** Theory of gamified learning. The sequences (D, C, B) and (A, C, B) are mediating processes. The influence of C in (A, B) is a moderating process. Directional arrows indicate theorized path of causality (Taken from [4]).

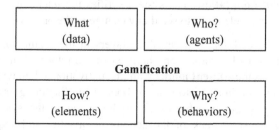

**Fig. 6.** Dimensions of the conceptual model for gamification in virtual learning environments (Taken from [13], translated by the authors).

- **Achievers:** points, levels and badges.
- **Socializers:** communication tools such as forums and chat.
- **Explorers:** hidden challenges.
- **Killers:** ranking, leaderboards.

The Model for Introduction of Gamification into Learning purposed by [14] presents and approach based on the phases of analysis, planning, development, implementation and evaluation to apply structural gamification.

1. **Analysis:** involves data colleting about pedagogical and technological issues, design, administration, people, learning material and gamification.
2. **Planning:** phase to define what, when and how will be developed.
3. **Development:** step in which the project is implemented in the virtual environment and the solution is tested.
4. **Implementation:** phase in which the solution is presented to the users and is monitored for adaptation with user feedback.
5. **Evaluation:** is the verification of the satisfaction and motivation of the user with the system to assess if the objectives of the project were fulfilled, verify the efficiency of the system, and to check the user learning experience.

The process flows in a linear way and consider elements of user experience: project management, user-centered design, usability evaluation, information architecture, interface design, interaction design, visual design, accessibility and web analytics. In addition, the authors list the following elements of gamification (game mechanics and dynamics) that can be incorporated to the learning process (Table 5).

The Framework for Intelligent Gamification presented by [15] aims to guide the development of structural gamification based on the following steps: information gathering, operation, assessment and adaptation.

1. **Information gathering:** data colleting about player profile, his psychological and behavioral attributes, gamification, psychological and interaction patterns.
2. **Operation:** adaptation of the interface to the game design elements provided by the student profile.
3. **Assessment and adaptation:** The system verifies the interactions of the students and the chosen game elements to see if any change in the process is needed (Fig. 7).

According to the authors, there are three layers in the Framework for Intelligent Gamification: the layer of gamification, the layer of the tutor and the data layer.

The data layer has the **student model** with his motivational, behavioral patterns, his attitudes, habits, interaction and information about his profile; the **gamification model**, with game mechanics and possible events to be added to the system, **interaction pattern** expected, to keep track of the actions in quantity and sequence; and the **psychological pattern** which provides information of the personality of the student during tasks.

The gamification layer refers to the interaction with the student to accomplish the motivational needs by the use of the operational modules for **assessment**, which analyses the actions of the student and make adaptations to the system; the **controller** component that establish data crossing in order to customize the gamification; and the **reasoner**, which evaluate system data and the interactions of the students to compare to the information pattern in user profile, interaction and psychological patterns.

Lastly, tutor layer provides decisions to provide better content and gamification customization according to the performance of the students.

**Table 5.** Gamification elements in learning (Adapted from [14]).

| Elements of gamification in learning | Game mechanics | Game dynamics |
|---|---|---|
| Rule-based system | Points | Rewards |
| Clear goals | Badges | Status |
| Small tasks | Levels | Achievements |
| Immediate Feedback | Challenges | Competition |
| Positive reinforcement | Virtual goods | Altruism |
| Rewards for accomplishing tasks | Leaderboards | |
| Measurable progressive challenge | Gifts | |
| Story behind | | |
| Voluntary participation | | |

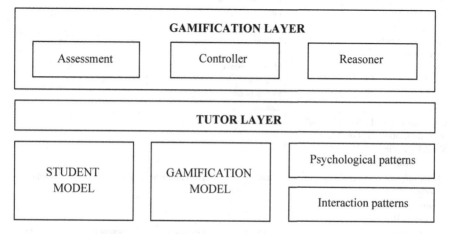

**Fig. 7.** Framework for intelligent gamification (Adapted from [15]).

# 4   Results

Based on the literature review, it was observed that frameworks, in a general way, are focused on structural gamification. Only one framework of the selected literature [9] meets the requirements to design both structural and content gamification.

During the framework comparison, it was noted the following phases and steps:
**Pre-production:**

1. Comprehension: step to analyze the context, user profile, technology and to identify the design needs, noted by the terms: context characterization; identify objectives; "what?, who?, why? how?"; data analysis; information gathering.
2. Design: includes defining the concept and the design of the gamification, with the determination of the behaviors to be achieved through the use of game design elements, reported as: insert content; select elements of games; define behavior, game elements and learning content; define behaviors, characteristics of games,

**Table 6.** Comparison between the nomenclature and phases of frameworks for designing gamification for education and learning.

| | Pre-production | | Production | Post-production | |
|---|---|---|---|---|---|
| | Comprehension | Design | Development | Application | Evaluation |
| Dynamical model for gamification of learning [9] | - | Define elements of challenge, fantasy and curiosity | - | - | - |
| Reference Model for Applying Gamification in Education [11] | Context characterization, identify objectives, data analysis | Insert content, select elements of games | - | Track activity | Evaluate outcomes |
| Model for social Gamification [12] | - | Define behavior, game elements and learning content | Implementation | Implementation | - |
| Theory of gamified learning [4] | - | Define behaviors, characteristics of games, instructional content | - | - | - |
| Conceptual Model for Gamification in Virtual Learning Environments [13] | What?, who? how? why? | What? how? | - | - | - |
| Model for introduction of gamification into learning [14] | Analysis | Planning | Development | Implementation | Evaluation |
| Framework for Intelligent Gamification [15] | Information gathering | Information gathering, operation | Operation | Operation | Assessment and adaptation |

instructional content; "what? how?"; define elements of challenge, fantasy and curiosity; planning; information gathering; operation.

**Production:**

3. Development: involve the production of the gamified system in which the game design elements are implemented or the application of those elements in an existing learning system, observed by the use of the terms: implementation; development; operation.
4. Application: step in which the gamified system is used by the students, verified by the terms: track activity; implementation; operation.

**Post-production:**

5. Evaluation: phase to verify the learning outcomes from the gamification use, noted by the use of the terms: evaluate outcomes; assessment and adaptation.

It was noted that some frameworks to design gamification are focused in determining the behaviors and goals to achieve by motivating students and defining game design elements for engagement. Those definitions occur in the pre-production, during the design phase.

In addition, some frameworks do not cover phases of production and post-production, lacking some steps of production, application and evaluation of the gamified solution. Hence, the identification that evaluation occurring only at the end of the process is problematic for the adaptation for learning. Those findings may indicate that the participation of the designer, teacher and student in the design process is limited.

The following table presents the comparison of the phases and its terminologies of the selected frameworks extracted from the literature review (Table 6).

# 5 Conclusion

The literature review indicates that there is no agreement by the consulted authors about the definition and reach of gamification in education – if the use of game elements which make the instructional content more game-like is or not gamification. This discussion can be taken to the epistemological field to confer if the magical circle[3] is considered to be an essential game element or not[4]. It is relevant to ponder that in the hypothesis of the gamification space does not look like a game, it is still a closed place, apart from the ordinary world. Thus, one of the most cited gamification characteristics – the use of game elements, is important in motivating actions and promoting behaviors. Based on this, it is possible to drive students to immersion in the gamification space during the process. So, it is possible to allege that the circle – as a closed space, isolated, in which some rule-based activities are practiced – still exists, either as a virtual learning environment or an application.

Nevertheless, studies have been published about both biases (structural and content gamification). The literature review of the frameworks showed that the majority of the models are for structural gamification design – although there are also models to design both structural and content gamification such as [9], and some authors report gamification design processes as game-based learning design processes [8] as well.

The identification of the phases of the frameworks for designing gamification for education and learning and its comparison was essential to comprehend the process. The gamification process concentrate efforts in the pre-production phase, especially during the design step. The most impacting lacunas were found in the production and post-production, with lack of application and evaluation procedures.

---

[3] The magic circle, in the context of play, according to [16], is a temporary world within the ordinary world, isolated hedged round, within which special rules obtain. This concept was expanded to the digital media by [17].

[4] Divergent points of view about this issue can be found in [18–22].

The literature review evinced that gamification for education and learning can be designed through many different approaches and methods. Lastly, the consulted authors agree that it is the designer's responsibility in collaboration with teachers and tutors to plan a model of gamification according to the learning context and user profile that may engage and help the student to reduce frustration of failure during the learning process by recognizing efforts through the use of elements available in the gamified system.

# References

1. ScienceDirect. https://www.sciencedirect.com. Accessed 10 Nov 2017
2. SciELO. http://www.scielo.org. Accessed 10 Nov 2017
3. Deterding, S., Dixon, D., Khaled, R., Nacke, L.: From game design elements to gamefulness: defining gamification. In: Proceedings of the 15th International Academic Mindtrek Conference: Envisioning Future Media Environments, pp. 9–15. ACM, New York (2011)
4. Landers, R.N.: Developing a theory of gamified learning: linking serious games and gamification of learning. Simul. Gaming 45(6), 752–768 (2014)
5. Zichermann, G., Cunningham, C.: Gamification by Design: Implementing Game Mechanics in Web and Mobile Apps. O'Reilly Media Inc., Sebastopol (2011)
6. Novak, J.: Game Development Essentials: An Introduction. Cengage Learning, Clifton Park (2011)
7. Kapp, K.M.: The Gamification of Learning and Instruction: Game-Based Methods and Strategies for Training and Education. Wiley, San Francisco (2012)
8. Kapp, K.M., Blair, L., Mesch, R.: The Gamification of Learning and Instruction Fieldbook: Ideas into Practice. John Wiley & Sons Inc., San Francisco (2014)
9. Kim, J.T., Lee, W.-H.: Dynamical model for gamification of learning (DMGL). Multimedia Tools Appl. 74(19), 8483–8493 (2015)
10. Nah, F.H., Telaprolu, V.R., Rallapalli, S., Venkata, P.R.: Gamification of education using computer games. In: Yamamoto, S. (ed.) HIMI 2013. LNCS, vol. 8018, pp. 99–107. Springer, Heidelberg (2013). https://doi.org/10.1007/978-3-642-39226-9_12
11. Simões, J., Redondo, R., Vilas, A., Aguiar, A.: Proposta de modelo de referência para aplicação de gamification em ambientes de aprendizagem social. In: Proceedings of the VIII International Conference on ICT in Education, Braga, Portugal, pp. 1117–1128 (2013)
12. Simões, J., Redondo, R.D., Vilas, A.F.: A social gamification framework for a K-6 learning platform. Comput. Hum. Behav. 29(2), 345–353 (2012)
13. Klock, A.C.T., Cunha, L.F., Gasparini, I.: A conceptual model for the gamification of virtual learning environments. Remote 3(1), 1–10 (2015)
14. Urh, M., Vukovic, G., Jereb, E.: The model for introduction of gamification into e-learning in higher education. Proc.-Soc. Behav. Sci. 197, 388–397 (2015)
15. Andrade, F.R.H., Mizoguchi, R., Isotani, S.: The bright and dark sides of gamification. In: Micarelli, A., Stamper, J., Panourgia, K. (eds.) ITS 2016. LNCS, vol. 9684, pp. 176–186. Springer, Cham (2016). https://doi.org/10.1007/978-3-319-39583-8_17
16. Huizinga, J.: Homo Ludens Ils 86. Routledge, London (2014)
17. Salen, K., Tekinbaş, K.S., Zimmerman, E.: Rules of Play: Game Design Fundamentals. MIT Press, Cambridge (2004)
18. Juul, J.: Half-Real: Video Games Between Real Rules and Fictional Worlds. MIT Press, Cambridge (2011)

19. Calleja, G.: Erasing the magic circle. In: Sageng, J.R., Fossheim, H.J., Larsen, T.M. (eds.) The Philosophy of Computer Games. POET, vol. 7, pp. 77–91. Springer, New York (2012). https://doi.org/10.1007/978-94-007-4249-9_6
20. Zimmerman, E.: Jerked around by the magic circle: clearing the air ten years later. Eric Zimmerman Publications (2012). http://www.ericzimmerman.com/publications. Accessed 11 Nov 2018
21. McGonigal, J.: I'm not playful, I'm gameful. In: Walz, S.P., Deterding, S. (eds.) The Gameful World: Approaches, Issues, Applications. The MIT Press, Cambridge (2014)
22. Stenros, J.: In defence of a magic circle: the social, mental and cultural boundaries of play. In: Transactions of the Digital Games Research Association, vol. 1, no. 2 (2014)

# Follow Me:
## The Impact of Opinion Majorities in Social Networks and the Role of Digital Maturity

Patrick Halbach[✉], Laura Burbach, Martina Ziefle, and André Calero-Valdez

Human-Computer Interaction Center, RWTH Aachen University,
Campus-Boulevard 57, 52074 Aachen, Germany
{halbach,burbach,ziefle,calero-valdez}@comm.rwth-aachen.de,
http://www.comm.rwth-aachen.de

**Abstract.** The emergence of social media platforms like Facebook and their success in connecting people changed not only the way people interact and socialize, but also allows for new forms of spreading opinion. The obstacles to share opinions and reaching many known and unknown others, decreased noticeably, bringing up an abundance of opinions on diverse topics. We investigated the interplay of the spiral of silence and the bandwagon effect in online contexts and performed a web survey with 163 participants, confronting them with opinion majorities in user comments on four diverse topics. Our results show, that both phenomena reoccur in online contexts. However, they were not traceable to our examined user factors. This indicates, that a large proportion of users could fall for online bandwagon effects and the spiral of silence.

**Keywords:** Spiral of silence · Bandwagon effect · Opinion change · Opinion majorities · Digital maturity · Human factors

## 1 Introduction

The internet simplifies the expression of opinion noticeably, as it gives the opportunity to spread content all over the world with a few clicks. Social media platforms such as Facebook serve as a source of information and possibility to share user content simultaneously [18]. Besides posting about daily life, social networking sites are also used for sharing individual opinions. Here, they introduce some simplifications compared to face-to-face communication due to their online context [5]. Simultaneously, platforms like Facebook are used more frequently by news organizations to share their media content, giving their followers the opportunity to conveniently express their opinion by marking the news post with a likes or commenting on them.

Hence, the topical posts in the users' news feeds are accompanied by a variety of opinions, which can influence the behavior of users regarding their participation in online discussions [16]. Majorities in opinion distributions can trigger the

© Springer Nature Switzerland AG 2019
V. G. Duffy (Ed.): HCII 2019, LNCS 11582, pp. 488–500, 2019.
https://doi.org/10.1007/978-3-030-22219-2_36

same influential effects as in offline contexts and may lead to silencing minority opinions, although the strength of this effect can differ [19].

In this way, perceptions of public opinion can be manipulated, as social network users are rarely able to verify the authenticity of other users' comments and further factors like the dissemination of disinformation through social bots emerge [20]. Altogether, the user can be tempted to change their opinion based on wrong assumptions, as it possibly happened after the Brexit debate [3].

Our exploratory approach examines the spiral of silence and the bandwagon effect in online social networks with regard to several user factors such as age, gender, personality traits, and social media expertise. In the following, the theoretical background of those effects and their relevance for current political affairs is described.

## 2    Related Work

In terms of opinion majorities, multiple phenomena interact that can influence the user's perception and evaluation of opinions on social network sites (SNS). Current research in particular considers the effects of the so-called *spiral of silence* and the *bandwagon heuristic*, which will be introduced with its relevant factors for our research in the following.

### 2.1    Spiral of Silence

The theory of the spiral of silence builds upon the fear of an individual to get isolated from a group with their minority opinion because of nonconformity in relation to the accepted public opinion [15]. This leads to muting divergent opinions of minority groups and enforcing a public opinion that is accepted by the whole group. This effect also occurs in online social networks like Facebook, where the users opinion concerning a topical post can be articulated through comments or reactions. However, there are certain particularities to consider, such as the change of privacy in online-contexts, the role of network size, and the high diversity of available opinions [7, 1420ff]. Kwon et al. found, that social network users in particular are afraid of relationship-specific isolation. They fear *isolation from offline contacts* and *isolation through breaking weak ties* when participating in a political online discussion and being confronted with diverse opinions. They further argued, that their measured willingness to self-censor is mostly determined by the uncertainty about the users opinion rather than of the wish for fitting into the social norm [7, 1430].

More concretely, Gearhart et al. state that the effects on opinion expression in social networks are consonant with the theoretical assumptions of the spiral of silence theory, as for example users who perceive more similar minded opinions are more highly motivated to share their own opinion than others who notice predominantly contradictory opinions [4,27]. Especially related to Facebook, they valued the reactions through likes or comments as either positive or negative influence on the self-censorship of a user. In line with other research, Gearhart et al. stated that if one receives positive feedback repeatedly for his input, they are also more willing to react positively to other users' posts [2]. On the other hand side they discovered, that the use of SNS in general alone increases the user's motivation for opinion sharing and lowers the ignorance of posts. This is interpreted as an effect of the lower perceived privacy in SNS environments [4].

Neubaum et al. investigated the implications of the fear of isolation on the user's attention for opinion cues. In their experiment they found evidence for a higher attention regarding opinions in user comments, when users show a stronger fear of isolation [14]. It could also be shown, that a perceived public opinion was constructed on the basis of user comments rather than on numerical reactions such as Facebook likes of a post. They conclude, that there is a relationship between the perceived user's opinions online and the perception of a public opinion in the real world [14]. Further effects on real world behavior were indicated by Kim, who inferred from the spiral of silence online to less political participation and opinion expression offline, especially for users with low levels of partisan belief [6]. This underpins the relevance for conducting research about the spiral of silence on Facebook, as it seems to gain influence on political participation processes and hereby also might alter the flows in our democracy.

## 2.2 The Bandwagon Effect

The so-called bandwagon effect was first defined by Leibenstein in 1950 and was referred to as the individual's lower or higher demand of a commodity directly connected to the appropriate demand of all other individuals regarding this commodity [11]. This definition resurfaces in online contexts as for instance, Lee et al. found, that the opinion majorities occurring in social media posts are skewed by the bandwagon effect. This effect shows its impact unattached to a specific topic area [10]. They argue, that the number of comments is utilized by the users for indicating an opinion majority, where not enough time has passed for the rise of an opinion majority.

Sundar et al. could show, that this effect also plays an important role for valuing the credibility of news articles, as users relied more on the articles chosen by other users rather than those chosen by experts [21]. Compared to other criteria for evaluating the quality of a news article, the bandwagon heuristic is competing against the freshness heuristic, which gives higher value to newer articles, and supports the credibility of an article with a sense of external validation [23]. Sundar et al. see this bandwagon heuristic also cued by Web 2.0 features like user-based recommendation algorithms that are used by online retailers and mechanisms for recommending the most shared articles on a news website [22].

Several researchers also examined the influence of the bandwagon effect on voting behavior. An early approach on measuring the mediating effects of the bandwagon was taken by Zech et al., who attested its impact on voters. Holding other influencing factors constant, they showed that users change their vote to a general favored candidate at each cost [26]. More recently, also Morton et al. were able to validate decreased participation and the occurrence of a bandwagon effect for elections depending on prior knowledge of possible outcomes through accessing exit polls. Voters who obtain this additional information about possible favorites during an election tend to be affected either by the bandwagon vote switching effect and vote contrary to their preferences or by the bandwagon turnout effect and only participate in the vote if their favored candidate is about to win [13].

Van der Meer et al. substantiate these findings by performing a large-scale survey experiment and found that not the result of an exit poll is the decision maker for appearing bandwagon effects, but the accentuation of which candidate is gaining the power to win the vote [12].

In conclusion, also the bandwagon effect plays an important role in democratic decision processes and will therefore be further object of investigation in our research.

### 2.3 Opinion Majorities in Social Media

We want to explore the interplay of the two previously introduced factors with concrete regard to perceived opinion majorities in posts in social networking sites, which arise through polarizing user comments on diverse topical posts. Previous research indicated, that dissonant user comments regarding a news article lead to higher distrust in the reliability of the news article [8], whereas positive comments were not beneficial for the trustworthiness [24].

It was also repeatedly shown, that comments have a higher impact on the reader's evaluation of news articles than the number of likes of a certain post [14, 24], wherefore we concentrated on user comments as influencing factor.

The following chapter will introduce the utilized research methods for obtaining further insights into opinion change behavior on the basis of influential user comments.

## 3 Method

To take a closer look on the previously described effects, we chose an empirical approach and conducted an online questionnaire for examining possible influences on opinion formation.

### 3.1 Online Questionnaire

After giving a brief welcome with stating the survey topic and informing participants about their anonymity and the duration of the questionnaire, the questionnaire started with requesting demographic factors such as age and gender. Afterwards, information about the social media habits and personality traits of our participants were collected. In the second part of the survey, we simulated opinion majorities and evaluated their effect on opinion change of the participants.

The social media habits were investigated by asking the users about their active use of social media services on the basis of six concrete examples (Facebook, Twitter, Instagram, Google Plus, Snapchat, Youtube) and their frequency of social media use in general (providing six answers from *multiple times a day* to *monthly*). In both cases, the users were allowed to give an additional free text answer.

We also wanted to assess the effect of personality on the user behavior in online social networks and therefore measured the Big Five personality traits *extraversion, openness* and *neuroticism.* Here, we provided a six-point Likert scale (from 1 = fully disagree to 6 = fully agree) instead of the originally used five-point scale to stay consistent with the previous questions.

**Fig. 1.** Requesting the initial opinion in form of a facebook post

For simulating opinion majorities in the context of online social networks, we chose four concrete questions:

1. Would you pay for using public toilets?
2. Do you agree with a tax reduction for healthy food and a tax rise for unhealthy food?
3. Do you like Christiano Ronaldo?

4. Do you agree with an obligation for installing smoke detectors in flats and houses?

These questions had the purpose to cover, on the one hand mainly neutral topics for which we expect that no polarized opinions exist. On the other hand, also topics were chosen that could involve clear opinions of the participants.

After a short introduction to our scenario that explained the social media context of the following tasks, a Facebook post was shown to the participants for each question containing a topic-related picture next to the initial question (see Fig. 1). The question would ask them whether they would agree or disagree with the opinion. Afterwards, these posts were presented again and now consisted of five additional comments from anonymized users.

By referring to their initial opinion, four of the comments contradicted the participants' opinion and only one of them matched it. Here, they were asked to choose the comment which they would most likely agree with. Those comments contained both rational and emotional arguments for and against the particular topic. The order of the comments was randomized for each participant to avoid possible sequence effects.

Finally, the participants had the possibility to leave further comments regarding the questionnaire. Our data was collected in December 2017 in Germany. Participants were acquired by sharing the hyperlink of the survey through mailing lists and social media.

### 3.2 Statistical Analysis

After the survey stage, the collected data was analyzed using IBM SPSS Statistics v24. We wanted to detect opinion changes and also their directions (from agree to disagree or reverse). Group differences were tested using T-tests for independent samples. Besides gender, we also performed group comparisons depending on the frequency of internet use and therefore separated the participants between those who answered to use social media services multiple times a day and the others who stated a lower usage. We chose a level of significance at $\alpha = .05$.

The influence of age and the measured personality traits on the opinion change behavior was examined by calculating Pearson correlation coefficients.

## 4 Results

In order to understand how our participants responded we first look into a descriptive statistics to characterize our sample. Next, we test differences and associations using both t-tests and correlations.

### 4.1 Sample Description

Our sample comprised of 163 participants in total of whom 60% were women and 40% were men. The mean age of the participants was 27.8 years ($SD = 9.37$) with a range from 16 to 77 between the youngest and oldest participant.

Regarding the social media expertise, Facebook was the most used social media service by our participants, followed by Youtube and Instagram (see Fig. 2). Each participant indicated to use at least one of the provided services and the mean amount of used services was 2.7 ($SD = 1.06$). 87% of the sample stated that they are using such services daily or even multiple times a day. Thus, it can be said, that our sample is very experienced in using social media services.

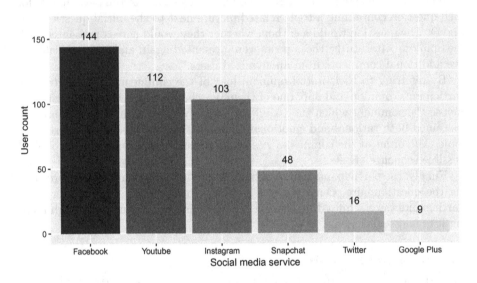

**Fig. 2.** Social media services used by the participants ($N = 163$)

We examined the personality of the participants by using the Big Five BFI-10 item set for the personality traits extraversion, openness, and neuroticism. The corresponding constructs consisted of 2 items each and showed useful reliability coefficients with exception of the construct for openness (see Table 1). Nevertheless, it will be used for further analysis, because the low reliability can be an effect of the imbalance of the sample regarding the age distribution compared to the sample used for standardizing the constructs. The values for extraversion and openness were slightly above the scale mean, whereas the value for neuroticism was subjacent.

**Table 1.** Dispersion and reliability of the Big Five items

|                  | Mean | Standard deviation | Reliablity    |
|------------------|------|--------------------|---------------|
| Big5 Neuroticism | 3.1  | 1.02               | $\alpha = .74$ |
| Big5 Extraversion| 4.3  | 1.02               | $\alpha = .73$ |
| Big5 Openness    | 4.4  | 0.92               | $\alpha = .39$ |

Concerning the initial opinion of the participants regarding the presented topics, the obligatory installation of smoke detectors gained the highest consistency of opinions. From our participants 88% agreed that it would be useful to make the installation of smoke detectors in flats and houses obligatory, whereas 12% were against it. The other questions showed weaker tendencies for one common opinion (see Fig. 3).

## 4.2   Opinion Change Behavior

The second round of the experiment, where the topics were shown with additional user comments, revealed interesting insights into the influence of majorities on the personal opinion.

We could show, that for all of the topics some participants tended to change their opinion because of a majority of comments with contradictory opinions. The highest amount of opinion change could be detected for the topics of usage fees for public toilets and the taxation of unhealthy food, whereas regarding the obligation of smoke detectors installation the fewest participants changed their opinion (see Fig. 3).

Falling back on paired-samples t-tests for comparing the initial opinion with the opinion influenced by the majorities shows, that the overall acceptance for usage fees for public toilets increases from initial ($M = 1.6$, $SD = 0.49$) to influenced opinion ($M = 1.9$, $SD = 0.34$, $t(162) = -5.1$, $p < .001$). In contrast, the opinion for taxation differences depending on food healthiness of food decreased significantly from the initial measure above mean acceptance ($M = 1.6$, $SD = 0.48$) to less acceptance ($M = 1.5$, $SD = 0.50$) after being confronted with the majority of contradictory opinions ($t(162) = 3.0$, $p < .01$). The opinion distribution regarding the topics Ronaldo and obligation of smoke detectors did not change significantly.

The direction of opinion change differed depending on the particular topic and could not be generalized. For the topics 1 and 3 the majority of the opinion changers switched from disagreeing to agreeing. For topics 2 and 4 it was the other way around (see Fig. 4).

Summarizing, only 14% of the participants did not change their opinion on any topic. A total of 72% are switching one or two times to the opinion majority and 13% withdraw their own opinion three or more times.

## 4.3   Influences on Opinion Change

We investigated the influence of age, gender, personality traits, and social media expertise as possible factors influencing the strength of the bandwagon effect.

Age and social media expertise did not show a relation with joining the opinion majority in our sample. Gender affected the opinion change for the topic of usage fees for public toilets. Concerning the public toilets, men changed their opinion significantly more often than women ($t(161) = 2.2$, $p < .05$).

The Big Five personality traits neuroticism, extraversion, and openness did not reveal arguable links to our research subject.

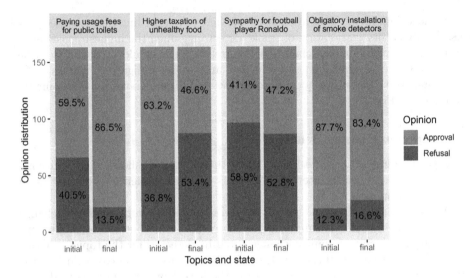

**Fig. 3.** Initial and final opinion distributions regarding the presented topics ($N = 163$)

## 5  Discussion

In our research, we focused our design on concrete conditions and wanted to explore influence factors on the user's opinion through opinion majorities. The taken approach aimed at implementing the theoretical concepts of the spiral of silence and facilitating the bandwagon effect for manipulating the user's decision making on various topics. Through presenting a majority of opposing comments after asking for an initial opinion, we could lead 86% of the participants to rethink their opinion and join the majority for at least one of the topics.

The chosen topics varied in terms of importance and prior opinion accordance. While almost 90% agreed to the obligation for installing smoke detectors, only about 40% indicated sympathy for the football player Ronaldo. This shows, that our topics covered diverse importance and relevance for our sample. While those two topics reached only marginal and not significant changes of opinion distribution, the other two topics concerning usage fees for public toilets and additional taxation of unhealthy food, obtained significant changes in opinion distribution through showing a majority of contradictory opinions. This could be a sign for differing decisiveness regarding the given topics. The direction of opinion change does not allow further assumptions for potential topic-related cues of opinion change. We should further question, which topics are suitable for examining the spiral of silence and the bandwagon effect, because it is almost inevitable to involuntary call further cues related to the individual with certain topics.

Further studies could tackle also the conviction of the user by including supportive majorities for preventing false-positives from users who were undecided for a certain topic or just forgot their initial choice. Lee et al. found for support-

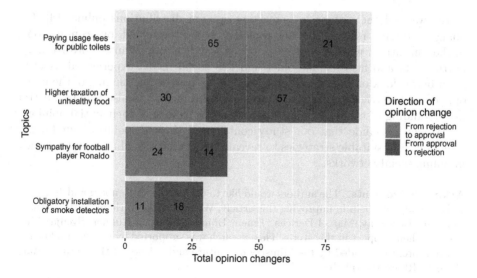

**Fig. 4.** Direction of opinion change

ing majorities, that the users tend to increase their rejection for a topic when they initially held a negative opinion. In contrast, supportive positive majorities showed no further polarizing effect [9].

As our study was designed to keep the answering effort low, we did not consider different semantics in our comments like Waddel et al. did in their experiment [25]. They found that the perception of user comments through their content can differ in authenticity.

Contrary to our findings and the aforementioned research, Porten-Cheé and Eilders doubt the transferability of the spiral of silence theory to user-generated content at social networking sites, as they did not find any relationship between the exposure of user-generated content with majorities of equal or contrasting opinion and the users' participation on these discussions [17], which demands for further consideration of our research topic.

## 5.1 Necessity of Gaining a Digital Maturity

Our study shows, that users of social network sites seem to be influencable through the presence of illusory opinion majorities in user comments. This finding calls for a need of action as social networking sites gain popularity in spreading political information and can hereby attain increased influence on democratic processes [28]. Moreover, a meta-analysis of studies dealing with the impact of social media use on offline political participation shows, that political engagement increases slightly with more frequent social media use, though not uncovering the underlying causal effects [1].

An appropriate way to deal with this issue would be to enhance the user's assessment of user-generated content on social networking sites so that they are more aware of the pitfalls in perceiving opinion distributions online [14]. For doing so, further research on this topic has to be conducted, overcoming some of the limitations which occurred in our study. It is important to involve more participants and also include older and less social media experienced users to get a better look on the overall picture. A more precise questioning of the users' opinion and conviction regarding the examined topics could also lead to a better understanding of the underlying reasons for the change of their initial opinion.

We can conclude that our study contributed through pointing out further directions and suitable strategies to reveal the peculiarities of opinion formation in online social networks.

**Acknowledgements.** The authors would like to thank Nils Plettenberg and Johannes Nakayama for his help in improving this article. We would like to thank Satvika Anantha, Kira Borowsky, Marcel Derichs, Tanem Dönmez, Marlien Rubner, Svenja Wimmers for their support in this study. This research was supported by the Digital Society research program funded by the Ministry of Culture and Science of the German State of North Rhine-Westphalia.

# References

1. Boulianne, S.: Social media use and participation: a meta-analysis of current research. **18**(5), 524–538. https://doi.org/10.1080/1369118X.2015.1008542. ISSN 1369-118X, 1468-4462

2. Chun, J.W., Lee, M.J.: When does individuals willingness to speak out increase on social media? Perceived social support and perceived power/control. Comput. Hum. Behav. **74**, 120–129 (2017). https://doi.org/10.1016/j.chb.2017.04.010. https://linkinghub.elsevier.com/retrieve/pii/S0747563217302480. ISSN 0747-5632

3. Del Vicario, M., et al.: Mapping social dynamics on Facebook: the Brexit debate. Soc. Netw. **50**, 6–16 (2017). https://doi.org/10.1016/j.socnet.2017.02.002. https://linkinghub.elsevier.com/retrieve/pii/S0378873316304166. ISSN 0378-8733

4. Gearhart, S., Zhang, W.: "Was it something i said?" "No, it was something you posted!" A study of the spiral of silence theory in social media contexts. Cyberpsychol. Behav. Soc. Netw. **18**(4), 208–213 (2015). https://doi.org/10.1089/cyber. 2014.0443. ISSN 2152-2715

5. Ho, S.S., McLeod, D.M.: Social-psychological influences on opinion expression in face-to-face and computer-mediated communication. Commun. Res. **35**(2), 190–207 (2008). https://doi.org/10.1177/0093650207313159. ISSN 0093-6502

6. Kim, M.: Facebook's spiral of silence and participation: the role of political expression on facebook and partisan strength in political participation. Cyberpsychol. Behav. Soc. Netw. **19**(12), 696–702 (2016). https://doi.org/10.1089/cyber.2016. 0137. ISSN 2152-2715

7. Kwon, K.H., Moon, S.l., Stefanone, M.A.: Unspeaking on Facebook? Testing network effects on self-censorship of political expressions in social network sites. Qual. Quan. **49**(4), 1417–1435 (2015). https://doi.org/10.1007/s11135-014-0078-8

8. Lee, E.J.: That's not the way it is: how user-generated comments on the news affect perceived media bias. J. Comput.-Mediat. Commun. **18**(1), 32–45 (2012). https://doi.org/10.1111/j.1083-6101.2012.01597.x. https://academic.oup. com/jcmc/article/18/1/32-45/4067495. ISSN 1083-6101

9.  Lee, M.J., Chun, J.W.: Reading others' comments and public opinion poll results on social media: social judgment and spiral of empowerment. Comput. Hum. Behav. **65**, 479–487 (2016). https://doi.org/10.1016/j.chb.2016.09.007. https://linkinghub.elsevier.com/retrieve/pii/S074756321630629X. ISSN 0747-5632

10. Lee, S., et al.: Understanding the majority opinion formation process in online environments: an exploratory approach to Facebook. Inf. Process. Manag. **54**(6), 1115–1128 (2018). https://doi.org/10.1016/J.IPM.2018.08.002. https://www.science direct.com/science/article/abs/pii/S0306457317307367?via%3Dihub. ISSN 0306-4573

11. Leibenstein, H.: Bandwagon, snob, and veblen effects in the theory of consumers' demand. Q. J. Econ. **64**(2), 183 (1950). https://doi.org/10.2307/1882692. https://academic.oup.com/qje/article-lookup/doi/10.2307/1882692. ISSN 0033-5533

12. Van der Meer, T.W.G., Hakhverdian, A., Aaldering, L.: Off the fence, onto the bandwagon? A Large-Scale survey experiment on effect of real-life poll outcomes on subsequent vote intentions. Int. J. Pub. Opin. Res. **28**(1), 46–72 (2016). https://doi.org/10.1093/ijpor/edu041. ISSN 0954-2892

13. Morton, R.B., et al.: Exit polls, turnout, and bandwagon voting: evidence from a natural experiment. Eur. Econ. Rev. **77**, 65–81 (2015). https://doi.org/10.1016/j.euroecorev.2015.03.012. https://linkinghub.elsevier.com/retrieve/pii/S0014292115000483. ISSN 0014-2921

14. Neubaum, G., Krämer, N.C.: Monitoring the opinion of the crowd: psychological mechanisms underlying public opinion perceptions on social media. Media Psychol. **20**(3), 502–531 (2017). https://doi.org/10.1080/15213269.2016.1211539. ISSN 1521-3269

15. Noelle-Neumann, E.: The spiral of silence a theory of public opinion. J. Commun. **24**(2), 43–51 (1974). https://doi.org/10.1111/j.1460-2466.1974.tb00367.x. https://academic.oup.com/joc/article/24/2/43-51/4553587. ISSN 0021-9916

16. Oeldorf-Hirsch, A., Sundar, S.S.: Posting, commenting, and tagging: effects of sharing news stories on Facebook. Comput. Hum. Behav. **44**, 240–249 (2015). https://doi.org/10.1016/j.chb.2014.11.024. https://linkinghub.elsevier.com/retrieve/pii/S0747563214006232. ISSN 0747-5632

17. Porten-Cheé, P., Eilders, C.: Spiral of silence online: how online communication affects opinion climate perception and opinion expression regarding the climate change debate. Stud. Commun. Sci. **15**(1), 143–150 (2015). https://doi.org/10.1016/J.SCOMS.2015.03.002. https://www.sciencedirect.com/science/article/pii/S1424489615000211?via%3Dihub. ISSN 1424-4896

18. Purcell, K., et al.: Understanding the participatory news consumer (2010)

19. Schulz, A., Roessler, P.: The spiral of silence and the internet: selection of online content and the perception of the public opinion climate in computer-mediated Communication Environments. Int. J. Pub. Opin. Res. **24**(3), 346–367 (2012). https://doi.org/10.1093/ijpor/eds022. ISSN 0954-2892, 1471-6909

20. Shao, C., et al.: The spread of low-credibility content by social bots. Nat. Commun. **9**(1), 4787 (2018). https://doi.org/10.1038/s41467-018-06930-7. ISSN 2041-1723

21. Sundar, S.S., Nass, C.: Conceptualizing sources in online news. J. Commun. **51**(1), 52–72 (2001). https://doi.org/10.1111/j.1460-2466.2001.tb02872.x. https://academic.oup.com/joc/article/51/1/52-72/4110134. ISSN 0021-9916

22. Sundar, S.S.: The MAIN model: a heuristic approach to understanding technology effects on credibility. In: Digital Media Youth Credibility, pp. 73–100 (2008)

23. Sundar, S.S., Knobloch-Westerwick, S., Hastall, M.R.: News cues: information scent and cognitive heuristics. J. Am. Soc. Inf. Sci. Technol. **58**(3), 366–378 (2007). https://doi.org/10.1002/asi.20511. ISSN 1532-2882

24. Waddell, T.F.: What does the crowd think? How online comments and popularity metrics affect news credibility and issue importance. New Media Soc. **20**(8), 3068–3083 (2018). https://doi.org/10.1177/1461444817742905. ISSN 1461-4448

25. Waddell, T.F.: The authentic (and angry) audience. Digit. Journal. 1–18 (2018). https://doi.org/10.1080/21670811.2018.1490656. ISSN 2167-0811

26. Zech, C.E.: Leibenstein's bandwagon effect as applied to voting. Public Choice **21**(1), 117–122 (1975). https://doi.org/10.1007/BF01705954. ISSN 0048-5829

27. Zerback, T., Fawzi, N.: Can online exemplars trigger a spiral of silence? Examining the effects of exemplar opinions on perceptions of public opinion and speaking out. New Media Soc. **19**(7), 1034–1051 (2017). https://doi.org/10.1177/1461444815625942. ISSN 1461-4448

28. de Zúñiga, H., Jung, N., Valenzuela, S.: Social media use for news and individual's social capital, civic engagement and political participation. J. Comput. Mediat. Commun. **17**(3), 319–336 (2012). https://doi.org/10.1111/j.1083-6101.2012.01574.x. https://academic.oup.com/jcmc/article/17/3/319-336/4067682. ISSN 1083-6101

# A Training System for Swallowing Ability by Visualizing the Throat Position

Nagisa Matsumoto[1(✉)], Chihiro Suzuki[2], Koji Fujita[2], and Yuta Sugiura[1,3(✉)]

[1] Keio University, Minato, Japan
{nkysc.1929.r, sugiura}@keio.jp
[2] Tokyo Medical and Dental University, Bunkyo, Japan
[3] JST PRESTO, Tokyo, Japan

**Abstract.** Our ability to swallow tends to decrease as we grow older. One reason for this is dysphagia, a condition that makes it difficult to swallow food well and causes malnutrition or food aspiration in severe cases. Therefore, preventing dysphagia is important in terms of maintaining quality of life. One way to prevent dysphagia is by using a throat raising exercise whereby we train our own throat muscles by consciously moving the throat. However, throat raising can be difficult because it is hard to see the motion of our own throat. In this work, we developed a system that helps users to move their own throat consciously. We designed a wearable device to visualize larynx position and a game to enhance user motivation. The proposed device measures the distance between skin surface and photo-reflective sensors and estimates the position of the larynx by means of a support vector machine. Experimental results showed that our proposed system can accurately estimate throat motion and that four out of five participants improved their ability to keep their throat in a high position for a long time by playing our proposed game. In future work, we will consider a system that can improve not only the muscle strength of the throat but also the comprehensive swallowing function.

**Keywords:** Exercise · Wearable sensor · Gamification

## 1 Introduction

The Health, Labour and Welfare Ministry of Japan reported in 2016 that the third highest cause of death is pneumonia according to demographics [1]. Among elderly patients with pneumonia, 70% suffer from aspiration pneumonia. Dysphagia is a condition that makes it difficult to swallow food well and causes malnutrition or food aspiration in severe cases. Therefore, preventing dysphagia is important in terms of maintaining quality of life.

Dysphagia is typically traced to three causes: structural, functional, and psychological. Structural causes stem from a structural problem that prevents the passage of food in the trachea, functional causes stem from a weakening of the muscles or nerves, and psychological causes are linked to psychogenic disease, such as anorexia by depression. In dysphagia stemming from the functional causes, the tongue and hyoid

V. G. Duffy (Ed.): HCII 2019, LNCS 11582, pp. 501–511, 2019.
https://doi.org/10.1007/978-3-030-22219-2_37

muscles strongly affect swallowing ability [2]. The hyoid muscles play an important role in the generation of tongue pressure by pushing the tongue from the bottom and also in pulling up the larynx by lifting from above. However, the hyoid muscles, especially the geniohyoid muscle, start to atrophy as people age [3]. This causes a decrease the hyoid muscles and a decrease in the raising up motion of the larynx. Raising the larynx closes the entrance of the trachea, which leads to the prevention of aspiration. This also affects the action whereby food passes through the pharynx. From these reasons, changes due to aging have a detrimental effect on the swallowing function. In order to prevent this, there are many rehabilitation methods to improve swallowing ability. Takehara et al. reported a training method for swallowing [4]. There is an exercise that opens the mouth while contracting the muscles as one way of strengthening hyoid muscles shown in this report. For improving the larynx raising movement, there is an exercise called Shaker where the patient lies with his or her back and shoulder to the floor and raises the head. Another exercise is the Mendelsohn method, where the throat is kept in a high position while swallowing. Uranagase proposed a similar throat exercise to consciously keep the throat in a high position [5]. As mentioned above, moving one's own throat consciously is important for training, but it can be difficult because it is hard to observe the motion of our own throat. For this reason, the training is monotonous and we are likely to feel bored and give up.

In this paper, we propose a system that helps users to move their own throat consciously. Specifically, we developed a wearable device to visualize the larynx position and prototyped a game to enhance user motivation.

## 2    Related Work

### 2.1    Measurement of Swallowing Motion

There have been several attempts to detect swallowing motion. Zhang et al. developed a shirt to detect swallowing motion [6] that comprises bio-impedance sensors around the neck and a pressure sensor behind the first shirt button. They found that the accuracy of the detection improved when the two kinds of sensors were used instead of just one. Iiduka et al. developed a sensor sheet to detect larynx movement in swallowing [7]. They arranged five piezoelectric pressure sensors on the sheet and were able to obtain the maximum rising velocity, the upper part staying period of the throat, and so on by the voltage signal. GOKURI [8] is a system that recognizes swallowing motion by microphone. This device analyzes the sound caused by swallowing and estimates whether the swallowing motion is normal or not. However, this system does not lead to any improvement of the action.

In swallowing motion, there has been some research that focused specifically on larynx movement. Ultrasonic diagnostic equipment [9] can evaluate the morphology of the muscles involved in swallowing or the swallowing movement by putting an ultrasonic probe around the throat. Shimizu et al. [10] stated that such inspection with ultrasonic diagnostic equipment is reliable; however, it is quite expensive and thus impractical for use in our daily lives. Taketani et al. [11] developed a system to evaluate swallowing motion by detecting larynx rising movement with a depth camera called Kinect. Kinect emits infrared light toward the larynx and then measures the distance between Kinect and the larynx. As another approach, Takahashi et al. developed a system called CODE that detect the larynx movement by photographs taken from the side [12]. CODE detects the throat outline by comparing the difference between the background and the jaw part. After removing noise and performing correction, CODE identifies the peak position from the differential values of the outline and obtains a larynx movement curve by plotting to a graph. However, these systems take time to set up and require a specialized environment for use. Sato et al. [13] developed a system that detects the larynx position with a photo-reflective sensor and then visualizes the position. This system can evaluate throat motion easily, but only for males with a protruding Adams's apple. Our proposed system is different in that we estimate the position of the larynx by machine learning even if user with not protruding Adams's apple.

## 2.2 Measurement Around the Larynx with Photo-Reflective Sensor

The photo-reflective sensor (PRS) measures the distance between itself and an object from the amount of reflected light. This type of sensor is small and inexpensive, and it has already been used in a few studies focusing on changes around the throat, including the research introduced in Sect. 2.1 [13].

Yasu et al. developed a wearable module equipped with six PRSs to measure pharynx position [16]. Their system estimates the pharynx position by measuring the peak position from the sensor values. Sakashita et al. developed an immersive telepresence system to transmit the body and facial movements of a performer into a puppet [17]. The performer wears a head mounted display (HMD) equipped with PRSs in the mask part that measure the condition of the mouth. The device proposed in this paper was developed with reference to these studies.

## 2.3 Gamification for Exercise

There has already been some research on introducing games for exercises. Masaki et al. developed a training game called Squachu for training oral function [14]. In this game, users train the muscles around the tongue and mouth by moving them around. Playing this game was shown to have a positive effect on training the throat muscles, and participants enjoyed playing the game.

Inoue et al. developed a voice input game to support the elderly in speaking [15]. It helps them to train strength to spit out food when food aspiration happens. This game was positively reviewed by elderly participants, who had comments like "I want to play it by myself if the operation is easy" and "I want to play it with my family".

On the basis of these previous studies, we apply similar gamification techniques to our system. Specifically, we developed a game to provide training on swallowing.

## 3    Proposed System

In our research, we visualize the motion of swallowing and use it for swallow training through the use of a game system. Our proposed system estimates the throat position between a natural throat state and a throat position raised to the maximum and visualizes it in real time.

### 3.1    Device

The wearable device we developed consists of 18 PRSs built into the module in a 6 × 3 formation of columns and rows, as shown in Fig. 1. This device was inspired by one proposed by Sato et al. [13] and Yasu et al. [16] that detects pharynx position. Each PRS measures the distance between the skin surface and itself. By arranging the sensors in the horizontal direction, the system can detect changes to the skin surface on the throat resulting from not only the throat position but also throat surface contraction. This enables the device to estimate throat position even if the position of the Adam's apple is not clear.

The outline from the center to the edge of the 3D printed module is fitted to the curvature of the neck. Users put on the wearable device so that the surface of the sensors face the throat and the upper part of the module touches under the chin. The device includes a reflector band in the belt part wrapped around the neck so that it can be put on without any specific tool.

There are individual differences regarding the bumps and dents of the throat, so we need to set the appropriate distance depending on the physicality of each user. In our device, we can change the distance from the throat to the sensors by replacing various parts with different heights.

photo-reflective sensor

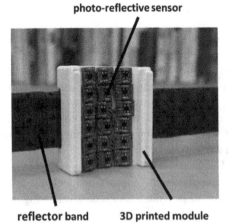 

reflector band        3D printed module

**Detail of wearable device**                    **Appearance of wearable device**

**Fig. 1.** Overview of proposed wearable device.

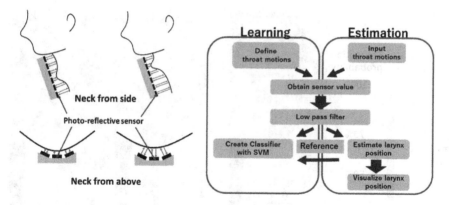

**Fig. 2.** Recognition overview.

## 3.2 Larynx Recognition

The proposed system estimates the larynx position in real time, as shown in Fig. 2. In the learning phase, two states of sensor values are learned: throat position in a natural state and throat position raised to the maximum.

In previous work [16], it has been reported that when we utter something with a high frequency voice, the throat position rises. Also, Hirai et al. [18] reported the position of the larynx moves up and down as frequency goes up and down. Therefore, we assume the throat position is raised to the maximum if user give out as high a voice as possible, we determine this position as the throat position raised to the maximum. We obtain 18 RPS values in each state and remove the noise using a low-pass filter. The laryngeal position is estimated with a support vector machine (SVM) that calculates probability for the two learned states. We got the estimation probability as ratio in measurement range, we determined the position of the larynx.

## 3.3 Visualizing and Game Design

In previous study conducted by Sato et al. [13], they reported visualizing the position of larynx is valid for training. In this research, we verify whether it is valid for training even if visualizing with gamification.

The estimation result is displayed in the form of an avatar positions on the game screen. When the avatar appears at Lv.0, the larynx position is in a natural state, and at Lv.4, it has risen to the maximum position. The level indication (Fig. 3) is the estimated larynx position divided into four stages according to the estimation probability of the maximum state provided by the SVM. Users can reference this indication as a guide to understand their rough throat position during play.

In the prototype game, users move an avatar up toward the sky by raising their own throat. The avatar moves vertically according to the estimation result; for example, when a user raises his or her throat, the avatar rises as well.

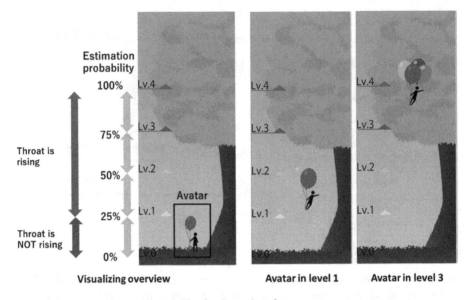

**Fig. 3.** Game interface.

The number of balloons the avatar holds increases as the larynx position gets higher, and the flying speed gets faster. When the total rising time reaches a designated limit, the game ends. The final arrival height is calculated as the sum-of-products of the level indication and the stay time at that level. Background music is always playing during the game, and every time a player levels up or finishes the game, a sound effect is played. The system records which level the avatar attained and how many seconds it stayed there. We performed two experiments to determine the effectiveness of the system, as described in the following sections.

## 4   Experiment 1: Estimation Performance

### 4.1   Overview

In the first experiment, we examined whether our proposed system can estimate throat motion. Four individuals (two males, two females) participated in the experiment. First they were taught the two throat states, natural state and maximum raising state. We instructed them to give out as high a voice as possible when learning the maximum rising state, and we recorded the sound pitch with a tuner. In the estimation phase, participants kept their throat at a natural state and gave out a voice depending on our instruction. We instructed them to give out the same voice as the learning phase, and we recorded the probability estimated by the SVM. With one of the participants (Participant 1), we recorded the estimation probability not only when giving out the same pitch but also when giving out a lower one than in the learning phase. This is because we check whether the estimated position of the larynx changes according to frequency.

## 4.2   Results

Figure 4 lists the estimation probability when each participant takes each action.

### Participant 1

| | Estimation | |
| | Natural state | Maximum state |
|---|---|---|
| Do Not raise throat | 84.2% | 15.8% |
| Vocalizing the same pitch as in learning phase | 5.3% | 94.7% |

_Action_

### Participant 2

| | Estimation | |
| | Natural state | Maximum state |
|---|---|---|
| Do Not raise throat | 85.0% | 15.0% |
| Vocalizing the same pitch as in learning phase | 10.7% | 89.3% |

_Action_

### Participant 3

| | Estimation | |
| | Natural state | Maximum state |
|---|---|---|
| Do Not raise throat | 82.6% | 17.4% |
| Vocalizing the same pitch as in learning phase | 14.6% | 85.4% |

_Action_

### Participant 4

| | Estimation | |
| | Natural state | Maximum state |
|---|---|---|
| Do Not raise throat | 84.7% | 15.3% |
| Vocalizing the same pitch as in learning phase | 10.9% | 89.1% |

_Action_

**Fig. 4.** Estimation probability in each state (%).

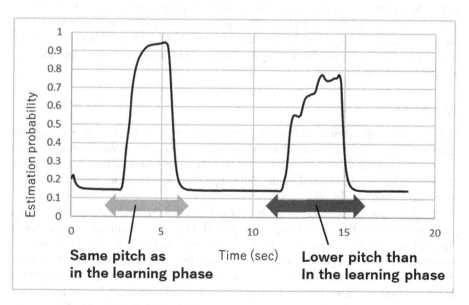

**Same pitch as in the learning phase**    Time (sec)    **Lower pitch than In the learning phase**

**Fig. 5.** Estimation probability changes of the estimated throat position.

Estimation probability was 84.1% when participants do not raise their throat. Estimation probability was 89.6% when participants gave out the same pitch as in the learning phase. This demonstrates that the proposed system can detect two states.

To go into further detail, Fig. 5 shows the continuously estimation probability changes for participant 1. The higher the estimation probability is, the closer to the state raised to the maximum the throat position is estimated. We found that the first increase showed the estimation probability from a natural state to the state she gave out at the same pitch as in learning phase, and the second increase showed that from a natural state to the state she gave out at a lower pitch than in the learning phase. This change corresponds to the continuous change of the larynx position. This result supports previous work showing that the higher the frequency we utter, the higher the throat position rises [16]. It also clearly demonstrates that our proposed system can estimate throat motion.

## 5   Experiment 2: User Performance

### 5.1   Overview

In this experiment, we examined whether users could raise their own throats consciously by repeatedly playing the proposed training game. Five individuals (three males, two females) participated in the experiment. First, participants learned the two states, natural state and maximum state, as in first experiment. They raised their own throats, and then checking the avatar movements to see whether their own throat motion was reflected. We told them that the higher they raised their own throats, the higher their avatar flying position would ascend when game finished. The game started whenever the participant was ready. This procedure was taken as one set, and we carried out one set every hour, for a total of six sets. When the total rising time of the larynx reaches a designated limit, the game ends. In this experiment, we determined the designated limit is 60 s.

### 5.2   Results

Figure 6 shows the total time that the larynx position was above level 3 during the game, and Fig. 7 shows the total time it was below level 2. However, around the third game of participant C, there seemed to be an estimation failure of the larynx position (all were below level 2) caused by the belt slipping during the game. Hence, this result is excluded from the figures.

As Fig. 6 shows, participants A, B, and E improved the total time that the larynx position was above level 3 each time they played the game. Specifically, participant A improved the throat raising time to 18 s, and participant B to 5 s. Participant E worsened from the first game to the second game, decreasing the rising time from 60 s to 22 s. However, he did improve his throat raising time, becoming able to keep it stably in a high position. There was no major change for participant D, and participant C tended to decrease the time to keep his own throat in a high position, but did improve the time from the first game to the second.

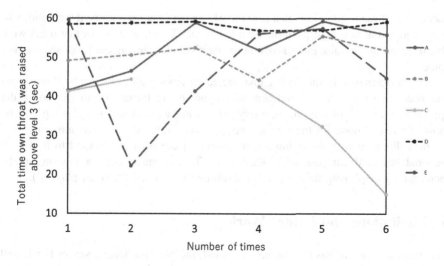

**Fig. 6.** Total time own throat was raised above level 3.

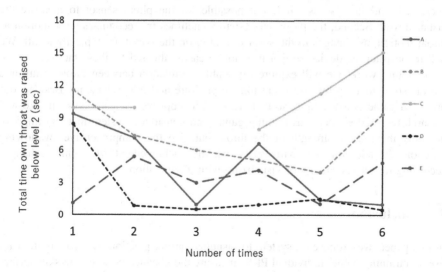

**Fig. 7.** Total time own throat was raised below level 2.

As Fig. 7 shows, participants A, B, D, and E decreased the time that the larynx position was below level 2 each time they played game. Participant C also decreased the time from the first game to the fourth game, although his time increased in the fifth and sixth games.

In other words, participants A, B, and E became able to keep their own throats in a high position for a long time, and the time in the low position got shorter. In regard to participant D, the time his throat was in a low position also got shorter, and the time that his throat was kept in a high position increased throughout the game. In conclusion, these results show that four out of five participants improved their ability to keep their throat in a high position for a long time. This demonstrates that users were able to learn how to raise their throat more effectively by playing our proposed training game.

The performance in the sixth game decreased among all participants. We assume this was caused by an accumulation of fatigue to the throat due to exceeding the appropriate amount of training in a day. Therefore, we feel that the training will be most effective if done for the appropriate amount of time and not overdoing it.

In addition, during the training game, some of the participants tried to beat their personal best and compete with other users. This suggests that motivation can be increased by displaying training scores (both one's own and the other players').

## 6   Limitations and Future Work

The proposed system has two limitations. First, the photo-reflective sensor is affected by skin color. This sensor measures the distance by the amount of infrared light reflected from the target. If the target color is dark, the amount of received light decreases, and in this case, it is not possible for the photo sensor to measure the distance well. Second, the proposed system sometimes misrecognizes neck motion as throat motion, as changes to the surface of skin on the throat are typically small. We will reconstruct the device so that it is not so easily affected by these factors.

In future work, we will explore a possible correlation between throat rising and muscle strengthening by measuring tongue pressure and other elements. Besides, our proposed game is too simple, so that we need to improve the game system. We will research required elements as training game, and consider a system that can improve not only the muscle strength of the throat but also the comprehensive swallowing function. In addition, we will verify whether achievement of training changes according to not visualizing or visualizing with gamification.

## 7   Conclusion

In this paper, we proposed a system to visualize larynx position by throat motion for use in a training game. Individual PRSs measure the distance between the skin surface and itself, and the laryngeal position is estimated by an SVM that calculates the probability for two learned states: a natural state and a throat position raised to the maximum state. Experiments showed that the proposed system could accurately estimate throat motion. We also found that when users played the proposed training game several times, they were able to improve their swallowing ability and keep their own throats in a high position. This demonstrates that participants learned how to raise their throats by playing our game.

In the future, we will explore a possible correlation between throat rising and muscle strengthening. We will also develop a training game to strengthen our comprehensive swallowing ability.

**Acknowledgments.** This work was supported by JST AIP-PRISM JPMJCR18Y2 and JST PRESTO JPMJPR17J4.

# References

1. 2018 vital statistics in Japan trends up to (2016). https://www.mhlw.go.jp/toukei/list/dl/81-1a2.pdf. Accessed 20 July 2018
2. Taniguchi, H., Magara, J., Inoue, M.: Dysphagia of the elderly. J. Jpn. Soc. Parenter. Enteral Nutr. **28**(5), 1069–1074 (2013)
3. Feng, X., et al.: Aging-related geniohyoid muscle atrophy is related to aspiration status in healthy older adults. J. Gerontol. A Biol. Sci. Med. Sci. **68**(7), 753–760 (2012)
4. The Japanese society of dysphagia rehabilitation medical review committee, summary of training aid (version 2014). Jpn. Soc. Dysphagia Rehabil. **18**(1), 55–89 (2014)
5. Uranagase, A.: Swallowing Ability Prevent 90% of Aspiration Pneumonia. Kadokawa, Japan (2017)
6. Zhang, R., et al.: A generic sensor fabric for multi-modal swallowing sensing in regular upper-body shirts. In: ISWC 2016 Proceedings of the ACM International Symposium on Wearable Computers, pp. 12–16. ACM, Heidelberg (2016)
7. Iizuka, M., Kobayashi, M., Hasegawa, Y., Tomita, K., Takeshima, R., Izumizaki, M.: A new flexible piezoelectric pressure sensor array for the noninvasive detection of laryngeal movement during swallowing. J. Physiol. Sci. **68**(6), 837–846 (2018)
8. GOKURI. http://www.ai.iit.tsukuba.ac.jp/gokuri/. Accessed 20 July 2018
9. FUJIFILM ultrasonic diagnostic imaging apparatus SonoSite M-Tubo. https://fujifilm.jp/business/healthcare/ultrasonography/sonosite_m_turbo/index.html. Accessed 26 Dec 2018
10. Shimizu, S., et al.: Retest reliability of ultrasonic geniohyoid muscle measurement. Jpn. J. Compr. Rehabil. Sci. **7**, 55–60 (2016)
11. Taketani, M., et al.: Evaluation of swallowing function using non-contact device of the Microsoft Kinect in healthy subjects. J. Health Sci. **14**, 103–113 (2017)
12. Takahashi, A., et al.: A study on the cervical outline detection method for measuring laryngeal movement -detection of differences in food textures-. J. Meikai Dent. Med. **44**(1), 92–97 (2015)
13. Sato, M., et al.: Training of laryngeal elevation for elderly people using a visual biofeedback of larynx movement. Jpn. Soc. Dysphagia Rehabil. **18**(1), 22–29 (2014)
14. Ando, T., et al.: A training game to improve oral function via a non-contact tongue-mouth-motion detection system. In: Proceedings of the 2018 International Conference on Advanced Visual Interfaces (AVI 2018), 26, 8 p. ACM, New York (2018)
15. Inoue, T., Ohsuga, M.: Development and assessment of serious games for elderly aimed at preventing dysphagia. Jpn. J. Ergon. **50** Spec. Number, 166–167 (2014)
16. Yasu, K., Inami, M.: Silent humming: a digital humming producing system using unvoiced sounds and throat motion. Laval Virtual (2012)
17. Sakashita, M., Minagawa, T., Koike, A., Suzuki, I., Kawahara, K., Ochiai, Y.: You as a puppet: evaluation of telepresence user interface for puppetry. In: Proceedings of the 30th Annual ACM Symposium on User Interface Software and Technology (UIST 2017), pp 217–228. ACM, New York (2017)
18. Hirai, H., Honda, K., Fujimoto, I., Shimada, Y.: Analysis of magnetic resonance images on the physiological mechanisms of fundamental frequency control. J. Acoust. Soc. Jpn. **50**(4), 296–304 (1994)

# Literature Review: The Use of Games as a Treatment for Obsessive Compulsive Disorder

Juliana Miranda[1,2], Vania Teofilo[3], Anthony Lins[2],
Bruno S. Oliveira[4(✉)], Fábio Campos[1], and Sergio Nesteriuk[4]

[1] UFPE - Universidade Federal de Pernambuco, Recife, Brazil
mirandaa@gmail.com. juliana@gmail.com, fc2005@gmail.com
[2] UNICAP - Universidade Católica de Pernambuco, Recife, Brazil
thonylins@gmail.com
[3] São Paulo, Brazil
[4] UAM - Universidade Anhembi Morumbi, São Paulo, Brazil
brunosoliveira@gmail.com, nesteriuk@hotmail.com

**Abstract.** Obsessive-Compulsive Disorder (OCD) is a chronic disease stated by United Nations as one of the 10 most disabling illnesses and key factor in decreased quality of life. It affects millions of people around the world, reaching a population equivalent of countries like Germany or Mexico. One of most used and effective treatment is Cognitive-Behavioral Therapy (CBT) but, its failure rate can be as high as 30%. Games have been greatly incorporated to everyday lives of millions of people, and because of that, are becoming a useful tool to help in healthcare - becoming what is called Games for Health (GfH). This literature review seeks to research academic papers that demonstrate the use of games to treat OCD - as games standalone or in conjunction with CBT. The main objectives of this literature review are to summarize the previous published works and to gather base knowledge in the area for future research developments.

**Keywords:** Games for Health · Obsessive-Compulsive Disorder · Cognitive-Behavioral Therapy

## 1 Introduction

In recent years, the development of digital technologies has made game creating easier. At the same time, the health area has been using these technologies to make games specially tailored to fit several areas of the healthcare system and several researches have shown the relevance of digital games, either as a support tool in the diagnostic process or during the treatment of various pathologies. Usually, these games are called Games for Health (GfH), they are health-related computer games, or similar computer applications that use software tailored to computer game development [1] and can have their focus on treatment, diagnosis, rehabilitation [2, 3]; on developing applications that implement games [4]; or on education, integration and socialization [5, 6]. When it comes to adapting new gaming technology for specialized health contexts, the scenario

© Springer Nature Switzerland AG 2019
V. G. Duffy (Ed.): HCII 2019, LNCS 11582, pp. 512–531, 2019.
https://doi.org/10.1007/978-3-030-22219-2_38

is full of interesting perspectives [7], a growing body of research indicates that GfH provide measurable health benefits [1].

Several kinds of games have been designed to support the training of health professionals, providing an environment for them to practice skills before embracing real situations. There is also a substantial variety in types of diseases considered by these training games, such as malaria [8], metabolic syndrome, diabetes mellitus, dyslipidemia, obesity [2], or diagnosis of breast problems [9]. However, all those efforts using technology to improve diagnosis can only succeed properly if the health system could be strong and fluid instead of a barrier [3].

Another relation between games and health is supporting treatments, for example, neurodevelopment treatment techniques for persons with traumatic brain injury [10]; a contrast-based game for treating both adults and children with amblyopia [11]. Games can also be part of preventive treatment, through an educational perspective, allowing the number of emergency clinical utilization to be reduced the longer patients spend playing and learning about their own self-care needs [12, 13].

Besides using games on health diagnosis or treatment, there is another possibility: Gamification, which means the "use of gameplay mechanics for non-game applications" [14], for example, adding game elements to standard computerized working memory (WM) to observe if it would enhance motivation and training performance of children with Attention Deficit Hyperactivity Disorder - ADHD [15].

The use of digital games specifically for treatments of 'mental health' began in the early 1990s with the use of high popular entertainment games such as Mario Bros series [16]; technology advances have facilitated, decades later, the development of specialized games, allowing researchers to apply games that can provide specific functions for treatments in psychotherapy [17, 18]; or even innovating through Patents of Methods to support psychological and emotional disorders [19]. Wilkinson [20] has observed a greater number of experiences through the offline games and highlights the potential of the online game in therapy because of the characteristics of the online game world which can both motivate, challenge and be governed by rules tailored by specific needs. Finally, one possible way to categorize the use of games on mental health context is games for prevention and games for health support [21]. Therefore, it is known that the use of smartphone applications increases the quality and results of behavioral health care [22].

## 2 Obsessive-Compulsive Disorder - OCD

Obsessive-Compulsive Disorder (OCD) is a chronic disease with periods of remission and relapse [23]. According to Veale and Roberts [24], OCD is the fourth most common mental disorder after depression, alcohol/substance misuse, and social phobia, and its global prevalence is estimated between 1.2 to 3% of the general population [25]. It occurs all over the world, and tends to be about one-and-a-half to two times more likely for women to meet criteria for OCD in their lifetime than men [26]. The first manifestations of OCD often appear between ages 8 and 11, with an increase in OCD diagnosis during puberty and again in early adulthood [25]. Also, persons with OCD were likely to have major depression or any other anxiety disorder as a comorbid condition [27]. The following, from the American Psychiatric Association, is the definition considered in this review [28]:

*"OCD is characterized by the presence of obsessions and/or compulsions. Obsessions are recurrent and persistent thoughts, urges, or images that are experienced as intrusive and unwanted, whereas compulsions are repetitive behaviors or mental acts that an individual feels driven to perform in response to an obsession or according to rules that must be applied rigidly. Some other obsessive-compulsive and related disorders are also characterized by preoccupations and by repetitive behaviors or mental acts in response to the preoccupations. Other obsessive-compulsive and related disorders are characterized primarily by recurrent body-focused repetitive behaviors (e.g., hair pulling, skin picking) and repeated attempts to decrease or stop the behaviors".*
(AMERICAN PSYCHIATRIC ASSOCIATION, 2013).

According to Bream [26], the individual with OCD, when in contact with certain triggers, have recurrent, specific thoughts, images, impulses, or doubts that remain against their will, and create awareness of the potential for danger which the person can cause or prevent, and these are called obsessions. As a result of them, the person performs actions that are also specific, which act as a ritual, a repetitive behavior in response to the trigger, that are intended to prevent danger of which the obsession has created awareness and to diminish the responsibility for its possible occurrence, or to undo or neutralize things which may have already happened, that generates a sense of relief at that moment, these are called compulsions [26]. Also, if in observing the patient, there is no clear relationship between the obsession and the compulsion, another diagnosis should be considered [29]. Treating OCD entails seeking to break these rituals, and then exchanging the reward system for the discomfort.

Obsessive-Compulsive Disorder is biologically assumed as result from abnormalities in the serotonin pathway and dysfunctional circuits in the orbitostriatal area and the dorsolateral prefrontal cortex, while in the cognitive-behavioral aspect of the obsessive-compulsive disorder, emphasizes the importance of dysfunctional beliefs in affected individuals [30].

The World Health Organization, once ranked OCD in the top 10 of the most disabling illnesses by lost income and decreased quality of life, and also states the disorder as the sixth largest contributor to non-fatal health loss globally [31]. People with OCD are less likely to be married, are more likely to be unemployed, to subsist on very low incomes, and to have low occupational status [26]. When the prevalence and the functional impairment acting together with the anxiety and distress individuals with this condition experience are considered, one recognizes that OCD represents a significant public health concern [25].

OCD is often regarded as a very heterogeneous disorder, and is usually classified by grouping patients according to similarities in their symptoms [32, 33]. According to Bream [26], patients with OCD can be classified into four broad categories or subtypes of symptoms that may have different implications for causation and treatment: contamination fears, checking and other forms of verification, rumination, and also ordering and symmetry. Until recently considered as a part of OCD, the process of hoarding has been observed in a different number of phenomenological and outcomes variables, leading to its new status as a stand-alone disorder in DSM-V [28].

Two common pathways in the treatment of OCD are medications or Cognitive-Behavioral Therapy (CBT), particularly 'Exposure with Response Prevention' (ERP), and/or cognitive interventions aimed at specific obsession beliefs structures, or serotonin reuptake inhibitor (SRI) medications [25]. Currently, it is common practice and not very controversial to opt for psychotropic medication concomitantly with psychoanalysis. Studies have shown the combination of CBT with drugs such as clomipramine since the early 1980s, and fluvoxamine and imipramine since the 1990s [34].

Treatment employing CBT is presently associated with large effect sizes for both ERP and CBT tailored to the condition. Relative to psychotherapeutic interventions, SRI medications have somewhat lower effect sizes for symptom relief [25]. A significant minority fails to respond to the available treatments with estimates of non response as high as 30% [25].

Sufferers of OCD often have other psychopathologies, and tend to have a high level of comorbidity during their lifetime: anxiety disorders (76%), depressive or bipolar disorder (63%), major depressive disorder (41%), obsessive-compulsive personality disorder (23%–32%), tic disorder (30%) [28]. Other disorders that occur more frequently in individuals with OCD than those without the disorder, include several obsessive-compulsive and related disorders such as body dysmorphic disorder, trichotillomania (hair pulling disorder), and excoriation (skin-picking disorder) [28].

## 3   Cognitive-Behavioral Therapy - CBT

Cognitive-Behavioral Therapy (CBT) is a practice that has been developed and used since the 1970s [35], it is a rich, complex, and evolving model of treatment that has been developed for and applied to a wide range of mental health and physical problems and disorders [35], it is an active and directive approach used in the treatment of disorders such as depression, anxiety, phobias, among others [36].

According to Hofmann and Asmundson [37], it is not a single treatment protocol, instead, it refers to a family of interventions, as well as a scientific approach towards understanding and treating psychiatric disorders and human suffering [37]. CBT is among the most studied forms of psychotherapy [37, 38]. A description of the various CBT protocols easy fills a 3-volume textbook series [39] and it has demonstrated efficacy in the treatment of OCD [35].

The term CBT refers specifically to treatments that change cognitions (such as thoughts and beliefs) that are influencing psychological problems [40]. Beck [41] and Ellis [42] were the early theorists in what would become the field of CBT [35], they both developed models during the 1970s in which cognitive assessment and cognitive change became the pivotal point for later behavioral adaptation and emotional success [35].

Nowadays, there is a range of terms that can encompass the CBT practice. For example, 'Behavior Therapy' is also called as 'Behavior Modification' or 'Cognitive-Behavioral Therapy' [40]; 'Cognitive Therapy' - which has been developed by Beck [41] - can be called 'Beckian CBT', or 'Formulation-Driven CBT' [37]; and anything that falls under the rubric of CBT can be regarded as (general) 'Rational Emotive Behavior Therapy - REBT' [43] - which has been developed by Ellis [41]. Researchers also refer to the 'Generic Cognitive Model of CBT' as the 'Case Formulation-Driven' or 'Case Conceptualization-Driven' approach to CBT [44].

There are records of effective treatments for OCD both through an isolated cognitive or behavioral approach alone [45]. Some researchers may argue about the merits of using a strictly cognitive or strictly behavioral approach, however, more pragmatic therapists view cognitive and behavioral methods as effective partners in both theory and practice [46].

Economic data consistently show that the provision of CBT for common mental disorders is more cost-efficient than pharmacotherapy or other interventions such as psychodynamic therapies [37]. The Britain National Institute for Clinical Excellence (NICE) recommends CBT more often than other therapeutic approaches in the treatment of a variety of psychological disorders [43]. Also, the results of many outcome trials and academic researches demonstrate the efficacy of CBT psychological treatments [47], and specifically in the treatment of OCD [48], likewise CBT approaches are the most commonly cited among evidence-based psychological treatments [43].

CBT is also indicated to treat individuals with comorbidity, who are those patients diagnosed with more psychological diseases than OCD. They may benefit from receiving one course of a 'Case Conceptualization-Driven' approach to CBT as opposed to receiving several courses of treatment from different treatments protocols [49], furthermore, CBT appear to have roughly equivalent results across several therapies for common problems such as Major Depression Disorder (MDD) and addictions [47]. It is also recommended for the treatment of problems such as sleep disorders and many of the anxiety disorders - including panic, OCD, social anxiety, and posttraumatic stress disorder (PTSD) - as well as specific phobias [47]. Also, it is prudent to train clinicians working within a managed care setting to use this efficient approach to therapy across the comorbidity [37].

# 4   Games for Health - GfH

Games are artifacts deeply rooted in human social development and it is possible to draw a comparison between them and current rites and ceremonies [50]. Although many news media and scientific groups tend to focus just on the worst aspects of games, like apology of violence [51] and gaming vice [52], games can be used in several positive ways for the good of the individual and/or society. As examples of this positive outcome are Zelda [53], World of Warcraft [54] and Eve Online [55]. The first one can be used to teach children and teenagers basic concepts of scientific process through the game cycle - find a problem, observe, search the environment, formulate a solution (hypothesis) and test it [56]. The second one, contributed to the research of epidemiology, especially about simulating human reactions in high epidemic disease cases, when an in-game disease spread in the game in a non-intentional event called 'Corrupted blood incident' [57].

Using a slightly different approach, Eve Online developers partnered with Human Protein Atlas Project, Massively Multiplayer Online Science, and Reykjavik University, forming the project Discovery [58]. Developers created a mini-game within the game where the players could observe molecules from a microscope, and with little training, classify the molecule shown in the microscopic image. There was no obligation to any player to do it, it didn't affect the gameplay, but those who actually did it were rewarded in in-game currency that could be used to buy spaceships and other in-game stuff.

Besides that, since the end of the 1970s and beginning of 1980s, many researchers and companies started to notice that the engaging power of games could be used to teach and/or train people [59]. This began what is today called 'Serious Games', but it didn't stop just in the educational and training areas, spreading to several other areas like health systems, military, etc. In the words of Wattanasoontorn [60], there's no common definition of Serious Games but, most researchers and developers agree that they are 'games used for purposes other than mere entertainment' [60].

When a serious game is used for health purposes, it can be called 'Game for Health' (GfH). The proper definition of this type of game crashes with multiple definitions of health concept [60]. Since health has several definitions, games for health have several applications and forms. However, looking at Sawyer and Smith [61]'s proposed game taxonomy; it is possible to verify the areas that games for health can encompass (as shown in Table 1).

**Table 1.** Sawyer and Smith games for health taxonomy Table (2008).

|              | Personal                         | Professional Practice                | Research/Academia | Public Health            |
| ------------ | -------------------------------- | ------------------------------------ | ----------------- | ------------------------ |
| Preventative | Exergaming Stress                | Patient Communication                | Data Collection   | Public Health Messaging  |
| Therapeutic  | Rehabitainment Disease Management | Pain Distraction Disease Management  | Virtual Humans    | First Responders         |
| Assessment   | Self-Ranking                     | Measurement                          | Inducement        | Interface/Visualization  |
| Educational  | First Aide Medical Information   | Skills/Training                      | Recruitment       | Management Sims          |
| Informatics  | PHR*                             | EMR**                                | Visualization     | Epidemiology             |

*Personal (or Patient) Health Record **Electronic Medical Record

The table columns divide the games by reasons to use and/or to make a GfH, while the rows divide the games by objectives within the health area. This bidimensional nature of the table allows an organic and flexible classification and, at the same time, shows how GfH's can be different depending on how they are used. Nevertheless, it is important to point out that, because games are a complex media, the divisions proposed by this taxonomy are not mutually exclusive. As an example, an allergy disease management game also brings elements from self-ranking and first aid [62].

Another point of Sawyer and Smith's taxonomy [61] is that it does not divide games by regular more usual game taxonomy, like platform type, or genre. That means it makes no difference if the game is digital or analogical, and, at the same time, it makes no difference if the game is an FPS (First Person Shooter), a board game, or a puzzle. Another very subtle or dubious type of game is the exergaming (and rehabilitation as consequence). Exergames are a type of game in which the player physically exercises while playing. To achieve that, a special device captures the player's movements and transforms them into game input (commands). The term Exergames comes from the words 'exercise and game', but several publications make use of the term in a broader way, simply meaning, games where the player make commands using special devices. This way, from the point of view of this paper's authors, it makes more sense to simply use 'exercise' instead of the term 'exergaming'.

Wattanasoontorn [60] also developed taxonomy of games after surveying several publications in the area (as shown in Fig. 1).

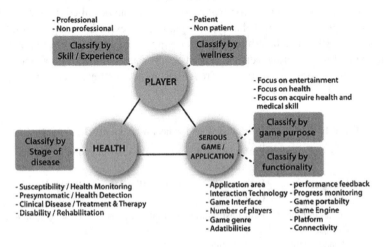

**Fig. 1.** Classification model proposed by Wattanasoontorn [60].

Wattanasoontorn's [60] classification is more complex than the one developed by Sawyer and Smith [61]. The starting point is based on three points of views to classify the game - 'Health', 'Player', and 'Serious Game/application' (the game *per se*). Each of these points of view has their own subdivisions, grouping the classifications in clusters. Although more complex and more complete, this classification mode lacks some classifications like 'research/academia' and 'public health', that were found in Sawyer and Smith's [61] model. This shows an interesting opportunity for further research and development but, for a while, this subject will be postponed since it is not entailed in the original scope of this research.

## 5   Literature Review

The purpose of this review of the literature is to summarize the previous published works and gather theoretical background material about using games as part of OCD treatment. Thus, the presentation is divided in two subsections: (i) Methodology, how the data was collected, selected, and analyzed; and (ii) Synthesis of the Literature Review, where the results were shown.

## 5.1  Methodology

The methodology used in this review happened in two steps: the first one was to find papers about the use of games on OCD treatment; the second, to refine the search, analyzing and sorting the results. The online bibliographic research (desk research) had the following parameters: only papers written in English available in the search engine Google Scholar [63]. The search terms used were "OCD treatment" and "game"; all the searches occurred during the period between December 2018 and January 2019.

Using these parameters, we found 335 results in Google Scholar. However, due to the criteria of relevance and repetition in more than one source, the sampling for this work was110 sources collected for analysis. After an initial analysis, only papers of academic research were considered for having more updated information. Thus, 45 papers were selected for the literature review, as presented in the Appendix. The other sources, distributed in 30 books, 28 internet pages, 1 as citation, 2 as a result not found and 4 repeated in more than one source, can be used in the next works related to the subject of this review.

The second part of the analysis of the selected academic papers was also divided into two steps: the first one consisted in the selection of the papers that met the criteria required to compose the sample intended by this review, i.e., fulfill the cross-field between OCD and the use of games on its treatment, preferably by CBT. The second step was a thorough analysis of the articles selected to compose the sample.

On step 1, the selection of sources occurred according to the following criteria: (i) if the source dealt with OCD; (ii) if the therapy used was CBT; (iii) if the use of games during the process, whether digital or analog, was identified; (iv) if sources did not meet the previous criteria, identify the relationship of the content with the search keywords;

Step 2 comprised of the analysis of articles that somehow used games and dealt with the treatment of OCD by CBT by reading all the papers and identifying the following aspects: (i) basic characteristics of the patients, that is, and if the treatment consisted only of therapy, medications, or both; and whether patients were adults, children or adolescents; (ii) Identifying how the digital artifact was included in the treatment and if it was applied for diagnosis, treatment, prevention or metrics, and evaluations; (iii) in case of use of games, identifying whether they were analog or digital; if the paper dealt with an educational artifact, whether it was an active part in treatment or a motivational complement; whether developed for the work in analysis or an existing commercial game.

The collection and analysis of these data are intended to provide a glimpse of the actual development and use of games as a treatment for OCD.

## 5.2  Synthesis of the Literature Review

For a better understanding, the data analysis will be presented following the same pattern used in the methodology.

## Step 1

When analyzing the 45 articles selected, 9 articles were extracted for a more in-depth analysis, since they met the criteria used in this review: games applied to the treatment of OCD, preferably by CBT. From the 9 (nine) articles [64–72], 8 (eight) met the criteria showed, and 1 (one) used ERP (exposure and response prevention), a therapy before CBT and that can be configured as one of its stages [73]. This ERP-based work was considered by similarity, but not selected for the sample later, because it did not contain use of game related to OCD.

Although there were 36 articles that did not meet the criteria for this research, they all went through a brief analysis to better understand the use of the term "game", aiming at a macro view of this research. Besides these, 4 results appeared duplicated in the search engine and 2 were not found for analysis. 3 papers did not deal with OCD, CBT and, therefore, not related games, and in these cases, it was the word 'game' used in another context.

Out of the 36 papers that did not enter the sample, 32 dealt with OCD, 21 of them using CBT, 1 using ERP and 11 did not use either. For purposes of understanding these results, the following terms were established, and the number of articles using each one is indicated in parentheses: playful digital artifact or application to aid treatment (2); video game and/or internet Addiction (6); 'game' used in another context (14); gamification (3); games universe used in the construction of metaphors for the therapy (5); game as a recreational activity at some point in the session, after its completion or as homework (5); defended the possibility of games in VRET - Virtual Reality Exposure Therapy [74] and reasons for not having many cases (1);

When observing only the results of papers treating OCD by CBT (or ERP), there is a recurrence of terms only in the use of the game universe in the construction of metaphors for the therapy (4) [75–78]; gamification (3) [79–81]; playful digital artifact or application to aid treatment (2) [82, 83]; game as a recreational activity at some point in the session, after its completion or as homework (4) [84–86].

## Step 2

The final sample, composed of the results that meet the research objectives of this review, has 9 results, 6 of which were applied in the treatment of children and/or adolescents, while 3 of adults. Only 2 used CBT and medications concomitantly for all patients, while 4 did not present a standard, having some medicated and others not, and one of the results did not show this information. The following items provide a preview of the 9 papers that make up the sample resulting from this review:

*Brezinka, 2013* [64]

Development and evaluation of a therapeutic digital game to support OCD treatment. The game mentioned in the article was applied specifically for treatment of OCD. There is no information about the type of OCD treated. The game covered psycho-education, the cognitive model of obsessive compulsive disorder, creating a symptom hierarchy, the use of externalizing techniques to cope with anxiety and unpleasant feelings, and exposure-response prevention exercises. 18 children, 6–12 years, some patients received medication (16) and others did not (2). As results, Therapists perceived the game as helpful for education and enhance motivation. 93.75% of the patients evaluated presented remarkably less severe OCD, but there was no control group to validate the role of the game on therapy. In order to achieve success on game tasks, sometimes the Therapist's or the parent's motivation was needed. The game did not covered parents and siblings' relation with the patient's rituals, but the author explained the importance of Therapist help to reduce adaptation and even participation (from family) in the child's rituals.

*Comer, Furr, Cooper-Vince, Kerns, Chan, Edson, Khanna, Franklin, Garcia, and Freeman, 2014 [65]*

Development of an Internet-based format for the delivery of family-based home-treatment for early-onset OCD. Real-time cognitive-behavioral therapy centering on exposure and response prevention to affected families through Video Conferencing and digital games. There is no information about the type of OCD treated. The game was played in session with parents and therapist to enhance the child understanding of treatment concepts. Games were both adaptations of previous works and new product created specifically for this experiment. 5 children, 4–8 years, none of the patients received medication. As results, all of the patients completed treatment and showed OCD symptom improvements and global severity improvements from pre- to post treatment, all showed at least partial diagnostic response, and 60% no longer met diagnostic criteria for OCD at post treatment. No participants got worse, the quality of services was perceived as "excellent." by all parents involved. The games used for teaching core treatment content and for alliance building, highly engaged and motivate the children while working with the therapist.

*Freeman, Garcia, Benito, Conelea, Khanna, March, and Franklin, 2012 [66]*

Randomized trial to compare efficacy CBT and sertraline and their combination to a placebo control condition of the pediatric OCD treatment. Family-based CBT. Family-based relaxation therapy. There is no information about the type of OCD treated. At relaxation therapy the game was part of engagement strategies such as drawing and variants of preexisting the card games; at CBT, therapists made exposure into a game where possible (having fun, playing games, doing silly things in the presence of a feared stimulus). 127 children, of 7–17 years old, some patients received medication and others did not. As results, games were not mentioned, but as a result, this trial could contribute with information about the comparability of this treatment program with CBT, but given a time.

*Haring and Warmelink, 2016 [67]*

Case study of five psychotherapeutic games using metacognition ("third wave" of CBT). OCD was treated by one of the five games, named Ricky and the Spider [87], previously mentioned and already described at these results. The paper offers design recommendations for future (metacognitive) psychotherapeutic games in general.

*Hong, Kim, Aboujaoude and Han, 2018 [68]*

A serious game to support OCD treatment based on ERP approach, aiming at validating if the symptom improvement would be associated with altered Functional Connectivity within Cortico-striato-thalamo-cortical. 15 adults, none of the patients received medication. There is no information about the type of OCD treated. The game was meant to ask subjects to perform behaviors. Subjects played the game for at least 30 min per day, 5 days per week, for 3 weeks. The game was created and pre-tested specifically for this experiment. As results, the game was shown to improve OCD symptoms and alter brain connectivity from the dACC to the DLPFC and to basal ganglia. The author suggests serious games as a less expensive alternative than ERP and self-administrated.

*Leib, 2001* [69]

Presents a multimodal method of treating OCD integrating psychoanalysis, psychopharmacology, and behavior modification. 1 adult received medication and CBT. The type of OCD was contamination fears. The game was mentioned at the sessions as of throwing things at each other to catch, a kind of exposure task through playing. There was neither digital nor board game. As results, the combined treatment was successful, but there is no mention about the use of game on it.

*March, Mulle and Herbel, 1994* [70]

Development and evaluation of a treatment Manual designed to facilitate patient and parental compliance, exportability, and empirical evaluation. There is no information about the type of OCD treated. The game was used only to engage the child's attention at the first session of therapy. 15 children and adolescents, all patients received medication. Because of its small contribution to treatment, the conclusions of the article did not mention the game, therefore, there are no relevant results about game on CBT.

*Miller, 2008* [71]

FRIENDS is a developmental, linear, classroom-formatted group activity curriculum based on CBT principles, that includes lessons (10 sessions) on identification of feelings, relaxation, problem solving, challenging negative or unhelpful thoughts, and exposure activities. There is no information about the type of OCD treated and, although the article mentioned OCD, the project aimed at treating anxiety disorders in general. The game was a quiz only for the last session to review the content and have fun on the last day. 373 Children from one school and 6 children (symptomatic), grades 4 through 6, with no age description, during 10 week and no medication informed. Although FRIENDS is called a prevention program, the game used at lesson 10 was a review quiz among CBT steps. As results, the author presents society needs about anxiety prevention, school environment as convenient do deliver treatment, the need for more validation, but there is no mention about the use of the game.

*Rocha, Alvarenga, Malloy-Diniz, and Corrêa, 2011* [72]

To evaluate the process of decision-making in patients with obsessive-compulsive disorder (OCD) using the Iowa Gambling Task (IGT), which is a card game. 214 adults (107 diagnosed with OCD and 107 healthy controls), some patients received medication (79) and others did not (22). There is inconsistent information about this sum, but it is registered here as it was in the original article. There is no information about the type of OCD treated. As results, the experiment found that OCD patients have significant deficits in their decision-making on the IGT, but also found that they performed equally well on several other tests that evaluate attention, different executive functions, memory and intelligence.

All outcomes that used game for educational purposes were intended for children and/or adolescents. And, of all results using games for educational purposes, only one was not developed for children and/or adolescents.

Concerning the use of digital artifact in relation to the treatment of OCD, 4 used it during the therapy sessions; 1 only at the end of the session; and 2 as homework; 2 did not use a digital artifact, but entered for analysis by using analog gaming. None of the 7 results using digital games was directed at prevention or diagnosis of OCD; however, 6 of them were used during the treatment and only 1 result recorded some type of metric.

About the use of games in relation to the sample, 8 of the 9 results, fulfilled the parameters aimed by this review, used game in the treatment of OCD by CBT. Among them, 5 applied a game developed specifically for this purpose and 4 applied commercial games, existing prior to the project. 1 result used game in the treatment of OCD by ERP.

Regarding the nature of the game and its positioning in the therapy, 4 of them were used for educational purposes; 6 as an active part in the treatment and one as a motivational complement, remembering that it is part of the beginning of the CBT, learning about OCD and its symptoms.

## 6 Final Conclusions

Veale and Roberts [24] say OCD is the fourth most common mental disorder. Its global prevalence is estimated between 1.2 to 3% of the general population [25]. Since worldwide population is around 7.5 billion [88], this prevalence corresponds to 90.6 to 226.5 millions of individuals suffering from OCD. This is roughly the population of countries like Germany (82.1 m), Mexico (129.1 m) and Pakistan (197 m) [88].

Since the fail rate of actual treatments is estimated as high as 30% [25], it means the window of improvement or search of alternative tools could improve the life of several million people around the globe. As games become more and more embedded in people's daily lives, they become increasingly attractive for the development of Games for Health in general. Given the large number of people affected with OCD and who do not respond to current treatments, the games appear as a promising idea to be studied.

Some authors agree with the role of Game as a facilitator in OCD-directed Cognitive-Behavioral Therapy [80, 89]. From this literature review, starting from 110 results analyzed, only 9 results met the predefined parameters in the methodology. This review shows data that is contrary to the theoretical indications regarding the use of games in the CBT for treating OCD due to the small number of cases: 4 cases of games in general, 4 digital games and one did not mention whether it was digital or not. This is a small number considering the initial sample of 110 analyzed results. There is, therefore, potential for research in the area involving Games related to OCD.

Among the results analyzed, even the articles that did not come to compose the sample brought information to this research, such as the interest of professionals in the universe of games, appropriating metaphors for their therapy [75–78], or using Gamification in the CBT [79–81].

Regarding the use of games in the treatment of OCD by CBT, the concern of professionals in choosing this alternative when the therapy was aimed at children and adolescents was evident. This shows an open possibility for designers to reach these professionals evidencing relations of consumption of games by adults, aiming to expand the use for all the ages.

Concerning the possibility of choosing between using a commercial game [66, 69, 70, 72] or developing one specifically for the purpose [64, 65, 67, 68], although the results point to close numbers, it is important to draw attention here to the fact that the development of a game meant a considerable high cost for research until the beginning of the years 2000. The ease and lower costs can influence adherence to this type of solution in the coming years.

# Appendix

1. Aboujaoude, E., Salame, W., Naim, L.: Telemental health: a status update. World psychiatry 14(2), 223–230 (2015).
2. Abramowitz, J. S., Blakey, S. M., Reuman, L., Buchholz, J.L.: New directions in the cognitive-behavioral treatment of ocd: theory, research, and practice. Behavior therapy 49(3), 311–322 (2018). https://doi.org/10.1016/j.beth.2017.09.002
3. An, S. K., Mataix-Cols, D., Lawrence, N. S., Giampietro, V., Speckens, A., Brammer, M. J., Phillips, M. L.: To discard or not to discard: the neural basis of hoarding symptoms in obsessive-compulsive disorder. Molecular psychiatry 14(3), 318 (2009). https://doi.org/10.1038/sj.mp.4002129
4. Bipeta, R., Yerramilli, S. S. R. R., Karredia, A. R., Gopinath, S.: Diagnostic stability of Internet addiction in obsessive-compulsive disorder: Data from a naturalistic one-year treatment study. Innovations in clinical neuroscience 12(3–4), 14–23 (2015).
5. Boger, K., Sperling, J., Potter, M., Gallo, K. P.: Treatment overview of an intensive group outpatient cognitive-behavioral therapy for youth anxiety disorders and obsessive-compulsive disorder. Evidence-Based Practice in Child and Adolescent Mental Health 1.2(3), 116–125 (2016). https://doi.org/10.1080/23794925.2016.1227947
6. Bouchard, S., Mendlowitz, S. L., Coles, M. E., Franklin, M.: Considerations in the use of exposure with children. Cognitive and behavioral practice 11(1), 56–65 (2004). https://doi.org/10.1016/s1077-7229(04)80007-5
7. Brezinka, V.: Ricky and the spider: a video game to support cognitive behavioral treatment of children with obsessive-compulsive disorder. Clinical Neuropsychiatry 10(3) (2013).
8. Cassano, M. C., Nangle, D. W., O'Grady, A. C.: Exposure-based treatment for a child with stabbing obsessions. Clinical Case Studies 8(2), 139–157 (2009).
9. Comer, J. S., Furr, J. M., Cooper-Vince, C. E., Kerns, C. E., Chan, P. T., Edson, A. L., Khanna, M., Franklin, M. E., Garcia, A. M., Freeman, J. B.: Internet-delivered, family-based treatment for early-onset ocd: a preliminary case series. Journal of Clinical Child & Adolescent Psychology 43(1), 74–87 (2014).
10. Cusimano, A.: Emdr in the treatment of adolescent obsessive-compulsive disorder: a case study. Journal of EMDR Practice and Research 12(4), 242–254 (2018).
11. Drake, K. L., Ginsburg, G. S.: Family-based cognitive-behavioral treatment of chronic pediatric headache and anxiety disorders: a case study. Child & Youth Care Forum. 579–598 (2012).

12. Falkenstein, M. J., Mouton-Odum, S., Mansueto, C. S., Goldfinger, G., Haaga, D. A. F.: Comprehensive behavioral treatment of trichotillomania: a treatment development study. Behavior modification 40(3), 414–438 (2016). https://doi.org/10.1177/0145445515616369

13. Foa, E. B., McLean, C. P.: The efficacy of exposure therapy for anxiety-related disorders and its underlying mechanisms: the case of ocd and ptsd. Annual review of clinical psychology 12, 1–28 (2016).

14. Freeman, J., Garcia, A., Benito, K., Conelea, C., Sapyta, J., Khanna, M., March, J., Franklin, M.: The pediatric obsessive compulsive disorder treatment study for young children (pots jr): developmental considerations in the rationale, design, and methods. Journal of obsessive-compulsive and related disorders 1(4), 294–300 (2012).

15. Hammond, D. C.: Neurofeedback with anxiety and affective disorders. Child and Adolescent Psychiatric Clinics 14(1), 105–123 (2005).

16. Haring, P., Warmelink, H.: Looking for metacognition. International Conference on Games and Learning Alliance. 95–106 (2016).

17. Havnen, A., Hansen, B., Haug, E. T., Prescott, P., Kvale, G.: Intensive group treatment of obsessive-compulsive disorder: a pilot study. Clinical Neuropsychiatry 10(3), (2013).

18. Herren, J., Brannan, E.: Clinical considerations for implementing exposure and response prevention for pediatric ocd. The Brown University Child and Adolescent Behavior Letter 34(6), 1–7 (2018).

19. Hong, J. S., Kim, S. M., Aboujaoude, E., Han, D. H.: Investigation of a mobile "serious game" in the treatment of obsessive–compulsive disorder: a pilot study. Games for health journal 7(5), 317–326 (2018). https://doi.org/10.1089/g4h.2017.0158

20. Kalra, S. K., Swedo, S. E.: Children with obsessive-compulsive disorder: are they just "little adults"?. The Journal of clinical investigation 119(4), 737–746 (2009).

21. Kendall, P. C., Beidas, R. S.: Smoothing the trail for dissemination of evidence-based practices for youth: flexibility within fidelity. Professional Psychology: Research and Practice 38(1), (2007).

22. Leib, P. T.: Integrating behavior modification and pharmacotherapy with the psychoanalytic treatment of obsessive-compulsive disorder: a case study. Psychoanalytic Inquiry 21(2), 222–241 (2001).

23. Lovato, L., Ferrão, Y. A., Stein, D. J., Shavitt, R. G., Fontenelle, L. F. Vivan, A., Miguel, E. C., Cordioli, A. V.: Skin picking and trichotillomania in adults with obsessive-compulsive disorder. Comprehensive psychiatry 53(5), 562–568 (2012).

24. Majchrzak, J. D.: Creative therapy in treating adolescent obsessive-compulsive disorder: a proposed therapeutic treatment. Meeting of Minds XVI Journal of Undergraduate Research 10, 107 (2003).

25. March, J. S., Mulle, K., Herbel, B.: Behavioral psychotherapy for children and adolescents with obsessive-compulsive disorder: an open trial of a new protocol-driven treatment package. Journal of the American Academy of Child & Adolescent Psychiatry 33(3), 333–341 (1994).

26. Matthews, A. J., Maunder, R., Scanlan, J. D., Kirkby, K. C.: Online computer-aided vicarious exposure for OCD symptoms: A pilot study. Journal of behavior therapy and experimental psychiatry 54, 25–34 (2017). https://doi.org/10.1016/j.jbtep.2016.06.002

27. Miller, L. D.: Facing fears: The feasibility of anxiety universal prevention efforts with children and adolescents. Cognitive and Behavioral Practice 15(1), 28–35 (2008).

28. Neziroglu, F., Fruchter, Y.: Manifestation and treatment of ocd and spectrum disorders within a pediatric population. Anxiety Disorders-From Childhood to Adulthood. (2018).

29. O'Neill, J., Schwartz, J.: The role of volition in ocd therapy: neurocognitive, neuroimaging, and neuroplastic aspects. Clinical Neuropsychiatry 1(1), 13–31 (2004).

30. Osgood-Hynes, D., Belmont, M. A.: Thinking bad thoughts. MGH/McLean OCD Institute.

31. Peterman, J. S., Read, K. L., Wei, C., Kendall, P. C.: The art of exposure: putting science into practice. Cognitive and behavioral practice 22(3), 379–392 (2015). https://doi.org/10.1016/j.cbpra.2014.02.003

32. Rocha, F. F. da, Alvarenga, N. B., Malloy-Diniz, L., Corrêa, H.: Decision-making impairment in obsessive-compulsive disorder as measured by the iowa gambling task. Arquivos de Neuro-psiquiatria 69(4), 642–647 (2011).

33. Rosa, A. C., Diniz, J. B., Fossaluza, V., Torres, A. R., Fontenelle, L. F., de Matthis, A. S., Rosário, M. da C., Miguel, E. C., Shavitt, R. G.: Clinical correlates of social adjustment in patients with obsessive-compulsive disorder. Journal of psychiatric research 46(10), 1286–1292 (2012). https://doi.org/10.1016/j.jpsychires.2012.05.019

34. Rowicka, M. Internet addiction treatment. Gambling and Internet Addictions: Epidemiology and Treatment. 55–64, (2016).

35. Sloman, G. M., Gallant, J., Storch, E. A.: A school-based treatment model for pediatric obsessive-compulsive disorder. Child psychiatry and human development 38(4), 303–319 (2007).

36. Tavares, H., Gentil, V.: Pathological gambling and obsessive-compulsive disorder: towards a spectrum of disorders of volition. Revista Brasileira de Psiquiatria 29(2), 107–117 (2007).

37. Thomsen, P. H.: Obsessive-compulsive disorder in children and adolescents. Clinical guidelines. European child & adolescent psychiatry 7(1), 1–11 (1998).

38. Tolin, D. F.: Alphabet soup: erp, ct, and act for ocd. Cognitive and Behavioral Practice 16(1), 40–48 (2009).

39. Valerio, C., Diniz, J. B., Fossaluza, V., de Mathis, M. A., Belotto-Silva, C., Joaquim, M. A., Miguel Filho, E. C., Shavitt, R. G.: Does anti-obsessional pharmacotherapy treat so-called comorbid depressive and anxiety states?. Journal of affective disorders 139(2), 187–192 (2012). https://doi.org/10.1016/j.jad.2012.02.002

40. Weidle, B., Skarphedinsson, G.: Treatment of a child with obsessive compulsive disorder with limited motivation: course and outcome of cognitive behavior therapy. Journal of clinical psychology 72(11), 1139–1151 (2016).

41. Wetherell, J. L.: Treatment of anxiety in older adults. Psychotherapy: Theory, Research, Practice, Training 35(4), 444 (1998).
42. Whiteside, S. P. H., Ale, C., Vickers, K. S., Tiede, M. S., Dammann, J. E.: Case examples of enhancing pediatric OCD treatment with a smartphone application. Clinical Case Studies 13(1), 80–94 (2014).
43. Wilson, R., Neziroglu, F., Feinstein, B. A., Ginsberg, R.: A new model for the initiation of treatment for obsessive–compulsive disorder: an exploratory study. Journal of Obsessive-Compulsive and Related Disorders 3(4), 322–337 (2014). https://doi.org/10.1016/j.jocrd.2014.08.003
44. Wilson, R. R.: The anxiety disorder game. Psychotherapy in Australia 12(2), 36–45 (2006).
45. Wu, M. S., Storch, E. A.: Personalizing cognitive-behavioral treatment for pediatric obsessive-compulsive disorder. Expert Review of Precision Medicine and Drug Development 1(4), 397–405 (2016).

# References

1. Kalapanidas, E., et al.: PlayMancer: games for health with accessibility in mind. Commun. Strat. **73**, 105–120 (2009)
2. Ozcan, A.: Educational games for malaria diagnosis (2014)
3. Small, P., Pai, M.: Tuberculosis diagnosis - time for a game change (2010)
4. Freitas, D.Q., et al.: Development and evaluation of a kinect based motor rehabilitation game. In: Simpósio Brasileiro de Jogos e Entretenimento Digital. SBC, Brasil (2012)
5. Baranowski, T., Buday, R., Thompson, D.I., Baranowski, J.: Playing for real: video games and stories for health-related behavior change. Am. J. Prev. Med. **34**(1), 74–82 (2008). https://doi.org/10.1016/j.amepre.2007.09.027
6. Bartolome, N.A., Zorrilla, A.M., Zapirain, B.G.: Can game-based therapies be trusted? Is game-based education effective? A systematic review of the Serious Games for health and education. In: IEEE Intelligent Systems, pp. 275–282. IEEE, New Jersey (2011)
7. Kharrazi, H., Lu, A.S., Ghargabi, F., Coleman, W.: A scoping review of health game research: Past, present, and future. Games Health Res. Dev. Clin. Appl. **1**(2), 153–164 (2012). https://doi.org/10.1089/g4h.2012.0011
8. Mann, B.D., Eidelson, B.M., Fukuchi, S.G., Nissman, S.A., Robertson, S., Jardines, L.: The development of an interactive game-based tool for learning surgical management algorithms via computer. Am. J. Surg. **183**(3), 305–308 (2002)
9. Sodre, C., Costa, A., Apolinário, J., Barros, F., Santos, A.: The metabolic race: an educational game. Revista de Ensino de Bioquímica **16**(7) (2018)
10. Sietsema, J.M., Nelson, D.L., Mulder, R.M., Mervau-Scheidel, D., White, B.E.: The use of a game to promote arm reach in persons with traumatic brain injury. Am. J. Occup. Ther. **47**(1), 19–24 (1993)
11. Vedamurthy, I., et al.: A dichoptic custom-made action video game as a treatment for adult amblyopia. Vis. Res. **114**, 173–187 (2015)
12. Brown, S.J., Lieberman, D.A., Gemeny, B.A., Fan, Y.C., Wilson, D.M., Pasta, D.J.: Educational video game for juvenile diabetes: results of a controlled trial. Med. Inform. **22**(1), 77–89 (1997). https://doi.org/10.3109/14639239709089835

13. Lieberman, D.A.: Management of chronic pediatric diseases with interactive health games: theory and research findings. J. Ambul. Care Manage. **24**(1), 26–38 (2001)

14. Kapp, K.M.: The Gamification of Learning and Instruction: Game-based Methods and Strategies for Training and Education. Wiley, Hoboken (2012)

15. Prins, P.J.M., Dovis, S., Ponsioen, A., Ten Brink, E., Van der Oord, S.: Does computerized working memory training with game elements enhance motivation and training efficacy in children with ADHD? Cyberpsychol. Behav. Soc. Networking **14**(3), 115–122 (2011)

16. Gardner, J.E.: Can the Mario Bros. help? Nintendo games as an adjunct in psychotherapy with children. Psychother. Theor. Res. Pract. Train. **28**(4), 667 (1991)

17. Brezinka, V.: Treasure Hunt-a serious game to support psychotherapeutic treatment of children. Stud. Health Technol. Inform. **136**, 71 (2008)

18. Coyle, D., Matthews, M.: Personal investigator: a therapeutic 3D game for adolescent psychotherapy. Interact. Technol. Smart Educ. **2**(2), 73–88 (2005). https://doi.org/10.1108/1741565058000034

19. Brown, S.J.: Method for treating medical conditions using a microprocessor-based video game. U.S. Patent No 5,918,603 (1999)

20. Wilkinson, N., Ang, R.P., Goh, D.H.: Online video game therapy for mental health concerns: a review. Int. J. Soc. Psychiatry **54**(4), 370–382 (2008)

21. Gamberini, L., Barresi, G., Majer, A., Scarpetta, F.: A game a day keeps the doctor away: a short review of computer games in mental healthcare. J. CyberTher. Rehabil. **1**(2), 127–146 (2008)

22. Luxton, D.D., McCann, R.A., Bush, N.E., Mishkind, M.C., Reger, G.M.: mHealth for mental health: Integrating smartphone technology in behavioral healthcare. Prof. Psychol. Res. Pract. **42**(6), 505 (2011)

23. Ayuso-Mateos, J.L.: Global burden of obsessive-compulsive disorder in the year 2000. World Health Organization. Global Burden Disease 2000, Draft 21-08-06 (2000)

24. Veale, D., Roberts, A.: Obsessive-compulsive disorder. BMJ **348**, g2183 (2014)

25. Abramowitz, J.S., McKay, D., Storch, E.A.: The Wiley Book of Obsessive-Compulsive Disorder, vol. 1. Wiley, Hoboken (2017)

26. Bream, V., Challacombe, F., Palmer, A., Salkovskis, P.: Cognitive Behaviour Therapy for Obsessive-Compulsive Disorder. Oxford University Press, Oxford (2017)

27. Sasson, Y., Zohar, J., Chopra, M., Lustig, M., Iancu, I., Hendler, T.: Epidemiology of obsessive-compulsive disorder: a world view. J. Clin. Psychiatry **58**(12), 7–10 (1997)

28. American Psychiatric Association: Diagnostic and Statistical Manual of Mental Disorders, 5th edn. American Psychiatric Association, Arlington (2013)

29. Franklin, M.E., Harrison, J., Benavides, K.: Treatment of childhood tic disorders with comorbid OCD. In: Storch, E., McKay, D. (eds.) Handbook of Treating Variants and Complications in Anxiety Disorders, pp. 135–148. Springer, New York (2013). https://doi.org/10.1007/978-1-4614-6458-7_9

30. Abramowitz, J.S., Taylor, S., Mckay, D.: Obsessive-compulsive disorder. Lancet **374**(9688), 491–499 (2009)

31. OCD—UK. https://www.ocduk.org/ocd/world-health-organisation/. Accessed 11 Dec 2018

32. Baer, L.: Standardized assessment of personality disorders in obsessive-compulsive disorder. Arch. Gen. Psychiatry **47**(9), 826–830 (1990)

33. Leckman, J.F., et al.: Symptoms of obsessive-compulsive disorder. Am. J. Psychiatry **154** (7), 911–917 (1997). https://doi.org/10.1176/ajp.154.7.911

34. Van Balkom, A.J.L.M., Van Oppen, P., Vermeulen, A.W.A., Van Dyck, R., Nauta, M.C.E., Vorst, H.C.M.: A meta-analysis on the treatment of obsessive compulsive disorder: A comparison of antidepressants, behavior, and cognitive therapy. Clin. Psychol. Rev. **14**(5), 359–381 (1994). https://doi.org/10.1016/0272-7358(94)90033-7

35. Wenzel, A., Dobson, K.S., Hays, P.A.: Cognitive Behavioral Therapy Techniques and Strategies. American Psychological Association, Washington, DC (2016)
36. Beck, A.T.: Cognitive Therapy of Depression. Guilford press, New York (1979)
37. Hofmann, S.G., Asmundson, G.J.G.: The Science of Cognitive Behavioral Therapy. Academic Press, Elsevier, Cambridge (2017). http://dx.doi.org/10.1016/B978-0-12-803457-6.00001-5
38. Butler, A.C., Chapman, J.E., Forman, E.M., Beck, A.T.: The empirical status of cognitive-behavioral therapy: a review of meta-analyses. Clin. Psychol. Rev. 26(1), 17–31 (2006). https://doi.org/10.1016/j.cpr.2005.07.003
39. Hofmann, S.G.: The Wiley Handbook of Cognitive Behavioral Therapy, 1st edn. Wiley, New Jersey (2014). https://doi.org/10.1002/9781118528563.wbcbt01
40. Spiegler, M.D., Guevremont, D.C.: Contemporary Behavior Therapy, 5th edn. Wadsworth, Cengage Learning, Belmont (2010)
41. Beck, A.T.: Cognitive therapy: nature and relation to behavior therapy. Behav. Ther. 1, 184–200 (1970). https://doi.org/10.1016/S0005-7894(70)80030-2
42. Ellis, A., Whiteley, M.M.: Theoretical and Empirical Foundations of Rational-emotive Therapy. Brooks/Cole, Monterey (1979)
43. Dryden, W.: Rational Emotive Behavior Therapy, 1st edn. Routhledge, East Sussex (2009)
44. Persons, J.B.: The Case Formulation Approach to Cognitive-behavor Theraphy. Guilford Press, New York (2008)
45. Chosak, A., Marques, L., Fama, J., Renaud, S., Willhelm, S.: Cognitive therapy for obsessive-compulsive disorder: A case example. Cogn. Behav. Pract. 16(1), 7–17 (2009). https://doi.org/10.1016/j.cbpra.2008.01.005
46. Wright, J.H., Basco, M.R., Thase, M.E.: Aprendendo a Terapia Cognitivo-comportamental. Artmed Editora, Porto Alegre (2009)
47. Dobson, D., Dobson, K.S.: Evidence-Based Practive of Cognitive-Behavioral Therapy, 2nd edn. Guilford Press, New York (2017)
48. Storch, E.A., et al.: Does cognitive-behavioral therapy response among adults with obsessive–compulsive disorder differ as a function of certain comorbidities? J. Anxiety Disord. 24(6), 547–552 (2010)
49. Persons, J.B.: Case formulation-driven psychotherapy. Clin. Psychol. Sci. Pract. 13(2), 167–170 (2006)
50. Huizinga, J.: Homo Ludens: O Jogo Como Elemento da Cultura. Editora Perspectiva, São Paulo (2001)
51. Goldbeck, L., Pew, A.: Violent video games and aggression. http://www.center4research.org/violent-video-games-can-increase-aggression/. Accessed 17 Dec 2018
52. Ng, B.D., Wierner-Hastings, P.: Addiction to the internet and online gaming. CyberPsychol. Behav. 8(2), 110–113 (2005). https://doi.org/10.1089/cpb.2005.8.110
53. Zelda. https://www.zelda.com/. Accessed 16 Nov 2018
54. Wow. https://worldofwarcraft.com/pt-br/. Accessed 16 Nov 2018
55. Eve. https://www.eveonline.com/. Accessed 16 Nov 2018
56. Johnson, S.: Tudo o que é ruim é bom para você. Zahar, Rio de Janeiro (2012)
57. Orland, K.: GfH: the real life lessons of wow's corrupted blood, 20 May 2018. https://www.gamasutra.com/php-bin/news_index.php?story=18571. Accessed 18 Feb 2018
58. Kelly, A.: How Eve Online players are helping medical science, 26 Apr 2016. https://www.pcgamer.com/how-internet-spaceships-are-helping-medical-science/. Accessed 22 Dec 2018
59. Prensky, M.: Aprendizagem Baseada em Jogos Digitais. Editora Senac, São Paulo (2012)
60. Wattanasoontorn, V., Boada, I., García, R., Sbert, M.: Serious Games for Health. Entertainment Comput. 4, 231–247 (2013)

61. Sawyer, B., Smith, P.: Serious games taxonomy. https://thedigitalentertainmentalliance.files. wordpress.com/2011/08/serious-games-taxonomy.pdf. Accessed 22 Dec 2018

62. de Vasconcellos, M.S., de Carvalho, F.G., Capella, M.A.M., Dias, C.M., de Araujo, I.S.: A Saúde na Literatura Acadêmica sobre Jogos: uma análise das publicações do SBGames. In: SBC – Proceedings of XV SBGames, SBC, Brasil, São Paulo (2016)

63. Google Scholar. https://scholar.google.com. Accessed 27 Jan 2019

64. Brezinka, V.: Ricky and the spider: a video game to support cognitive behavioral treatment of children with obsessive-compulsive disorder. Clin. Neuropsychiat. **10**(3) (2013)

65. Comer, J.S., et al.: Internet-delivered, family-based treatment for early-onset ocd: a preliminary case series. J. Clin. Child Adolesc. Psychol. **43**(1), 74–87 (2014)

66. Freeman, J., et al.: The pediatric obsessive compulsive disorder treatment study for young children (pots jr): developmental considerations in the rationale, design, and methods. J. Obsessive-compulsive Relat. Disord. **1**(4), 294–300 (2012)

67. Haring, Priscilla, Warmelink, Harald: Looking for Metacognition. In: Bottino, Rosa, Jeuring, Johan, Veltkamp, Remco C. (eds.) GALA 2016. LNCS, vol. 10056, pp. 95–106. Springer, Cham (2016). https://doi.org/10.1007/978-3-319-50182-6_9

68. Hong, J.S., Kim, S.M., Aboujaoude, E., Han, D.H.: Investigation of a mobile "serious game" in the treatment of obsessive–compulsive disorder: a pilot study. Games Health J. **7**(5), 317–326 (2018). https://doi.org/10.1089/g4h.2017.0158

69. Leib, P.T.: Integrating behavior modification and pharmacotherapy with the psychoanalytic treatment of obsessive-compulsive disorder: a case study. Psychoanal. Inquiry **21**(2), 222–241 (2001)

70. March, J.S., Mulle, K., Herbel, B.: Behavioral psychotherapy for children and adolescents with obsessive-compulsive disorder: an open trial of a new protocol-driven treatment package. J. Am. Acad. Child Adolesc. Psychiatry **33**(3), 333–341 (1994)

71. Miller, L.D.: Facing fears: The feasibility of anxiety universal prevention efforts with children and adolescents. Cogn. Behav. Pract. **15**(1), 28–35 (2008)

72. da Rocha, F.F., Alvarenga, N.B., Malloy-Diniz, L., Corrêa, H.: Decision-making impairment in obsessive-compulsive disorder as measured by the iowa gambling task. Arqu. Neuropsiquiatr. **69**(4), 642–647 (2011)

73. Havnen, A., Hansen, B., Haug, E.T., Prescott, P., Kvale, G.: Intensive group treatment of obsessive-compulsive disorder: a pilot study. Clin. Neuropsychiatry **10**(3) (2013)

74. Aboujaoude, E., Salame, W., Naim, L.: Telemental health: a status update. World Psychiatry **14**(2), 223–230 (2015)

75. Cassano, M.C., Nangle, D.W., O'Grady, A.C.: Exposure-based treatment for a child with stabbing obsessions. Clin. Case Stud. **8**(2), 139–157 (2009)

76. Wu, M.S., Storch, E.A.: Personalizing cognitive-behavioral treatment for pediatric obsessive-compulsive disorder. Expert Rev. Precis. Med. Drug Dev. **1**(4), 397–405 (2016)

77. Abramowitz, J.S., Blakey, S.M., Reuman, L., Buchholz, J.L.: New directions in the cognitive-behavioral treatment of ocd: theory, research, and practice. Behav. Ther. **49**(3), 311–322 (2018). https://doi.org/10.1016/j.beth.2017.09.002

78. Herren, J., Brannan, E.: Clinical considerations for implementing exposure and response prevention for pediatric ocd. Univ. Child Adolesc. Behav. Lett. **34**(6), 1–7 (2018)

79. Sloman, G.M., Gallant, J., Storch, E.A.: A school-based treatment model for pediatric obsessive-compulsive disorder. Child Psychiatry Human Dev. **38**(4), 303–319 (2007)

80. Peterman, J.S., Read, K.L., Wei, C., Kendall, P.C.: The art of exposure: putting science into practice. Cogn. Behav. Pract. **22**(3), 379–392 (2015). https://doi.org/10.1016/j.cbpra.2014.02.003

81. Wilson, R., Neziroglu, F., Feinstein, B.A., Ginsberg, R.: A new model for the initiation of treatment for obsessive–compulsive disorder: an exploratory study. J. Obsessive-compulsive Relat. Disord. **3**(4), 322–337 (2014). https://doi.org/10.1016/j.jocrd.2014.08.003
82. Whiteside, S.P.H., Ale, C., Vickers, K.S., Tiede, M.S., Dammann, J.E.: Case examples of enhancing pediatric OCD treatment with a smartphone application. Clin. Case Stud. **13**(1), 80–94 (2014)
83. Matthews, A.J., Maunder, R., Scanlan, J.D., Kirkby, K.C.: Online computer-aided vicarious exposure for OCD symptoms: A pilot study. J. Behav. Ther. Exp. Psychiatry **54**, 25–34 (2017). https://doi.org/10.1016/j.jbtep.2016.06.002
84. Foa, E.B., McLean, C.P.: The efficacy of exposure therapy for anxiety-related disorders and its underlying mechanisms: the case of ocd and ptsd. Annu. Rev. Clin. Psychol. **12**, 1–28 (2016)
85. Neziroglu, F., Fruchter, Y.: Manifestation and treatment of ocd and spectrum disorders within a pediatric population. Anxiety Disorders-From Childhood to Adulthood (2018)
86. Bouchard, S., Mendlowitz, S.L., Coles, M.E., Franklin, M.: Considerations in the use of exposure with children. Cogn. Behav. Pract. **11**(1), 56–65 (2004). https://doi.org/10.1016/S1077-7229(04)80007-5
87. Rick and the Spider. https://rickandthespider.uzh.ch. Accessed 15 Jan 2019
88. UN: World Population Prospects 2017. Data Booklet (2017)
89. Brezinka, V.: Computer games supporting cognitive behaviour therapy in children. Clin. Child Psychol. Psychiatry **19**(1), 100–110 (2014)

# Exergames: Game Prototype Using Maker Movement Assets

Bruno S. Oliveira[1($\boxtimes$)], Vania Teofilo[2], Juliana Miranda[3,4],
and Sergio Nesteriuk[1]

[1] UAM - Universidade Anhembi Morumbi, São Paulo, Brazil
brunosoliveira@gmail.com, nesteriuk@hotmail.com
[2] São Paulo, Brazil
[3] UFPE - Universidade Federal de Pernambuco, Recife, Brazil
mirandaa.juliana@gmail.com
[4] UNICAP - Universidade Católica de Pernambuco, Recife, Brazil

**Abstract.** The world population is expected to grow until the year 2100. Also, the number of senior individuals is expected to surpass the number of children and teens in the populations. This growth in the raw number and number of seniors creates huge challenges for countries - especially in cost terms. It's well known that preventive healthcare could smooth those impacts through preventing disease. One of the most effective and easy to implement tools healthcare programs of this scope use is exercise. However, many individuals lack motivation for the practice. Since gaming is one of most used entertainment form, it seems a good way to attract and maintain people into exercise routines. Games of this type, that require the user movement as part of playing, are called 'Exergames'. This paper is consequence of a larger research towards game design methods for this specific type. Since initial surveys showed some lack of information about this subject, the need for this project emerged. A problem found along the research development was which device would be used to conduct further testing with design methodologies. Therefore, this paper shows the process of using maker movement assets to create an open source device capable of transforming body movement through cycling into command input to a platform game.

**Keywords:** Exergames · Health care · Maker movement

## 1 Introduction

In the last decades the world population has been growing constantly. According to predictions, we will reach 9.8 billion inhabitants by 2050, when the global population of people older than 60 is expected to jump to 2 billion [1]. This growth is expected to stabilize around the year 2100, when we expect to reach the number of 13.2 billion people [2]. In addition, the distribution of the population by age groups has taken a very different form from the past. This is due to declining birth rates and mortality rates. Thus, the distribution that could previously be represented by a pyramid (in which the base is much wider than the top) is gradually shaped into a column. As a result, the proportion of people over 60 years of age in the population has increased

© Springer Nature Switzerland AG 2019
V. G. Duffy (Ed.): HCII 2019, LNCS 11582, pp. 532–549, 2019.
https://doi.org/10.1007/978-3-030-22219-2_39

significantly, to the point that, excluding the African continent, it has surpassed the number of children between 0 and 14 years [2].

This aging of the population has a direct impact on the cost of health and on the existing structure of the health systems of countries [1]. In a traditional healthcare system, focused on reactive treatment services, this population increase should accentuate problems related to hospital and outpatient structure, health personnel, equipment, etc. One way to alleviate this rising cost is to invest in preventive health programs to reduce the frequent demand for hospitals and clinics [3].

However, a problem in implementing this type of approach is the culture and habits of the population. For example, it is commonly known and scientifically demonstrated that exercise practice prevents the onset of various diseases. However, about 10–50% of people who start structured exercise programs give up in the first six months, with most of these withdrawals occurring within the first three months [4].

From the point of view of this research, it is believed that it is possible to minimize this resistance to exercises if these are done concomitantly to the practices of entertainment and fun. To play is part of the human essence, in the course of history and in all cultures we find various manifestations of games spread across different regions and countries [5]. In the last decades, electronic games have increased in popularity due to the expansion of Internet access, the popularity of computers - especially smart phones [6]. Digital games, notably entertainment games, draw the attention of the media and researchers to the increasing spread of their use - thereby bringing about an equally increasing volume of capital movement [6]. Despite stereotypes, gamers come from all walks of life. Today, there are over two billion gamers worldwide - and they all play across a wide variety of genres and platforms. About 59% of gamers are males, and 41% are females - and the average age of a gamer is 38 years old [7].

Due to the immersive capacity and attractiveness of digital games, they have also been used for practical and serious applications, such as education, health, and for specific skills training - simulation games - thus being designated serious games [8]. Among these applications, we highlight serious games for health as the focal point of our research, due to the possibility of their application in the achievement of wellbeing for people of any age, gender, race, or social class.

The term 'Games for Health' (GfH) refers to games used in health and fitness treatments [9]. In the same way that the concept of health covers a wide range of areas [10], games in this segment have applications in a wide range of areas, such as: aid for the training of health professionals [9], physical rehabilitation [11], health education [12], and even aid in diagnosis [10].

Among the games used directly in treatments, there are two subtypes: those that work for mental and cognitive health, and those that care and treat the body, requiring the user to effectively perform some type of physical exercise [9]. Games of this second type are commonly known as Exergames - term from the union of the words exercise and game. These games require that the user execute movements with the body or members as an effective part of the game play.

This research began in 2016, with the accomplishment of a bibliographical review of academic works related to the Exergames, using works published in Brazilian and international journals as source. This sampling demonstrated the lack of methods and tools for the design process of Exergames [13]. Therefore, the main objective of the research was to explore several design methods and tools and, if necessary, create new ones specifically for this game genre.

However, as the research went on, it was clear that a device platform had to be developed before studying game design methodologies so that the specificities of the health area could be met. Thus, the research was directed to look for ways to create or adapt an equipment keeping it cost accessible and easy to use so that it made the application of Exergames more extensively available to a greater part of the population in the scenario of a developing country.

After considering many options, the path chosen was to use the tools from maker movement which could allow the construction of a device prototype based on an Arduino system. Also, using the maker movement bases, the research could make results more accessible through an open source and keep it low cost. All of this is aligned with goal #3 from United Nations 'Goals for a Sustainable Future' [14].

## 2 Health

Health is a term that has different definitions or interpretations, being considered as a simultaneously philosophical, scientific, technological, political, and practical issue [15]. Within the scope of this research, we understand that health is the second most important point for safety and security in the pyramid of Maslow's hierarchy of human needs [16], and also consider United Nations Sustainable Development Goal 3, which states that "*Ensure healthy lives and promote well-being for all ages*" is the third most important point to be worked towards developing a sustainable world [14].

The improvements in nutrition, hygiene, sanitation and a better health system achieved in the last decades have resulted in an increase in the longevity of populations, leading to a considerable escalation of the prevalence of chronic diseases in society, leading them to be considered the challenge of public health in the 21st century [17].

One of the ways to address this problem is to change the way people care for their health by changing people's health habits from a reactive approach to a proactive approach, by encouraging people to take basic care of themselves and become protagonists of their health. This can be accomplished with participation from health providers to encourage the patients to exercise, take prescribed medications and vitamins correctly, drink water, watch their weight, eat healthily, and schedule regular wellness exams with primary care physicians [3].

This new approach has the potential to change cost perspectives in the area around the world, considering that health occupied, in average, about 10% of the GDP (Gross Domestic Product) of the nations in 2014 - 8.3% in Brazil. There is also a tendency to a growth in this percentage, with an increase of about 1.5% in GDP revenue in the last two decades, as well as in the average value of investment per capita [18].

Prevention in health is defined as an anticipated action based on the knowledge of the natural history of the disease [19]. It is comprised of three phases: [a] Primary Prevention, corresponding to the actions performed in the pre-pathogenesis period, 'health promotion' and 'specific protection'. [b] Secondary Prevention, dividing between 'early diagnosis and treatment' and 'disability limitation', and finally [c] Tertiary Prevention corresponding to 'rehabilitation' actions [19].

## 3    Games for Health and Exergames

The percentage of the population with access to computers and the Internet has grown worldwide in the last decades. To illustrate this, in Brazil, according to IBGE - Brazilian Institute of Geography and Statistics, Internet access by computers increased from 6.3 million households in 2004 to 25.7 million in 2012 [20]. In this regard, it seems valid to think of a possible point of convergence among these three trends - increasing life expectancy in the world population, increasing gamer population, increased access to digital media that allow playing.

Some of the examples of the roles Games for Health can play are the training of doctors [21]; patient awareness [22], improving health [23]; and rehabilitation treatments [24]. This research proposes the study of these last two types of applications by design bias: the Exergames.

The term Exergames comes from the union of the words exercise and game, and covers a wide range of games that similarly require the user to perform some type of physical effort. Other terms used to define games of this type are: Active Video Game, Active Gaming, Movement Controlled Video Game, and Exertion Game.

It should be noted that many games that, at first glimpse, would not be qualified as Exergames, can be used for these purposes, even though they have not been created for this intention. As examples we have the series Wii Sports [25], also used in experiments of improvement of physical conditioning [11], and Pokemon Go [26], which was already pointed out as possible cause of the weight loss of some of its users.

The term Exergames should be understood, in the scope of this study, as digital games created with the primordial and main intention of physical exercise to improve some aspect of health - either for the physical-motor rehabilitation or improvement of the physical condition of its player.

### 3.1    Brief History of Exergames Devices

The first known device for Exergames was the Atari Puffer [27]. It was planned by Atari in the early 1980s when the company realized an opportunity to market entertainment games to exercise on exercise bikes. The project had three specific models, aimed at different markets: Pro model, for gymnasiums; Arcade Model, for arcades stores; and, Home Model for home use, with a more affordable price. The project ended up being filed due to the bankruptcy of the company.

Following this device, two other projects involving stationary bikes and games were developed - Autodesk HighCycle and RacerMate CompuTrainer. Few technical references exist about Autodesk HighCycle - just images of bike racing simulators. The RacerMate CompuTrainer was developed by a fitness equipment company, known to have an electromagnetic exercise load system, different from the conventionally used straps. This electromagnetic system allowed the sending of data to a computer [27].

Still in the 1980s, Nintendo entered the market with PowerPad and PowerGlove. The PowerPad was a rug with built-in buttons to be fired with the users' feet, consisting of 3 rows with 4 columns of buttons each, totaling 12 buttons. The use could be individual or double, the buttons were marked half blue and half red, signaling the ones that should be used by player 1 and player 2 in the case of double matches. The most well-known game of this device was the 1989 Dance Aerobics, a dance game that is considered the forerunner of Dance Dance Revolution, mentioned later in this section.

Nintendo PowerGlove was basically a glove with joystick-like buttons and sensors that sensed the movements made by the user's hand. There are reports that the device did not work very well, even when used in conjunction with a game developed especially for the glove – Myke Tyson's Punch Out [27]. Entering the 90's, Tectrix VR Bike and VR Climber were respectively a bicycle ergometer and a step device (simulating something between walking and climbing steps of a ladder). Both had a computer and CRT monitor coupled and came with six games, loaded via CD-ROM. Both had special versions of games developed for the use of the American military, and the price for the public was around USD 28,000.00 [27].

Dance Dance Revolution (DDR) is considered the first successful exergaming system [28]. Created by Bandai, based on concerns about growing obesity among young Japanese, DDR consisted of a dance-themed game running on an arcade device with push buttons to be triggered. These were arranged in a matrix of $3 \times 3$ buttons with the central neutral position (without drive) in which the player was initially stopped. In this way, the eight drive positions were around the player. The player during the match should fire the buttons at the correct time according to the song and the level of difficulty chosen - thus gaining points. This rhythmic drive together with music formed the central theme of dance.

Using a different approach, two command-trigger devices were created to replace the joysticks, the CatEye Game Bike, and the Bodypad for Fighting Games, which operated on conventional consoles such as PlayStation 2, being used instead of the original joystick [27]. The Cat-Eye Game Bike was a stationary bicycle geared towards racing games, where pedaling replaced the acceleration command of the joysticks. The Bodypad for Fighting Games was a series of sensor clamps that the user could use to capture the movements. A receiver received the data and converted it into blows from the fighting games.

### 3.2   Current and Near Future Devices

As current devices, the most popular and well-known are the Nintendo Wii and Microsoft Kinect. Through research, we verified the existence of other devices, which are not available in Brazil such as Expresso bikes, Goji Play and the Holodia VR system. Nintendo Wii was released in 2006 and discontinued in 2013 [25], for purposes of this approach, it is considered current because it is still used by rehabilitation clinics such as the Lucy Montoro Clinic [29].

The novelty of the device was to use sensors embedded in the joystick, allowing the console to calculate the spatial positioning (X, Y and Z axes) the joystick was in, thus perceiving changes in its positioning, which was then converted into action in games. Hence, the act of playing on Wii approached real actions such as boxing, bowling or sword fighting. Due to popularity and low cost, the console has been used in research for use in rehabilitation, child obesity [11] and physical education [30, 31].

To compete with Nintendo Wii, Microsoft introduced the Kinect in 2010 as an accessory to the Xbox 360 console [32]. Equipped with special cameras and microphone, the accessory could capture the body of the users and verify changes in the positioning of this or the limbs and head. A new version of the system was released in 2013 for the Xbox One and for PC (Personal Computer). The use with PC allowed the appearance of several studies and projects related to the use of Kinect for different applications from the evaluation and rehabilitation of motor deficit [33] to the improvement of balance in the elderly [34]. Microsoft Kinect had its production stopped in the second quarter of 2017 and a new version was presented in the second quarter of 2018 [35]. Once the technical features were released, this new version of Kinectic shows that Microsoft's mindset was quite similar to our approach, making this new version directed to makers and tinkers. This subject will be further commented in the Sect. 5 of this paper.

The bicycles of the brand Expresso [36] have a closed system with a monitor and computer docked. Roughly speaking, it can be considered an evolution of Tectrix VR with updated hardware and software. During the survey, a user of a US fitness club who has a model of the brand was contacted. In an initial conversation, he offered to informally interview some instructors of the gym about the use of the Expresso. They said that the equipment is little used and believe that the system is uninteresting for the local reality because the game consists of a simulation of cycling in streets. According to the comments of these instructors, the public of the gym prefers to ride bikes outdoors, in parks and streets instead of trying to simulate an immediate reality.

Another system found in the research was the Goji Play [37]. This consists of two small buttons that can be attached to the bicycle handlebars and can communicate with mobile devices. The company website features examples of various games that can be used with the system. In the first version of Gojy Play, only handsets running iOS were supported. The current version supports both iOS and Android. The company has VR system ads, but at the time the search was made, there were no available further details.

The Holofit [38] of the company Holodia is the most recent release found in this research. According to data from the manufacturer, Holofit integrates with modern stationary bikes, rowing, and step devices, providing integrated experiences in virtual reality.

## 4 Proposal: Use of Maker Movement Technology

For the study of methods and tools for Exergames Game Design, it is necessary to define the device to be used for capturing user movements. Points to consider for this choice are: [i] device availability - that is, if it is currently in production and sale; [ii] the system allows for easy development, not being blocked or in need of expensive/specific development kits; [iii] ease of device reproduction and replacement of parts; [iv] availability for use in social projects, thus increasing the impact that Exergames can have on improving the health of the population.

Considering the points discussed above, a decision was made to use a prototype exercise device for Exergames, a common stationary bicycle, modified using the technology of the Maker Movement to provide communication with the computer and/or mobile device. This section is subdivided into four parts relating: the Maker's Movement, the process of choosing the stationary bicycle, the prototyping of the platform game, and the comments on the results obtained.

## 4.1    Maker Movement

Vilém Flusser was a philosopher whose thought approached what he called Homo Faber, that is, the human that becomes human through doing. For Flusser, the factory of the future will be a place where the potentialities of Homo Faber can be realized [39]. Also, from this perspective, everyone can take ownership of existing things, transform, and use them.

Flusser passed away in 1991, but his texts anticipated the change in the concept of factory in at least a decade. Only in 2001, with the implementation of the first FabLab at MIT (Massachusetts Institute of Technology), did these Flussian concepts begin to appear [40]. The FabLabs are a laboratory-factory model that makes CNC machines (computer numerical control) that receive instructions directly from the computer available to the general public. The operating system of the FabLabs has ideological foundations in what is now known as the Movement Maker.

According to Anderson [41], this movement has in its foundations the practice of Do-It-Yourself (DIY) that involves the unprofessional development of manufacturing skills - commonly regarded as a hobby. It covers the term a wide variety of activities, from crafting practices such as woodworking, to the use of high-tech electronics.

Practitioners of this movement are popularly known as Makers. Anderson [41] points out two aspects that separate these from the makers and inventors of the past: [i] they are using digital tools - projecting on the screen, and manufacturing them using computerized machinery; and, [ii] they are sharing their creations over the internet. These, in turn, promote the democratization of innovation around bits (digital archives) just as fast prototyping machines, such as 3D printers and laser cutting machines, provide the democratization of innovation in the physical-material plane. Briefly, the Maker Movement is characterized by:

- Use of digital tools to design new products and to prototype them (called 'digital DIY' by Anderson);
- Common sense in distributing and collaborating on collective projects through online communities;
- Use of a standardization in these files that allows anyone, if he so desires, to send those files to companies with the intention of manufacturing these products in any desired quantity - as easily as producing it on the bench itself [42].

Although, in general terms, the Makers use any available material or technology, observing the application list of FabLabs [42], we can observe that they must have Computer Numerical Control (CNC) cutting machines of different types, additive manufacturing machines (popularly known as '3D printers'), and electronic equipment of the Arduino type.

CNC cutting machines can receive commands directly from computers, making cuts with precision and speed. There are both those that use cutter-type cutters (cutting and beveling), depending on the profile of the cutter, as well as laser cutting machines - used both for sheet cutting of various materials and for engraving textures on surfaces of materials.

Additive Manufacturing (AM) Machines also receive commands via computer and function by principle of depositing material to form the desired object - as opposed to the traditional method of removing material to achieve the final shape of the object. There are several types of AM machines, varying the material type, speed, final object precision, etc. In recent years, the price drop has made the equipment more affordable. One of the most popular types is the filament AM machine, which is fed by a plastic coil to produce the objects. An example of this type, is the Arduino Materia 101 [43] which costs close to US $ 800.00.

As for electronics, one of the most popular systems is the Arduino. This is an open source electronic platform that is easy to assemble and easy to program. Arduino is capable of receiving electro-electronic pulses either through sensors, buttons or even a message via Twitter and turn it into a command to drive a motor, connect a LED lamp etc. [44]. For example, with Arduino it is possible to create an automatic irrigation system of the gardens of a house [45].

Given the possibilities of creation provided by the technologies used in the Maker Movement, in the understanding of this research, it is believed that the use of these technologies are quite feasible and bring two important factors for the application of Exergames in Brazil: cost and dissemination. Considering cost, the materials are considerably more affordable when compared to closed systems. As for dissemination, the principles of the Maker Movement favor the reproduction of the experiments to be carried out during this research, not only by teaching and research institutions, but also by companies of different sizes and individuals from different parts of the country - thus increasing the possibility of dissemination of Exergames in our society.

## 4.2    Device Selection: Ergometer Bicycles

For the equipment, a stationary bicycle was chosen. Factors that led to the choice were: [i] acquisition cost, [ii] the amount of basic electronics shipped, [iii] equipment popularity, and [iv] the possibility of future expansion adding new functionality.

In terms of acquisition cost, models ranging from USD 125.00 to USD 1,750.00 were surveyed. The main factor of this big cost difference is in the structural part of the bicycles that, due to several reinforcements, end up bringing up the cost of the models destined to clinics and gymnasiums – which have a very high daily load of use. It was noticed that even the most basic bicycles had basic electronics and had an on-board computer in which data such as speed, distance traveled, spent calorie, and heart rate are shown.

As for the popularity, it was noticed in visits to gymnasiums that had bicycles among their equipment. These are offered both in the upright pedaling position (also called spinning position, similar to racing bikes, where the pedals are under the seat) and in a seat configuration similar to a common chair (known as horizontal model, in which the pedals are in front of the chair). Rehabilitation clinics such as the pulmonary disease treatment laboratory at the University of São Paulo Medical School Hospital (HCFM-USP) and the Lucy Montoro Clinic, have been found to use bicycles (horizontal model) in the physical treatment of patients.

Lastly, the possibilities of scope expansions of the device were considered - that is, the possibility of introducing new features to the project. At this point, we highlight new technologies such as wearable's (clothing and accessories with built-in computing) and virtual reality equipment (VR gear), the latter being particularly interesting given the great interest of the media and the devices that are being developed by companies.

Taking into account all these factors, a KIKO brand bicycle, model KV31i [46] was purchased with the authors' own resources, with an acquisition cost of around USD 250.00. It contained embedded electronics (on-board computer); integrated heart rate monitor and vertical pedaling position. Also, we considered this model since in conversations with some local gym instructors the brand was one of the recommended for its quality and reliability.

### 4.3 Bike Prototype for Exergame

This section describes the steps of the prototype of the bicycle and is divided into two sub-sections. In the first one, a complete planning of the stages of this research is presented.

In the second section, we present the work done until now, which consists in the first stage of this study, resulting in a prototype, where we show what was worked on the electronics using Arduino, C# programs, and the game platform developed to validate the game idea using only the pedaling as input.

**Complete Planning Steps for this Research**
For the complete development of the bicycle for Exergames, we adopted system of development in stages, in which a new characteristic or functionality would be added to the device in each step. Thus, the research is developed in six stages, the first of which has its completion described in this paper.

For the planning of the stages, the know-how of the researchers, the acquisition of equipment, and the maturity of the technologies involved were taken into consideration. Thus, the planning of the stages went from the simplest functionality – verifying the speed of the user's pedaling – to the most complex – virtual/augmented reality addition. The stages are shown in Fig. 1 and described below.

# Development Stages

1 Pedal control

2 Heart beat sensor

3 Intensity control

4 Tablet / mobile suport

5 Bike handlebar with joystick buttons

6 VR Gear support

**Fig. 1** The schematic of all planned project stages.

- 1st Stage (complete) - the capture of the most basic movement of the bicycle was defined: the movement of the pedal. This was then sent to a computer, so that communication with Unity for the development of games was possible;
- 2nd Stage - capture the heart rate using the sensor built into the bike itself. Through this monitoring, it will be possible to carry out prototypes and tests with users;
- 3rd Stage - measurement of the load (pedaling effort). For this, we'll need to study and test different types of sensors, since bikes in this price range have no native sensors;
- 4th Stage - the development of support for mobile devices. The idea is that this support is printed on machines of additive manufacture so that it is easy to reproduce, in the molds of the Maker Movement. Larger tests with more users should start at this stage, because at this point the bike will work with games running on tablets or smartphones, making it easier to move and use;
- 5th Stage - tests on the modification of the bicycle handlebar for the addition of extra buttons, of the type found on joysticks. This addition can be in two ways: adding a new "handle" on the handlebar, with the buttons built-in (in a similar concept to Goji Play); or redesigning the entire handlebar, adding the buttons and with the option to make the handlebar moveable, adding a turn sensor for control of left-right turns;
- 6th Stage (Final) - VR technology will be added to the system. Regarding this aspect, it is important to highlight the concern with the use of this technology for health applications, especially around sickness and malaise that have been reported and studied.

VR technology has returned after a long hiatus since its rise in the 1990s. Recent technological developments have made HMD (head-mounted display) smaller, lighter, cheaper, and faster response devices [47]. Despite all technological advancement, most virtual reality helmets still depend on computers to process images, and power cables, and image transmission connecting the computer to the helmet, what ends up limiting users' movements, which would hinder performance and ergonomics of the project.

In 2015 the company Google launched the Cardboard, a product to bring virtual reality to the public with a cost around USD 15.00. The idea is that almost everyone carries a virtual reality device in our pockets: our own smartphone. The Cardboard is nothing more than a pair of lenses coupled to a cardboard structure in the shape of a helmet, which is attached to the user's head through an elastic strap.

In parallel to the development of the Cardboard, the Korean company Samsung developed a more advanced option of helmet that uses the mobile device called Gear VR [48]. With better construction material, it has superior image quality and is more robust. Gear VR and Cardboard are the two viable options for the project, both of which have applications developed through the Unity gaming engine, and is easily portable so that it can be used on different platforms. The choice of the virtual reality device would end up being guided by the cost or the mobile device of the user, since the Gear VR requires the use of a Galaxy line phone.

Virtual reality in mobile handsets creates challenges that are more easily transposed when target platforms are computers. Because of the lower graphics processing power of mobile devices, care is required regarding application performance so that it maintains an update rate of 60 fps (frames per second), which is the recommended minimum value. Another important factor in choosing Gear VR is that it has a latency of less than 20 ms, which reduces cybersickness, which is a kind of motion sickness or movement caused by user exposure in virtual reality environments. According to Carmack [49], cybersickness is one of the biggest impediments to a greater adoption of virtual reality in the gaming industry.

The exercise bike is safer than an electric treadmill, for example. Cybersickness can pose a threat to the balance of users who are more susceptible to motion sickness, who are prone to seasickness when reading while traveling by car, or with the uneven movements of a boat trip [50].

Due to all these factors, the development with VR was left to the last stage of the project in view of the longer time for studies and the development of new hardware and software by the industry.

**Making the 1st Stage Prototype**

The elaboration of the prototype of the 1st Stage had three phases:

- Hacking the basic electronics of the bicycle;
- Handling of the bike data for use in Unity;
- The confection of the platform game in Unity.

For the hacking of basic electronics, the bike was first taken to the FabLab Livre of São Paulo City Hall, in the São Paulo Cultural Center unit. There, the initial tests of the general functioning of the bicycle and of the original electronics were made. After this verification, measurements of the working voltages of the sensors of the bicycle were made, obtaining values below 0.5 V. With this value, it would not be necessary to put resistors to decrease the voltage because they were within that which is supported by the Arduino Uno board.

Since the normal working voltages of the bicycle sensors were safe for the electronic part, the bicycle wiring was connected to the sold-board and from the Arduino board to a PC running Linux through the USB port. The programming part was done with the Arduino IDE [44]. Once the connection was established, the voltages were shown by the Serial Monitor screen of the Arduino IDE.

To facilitate the visualization of the values, Processing [51] was used to construct a light graphic application. An image of the type of graph obtained is shown in Fig. 2. The chart roughly resembles an electrocardiogram in which each time the plotted graph reached zero, it meant that the pedal of the bicycle had taken a turn.

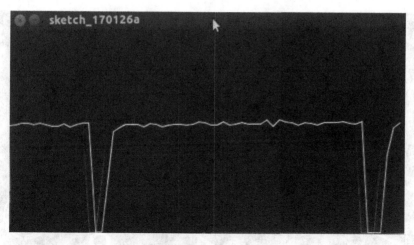

**Fig. 2** Graphic plotted by processing program, showing the electric signals sent by bicycle through Arduino to the computer.

For the second phase, the bicycle was then transferred to the Games Laboratory of the Anhembi Morumbi University. The goal at this stage was to process data that were required for the use of electric bicycle signals by the Unity gaming suite [52]. Adjustments had to be made using Microsoft's Visual Studio [53] because some of the features needed were not supported by the Unity code editing tool.

There was also a need to make some Unity configuration adjustments to allow communication with the C# tool (reads C Sharp). The developed program was used to pick up the electrical signal sent by the Arduino card through the USB port and rework the signal as a time count between the interruption of one signal and another, thus calculating factors such as time and speed of pedaling. In this way, the C# tool allows Unity to receive the data and use it.

In the third phase of the prototype, the development of the game prototypes was carried using the Arduino-bicycle interface developed in the previous phases. The project group was composed of three undergraduate students in digital games divided into 3 main expertises: game design, programming, and art. The students were briefed that the game should demonstrate the use of a different scenario from a real race simulation, since several applications of the type were already found. The students had total freedom of creation in the other options of game type and ambiance.

For game and theme choice, students gathered and brainstormed ideas and outlining concepts. From these meetings, they came to the concept of a 3D platform game, in which the character would move jumping from platform to platform until reaching the goal. The students used some Wii games as initial inspiration for game mechanics. A first draft of the project can be seen in Fig. 3.

**Fig. 3** Early game prototype (draft), testing the game mechanics.

The prototype then received textures and the final character. Students sought various thematic references and adjusted the intended plot in free brainstorming meetings for their elaboration. As a result, they came to an environment inspired by the game Limbo [54]. The plot chosen was a person trapped in a dream world whose foundations are eroding and he must find the way out. The Figs. 4 and 5 show the final result of the prototype with the textures and the character.

**Fig. 4** Final game prototype, showing the character midair during a jump.

**Fig. 5** Final game prototype, showing energy circle in red and timer (little clock). (Color figure online)

The game play happens as follows: the character finds himself inside a nightmare standing on top of a column. In front of him, there are a series of columns, and to jump, the player must pedal the bike within a certain speed range. This way, the speed is converted into the logic of the game to boost the character to make the leap forward - and for this there is a time count. If the user does not pedal and/or pedal out of the speed range, the character does not gain sufficient momentum and, in the fantasy of the nightmare story, ends up being thrown back to the previous column. The victory condition in the stages is pedaling within certain speed ranges before the time runs out.

### Results Achieved and Future Steps

The results of the survey have been satisfactory so far. As for the 1st Stage of the bike, the Arduino system proved to be very practical and adaptable. There are some communication problems between the signal sent by the board and Unity, which was bypassed with the C# counter and changes to the default configuration of the program.

In this regard, future steps will be to improve this Arduino-Unity communication whether through new Arduino tests, new circuits and components, or through add-ons (called assets) by Unity that could improve such communication and make application creation easier.

The future step in relation to the game is precisely the creation of levels (level design) and expansion of the scope to include cardiac monitoring in gameplay. The platform-type gameplay mechanics enables specific adjustments such as:

- Exercise intensity (speed + pedal loading);
- Exercise time;
- Time scheduling of intervals between exercises;
- Self-tuning of the game through feedback with heart rate, changing previous factors.

These adjustments would compose the elements for tests with users around the problematic of dual flow [55].

## 5  Final Considerations

This article presents the partial results of an ongoing research on methodologies for the design of Exergames, arising from a problema raised in an article presented in SBGames 2016 [13], one of the first issues that surfaced early in the process was the inquiry into which device would be ideal to be used for experimenting with these methodologies.

Research into the devices for Exergames has paved the way from the early models to those still in the developmental stage by the industry. During this historical research process, the possibility of using open source technologies, of the so-called Maker Movement, was developed to create a device of its own.

An interesting fact, the new Microsoft Kinect model was released as a tool for developers powered by a more sophisticated camera module and Microsoft's cloud-based AI technology, especially targeted for hackers and tinkerers [35]. This approach shows a similar path this research took in the sense of developing a pure game device, but a platform that allows the creation and use by a wide range of applications from games and simulators to rehab systems.

At this point, the research has been done around the maker technologies and the choice of an exercise apparatus to be adapted for use with Exergames. As a result, it was chosen to use an ergometer bicycle adapted with the Arduino system, in order to create a communication protocol between the exercise apparatus and a computer.

Once the bike was chosen and the means adapted, a six-stage construction plan was developed, from the basic pedal movement to the insertion of virtual reality technology. This article presents the 1$^{st}$ Stage of this project - the process of constructing the first stage of the ergometric bicycle for Exergames, and the subsequent creation of a prototype of game platform for system testing.

Thus, within the scope of this research, the results have been promising in the sense of creating a platform to test the design methodologies for Exergames of reduced cost and with great possibility of dissemination through the practices of the Maker Movement and open source technologies.

This research intends to carry the next five developments on the ergometric bicycle, and once they are completed, to use it to elaborate Exergames prototypes using selected design methodologies through bibliographic research. From this process of prototyping, it is expected to extract data that validate the selected methodologies or, if not, point a direction to the development of specific methodologies.

## References

1. Haseltine, W.A.: Aging populations will challenge healthcare systems all over the world. Forbes (2018). https://bit.ly/2FqrUma. Accessed 14 Jan 2019
2. UN: World Population Prospects 2017. Data Booklet (2017)

3. Friedeman, J.: Prevention is better than a cure: an in-depth look at proactive health (2017). https://www.evariant.com/blog/in-depth-look-proactive-health. Accessed 14 Jan 2019
4. Tak, E.C.P.M., Van Uffelen, J.G.Z., Paw, M.J.C.A., van Mechelen, W., Hopman-Rock, M.: Adherence to exercise programs and determinants of maintenance in older adults with mild cognitive impairment. J. Aging Phys. Act. **20**(1), 32–46 (2012)
5. Huizinga, J.: Homo Ludens: O jogo como elemento da cultura. Editora Perspectiva, São Paulo (2001)
6. Chikhani, R.: The History of gaming: an evolving community (2016). https://techcrunch.com/2015/10/31/the-history-of-gaming-an-evolving-community/. Accessed 10 Jan 2010
7. Desjardins, J.: How video games became a $100 billion industry (2012). https://www.businessinsider.com/the-history-and-evolution-of-the-video-games-market-2017-1. Accessed 10 Jan 2019
8. Prensky, M.: Aprendizagem Baseada em Jogos Digitais. Editora Senac, São Paulo (2012)
9. Wattanasoontorn, V., Boada, I., García, R., Sbert, M.: Serious games for health. Entertain. Comput. **4**, 231–247 (2013)
10. de Vasconcellos, M.S., de Carvalho, F.G., Capella, M.A.M., Dias, C.M., de Araujo, I.S.: A Saúde na Literatura Acadêmica sobre Jogos: uma análise das publicações do SBGames. In: SBC – Proceedings of XV SBGames, SBC|Brasil, São Paulo (2016)
11. Staiano, A., Abraham, A., Calvert, S.: The Wii Club: gaming for weight loss in overweight and obese youth. Games Health J. Res. Dev. Clin. Appl. **1**(5), 377–380 (2012)
12. Ito, M.: Uma alternativa de conscientização sobre prevenção odontológica: desenvolvimento e avaliação do protótipo de um serious game. CEETEPS (2011)
13. Oliveira, B.S., Nesteriuk, S., Queiroz, P.: Exergames: Amostragem da Produção Acadêmica entre 2010 e 2015. In: Proceedings of XV Simpósio Brasileiro de Jogos e Entretenimento Digital, pp. 714–717. SBC|Brasil, São Paulo (2016)
14. Almeida Filho, N.D.: O que é Saúde? Ed Fiocruz, Rio de Janeiro (2011)
15. Maslow, A.H.: Maslow's hierarchy of needs. Psychol. Rev. **50**, 370–396 (1943). http://www.researchhistory.org/2012/06/16/maslows-hierarchy-of-needs/. Accessed 8 Jan 2019
16. UN: Sustainable Development Goal 3 (2018). https://sustainabledevelopment.un.org/sdg3. Accessed 10 Jan 2019
17. CDC: The Power of Prevention (2009). https://www.cdc.gov/chronicdisease/pdf/2009-Power-of-Prevention.pdf. Accessed 3 Jan 2019
18. HEALTH expenditure. The World Bank. http://data.worldbank.org/indicator/SH.XPD.TOTL.ZS?end=2014&name_desc=false&start=1995&view=chart>. Accessed 29 Aug 2016
19. Czeresnia, D., de Seixas Maciel, E.M.G.: Os Sentidos da Saúde e da Doença. Ed Fiocruz, Rio de Janeiro (2013)
20. IBGE: Pesquisa Nacional por Amostra de Domicílios - Acesso à internet e à televisão e posse de telefone móvel celular para uso pessoa 2014. IBGE, Rio de Janeiro (2016)
21. Diehl, L., Souza, R., Alves, J., Esteves, R., Gordan, P., Jorge, M.L.: A game for training medical doctors on insulin use for diabetic patients. In: Simpósio Brasileiro de Jogos e Entretenimento Digital. SBC|Brasil, Porto Alegre (2011)
22. Theng, Y.L., Lee, J.W.Y., Patinadan, P.V., Foo, S.S.B.: The use of videogames, gamification, and virtual environments in the self-management of diabetes: a systematic review of evidence. Games Health J. Res. Dev. Clin. Appl. **4**(5), 352–361 (2015)
23. Barros, M., Formiga, R., Neves, A.: Exergame Peggo – desenvolvimento de jogos de exercício físico-funcional para auxílio no combate da obesidade infantil. In: Simpósio Brasileiro de Jogos e Entretenimento Digital. SBC|Brasil, Porto Alegre (2013)
24. Passos, N.R.S, et al.: Siirius Surfer – Utilizando jogos sérios na reabilitação de tronco de pacientes pós-AVC. In: Simpósio Brasileiro de Jogos e Entretenimento Digital. SBC|Brasil, Porto Alegre (2013)

25. Wii, N.: https://en.wikipedia.org/wiki/Wii. Accessed 14 Dec 2016
26. Jeffery, M.: Pokemon GO helped player lose 85 pounds (2017). https://gamerant.com/pokemon-go-weight-loss/?fbclid=IwAR0IotbNFky3REEABaGmgG5bmvAOf9Gck8uIDtD2XsxDc3iSaEIXKLGgJ-w. Accessed 3 Jan 2019
27. Johnson, J.: From Atari Joyboard to Wii Fit: 25 years of "exergaming" (2008). http://gadgets.boingboing.net/2008/05/15/from-atarijoyboard.html. Accessed 4 Aug 2017
28. Barros, M.: Exergames: o papel multidisciplinar do design no desenvolvimento de jogos de exercício físico-funcional para auxílio no combate da obesidade infantil. Universidade Federal de Pernambuco (2012)
29. Equipamentos de Reabilitação Lucy Montoro. http://crlmsjc.spdmafiliadas.org.br/equipamentos-de-reabilitacao/. Accessed 4 Aug 2017
30. Vernadakis, N., Gioftsidou, A., Antoniou, P., Ioannidis, D., Giannousi, M.: The impact of Nintendo Wii to physical education student's balance compared to the traditional approaches. Comput. Educ. 2(59), 196–205 (2012)
31. Vaghetti, C., Vieira, K., Mazza, S., Signori, L., Botelho, S.: Exergames no currículo da escola: uma metodologia para as aulas de Educação Física. In: Proceedings of XII Simpósio Brasileiro de Jogos e Entretenimento Digital. SBC|Brasil, São Paulo (2013)
32. Kinect. https://en.wikipedia.org/wiki/Kinect. Accessed 14 Dec 2016
33. Balista, V.: PhysioJoy: Sistema de Realidade Virtual para Avaliação e Reabilitação de Déficit Motor. In: Proceedings of XII Simpósio Brasileiro de Jogos e Entretenimento Digital. SBC|Brasil, São Paulo (2013)
34. Rossito, G., Berlim, T., Hounsell, M., Vinicius, A.: SIRTET-K3D: a serious game for balance improvement on elderly people. In: Proceedings of XIII Simpósio Brasileiro de Jogos e Entretenimento Digital. SBC|Brasil, Porto Alegre (2014)
35. Cranz, A.: Microsoft Kinect Refuses to Die (2018). https://gizmodo.com/microsoft-kinect-refuses-to-die-1825847023. Accessed 21 Oct 2018
36. Expresso Bikes. https://expresso.com/Home. Accessed 4 Aug 2017
37. Goji Play. http://www.bluegoji.com/gojiplay. Accessed 4 Aug 2017
38. Holofit. http://www.holodia.com/. Accessed 4 Aug 2017
39. Flusser, V.: O mundo codificado: por uma filosofia do design e da comunicação. Editora Cosas Naify, São Paulo (2007)
40. Mikhak, B., Lyon, C., Gorton, T., Gershenfeld, N., McEnnis, C., Taylor, J.: Fab lab: an alternate model of ICT for development (2002). http://cba.mit.edu/events/03.05.fablab/fablabdyd02.pdf. Accessed 4 Aug 2017
41. Anderson, C.: Makers: the new industrial revolution. Crown Business (2012)
42. Fablab: Hardware and Software. http://fabfoundation.org/index.php/the-hardware-andsoftware/index.html. Accessed 4 Aug 2017
43. Arduino Materia 101. https://store.arduino.cc/usa/arduino-materia-101-assembled. Accessed 4 Aug 2017
44. Arduino Introduction. https://www.arduino.cc/en/Guide/Introduction. Accessed 4 Aug 2017
45. Moraes, M.: Arduino sistema de irrigação (2013). https://arduinobymyself.blogspot.com.br/2013/09/sistema-deirrigacao.html. Accessed 4 Aug 2017
46. Kiko's KV3.1li. http://www.kikos.com.br/item/produto/bike-kikos-kv-31i. Accessed 4 Aug 2017
47. Barfield, W.: Fundamentals of Wearable Computers and Augmented Reality, 2nd edn. CRC Press, Boca Raton (2001)
48. Manual do usuário Samsung Gear VR SM-R322. http://www.samsung.com/br/support/model/SMR322NZWAZTO. Accessed 3 Aug 2017

49. Carmack, J.: Keynote Oculus Connect (2014). https://www.youtube.com/watch?v= nqzpAbK9qFk. Accessed 17 June 2017
50. Riccio, G., Stoffregen, T.: An ecological theory of motion sickness and postural instability. Ecol. Psychol. **3**(3), 195–240 (1991)
51. Processing. https://processing.org. Accessed 4 Aug 2017
52. Unity. https://unity3d.com/pt. Accessed 4 Aug 2017
53. Microsoft Visual Studio. https://www.visualstudio.com/pt-br/. Accessed 4 Aug 2017
54. Limbo on Steam. http://store.steampowered.com.app/48000/LIMBO/. Accessed 4 Aug 2017
55. Sinclair, J., Hingston, P., Masek, M.: Considerations for the design of exergames. In: Proceedings of the 5th International conference on Computer and Interactive Techniques in Australia and Southeast Asia. ACM, USA, Perth, Australia, pp. 289–295 (2007)

# An Empirical Study on the Influential Factors of User Loyalty in Digital Fitness Community

Yao Shen[(⊠)]

School of Design, Shanghai Jiao Tong University, Shanghai, China
18317000160@163.com

**Abstract.** Nowadays, consumption of self-healthy and figure management is developing rapidly. Scholars have studied the impact factors of long-term use of wearable fitness devices. However, a holistic loyalty impact analysis of the applications they are associated with is rarely seen. Based on the individual cognitive model of perception-emotion-intention, seven hypotheses are proposed to verify the relationships among transaction cost, motivation, usability, trust and loyalty. The results show that transaction costs have significant adverse effects on loyalty. Trust has significant positive effect on loyalty, partial mediating effect in transaction costs, and complete mediating effect in motivation and usability on loyalty.

**Keywords:** Fitness APPs · Self-healthy management · Loyalty

## 1 Introduction

### 1.1 Background

Internet and technology have accelerated the development of wearable fitness device and fitness APP market, providing convenience and fitness guidance for users' self-healthy management. In China's fitness app market, 75% fitness APPs did not match wearable devices, Only 25% matched [1, 2]. The physical comfort and aesthetical of wearable devices satisfied users both physically and mentally. However, the associated application also affects the overall user experience. In addition to the real-time tracking of sports data and body physiological data, most of the visual display of self-information and fitness reports mainly depends on the related mobile application. Therefore, the paper aim at Fitness Guide App as the research object.

### 1.2 Research Significance

At present, most research on user loyalty focus on traditional online shopping [3, 4], and some scholars have also studied on the factors that influence the loyalty of using wearable fitness devices [5–7]. However, a holistic loyalty impact analysis of the applications they are associated with is rarely seen. This paper will study the factors that influence the user loyalty in the mobile fitness community and validate four related

© Springer Nature Switzerland AG 2019
V. G. Duffy (Ed.): HCII 2019, LNCS 11582, pp. 550–559, 2019.
https://doi.org/10.1007/978-3-030-22219-2_40

factors to loyalty: Transaction costs, Motivation, Usability, trust [6] to provide specific case studies for relevant practitioners and academic researchers.

## 2 Theoretical Framework

The research framework of this paper draws on the individual cognitive model of perception-emotion-intention [2, 8]. It has three stages: perceive information, forms preference and finally constitutes the corresponding intention. On the basis of this research framework, this paper analyzes the mediating effect of trust on loyalty, verifies the relationship between Transaction costs, motivation, usability, trust [6], and loyalty, among the four factors.

### 2.1 Perceived Elements

According to the literature research, this paper sums up three elements of perceived content: transaction cost, usability and motivation. When choosing store or brand, users need to consider the transaction cost and risk. Traditional asset specificity has different forms, including manpower attribute, time attribute, money attribute, location attribute and so on. Usability is user's impression and experience of using product, which is changed through time. There is no denying that UED is one of the elements to win user's trust. Usability has always been one of the most important research issues in human-computer interaction. Structure arrangement, interface and interaction design all affect user's product perception. Normally, the use of products is driven by different motives. The theory of motivation is very rich, contain Maslow's hierarchy of needs and Aldrich's erg theory. The other is process motivation theory, which focuses on the psychological changes between motivation and behavior, contains the theory of reinforcement motivation, goal incentives, expectations and rewards. They have gradually been used and become one of the important theoretical foundations of the human-computer interaction behavior analysis.

### 2.2 Emotional Element

The emotional element is expressed as trust. Trust is the relationship between user and product, which means contact with producer, service provider and program builder. Trust creates loyalty to attitude and action. Researchers have suggested that trust is an important factor that affects brand loyalty [6]. Brand trust can bring loyalty, the needs of designing trust and motivation mechanism is just as important as usability assessments.

### 2.3 Intentions

The establishment of e-commerce loyalty is a complex and cumulative process. The measure of loyalty includes two aspects: behavior intention and attitudinal intention. Blackman and Crompton propose that behavior of loyalty including: direct consumption, preferences and making recommendations to others; attitudinal loyalty shows as being immunity to other competing brands and having high price tolerance.

## 3 Hypothesis Based on SEM Model

### 3.1 The Influence of Transaction Cost, Usability, Motivation, Trust on Loyalty

The cost of using a new App or buy related product in a new online store includes not only the price of the product, but also the time costs to compare different brands and confirm the process before purchasing [9]. Werner websphere and Ratchford proposed that the construction of nontransferable skills need to be taken into consideration when talking about loyalty. In the case of fitness app, similar perform regulations can reduce the cost of learning. And users prefer to use the current product when competitors have the similar interface design.

H1a: Low transaction cost of fitness guidance bring more loyalty for fitness APPs.

Nielsen believes usability means that people can easily and efficiently learn and use the basic functions of the App. According to ISO/IEC 9126-1, Usability is attractive and easy to use which related to the properties of product [10]. Searching, shopping or inputting information online, every decision is a reaction from interface and functional design [11]. Bevan believes usability is a determining factor in end-brand loyalty.

H2a: Usability of mobile fitness Apps has an attractive influence on loyalty.

Snakin believes that human behavior is a function of received stimulation. If the stimulation was benefit to him, the behavior would repeat; If it is to his disadvantage, it will weaken and even disappear. Users who aim to lose weight are more likely to use the practice function, while those who focus on social motivation are more likely to use the fitness activity recording that can be shared. Online fitness community users are more likely to be goal-driven than non-OFC users and are more focused on goal - achievement [12]. Therefor according to different goal setting, various motivational reinforcement methods can be adopted to help people adjust their behavior and realize their self-achievement.

H3a: Motivation stimulated user's loyalty of fitness APPs.

Cha argued that the trust mechanism of e-commerce has three independent dimensions: consumer behavior dimension, institutional dimension and technical dimension. Depending on users' cultural background, the degree of uncertainty about risk avoidance varies [13]. Bivouque and Brislin found that the characteristics of the western members under the influence of individualism were self - reliance, competition, trust of others, and utilitarianism in exchange and competence [14]. Utilitarianists have a high tendency to trust, and individualists believe in others until there is a reason to distrust them [15]. However, under the guidance of collectivism, the Oriental users prefer to trust the people in the group. So, their trust will easily be affected by the experience and evaluation of their relatives, friends and colleagues. Products in different cultural backgrounds should adopt different trust-building systems.

H4: The trust of fitness Apps has attractive effect on user loyalty.

## 3.2 The Relationships Among Transaction Cost, Usability, Motivation and Trust

Other people's using experience can influence self-willingness to buy and use [16]. EWOM (Feedback and Evaluation of Other Buyers) can help to dispel user's doubts and reduce the cost of searching information and moral hazard [17]. When a product or service offers a price discount and sales, the user perceives that the cost of the transaction is reduced, and the willingness to purchase and use increases [18]. For example, filters with costs provided by photo-social networking sites are free for seven days' trail, reducing the cost of investing.

H1b: Low transaction cost of fitness guidance bring more trust on fitness APPs.

Friendly interface design, high quality fitness content, in-time feedback will bring pleasure and satisfaction to users. Obvious entrance of function, fluent using and creative interface design attracted more users' trusty. Fast shopping processing and visualized information can increase trust effectively. Today, the main parts of fitness App contains video or graphic teaching, data tracking, planning and management, sporting, online malls. The reasonable organization of these resources makes it easy for users to use. In the models presented by Werner Derech and Ratchford, products also need to add non - transferable skills to maintain users' loyalty on the product [9].

H2b: The usability of mobile fitness App has an attractive effect on trust.

Motivation-hygiene theory (Frederick Herzberg 1966) pointed out that the motivational factor is easy to satisfy users, but without it, the user will not be dissatisfied. Conversely, when hygiene is absent, users quickly feels dissatisfied. Japanese scholars have proposed that H factor is the necessary condition of user's emotion identification, and M factor is the charming condition of enhancing emotion recognition. [6] Rupp considered motivational support and technical trust to be important factors in the continued use of wearable fitness devices. In the aspect of structure and visual design of the product, considering how to stimulate the user's motivation. Making the user use continuously, even become the nontransferable user's skill. It is very important to keep the loyalty of the product from the beginning to the end.

H3b: Motivation has a positive effect on fitness APPs trust.

Researchers have discussed the determinants of loyalty in different areas [6]. This paper makes minor modifications to their research and presents the relationship between trust, motivation, transaction cost, usability and loyalty for fitness Apps, and seven hypotheses are presented as the below table (Table 1).

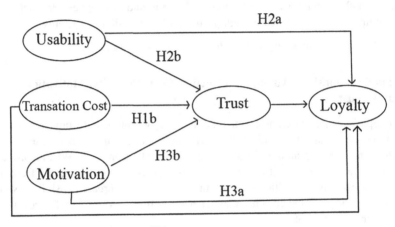

**Table 1.** Hypotheses model

H1a

## 4  Research Methodology

### 4.1  Measurement of Variables

There are five variables in this study, trust [6], motivation [7], Transaction costs (Williamson 1985) and usability, four exogenous variables, loyalty is endogenous variable, Questionnaire test is used to collect data contained 27 items, seven of which were basic personality information problems about the sample, including sex, career, whether using fitness software. The rest of 20 questions were investigated by Likert Five Scale, and each variable is tested by four items. In order to ensure the reliability and rigor of the study, the scale was designed referring previous study. Using Amos to analyze the structural equation of the theoretical mode, which is convenient to deal with the sample with small data quantity accurately (Table 2).

**Table 2.** Question scale

| Variable | Scale | Resource |
|---|---|---|
| Transaction cost | 1.1 The simple online shopping process saves time | [16, 17] |
| | 1.2 Fitness APP offers additional benefits | |
| | 1.3 Fitness APP course plan trial reduced my investment risk | |
| | 1.4 Transparent transaction records and fast order processing | |
| Usability | 2.1 Fitness data tracking is satisfactory | [9, 10] |
| | 2.2 I can quickly get the fitness content I want | |
| | 2.3 The fitness APP content module is clear and easy to use | |
| | 2.4 The shopping communication on the fitness APP is convenient | |

*(continued)*

**Table 2.** (*continued*)

| Variable | Scale | Resource |
|---|---|---|
| Motivation | 3.1 Timed reminders can increase your fitness frequency | (Rupp et al. 2016) |
| | 3.2 A scientific diet and fitness program make me determined | |
| | 3.3 Often use online fitness APP to assist with fitness activities | |
| | 3.4 I can get more fitness knowledge in the fitness app | |
| Trust | 4.1 The content on the fitness APP is scientific and true | [4] |
| | 4.2 Fitness APP protect my privacy | |
| | 4.3 The paid course on the fitness software is trustworthy | |
| | 4.4 The service quality of this fitness software is trustworthy | |
| Loyalty | 5.1 I am willing to purchase paid courses on fitness platform | Gronhold (2000) |
| | 5.2 I often share my fitness record and experience | |
| | 5.3 I once recommended family and friends to use this APP | |
| | 5.4 This software is preferred when I do fitness activities | |

## 4.2   Data Collection

With the help of the questionnaire star system platform, the distribution and recovery of the questionnaire were carried out. Consumption is the primary indicator of e-commerce, however, as for fitness activities, to some extent, is pursuing self-respect. Chinese scholars used the Answer Tree model to investigate and find out that the difference of using fitness Apps is strongest effected by education background, secondly, region. The utilization rate in urban areas and above is higher than that in counties. Therefore, the sample of this paper comes from Shanghai and Guangzhou, two first-tier cities in China. 500 responses were received, excluding those uncompleted, 456 responses valid. 28.9% of valid samples were male and 71.1% were female, 75.6% have the experience of using fitness App.

# 5   The Experimental Analysis

## 5.1   Reliability and Validity Analysis

By using spss software, the internal consistency reliability of the questionnaire is analyzed, and the coefficients are calculated as shown in the table below (Table 3).

**Table 3.**  Reliability statistics

| Cronbach's Alpha | No. of items |
|---|---|
| .875 | 27 |

According to the reliability test of the variables studied, cronbach's value is 0.875, which is greater than 0.8. It can be seen that the measurement indexes of variables have higher internal consistency reliability.

The validity of the data was tested by KMO and Bartlett sample measure. The closer KMO is to 1, the more efficient the data. Experience shows that KMO is greater than 0.9, indicating that the data is very efficient, KMO between 0.8 to 0.9 indicates that the data is valid, while under 0.5 the data need to be re-collected (Table 4).

**Table 4.** KMO and Bartlett's test

| Kaiser-Meyer-Olkin measure of sampling adequacy | | .845 |
|---|---|---|
| Bartlett's test of sphericity | Approx. Chi-Square | 3571.244 |
| | df | 190 |
| | Sig. | .000 |

The validity value of KMO is 0.845, which is more than 0.8, indicating that the research data is quite effective. The significance value of bartlett's spherical test was 0.000, less than 0.01, therefore the relationship between variables is strong and the data validity of this study is good.

## 5.2    Confirmatory Factors Analysis

In this study, the maximum likelihood method is used for confirmatory factor analysis. In the evaluation of model adaptation degree by confirmatory factor analysis, it is advisable to consider simultaneously the indicators of Absolute Fit, Value-added Fit and Reduced Fit: (1) Generally speaking, X2/df is between 1 and 3 to show that the model has the degree of reduction and adaptation, and more strict adaptation criterion is between 1 and 2. (2) The value of RMR should be as small as possible, and RMR < 0.1 is an acceptable adaptation model. (3) The three indexes of value-added adaptation, TLI, IFI and CFI, are all good for model adaptation with >0.8. (4) The other two indicators, PGFI and PNFI, are all expressed as acceptable models in the range >0.5 (Table 5).

**Table 5.** Multi-factor structural validity analysis

| Adaptation test indicator | Ideal standard | Result | T/f |
|---|---|---|---|
| CMIN/DF | <3.00 | 2.503 | T |
| RMR | <.01 | 0.043 | T |
| CFI | >.80 | 0.933 | T |
| IFI | >.80 | 0.934 | T |
| TLI | >.80 | 0.920 | T |
| PNFI | >.50 | 0.748 | T |
| PGFI | >.50 | 0.606 | T |

It can be seen that all the hypothesis models are within the acceptable range and reach the ideal standard. Therefore, the theoretical model can fit the empirical data structure, and the adaptability of the model is good.

## 5.3   Analysis Path Factors for the Model

The path coefficients between indexes are estimated by the variance calculation and covariance calculation of variables. In the selection of the model, recursive form is generally adopted, and the observed scalars in the regression equation are generally linear, then all path coefficients can be estimated by maximum likelihood estimation method. Using Amos software to calculate the coefficients is as follows (Table 6).

**Table 6.**  Standardized regression coefficient and significance test

|  | Estimate | S.E. | C.R. | P | Label |
|---|---|---|---|---|---|
| Trust ← Transaction cost | 0.230 | .062 | −3.771 | *** | |
| Trust ← Motivation | 0.471 | .074 | 6.472 | *** | |
| Trust ← Usability | .134 | .039 | 2.904 | .004 | |
| Loyalty ← Transaction cost | −.215 | .031 | −4.694 | *** | |
| Loyalty ← Motivation | .017 | .026 | .417 | .676 | |
| Loyalty ← Usability | .006 | .042 | .139 | .889 | |
| Loyalty ← Trust | .227 | .131 | 2.607 | .009 | |

The fourth column, C.R., is the test statistic (critical ratio) and the critical ratio is the t value of the t-test. When this value is greater than 1.96, the preceding regression coefficient has reached a significant level of 0.05, The value of p in the fifth column is significant. If $p < 0.001$, it is denoted by the symbol "***", and if p is $>0.001$, the value of p is directly rendered. As can be seen from the table, there are 5 hypotheses are correct (Table 7).

**Table 7.**  Results of hypotheses model

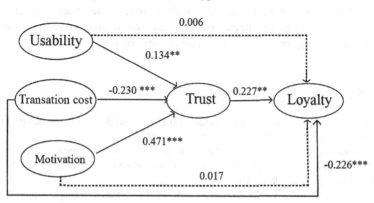

***:p<0.001   **:p<0.01   *:p<0.05

From the above table, P value of motivation and usability is more than 0.05, indicating that motivation and usability have no significant effect on loyalty. However, usability (0.134, $P < 0.01$), motivation (0.471, $P < 0.001$) had positive effect on trust, motivation had the greatest influence on trust. Transaction cost ($-0.230$, $P < 0.001$) had negative relation to trust, meanwhile had a significant negative impact ($-0.230$, $p < 0.001$) on loyalty. Trust (0.227, $p < 0.05$) had a significant positive effect on loyalty. In conclusion, for transaction cost, trust has a partial mediating effect on loyalty. As for motivation and usability, trust has a complete mediating effect on loyalty.

## 6    Results and Discussions

In the observation index, behavior intention has better effect on loyalty than attitude intention. Purchasing paid courses and fitness device on fitness Apps is the best expression of loyalty. The experimental results agree with our previous hypothesis that transaction costs have the greatest effect on loyalty. Reduce the transaction costs will increase loyalty and trust.

The effect of usability on loyalty is not significant. It might because, with the popularity of smartphones, Apps' interface design is mature and has become the basic element of user loyalty, not the charm condition. As for the result that motivation does not significantly influence the trust, it may be affected by personality, educational background and self-recognition, which are unconcentrated in this paper. The small sample size of the experiment, of course, does not represent all people's views on loyalty. However, this paper can serve as a case study and reference for academics and fitness software practitioners.

Today's mobile fitness APPs can not only track users' movement timely, but also intelligently recommend fitness information and instructions that meet the different needs of different users. In addition to well-conduct online fitness platform operation, online fitness platform is also gradually developing offline fitness sphere. How to maintain the relationship between community users and products will affect the development of online fitness community in the future. In the future research, we can study these potential variables affected by time and other regions to complete the theory and provide case study of digital fitness community loyalty.

## References

1. Zhang, H., Liu, X.: Investigation and research on fitness guidance APP resources and usage behavior. J. Wuhan Inst. Phys. Educ. **51**(10), 37–42 (2017)
2. Liu, L., Zhang, N.: Research on the relationship between customer perceived value, satisfaction and loyalty-empirical analysis in e-commerce environment. J. Inf. Resour. Manag. **6**(03), 50–57+106 (2016)
3. Deng, A., Tao, B., Ma, Y.: An empirical study on the factors affecting customer loyalty in online shopping. Chin. Manag. Sci. **22**(06), 94–102 (2014)

4. Cha, J.: Research on the relationship between B2C e-commerce customer value and customer loyalty. Zhejiang University (2006)
5. Sallis, J.F., et al.: The development of scales to measure social support for diet and exercise behaviors. Prev. Med. **16**(6), 825–836 (1987)
6. Rupp, M.A., et al.: The role of individual differences on perceptions of wearable fitness device trust, usability, and motivational impact. Appl. Ergon. **70**, 77–87 (2018)
7. Ba, S., Wang, L.: Digital health communities: the effect of their motivation mechanisms. Decis. Support Syst. **55**(4), 941–947 (2013)
8. Koo, D.-M., Ju, S.-H.: The interactional effects of atmospherics and perceptual curiosity on emotions and online shopping intention. Comput. Hum. Behav. **26**(3), 377–388 (2010)
9. Murray, K.B., Haubl, G.: A human capital perspective of skill acquisition and interface loyalty. Commun. ACM **46**(12), 272–278 (2003)
10. Lee, D., et al.: Antecedents and consequences of mobile phone usability: linking simplicity and interactivity to satisfaction, trust, and brand loyalty. Inf. Manag. **52**(3), 295–304 (2015)
11. Bevan, N.: International standards for HCI and usability. Int. J. Hum. Comput. Stud. **55**(4), 533–552 (2001)
12. Stragier, J., Vanden Abeele, M., De Marez, L.: Recreational athletes running motivations as predictors of their use of online fitness community features. Behav. Inf. Technol. **37**(8), 815–827 (2018)
13. Park, J., Gunn, F., Han, S.-L.: Multidimensional trust building in e-retailing: cross-cultural differences in trust formation and implications for perceived risk. J. Retail. Consum. Serv. **19**(3), 304–312 (2012)
14. Bhawuk, D.P.S., Brislin, R.: The measurement of intercultural sensitivity using the concepts of individualism and collectivism. Int. J. Intercult. Relat. **16**(4), 413–436 (1992)
15. Yamagishi, T., Yamagishi, M.: Trust and commitment in the United States and Japan. Motiv. Emot. **18**(2), 129–166 (1994)
16. Keaveney, S.M., Parthasarathy, M.: Customer switching behavior in online services: an exploratory study of the role of selected attitudinal, behavioral, and demographic factors. J. Acad. Mark. Sci. **29**(4), 374–390 (2001)
17. Cheung, M., et al.: Credibility of electronic word-of-mouth: informational and normative determinants of on-line consumer recommendations. Int. J. Electron. Commer. **13**(4), 9–38 (2009)
18. Zeithaml, V.A.: J. Marketing 2 (1988)

# Author Index

Printed in the United States
By Bookmasters